THE
CULTURAL
POWER
OF
PERSONAL
OBJECTS

SUNY series in American Philosophy and Cultural Thought
―――――――
Randall E. Auxier and John R. Shook, editors

THE CULTURAL POWER OF PERSONAL OBJECTS

TRADITIONAL ACCOUNTS AND NEW PERSPECTIVES

EDITED BY
JARED KEMLING

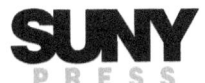

Published by State University of New York Press, Albany

© 2021 State University of New York

All rights reserved

Printed in the United States of America

No part of this book may be used or reproduced in any manner whatsoever without written permission. No part of this book may be stored in a retrieval system or transmitted in any form or by any means including electronic, electrostatic, magnetic tape, mechanical, photocopying, recording, or otherwise without the prior permission in writing of the publisher.

For information, contact State University of New York Press, Albany, NY
www.sunypress.edu

Library of Congress Cataloging-in-Publication Data

Name: Kemling, Jared, editor.
Title: The cultural power of personal objects : traditional accounts and new perspectives / Jared Kemling, editor.
Description: Albany : State University of New York Press, [2021] | Series: SUNY series in American Philosophy and Cultural Thought | Includes bibliographical references and index.
Identifiers: ISBN 9781438486178 (hardcover : alk. paper) | ISBN 9781438486185 (ebook) | ISBN 9781438486161 (pbk. : alk. paper)
Further information is available at the Library of Congress.

10 9 8 7 6 5 4 3 2 1

Contents

Acknowledgments ix

Introduction 1

Part 1: Traditional Accounts

Chapter 1
Mereology: Wholes, Parts, and the Big Thicket 11
   Pete A. Y. Gunter

Chapter 2
Personality in Seagoing Ships 27
   Marc M. Anderson

Chapter 3
Personified Objects and Objectified Persons in Ancient Egypt 53
   Martin Pehal

Chapter 4
Seeing and Time: Personal Divinity in the Object of
Hindu Devotion 75
   John W. August III

Chapter 5
Convergence and Divergence of Spirit: *Tsukumogami* and the
Personality of Objects 95
   Kevin C. Taylor

Chapter 6
The Journey of the Javanese *Keris* — 105
    Alan G. Maisey

Chapter 7
Cherokee Nonhuman Persons in Dual Realms — 119
    Carrie McLachlan

Chapter 8
The Quilt as Personal Object — 143
    Sasha L. Biro

Part 2: New Perspectives

Chapter 9
The New Materialism: A Critique — 165
    Michael Jackson

Chapter 10
Constituting Personal Objects, Constituting Persons — 185
    Dwayne A. Tunstall

Chapter 11
A Personalized Cultural World: A Cassireran Phenomenology of Personalized Intuition — 197
    Jared Kemling

Chapter 12
The Comfort of Things: Personal Objects, Possession, Dwelling, and the Desire to Be God in Sartre and Levinas — 221
    James McLachlan

Chapter 13
Have We Effectively Made Money a Person and Ourselves Its Corporeal Embodiment? — 241
    Helen Grela

Chapter 14
Wampum, Person, and the Life of Exchange — 267
    Randall Auxier

Chapter 15
How My Piano Uses Gendlin's Focusing Method 303
Ralph D. Ellis

Chapter 16
Meditating on the Vitality of the Musical Object: A Spiritual
Exercise Drawn from Richard Wagner's Metaphysics of Music 319
Eli Kramer

Chapter 17
Bring Out Your Dead: Human Bodies, Cultural Objects,
and Personality 341
Laura J. Mueller

Chapter 18
Sex Robots and Solipsism: Towards a Culture of Empty Contact 367
Charles W. Harvey

Contributors 385

Index 391

Acknowledgments

I would like to thank the anonymous reviewers who saw the value in this project and provided helpful feedback on how to improve it. I would also like to thank the editorial and production staff at SUNY; without them this volume simply would not exist. Versions of several chapters in this volume have been published elsewhere, and I would like to thank those publications for their permission to include the following works in this volume:

An earlier version of chapter 9, Michael Jackson's "The New Materialism: A Critique," was originally published as "The New Materialisms," in *Critique of Identity Thinking* (Berghahn: New York, 2019): 56–72.

An earlier version of chapter 16, Eli Kramer's "Meditating on the Vitality of the Musical Object: A Spiritual Exercise Drawn from Richard Wagner's Metaphysics of Music," was originally published in *Eidos. A Journal for Philosophy of Culture* 3, no. 3 (2019).

An earlier version of chapter 18, Charles W. Harvey's "Sex Robots and Solipsism: Towards a Culture of Empty Contact," was originally published in *Philosophy in the Contemporary World* 22, no. 2 (Fall 2015/Spring 2016).

On a personal note, I would like to thank my wife Larissa and my daughter Florence for their tremendous love, support, and guidance. Every day they inspire me, and gently remind me of the true value of philosophy.

Jared Kemling
December, 2021

Introduction

The first question that a reader might reasonably have when opening this volume is: What do you mean by personal object? As it turns out, that is a very good question. It is also a very difficult question to answer—difficult enough to prompt us to create this volume. There is no single English term that encapsulates the whole of this concept; and different terms are liable to introduce different misunderstandings. I have chosen to call these experiences of "personal" objects because the word "personal" retains its connection to the concept of "person"—put succinctly, we wish to discuss "objects" (or at least, experiences usually labelled as objective) that are also persons. Depending on the case, these objects might be understood to truly be person in the fullest sense, or they may be objects that are metaphorically "person-like," at least enough so as to be philosophically interesting. In other words, these objects might literally be a person in the full personalist sense (whether understood as possessing Kantian dignity, or various other conceptions of person). Or they might be understood as possessing a "persona" or a "personality" that gives them an aura unlike other objects.

The downside of choosing the term "personal" (as opposed to "vital objects" or "anthropomorphized" or similar) is that to the modern English speaker the term might connote "possession." For example: that car is my personal property. While there is an interesting relationship between private property and personal objects (see for example chapter 13 of this volume), we do not want to limit our conversation to just this sense of the term. Somewhat closer to our usage is the sense of "personal" as a marker of importance and value: this car is personal for me because it was my mother's. Why are certain objects more personal to us than others? Why do we so often give names to our cars (and ships, and weapons, and so on)? How is the experience of a personal object distinct from experiences of other objects? Personal objects are present in nearly every culture (as this volume will demonstrate), and they play a powerful role in our experience of the world. Further, these objects often have important cultural and sociological functions: whether religious, economic, ethical, aesthetic, or political. However, philosophy has not done an adequate job in addressing this aspect of the human experience.

The narrative of "modern" philosophy since Descartes, at least as it is commonly understood, has been the story of increasing dominance by a certain form of scientific and mathematical understanding of the world—an understanding that has taken a certain view of subjects and objects, which prioritizes quantifiable (mathematizable and measurable) articulations of experience. The benefits of this worldview have been great, but the detriments have at times been less emphasized. Questions concerning our Cartesian heritage (a broad term I take to mean not just Descartes but the style of philosophy that followed him) proliferated in the twentieth century: such questions were brought to crisis by the tragedies of the two world wars and the Cold War.

Now we live in a transitional time in which the dominance of that modern worldview has tilted (which is not to say that it does not remain incredibly influential). We are not yet sure if it will right itself, or if something new will rise in its place. It is not enough simply to critique the tradition or lose ourselves in skepticism; either solutions must be offered, or alternatives must be proposed. In the midst of this struggle, large sections of the academy are either struggling for new worldviews to articulate, or seeking to look back and reclaim something of what has been covered up by the dominance of Cartesian "modernism."

It is in the spirit of both of these efforts that we have written this volume. Ironically, science itself has already in many ways outgrown "modern" philosophy—modern philosophy has failed to keep up. More critically, however, human cultures (especially Western European dominated cultures) have also failed to keep up. While work has been progressing on quantum physics and non-Euclidean geometries for over a century, culture at large is still firmly Cartesian. The effects of that influence are not aging well.

This volume attempts to broaden and reinvigorate our understanding of cultural meaning and experience. Personal objects—objects with significant cultural value (with personality)—are a class that cannot be understood from the standpoint of the dominant mathematized modern worldview. And yet, experiences of this sort are incredibly pervasive and appear throughout almost every culture. Most readers are bound to recognize their own experiences in depictions of different personal objects: for example, your grandfather's watch is not just any watch. It has a personality that other (even materially identical) watches do not.

These experiences cannot be denied, and yet they also cannot be accommodated by the dominant cultural form. As a result, work is necessary either to adapt the dominant form or propose alternative forms of understanding. That is precisely what this volume seeks to do. Some authors look to existing or historical cultures for examples, while other authors propose new systems of cultural thought. Many chapters in the volume feature some blend of both approaches.

This volume has three aims. The first aim is simply to articulate what it means to have an experience of a personal object—so that readers can recognize this experience in their own lives. The second aim is to provide an overview of some historically or culturally significant examples of personal objects. While it is impossible to provide a complete listing of culturally significant personal objects, we have provided a representative sample that draws from geographically and historically diverse sources. The third aim of the volume is to provide a variety of theoretical frameworks that can help the reader to understand the existence and purpose of personal objects. These interpretative positions are varied: some argue for the positive value of personal objects, and others are less optimistic.

Nearly every article in the volume contributes in some way to our first aim: providing descriptions of the experience of personal objects. For that reason, we have not provided a separate section dedicated solely toward that aim. Instead, the volume has been divided into two major sections, roughly in accordance with our second and third aims (historical and theoretical, respectively). Thus part 1, "Traditional Accounts," features articles that primarily articulate and reflect on personal objects that have appeared in various historical cultures and times. Part 2, "New Perspectives," contains articles whose primary purpose is to provide new philosophical frameworks from which to understand the experience of personal objects.

It is important to note that while some articles fit relatively easily into this artificial division, almost every article features at least some blend of these two aims. Certain articles could easily have been placed in either category; some subjective decisions had to be made in order to decide which aim (historical or theoretical) any particular chapter was most engaged with. Thus, the reader should be sure to understand that chapters in part 1 often have significant theoretical value, while chapters in part 2 are often carefully situated in cultural and historical contexts.

The chapters internal to part 1 have been arranged roughly "historically" (in a broad sense), with objects with a long tradition of personalization (natural objects, ships, religious objects, weapons) followed by more recent traditions and contexts (for example in Native American and modern American cultures). The chapters internal to part 2 begin with a set of four chapters that are more general in scope, providing broad philosophical reflections on the topic of personal objects and serving as a starting point for our theoretical perspectives. The final six chapters tackle more specific issues, with two chapters on economic themes, two chapters on aesthetic (musical) themes, and the final two chapters dealing with the ethics of human (and robot) bodies. Each chapter will begin with an editorial note to provide context on the place of the work within the overall volume—hopefully, this will help to keep the reader orientated and give a sense of how it contributes to the project as a whole.

In chapter 1, Pete A.Y. Gunter discusses the mystery that is a subregion of East Texas called the Big Thicket. If it were a swamp (like the Everglades) or a mountain chain (like the Smokies) there would be no problem. What is a plant growth community or, more inclusively, an ecosystem? Are they simply aggregates of individual plants and/or animals? Or are they, as some have argued, organisms? In summary, he is asking if an entire ecosystem can have personality.

In chapter 2, Marc M. Anderson argues that personality is the result of certain acts, vocal and visible, which transform the average human into something that is not the average—transformation *toward* something divine. He argues that the tendencies toward personality (which he enumerates) that are at work on the human level are also at work on the level of nonhuman objects, and the best example of that is seagoing ships.

In chapter 3, Martin Pehal discusses how, for the ancient Egyptians, certain objects (such as statues, mummies, etc.) could in certain contexts (temple and funerary rituals) be animated by powers or entities that would enter into or interact with them. In order to outline the context of such a worldview, he first explains the basic principles of ancient Egyptian thought as reflected in the rules governing their scriptual tradition—hieroglyphics. He then outlines the basic concepts of the *ka* and *ba*—constituent elements of "personhood" in a very broad sense as it also concerned deities. The final part of the essay is devoted to the description of the rituals that activated this transference.

In chapter 4, John August explores one way in which a special mode of cognition (the mode of cognition that judges persons as such), can transform the relation between the cognizer and the cognized so that a new horizon of possibility opens up to the cognizer. Specifically, he inquires into the development of the relationship between the Brahminical devotionalist and the divine object, that is, the divine image as embodied in some medium, such as a statue, painting, or some other depiction of the divine.

In chapter 5, Kevin Taylor focuses on the personality of Japanese objects such as *tsukumogami*. It is therefore a paper on *kami*; it is his hope that this topic will problematize those who, in his research, write "there is no personalism in Japan." He aims to demonstrate that the ways in which we treat objects as alive enrich and reorient our praxis to intensify personal experience.

In chapter 6, Alan Maisey argues that throughout history the object that has probably had the closest connection with any man has been that man's personal weapon. More than 1000 years ago in the Island of Java, a weapon known as a *keris* (or *kris*) appeared that became perhaps the ultimate expression of what a personal object can become. Maisey outlines the history of this weapon and how it became so central to Javanese culture.

In chapter 7, Carrie McLachlan discusses the idea of nonhuman persons in Cherokee traditions. She focuses her discussion on two types of Cherokee nonhuman persons who fit into two categories of person for the Cherokee: they are both this world and "sky" world persons. She examines a mid-eighteenth-century document that establishes the identity of the Cherokee "Corn Mother" as simultaneously an earth and sky being. Then she suggests that other nonhuman persons also fit this category and offers as an example the Cherokee River (Long Person, Yvwi Gunahita).

In chapter 8, Sasha L. Biro utilizes the work of Georges Bataille as a lens through which to critically examine the economy of the quilt, whereby as blanket it serves a utilitarian function as project object, but later it becomes more than just object, taking on cultural power as a personalized narrative experience. The quilt is a tangible and tactile object that also holds and transmits personal memories.

In chapter 9, the first chapter of part 2, Michael Jackson explores the existential conditions under which things *appear*, by turns, inert or vital, objects or subjects. Drawing on traditions as diverse as object relation theory and Marxism, Jackson shows what motivates humans to treat their environment as personalized. However, he argues that personalized experience should be understood as a defense against the unresponsiveness of matter in an age when our waning powers to sustain life on earth make this issue more vexed than it may have ever been before.

In chapter 10, Dwayne Tunstall investigates the phenomenological sense of constituting personal objects from the perspectives of an unapologetic idealist, Josiah Royce. Tunstall contends that there are phenomenological clues in Royce's theory and the resulting account of individuality that we can use to formulate a phenomenological account for how we constitute personal objects and, by extension, constitute our world.

In chapter 11, Jared Kemling provides a phenomenology (in the spirit of Ernst Cassirer) of the way in which personalized experience becomes intuitive (i.e., assumes spatiality, temporality, and numerality). He argues that personalized experience spatializes in a mode of "responsibility," that it temporalizes in a mode of "hope," and that it numeralizes in a mode of "community." Each of these modes has a dynamic tension between integrative and differential movements. While outlining his phenomenology, Kemling discusses several concrete examples of personal objects, including: a wedding ring, and the character of Alice from Lewis Carroll's *Alice in Wonderland*.

In chapter 12, James McLachlan delineates the similarities and differences between Levinas's and Sartre's approaches to possession and personal objects and how the relation to the object does not constitute the otherness of the face. By tracing both Sartre and Levinas's responses to Descartes, he shows the difficulty of understanding objects as fully "person" for both thinkers.

In chapter 13, Helen Grela considers whether, as a society, we might have unwittingly turned money into a person (as Marx implies) and ourselves into its corporeal embodiment. To do so, she explores how our social imaginary is based on certain flawed or inconsistent concepts that both obscure and enable such a reality. These concepts include: our reflexive beliefs that money is a naturally arising and neutral tool in economic transactions; that our economic system protects the universality of natural rights of life, liberty and property; and that our legal system supports our common understanding of the person as the bearer of these universal rights.

In chapter 14, Randall Auxier discusses how King Philip's War was the deadliest in North American history, so far as records extend. Lying at the base of this war was the collapse of the wampum economy that had been adapted to the needs of poorly supplied colonizers in Plymouth and Massachusetts Bay. This odd cultural institution of wampum fulfills political, economic, religious, artistic and even legal roles (especially as they affect rituals of war and peace). Auxier argues that wampum was "person" in a higher sense than any individual or even any single community. Unfortunately, it would not yield to the pressures of quantification that even the rudimentary Plymouth and Massachusetts Bay forms of economy required.

In chapter 15, Ralph D. Ellis discusses the uncanny personality of his piano and ties this unique instrument into a larger conversation about jazz music, hermeneutics, ambiguity, and the "focusing method" of Eugene Gendlin. He argues that his piano literally mirrors Gendlin's focusing process: in the sense that it does it in reverse.

In chapter 16, Eli Kramer discusses how, in 1870, Wilhelm Richard Wagner (1813–1883) wrote an essay to celebrate the centennial of Beethoven's birth. In this essay, Wagner made the case that music is, unlike any other object we create or are attentive to in experience, in an immediate analogical relationship with the activity of the Schopenhauerian "will" and is always enlivened. By drawing on this idea, we can not only conceive of music as in an immediate analogical relationship with our personal experience, but as perhaps the only object of cognition that is in a constant state of personal vitality. It is by that very continuous vitality that it can return us to our own personhood with deeper insight and perspective. The chapter concludes by exploring how attending to the musical object as a spiritual (existential) exercise might reconnect us to our roots in *sensus communis*, educate us on our common personhood, and play an ethical role in our lives.

In chapter 17, Laura J. Mueller investigates the link between the sublime moral *person* and personalized *objects* of the world around us. Using Kant's foundational argument on philosophical personhood and the criteria thereof (intersubjectivity and self-consciousness), she argues that multiple kinds of personality derive from the philosophical person, including object-personality and personal-personality. Cultural objects are, she argues, objects formed by intersubjectivity but without self-consciousness, thus giving them a special status of personality. She concludes by examining the role of mythic thought in this formation of personality, using a Cassireran methodology.

In chapter 18, Charles Harvey presents and reflects upon rapidly evolving developments in human-robot relations. He argues that psychological, phenomenological, and neuro-physiological evidence suggests that our new media-saturated environment is eroding the human capacity for deep and prolonged concentration, empathy, and attachment. As machines become more human-like, humans become more machine-like: objects become more personal, and persons become more objectified. This sets the stage for diminished relations between humans.

Jared Kemling
December, 2021

PART 1

TRADITIONAL ACCOUNTS

Chapter 1

Mereology

Wholes, Parts, and the Big Thicket

PETE A. Y. GUNTER

Editor's Note: In one sense, this chapter is the most contemporary of the volume's historically focused chapters: after all, it deals with a conservational movement that is still very much alive today. However, while it focuses on the Big Thicket region of Texas in particular, at a general level, the chapter raises the question of whether natural objects (plants, environmental systems, and so on) should be understood as personalized. Since the personalization of nature is, seemingly, as old as human culture itself, it seemed fitting to begin the volume with this discussion. Furthermore, Gunter provides a helpful mereological discussion of the concept of "living" organisms, which will provide a usefully broad ontological backdrop for the following chapters.

Posing a Problem

All my adult life I have been trying to save something. The really sad thing is that I don't know what it is. That is, along with many others, I have been trying to "save" a subregion of east Texas called the Big Thicket. But what is it?

If it were a swamp (like the Everglades) or a mountain chain (like the Smokies), there would be no problem. We could go to a topo map and look up the boundaries. But what is an extraordinarily diverse plant growth region? What is a plant growth community or, more inclusively, an ecosystem? Are they simply aggregates of individual plants and/or animals? Or are they, as some have argued, organisms?

Such questions are, I insist, not the mere quibbling of those most obscure generalists, the philosophers. They cut to the heart of biology and what is meant by some central biological terms. As different as philosophy and science are, I can find no absolute boundary between them. Philosophical ideas seep into the sciences; scientific ideas creep into philosophy. The following chapter pursues this foggy boundary to the bitter end.

The Thicket: A First Look

So, to continue. What is the Big Thicket, and where? Some have called it Lapland: where Louisiana laps over into Texas. It is the part of Texas that looks entirely unlike what the state is supposed to look like. Technically it is the southwestern-most extension of the Southern Evergreen Forest: Deep South. If some parts of this extension are open (sandhills, pine savannahs, prairies), most, as its name suggests, are dense and impassible (swamps, seeps, baygalls, palmetto jungles).

Besides the biological definitions of the region, there are folklore definitions. These often disagree with each other. Unsurprisingly, they also may disagree with biological definitions. If folklore on the Thicket is diffuse, scientific writings on it are sometimes hard to deal with. That is, alternative scientific definitions of the area are proposed. Attempts to define the region exhibit both strong scientific difficulties and a dramatic conflict between *mythos* and *bios*. These divergences made conservation in the area all the more difficult.

We do not know, for example, who first called the area the Big Thicket. Nor are we sure how the vague, persistent presence of the Thicket came, very early on, to be lodged in the collective consciousness of Texas and adjacent states. Somehow it was simply *there*: a remote place where, in the words of folklorist J. Frank Dobie, men went "to forget and be forgotten." The 1936 Big Thicket Biological Survey states:

> Just who first made reference to it is unknown. The Spanish Padres in visiting the Missions in the Nagcogdoches country record that between the Missions and the sea there existed a forest so thick that it was impossible to traverse it even afoot and that Indians in travelling from the Missions to the sea went by canoe as there were no trails by land.[1]

Early settlers arriving in Texas from states to the east skirted the Big Thicket on both its northern and southern borders, leaving the densely vegetated area to its own devices.

There grew up a dark mythology of a place entirely word-lost, forsaken, and threatening. Historical events reinforced this image. Just to its east, on the Louisiana side of the Sabine River, lay the Neutral Ground,[2] a many-county area belonging neither to Spain nor to the United States, a no man's land occupied by drifters, fortune seekers, escaped criminals, highwaymen, feral vice presidents, escaped slaves, and Indians. When the Neutral Ground was annexed in the 1821 by the United States, many of its inhabitants spilled over into southeast Texas. Thus, if the area started with a reputation for natural wildness and danger, a reputation for violent untrustworthy people soon was added to it. The Big Thicket now had Bad Blood.

Detour: Remarks on Mereology

Mereology is the discipline that deals with the relations of parts to wholes and between parts within wholes. It must deal with what is meant by a "whole" and, e.g., whether parts can be wholes on their own. It must also address the problem of definition. One must, if there are wholes, be able to state their essential characteristics and to single them out. Presumably, one would not be able to show that an organism is a whole unless you could say what you mean by "organism." What follows is less an application of mereology than a series of reflections on it.

Here one meets with a puzzle. There is no universally accepted definition of "life" or "living thing." There is a commonsense working definition, however. A living thing must be able to both reproduce and contain a complex, integrated metabolism. But this definition consists of two definitions, not one, and that in any case the second component might be stated differently, probably to include structure. This puzzle leads to a second.

The term "life" is taken here as an example of what we call intension. The intension of a term is its definition or meaning. Extension by contrast refers to the individual entities covered by the intension. Particular instances of the term rectangular might include tables, envelopes, and calling cards. The problem is that, in the case of "life," we have a term that covers, by extension, all and only organisms. Anything not an organism cannot be termed "living." Anything not living cannot be termed an organism. The problem then arises: If we cannot define life, then how can we single out entities called organisms? If we cannot define "life," to take the matter a step further, how can we define organism: which is the fundamental issue dealt with in this chapter.

Perhaps an organism is simply a living cell or a multicellular entity. But there is the recent discovery of viruses carrying genetic elements, viruses which are more complex than the simplest living cells.[3] It can be argued that such viruses are living things, even if they cannot reproduce outside of a host organism. If so, one cannot define organisms simply by pointing at a cell.

So what is an organism? What are its wholes and parts?

Forests as Wholes

Here are some examples, involving not unicellular organisms or viruses but forests. In the last two decades, it has been discovered that the trees in the forest are profoundly and systematically connected at the roots.

In Utah there is a grove of quaking aspen (*Populus tremuloides*) whose roots literally grow together to make one root. The roots of one tree have grown into the roots of the next, and that root into the next, and so on, indefinitely. Then if one aspen sends out a message through its roots asking for water and/or nutrients, other trees will send the raw materials back through their roots in reply. When the generous sender trees signal for help, the favor is returned. Water or nutrients are shifted to the tree in need. The Utah forest totals 108 acres.[4] It is also claimed to be 80,000 years old and to weigh 6000 metric tons. The genes in each tree are identical.

Is it, therefore, a 108-acre organism? Many biologists insist that it is.

Most tree species do not intergrow their roots. The really striking recent discovery is that mycelial fungi do the job for them. These fungi interconnect adjacent tree root systems, growing *into* the tips of one set of tree roots and then into the tips of *other* nearby roots, linking not just one tree but many. These fungi explore the forest, horizontally and vertically, effectively enlarging the rootweb area which assists the trees.[5]

If the roots of the forest trees are part of a (fungal) network that, literally, connects one root system to another through a conduit, a conduit through which water and nutrients can be transported, then can we say that, as claimed in the case of the aspen forest, we are dealing here too with a single forest organism?

Finally, in India, there is a *Thimmana marimanu*, a banyan tree, which sprouts some four hundred tap roots, each of which grows up as a tree. The tree, famous in India as a terminus of pilgrimage, covers five acres.[6] Can we deny that *this* is an organism?

I would like to add two more examples that show how widespread networking is in nature. These involve not trees but fungi. In the upper peninsula of Michigan, a fungus (*Armillaris bulbosa*) covers around thirty acres and has been hailed as the world's largest organism.[7] In Switzerland, a honey fungus covers nearly 120 acres and is approximately one thousand years old.[8] Three other examples of such multiple, strongly interrelated systems are massive fungal mats in Oregon, a system of ancient creosote bushes, and *Posidonia oceanica*, a clonal marine plant in the Mediterranean Sea.[9] I have no doubt that innumerable other such plant growth communities will be found as people come to the realization that such things actually exist.

I cannot resist adding another significant discovery, reported by the biologist Susan Simard. The first realization of mycelial webs can link tree root systems happened in the Pacific Northwest around 1998 in an effort to explain "the remarkable fertility of these forests." Shortly after, something else was discovered. The extirpation of paper birches there was, surprisingly, followed by a general decline in the health and productivity of the Douglas fir. Far from being a useless and eliminable species, the birches turned out to be busy "feeding the soil and helping their coniferous neighbors."[10] That is—a point that has more than a little significance in the South where pine monoculture has increasingly replaced the diverse native forest[11]—it might lead to the realization that pines grow better along with other tree species rather than they do growing alone, in a biological desert.[12]

One is thus confronted with (1) One tree (in India) that has "branched out" to create new trunks, each a tree; (2) a forest, probably generated from a single tree, with each new tree clearly a distinct organism but interconnected by the roots; and (3) forests whose roots are conjoined by microrizal fungi, a fungal "pipeline," which creates a unity of information, water, and nutrients among distinct trees, some of different species.

These examples ground a classical "slippery slope" argument. The banyan tree is clearly an organism. It is a tree, and any tree is, by general agreement, an organism. But, next, we have a forest (the aspen forest) also generated originally by one tree, all of whose outposts are strongly connected to the original organism and bound to each other by interconnected roots. It is not difficult to describe this as an organism, though it does stretch our usual conceptual schemes. But if this is an organism then how can we fail to treat forest trees decisively linked by microrizal fungi, which exchange information, water, and nutrients in exactly the same way, as organisms? If we accept the first example as an organism, don't we have to accept the second and then the third?

But if we accept the third, then perhaps we should extend the notion of organism to include, e.g., plant growth communities, ecosystems, or even more.

Some Philosophical Reflections

The problem of the whole and its parts is a particular instance of what Samuel Taylor Coleridge called the "world-knot": the problem of the one and the many.

Those familiar with the travails of philosophy will recognize that the knot to which Coleridge referred is a Gordian knot: a knot so complex that, to date, no one has satisfactorily been able to untie it.

Nonetheless, inescapably, a philosopher will make the try.

I would like to begin by sketching a contrast between philosophers who give us the One (and nothing but the one) and those who give us an irreducible Many. I will presume that for the latter the One is an immense Whole, while the many constitute many parts (which, however, may never constitute wholes).

On the side of the Whole, we have Parmenides, Spinoza, Hegel, and (to bring us up to the twentieth century) F. H. Bradley. On the side of real, irreducible plurality we have Democritus, Newton, and Leibniz.

This set of oppositions contrasts those who believe there is nothing but one whole with those who hold there are nothing but (many) parts. What fascinates me is not only the dramatic opposition between the two but the way in which both—seemingly so different in their thinking—agree absolutely on the fundamental characteristics they ascribe to their wholes and/or parts.

That is, both agree that any true whole or part (1) can neither be added to nor subtracted from (2), cannot be changed by its relations to anything else if there is anything else, (3) is absolutely unchanging and unchangeable, (4) is perfectly whole, and (5) is perfectly what it is. A whole must be perfectly a whole, or it is nothing. The same with parts.

This way of thinking is as old as the Greeks, but it did not end with them. It is still with us, and I believe, gets in our way when we try to think about organisms, cells, life, and plant growth communities. And atoms, and subatomic "particles."

What is a "thing"? What is a "whole"? Is it possible that there are degrees of wholeness? Is it possible that a thing can be a whole without being perfectly or timelessly a whole?

I have always been fascinated by F. H. Bradley's *Appearance and Reality*.[13] To cut short what could be a very long discussion, it is clear to me that in this book Bradley provides the case *par excellence* of a whole (the Absolute, or Absolute Mind) that ablates its parts: does away with them, making them at best aspects of itself. The same can be said of Spinoza and of Hegel (though this will doubtless be disputed). For Spinoza all particular entities, including human beings, are finite modes of an infinite substance. One notes that finite and infinite are incommensurable.

Exactly the same holds for the atoms of Democritus, the mass particles of Newton, and the monads of Leibniz. Each is an isolated island that cannot be influenced by any other. Each is absolutely identical with itself, so much so that any whole of which they are parts could not be a whole. It would only appear to be.

So traditionally, when we have looked for wholes, we have looked for absolutes. But as I hope the forest examples cited above illustrate, it is not at all clear that in biology or ecology there is any such thing.

Rather, we keep running into, not absolutes, but matters of degree. Is an aspen forest an organism? But root interconnectivity is a loose form of organization compared to the dynamic interdependencies of, say, a nucleated cell.

Hence, should our inability to find the glassy essence of "life" or of "organism" be conceived as defeating or simply as the flip side of the real limits of our thought, limits that, if we understand them, can help us, not hinder us in our thinking.

Kinds of Organisms

Here we introduce a distinction, which I derive from the thought of Alfred North Whitehead between colonial organisms and monarchical organisms.[14] A colonial organism has no central command post. Its behavior, if we can call it that, is broadly distributed and consists largely in growth. A monarchical organism, by contrast, can, consistently with its central nervous system, centrally control its behavior. Examples: birds, mammals, reptiles.

Perhaps the reader guesses where this is heading. The notion of a colonial animal approximates that of a plant growth community. It contains—as we are beginning to see more clearly—persistent coordination between the species that make it up, to the extent that we can now conceive of it as one entity. Yet we can find no centralized behavior in such an entity. Mobility in space is largely a matter of seed dispersal or growth at the apical meristem: the tips of limbs. Animals move around and direct their behavior as a whole.

On the other hand, it is a bit strange to lump such a plant growth community together with trees, as organisms. A tree has a far more singular location than a plant growth community, has greater genetic unity, has a far more single pattern of existence.

I propose, to resolve this problem, that we should distinguish two sorts of colonial organisms. One (consisting of trees, shrubs, vines, etc.) to be called *simple locus* organisms, the other (consisting of plant growth communities, ecosystems, even plant growth regions) to be called *multiple locus* organisms. For the great majority of biologists, this would be to extend the concept of organism beyond its present boundaries. Whitehead, incidentally wanted to extend the notion of organism to include even molecules, atoms, and subatomic entities. For Whitehead, every actual entity in nature is an organism.

The fundamental image behind the idea of multiple-loci organisms is for me that of a tissue. The sort of tissue (out of the four different sorts of tissues)[15] that best illustrates such organisms is epithelial tissue (for example, skin).[16] The notion of "tissue" was introduced into physiology by the French scientist Bichat in 1801.[17] It is interesting that the word "tissue" in French is intimately connected to the notions of cloth and weaving. Thus, a cloth with open weave in French is *tissue lâche*, while a closely woven cloth is *tissue serré*. The word "tissue" for Bichat thus is derived from weaving: The French for "weaving" is *tissage*. It is interesting that, as in forest systems, cells in tissues contain junctions make communication possible between adjacent cells.

A single-locus colonial organism has a unified location with tightly organized structure. A multiple-loci colonial organism has a plural location with a more diffuse, less "architectural" structure. Like epithelial tissues or loosely woven cloth, its organization sprawls by its very nature. Rather than being centered in one place, it reaches out to cover many places. Its existence will also be a matter of the longer time periods required to pass information or raw materials from one *locus* to another.

It is helpful in this context to consider an ordinary organism, the lichen. These "patches" are found on rock outcrops, tree trunks, and branches from the tropics to the subarctic. They consist of two unicellular organisms: a fungus and a chlorophyll-bearing plant. The fungus shelters the plant, and the plant supplies the fungus with nutrients. This is an example of symbiosis or mutualism. But the mutualism of the yucca moth and the yucca plant—without which neither survives—is intermittent, involving simply a nutrition-pollination tradeoff. The mutualism of the lichen however involves a life-long very close physical relationship between fungus and algae. Hence biologists term lichens organisms.

But if we can call a lichen an organism, then it is all the more plausible to extend the term to include similar plant communities, including forests. An analogous loosely woven fabric that we find in lichens we now discover to exists in forests.

The reader will perhaps begin to suspect that this article presents a broader preoccupation than simply the question of how many biological entities can be called organisms. The ultimate question approached here is more broadly, what sorts of things can we call real? Or (though it is somewhat misleading) what sorts of "things" are we willing to call *things*? I believe, as the examples of Spinoza and Newton and Leibniz show, that we approach this question with a prejudice: we conceive a real *thing* to be perfectly one, to be simply located, and I think, that we want things to be such that, at least in principle, we could grasp and manipulate it them.

But the cell, and the tree only exist in a context to which they are significantly interrelated, on which they depend, and to which they contribute. To conceive them with no intrinsic relations to their environs is to fail to see them for what they are: relational existences, but no less real for that. It is also to inherently fail to see, to take into account and explore, any number of important facts which help explain them. It is, in my opinion, to violate Peirce's maxim: Never Block Research. What I am talking about is in its broadest reaches, metaphysical. But in its particular applications, it is scientific.

I find myself unexpectedly able to appreciate more fully William James's extended criticism of F. H. Bradley's idealist monism.[18] Why, James repeatedly objected, in order to think correctly about the world, do I have to end in a unitary, unchanging, closed Absolute? The consecutive relations between things and the way that they hang together without attaining perfection surely provide a sufficiently realistic approach to the real. James, in formulating his pluralism, held that there are many degrees of unity in the world that both science and common experience reveal to us. I think he would have liked the idea of a multiple-locus colonial organism.

The Big Thicket: A Second Look

First, something more needs to be said about attempts to define and locate the Big Thicket. In the years in which environmentalists tried to save the sprawling forest,[19] any counter-claims they made on its behalf were immediately countered by the lumber companies with the claim that the "Thicket" was "mere folklore" or worse, "a mere state of mind." This was a persuasive argument, precisely because conservationists had a hard time responding to it. As mentioned above, there had been a Big Thicket Biological Survey in the 1930's,[20] but its proposed locations for the region were exaggerated. Not till the late 1960s was there a well-founded floristic study of the area. Claude McLeod's *The Big Thicket of East Texas*[21] describes a single "matrix vegetation" stretching through the entire Big Thicket and defining it: in its upper region, loblolly pine, southern magnolia, and beech; in its lower part, loblolly pine, southern magnolia, and swamp chestnut oak.

It follows form this that the loblolly pine and the southern magnolia, connected at the roots by microrhizal fungi, and hence constitute a single organism, make up an organism is 105 miles long (east-west), 60 miles wide at the widest (north-south), and covers 1,854,000 acres. I hope no one will ever try to calculate its weight in metric tons.

I add a note here that strengthens the case for the existence of the Big Thicket (though not necessarily for its being an organism). That is, it has been possible to collect facsimiles of all the maps that have over the years been proposed to demarcate the region. Some of these are provided by backwoodsmen, some by folklorists, some by industrial ecologists, some by floristic ecologists, and some by biologists *per se*. Those by backwoodsmen tended to be localized depicting only the area with which they were familiar. Those backwoodsmen who had traveled widely in the Thicket, however, escaped this sort of provincialism and described boundaries for the Thicket that approximated those of the biological community. The point is this: when all of the maps proposed for the region are superimposed,[22] *they cover the same area*: a roughly pie-shaped wedge that I have mentioned beginning near Conroe, Texas, on I45 and gradually broadening as it sprawls eastwards towards the Louisiana border.

This has two results. As noted, it strengthens the case for the existence and extent of the Big Thicket. It also heals the gap between *bios* and *mythos* that made conservation so difficult originally. A knowledgeable backwoodsman and a trained environmental biologist are not necessarily in conflict. Their maps converge on the same area.

I want to point out here that the struggle to save the Thicket has had a positive outcome, namely the creation in 1984 of the Big Thicket National Preserve. The result of an exhausting ten-year campaign, the national preserve was the first example of such a preserve in the history of the National Park Service. It marks a shift from the aesthetic and religious values of prior American conservation to the effort to conserve biology *per se*. Equally, its clustering of biological sanctuaries along stream corridors (creeks, rivers, bayous) added a new approach to the Park Service's arsenal of approaches to the environment.

Originally consisting of 84,550 acres, it has since been enlarged to over 105, 000 acres, along with an additional 20,500 acres of related wilderness areas.[23] These acres cover a profound richness in plant growth communities, plant and animal species, and topographies. They are—since we continue to add to them—one of America's finest works in process.

Concluding Quasi-Scientific Conclusions

Much more can be said about any of the topics explored in this brief chapter. I would like here, in concluding, to deal with two of these in greater detail: the question of whether some sort of distinction needs to be made between two or more types of monarchical organisms, and the very broad question of how our "intuitions" of the forest as having a life and a unity of its own (a personality? moods?) can relate to what we know about forests. Treatment of the first of these will be brief, leading to an open question. Treatment of the second will be longer: in an attempt to frame questions that nonetheless will retain a quaint aura of vagueness.

One problem that I have not dealt with above is that of what are sometimes called superorganisms. What, for example, would Whitehead make of a beehive or a termite mound: entities often called superorganisms. He nowhere tells us. This is unfortunate for on his terms a bee is a regnant or monarchical organism that lives only in what he would have been inclined to call a colonial organism: it is part of the bee colony and cannot live without it. Perhaps he would have called a beehive a hybrid monarchical/colonial organism: but oddly, with the colonial organism having the last word.

Whitehead's distinction between monarchical and colonial organisms is nowhere fully developed. He suggests that lower animals are not (doubtless because their nervous systems are not fully developed) monarchical but colonial. This would certainly fit sponges and coral reefs. To what extent it fits unicellular organisms, however, is a question he never considered. Some unicellular organisms simply perform photosynthesis. Others, however, are carnivorous. In a centered, monarchical way, they move and predate, hunt and gather. Unicellular organisms constitute by far the majority of the planet's biomass. Whitehead's distinction between kinds of organisms does not apply to them.

This chapter begins with the question of what one has saved when one has saved a forest or other plant growth community. The bulk of the chapter is focused on showing that one has protected something that is far more interrelated and independent than we have generally believed. In communicating and sustaining each other, forest species act as if they had signed some kind of Lockean social contract, willing to give up some of their own substance for others, on the assumption that the others will do the same. Root talk demonstrates this communal character dramatically. But it only adds to what we already know about the many supportive relationships that help secure the forest's continued existence. Without the forest, its understory would vanish. Without the soils that the forest produces, the next stage in ecological succession could not occur.

When I enter a forest, I have a strong sense of the forest as such. I am confronted, then enveloped, by something that presents itself as real, even substantial. This sense of the "wholeness" refuses to leave. Indeed, the more I explore the woods, the more time I spend there, the more pronounced is the sense of the forest as such. I cannot put my finger on precisely what that is, this *as such*. You cannot produce or even describe a substantive *it*, a forestrial glassy essence, that I am chasing a metaphysical will-of-the-wisp. But for there to be something there surely what the forest provides is sufficient: an interconnected, vast, interdependent life. Enough unity to constitute an entity without its being an "atom," enough diversity to enable vitality.

One virtue of looking at the issue this way—of insisting that an interactive real is no less real for its not being a singly located "thing"—is that it brings our intuitive sense of the world closer to our scientific knowledge of it. Sensibility and scientific insight on this view approximate each other. What the biologist can now tell me about the forest makes all the more plausible my feeling of the forest as a persisting presence not even conceivable as an aggregate, in no way reducible to an aggregate of individual trees. The poet's or the photographer's efforts to capture the forest's sort of wholeness are not merely subjective. I once heard Robert Frost reply to a reporter who said that poetry is only so much emotion, that poetry gets life by the throat. On the view presented in this lecture, the poet too is literally in the interaction man-nature, and the more seriously he or she attempts to participate in the given, the more real and the more effective is the result?

So that if the reader and this writer were kayaking in the Big Thicket Preserve, say, down the winding world-lost shadows of Pine Island Bayou, our sense of being cut off from the patchwork suburbs and cutover pinelands on the "outside" and existing within a sprawling, seeming endless reality—a different reality but still real—would not be some merely emotional experience but a real encounter of one sort of creature with yet another, slower, more decentered organism. Its slow, primitive rhythms would penetrate us, as we participate in them, in the complaint of a great blue heron breaking with dark tea water, and in the constant drumbeat of the insects.

I think it is possible to show that a forest has states similar to moods, that it confronts us with what the French call "presence," and what for lack of a better word I would call "personality." In making this claim, I will struggle to escape anthropomorphism. The forest is not a big human being, even a ghostly one. But its life is in some respects similar to our own.

A mood is a sustained emotional state. In people, these are widely diverse: moods of depression, of expectation, or of contentment are man's common lot. Would it be stretching things too far to suggest that a forest in the spring embodies a quickening of tempos, a future-oriented, renewed vitality analogous to our own rebirths of lived pleasure and lived intensity? If so, the human rebound from winter's suspended animation and the forest's recovery from winter's stasis would be taken as objectively similar. The sustained, constant vitality of a forest in summer could be taken as embodying a kind of contentment.[24] The reader will doubtless notice the shift here from spatial relatedness to an emphasis on temporality. The shift is intended. Communication between root networks is "timed" to take advantage of the needs and capacities of trees. But growth, development, decay, and procreation in the forest are rhythmic and essential. In an editorial in *Science* magazine, Denis Duboule insists:

> Animal development is in fact nothing but time. From the cell cycle to the beating of the heart, our own lives are composed of a multitude of microscopic and molecular oscillations. For developmental biology, the study of causal relationships implies the examination of two time

points: inducing the cause and looking at the effect. We are generally ignorant of the temporal rules governing this transformation.[25]

As for what I have called "personality," it is easy to turn for examples to the Big Thicket Preserve, which was created so as to conserve all the forest types of southeast Texas. One can easily trek there from a cypress swamp to a long-leaf-pine savannah, from the savannah to a pine-magnolia forest and assuming that one had a feeling, not only for its visual appearance but for the massive persistent rhythms of birth, development, growth and senescence which are its fundamental character, one will find three different vital signatures, forms of life "personalities"—for lack of a better term. A prolonged and thoughtful acquaintance with them—Thoreau's painstaking study of the forests around Concord provide a nice example—will lead to acquaintance with their fundamental life. A visual forest is frozen music. The living music is what keeps it alive—and renders it "personal."

The notion of "presence" follows from those of mood and personality. It suggests something like a profound personal awareness, hard to "unpack," that is, to verbalize. I think of Martin Buber's I-Thou relationship, Whitehead's primitive prehensive act, Bergson's intuition. None of these quite fit. Perhaps one's encounter with a forest is best filed under William James's radical empiricism, a view of experience that excludes nothing, vague or distinct. It is the sense of a vast, slow life, a dull ceaseless existence, persistently renewing itself and if conscious, conscious somewhere on the borders of unconsciousness.

By treating only the overstory of the forest and worse, only the dominant species (like the pines and magnolias that make up the Thicket's matrix vegetation) I am guilty of the same offence and would commit by writing about a full symphony and only mentioning parts of the percussion section or the bassoons. The forest, as a plant growth community, includes both the understory and the overstory (the smaller trees other plants that live in the overstory shade).[26] Add the myriad animal species that make the plant growth community and ecosystem and one adds innumerable temporalities to the orchestra, from the biological rhythms of birth, persistence, and death to the cries of birds, the howling of coyotes, the scuffing of mice.

It is a full orchestra indeed that one encounters in the deep woods. If I am right, our sense of sheer encounter, of participating in a life and a complex of lives other than our own, is not a subjective illusion but a grounded fact: though not a fact as obvious as a meter reading of a microscope slide.

To conclude: the sadness mentioned at the beginning of this article has vanished. For it is clear what those of us who struggled so long to "save" the Big Thicket had indeed saved something real. We had saved a life.

Notes

1. H. B. Parks and V. L. Cory, *Biological Survey of the East Texas Big Thicket Area* (Huntsville: Sam Houston State Teachers College, 1936), 3.

2. Cf. Francis E. Abernethy, "Big Thicket" in *Handbook of Texas, Online Version*. https://www.tshaonline.org/handbook/entries/big-thicket. Roughly thirty miles wide and one hundred miles north to south (from the Gulf of Mexico to the place where the Sabine River ceases to be a border between Louisiana and Texas and passes into Texas *per se*), it included eleven Louisiana parishes. So lawless was this area and so well organized were its criminal elements that in 1810 and 1812 joint Spanish and American military operations had to be mounted against it.

3. Elizabeth Pennisi, "Ever-bigger Viruses Shake the Tree of Life," *Science* 341 (July 19, 2013): 226–227; Mitch Leslie, "Cell-Like Giant Viruses Found," *Science* 356, no. 6143 (April 7, 2017): 15–16; Sam Wong, "Giant Virus May Just Be a Small-Time Crook," *New Scientist* 3121 (April 15, 2017): 12.

4. "Pando," *Wikipedia The Free Encyclopedia* (accessed May 1, 2017). https://en.wikipedia.org/wiki/Pando_(tree); Michael C. Grant, "The Trembling Giant," *Discover Magazine* (October 1, 1993).

5. Marcel G. A. van der Heijden, "Underground Networking: Fungal Networks Transfer Carbon between Forest Trees," *Science* 352, no. 6283 (April 15, 2016): 290–91; Cf. Tamir Klein et al., "Belowground Carbon Trade among Tall Trees in a Temperate Forest," *Science* 352, no. 6283 (April 15, 2016): 342–44; for a best seller devoted to this topic, see Peter Wohlleben, *The Hidden Life of Trees* (Vancouver-Berkeley: Greystone Books, 2015), 271.

6. Ben Crair, "The Fig and the Wasp," *Smithsonian* 48, no. 1 (April, 2017): 64–69.

7. M. L. Smith, J. N. Brun, and J. B. Anderson, "The Fungus *Armillaria bulbosa* Is among the Largest and Oldest Living Animals," *Nature* 356, no. 6368 (1992), 428–31; cf. New York Times, December 21, 1992.

8. Peter Wohlleben, *The Hidden Life of Trees*, 50.

9. "Posidonia Oceanica," *Wikipedia, The Free Encyclopedia* (accessed May 1, 2017). https://en.wikipedia.org/wiki/Posidonia_oceanica. This article is not paginated.

10. Susan Simard, "Note From a Forest Scientist," in *The Hidden Life of Trees*, Peter Wohlleben (Vancouver, Berkeley: Greystone Books, 2015), 247–50.

11. The massive intrusions of pine plantations into Southeast Texas was the reason for the second Big Thicket conservation movement, which began in the 1960s. C.f. Pete A. Y. Gunter, *The Big Thicket: A Challenge for Conservation* (Austin: Jenkins, 1972).

12. Ned Fritz, *Clearcutting: A Crime against Nature* (Austin, Texas: Eakin Press, 1989), 124.

13. F. H. Bradley, *Appearance and Reality*, 2nd ed (Oxford: Oxford Press, 1963), 578.

14. I have not found a passage in which Whitehead introduces the distinction in exactly these terms. The distinction, however, correctly conveys the terms that Whitehead opposes between "regnant" and "subordinate," "dominant" and "subservient," "monarchical" and "democratic." I prefer the term "colonial" to the term "democratic" because it avoids highly misleading political connotations. Cf. Alfred North Whitehead, *Modes of Thought*

(New York: Capricorn Books, 1938), 33–39; Alfred North Whitehead, *Process and Reality* (New York: The Free Press, 1978), 102, 107–109.

15. These are nerve, muscle, connective, and epithelial.

16. Epithelial tissues also include those which serve as covering for various organ systems within the body besides serving as the covering of the body *per se*.

17. Marie F. X. Bichat, *Traité des membranes* (Paris: Meguignon-Marvis, 1816), 328.

18. T.L.S. Sprigge, *James and Bradley: American Truth and British Reality* (Chicago and La Salle: Open Court, 1993), 648.

19. There had been more than one such effort. Cf. Pete A.Y. Gunter, "R. E. Jackson and the Early Big Thicket Conservation Movement," *East Texas Historical Journal* 37, no. 2 (1999), 1–24.

20. H. B. Parks and V. L. Cory, *The Fauna and Flora of the Big Thicket Area* (Texas Agricultural Experiment Station, 1936), 51.

21. Claude A. McLeod, *The Big Thicket of East Texas: Its History, Location and Description* (Huntsville, Texas: Sam Houston Press, 1967), 33.

22. Cf. Pete A.Y. Gunter, *Finding The Big Thicket: A Cartographic Approach* (Create Space: 2015).

23. These include Village Creek State Park (4,000) acres; a 12,000-acre National Heritage Site, and a 4,500-acre wilderness area on Village Creek owned by Nature Conservancy. Effectively the Preserve is now half again as large now as when it was originally created.

24. The analogous circadian rhythms of a forest and of human beings make possible similar comparisons, and participations.

25. Denis Duboule, "Editorial: Time for Chronomics?" *Science* 301, no. 5631 (July 18, 2003): 277.

26. And for that matter, the plants that live in the forest's soils.

Bibliography

Abernethy, Francis E. "Big Thicket," *Handbook of Texas, Online Version*. https://www.tshaonline.org/handbook/entries/big-thicket.

Bichat, Marie F.X. *Traité des membranes*. Paris: Meguignon-Marvis, 1816.

Bradley F. H. *Appearance and Reality*. 2nd ed. Oxford: Oxford Press, 1963.

Crair, Ben. "The Fig and the Wasp." *Smithsonian* 48, no. 1 (April, 2017): 64–69.

Duboule, Denis. "Editorial: Time for Chronomics?" *Science* 301, no. 5631 (July 18, 2003): 277.

Fritz, Ned. *Clearcutting: A Crime against Nature*. Austin, Texas: Eakin Press, 1989.

Grant, Michael C. "The Trembling Giant." *Discover Magazine*. October 1, 1993.

Gunter, Pete A.Y. *The Big Thicket: A Challenge for Conservation*. Austin: Jenkins, 1972.

———. *Finding the Big Thicket: A Cartographic Approach*. Create Space: 2015.

———. "R. E. Jackson and the Early Big Thicket Conservation Movement." *East Texas Historical Journal* 37, no. 2, 1999, 1–24.

Klein, Tamir et al. "Belowground Carbon Trade among Tall Trees in a Temperate Forest." *Science* 352, no. 6283 (April 15, 2016): 342–44.

Leslie, Mitch. "Cell-like Giant Viruses Found." *Science* 356, no. 6333 (April 7, 2017): 15–16.
McLeod, Claude A. *The Big Thicket of East Texas: Its History, Location and Description*. Huntsville, Texas: Sam Houston Press, 1967.
New York Times. December 21, 1992.
"Pando." *Wikipedia: The Free Encyclopedia*. May 1, 2017. https://en.wikipedia.org/wiki/Pando_(tree).
Parks, H. B., and V. L. Cory. *Biological Survey of the East Texas Big Thicket Area*. Huntsville: Sam Houston State Teachers College, 1936.
———. *The Fauna and Flora of the Big Thicket Area*. Texas Agricultural Experiment Station, 1936, 51.
Pennisi, Elizabeth. "Ever-Bigger Viruses Shake the Tree of Life." *Science* 341, no. 6143 (July 19, 2013): 226–227.
"Posidonia Oceanica." *Wikipedia: The Free Encyclopedia*. May 1, 2017. https://en.wikipedia.org/wiki/Posidonia_oceanica.
Simard, Susan. "Note from a Forest Scientist." In *The Hidden Life of Trees*. Peter Wohlleben. Vancouver, Berkeley: Greystone Books, 2015.
Smith, M. L., J. N. Brun, and J. B. Anderson. "The Fungus *Armillaria bulbosa* Is among the Largest and Oldest Living Animals." *Nature* 356, no. 6368 (1992): 428–431.
Sprigge, T. L. S. *James and Bradley: American Truth and British Reality*. Chicago and La Salle: Open Court, 1993.
Van der Heijden, Marcel G. A. "Underground Networking: Fungal Networks Transfer Carbon Between Forest Trees." *Science* 352, no. 6283 (April 15, 2016): 290–91.
Whitehead, Alfred North Whitehead. *Modes of Thought*. New York: Capricorn Books, 1938.
———. *Process and Reality*. New York: The Free Press, 1978.
Wohlleben, Peter. *The Hidden Life of Trees*. Vancouver, Berkeley: Greystone Books, 2015.
Wong, Sam. "Giant Virus May Just Be a Small-Time Crook." *New Scientist* 3121 (April 15, 2017): 12.

Chapter 2

Personality in Seagoing Ships

MARC M. ANDERSON

Editor's Note: Anderson's chapter transitions from the broad ontology found in the previous chapter by providing an etymology of the term "person" and then giving a multifaceted analysis of what he calls "personalizing tendencies." This theoretical section is then followed by a thorough demonstration of how his analysis can be applied to the concept of a sailing ship. While this chapter could easily have been placed in the more theory-focused section of the book, I have chosen to place it here because it addresses another very ancient class of personalized objects: those relating to movement and travel. It is telling that ships (and trains, planes, and so on) are often, still to this day, given personal names—with many people even naming their cars. Anderson provides an interesting theory as to why such objects are so often personalized. While it is debatable whether ships have been personalized for longer than some of the objects discussed in later chapters (Anderson asserts a 9000-year history), I believe this chapter works well in conjunction with chapter 1: moving from humanities' awe at the natural world, and into our early attempts to harness nature.

"Person" has an interesting origin. It can be traced back through Old French to the Latin *persona*, meaning mask or character, from which our modern use of the word "persona." Somewhere along it branched out in Old French to culminate in the modern word "parson"—a clergyman—as well. But what does "person" have to do with "parson"?

"Persona" invokes a public image or mask. We tend to think of masks as hiding the face, as helping someone blend in. Think of the contemporary Anonymous masks used these days at mass protests. This is a contemporary innovation, however. Up until recently, perhaps two hundred years ago, masks appear to have been used to emphasize rather than to disguise.

Masks go with actors, in ancient Greece, in European theater, and still in Chinese opera. A glance at ancient Greek masks shows the outlandish exaggerated caricatures the Greeks favored. The bad guy mask looked like a complete madman, the good guy was stern and kingly, and the scared woman was terrified. In taking on a certain physical appearance and speaking, the actor became what he was not.

"Parson" perhaps branched from this trend. Masks have been used to represent the god in human rituals perhaps longer than acting as such, in its secular sense. The first act may have been for a shaman to represent a god, to look like and to speak the words of the god. A clergyman in medieval Europe gave up the facial mask of the god, but he took on other vestments that represented the god. And he spoke—in some cases did nothing but speak—week after week, the word of the god. So he became a *personality* in the village.

From this, one can begin to get a sense of what person and thus personality entail. As a working definition, personality is the result of certain acts, vocal and visible, which transform the average human into something which is not the average. If my supposed connection of person and parson is any guide, that transformation is *toward* something divine.

What kind of acts? This is the question that concerns me here, rather than the final character of divinity that is taken on. We do well to look to *actors* first, to attempt an answer.

Actors often portray a "personality," in one of our contemporary senses of the term. Our fascination with personalities is ancient. In Shakespeare's plays, you have actors who display everyday people, e.g., Romeo and Juliet, but in such plays, the people are often less important than the circumstances. When Shakespeare concentrates on circumstances, he uses types: Falstaff, Shylock, Romeo, and so on. More interesting to him though are personalities: Henry V, Caesar, Macbeth, Cleopatra, Brutus. When personalities are involved, his plays revolve around them.

So a personality can be created by an actor. Yet if it can be created by an actor, it can no doubt be created by a nonactor. In fact, it is so created constantly by a great many nonactors among us, the difference with the actor proper being that the latter reverts to a blank slate *qua* actor—even this is sometimes difficult—in order to take on a new personality as the job requires.

We are all acting a part in the play of our lives, so to speak. Some are doing it more successfully than others. They become the personalities of human history. They reach toward the divine.

This does not mean that every person gains personality solely by her own act; far from it. The environment of such personalities matters and gives active impulses to the center of action, which develops the personality.

Moreover, the personality becomes a personality *relative* to his or her environment. A professor may be the personality within a lecture hall setting, but place him or her among other professors at a conference, and *that degree* of personality is relatively lost.

Likewise, a Hollywood star is a personality on an average city street, but that quality fades a bit when surrounded by the glamour of Oscar night, where relative blandness of actors among their own kind is sometimes painful to watch.

Certain tendencies are thus at work, relative to act and environment. If we can uncover them in their relation to the human object, we may come to a valuable insight regarding the nonhuman object. To that end, the opposite of human personality, human materiality, also deserves reflection.

When we pass to material objects, the plot thickens, literally. The quality of materiality is a certain "deadness," relative to the life of act as we know it. The dead human body for example has reverted to materiality, lost the living action that drives it, that makes it personal. If you doubt this, look at old or new pictures—if you can stomach it—of mass killings or mass graves. Here the human body is reduced to extreme materiality. Parts blend together as a relatively immovable mass.

A lesser degree of that materiality can be felt in any stifling crowd though, on a busy city street for example or a subway system entrance. Sheer numbers of people, relatively undistinguished, moving in relative unison, bear a weight, an undeniable mass, which can be felt[1] and which is repellent in a way that the "virgin" materiality of say piled earth, is not because it has never been *known* to us as being active.

Phrases such as "unwashed masses" strike a chord because they draw out what is felt in the presence of humanity as a relative *reversion* to the merely material, namely, that the unwashed are dirty and that dirtiness is akin to dirt, which is in turn a mere accumulation of material in quantity through the relative loss of action, which is accumulation.

Dirt, which has only ever been dirt—think of the alternative word, "soil"—or which is the *outcome* of activity, is less guilty of sin than dirt in its other sense which is the product of cessation of act, e.g., a house filled with dust balls. It has a certain value out of act, the value of "a honest day's work," for example.

Dirt by mere accumulation, by settling, the *devaluating* tendency, is another thing. It is the horror of reversion from act to inaction, which repels us, of active object reverting to mere material, just as conversely good soil holds the promise of exceptional growth for plants.

Materiality is a sort of "sedimentation" of experience brought about by a relative cessation of action. In human terms, Everyman produces this materiality insofar as he remains a mere number; he produces human materiality in its unpleasant aspect, insofar as he tends toward mere mass. Cities, for all their teaming activity, produce "dirt," both figuratively and literally: garbage dumps, uncleaned public bathrooms, cigarette butts and chewing gum at the bus stop, and on and on, through the averaging out of that activity into similar types tending to mere quantity.

Yet "flowers" grow out of this human mass. Tendencies of act creative of personality escape this materiality, though always in a relative manner. Take some of the great personalities in history—Lincoln, Churchill, Einstein—and try to tease out what made them so. The main tendencies are clear enough. They can be outlined, in a not exclusive manner, under certain headings. Each of the tendencies cooperates with the others.

I will outline them. I will then consider whether they apply to nonhuman objects as well. My suggestion will be that the tendencies that are at work on the human level are also at work on the level of nonhuman objects. Certain kinds of objects lack personality because these tendencies are not at work in them. Others take on relatively high degrees of personality through these tendencies, and the best example of them is seagoing ships.

Some Personalizing Human Tendencies

MOVEMENT

I will call the first tendency *personality as movement*. Movement bestows personality. The more the movement, the more personality it bestows. Lincoln's life was one of steady movement. His birth in a backwoods is followed by an active childhood into further reaches of wilderness—the pioneer life—then by various moves to larger towns and new states, then the great move to Washington, and finally the movements of a war leader.

Churchill begins in Britain, journeys to Cuba, India, Turkey, South Africa, back to Britain, into the trenches of WWI, back to Britain again, to the halls of leadership and many adventures of WWII, ultimately around the world.

Einstein's life moves from Ulm to Munich to Zurich, to Bern, to Prague, back to Zurich, on to Berlin, to New York, Asia, Palestine, and ultimately to live in America.

The reverse of the tendency to movement tends to strip personality. Kant, for example, who never ventured very far beyond Königsberg, loses in personality thereby. His personality is smothered in the rigid embrace of an intellect whose movement merely revolves internally. In Kant, one encounters less a man than a mind, less a personality in any objective sense than an idea. He does not bear personality on the level of a Churchill or an Einstein.

The loss of personality in lack of movement has been understood and displayed well enough in fictional work. Thurber's *Walter Mitty* gives us the depersonalized common man, the man of the unwashed masses. Goncharov's *Oblomov* gives us the extreme of a living death, soon to dissolve back into dirt. These often fascinate us nonetheless, because their lack of personality in this relative reversion toward materiality repels us.

ADJUSTMENT AND CORRECTION

But beyond mere movement, there is also *personality as adjustment and correction.* If a life is adjusted, preferably from within, it adds personality.

Even adjustment from without is promising for personality, though it sometimes cannot be maintained long when adjustment stops. A Tom Sawyer who slumps into lollygagging once passed beyond the constant adjustment of an Aunt Polly, illustrates the usual end of many an external adjustment of personality. What Tom loses in adjustment he redeems a good deal in movement though.

Personality is proportional to the making of mistakes and the learning and correcting thereby, in other words to the grasping of and response to new and changing circumstances, environments, times, and acquaintances.

Lincoln again illustrates this well. It took some time for him to learn what path in life suited him, and he tried many things, from river boatman, to shopkeeper, to militia captain, to lawyer, so that it is often said that he failed at many things. He did fail, but each time he corrected himself and adjusted his actions. This adjustment becomes the story of a life, with its many twists and turns, a thing of great interest to us.

GROWTH AND DECAY

Personality as growth and decay means for us a growth and decay in its localized sense, as periods of growth and decay here and there within a life. The phrase "ups and downs of life" captures it well enough.

Churchill, for example, had these ups and downs aplenty, these setbacks from which he recovered himself and expanded even further, like waves upon a beach. His daring dash in the Boer War and resulting fame were a long period of initial growth. The ill-thought-out Gallipoli campaign of 1915 effectively cast him out of government, the decay of a line of action. Rebuilding followed, as a soldier among men—without the daring dash. In effect, he had to initiate growth along another line, as a steadier and more grounded leader. And he grew again.

Opposition to various British policies then led to his becoming a relative political outcast in the 1930s, his "wilderness years." Another line of action leading to decay—the refusal perhaps to recognize a changing world—was then turned to the growing recognition of the effort that would have to be made to see mankind through that change.

A third period followed the success of that guidance through the depths of WWII. Disillusionment and depression followed the loss of the 1945 election. He soon picked himself up, re-adjusting from the hopeless task of defender of the British Empire to promoter and prophet of future world relations.

Circumstances must allow for these periods of growth and decay, but the man himself, or the woman, must grasp them as they come and learn from them.

AGING AND LIABILITY TO AGING

In order to have growth and decay of any significance, however, one must be subject to temporality. One must be liable to aging, and one must age, thus the tendency of *personality as aging and liability to aging*. In aging the record of successes and reverses is kept.

By aging, I do not only mean the change of the physical body, which changes faster or slower depending upon genetics, environment, and the habits of life. This change of the physical body is indeed *liability to aging*, and personality is bound up with it.

An ageless body would lose personality in proportion to its agelessness. The elves in Tolkien's *Lord of the Rings*, for example, are archetypes rather than personalities *with respect to objectification*. They do indeed age, but in thought and experience. When Master Elrond says, "My memory reaches back even to the Elder Days . . . I have seen three ages in the West of the world, and many defeats, and many fruitless victories,"[2] one can dimly feel—if one can imagine what the full memory of the experience and interpretation of 6000 years of history would be like—a great weight of personality.

But that personality is not "here" in human and objective terms—the kind that are at play in personal objects—because its active interpretation has left no traces "here." The bodies of the elves are not liable to aging. The elves have personality on another level of complexity, which must remain archetypal to those on this level.

Hence there must be liability to aging to have personality as we know it. By aging itself, however, I mean rather the tendency of *the willingness to embrace and work with that liability to aging*.

Understanding this tendency is helped by looking at its opposite: the effort to retain personality by denying the changes of the body, the urge to eternal youth along with the urge to retain the personality as bound up with youthfulness.

Personality must age. And for us—not being elves—it must age in concert with the aging of a body. In our world, the ageless personality is already dead as personality. Rock stars of the 1970s and 80s clinging to personas invented fifty years ago epitomize the failure to age.

Actors are also particularly liable to the fighting of this tendency of healthy personality to age. Not ironically, a number of famous acting personalities have cemented "ageless" personalities and avoided the decline of living personality through an early death.

Marilyn Monroe remains the personified symbol of the fullness of youthful female sexuality by having exited at a point beyond which an aging body would have stolen away that symbolism. Other actors fare less well. Unable to escape the changes of the body, and denying those changes, they make vain efforts, abetted by plastic, to retain the personality in a steady state, often pitiful to behold.

When aging is respected and allowed to proceed, it builds personality. Whatever Lincoln may have thought of his aging, he was not afraid to let himself age. Thin faced and younger looking before 1860, growing a beard transformed him into a patriarch, a modern Methuselah, mirroring the personality of the man underneath: as a weather-beaten rock holding up in a storm. To see that face in its "beautiful ugliness" is to see the other tendencies of personality preserved as a history of living.

Einstein, perhaps best of all, epitomizes this tendency of aging to build the personality. He does it with such ease as to make us envious. He passes from the dapper young man of the early twentieth century just becoming known to the world, to the stately Nobel prize winner of 1921 posing for official portraits, to the world-renowned mad genius in his fifties seeking a new life in America, to the aged prophet of the 1940s and 50s, the funny little old man with thinning wild hair, dropping pearls of wisdom, a real-world Yoda, who playfully embraces his role.

The child is playful because the body is developing. The feeling of the body's growth and change stimulates action, which makes the best of—interprets—that growth and change. The constant discovery in a child of its own new strengths, increasing size, and new external appearance naturally prompts the use and testing of the new capacities. The unrestrained child lives in active concert with its own changes. Children—puppies and kittens too—are never so much personalities as when they are playing with the discovery of their own aging process.

Likewise, the changes of growing old: changing appearance, loss of strength, of capacities, of physical and mental stature, all lead to the building of personality when they are accepted and actively interpreted. Playfulness in senescence is response to change. If you can no longer act as you once did because of bodily changes, you have to take alternate routes, playfully, like a child. Otherwise, there is a calcification of activity, which, while it may fascinate us at its extreme is nonetheless an *undoing* of personality. Mr. Wilson must become more like Dennis the Menace, not retreat grumbling into his shell.

AMENABILITY TO MULTIPLICITY OF INTERPRETATION

Finally, the above tendencies are gathered into a higher tendency, that of *personality as amenability to multiplicity of interpretation.*

Can a person be *variously* interpreted by others and by how many others? This is the question to be answered. With another emphasis, how many facets—literally *little faces*—does the person have? The more faces he or she has, the more *personas*, the more a person he or she is. These facets are the personal "possessions"—in the sense evoked in "personal property"—of she who can gain them.

Through its movement, its adjustments and corrections of itself, its growth and decay, and its aging and liability to aging, great human personality can be many things to a great many people. It is variously interpretable to many, including itself.

Being interpretable to a high decree, it forms the nucleus of logical, and thus objective, community, including *a community of its own selfhood*. The acts of the life are bound together around "that which moved," "that which adjusted itself," "that which grew and regressed and grew again," and "that which aged." The person has been built as the locus of these tendencies and the value of the person is visible in the wealth of facets of interpretation she consequently shows off.

The great personality is more than just an adventurer. The mere adventurer who has "done it all" will always be more of a personality relative to those who haven't done it all. Fairy tales love the mysterious traveler who comes to town. But the higher adventurer whose adventures of experience are woven into a larger thread of purpose takes on much greater personality.

The reason for this should be clear from what we have suggested already: the random adventurer must have a locus that connects the experiences, as a jewel of many facets must be one jewel underneath. If other connections are lacking, that locus must be located in the body as a relative object, as a mere body.

If other connections—a career, a love, a quest, a mission—unite the experiences, then the multiple interpretations of the facets of the person can expand beyond the objectified body and become more valuable because of it. The Lincolns, Churchills, and Einsteins of human history have this higher connection of experiences.

The great personality is thus highly interpretable, a deep well that everyone can drink from to quench different thirsts. It never runs dry.

We can for example—a favorite pastime for many of us—interpret our own past or hypothetical future actions to the great personality. Take Lincoln for example. Have I labored in some outdoor job? Then I interpret myself to Lincoln for he too was a rail-splitter and a wood cutter, and so my work is worthy too. Did he rise higher? Yes, so he becomes a model for my future striving.

We can interpret the past of the great personality to his or her own future, and the more endlessly so as the person built diversity into that history through initiating all the tendencies above rather than merely a few. We can read the book of the life and compare the chapters to one another.

Did the person move about? All the better for me, as a scholar perhaps, or a globetrotter, to interpret the change of his outlook with respect to the various towns he lived in. What did Einstein think of his life in Switzerland in comparison with his life in Germany or of his life in Switzerland with the life he lived in America? What did others think of him in each of these places? What stresses did these moves put on his work at different times?

When the personality is great, you find that communities develop around the personality. They are often able to retain their cohesion after the bodily death of the person. Such communities, the numerous Churchill, Lincoln, and Einstein societies for example, continue to interpret the life of the personality often engaging in action in the spirit of the acts the personality engaged in.

From Human Person to Objective Personality

This seems too simple perhaps. In fact, there are other tendencies that I have left unexamined, the tendency to communication for instance, which also works to build personality.

But here I will concentrate on the suggestion that *the tendencies that build human personality are operative all through experience, so that the very same tendencies externally applied in our creative efforts engender personality proportionally in the objects we make.*

A caveat though: objects cannot bear personality to the degree of human personality. Their nature as mere objects, whose object-hood is worked upon from without, prevents it. So the question is: How much personality can an object bear?

Consider the personal objects of famous personalities, that is, their *stuff*. The thing that damns great human personality most, when its source is misunderstood, is to find out that the great person's stuff is often just stuff like a lot of other stuff.

We want to know for example what Napoleon did for a pastime or see the clothes he wore perhaps, but when, expecting seven-league boots, we see a rather plain pair of riding boots and a rather small felt hat beside them, our sense of the personality wearing them often takes a hit.[3]

To say it plainly: the boots do not make Napoleon, but neither does Napoleon make the boots, because their characteristics are heavily on the material side. They probably aren't much different from Marshall Ney's boots, or those of other generals of the period. Napoleon's personality cannot "rub off" on his boots except in a weak manner. The boots won't bear it.

Lots of people would like to have Napoleon's boots of course, or Einstein's pipe, or Lincoln's hat. Yet while these objects might allow us to interpret the respective personalities to some degree, they would not necessarily have great personality as objects. This is easiest to see if we apply the test of the final tendency, the test of multiple interpretation. Can Lincoln's hat be variously interpreted by many?

As soon as you ask this you see that it can be interpreted by a number of people, but not according to multiple facets, and not to all that many people really. The hat's main function, built into it, is to be worn. If the hat were passed around to be truly worn by many, it would soon wear into tatters. If it has other potential uses—a church collection platter, a Frisbee, scooping water from a river, serving as a source of chemical analysis of nineteenth-century felt, sitting on a scarecrow's head—they would all wreck it pretty quick.

The hat can be moved, it can be adjusted somewhat, it will age somewhat, and it will decay. But it isn't made to move of itself, it isn't made to age (rather to be replaced when worn out), and it will not grow. A little of some of our five tendencies have gone into it, and none at all of one of them. In short, it is not *made* to be multiply interpretable to any great degree. It will lack *its own* personality proportionally, despite being Lincoln's hat.

Personal Objects

We have passed from the personal as human to a search for the personal object. That search is unfulfilled in the *mere* connection of an object with human personality.

Yet just as the human can tend toward object-hood—in pornography for example—the object can tend toward personality. It does that according to the very same tendencies that apply to human personality. These tendencies are not exclusive to the creation of human personality; *they are general tendencies of an interpretable world.* [4]

Before suggesting my main example of such highly personal objects, I'll consider briefly through the above five tendencies a counter-example, a highly impersonal object: an iPad.

Our first tendency was movement. Has movement been built into this object? Decidedly not. The iPad moves as a whole only if you carry it. It lacks moving parts. What movement it has is built into whatever is occurring on its screen; for the most part, nothing is occurring unless deliberate efforts are made. Those efforts are made to be as minimal as possible; the tiniest motions of one or two fingers will accomplish nearly everything that can be done.

Our second tendency was adjustment and correction. All of the iPad's adjustments and corrections are meant to be internal. You press a button in agreement, and it updates itself regularly. There is little to adjust. The machine—staying within certain boundaries—discourages manipulation of its software structure. So it hardly goes wrong, unlike older computers, which needed regular adjustment. You may change the display background, the colors, the sounds, but on the whole, the object is built to do away with adjustment.

The third tendency was growth and decay. The iPad is not made to grow. Unlike older computers, it has no slots to upgrade its memory, its visual display, or its speed. Its software architecture never seems to undergo any *noticeable* growth. Despite regular updates, its capabilities remain fairly constant. Nor is it made to grow in its internal structure by an active engagement of the user. Decay is foreign to its internal and external structure in regular use.

The fourth tendency was that of aging and liability to aging. Does the iPad age? Not noticeably. In an internal environment or fine weather, it never seems to change physically. To put it in a rougher external environment would be to destroy it soon enough except as a small chunk of glass and metal. The surface never really wears under normal use (the back might scratch). It is ageless relative to the creative intention behind it.

Finally, as to being variously interpretable to multitudes, the iPad's possibilities are limited. It is used by multitudes, but not variously. It tends to be used in relatively the same way by each user with regard to its object-hood. Each will browse the internet, use applications, manipulate its brightness or sound, swipe the screen in similar ways, tap the screen in similar ways, hold the iPad in similar ways, and so forth. One could imagine impromptu uses it might be put to—a vanity mirror perhaps, a paperweight—but none are very likely. Certainly, the object does not encourage them. Other uses would begin to take it apart and refashion it or destroy it quickly enough, for example, a crude knife made from the casing, a club of sorts, a kitchen cutting board, or a nice surface to divide cocaine on.

The iPad is nearly the perfect impersonal object. A box of matches has more objective personality than an iPad. The matches burn, they get damp and decay, they scatter if thrown, they can build matchstick houses, the striking strip wears. The matches diminish. They strike in different ways and can light a fire in many places. Each one smells and sounds and burns in different ways.

Lincoln's hat lies at the lower end of the scale of personality in objects in interpretability to a human person, but it is ahead of Lincoln's iPad, which would have been lower still. Lincoln's iPad would have been mostly indistinguishable from Grant's iPad, unless he had carved his name on it. Lincoln's hat would at least have taken on wear relative to the shape of Lincoln's head and would have picked up some of his hairs in its lining. The iPad is relatively dead as a personal object, even in comparison to a hat.

Perhaps I've exaggerated the poverty of personality in the iPad to make the point. The personality of any object is always relative to other such objects, but just how relative can be seen by taking a very different object, the ocean-going ship, more specifically the sailing ship.

The Sailing Ship as a Personal Object

The age of great sailing ships is past as an age, though it remains as a hobby. We would be wrong to think it long past, because "long" would be relative to an age whose height of complexity spanned 300 years, but whose history spanned perhaps 9000 years, so far, and though it ended about 150 years ago, sailing ships were still in widespread use up to 100 years ago.

Ships in general are somewhat less personal than sailing ships, as we shall see, but nonetheless more personal than most objects. Generally, the personality of such objects, large or small, varies only within some small range for all are imminently personal by intent and design.

My own experience with ships is considerable if not vast, enough so to perhaps strengthen the argument by mentioning it. From the age of nine, I worked for twenty-five years on the Lower North Shore of the Gulf of St. Lawrence, between the shores of Quebec and Newfoundland, on ships and boats of various sizes, as a commercial or deep-sea fisherman of codfish, snow-crab, and later turbot. I built several small sailing craft as well in those days, one of 18-foot and another of 21-foot length, and sailed them. I built larger boats with my father, brother, and grandfather, and participated in the traditional ways of launching, mooring, and so forth. I lived the traditional migratory journey to our summer island to fish each year. In general, I grew up on the salt tales and practices left over from an older era of the 1930s and 40s that remained strong in a place that in those days was fifty years behind the rest of the developed western world.

The sense of ships as personal objects has thus always seemed particularly clear to me in ways that I will try to express within the framework of my argument. A full—if not the fullest—development of the five tendencies of personality given above is to be seen in ships, and particularly sailing ships.

MOVEMENT

The great poet John Masefield can have the first word:

> I march across great waters like a queen,
> I whom so many wisdoms helped to make;
> Over the uncruddled billows of seas green
> I blanch the bubbled highway of my wake
> By me my wandering tenants clasp the hands,
> And know the thoughts of men in other lands.[5]

Our first tendency was movement. The ship has it through and through. It moves. As Masefield shows, it moves because it is made to move to "other lands." The great ships of the Age of Sail were made to travel the whole world, and they did.

A ship's movement is unfettered in its domain. The whole ocean is the domain of a seagoing ship, the larger part of the globe. That domain is fully interpretable in the sense that any part of it is a potential journey of the ship. Even the voyages of a small boat are theoretically nearly endless, with skill, decent conditions, and a little luck, as witnessed by the tens of thousands of miles sailed by Captain Thomas Drake out of Seattle, in boats little more than thirty feet long.[6]

Compare this to an airplane. A large airplane might have the whole of a region of earth airspace at its command. But it cannot *stay* in that region. It isn't wholly made for that region. Where the seagoing ship is at home in its domain, the airplane is just visiting. The intent behind the airplane is for the most part not for the object to move in itself with regard to its domain, to merge with that domain. It is rather to transport another object. The airplane is not properly called a ship—an airship—in the same sense as a seagoing ship at all. It lacks—proportionally—the movement tendency embodied in the latter. To gain the fullness of that tendency, it would need to be fully at home in its element.

The dirigible airships of steampunk fantasy-fiction, which can stay airborne, approach closer to this tendency of personality, and indeed the dirigibles of the mid-twentieth century are the closest we have come to the true airship as personality. If and when there are spaceships in the proper sense, they will bear personality closer to that of sea-going ships. The *Enterprise* of Star Trek fame has her fictional personality on the level of a sailing ship, precisely because she is at home in her element. The Nasa space shuttles, individually named, came closer to the level of personality of sea going ships than contemporary airplanes for these reasons.

Yet ships have more of movement in them than that of their routes. They move constantly in other ways. First of all, the body of the ship, particularly wooden ships, is in a continual state of flexing, one way or another. This is brought to consciousness most in a modern boat—even of fiberglass—when the engine stops and in a wooden sailing boat even more so, a continual creaking and cracking of gaffe and boom, of blocks, of plank and timbers, of rudder pintles, and so forth.

Laid upon this internal flexing is the constant motion of the vessel as she responds to the waves. Apart from dead calm, rare enough, the ship makes constant little motions as she rolls to waves and heaves to swells. She cannot be still, no matter if moored or docked.

You can get some sense of the personality a ship accrues in this movement by considering the most miniature and impromptu version of a ship, without human passengers or crew, yet possessing the creative intent to movement: the message in a bottle. The mystery and interest of something unique that a message in a bottle evokes captures the result of this intent to movement. Over what expanses of ocean has it traveled, in what conditions, over how many faded years, bobbing, drifting, moving constantly? The simple intent that the creator of the message imparts to its vessel retains the answers, visibly but secretly.

ADJUSTMENT AND CORRECTION

Turning to adjustment, we add another essential facet of the personality of a ship. Ships have a life of their own. They move where you want them to mostly, but they always take you there by moving where and how *they* want to in some degree. You may set the wheel, but the wind knocks you off. The current pushes you off your course, or the steering is cranky with more or less weight aboard. The need for adjustment is more or less constant and relative to a host of conditions: objects in the water, other ships, waiting on low and high tides, cargo, current, wind, wave, swell, visibility, day and night. Your road today will differ from your road tomorrow; in fact, you do not have a true road.

Compare this to a car. In normal conditions you drive a car directly where you want upon roads. The car—SUV commercials notwithstanding—is bound to its road, and the road is where it is because it is the most efficient route, and generally the fastest route. Speed is made possible through a lessening of the need to interpret, but it deprives the car object of personality proportionally. The car needs adjustment still of course, but *far* less than the ship.

Where every car of the same model is more or less the same and gives the same feel in the beginning and for long after, no two ships are exactly alike. This is due to the process of manufacture you may say. You would be right. But that is just the point being made, that the type of active intent that has gone into the object—here the car—has tended to reduce its personality. Small differences in the building of ships not merely machine built make them act in different ways. The first thing an experienced seaman looks for is how a ship "behaves" in the water, how she acts in different scenarios of wind and wave. Different ships will need different handling, different adjustment.

And such adjustment of movement by *steering* is only one of the many adjustments to be made in a ship. The ships of the great Age of Sail needed constant adjustment: the amount of sail, the set of the sail, the tightening of lines, the stowing and unstowing of gear, the positioning of cargo, and on and on.

Captain John Whidden describes his confusion as a young sailor:

> Suddenly I was startled by a hoarse cry of "All hands on deck! Reef Topsails!" In a few minutes the watch below came tumbling up, the topsail yards were lowered on the caps, reef tackles hauled out, spilling-lines and buntlines bowsed taut, the men laid aloft to take in a double reef . . . all this was new to me . . . while from out of the darkness overhead, after they had laid aloft, the stentorian voice of the second mate roared out to "Light over to wind'ard," followed by "Haul out to leeward," terms which at that time were so much Greek to me.[7]

Diesel motors simplified things greatly of course in my day, just as steam had simplified them after Whidden's time, but only *so* much. In our fishing boat the steady bearing still had to be checked and greased, the water intake had to be cleared of "goose grass," pumps cleared, bilge checked regularly in rough weather to see if the boat was taking on water, mooring lines coiled, heavy items lashed down, and on and on. A boat remains a boat, with always a thousand things to adjust.

GROWTH AND DECAY

Growth and decay in a ship takes many forms. Ships constantly undergo decay as a whole process. A continual cycle of decay and regrowth, of damage and repair, takes place. Larger ships of the Age of Sail thus shipped a carpenter, which made the ship a self-repairing object, but also an object that could grow into new tasks as needed by being modified, sometimes substantially.

So, for example, Captain Bligh's cabin on the *Bounty* was converted into a specialized floating nursery for breadfruit plants before the ill-fated voyage:

The great cabin was appropriated for the preservation of the plants, and extended as far forward as the after hatchway. It had two large sky-lights, and on each side three scuttles for air, and was fitted with a false floor cut full of holes to contain the garden-pots, in which the plants were to be brought home. The deck was covered with lead, and at the foremost corners of the cabin were fixed pipes to carry off the water that drained from the plants, into tubs placed below to save it for future use.[8]

The tendency to growth and decay was lost a bit, and personality lost proportional to it, in more modern "ageless" ships, of iron, steel, and now fiberglass. But the nature of a ship as being water-bound ensures that even modern ships suffer constant minor damage to their hulls: iron rusts, fiberglass degrades in sunshine, surfaces must be painted, patches applied. Decks need repainting, or refinishing. Portholes and windows need caulking and sometimes replacing. Cabins need cleaning. Carpentry may be needed to fit a cabin, a fish hold, or some other part, for a different use. This was the ritual of spring—the cycle as growth—I took part in for twenty-five years, lasting anywhere up to two months and involving the repair of up to five different boats.

Large modern ships still need large repairs, despite their strength and materials. I once spent an afternoon on a Russian bulk grain carrier of perhaps 80,000 DWT capacity at the Port of Quebec in what was at that time still the Soviet era. The ship's doctor showed me the damage from a rogue wave that had sheared off the starboard bridge wing as the ship left the English Channel, leaving the doctor in the most ridiculous—and the luckiest—of possible outcomes: trapped in the shower with a dizzying drop down to the ocean waiting for her just outside the door. Such damage, not being fatal to the ship, is repaired, however, and growing, and regrowing, out of it, the ship carries on.

The ship thus goes through a regular cycle of decay and regrowth and gains personality commensurate.

AGING AND LIABILITY TO AGING

The aging and liability to aging of a ship as an object mesh naturally enough with its growth and the decay. A ship can be said to have a youth, a middle age, and a senescence into old age.

The British naval ship *Bellerophon*, with personality enough to have its name copied four more times by British navy ships, illustrates these life periods well enough. The ship was begun in 1782 in the shipyard at Frindsbury, England, and launched—born—in 1786, in haste, after her cradle threatened to collapse in an autumn gale.[9]

She lay in reserve, moored for six months, without masts or rigging, Britain being "between wars," with a small caretaking compliment of a dozen men aboard. [10]

She was then fitted out as tensions with Spain increased and received her first captain, who slowly made up the 550 men that she needed. Sailing for Spithead, she was active one month and then put back in reserve after tensions abated. It was 1790.

Events were afoot in France, however, and she was soon outfitted again. Collision and damage followed near the Scilly Isles, when another ship of the fleet crossed her bows in a gale and tore away her bowsprit and with it a good portion of her topmast, sending her back for repairs.[11]

She then took up her station patrolling off the west coast of France and there earned in racing exercises her personalizing epithet: *the Flying Bellerophon*. Shortly after, in 1794, she participated in the battle of the Glorious First of June. She had passed her youth.

In middle life, over the next ten years, she served in the Atlantic, West Indies, Mediterranean, and Baltic, in various capacities, taking part in the great sea battles of the age—the Battle of the Nile in 1798, the Battle of Trafalgar in 1805—undergoing cycles of damage and repair each time.

After this, the senescence of the ship began, with blockade duty in mainly northern waters, apart from several voyages across the Atlantic to Newfoundland and the British Caribbean. The end of this period culminated in the events of July 1815. Napoleon, beaten at Waterloo and weighing his options on the French coast, was shadowed by the *Bellerophon*, on blockade duty. Having decided that escape was hopelessness, Napoleon boarded *Bellerophon*, where he spent the next four weeks off the English coast.

Bellerophon was to take the former emperor to far away St. Helena, but as Cordingly writes: "there were problems with the ship which was to take Napoleon to St Helena. The Admiralty had decided that the 29-year-old *Bellerophon* was not up to the 5,000-mile voyage to the South Atlantic and had selected the 74-gun ship *Northumberland* to take her place."[12]

Thus, Napoleon sailed off in the *Northumberland*, and the aged *Bellerophon* sailed into Plymouth and into her later fate as a prison hulk from 1817 to 1836. Her peers of Nelson's navy had similar but varied fates in retirement:

> Many were converted into receiving ships: these were used as floating barracks for sailors between commissions or for the accommodation of volunteers and pressed men before they were assigned to a warship. Some of the hulks became store ships for coal or gunpowder. Some were converted into floating hospital ships or convalescent ships or were used as quarantine ships (called lazarettos) for men suspected

of having infectious diseases. A few became sheer hulks or floating cranes, and several were even used as breakwaters.[13]

The life of the *Bellerophon* is thus illustrative of the aging tendency intentionally built into the objects that we call ships. Not all ships end up being put to uses that are as "humiliating"—Cordingly's term—as the final fate of the *Bellerophon*. Her use as a convict ship may be a questionable use, but that a ship most often *has* a use consistent with her age is one of the great personalizing tendencies of ships.

For the most part, we make the plane and car to be retired; they run or they don't. Their duties can be changed somewhat to fit their aging circumstances of course, but not like those of a sea ship.

Ships have been used for harbor service, for coastal service, placed in reserve (naval), used for training, and in general given age-appropriate tasks. The Canadian schooner *Bluenose,* begun as a fishing schooner, became essentially a racing schooner and ended as a coastal freighter. Aging small boats in my youth were used as tenders between our larger boats.

Old boats have been used for still odder purposes. My brother and I, when little, had an aged *flat*—a skiff—perhaps eighteen feet in length, nestled in a hollow not far from our summer house, as a toy. There in our "ship," we had a variety of imaginative adventures. Another old unseaworthy flat-bottomed scow was requisitioned for local adventures in the great freshwater pond on our island. Cousins on a neighboring island had a retired old outboard motorboat for boyhood adventures, complete with a cabin they had built to accommodate visiting guests.

This is the fascinating nature of ships. Where the ship has been and what she has done—accruing through the movement tendency—naturally comes to make up part of her aging. Here—unlike the earlier example of the hats—*the object can bear its age*, to a high degree. The ship has aged by traveling to this or that port, sailing this or that sea, having this or that success or mishap, taking up this or that task. Her "lifetime" in various uses becomes her personality.

I have known larger ships that had respectable uses in old age. Two aged boats that were draggers in their youths, the *Kecarpoui* and the *Musquaro*, remain prominent in my memory as fish collecting boats that made the daily round from Harrington Harbor, where we sold our catch, near our island summer home, to the fish plant at La Tabatière, fifty miles away. Regular renewal in paint and repairs notwithstanding, their pitted and splintered gunwales and ironwork, rugged and seamed bluff black bows, and smoke-stained white wheelhouses betrayed their adventures, giving them personalities evocative of old bulldogs—not unlike Churchill.

In fact, the end of life for many ships comes in an objective and extremely personalized death, which casts a long memory in man, their builder. Any ship that has sunk, that has "gone to her watery grave," so that the object even in death locates and displays the effects of aging—from the *RMS Titanic* to the schooner *Sweepstakes*—remains as a record of all the personality that is possible in an object. This in just the same way and according to the same tendencies by which we accentuate the human personality out of the mere object-hood of material death with all the paraphernalia of tombs and mausoleums, that is, with a final interpretable record of the objective aging process.

AMENABILITY TO MULTIPLICITY OF INTERPRETATION

Our final tendency, amenability to varied multiplicity of interpretation, is built upon the earlier tendencies. It issues in a hodgepodge of ways in which a multiplicity of people can interpret the objects that are ships. No complete list could easily be given for the degree of interpretability of ships as objects tends to defy completion; the more obvious ways are easy enough to locate, however.

Most prominently, ships tend to have crews, and each member of the crew may have multiple tasks, change tasks, and grow into new tasks. In the great Age of Sail, ships had quite varied crews. There were men to cook and to help cook, clean, splice rope, and sow sails carpenters and their helpers, doctors and their helpers, men to steer, mapmakers, navigators, botanists and naturalists—as on the *Bounty*, *Endeavour*, and *Beagle*—guards, men for away parties, pursers, chaplains, musicians, men to reef and set sail, men to direct (the captain and mates). Each of these often had multiple and differing tasks depending upon the need.

The great ships of our day may incorporate tendencies that reduce certain facets of interpretation while increasing others, relative to the history of ships. Thus, the modern aircraft carrier loses personalizing facets of interpretability in its physical form by the flatness of its upper deck, relative to the great complexity and busy-ness of masts and sails of a Napoleonic ship of the line.[14] But on the other hand it gains by the interpretable complexity of its fleet of aircraft. As Lt. Cmdr. Max Miller put it, in terms of the changing purpose of the ship:

> Even as with our own lives, ships also have their own days which cannot be segregated into continuity. Too many things overlap within any given hour. The pattern of the day may be left suspended and without borders. A design may be there in the weaving, but the design is only a suggested one and may turn out to be something else entirely. Threads which should be finished are left unfinished, and through nobody's fault. Other threads may come to a quick end even before

they get started ... a carrier's pattern of operations ... continues to be a sort of fourth-dimensional one even during an engagement. The pattern reaches beyond the surface, and it extends ... but the carrier nevertheless remains the core of her own pattern. From her it is that the threads are started, and it is to her that they intermittently return. Back and forth they go, and in and out, and yet the weaving is so spacious and so complex that no individual can hope to follow each strand of it.[15]

This quality of multiple interpretability is what gives ships their living personality; all the more in a ship because the crew may be from all over. As Miller noted of his American carrier, "a state cannot be named which is not represented in her somehow. The men aboard are from all these states likewise."[16]

In ships of the Age of Sail, crews often hailed from various countries. The crew of the *Bellerophon* in midlife were "English (49 per cent), and the rest were made up of a large contingent of Irishmen (24 per cent); a number of Scotsmen (12 per cent), and Welshmen (7 per cent); and a variety of foreigners (8 per cent). The foreigners included 13 black sailors (9 from the West Indies, 3 from Africa, 1 from America) as well as 2 Dutchmen, a Frenchman, a Swede, a Portuguese, a Maltese, a Bengal Indian, one man from Guernsey and one from the Isle of Man."[17]

All of them might be active interpreters of their own culture to the community of the ship. Where the large modern airplane might have a variety of cultures aboard *in latency*, the seagoing ship could have them aboard *in active interpretation*, for the bearers of those cultures, being not merely "cargo" had definite tasks in the ship which sooner or later would bring their cultural background into interpretation with other interpreters of the ship.

Ships are objects in and around which cultural stories can easily be told because they themselves serve as the loci and bearers of stories; they are the type of object that can bear the active interpretation of culture.

The ship is a personal object because of the capacity imparted to it as "personalizable," the capacity to gather up human personality from its creation and its ongoing process, into a living community of personality. This is the cultural power of ships as personal objects: *the power to blend culture into community and thereby accrete personality for themselves.*

Despite our carrier example, *size* is not the true driver of this living state of a ship, except insofar as *mere multiplicity* truly gives way to *variety of interpretation*. A Grand Banks schooner of the 1920s and 30s such as *Bluenose* incorporated a good deal of the interpretability of a carrier, with her dozen dories coming and going each day.

On the other hand, a large contemporary airplane may carry four hundred people, but the relative sameness of the actions of all but half a dozen, as mere baggage sitting to be transported from point A to B, works against the object as a living personalized object. Likewise, a small town of five thousand may contain a number of people equal to a modern carrier, but the carrier is alive in a way such as only movement can add to other tendencies, in personalizing her as an object—she is a *moving town.*

A fishing boat with a crew of three or four, such as I worked on, has less variety but always plenty and varied tasks for each of her crew. Even a *toy* ship such as the homemade square rigger I loved to build up, tinker with, and sail on ponds, as a boy, has multiplicity of interpretation incorporated in it as an object, despite *carrying* no crew, through the many possible configurations of its masts, its rigging, the stowing of various "cargos," and so on.

Moreover, ships are bought, sold, transferred between owners, between corporations, between countries. Other objects such as houses are liable to such actions of course, but not to the same degree as ships. A ship thus serves as a locus of interpretation external to herself—beyond the interpretations of her crew—as well, precisely because of the variety of movements she makes and the uses to which she can be put. These movements and tasks give her a personalizing history.

Thus, she may change names over her history concomitant to her changes of personality or in some cases even undergo personalization of her name, as we saw for the *"Flying" Bellerophon.*

HMS J-826, a British minesweeper built in America in 1941, and used through WWII, became *BYMS-2026* in 1944. She then became the *Calypso G[ozo]* in 1950, a ferry on the Maltese coast, and finally the famous *RV Calypso* of Captain Cousteau, serving for forty years of research and adventure.

Objects that tend to have proper names have them because they can bear personalization. We name our pets because—although they can be objectified—animals start out far beyond mere objects in being able to accrue personality. Most often objects that otherwise lack the higher capacities for personalization are given names because a use is foreseen for them which incorporates some special mode of interpretation beyond the average. Thus, the special purposes of Lindbergh's *Spirit of Saint Louis*, or that of the *Enola Gay*, were recognized in the personalizing of the respective aircraft by names.

If names come naturally to seagoing ships most of all, it is because their builders and those who used them have felt and understood the interpretive possibilities inherent in them which bring them further beyond being mere objects than any other objects which humanity has yet attempted to create.

Conclusion: Or Why a Ship Is "She"

I have shown how personalization follows certain tendencies or principles. These tendencies are readily identifiable in the building up of human personality. We see them at work in strong human personalities, the consideration of which can help us clarify them as movement, adjustment and correction, growth and decay, aging and liability to aging, and amenability to varied multiplicity of interpretation.

There are other related tendencies that space does not permit my considering here but that apply in varying degrees to ships as well. Among these can be mentioned communication and physical curvature. The latter in particular, the curvature of hulls and sails, imbues a ship with the capacity for constant movement in the water environment, leading to value.

The five tendencies elaborated upon, however, capture a great deal of what gives human personality and in turn what gives personality in sea-going ships.

The difference between human personality and that of an object is that human personality arises through the tendencies being followed or driven *from within*, while the capacity for personality in an object is incorporated into it *from without* through the creative foresight to make the object such that its use will provoke and allow the tendencies in question.

As a side note, insofar as we can step back from our own bodies and see them as objects to be personalized through this creative foresight, we build our own personalities, i.e., our bodies become the created vehicles of our personalities. The human makes him or herself a personality by following the tendencies in question—among others. Humanity which fails to follow these tendencies tends—proportionally—toward object-hood.

In other words, and here is the practical side of the matter, if you can create objects with and in which the above tendencies are made possible, then your objects will begin to take on personality.[18]

Sea-going ships have always been such objects. They accrue personality, as I have shown, because they are created such as to have a capacity for it. Ships are what might be called *high interpretive value objects* in contra-distinction to something like iPads which are *high quantitative value objects*.

But quantitative value is simply a very weak form of interpretive value; it is an attempt to create value without a clear understanding of value. The iPad is designed to give us access to an experience which is only very weakly interpretable by us—millions of pages of internet to mostly *see*—but to give us a very great quantity of it. It is a premature picking of the fruit of value.

The iPad seduces us with the false promise of having an experience beyond our bodily object-hood—as the earlier mentioned elves do—without having gained that experience through the hard work of a creative use and integration of our bodies relative to that experience. Personality wise, the iPad is to the sea-going ship what Kant is to Churchill.

The iPad seems to allow us to move, the ship really allows us to move; the iPad seems to give access to an age, the ship really ages; the iPad seems to be adjustable, the ship really is adjustable, and so on. Anyone who takes time to compare the two experiences will easily feel this difference.

The ship thus acts as a locus of interpretive activity. In fact, it acts as a locus of community, for it facilitates all the tendencies needed for community: combined action, evolving goals, the need for a variety of active skills, the retention of the history of the community. The community is comprised of any and all who work on the object in a multitude of varying ways. All who do so personalize the object.

They can only personalize the object, however, because the object will bear it. An object such as a ship begins to have personality because those who imagine and build it abide by some of the varying tendencies given above in a greater degree. They know how to create a skeleton upon which the flesh of personality can grow. The object is thus born personalized to some degree. It gains further personality by variability of use by many because it inspires such use.

The understanding of this creativity does not come accidentally. If human personality is created through a consistent use of such tendencies, in response to an environment that goads the use of those tendencies, that is, the ebb and flow of busy and varied human society, then object personality is created likewise in relation to a different media of experience.

The English were arguably the most nautical culture the world has ever produced. Trapped on their little island, they must interpret the sea about them or wither and die culturally. In interpreting the sea, they personalized themselves as a culture, and they learned to create objects that reached the heights of personalization, objects that had the capacity to serve as loci of communities. The use of the feminine gender for sea craft became natural to them for these reasons.

In terms of the object-hood of living things—both human and animal bodies—the body of the mother in nearly all species is the nearest and most original source for our sense of an object which serves as a locus of interpretive community. The mother's body begets and then nurtures to personality all those offspring who continually come and go from her, moving in search of food and new experience, growing, adjusting themselves and being adjusted, aging, and ultimately interpreting her along with their siblings as the locus of community. The ship, naturally and through evolving creative skill, mimics this motherhood. The concept of a "mother-ship," in life and fiction, is no accident.

Being imbued with personality from the beginning, a ship gives birth to personality in herself and in her human interpreters. The journey and experience of a sailor are a birth of personality, tied to an object capable of nurturing it. By another name it can be called an object for building character. Thus, a ship is very naturally *she* in the same sense as mother, for any culture with the environment and experience sufficient to recognize and create one. Sailors are children of the ship.

I will give the last word to Masefield:

You should have seen, man cannot tell to you
The beauty of the ships of that my city.

That beauty now is spoiled by the sea's pity;
For one may haunt the pier a score of times;
Hearing St. Nicholas bells ring out the chimes,
Yet never see those proud ones swaying home
With mainyards backed and bows a cream of foam,
Those bows so lovely-curving, cut so fine,
Those coulters of the many-bubbled brine,
As once, long since, when all the docks were filled
With that sea-beauty man has ceased to build

Yet, though their splendour may have ceased to be,
Each played her sovereign part in making me;
Now I return my thanks with heart and lips
For the great queenliness of all those ships.[19]

Notes

1. Sartre and the existentialists were on to this. Their mistake was to remain swimming in the realm of mere feeling.

2. J. R. R. Tolkien, *The Fellowship of the Ring: Being the First Part of the Lord of the Rings* (London: Allen & Unwin, 1954; London: HarperCollins, 1994), 318. Citations refer to the HarperCollins edition.

3. They can be seen at the Montreal Museum of Fine Arts.

4. Within these tendencies is a logic of interpretation. See my book on the subject: Marc Anderson, *Hyperthematics: The Logic of Value* (Albany: SUNY Press, 2019).

5. John Masefield, "The Ship and Her Makers," in *Salt-Water Poems and Ballads*. Illust. Charles Pears (New York: Macmillan, 1916; Reprint, New York, Macmillan, 1967), 122. [Hereafter *Salt-Water Poems*]

6. W. L. White, *The Log of the Lone Sea Rover: Being the Story of an 8000 Mile Voyage Alone* (N.p.: N.p., 1917)

7. John D. Whidden, *Ocean Life in the Old Sailing-Ship Days: From Forecastle to Quarter-deck* (Boston: Little Brown, 1914), 13–14.

8. William Bligh, *A Voyage to the South Seas, undertaken by command of His Majesty, for the purpose of conveying the breadfruit tree to the West Indies in His Majesty's Ship the Bounty* (London: G Nicol. 1792), 2.

9. David Cordingly, *The Billy Ruffian: The Bellerophon and the Downfall of Napoleon, the Biography of a Ship of the Line, 1782–1836* (New York: Bloomsbury Publishing: 2003), 26–30.

10. Ibid., 39–40.
11. Ibid., 59.
12. Ibid., 273.
13. Ibid., 283.
14. Max Miller, *Daybreak for our Carrier* (New York: McGraw-Hill, 1944), 16–17.
15. Ibid., 90–91.
16. Ibid., 2.
17. Cordingly, 210.
18. The cash value of this, as William James would say, is that objects with personality can be deliberately created. For more on this see my *Hyperthematics*.
19. Masefield, "Ships," in *Salt-Water Poems*, 129.

Bibliography

Anderson, Marc M. *Hyperthematics: The Logic of Value*. Albany: SUNY Press, 2019.

Bligh, William. *A Voyage to the South Seas, undertaken by command of His Majesty, for the purpose of conveying the breadfruit tree to the West Indies in His Majesty's Ship the Bounty*. London: G Nicol, 1792.

Cordingly, David. *The Billy Ruffian: The Bellerophon and the Downfall of Napoleon, the Biography of a Ship of the Line, 1782–1836*. New York: Bloomsbury Publishing, 2003.

Masefield, John. *Salt-Water Poems and Ballads*, Illustrated by Charles Pears. New York: Macmillan, 1916. Reprint, New York: Macmillan, 1967.

Miller, Max. *Daybreak for our Carrier*. New York: McGraw-Hill, 1944.

Tolkien, J. R. R. *The Fellowship of the Ring: Being the First Part of the Lord of the Rings*. London: Allen & Unwin, 1954. Reprint, London: HarperCollins, 1994.

Whidden, John D. *Ocean Life in the Old Sailing-Ship Days: From Forecastle to Quarter-Deck*. Boston: Little Brown, 1914.

White, W.L. *The Log of the Lone Sea Rover: Being the Story of an 8000 Mile Voyage Alone*. N.p.: N.p., 1917.

Chapter 3

Personified Objects and Objectified Persons in Ancient Egypt

MARTIN PEHAL

Editor's Note: If the first two chapters dealt with the "natural" world, the next three will deal with the "spiritual" or religious world. In chapter 3, Pehal discusses some of the personalized religious objects found in ancient Egypt. He describes the Egyptian's "aggregate" concept of personhood and demonstrates how these religious objects, including the bodies of the dead, came to be personalized through certain rituals. This chapter transitions from the more general discussions found in chapters 1 and 2 and provides a very concrete example of how personalized objects can arise within a specific historical and cultural context.

Introduction

Given the philosophical perspective of many chapters in the present volume, it might be useful to provide a brief introduction to how ancient Egyptian symbolic thought relates to a more rationalist, philosophical position to contextualize the examples from ancient Egypt included in this chapter, which are an example *par excellence* of associative aspects of symbolic thought.

In a dualistic manner so typical of his overall method, Claude Lévi-Strauss remarked on the stark difference between the "wild" mind of various peoples on the one hand, and the domesticated mind of the "philosopher" on the other by liking the first to a rainforest and the other to a domesticated, single-variety agricultural field.[1] The philosophical mind, Lévi-Strauss claims, is akin to a domesticated field: it focuses on thought-effective, high-yielding crops of rationalist intellectual processes during which individual thought specimens are isolated from among a number of other possible varieties, laid out in logical rows and then harvested by similarly specialized "machinery" of philosophical discourse. It is a logically coherent, effectively straightforward, and a spatially lucid strategy.

On the other hand, the "wild" symbolic mind, prevalent in many archaic religious systems, rather resembles a multitier rainforest ecosystem, swarming with a variety of diverse life forms where harvesting mechanisms of the domesticated landscape prove ineffective or even destructive. A rainforest mind interconnects the immense variety of intellectual species coexisting in the human mind through metaphor, metonymy, and other tropes. Thus, the individual human body and its very individual physiological processes become a microimage of the macrocosmos, of the movement of celestial bodies, ebbing of the tide, and of the society at large. The rainforest mind understands these experiential fields (physiological, ecological, economical, cosmical, ethical, etc.) as inextricably interconnected and constantly influencing each other. The rainforest mind tends to personify abstract concepts and societal dynamics, transforming them into entities that then interact with one another in mythological paradigms (in either narrative or non-narrative forms) and through performative templates ("rituals").

Needless to say, Lévi-Strauss's strict opposition is more of an ideal-type setting, representing extreme positions of a scale. In day-to-day life, these two basic mind-sets are inclusive, always coexisting and influencing each other in a large variety of combined forms, often on an idiosyncratic level.

Ancient Egyptian society is an example of a complex system for which the symbolic mind and its governing principles was constitutive. The idea that certain objects (such as statues, mummies, etc.) could in special contexts (temple and funerary rituals) be animated by powers or entities that would enter into or interact with them was natural. In order to outline the context of such a worldview, I will outline the basic concepts of the *ka* and *ba*—constituent elements of "personhood" in a very broad sense as it also concerned deities. These elements, at the same time, represented the medium of animation as they enabled the transference of certain aspects of life between various cosmological spheres (here and the beyond) taking full advantage of the symbolic potential offered by the hieroglyphic system (graphic punning). The final parts of the chapter will be devoted to the description of ritual means (Daily cult ritual and Opening of the mouth ritual) which activated such transference, thus establishing an intricate social and symbolic web between various parts of the ancient Egyptian cosmos.

Statues of Gods and the Deceased as Manifestations of the Divine

Statuary in ancient Egypt was much more than a piece of decorative art. Made from precious metals (silver, gold), exotic wood (cedar) and minerals (lapis lazuli, turquoise), and other valuable materials, statues were primarily considered as having the ability to somehow carry the living essence of a certain deity and as such serve as the object of cult worship.[2] A text carved on a slab of black granite (reused as a millstone) sometimes labeled as the "Memphite Cosmogony"[3] describes one of the several cosmogonical accounts that have survived from ancient Egypt. According to this composition, the creation of the cosmos and all within it was the result of an intellectual process beginning in the heart of the god Ptah.[4] By his pronouncement, things came into existence. Among other things were statues of gods:

> *Shabaka Stone, columns 59–61*[5]
> And then Ptah rested after having made everything and every divine word, having given birth (*mesi*) to the gods, having created all the cities, having founded the nomes (administrative districts), having placed the gods in their cult-places, having established their offerings and having founded their shrines, having made their statue-bodies according to the wishes of their hearts. So have the gods entered their bodies of all kinds of wood, all kinds of minerals, all kinds of clay, and of everything that grows on him,[6] in which they took form.

This text makes a clear distinction of the cultic divine "bodies" (statues) and the process of "in-dwelling,"[7] which enables their animation by the gods. As Assmann stresses very clearly: "*The statue is not the image of the deity's body but the body itself.*"[8] It "in-forms" the deity in an identical way as the deity could be "in-formed" in an animal or a natural phenomenon. In line with the basic principles of the symbolic mind as described in the introduction, statues were "born" (*mesi*) in the same way as human beings. What was the role of such statues? How did they fit in within the whole ideological system? Assmann provides a most useful overview of several relevant texts illustrating this phenomenon.[9] At the entrance of the temple of Edfu, we learn that the god Horus, who often takes on a full falcon form or a falcon head:

> [. . .] comes from heaven each day to behold his image (*bes*) on its Great Seat (i.e., the Holy of Holies). He descends (*hai*) on his image (*sekhem*[10]) and joins (*sensen*) his cult images (*akhemu*).[11]

However, the god could enter or inhabit not only statues but by virtue of association also depictions on the walls as is the case of the goddess Hathor and of Osiris in the temple of Dendara:[12]

> She (Hathor) unites (*khenem*) with her forms (*kheperu*)
> that are carved (*kheti*) in her sanctuary (*khem*).
> She alights (*kheni*) on her forms (*bes*) that are carved (*kheti*) on
>   the wall.[13]

In a text of the so-called Vigil for Osiris/Hourly vigil (*Stundenwachen*) in Dendara, Osiris's descent to join his cultic images is described:

> Osiris (. . .) comes as a spirit (*akh*) to unite with his form in his
>   sanctuary.
> He comes from the sky flying like a sparrowhawk with glittering
>   feathers,
> and the *ba*s of the gods with him.
> He descends as a falcon on his chamber in Dendara (. . .)
> In peace, he enters his august chamber with the *ba*s of the gods
>   who are around him.[14]
> He sees his mysterious form (*seshta*) depicted in its place (*sesh*),
> his figure (*bes*) engraved on the wall;
> he enters into his mysterious form, alights on his image (. . .)
> and the *ba*s of the gods take their places beside him.[15]

In this chapter, I shall explain the basic terminology (*ka*, *ba*, *akh*, etc.) and the animating principles that enabled such a transference of vital qualities within the ancient Egyptian cosmos and the ritual and religious contexts in which they were evoked and utilized. I will also explain in what way these very principles were used to conceptualize not only the process of the emanation of the divine, but also as the sustaining principles of human interaction within both realms of the living and the dead. Just as the living were in constant relationship with their gods, so were they entangled in a reciprocal web of ties with the deceased.

Ka and *Ba*—Vehicles of Syncretism and Group Identity

To understand how a statue or any other object could become a manifestation of a certain entity or power, we must have a look at two constituent notions, namely, the *ka* and the *ba*. Together with other concepts such as the heart, the body, the name, and the shadow, they are used to define the notion of personhood that was essentially aggregational. During life, these powers formed a whole but became dissociated with the moment of death. The main goal of funerary rituals was the reconfiguration of these parts into a new complex.

KA

Very generally, *ka* symbolizes the force that provides a direct link between various generations and also enables crossing the ultimate border between life and death.[16] *Ka* is sometimes thought of as a "twin" of a person born simultaneously. "It was soul, protective spirit and doppelgänger, all rolled into one."[17] The general idea of a good death therefore meant that one "went to his *ka*"—that is, was not only reconnected with it but was simultaneously integrated into the community of his forebearers.[18] The *ka* is also a homonym for "bull." This is associated with the central concept of a force that passes from father to son through embrace[19] and is thus a conceptualization of their mutual dependence—the hieroglyph for the *ka* ⎵⎿ depicts two outstretched arms.[20] The father is dependent on his son for the maintenance of his mortuary cult and the preservation of his good name, but it is the father who provides legitimacy to his successor (through maintenance of his father's mortuary cult).

> *PT 356, §582c–d*[21]
> O Osiris N.,[22] Horus has intervened for you,
> he has acted on behalf of his *ka* in you,
> that you may be satisfied in your identity "Satisfied *Ka*."

This constellation is modeled on the mythic precedent of Horus helping and defending his deceased father, Osiris, from his enemies (chiefly Seth),[23] the son being in reciprocity legitimized as the rightful heir to the throne of Egypt/head of family household, which only again strengthens his ability to create respect for his father:

> *Coffin Text 312, 68a–69g*[24]
> O Horus, come to Djedu (Busiris),[25]
> (. . .) that you may see my form (*iru*) and extol my *ba*!
> Spread fear (*senedj*) of me, create awe (*shefshef*) of me,
> so that the gods of the netherworld fear me,
> so that they defend their gates for me,
> so that the one who harmed me (Seth) not draw near to me (. . .)

BA

The notion of the *ba* developed across the millennia of Egyptian history.[26] The quintessential characteristic of the *ba* was its freedom of movement—especially between this world and the next. In the case of the deceased, the *ba* first had to leave the body and ascend to the sky: "Your *ba* to the sky, your corpse (*khat*) to the netherworld!"[27] only to return to it whenever necessary. The mythic precedent for this concept was sometimes sought in the cycle of the sun, which traverses the sky during the day to visit its corpse (Osiris) resting in the netherworld during the night.[28] Through this union, the *ba* renewed itself so as to "rise" the next day. The individual could take part in this cosmic cycle as long as the body in the form of a mummy existed enclosed within the tomb, which represented the netherworld. The body and the *ba* were therefore an inseparable pair—one needed the other (see figure 3.1).

SUMMARY

Even though it is tricky to strictly divide the notions behind the *ka* and *ba* as they can overlap in a sense, we may say that the freedom of movement was an essential aspect of the *ba* and played no major role in relation to the *ka*. The *ba* moved freely within different spheres of the cosmos and around in the tomb forming a "general presence" and being directly related to the mummy with

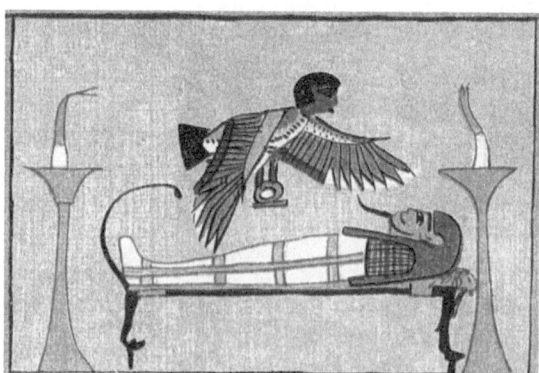

Figure 3.1. Facsimile of a vignette from the *Book of the Dead* of Ani (ca. 1250 BC). The *ba* of the deceased Ani hovers over his mummy as it lies on a bier. Original facsimile by E. A. Wallis Budge (1890). Photo: J. Wasserman on Wikimedia Commons (https://commons.wikimedia.org/wiki/File:BD_Mummy_and_Ba.jpg), under the public domain.

which it formed a unit. The *ka*, on the other hand, had nothing to do with the corpse but was rather focused on the statue of the deceased as the means of re-establishing and upholding social relationships between the deceased and the living (through the offerings—*kau*—and through the principle of patrilineal succession) and also with the forefathers whose community the deceased joined.[29]

In relation to the gods, it was the *ba* through which the deities could merge not only with objects (statues, reliefs, temples) but also with each other. The *ba* represents the "power" of a certain god, and if need be, these powers could combine forming a more or less temporary union resulting, among other things, in syncretistic iconography and names of these "new" entities.[30] The syncretic deity Atum-Cheper-Re thus represented the sun in its three forms: the nocturn sun (Atum), the new-born sun (Cheprer), and the sun at its strongest at noon (Re). This syncretistic principle applied also to the deceased to some extent. They too entered the divine and through their *ba* could "animate" or "enliven" their statues, tombs, and other cultic objects.

We can therefore conceptualize the *ka* as an intergenerational, reflexive principle operational among both the gods and the mortals in which one generation provides nutrition and sustenance (in the form of offerings) to receive social (divine) legitimacy in return. The *ba* is the vehicle through which the connection between the world of men and the world of gods was achieved with the deceased becoming part of the divine world through ritual transformation (mummification).

Ancient Egyptian Temple Rituals

Even though the ancient Egyptians developed cultural notions such as the *ka* and *ba* to conceptualize the interaction between entities populating the ancient Egyptian cosmos, it is very important to realize that their religion was primarily that of ritual performance focusing especially on the daily cult of divine statues, whose abodes were temples.[31] This service—supported by vast temple complexes and staff within[32]—were at the heart of ancient Egyptian religious experience.

As Assmann correctly stresses, we must conceive of this phenomenon—through which a god, a powerful entity, animated a certain image in the form of "uniting," "embracing," "indwelling"—as a process rather than as a state;[33] that is, the gods do not "live" in this world, but they "install" themselves, again and again. They must, however, be coerced to do so through ritual means, the most important of which were festivities and the daily cult ritual.[34] In case of festivities, which focused on the interaction with the cult statue mainly through processions, the deity could be perceived as "active" for example by providing prophecies revealed through its statue. The rites were often accompanied by strong and joyful emotions as statues left their hidden temple abodes and were presented to the general public.[35] The daily cult ritual, on the other hand, was a rather intimate event that took place within the innermost chamber and was attended by a very limited group of ritualists. The basic idea of the daily cult ritual was a very intuitive one: the main deity of a certain temple resides within this structure in the same manner as the pharaoh (himself directly partaking of divinity) rests in his palace or—for that manner—the head of a household in his home. Their needs must be addressed to make the deity "satisfied" (*hetep*) through "offerings" (*hetepu*). They are therefore awakened, washed, clothed, fed, and anointed three times a day. The deity descends into the statues and images in the form of the *ba* to partake of these ritual events, which accompany and, in a way, confirm the deity's connection to the given cultic statues or other objects.[36]

Mythic Precedents of the Daily Cult Ritual

Even though the daily cult ritual is concerned with satisfying the specific needs of a specific cult statue, the mythic precedents to which the activities are related to create an intricate web of meaning especially alluding to the mythological complex of the Osirian Cycle. Every offering can therefore be considered the "Eye of Horus," that is, the life force that the living son (Horus) provides to his deceased father (Osiris) thus revivifying him in the Netherworld: "Your natron[37] is on your mouth: you should clean all your bones and end what is (bad) against you. To you have I given the eye of Horus" (*Pyramid Text* 36, §29a–b); "Take the eye of Horus (i.e., a *depet*-cake), which you are to taste!" (*Pyramid Text* 51, §38a).[38] The ritual interaction attested in relation to these statues was therefore of an interdivine and not of human-divine character. Thus, when the ritualist approaches the inner sanctuary in which the divine statue rests, he positions himself variously as the pharaoh (whose nature is also divine) or directly as Horus. When he breaks the seal and removes the bolt holding the doors of the naos together, he removes the finger of Seth from Horus's eye thus repeating the healing event through which the eye became whole—an *udjat*-eye (from the root "to be healthy")—and a mediator of power. This in fact means that not only is the officiant assimilated to Horus, but through this act also the deity inside the naos (in this case Amun-Re) is structurally positioned as Horus: "It is to you that I have come and brought the Eye of Horus: your Eye is yours, o Horus."[39] The significance of the eye (*iret*) motif can be highlighted also through the punning principle. Thus the eye (*iret*) is often used as a pun on words deriving from the verb *iri* "to make/do," which can refer to "something that is made"/"deed," a ritual act or an offering, but also to the *iru* "that which acts" in the sense of the active aspect of the visible manifestation of a deity.[40] This is but a taste of the intricate web of meanings and associations that—through the similarity of these words on the phonetic and graphic level—functioned as the interpretative key.

Opening of the Mouth Ritual (*wepet-ra*)[41]

The daily cult ritual was practiced once a statue was established within a certain cult. Outside of creating the statue, it also had to be ritually activated—its mouth (and eyes) needed to be "opened" to make it an adequate medium for the deity. From the sources available to us, it seems that this particular ritual was practiced extensively on a varied group of objects—statues of gods, living kings and dead people, mummies (ritually equivalent to statues of gods), Apis bulls,[42] coffins, temples, sacred boats, amulets (heart-scarabs), and names[43]—and in a wide range of contexts (in the embalming workshop to conclude the mummification, at workshops where statues were made, in temples and sanctuaries). Even though we have textual mentions of this ritual dating back to the Old Kingdom (tomb of Metjen, approx. 2600 BC),[44] the oldest depictions of its individual scenes are attested later from the New Kingdom, especially from the Theban area.[45] An important detail is that these sources are part of the decoration of tombs. The funerary context of this ritual is crucial as we shall see further on. D. Lorton provides a very concise description of the crucial stages of the ritual:

> After purifications and the awakening and dressing of the *sem*-priest,[46] the artisans are brought before the statue. The next significant stages comprise [. . .] the presentation to the statue of the foreleg and heart of a slaughtered bull. Then follows the touching of the mouth with various implements that were evidently artisans' tools, as well as with the little finger of the *sem*-priest. One of these, the touching of the mouth with the adze called *netjerty*, was evidently of such importance that the entire ritual could be called to mind by the representation of this scene alone. This might have less to do with the object itself as an artisan's implement than with its name, which is formed from the root *netjer* "god": to show it touched to the statue's mouth symbolizes the purpose of the entire ritual, which was to make the statue a fit object for the cult.[47]

Once performed, the statue or any other object became ritually operative, that is, it could receive offerings, and in the case of statues connected with the funerary cult of an individual, operate on behalf of the deceased. In relation to statues of divinities, the idea was identical—once "born" (*mesi*), a statue could serve as physical means through which divine power manifested in physical form. The ritual was aimed at evoking the god, calling him/her to earth and preparing a body which the god could "enter" and "enliven."[48] In this sense, it is quite understandable that the ritual could be performed on whole temples as the function of an abode for the gods was also their primary reason.

Provided one had the means, ancient Egyptians equipped their tombs with several statues. Some were accessible to the living, whereas others were hidden (for example in the burial chamber). The most important statue—often in the form of a seated person—was that which served in the funerary cult and before which offerings were presented. The primary importance of statues in the mortuary cult of the deceased (tomb TT 82 of Amenemhet, dating to the reign of Thutmose III, 1479-1425 BC) is evident: "May your name endure inside your mansion (*hut*), may your images (*tutu*) be in their chapels, may your *ba* be living, your corpse (*khat*) [established] in your tomb of the necropolis, [your name being established] and lasting in the mouth(s) of your children forever."[49] This inscription informs us about the crucial prerequisites of a fortunate postmortem existence—a well-furnished tomb (statues in their chapels) in which the mummy had been provided with the necessary mortuary rituals (so as to enable the *ba* to "live," that is, mediate between this world and the beyond) and regularly serviced by his kin through mortuary rituals. (Only by being remembered through his name by the living can one continue an existence in the netherworld.) The statue functioned as a mediator in the interaction between the living and the transfigured dead in a very similar fashion as the statue of a god in a temple. After all, the deceased did attain a god-like nature by becoming an *akh* ("effective spirit") once the appropriate rituals were carried out.[50]

The statue focused on the deceased's continued life on earth after death, his/her cultic presence respectively.[51] The ritual prepares the deceased's statue to become a hierophanic vehicle for the life-force (*ka*):

> O my statue, you are before the lords of the sacred land;
> place yourself as the memory of my name in the domain of the Lords of Tawer,
> for you are here for me as an abode(?); you are my true body;
> for the *ka* of . . . Panehsy, true of voice.[52]

It is very probable that the opening of the mouth ritual was first enacted in a limited version in the workshop right after the statue was completed[53] in a manner very similar to the situation when the mummy was finished in the embalmer's workshop.[54] In both cases, the "objects" were made ready for cultic use and henceforth could start ritually "living." Very probably, the ritual was then fully carried out again during the funeral itself in the forecourt of the tomb.[55] However, we also know that the ritual (again possibly in a shorter version) was then repeated on special occasions, among which was the annual mortuary feast and the Feast of the Valley. On these and other occasions, the statues of the deceased were paraded through the necropolis in an Amun-procession.[56] The general idea was probably to ascertain the desired fate of the deceased after death and safeguard the communication channel with the living relatives. The relationship between the dead and the living is then mediated through food offerings (*kau*), which are presented to the *ka*-statue at both regular and festive occasions.[57]

The ritual of the opening of the mouth was carried out not only on the deceased's statue(s) but also on the mummy and the coffin(s) of the deceased. We have already seen that a mummy of an individual was classified in the same category as a (divine) statue. The ritual of the opening of the mouth corroborates this but from a ritual perspective. According to R. B. Finnestad, there was a rationale as to why these three "objects" (statue, mummy, coffin) were the main focus of the funerary rituals.[58] If the mummy becomes the object of the ritual, the focus is on the transcendental aspect of the deceased. The existence of the mummy founds the existence of the deceased's cult as the mummification process transforms the decaying flesh into an object of reverence. "The mummification is a divinization, a transmutation of the human body to a god's body."[59] This directly relates to the mythic precedent of Osiris being evoked to become present through his *ba*—sometimes depicted as a bird flying in and out of the burial chamber—in the sanctuary, not in any specific place or dependent on any specific cultic events, but rather as a general presence. The ritual thus manages to transform the mummy into a ritually operative object (see figure 3.2). The deceased becomes a deified individual, whose new ontological status is based on that of Osiris. "Hidden in the burial chamber the mummy represents this divine being who is met in the shrine in the statue. Thus, the tomb is like a temple of Osiris."[60] Furthermore, the central part of the whole ritual—the offering of the heart and leg—very aptly illustrates the idea of the transference of "vital" energy to the deceased[61] even though its form might seem rather ghastly to us today. At one moment, a calf and its mother are brought to the ritual space. The foreleg and heart of the living calf is cut out while its mother is standing behind and bellowing. Immediately, these parts are rushed to the mummy in an effort to open the mouth and eyes of the deceased through the warm vital energy streaming from the still quivering flesh:

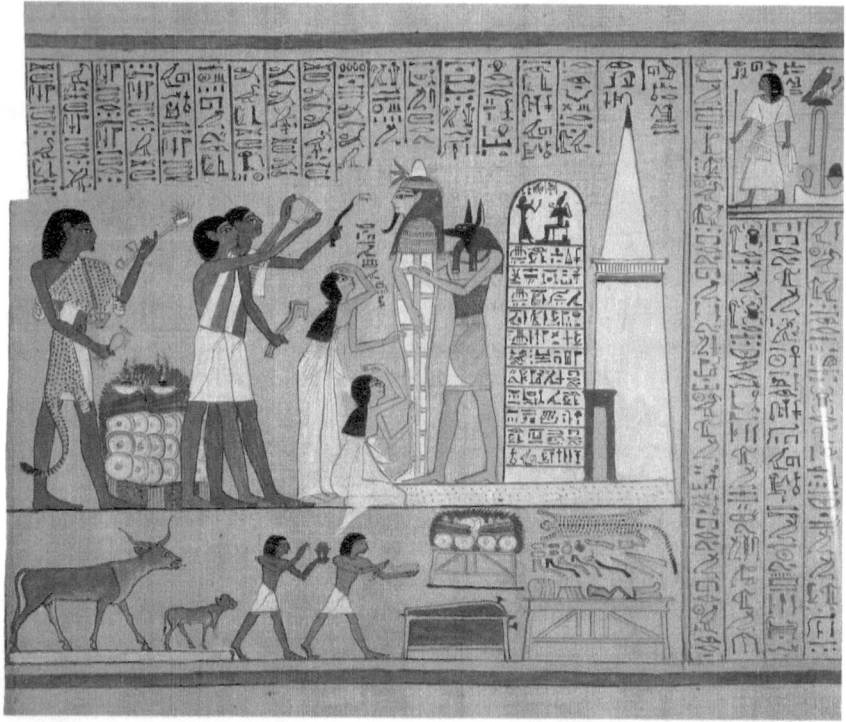

Figure 3.2. Vignette from the *Book of the Dead* of Hunefer (ca. 1275 BC). Opening of the mouth ritual performed in front of the deceased's tomb. Photo courtesy the British Museum, published on Wikimedia Commons (https://commons.wikimedia.org/wiki/File:Opening_of_the_mouth_ceremony.jpg), under the public domain.

Scene 44

[. . .]

Recitation: Oh N.! Take the leg, the Eye of Horus!

I have brought you the heart belonging to him (i.e., Seth). Do not approach(?) that god![62]

Scene 45

[. . .]

Recitation: Oh N., I have come in search of you/to embrace you! I am Horus.

I have supplied your mouth. I am your beloved son, and I have opened your mouth for you.

He (Seth) is slain for his mother, who bewails him, he is slain for his companion (i.e., Osiris/Horus).

[. . .]

O N.! I have opened your mouth for you with the leg/Eye of Horus![63]

The mythic precedent to this ritual act of course refers again to the Osiris-Seth constellation. The calf is likened to Seth, who is punished for his crime against Osiris. The body parts are pronounced to be the Eye of Horus, that is, the archetypal medium through which vital energy is channeled.

By being performed on a coffin, the ritual confirms and activates its protective function. By protecting the mummy, the coffin partakes of its sacred status, which is nicely reflected in case of the anthropoid-shaped exemplars. They look like the transformed deceased who has acquired divine nature. Just like the bodies of gods, they can be made of gold, silver, turquois[64] and they can be tripled (in a *matryoshka* manner), three being the number of wholeness and eternity.[65] Through its protective function, it enables the mummy (and therefore the deity) to remain in the sanctuary.

Conclusion

We began this text with an account of the principles that enabled the animation of various objects by divine powers, and we end with the description of a ritual that has the ability to transform a body of a deceased person into a cultically active object on a par with the statues of gods. In ancient Egypt, an individual hieroglyph was called *teet* (sign, image, icon), which also means "the image of a God."[66] Hieroglyphs were "images of the divine" in the same way as a transfigured (mummified) individual. The moment that enabled the transformation of a living individual into a unit of the Egyptian universal onto-semiotic system was the moment of death and subsequent mummification.

Having looked into these mechanisms in some detail, we still have to find and answer the question as to why have the ancient Egyptians gone to such lengths to create such a sophisticated symbolic framework that consumed and literally entombed immense amounts of both material and human resources?

Maurice Bloch and Jonathan Perry offer a rather interesting interpretation through their concept of two transactional orders, even if their neo-Marxist position poses serious limitations to their conclusions.[67] According to them, the short-term order is associated with the everyday, perishable, individual acquisitive transactions of goods and services. The long-term order, on the other hand, focuses solely on the reproduction of the social and cosmic order. This long-term order is often conceptualized through the image of some shared cultural identity ("immortal chiefdom," ancestral spirits, "nation," *ka* in case of ancient Egypt); on the material level, it can be represented through more or less lavish tomb structures that performatively enact its desired enduring character. As much as these two orders are in opposition, they are organically intertwined: "What we consistently find, then, is a series of procedures by which goods which derive from the short-term cycle are converted into the long-term transactional order."[68] These processes, as Bloch and Parry show, are often framed as a cultural transformation of an amorphous mass of organic matter, often expressed through the alimentary idiom of cultural "cooking" of "raw" substances.[69] In the case of ancient Egypt, the raw "substance" would be the body of the deceased, which, prior to the embalming rituals, was viewed as a lump of rotting meat (as indicated by the hieroglyph of a dead fish appended at the end of the Egyptian word for "corpse"). Funerary rituals physically transformed this "raw" material into a mummy—a precious, "cultural" object capable of channeling transcendental forces of the divine. As the opening of the mouth ritual shows, a mummy was considered equivalent to the statues of gods located in Egyptian temples, and, as the texts show, the dead person was addressed as Osiris, the paradigmatic divine deceased. Through death and transfiguration rituals, even a non-royal person entered the sphere of the eternal.

Notes

1. Claude Lévi-Strauss, *The Savage Mind*, 2nd edition (London: Weidenfeld & Nicolson, 1968).

2. David Lorton, "The Theology of Cult Statues in Ancient Egypt," in *Born in Heaven, Made on Earth: The Making of the Cult Image in the Ancient Near East*, ed. Michael B. Dick (Winona Lake: Eisenbrauns, 1999), 123–210; Jan Assmann, *The Search for God in Ancient Egypt*, trans. David Lorton (Ithaca: Cornell University Press, 2001), 41–47; Nicola Harrington, *Living with the Dead: Ancestor Worship and Mortuary Ritual in Ancient Egypt* (Havertown: Oxbow Books, 2012), 40–49.

3. The text is preserved in one copy only from Dynasty 25 from the reign of King Shabaka (approx. 716–702 BC) and was written in a then very archaizing form of Old Kingdom Egyptian claiming that it was copied from a text "that the predecessors had made, worm-eaten and unknowable from beginning to end."

4. Joshua J. Bodine, "The Shabaka Stone: An Introduction," *Studia Antiqua* 7, no. 1 (April 2009): 1–21; Ragnhild Bjerre Finnestad, "Ptah, Creator of the Gods: Reconsideration of the Ptah Section of the Denkmal," *Numen* 23, no. 2 (1976): 81–113.

5. Original published by James Henry Breasted, "The Philosophy of a Memphite Priest," *Zeitschrift für ägyptische Sprache und Altertumskunde* 39, no. 1 (December 1,

1901): 39–54. Translation based on Kurt Sethe, *Dramatische Texte zu altägyptischen Mysterienspielen* (Leipzig: J.C. Hirnsch, 1928), 68–70. See also Assmann, *The Search for God in Ancient Egypt*, 46; James P. Allen, *Genesis in Egypt: The Philosophy of Ancient Egyptian Creation Accounts* (New Haven: Yale University, 1988), 44.

6. Earth, personified by the god Geb, was masculine.

7. English translation of the German term *Einwohnung* coined by Herman Junker for the description of the special type of interaction between powers and entities within the ancient Egyptian cosmological universe.

8. Assmann, *The Search for God in Ancient Egypt*, 46.

9. Assmann, *The Search for God in Ancient Egypt*, 41–42.

10. *Sekhem* means "power" or any element that has the ability to exude power, for example an "image."

11. For the text and translation, see Aylward M. Blackman and Herbert W. Fairman, "A Group of Texts Inscribed on the *façade* of the Sanctuary in the Temple of Horus at Edfu," in *Miscellanea gregoriana raccolta di scritti publ. nel i centenario dalla fondazione del Pont. Museo Egizio (1839–1939)* (Vatican: Tipografia poliglotta vaticana, 1941), 398–99, nn. 6–9, fig. 2, text B.; also Siegfried Morenz, *Egyptian Religion* (Ithaca: Cornell University Press, 1992), 152.

12. Françoise A. F. Mariette, *Dendérah: Description générale du Grand temple de cette ville* (Paris: A. Franck, 1870), 29c, 87a.

13. Morenz, *Egyptian Religion*, 152, nn. 61–62. We can see the similarity of the roots of these words, which is one of the important principles of ancient Egyptian religious speculation.

14. Ancient Egyptian temples housed not only the main god or goddess but accommodated a whole pantheon of (regionally relevant) deities. Outside having individual cultic statues, their depictions were also carved on the temple walls.

15. Assmann, *The Search for God in Ancient Egypt*, 42.

16. For a survey of the history of research on this term, see Andrey O. Bolšakov, *Man and His Double in Egyptian Ideology of the Old Kingdom*, rev. transl. of the Russian ed. (Wiesbaden: Harrassowitz Verlag, 1997), 123–32. A concise account is to be found in Jan Assmann, *Death and Salvation in Ancient Egypt* (Ithaca: Cornell University Press, 2005), 43–44, 96–102.

17. Assmann, *Death and Salvation in Ancient Egypt*, 97.

18. Assmann, *Death and Salvation in Ancient Egypt*, 99.

19. On the concept of the embrace of *ka*, see Jan Assmann, Martin Bommas, and Andrea Kucharek, *Altägyptische Totenliturgien. Bd. 2., Totenliturgien und Totensprüche in Grabinschriften des Neuen Reiches* (Heidelberg: Universitätsverlag C. Winter, 2005), chapter 7, § 17, pp. 491–492.

20. Ancient Egyptians depicted distinctive elements of an object regardless of the perspective. For an overview of the basic principles, see Paul J. Frandsen, "On Categorization and Metaphorical Structuring: Some Remarks on Egyptian Art and Language," *Cambridge Archaeological Journal* 7, no. 1 (1997): 71–104.

21. Translation based on James P. Allen, *A New Concordance of the Pyramid Texts*. Brown University 2013, on-line source (http://ancientworldonline.blogspot.com/2013/07/a-new-concordance-of-pyramid-texts.html).

22. "N." is standardly used instead of the name of the specific individual who is written out in full in the original text.

23. In its totality written down in a coherent narrative only rather late by the Greek historian Plutarchos, the motif of the murder of Osiris from the hand of his brother Seth, posthumous engendering of Horus through Isis's cunning and the subsequent contendings of Horus and Seth for the throne of Egypt during which both opponents are maimed (Horus loses his eye/s, Seth his testicles) and then healed and reconciled (Osirian Cycle), were repeatedly alluded to already since the oldest extent corpus of mortuary texts located in the underground chambers of some pyramids. For a classic work on the topic focusing also on ancient Egyptian sources, see J. Gwyn Griffiths, *Plutarch's De Iside et Osiride* (Cardiff: University of Wales Press, 1970); most recently, Mark Smith, *Following Osiris: Perspectives on the Osirian Afterlife from Four Millennia* (Oxford, New York: Oxford University Press, 2017).

24. For the hieroglyphic text, see Adriaan de Buck, *The Egyptian Coffin Texts. T. 4, Texts of Spells 268–354* (Chicago: University of Chicago Press, 1951).

25. A cultically important city located in the Nile delta.

26. Boyo Ockinga, "Hatshepsut's Election to Kingship: The Ba and the Ka in Egyptian Royal Ideology," *The Bulletin of the Australian Centre for Egyptology* 6 (1995): 89–102; Jiří Janák, "Ba," ed. Willeke Wendrich and Jacco Dieleman, *UCLA Encyclopedia of Egyptology*, May 8, 2016 (http://digital2.library.ucla.edu/viewItem.do?ark=21198/zz002k7g85).

27. Louis V. Žabkar, *A Study of the Ba Concept in Ancient Egyptian Texts* (Chicago: University of Chicago Press, 1968), 111, n. 139.

28. The tomb of Nefertari (Queen Valley 66, Thebes) contains a splendid scene illustrating the *unio mystica* of the sun god Re and Osiris in the form of one being. Terence duQuesne, "The Osiris-Re Conjunction with Particular Reference to the Book of the Dead," in *Totenbuch-Forschungen: gesammelte Beiträge des 2. Internationalen Totenbuch-Symposiums, Bonn, 25. Bis 29. September 2005*, ed. Burkhard Backes, Irmtraut Munro, and Simone Stöhr (Wiesbaden: Harrassowitz, 2007), 23–33. For a color photograph, see Gertrud Thausing and Hans Goedicke, *Nofretari. Eine Dokumentation der Wandgemälde ihres Grabes* (Graz: Akademische Druck- u. Verlagsanstalt, 1971), 41.

29. Assmann, *Death and Salvation in Ancient Egypt*, 96.

30. Hans Bonnet, "On Understanding Syncretism," trans. John Baines, *Orientalia* 68, no. 3 (1999): 181–98; John Baines, "Egyptian Syncretism: Hans Bonnet's Contribution," *Orientalia* 68 (1999): 199–214; Erik Hornung, *Conceptions of God in Ancient Egypt: The One and the Many* (Ithaca: Cornell University Press, 1982), 91–99.

31. Katherine Eaton, *Ancient Egyptian Temple Ritual: Performance, Pattern, and Practice* (New York: Routledge, 2013); Lorton, "The Theology of Cult Statues in Ancient Egypt"; Assmann, *The Search for God in Ancient Egypt*.

32. For example, the property associated with the cult of the god Amun in Thebes in its heyday during the New Kingdom included 81,322 staff, 421,362 beasts, 433 gardens, 924 sq. miles (239 ha) of fields, 83 boats, 46 work yards and 65 market towns. See Serge Sauneron, *The Priests of Ancient Egypt*, new ed. (Ithaca, N.Y.: Cornell University Press, 2000), 55.

33. Assmann, *The Search for God in Ancient Egypt*, 43.

34. The main sources for the study of this ritual are wall reliefs with accompanying hieroglyphic inscriptions in the temple of Abydos dedicated to the cult of king Seti I (1290-1279 BC). Later sources on papyri—originating in Eastern Thebes (but lacking depictions)—provide a full record of the words of the cult dedicated to the god Amun and the goddess Mut at Karnak (first part of Twenty-second Dynasty, approx. 945-800 BC).

35. Richard H. Wilkinson, *The Complete Temples of Ancient Egypt* (New York: Thames & Hudson, 2000), 95-99.

36. As we shall see later, the very same principle holds true for the *ba*s of deceased private individuals: "Your *ba* ascends to the sky in the company of the *ba*s of the gods and descends again on your mummy in the cemetery." (For the translation, see Žabkar, *A Study of the Ba Concept*, 133, n. 48.)

37. A substance—naturally occurring mixture of sodium carbonate decahydrate (a kind of soda ash)—used for desiccating and thus cleansing the body. Natron was in Egyptian called *senetjer*, that is, "that which divinizes."

38. Allen, "A New Concordance of the Pyramid Texts."

39. Alexandre Moret, *Le rituel du culte divin journalier en Égypte: d'après les papyrus de Berlin et les textes du temple de Séti Ier, à Abydos* (Genève: Slatkine Reprints, 2007), 35-36.

40. Such as was the main focus of the famous Litany of Re, A funerary New Kingdom composition describing and depicting the ninety-nine forms (*iru*) the sun-god Re is able to take on himself; see Alexandre Piankoff, *The Litany of Re* (New York: Bollingen Foundation, 1964).

41. Reference works on the topic include Eberhard Otto, *Das ägyptische Mundöffnungsritual*, vol. 1—Text, vol. 2—Kommentar (Wiesbaden: Harrassowitz, 1960); Jean-Claude Goyon, *Rituels funéraires de l'ancienne Égypte: le rituel de l'embaumement; Le rituel de l'ouverture de la bouche; les livres des respirations* (Paris: Cerf, 1972), 86-187; Hans-W. Fischer-Elfert, *Die Vision von der Statue im Stein: Studien zum altägyptischen Mundöffnungsritual* (Heidelberg: Universitätsverlag C. Winter, 1998).

42. Sacred bull worshipped especially in the area of Memphis (apex of the delta) associated primarily with Ptah and Osiris; see Jean Vercoutter, "Apis," in *Lexikon der Ägyptologie, Bd. 1*, ed. Wolfgang Helck and Eberhard Otto (Wiesbaden: Harrassowitz, 1976), cols. 338-350.

43. Ragnhild B. Finnestad, "The Meaning and Purpose of Opening the Mouth in Mortuary Contexts," *Numen* 25, no. 2 (August 1978): 118-119.

44. Otto, *Das ägyptische Mundöffnungsritual*, vol. 2—Kommentar: 1.

45. Finnestad, "The Meaning and Purpose of Opening the Mouth in Mortuary Contexts," 118. This does not mean that the ritual was practiced primarily in this region; it is rather informative of the state of preservation of archaeological evidence.

46. A ritual specialist distinctively dressed in leopard skin. During the opening of the mouth ritual, his structural role was that of the son of the deceased. Bettina Schmitz, "Sempriester," in *Lexikon Der Ägyptologie, Bd. 1*, ed. Wolfgang Helck and Eberhard Otto (Wiesbaden: Harrassowitz, 1976), cols. 833-835.

47. Lorton, "The Theology of Cult Statues in Ancient Egypt," 148–149.

48. Finnestad, "The Meaning and Purpose of Opening the Mouth in Mortuary Contexts," 133. In this respect, the practice is comparable to a similar Mesopotamian *mīs pî* ritual. See Christopher Walker and Michael B. Dick, "The Induction of the Cult Image in Ancient Mesopotamia: The Mesopotamian Mīs Pî Ritual," in *Born in Heaven, Made on Earth: The Making of the Cult Image in the Ancient Near East*, ed. Michael B. Dick (Winona Lake: Eisenbrauns, 1999), 55–121.

49. Peter Der Manuelian, "Semi-Literacy in Egypt: Some Erasures from the Amarna Period," in *Gold of Praise: Studies on Ancient Egypt in Honor of Edward F. Wente*, ed. Emily Teeter and John A. Larson (Chicago: University of Chicago, 1999), 288.

50. Jiří Janák, "Akh," ed. Jacco Dieleman and Willeke Wendrich, *UCLA Encyclopedia of Egyptology* (February 20, 2013), on-line source http://digital2.library.ucla.edu/viewItem.do?ark=21198/zz002gc1pn.

51. The issue of women and funerary rituals is more complicated as the main mythic precedent was a strictly masculine one concentrating on the relationship between a dead father and his son as a rightful heir. For a most interesting analysis of the subtle work with this masculine template in case of some deceased women, see Kathlyn M. Cooney, "The Problem of Female Rebirth in New Kingdom Egypt," in *Sex and Gender in Ancient Egypt: "Don Your Wig for a Joyful Hour,"* ed. Carolyn Graves-Brown and Kathlyn M. Cooney (Swansea: Classical Press of Wales, 2008), 1–25.

52. Elizabeth Frood and John Baines, *Biographical Texts from Ramessid Egypt* (Atlanta: Society of Biblical Literature, 2007), 170.

53. Assmann, *Death and Salvation in Ancient Egypt*, 272.

54. Marianne Eaton-Krauss, *The Representations of Statuary in Private Tombs of the Old Kingdom* (Wiesbaden: Harrassowitz, 1984), 75–76.

55. For a spatial reconstruction of the ritual setting outside the tomb entrance, see Harrington, *Living with the Dead*, 105–108, fig. 37.

56. The celebrations took place within a larger religious framework, which included a procession of the god Amun from the main temple in Karnak (Thebes). Part of these celebrations was the presentation of flower bouquets—among other things—consecrated directly in Amun's temple. Temple archives attest the vast extent of this practice: in almost three years, nearly 4.8 million flower offerings were presented (and recorded) at the Great Temple of Amun. Richard H. Wilkinson, *The Complete Temples of Ancient Egypt* (New York: Thames & Hudson, 2000), 97.

57. Andrew H. Gordon, "The *ka* as an Animating Force," *Journal of the American Research Center in Egypt* 33 (1996): 33–35.

58. Finnestad, "The Meaning and Purpose of Opening the Mouth in Mortuary Contexts," 134.

59. Finnestad, "The Meaning and Purpose of Opening the Mouth in Mortuary Contexts," 128.

60. Finnestad, "The Meaning and Purpose of Opening the Mouth in Mortuary Contexts," 128.

61. Assmann, *Death and Salvation in Ancient Egypt*, 324–329; Andrew H. Gordon and Calvin W. Schwabe, " 'Live Flesh' and 'Opening-of-the-Mouth': Biomedical, Ethnological, and

Egyptological Aspects," in *Proceedings of the Seventh International Congress of Egyptologists, Cambridge, 3–9 September 1995*, ed. Christopher Eyre (Leuven: Peeters, 1998), 461–69.

62. Otto, *Das ägyptische Mundöffnungsritual*, vol. 1—Text: 100–101; vol. 2—Kommentar: 104–105.

63. Otto, *Das ägyptische Mundöffnungsritual*, vol. 1—Text: 102–104; vol. 2—Kommentar: 106.

64. See for example the exquisite examples of the coffins of the pharaoh Tutankhamun found by Howard Carter in the pharaoh's tomb in the Valley of the Kings in Thebes.

65. Hornung, *Conceptions of God in Ancient Egypt*, 218–219.

66. Adolf Erman and Hermann Grapow, eds., *Wörterbuch der ägyptischen Sprache*. Bd. 5 (Leipzig: J. C. Hinrichs'sche Buchhandlung, 1931), cols. 239–240, A I, B I, C.

67. Jonathan P. Parry and Maurice Bloch, "Introduction: Money and the Morality of Exchange," in *Money and the Morality of Exchange*, ed. Jonathan P. Parry and Maurice Bloch (Cambridge: Cambridge University Press, 1996), 23–30.

68. Parry and Bloch, "Introduction: Money and the Morality of Exchange," 25.

69. A similar idea was expressed by Claude Lévi-Strauss, *The Raw and the Cooked: Introduction to a Science of Mythology*, trans. Doreen Weightman and John Weightman, 1st. U.S. edition (New York: Harper & Row, 1969).

Bibliography

Allen, James P. *Genesis in Egypt: The Philosophy of Ancient Egyptian Creation Accounts*. New Haven: Yale University Press, 1988.

———. A New Concordance of the Pyramid Texts. Brown University 2013, on-line source (http://ancientworldonline.blogspot.com/2013/07/a-new-concordance-of-pyramid-texts.html).

Assmann, Jan. *Death and Salvation in Ancient Egypt*. Ithaca: Cornell University Press, 2005.

———. *The Search for God in Ancient Egypt*. Translated by David Lorton. Ithaca: Cornell University Press, 2001.

Assmann, Jan, Martin Bommas, and Andrea Kucharek. *Altägyptische Totenliturgien. Bd. 2., Totenliturgien und Totensprüche in Grabinschriften des Neuen Reiches*. Heidelberg: Universitätsverlag C. Winter, 2005.

Baines, John. "Egyptian Syncretism: Hans Bonnet's Contribution." *Orientalia* 68 (1999): 199–214.

Blackman, Aylward M., and Herbert W. Fairman. "A Group of texts inscribed on the façade of the sanctuary in the temple of Horus at Edfu." In *Miscellanea gregoriana raccolta di scritti publ. nel i centenario dalla fondazione del Pont. Museo Egizio (1839–1939)*, 397–428. Monumenti Musei e Gallerie Pontificie. Vatican: Tipografia poliglotta vaticana, 1941.

Bodine, Joshua J. "The Shabaka Stone: An Introduction." *Studia Antiqua* 7, no. 1 (April 2009): 1–21.

Bolšakov, Andrej O. *Man and His Double in Egyptian Ideology of the Old Kingdom*. Rev. transl. of the Russian ed. Wiesbaden: Harrassowitz, 1997.

Bonnet, Hans. "On Understanding Syncretism." Translated by John Baines. *Orientalia* 68, no. 3 (1999): 181–198.
Breasted, James Henry. "The Philosophy of a Memphite Priest." *Zeitschrift für ägyptische Sprache und Altertumskunde* 39, no. 1 (December 1, 1901): 39–54.
Cooney, Kathlyn M. "The Problem of Female Rebirth in New Kingdom Egypt." In *Sex and Gender in Ancient Egypt: "Don Your Wig for a Joyful Hour,"* edited by Carolyn Graves-Brown and Kathlyn M. Cooney, 1–25. Swansea: Classical Press of Wales, 2008.
De Buck, Adriaan. *The Egyptian Coffin Texts. T. 4., Texts of Spells 268–354*. Chicago: University of Chicago Press, 1951.
DuQuesne, Terence. "The Osiris-Re Conjunction with Particular Reference to the Book of the Dead." In *Totenbuch-Forschungen: Gesammelte Beiträge des 2. Internationalen Totenbuch-Symposiums, Bonn, 25. bis 29. September 2005*. Edited by Burkhard Backes, Irmtraut Munro, and Simone Stöhr, 23–33. Wiesbaden: Harrassowitz, 2007.
Eaton, Katherine. *Ancient Egyptian Temple Ritual: Performance, Pattern, and Practice*. New York: Routledge, 2013.
Eaton-Krauss, Marianne. *The Representations of Statuary in Private Tombs of the Old Kingdom*. Wiesbaden: Harrassowitz, 1984.
Erman, Adolf, and Hermann Grapow, eds. *Wörterbuch der ägyptischen Sprache. Bd. 5*. Leipzig: Hinrichs'sche Buchhandlung, 1931.
Finnestad, Ragnhild Bjerre. "The Meaning and Purpose of Opening the Mouth in Mortuary Contexts." *Numen* 25, no. 2 (August 1978): 118–134.
———. "Ptah, Creator of the Gods: Reconsideration of the Ptah Section of the Denkmal." *Numen* 23, no. 2 (1976): 81–113.
Fischer-Elfert, Hans-W. *Die Vision von der Statue im Stein: Studien zum altägyptischen Mundöffnungsritual*. Heidelberg: Universitätsverlag C. Winter, 1998.
Frandsen, Paul J. "On Categorization and Metaphorical Structuring: Some Remarks on Egyptian Art and Language." *Cambridge Archaeological Journal* 7, no. 1 (1997): 71–104.
Frood, Elizabeth, and John Baines. *Biographical Texts from Ramessid Egypt*. Atlanta: Society of Biblical Literature, 2007.
Gordon, Andrew H. "The *ka* as an Animating Force." *Journal of the American Research Center in Egypt* 33 (1996): 31–35.
Gordon, Andrew H., and Calvin W. Schwabe. "'Live Flesh' and 'Opening-of-the-Mouth': Biomedical, Ethnological, and Egyptological Aspects." In *Proceedings of the Seventh International Congress of Egyptologists, Cambridge, 3–9 September 1995*, edited by Christopher Eyre, 461–469. Leuven: Peeters, 1998.
Goyon, Jean-Claude. *Rituels funéraires de l'ancienne Égypte: le Rituel de l'embaumement; Le Rituel de l'ouverture de la bouche; les Livres des respirations*. Paris: Cerf, 1972.
Griffiths, J. Gwyn. *Plutarch's De Iside et Osiride*. Cardiff: University of Wales Press, 1970.
Harrington, Nicola. *Living with the Dead: Ancestor Worship and Mortuary Ritual in Ancient Egypt*. Havertown: Oxbow Books, 2012.
Hornung, Erik. *Conceptions of God in Ancient Egypt: The One and the Many*. Ithaca: Cornell University Press, 1982.

Janák, Jíří. "Akh." Edited by Jacco Dieleman and Willeke Wendrich. *UCLA Encyclopedia of Egyptology*, February 20, 2013, on-line source, http://digital2.library.ucla.edu/viewItem.do?ark=21198/zz002gc1pn.

———. "Ba." Edited by Willeke Wendrich and Jacco Dieleman. *UCLA Encyclopedia of Egyptology*, May 8, 2016, on-line source, http://digital2.library.ucla.edu/viewItem.do?ark=21198/zz002k7g85.

Lévi-Strauss, Claude. *The Raw and the Cooked: Introduction to a Science of Mythology*. Translated by Doreen Weightman and John Weightman. 1st US edition. New York: Harper & Row, 1969.

———. *The Savage Mind*. 2nd edition. London: Weidenfeld & Nicolson, 1968.

Lorton, David. "The Theology of Cult Statues in Ancient Egypt." In *Born in Heaven, Made on Earth: The Making of the Cult Image in the Ancient Near East*, edited by Michael B. Dick, 123–210. Winona Lake: Eisenbrauns, 1999.

der Manuelian, Peter. "Semi-Literacy in Egypt: Some Erasures from the Amarna Period." In *Gold of Praise: Studies on Ancient Egypt in Honor of Edward F. Wente*, edited by Emily Teeter and John A. Larson, 285–298. Chicago: University of Chicago Press, 1999.

Mariette, Ferdinand. *Dendérah: description générale du grand temple de cette ville*. Paris: A. Franck, 1870.

Morenz, Siegfried. *Egyptian Religion*. Ithaca: Cornell University Press, 1992.

Moret, Alexandre. *Le rituel du culte divin journalier en Égypte: d'après les papyrus de Berlin et les textes du temple de Séti Ier, à Abydos*. Genève: Slatkine Reprints, 2007.

Ockinga, Boyo. "Hatshepsut's Election to Kingship: The ba and the ka in Egyptian Royal Ideology." *The Bulletin of the Australian Centre for Egyptology* 6 (1995): 89–102.

Otto, Eberhard. *Das ägyptische Mundöffnungsritual*. Vol. 1—Text. Wiesbaden: Harrassowitz, 1960.

———. *Das ägyptische Mundöffnungsritual*. Vol. 2—Kommentar. Wiesbaden: Harrassowitz, 1960.

Parry, Jonathan P., and Maurice Bloch, eds. *Money and the Morality of Exchange*. Cambridge: Cambridge University Press, 1996.

Piankoff, Alexandre. *The Litany of Re*. Bollingen Series. New York: Bollingen Foundation, 1964.

Sauneron, Serge. *The Priests of Ancient Egypt*. New ed. Ithaca, N.Y: Cornell University Press, 2000.

Schmitz, Bettina. "Sempriester." In *Lexikon Der Ägyptologie, Bd. 1*, edited by Wolfgang Helck and Eberhard Otto, 833–35. Wiesbaden: Harrassowitz, 1976.

Sethe, Kurt. *Dramatische Texte zu altägyptischen Mysterienspielen*. Leipzig: J.C. Hirnsch, 1928.

Smith, Mark. *Following Osiris: Perspectives on the Osirian Afterlife from Four Millennia*. Oxford, New York: Oxford University Press, 2017.

Thausing, Gertrud, and Hans Goedicke. *Nofretari. Eine Dokumentation der Wandgemälde ihres Grabes*. Einleitung: Gertrud Thausing. Kommentar: Hans Goedicke. Graz: Akademische Druck- u. Verlagsanstalt, 1971.

Vercoutter, Jean. "Apis." In *Lexikon der Ägyptologie, Bd. 1*, edited by Wolfgang Helck and Eberhard Otto, 338–350. Wiesbaden: Harrassowitz, 1976.

Walker, Christopher, and Michael B. Dick. "The Induction of the Cult Image in Ancient Mesopotamia: The Mesopotamian *mīs pî* Ritual." In *Born in Heaven, Made on Earth: The Making of the Cult Image in the Ancient Near East*, edited by Michael B. Dick, 55–121. Winona Lake: Eisenbrauns, 1999.

Wilkinson, Richard H. *The Complete Temples of Ancient Egypt*. New York: Thames & Hudson, 2000.

Žabkar, Louis V. *A Study of the ba Concept in Ancient Egyptian Texts*. Chicago: University of Chicago Press, 1968.

Chapter 4

Seeing and Time

Personal Divinity in the Object of Hindu Devotion

JOHN W. AUGUST III

Editor's Note: In chapter 4, August discusses the Brahminic concept of darśan *and describes devotional practices that serve to create personality in divine images and objects. The chapter serves as an important complement to the previous chapter in several ways. First, it moves us from Ancient Egypt to the Indian subcontinent and allows us to explore the idea of personalized objects in another historical and cultural context. Furthermore, while chapter 3 focused on the religious objects and rituals themselves, this chapter draws attention to the role of the devotional practitioner. Thus, generalized from these two chapters, we can reflect on the differences between ritual and devotional objects: one associated with priestly (and therefore possibly larger social) functions, and the other with existential modes of individual spiritual practice. This chapter is the first of three that will focus on Asian traditions of personalized objects.*

When we cognize objects, we do so in various modes.[1] These modes of cognition lead to corresponding types of action. That there are multiple ways of cognizing objects means there are different forms of judgment that have as their basis specific kinds of acts that can be performed on or in relation to objects. Almost all of the various kinds of judgments we perform in the synthesis of objects are directed toward a specific kind of utility that particular objects have for us. For example, we may cognize an object in the economic mode when we anticipate acting on the object as one that we intend to perform an act of exchange (or consider the object in light of this kind of act). Or, alternatively, we may cognize an object in the scientific mode when we desire to measure (in a broad sense) the object for the sake of knowing objects like it. The judgment of an object in one of mode of cognition is reliant upon an exclusion of the other possible ways we could act upon it. The exclusion of some kinds of actions and emphasis of others shapes the horizon of possibility within which we choose an action appropriate to the utility of an object we find within a specific context.

As creatures of habit, we find that we have a tendency to cognize objects in our world in one or a few modes of cognition, while, at the same time, we often neglect other modes. That is not to say that we do not cognize objects in all the modes at various times. What I mean to say is that, over time, we, as individuals, develop the skills that are required to cognize objects in highly advanced ways in fewer and fewer modes of cognition. In this chapter, we will explore one way in which a special mode of cognition (the mode of cognition that judges persons as such), when it is applied to objects that would otherwise be judged in some other mode of cognition, can transform the relation between the cognizer and the cognized in such a way that a horizon of possibility opens up to the cognizer that was not apparent before. Specifically, we will inquire into the development of the relationship between the Brahminical devotionalist and the divine object, that is, the divine image as embodied in some medium, such as a statue, painting, or some other depiction of the divine.

Before we engage in this inquiry, I want to clarify how I shaped this investigation on several fronts. First, I do not intend to promote the hypothesis that the interpretation of the object as personal is the sole mode of cognition that might promote the transformation of the subject-cognizer. Rather, as Cassirer would note, modes of cognition are tyrannical. That is, the frequency of judging in particular modes of cognition determines the subject's disposition toward objects in general. For example, a person that habitually cognizes objects in the historical mode will, generally speaking, have a tendency to cognize all objects as such. So, regardless of the mode in which objects are cognized, all modes of cognition are transformative. Our interest in this particular investigation is the transformative acts of judgment that occur when the personal mode of cognition is habituated.

The second point of the preamble to our inquiry is related to the actual nature of the world as it plays a part in the transformation of the subject. For the sake of *this* inquiry, we are not required to take a particular stand on whether or not the divine object *is* or *could be* personal. Because the question of a personal divine object is not the focus of this investigation, I will remain humbly agnostic about the actuality or possibility of the divine personal object. The emphasis in this inquiry is on the transformation of the subject as she engages with the object that she interprets to be both personal and divine. The results of such an inquiry, then, do not necessitate a position regarding the personality or the divinity of the object without the subject. With this agnosticism in mind, I propose that we refrain from locating the personal relation merely in the subject or in the object. At times, I may make statements that appear to lean in the direction of an actual personal and divine object. Where deviations from agnosticism appear, I ask that we understand such statements as presented in the way they are for the ease of description rather than as an indication of some metaphysical or ontological commitment.

Next, given that I am not a practitioner of devotionalism, this chapter ought to be regarded as merely a precursor to further work done by those who have devoted much more time to scholarship in this area. Despite my shortcomings in studied servitude to Brahminical devotionalism, I do feel that I provide something substantial to the conversations that occur in and around our topic of investigation that may be useful for several different disciplines. These areas of study may include phenomenology, hermeneutics, ontology, religious studies, process studies, and personalism. Needless to say, this list is not exhaustive.

Finally, the varieties of metaphysical conjecture, religious belief and ritual, and the praxes that develop out of Hindu thought create an overwhelming tension between the multitude of traditions that contribute to the plurality of religious practices that are termed "Brahmanism." Organizing the wide array of traditions into a single concept is problematic at best. For our purposes, I will be working within devotionalistic variations of the Brahminical traditions. The sources that I draw from are not restricted to a specific region or set of beliefs by a particular culture or subculture. What I attempt here is to glean some common features of these traditions (as they utilize the greater traditions holy texts, primarily from the *Gita*) in order to produce general hypotheses from these different sources. The hope for this presentation is that it describes, generally speaking, what the lived experience of the person genuinely disposed toward the possibility of personal divine objects might be like.

The Argument

As for the structure of this chapter, the argument takes the conditional form, where the consequent portion is derived from the empirical research completed in order to present the initial portion of the chapter. This means that the research-oriented portion (which will be presented first) of this work forms the necessary conditions for the possibility of the kind of experience that might be available to the practitioner of devotionalist Brahminic thought. The latter portion of the presentation utilizes the research as a ground for speculation about the lived experience of the practitioner in terms of the transformation of her disposition and, thus, about what she is capable of seeing. The most important thing, I think, to take note of in the formation of this argument is that the speculative portion of the text, found in the latter half of the presentation, is only a possible way that the practitioner's experience might unfold and, thus, is not an account of what will necessarily happen.

In terms of content, this inquiry has two major hypotheses (and several minor ones). The first makes the broad claim that, through a radical reordering of perceived (though not necessarily cognized) possibility, the actual disposition of an individual person can also be radically reordered. This hypothesis, while I think it is important, will not receive much attention here. In effect, it is a generalization of the second hypothesis.

The second, and more important, hypothesis claims that, through practices of humility and care directed toward the divine object, the practitioner of devotionalism exhibits a desire for a new way of seeing (and being seen) that acts as a call to the divine for edification. These practices reorient the devotionalist's habits of cognition that might then reshape her horizon of experience to include the possibility of personal interaction with the divine. The ultimate result of such practices directed toward divine objects or images may be found in a divine and personal world. That is, the divinity of the object may come to permeate the rest of her experience, the divine no longer concentrated merely in the object of the practitioner's devotion.

Darśan

Diana Eck names the experience of the divine personal object using the colloquial Indian term *darśan*. She writes, "The central act of Hindu worship, from the point of view of the lay person, is to stand in the presence of the deity and to behold the image with one's own eyes, to see and be seen by the deity."[2] *Darśan*, as Eck notes, is commonly translated as "auspicious sight."[3] For the devotionalist, to engage with a divine object is to engage with the embodied deity him- or herself. Thus, it is an exchange of vision between the divinity and the individual that forms the heart and soul of Brahminical devotionalism. Primarily, we are interested in how the practitioner of devotionalism anticipates and prepares for *darśan* with an eye to how these practices alter the devotionalist's outlook. However, to appreciate the practices that are performed in preparation for divine insight, it behooves us to understand these activities in relation to their aim. Thus, to appreciate the fuller process that culminates in *darśan*, we begin with an account of divine insight itself. From there, we will work backward to understand the processes that open up the possibility of *darśan*.

Unfortunately, human beings do not have the wherewithal to see the divine on their own merit. This initial incapacity to see the divine is prevalent in most Hindu cultures. There are some exceptions, however, that explain that humans did, at one time, have the ability to see the divine. Through some kind of mishap or misfortune, however, we lost the ability. For example, a Balinese legend explains the mishap that leads to humanity's loss of divine sight. Wiener writes:

> According to a story people tell in Bali, there was once a time when divinities and spirits were knowable through ordinary human perception. In those days humans had completely black eyes, like those of dogs or other animals, and, like dogs, they could see spirits. More important, being superior to dogs, they could see divinities. . . . One day, a fellow was shitting in the woods when a god (which one isn't mentioned) walked by. Without thinking, he called out cheerfully the usual friendly Balinese greeting, "Betara, where are you going?" Such impertinence could not be allowed to recur. By covering the larger part of the human eyes with a white membrane, the gods made it impossible for people to see them, and so matters have remained to this day.[4]

Thus, the present human condition appears to entail initial blindness to the divine. Fortunately, this blindness can be resolved. The *Gita* provides us with an example of a resolution to this blindness:

> Kṛṣṇa: O son of Pritha, behold My forms, a hundredfold, a thousandfold, of varied kinds, divine, many-colored and many-shaped. Behold the Ādityas, the Vasus, Rudras, Ashvins, as also the Maruts. Behold, O descendent-of-Bharata, many wonders never seen before. Behold now, O Gudākesha, the whole universe, moving and unmoving, abiding as one here in My body, and whatever else you desire to see. Yet, you will not be able to see Me with this your own eye. I will give you the divine eye. Behold my Lordly Yoga.[5]

In this passage, Kṛṣṇa gives Arjuna the capacity to have *darśan* by bestowing him with the divine eye. As the quotation notes, before Arjuna can have his *darśan*, he must be granted the capacity by Kṛṣṇa.

The above passage describes a precursor to the Arjuna's *darśan*. If we read the passage closely, we find that it acts as an invitation to see the god through auspicious sight and as an indicator that, in Arjuna's present state, he is incapable of doing so. What, we might ask, prepares Arjuna for *darśan*? The answer to this question is provided in a passage immediately prior to Kṛṣṇa's invitation.

Arjuna says, "Even as you have described [Your] Self, O Supreme Lord, thus do I desire to see Your Lordly form, O Supreme Spirit. If, Lord, You think it possible for me to see that [form of Yours], O Lord of Yoga, then do reveal to me [Your] immutable Self."[6] From this passage, we find that the initial condition for Arjuna's *darśan* is found within Arjuna himself. He *desires* to see, and, thus, he is open to the possibility of divine sight. By "openness" I mean something akin to James's concept of a live option. In response to this openness and desiring, Kṛṣṇa invites Arjuna to behold him in his real nature.

One thing to note about Arjuna's desire for and openness to *darśan* is that both of these characteristics are directed toward a personal being. Arjuna is engaged with Kṛṣṇa, a being capable of personal interaction. It is true that Arjuna laments and apologizes for treating Kṛṣṇa as a person after he realizes (a realization that occurs because of his *darśan*) his charioteer is in fact a god. He says, "That [I], ignorant of Your majesty, through my heedlessness or perhaps out of fondness and thinking importunely [that You are my] friend, saying [impolitely] 'Hey Krishna! Hay Yādava! Hey, friend!' And that in jest [I showed] disrespect to you, [while] playing, reposing, sitting, or eating, alone or in the presence [of others]—[for] that, O Acyuta, I beg Your pardon, [you who are] unfathomable!"[7] Some contend that this passage is an indication that Kṛṣṇa is not to be regarded as a person. I believe such an assertion is a mistake. Arjuna is distraught that he teased Kṛṣṇa in a way that would otherwise be considered disrespectful to a god. Upon realizing the divine nature of his charioteer, he apologizes for playing with Kṛṣṇa as he would any other person. That is, Arjuna is deeply troubled by his treatment of Kṛṣṇa as a *regular* person. His apology should not be read as an indication that Kṛṣṇa is not a person. Rather, Kṛṣṇa is the most venerable and enlightened person, one who is worthy of Arjuna's undying devotion.

Just as personal beings communicate with personal messages, Arjuna's *darśan* is personal (though it is personal with qualification). We shall see this later. However, there do appear to be cases in which mortals do develop unusual (and possibly divine) capacities for extraordinary sight. In the *Mahabharata*, we find instances of extraordinary sight that would better be described as impersonal. For example, Sanjaya, the advisor of Dhritarashtra, relates the events of the war of Kurukshetra (including the fight between the Kauravas and the Pandavas) to Dhritarashtra through an act of seeing at a distance. Sanjaya tells of these events as though he were present at the scene of the fighting. Sanjaya, like Arjuna, did not originally have this gift of sight. It was gifted to him by Vyasa, one of the seven immortals. Another example of gifted sight in the *Mahabharata* is found in book 11, section 16. In this section, we find Queen Gandhari (who also received the gift of sight from Vyasa) looking upon the happenings of the battlefield in the aftermath of the war:

> Gandhari, though staying on that spot which was distant from the field of battle, beheld, with her spiritual eye, the slaughter of the Kurus. Devoted to her lord, that highly blessed lady had always practiced high vows. Undergoing the severest penances, she was always truthful in her speech. In consequence of the gift of the boon by the great *rishi* Vyasa of sanctified deeds, she became possessed of spiritual knowledge and power. Piteous were the lamentations in which that dame then indulged. Endued with great intelligence, the Kuru dame saw, from a distance, but as if from a near point, that field of battle, terrible to behold and full of wonderful sights, of those foremost of fighters.[8]

The extraordinary visions of Sanjaya and Gandhari help to distinguish personal from impersonal visions. In impersonal divine sight, of which Sanjaya and Gandhari partake, the ability seems to allow the seer to remotely view events that are presently occurring at a distance. Both Sanjaya and Gandhari are watching things occur as they happen from quite some distance away. Sanjaya sees the events of the war, and Gandhari sees the aftermath of that war. While these kinds of vision should be classified as extraordinary, they do not contain one of the crucial elements, *being seen*, that is included in *darśan*. Because they lack the crucial element of being seen by divinity in a personal way, a reciprocal of the seeing of the divine found in *darśan* proper (and it is this reciprocation that makes the *darśan* personal), I will refrain from including these as instances of the kind of *darśan* that we are including in our analysis.

One thing, however, that we can glean from all of the examples of extraordinary vision provided so far, both personal and impersonal, is that these extraordinary ways of seeing all share in the characteristic that they are unavailable to ordinary mortals. Arjuna, Sanjaya, and Gandhari all receive this capacity from another. Arjuna receives his *darśan* from Kṛṣṇa, and Sanjaya and Gandhari both receive their gifts from Vyasa. In the case of Arjuna, the gift of sight provided by Kṛṣṇa appears to be a one-time affair. His vision is provided to him directly by Kṛṣṇa for the sake of directing him toward the virtuous path in the coming battle. The gifts of Sanjaya and Gandhari, on the other hand, are given to them on account of their established virtuousness. While the gift of *darśan* may be granted to practitioners by the gods or some celestial being, our ordinary way of seeing is not *darśan*. However, as we shall see, for the Brahminical devotionalist, sight of the more mundane kind is the basis upon which *darśan* is pursued.

Mundane seeing in Indian culture is related to both touching and knowing. Kramrisch writes, "Seeing, according to Indian notions, is a going forth of the sight toward the object. Sight touches it and acquires its form. Touch is the ultimate connection by which the visible yields to being grasped. While the eye touches the object, the vitality that pulsates in it is communicated."[9] Seeing, then, is an extension of tactile sensation. It connects us to the objects of sensation through an illumination of the world around us. This illumination, in turn, provides the initial basis for an experience of truth, divine or otherwise. In contrast to the historical mistrust of the senses that characterizes many philosophies in the West, seeing, for many Indians, facilitates an immediate connection to the material world. This basic trust of the visible lends itself to an epistemic disposition that demands a seeing, although seeing must presumably be done appropriately, at the basis of Indian knowledge.

The way that Indian culture and its wide variety of philosophies understand sight can be contrasted against the traditional understanding of perception that has arisen in the West. For most of Western history, perception has been understood as originating in an outer world that comes to affect the sense organs. This theoretical understanding that moves from the outside into the subject is reversed in Indian thought. According to King, "In the early *Upaniṣads* perception is explained in terms of the self (*ātman*) as an inner light which shines outward (through the eyes) and illuminates the objective world."[10] This Eastern understanding of perception finds no analogous account in Western thought until the development of the critical philosophy by Kant.

Ordinary sight, as Kramrisch notes, is the ultimate connection to the visible. It provides us with our connection to the vital impulse of the sensuous world. However, *darśan* is divine vision, the seeing of the invisible or subtle and enduring truth of the world that lies beyond mere sensuous experience. Thus, a further distinction can be drawn between the visions of Sanjaya, Gandhari, and Arjuna. Gandhari had a basic sensuous vision. While it was horrific and unnerving, it was mundane in the sense that it was of the merely sensuous events that were occurring on the battlefield after the carnage. The unusual characteristic of both Gandhari and Sanjaya's gifted sights was their capacity to see at a distance. What she saw, however, were events occurring in the visible realm. Her gift of vision did not, at least in this instance, provide her with access to subtle or invisible reality.

Sanjaya, on the other hand, did see what Arjuna saw when Kṛṣṇa gifted him with divine vision, as the *Gita* notes. "Having spoken thus, O king, the great Lord of Yoga, Hari, then revealed, supreme lordly form to the son-of-Pritha. Many mouths and eyes, many wondrous appearances, many divine adornments, many divine upraised weapons, wearing divine garlands and garments, anointed with divine fragrances, all-wonderful. God, infinite omnipresent."[11] Sanjaya is performing double duty in his vision. He is watching events unfold at a distance *and* he is seeing "into" the subtle realm. Unlike Gandhari's vision, Sanjaya is capable of seeing the vision that Arjuna is privy to along with him.

We understand, then, that divine sight is a gift. Further, we understand that the devotionalist begins with mundane sight as the basis from which she cultivates the possibility of auspicious sight. We are left with an interesting problem, though. How can ordinary seeing act as a cultivating factor in the development of the possibility of *darśan*? How can the devotionalist use ordinary vision as part of a method to access divine gifts? In a peculiar way, ordinary seeing is already connected to seeing the invisible. As inquirers, we investigate the world through our senses, and we understand it via our capacities as mindful beings. We see, taste, touch, hear, and smell our world (among other ways of being intimately connected with it) and we understand this world in certain ways according to syntheses that our minds provide. This is one of the most important insights that Kant contributes to Western philosophy. This capacity for understanding could be seen as a special way of seeing. In fact, our *understanding* of the world shapes what and how we see. The reciprocal relation between seeing and understanding, I suggest, illuminates something about the Brahminical devotionalist's methodocial approach toward *darśan*. That is, to see the divine the devotionalist must understand at least some objects in the world to be divine. The question, then, is how the devotionalist reshapes his understanding through seeing in such a way that it opens up the possibility of *darśan*. If we have followed the trail of the inquiry correctly, then the question of *darśan* is a question of practice. This is discussed in more detail later. For the moment, however, we step back and inspect *darśan* more closely.

Anticipations of Darśan

Instead of immediately pursuing the question of practice regarding preparation for *darśan*, we move to understand the *darśan* experience itself. In order to do this, we ask, "What can be seen in *darśan*?" To find our answer, we return to the *Gita* to provide some insight. There we find Arjuna describing what he sees in his *darśan*. Arjuna says:

> O God, in your body I behold the gods and all the kinds of beings, Lord Brahma seated on the lotus seat, and all the seers and divine serpents. Everywhere, I behold you of endless form, many arms, bellies, mouths, eyes. I see in You no end, no middle, and also no beginning, O All-Lord, All-Form! I behold You [with] diadem, mace, and discus—a mass of brilliance, flaming all-around. Hard-to-see completely, an immeasurable blazing radiance of sun-fire. You ought to be known as the Supreme Imperishable. You are the supreme

receptacle of all this. You are the Immutable, the Guardian of the eternal law. You are the everlasting Spirit. [This is my conviction]. Without beginning, middle, or end, of infinite vitality, infinite arms [and with] moon and sun [as] eyes.[12]

In his vision of Kṛṣṇa, Arjuna is overwhelmed by the greatness of the deity. He is awestruck by the immensity of Kṛṣṇa and the complex plurality of manifestations that arise out of this imperishable and infinite being. Through his vision, Arjuna is granted immediate access to the divine and the cosmos produced through him. What Arjuna sees in his divine vision is all of actuality in Kṛṣṇa. This actuality, however, is not a mere static image of the cosmos. It is a dynamic and unfolding universe embraced and pervaded by Kṛṣṇa, who illuminates the totality by his beaming and seeing, face. The dynamicity of Arjuna's vision means that he is seeing the actual cosmic totality as it unfolds through the actualization of manifesting possibilities. He is watching, it would seem, the grandest show of all.

In addition to his vision of the cosmic totality, *darśan* provides, according to the Gita, insight of a more personal kind. The first constituent of the personal insight one receives is dependent upon the practitioner's approach toward the divine. Speaking to Arjuna, Kṛṣṇa says, "Just as these [*yogins*] resort to Me, so do I love them [in turn]."[13] Eck states that "in that way I do love them" (from "so do I love them [in turn]" in the translation used here) could be translated as "in that way do I share myself with them."[14] The "as," then, in "Just as these [*yogins*] resort to Me," is not intended to convey only a temporal meaning. Rather, the meaning is intended to indicate that God reveals himself in whatever way we are inclined to see him, so long as we are inclined to do so. So, in one sense, in whatever way one approaches the divine, the divine will reveal itself to her in that way.[15] Many of the Brahminical gods take on different forms, but the form of God that one experiences in *darśan*, according to this passage, is dependent upon and governed by the individual's way of approaching the divine. This personal constituent of *darśan* is further shaped by the second mode in which God reveals himself to the devotionalist in a personalistic manner.

When a practitioner approaches the divine, she does so as finite being with finite vision of the world. The very fact of her finitude, it would seem, is the basis of her desire to have a vision of the transcendent (and simultaneously immanent) order of the world. While there may be various reasons *why* she seeks *darśan* and many ways she may approach him, she will always do so on the basis of a desire for edification, guidance, and, perhaps, comfort. The makeup of the personal revealing, where the first constituent indicates that the divine reveals himself in a way that is conducive to the practitioner's approach, also includes a meaningful edification that gives the practitioner guidance specified to herself. To illustrate this point, we return to Arjuna's *darśan* in the *Gita*. After receiving the revelation of Kṛṣṇa's supreme cosmological totality, Arjuna's *darśan* turns quite grim. He begins to see Kṛṣṇa manifest in a way that causes him great fear. His divine vision transforms from one that is awesome and all-pervading to one that is unbearably horrifying. Arjuna says:

> I behold you—[Your] blazing mouth[s] eating [everything as an] oblation—burning up all this with your own brilliance. By You alone this [space] between heaven and earth pervaded, and all the quarters [too]. Seeing this wondrous, terrifying form of Yours, the triple world shudders, O Great Self. Yonder, these hosts of deities enter into You. Some, terrified, praise [You] with *anjali* [-gesture]. Crying out "Hail! the multitude of great seers and perfected-ones laud You with plenteous hymns-of-praise. Rudra, Ādityas, Vasus and Sādhyas, the Vishve, the Ashvins, the Maruts and the quaffers-of-steam, and the hosts of the Gandharvas, Yakshas, Asuras, and perfected-ones—[they] all behold you, [utterly] astounded. Beholding [that] great form of Yours, many mouths and eyes, O mighty-armed [Krishna], many arms, thighs, feet, many bellies, many formidable fangs—the worlds shudder; so [do] I. Touching the world-sky, flaming many-colored, gaping mouths and flaming vast eyes—beholding You, [my] inmost self quakes, and I find no fortitude or tranquility, O Vishnu. And seeing Your mouths [studded with] formidable fangs resembling the fire of time, I know not where-to-turn, and I find no shelter. Be gracious, O Lord of the gods, O home of the universe! And all these sons of Dhritarāshtra together with hosts of protectors of the earth—Bhishma, Drona, as well as the son of the charioteer and also our leading warriors—they swiftly enter Your mouths with formidable fear-instilling fangs. Some are seen with pulverized heads sticking in between [Your] teeth. Slain by various kinds of men, they enter Your mouth[s] of inconceivable form—all the fighting followers-of-Yudhishtira and the followers-of-Dhritarā are cut down by diverse weapons and all are surely annihilated by your radiance: thus these [men] presently enter Your body. As many rivers and water torrents flow headlong into the ocean, so do these heroes of the world of men enter Your flaming mouths. As moths in profuse streams enter a blazing flame to [their own] destruction, so do the worlds in profuse streams enter Your mouths for [their utter] destruction. With the flaming mouths, You lick up, devouring, all the worlds entirely. Filling the entire universe with [Your] brilliance,

> Your dreadful rays scorch [all], O Vishnu. Tell me who You are of dreadful form. May salutation be to You! O Best of gods, have mercy! I wish to know You [as You were] in the beginning. For I [do] not comprehend Your [divine] creativity. [16]

Where the beginning of Arjuna's *darśan* beautifully illustrates the harmony of the cosmic totality of Kṛṣṇa, the latter portion of it is violent and utterly destructive. Because of this dramatic change in the content of Arjuna's *darśan*, I propose that Arjuna really has two visions rather than one. While these two visions are indistinct, in that they are continuous, they are distinguishable by their difference in content. I propose that the first *darśan* is that of the cosmic totality, of the actual unfolding totality in manifesting divine actualities. The second one, which is more personal, is different. This "second" *darśan* is still actuality unfolding, but it is something less than the totality vision that Arjuna saw before. That is, the personal communication between Kṛṣṇa and Arjuna is the product of an inclusion of specific sights by the exclusion of irrelevant sights that are not specific to the actions Arjuna is supposed to perform. If we consider this grim transformation of Arjuna's *darśan* in light of what personal communication (divine or otherwise) entails, this becomes clearer.

The purpose of this second vision of the divine is made clear in Kṛṣṇa's response to Arjuna's plea for a return to the original and more appealing vision that Kṛṣṇa manifests earlier.[17] Kṛṣṇa responds to Arjuna,

> I am time, mighty wreaker of the world's destruction, engaged here in annihilating the worlds. Except for you, all these warriors arrayed in the opposing armies shall not be [alive after this battle]. Therefore, you arise [and] win glory! Conquering the enemies, enjoy a prosperous kingdom! Verily, they are slain already by Me. Be [My] mere instrument, O Savyasācin![18]

In this passage, Kṛṣṇa reveals to Arjuna the role he ought to play according to the divine order. In addition to a vision that is adapted to the seer's approach to divinity, then, divinity also provides moral guidance with the gift of *darśan*.

The gift of *darśan* appears to answer two questions for the practitioner. These questions are "What is?" and "Whom ought I become?" The first question is answered in two ways. Initially, the question "What is?" is answered in an impersonal way that transcends the approach of the practitioner and gives insight into the divine along with the whole of creation. This impersonal answer to the question is illustrated when Arjuna receives the grandiose vision of Kṛṣṇa in the totality form. This *darśan* is a massive dilation of Arjuna's vision, illuminating the invisible where he beholds the dynamic unfolding of the totality of the cosmos. The second way the question is answered is more personal. It addresses the approach of the practitioner toward divinity according to who she is. We see this personalized vision of the deity in the darker revelation of Kṛṣṇa to Arjuna. In this *darśan*, Arjuna receives a "filtered" view of the totality that is restricted by a criterion of relevancy in relation to Arjuna himself. This personalized vision reformulates the question "What is?" into "Who am I?" and the auspicious sight transforms from the totality form into the filtered form as it answers the latter question. Arjuna is a *Kshatriya* (a member of the warrior caste). Although he is a questioning warrior, he is a warrior, nonetheless. His status as a Kshatriya is the reason for Kṛṣṇa's appearance as the destroyer. His *darśan* reminds him of that role and, although it terrifies him, provides the basis for the second question. This question, "Whom ought I be?" is appropriately answered in the personal form through the divine edification of the practitioner. Arjuna's struggle is to find the right path of action on the field of battle. On the one hand, he has family responsibilities to adhere to (i.e., not killing them), and, on the other, he has social responsibilities to his community (i.e., to rule and ensure justice, violently if necessary). Arjuna worries that he will be unjust to his family if he engages in battle with them. Thus, he is reluctant to pursue the course of violent action. Kṛṣṇa is trying to convince him that his social responsibilities are of greater importance than any responsibilities he has to his family. The *darśan* of Arjuna seems to be clear. He ought to fight to restore justice.

Beyond understanding what is seen in *darśan*, we also have, based upon our investigation into the prior question, a basic account of the process of *darśan*. This overall process has three major components. The first is a desire for *darśan*. This process opens up the possibility of divine vision. The second is an invitation to be seen, as illustrated by Kṛṣṇa when he beckons Arjuna to behold him in his true form. Presumably, this invitation is extended only to those who are worthy of divine sight. Finally, is the gifting of the sight by the divine to the seer. All of these components need further attention in order to understand the overall process of *darśan*. However, we need to address one more point before we can begin the last portion of our inquiry.[19]

Preparation for Darśan

Now that we understand what can be anticipated in *darśan*, we move to understand how the devotionalist practitioner prepares for it. The centerpiece of Brahminical devotionalism is divine images. These images vary widely. They can be found in temples, in bizarre or majestic landscape features, or in the home at altars.

According to some Brahminical thinkers, the role of the divine image is as a tool for meditation. Through meditation upon the image, in this view, devotionalist practitioners prepare for auspicious sight. I contend that the role of the divine image as a focus of concentration ought to be understood in the greater context within which the image plays a role as divine object in the practitioner's everyday life. While it may be true that the image facilitates a connection between the human and the divine by acting as a focus for meditation, I would like to put forth the hypothesis that the ritualistic day-to-day relationship between the individual and the divine image (especially those images found in the home) is just as important, if not more so, as those moments of meditative concentration on the image. It is through the day-to-day non-meditative practices, I propose, that the practitioner of devotionalism creates a relation between himself and the divine image that prepares him for *darśan*.

For the devotionalist practitioner, the day-to-day relationship with the divine image is performed through frequent contact and physical interaction with the image. According to Eck, these nonmeditative activities of devotion performed by the practitioner "are gestures of humility, with which a servant approaches his master, or a host his guest—gestures such as bowing, kneeling, prostrating, and, in the Hindu world, touching the feet of a revered superior."[20] These acts of humility before the image, which are performed several times daily, shape the practitioner's disposition toward the image and imbue the practitioner with reverence for the image. The result of such activities highlights, for the practitioner, the religious value of the image and provide a basis for an intimate connection to the divine.

In addition to cultivating a relation of humility toward the divine image by the practitioner, the devotionalist engages in acts of affection or caring for the image. Eck writes, "In observing Hindu worship, in the home or in the temple, many Western students are baffled by the sense in which it appears to be an elaborate form of 'playing house' with God."[21] The ritual performance of "playing house" with the image promotes the development of a form of intimacy that opens up the practitioner to the possibility of *darśan*. Eck continues, "The image is wakened in the morning, honored with incense and song, dressed, and fed. Throughout the day, other such rites appropriate to the time of day are performed until, finally, the deity is put to bed in the evening."[22] Initially, the practitioner, who intellectually understands the image as representative of the infinite divine, does not (presumably) regard the divine image as personal.[23] Seeing the image as personal occurs as a result of the process of engaging the object in a way that she would a person (i.e., through acts of reverence and care for the divine object). The practices of humility and care transform the disposition of the practitioner.

That is, as the primary hypothesis stated, the radical reordering of possibility as perceived by the practitioner results in a radical reorganization of her disposition.

The clue that provides us with an indication of one of the more interesting features of preparation for *darśan* is found in the phenomenon of personhood itself. Some of what makes persons recognizable are the habits they accumulate. However, while we do grow to know one another in such ways that we are better able to make general predictions about each other, there is always something left over that is fundamentally mysterious about them. As we intellectually develop, we become accustomed to objects in relation to the quality of mystery that constitute them for us. Through this process, we begin to mark out territories of experience that we then identify as personal or impersonal. We never truly know where to draw the line between person and nonperson. Nevertheless, experience directs that we habituate a particular perspective that facilitates distinguishing between person and nonperson. What I would like to suggest is that the practice of preparing for *darśan* alters, perhaps even eradicates, our habituated interpretation of the personal that acts as a ground for judgment regarding what is and what is not a person. If this hypothesis is correct, then part of the result of the preparation for *darśan* alters our way of seeing and, through this process, opens up the possibility of a new way of distinguishing between the personal and the impersonal. In this new way of seeing, divine objects are laden with the possibility of personhood. Once the possibility of personhood appears in the divine object, the practitioner of devotionalism has prepared herself for the possibility of *darśan*. Her preparation for *darśan* is a manifest exhibition of her desire for auspicious sight. Just as Arjuna expressed his desire for *darśan*, the practitioner illustrates her openness and desire for divine insight through the practices of humility and care.

Prepared for Darśan

In order to illustrate the genetic transformation of the practitioner, I would like to draw upon a metaphor. The pupil of the human eye is like the aperture of a camera. The function of the pupil of the eye and aperture of the camera is to allow enough light in to a receptacle so that a visual image can emerge through the effect of the light on the sensory receptors at the back of the eye or on the film in an analog camera.[24] The more available light there is, the smaller the pupil or aperture needs to be in order for an image to emerge. Conversely, the less available light, the larger the pupil or aperture needs to be for an image to form. The tradeoff in expanding the aperture to allow more light in is that the depth of field (i.e., the measure of the depth of the spatial zone where distinct objects appear) is reduced in relation to the size of the aperture. A small aperture, then, gives a deeper zone of clarity while a large aperture provides a much shallower zone.

The reason for the difference between the depth of clarity in the large and small openings is based upon the difference in the pattern of light that occurs in each case. In a small opening, the light that enters is constricted into patterns where the light, more or less, runs in a straight line (i.e., where the photons run parallel with each other). In contrast, when the aperture is large, the light patterns are less constrained, and the light that enters the opening is more diffuse, running in lines that have a much wider range of difference in direction.

When the practitioner of devotionalism engages in a praxis of care and humility with the divine object, one in which she both reveres and nurtures the object, she does something akin to dilating what we might call her "third eye." That is, the common interpretation that affords us the capacity to distinguish between persons and nonpersons becomes unsettled. Through the many acts of humbling herself and caring for the divine image, the possibility of personhood in the divine object appears within the horizon of her experience. As the practitioner habituates practices of humility and care, the possibility of personhood becomes concentrated in the object of her devotion. The concentrated possibility in the object intensifies the mysteriousness of the object. In this expansion of the mysterious, the practitioner anticipates the inevitable characteristic of surprise that appears wherever persons are seen. When the mystery of the divine object reaches a certain threshold, the practitioner reopens the question of the appropriate interpretation of personhood. That is, the divine image becomes a focus for an inquiry into the possibility that objects previously considered to be impersonal might, in fact, be personal. The reopening of the question of personhood destabilizes the habituated interpretation that acts as a fulcrum upon which the judgment of the personal and impersonal is made.

When the devotionalist has accomplished the destabilization of his habituated interpretation of the delineation between the personal and the impersonal and the divine object is infused with the quality of mysteriousness, the practitioner is ready for *darśan*. His openness to the experience and commitment to care for the image as a person has opened up the possibility of interpreting personhood in the object, and this possibility is concentrated in the object itself. At this point in the development of the practice, the practitioner must wait for the divine invitation. His desire for the experience has been exhibited in practice, and he simply awaits his opportunity for *darśan*.

We have already laid out, in general, what the practitioners *darśan* will include. However, we have not yet spoken of the effects of divine insight have on the practitioner after the gift of sight into the invisible has been extended to her. Presumably, there will be many aftereffects of *darśan*. Such events, of course, would likely have many unforeseeable life-changing consequences. In the main, these consequences stem from the "intimate" connection that is established in the totality form of *darśan* and, further, in the diminishment of the mysteriousness of the devotionalist to herself in the second phase of her vision. These effects would seem to be transformations of the practitioner herself.

What, then, is left over? Having had her *darśan*, has the practitioner completed her work? I would suggest that she has not. There is a twofold world change (changes that transform the world in which the practitioner lives) that occurs after *darśan*. The first, and most apparent, transformation occurs in the image itself. Prior to the practitioner's *darśan*, the question of personhood is reopened, and this question is concentrated in the image. After her divine seeing, the question is no longer a question, as the inquiry has come to fruition in *darśan*. The divine image has become personal.

The second world change follows from the first. To illustrate this change, I draw once more from the *Gita*. Prior to Arjuna's *darśan*, Kṛṣṇa explains to him what he will come to understand in his vision of the god. Kṛṣṇa says:

> I am the rite. I am the sacrifice. I am the oblation. I am the herb. I am the mantra. I am the clarified-butter. I am the fire. I am the offering. I am the father of the universe, the mother, the supporter, the grandsire, [all that is] to-be-known, the purifier, the syllable OM, and the *Rig-, Sāma-* and *Yajur-*[*Veda*]. [I am] the course, the sustainer, the Lord, the witness, the home and refuge, the friend, the origin, dissolution and ultimate state, the receptacle, the immutable seed [in all beings]. I burn [like the sun]. I hold back and pour forth the rain. I am immortality and death, the existent and the nonexistent, O Arjuna.[25]

Arjuna is pleased to hear these things, but he desires to see them with his spiritual eye rather than hear them spoken to him. Arjuna cognitively understands Kṛṣṇa as saying that he is *All* things. The totality vision of Kṛṣṇa exhibits to Arjuna the truth of his pervasiveness that cannot be expressed in words. For the practitioner, when the inquiry into the question of personhood in the divine object has come to a close, the inquiry is not finished. Rather, as with all good inquiries, new questions emerge from answers to prior inquiries. A central question appears as a result of closing the investigation into the personhood of the divine object occurs when the actuality of the personal divine image is gifted to the practitioner. This question appears when the actuality of the personal divine image converges on the appreciation that all manifestations in experience are results of the divine vitality that underlies them. If this appreciation occurs to the practitioner, the result is (likely to be) an outward expansion of that concentrated actuality of personhood in the divine object as new possibility (it is not expanded as actuality because it comes to the practitioner in the form of a question). This new inquiry reopens (again) and disperses the question of personhood across all of experience.

To locate the final transformation of the experience of the devotionalist, we return to the anticipations of *darśan*. The practitioner's world, now engorged with the possibility of personhood, also contains those possibilities that first attracted the practitioner to her *darśan*. When she first approaches the divine object in hopes of *darśan*, she anticipates that her divine vision will not only reveal to her cosmic knowledge, but will also speak to her in terms of her own individuality, illustrating her highest self to her, just as Kṛṣṇa did for Arjuna, and, additionally, give her direction in her life. The practices that prepared the devotionalist for her initial *darśan* were initially focused on a particular divine object. The inquiry into the possibility of the personal, divine, particular object has been resolved and has now opened up a new line of inquiry in which all of experience is saturated with the possibility of divinity and personhood. The connection between the actual, divine personal object and the possibility of a divine personal world is found in practice. If the practitioner makes this connection, she realizes that the humility and nurture that she offered the divine object in her preparation for *darśan* must be repeated in similar rituals of humility toward and nurture for all of her experience. It is, presumably, only through these practices that she opens her horizon of possibility to include the possibility of world *darśan*, or, perhaps, more appropriately, *darśan* world. Once the practitioner sees in this new way, her world becomes dramatically transformed into one that is more meaningful, more personal, and, ultimately, more mysterious. Speculatively speaking, for the devotionalist, the practices of humility and nurture take on a new shade of meaning that colors her whole active life. She becomes an inquirer into the world as permeated by the divine. That is to say, in a certain kind of way, she begins where she started with a revised scope of her practices of care and nurture. This new scope is inclusive of all her experience.

Notes

1. For more information on modes of cognition, see Cassirer's writings on symbolic forms.

2. Diana L. Eck, *Darśan: Seeing the Divine Image in India*, 3rd ed. (New York: Columbia University Press, 1998), 3.

3. Diana L. Eck, *Darśan: Seeing the Divine Image in India*.

4. Margaret J. Wiener, *Visible and Invisible Realms: Power, Magic, and Colonial Conquest in Bali* (Chicago: University of Chicago Press, 1995), 76.

5. *Bhagavad Gita*, trans. Georg Feuerstein and Brenda Feuerstein (Boulder: Shambhala Publications, 2011), 221–23. The Feurerstein's translation provides bracketed text in their translation to bring clarity to the reading. I tend to not include these additions. However, where they are especially helpful to the reader, I add them to the quotations. All bracketed texts in quotations from the Feurerstein translation are the translators' additions.

6. *Bhagavad Gita*, trans. Georg Feuerstein and Brenda Feuerstein, 221.

7. *Bhagavad Gita*, trans. Georg Feuerstein and Brenda Feuerstein, 239.

8. *The Mahabharata*, trans. Kisari Mohan Ganguli, *sacred-texts.com*. Accessed 04/15/2017. www.sacred-texts.com/hin/m11/m11015.htm.

9. Stella Kramrisch, *The Hindu Temple* (Delhi: Motilal Banarsidass, 1946), 136.

10. Rich King, *Indian Philosophy: An Introduction to Hindu and Buddhist Thought* (Washington, DC: Georgetown University Press, 1997), 147.

11. *Bhagavad Gita*, trans. Georg Feuerstein and Brenda Feuerstein, 223.

12. *Bhagavad Gita*, trans. Georg Feuerstein and Brenda Feuerstein, 227.

13. *Bhagavad Gita*, trans. Georg Feuerstein and Brenda Feuerstein, 137.

14. Diana L. Eck, *Darśan: Seeing the Divine Image in India*, 3rd ed. (New York: Columbia University Press, 1998), 46.

15. I would like to point out here that the controversial position of the personal nature of the gods could be resolved through this passage in the *Gita*. Those who experience the divine as impersonal could be explained by this passage. The *Gita* suggests that the impersonalistic understanding of the nature of God as held by the practitioner is why the impersonal divine appears to him in the way it does.

16. *Bhagavad Gita*, trans. Georg Feuerstein and Brenda Feuerstein, 227–33.

17. It is unclear whether Arjuna's request implores Kṛṣṇa to return to the original divine vision (the actual unfolding totality) or to return to his visible self that can be perceived through mundane vision. Arjuna provides his reason for the request when he says, "For I [do] not comprehend Your [divine] creativity." The inclusion of the term "divine" in this translation could indicate that Arjuna wants his *darśan* to end. However, Kṛṣṇa's response to Arjuna would seem to indicate that that author of the *Gita* intends to convey why Kṛṣṇa has taken the second darker form. Further, Arjuna's response to Kṛṣṇa's explanation of the role of his appearance in destructive form seems to indicate that Arjuna's *darśan* transforms again into the original "totality" form. If we return to Kṛṣṇa's invitation to Arjuna to see him in his divinity, we find something interesting. Kṛṣṇa says, "Behold now, O Gudākesha, the whole universe, moving and unmoving, abiding as one here in My body, and whatever else you desire to see." It appears as though Arjuna sees whatever it is that he desires to see. That is, in a sense, he is in control of his own *darśan*. If this is the case, it is an indicator that Arjuna's request to Kṛṣṇa is to return to his totality form.

18. *Bhagavad Gita*, trans. Georg Feuerstein and Brenda Feuerstein, 233.

19. I would be remiss if I did not at least mention that being seen by the divine is emphasized in contemporary Brahminical devotionalism. According to Dr. Kenneth Valpey, whom I discussed this work with, being seen is, for most contemporary practitioners

of devotionalism, the more important constituent of *darśan*. Given this emphasis, it is unfortunate that we have very little textual evidence to draw upon in order to produce a more robust understanding of the process of being seen by the divine. Fortunately, however, the emphasis of our overall inquiry is devoted to the process of the transformation of the practitioner in preparation for *darśan*.

20. Diana L. Eck, *Darśan: Seeing the Divine Image in India*, 3rd ed. (New York: Columbia University Press, 1998), 47.

21. Eck, *Darśan: Seeing the Divine Image in India*, 46.

22. Eck, *Darśan: Seeing the Divine Image in India*, 46–47.

23. From a Western perspective, the transformation of an object into a possible person seems to be the "natural" progression for devotional practices. However, viewing this process as the typical progression of transformation could include the implicit denial of the possibility that there is a way of living that regards the divine object as a person already. I will not weigh in here as to whether or not this "denied" possibility is the case. However, I would like to point out that that a different cultural understanding of the divine object, where the object is always already regarded as personal, appears to be possible.

24. It should be remembered that, for Indian thinkers, perception is understood as illumination that originates from the interior of the self rather than the exterior.

25. *Bhagavad Gita*, trans. Georg Feuerstein and Brenda Feuerstein, 195.

Bibliography

Bhagavad Gita. Translated by Georg Feuerstein and Brenda Feuerstein. Boulder: Shambhala Publications, Inc. 2011.

Eck, Diana. *Darśan: Seeing the Divine Image in India*. New York: Columbia University Press. 1998.

Hiriyanna, M. *Outlines of Indian Philosophy*. Delhi: Motilal Banarsidass. 2000.

King, Richard. *Indian Philosophy: An Introduction to Hindu and Buddhist Thought*. Washington D.C.: Georgetown University Press. 2007.

Kramrisch, Stella. *The Hindu Temple*. Delhi: Motilal Banarsidass, 1946.

The Mahabharata. Translated by Kisari Mohan Ganguli. *sacred-texts.com*. Accessed 04/15/2017. www.sacred-texts.com/hin/m11/m11015.htm.

Valpey, Kenneth Russell. *Attending Kṛṣṇa's Image: Caitanya Vaiṣṇava Mūrti-sevā as Devotional Truth*. New York: Routledge. 2006.

Wiener, Margaret J. *Visible and Invisible Realms: Power, Magic, and Colonial Conquest in Bali*. Chicago: University of Chicago Press. 1995.

Chapter 5

Convergence and Divergence of Spirit
Tsukumogami and the Personality of Objects

KEVIN C. TAYLOR

Editor's Note: From brahminic India, we move to medieval Japan, continuing our survey of personalized objects in religious and spiritual practices. Taylor discusses the complex spiritual tradition of Japan, where Shinto, Buddhism, Confucianism, Daoism, and other traditions all intermix. He describes how the concept of tsukumogami *arises out of this syncretic history: household objects that, if they are old enough, are said to come to life. Tsukumogami are often ordinary household objects, but they are also firmly embedded in the spiritual traditions of Japan. For that reason, this chapter provides a nice transition out of the religiously focused chapters and into the discussions of household and everyday objects that will be the focus of the next several chapters.*

Japanese religious philosophy is a syncretic tradition. To talk about Buddhism or Shintoism without reference to one another, let alone Confucianism, Daoism, or any of the cultural factors that played a role in their developments would be not only a disservice but also difficult or impossible. This chapter focuses on Japanese animated household objects known as *tsukumogami*. This subject matter involves *kami*, spirits associated with later developments of Shintoism, but the folklore scroll that introduces *tsukumogami* is of Buddhist origin. But even here, the first lines of the scroll attribute belief in *tsukumogami* to a little-known text, Miscellaneous Records of Yin and Yang, and one of the principal characters of the scroll is Confucian.

By focusing on animate objects in the *tsukumogami* scroll (*tsukumogami-ki*), this chapter becomes situated in the Muromachi period (1336–1573) and early Edo period (1603–1868), politically Confucian and religiously Buddhist but never without strong Daoist and *kami* presence. Since kami and Buddhism are closely intertwined it will be necessary to give some philosophical development to fully appreciate the difficulty in sorting the Buddhist elements from *kami* elements. I will then discuss the role of *kami* in terms of the person and then objects with some acknowledgment of the Buddhist role in this development. It was, after all, a scroll intended to demonstrate the superiority of Buddhism over *kami* worship, but in so doing, Buddhism amplified and popularized a normative approach to object veneration in the wider Japanese culture that persists to this day. It is my hope that this work demonstrates that the ways in which we treat objects as alive enrich and reorient our praxis to intensify personal experience.

Buddhism and the Path East

Buddhism as a product of Indian philosophy carries with it many cultural, religious, and philosophical assumptions but the lynchpin for a radical break from the brahminical traditions rests mostly on the notion of *atman/anatman* (self/no-self). Whereas Indian philosophy was largely concerned with the unchanging, eternal self, known as *atman*, Buddhism rejected the concept and posits that everything is subject to change and impermanence, and utterly without self (*anatman*). As Buddhism began to flourish, its teachings moved east into China where a strong Confucian tradition was already well established. The story could end here since the Confucian world-view is strongly unsympathetic to Buddhist notions of life characterized by suffering, the emphasis on reincarnation, and the all-too-frequent accusation that Buddhism is a world-renouncing religion. However, Daoism is often credited with the successful promulgation of Buddhism among folk religions with Buddhism and Daoism borrowing/co-opting one another. In the fourth and fifth centuries, when Mahayana Buddhism was introduced to China, Daoism, despite its long history, was still developing. Sympathetic to its teaching Daoism provided a way in to China, however, Christine Mollier notes identical usage of sutras and literary works variously plagiarized by both Buddhists and Daoists.[1] Slowly various Buddhist sects took root in Northern and Southern China and while Buddhism first entered Japan in 552 AD, Kūkai's study of Chinese Buddhism from 804–806 was the first among several defining moments for Japanese Buddhism. Kūkai founded the esoteric Shingon sect of Buddhism and a companion on a separate ship from the same trip to China, Saichō, would become the founder of the exoteric Tendai-sect of Buddhism which was the more influential occupying a privileged space in the capital at Kyoto and out of which the Muromachi sects all emerge (Dōgen, Nichiren, and Hōnen). Saichō was the first to use the term *mokuseki bussho*, "The Buddha nature of trees and rocks," in Japan, but Kūkai made substantially greater contributions, which would promulgate throughout future students coming out of the Tendai-sect on Mount Hiei.

Kūkai and Saichō mark a significant development in Buddhist thought from India to Japan. Indian Buddhist practices insisted the Buddha nature was something to be attained through hard work and spiritual development. Kūkai and Saichō introduced the concept of *hongaku*, "original enlightenment," arguing that all sentient beings already have Buddha nature, "insofar as our interdependent relationship with others and nature can, at any time, be authenticated by perceiving the world from a nondiscriminating mode of awareness."[2] The extent of *hongaku* thought varies from thinker to thinker always including sentient beings but privileging humans. In the Japanese Buddhist cosmological view of reincarnation, *rokudō* or six realms, only the human realm can attain Buddha nature, whereas those in *akudō*, the evil or unfortunate realms, must improve their karmic merit in order to be reborn in the human realm while the gods and *asuras* of higher realms must burn off some of their karma in order to be reborn as humans.

Kami in the concept of *rokudō* find themselves at the whims of the rapidly dominant Buddhist tradition. As early as 901 AD the term *honji suijaku*, "original ground manifest trace," was employed to explain the relationship between Buddhist deities and local *kami*. The term was codified by the majority of temples during the Kamakura period (1185–1333), and it was understood that *kami* were manifestations of Buddhist deities resulting in the temple-shrine complexes where *kami* and buddhas were worshipped side by side. This interpretation came to be questioned by Tendai monks as *inverted honji suijaku*, *kami* are original and Buddhas were outsiders who took over. This trend gets repeated throughout the Muromachi and Edo periods as Buddhist support by the government shifts towards Confucianism which aligned with Shinto and attacked Buddhism as foreign and later still in the 1900s when state Shinto was dominant.

Until now I have avoided the use of the word "Shinto" preferring instead to refer to *kami* worship. Shinto as a religious system has its origins in the fourteenth century: "The term Shinto developed from a simple word meaning '(the realm of) the kami' into a more sophisticated concept meaning 'the kami Way' in the course of the medieval period, and evolved into an autonomous ritual system from there."[3] The text I will be referring to, the *Tsukumogami-ki*, is dated to have originated from Muromachi period, when a unified Shinto would be forming and therefore not widely understood as a religious system. The advantage is that the "particularistic, centrifugal pantheon of the kami has always stood in opposition to all centralizing conceptions, be they Buddhist or Shinto."[4] Such an approach should serve to highlight the dynamics involved in a text that comes from a background of Confucian governance, Buddhist religion, and *kami* culture with some Daoist and Yin-Yang elements, *onmyōdō*, rising throughout.

Kami and *Tsukumogami*

According to kami worship, *kami* express themselves in the human realm as natural objects like rocks, trees, and animals, and as man-made objects like tools and everyday artifacts. *Kami* can be humans as well, such as the emperor of Japan or Sugawara no Michizane (845–903). Michizane was a famous poet and scholar who served the emperor until he was deposed and exiled in 901. After his death two years later, plague and drought spread, the sons of Emperor Daigo died in succession, and lightning repeatedly struck the palace as rainstorms flooded the city. These events were attributed to the angry spirit of Sugawara, so the imperial court built a shrine dedicated to him and later deified him as Tenjin-sama, a *kami* of scholarship (many shrines are dedicated to him). Of course, not all *kami* are so grandiose; ancestors are said to become *kami*, and the Yasakuni Shrine is said to hold 2.5 million *kami*. *Kami* come in a variety of shapes and sizes, but they are generally understood to be expressed in objects that are particularly striking, such as an ancient camphor tree or Mount Fuji.

Not only does nature find itself imbued with *kami*, but the line blurs between man and nature with *kami* in man-made objects such as the *tsukumogami* 付喪神 (animated household objects). Introduced in the *tsukumogami-ki* 付喪神記 (Record of Tool Specters), a *tsukumogami* is a type of *yōkai* 妖怪, "variously translated as monster, spirit, goblin, ghost, demon, phantom, specter, fantastic being, lower-order deity, or, more amorphously, as any unexplainable experience or numinous occurrence."[5] When an object becomes one hundred years old, it attains a spirit and becomes an animated object known as a *tsukumogami*. As *yōkai*, *tsukumogami* are not quite *kami* and not quite *oni* (demons), and this is attributable to a demarcation between these three types of spirits:

> Orikuchi Shinobu suggests that there may have been no clear demarcation between an *oni* and a *kami* in Japan's ancient past. Both were "awesome" beings, although the *oni* may not have been worshipped. Orikuchi asserts as well that the negative and fearful aspects of kami came to be considered *oni*. He writes that the *oni* concept before the introduction of Buddhism was a variation of *tokoyo-kami* (kami who live in the other land or the land of the dead) or *marebito* (foreign

travelers, kami who visit villages) who give blessings on the lunar New Year's Eve and/or New Year's Day for the coming year.

Komatsu Kazuhiko explains that supernatural deities worshipped by Japanese are known as *kami* while those that are not worshipped are called *yokai* (hobgoblins/monsters), and the *yokai* with the most negative association are *oni*.[6]

The concept that one-hundred-year-old objects can develop spirits of their own was an outgrowth of the *kami* worship and reverence for objects and sacred spaces but was also connected to a practice from late tenth-century year-end housecleaning event known as *susuharai* 煤払 (sweeping soot, housecleaning):

> *Susuharai* is not only a large annual housecleaning event, but also a part of the preparation rituals for welcoming a Shinto god of the coming year, or a harvest god. It is the day to remove the accumulated misfortunes of the year (*yaku* 厄), as well as to expunge one's defilements and crimes . . . An entry for the sixth day of the twelfth month of 1236 in *Azuma kagami* 吾妻鏡 (Mirror of the east, ca. thirteenth century) records the *Susuharai* event at the Kamakura military court. It also recounts that *Susuharai* activities were not carried out in a newly built residence for three years (kt 33, 185). Later, commoners are said to have followed this custom.[7]

The *tsukumogami-ki* was written to promote Shingon Buddhism, and we can see the blending of *kami* worship and Buddhist beliefs throughout the text. Shortly after they are discarded, the objects begin speaking among themselves. Angry at the extravagance of wealthy families and for receiving no reward for their years of service, they consider taking revenge. Ichiren, the Buddhist rosary, concedes that their human owners treated them with hostility and yet tries to dissuade the others from taking revenge on humans (insisting that it must be their karma). The objects reject Ichiren but listen to Kobun sensei, professor of classical (Chinese) literature depicted as a hand scroll. Kobun sensei explains some principles of animism via *onmyodo*, the way of yin and yang, and leads them to *kami* worship and the practice of Confucian virtues:

> Japan is a divine country where everyone believes in Shinto. While we have already received our forms from the creation god, we have not worshipped him, and this is as if we were nonsentient beings like trees and rocks. I propose that we make the creation god our patron and worship him. That way we will be sure to have a long life with abundant posterity.[8]

Living just outside of Kyoto, the *tsukumogami* took their revenge as they robbed, killed, and ate all kinds of animals and humans. The *tsukumogami's* cruel actions led to an intervention by Buddhist deities who offered them the opportunity to convert to Buddhism. In the end, the *tsukumogami* returned to Ichiren, who teaches them Buddhism, and they all eventually attain Samadhi. The record concludes attributing specific tools to specific Buddhist deities (*honji suijaku*). It also states that whereas some sects advocate "only *sōmoku jōbutsu* 草木成仏 (the enlightenment of plants), the teaching of the Three Mysteries of the Shingon sect alone goes so far as to say *sōmoku hijō hosshin shugyō jōbutsu* 草木非情発心修行成仏 (plants and nonsentient beings become Buddhas by arousing the desire for enlightenment and performing ascetic and religious practices)."[9] The *tsukumogami-ki* was a story to promote Shingon Buddhism portraying Chinese philosophy and *kami* worship as legitimate although inferior to Buddhist doctrine and rival Buddhist sects as inferior for their narrow views on Buddha nature.

The idea of animated household objects continued into the early sixteenth century in the form of *Hyakki yako emaki* (lit., "illustrated handscrolls of night processions of one hundred demons"),[10] although the "ki" in Hyakki could also be written or pronounced *hyakki yagyō* 百器夜行, "the night procession of one hundred tools" since the words for demon (鬼 *oni* and *ki*) and tool (器 *utsuwa* and *ki*) are homonyms. In these scrolls, animated household objects parade at night and wreak havoc on anyone who crosses their paths.

While the *Tsukumogami-ki* singles out extravagant families as the source of their anger, the popularity of *tsukumogami*, a popularity that is enjoying a resurgence even now, may have been a by-product of the increase in commerce and industry. Komatsu Katsuhiko speculates:

> Perhaps because people were becoming more separated from nature with this increased production, they started to believe that tools not treated with respect would come to life and seek revenge. Many people in medieval Japan apparently believed that man-made objects can possess a spirit, and that tools must consequently be handled with reverence. This attitude still survives, at least to some ex-tent.[11]

A modern-day ritual known as *ningyō kuyō* collects unwanted but not unloved dolls and, in a kind of mock funeral, prays for and thanks the dolls for years of fond memories. Even though the dolls are not *tsukumogami*, a ritual is performed to purify and drive out the spirits within. Both Shinto and Buddhist sects perform the ritual, though funerals are typically the realm of Buddhist priests. In an interview with NPR, Ian Reader explained: "The general perception is that you do need rituals to be done, to help the passage of the spirit from the realm of the living to the dead and also to separate the spirit from this realm."[12]

The Japanese reverence for objects is commonly exemplified in katana, teapots, and calligraphy brushes, but also in more mundane items such as pencils boxes, *shōji* (delicate paper sliding doors) and umbrellas (all of which have been represented as animated objects at some point). More than just a religious justification, there is also a practical reasoning behind this reverence for objects. *Shōji* are fragile, and umbrellas are more common and necessary in an island country where rainfall is plentiful.

The personality of these animated objects is often related to their intended purpose: Ichiren being a Buddhist rosary was a monk, and Kobun sensei was a scroll. In other tales, the swordsmith Muramasa was thought to be unstable and bloodthirsty, traits that were said to be passed on to his blades. His blades eventually fell out of popularity after Shogun Tokugawa Ieyasu's father and grandfather were killed with Muramasa blades and even he was cut but a *yari* blade while inspecting the weapon. What becomes difficult in analyzing tales of animated objects is delineating their intended meaning from their unintended meanings that take on a life of their own as they increase in popularity. The Shingon priest may tell us that these tales employed folk religion to attest to the exceptional power of their Buddhist sect and their superior understanding of Buddha nature as opposed to other Buddhist sects. But in telling this story, they also caution against carelessly tossing away objects because spirits inhabit everything around us, and they must be treated with respect. Muramasa could transfer his instability to his blades thus perpetuating a negative karma through generations. But this Buddhist message is communicated with a strong *kami* worship foundation. Part of what is at work here is what Lafcadio Hearn calls "cult-craft." Guild apprentices were adopted not only in a craft, but into a cult. Guilds of weavers, weapon makers, and other tradesmen were affiliated with worship of a tutelary deity. According to Hearn:

> The servant could not dare to forget the presence of the deities of the cooking range, the hearth, the cauldron, the brazier . . . the sewing girl was taught to respect her needles . . . in samurai families the warrior was commanded to consider his armour and his weapons as holy things.[13]

Odate Toshio states that the objects created by craftsmen have a soul and describes a ritual dedicated to the spirits of their tools:

> At the end of every year, the *shokunin* [craftsman] cleans and oils his tools. My master and I would honor our tools on New Year's Eve [with a simple gesture that] was a traditional way of thanking the tools for their hard work on our behalf and for the crucial part they play in the *shokunin's* life.[14]

Religious practices related to trades craft continue to this day along similar lines to the aforementioned doll-burning ceremonies. Other fire or funeral ceremonies or relate specifically to trade items like sewing needles which may be burned or jabbed into a piece of tofu representing their increasingly blunted character so that they no longer fulfill the purpose of their craft.

I have argued in the past that this reverence for objects can be understood with the concept *mottainai* meaning both what a waste and don't be wasteful.[15] Kenyan activist Wangari Mathaii has described the *mottainai* concept as including the three Rs of recycle, reduce, reuse but she adds a fourth concept of respect. Indeed, the Buddhist proclivity for frugality permeates their monastic tradition and one of the unintended consequences of the Shingon Buddhist tale of *tsukumogami* is what becomes a normative environmental ethic to mindfulness of the material goods that make life meaningful.

The *tsukumogami* scroll starts as a Buddhist text to emphasize the superiority of Buddhist teaching over local kami worship. In so doing they demonstrated the strength of the syncretic tradition that incorporated Buddhist, *kami*, yin yang, and Confucian elements. The *tsukumogami* scroll also became a cautionary tale warning us that tools and treasured belongings are more than mere items. *Kami* worship was integrated with household objects and the crafts of tradesmen, so that old items (one-hundred-year-old objects) develop a soul but so too did the objects invested with care by their creators. Contemporary Japan is seeing a resurgence in these concepts with the popularization of *mottainai* as an environmental ethic both reviving old notions of ensouled items and reminding us that culturally speaking, the belief never actually went away.

Notes

1. Christine Mollier, *Buddhism and Taoism Face to Face: Scripture, Ritual, and Iconographic Exchange in Medieval China* (Honolulu: University of Hawaii Press, 2009), 11–12.

2. David Edward Shaner, "The Japanese Experience of Nature," in *Nature in Asian Traditions of Thought: Essays in Environmental Philosophy*, ed. J. Baird Callicott (Albany: State University of New York Press, 1989), 174.

3. Mark Teeuwen and Bernhard Scheid, "Tracing Shinto in the History of Kami Worship," *Japanese Journal of Religious Studies* 29, nos. 3–4 (2002): 199, https://nirc.nanzan-u.ac.jp/nfile/2780.

4. Teeuwen and Scheid," 199.

5. Michael Dylan Foster, *Pandemonium and Parade: Japanese Monsters and the Culture of Yōkai* (Berkeley: University of California Press, 2009), 2.

6. Noriko T. Reider, *Japanese Demon Lore: Oni, from Ancient Times to the Present* (Logan, Utah: Utah State University Press, 2010), 3.

7. Noriko T. Reider, "Animating Objects: *Tsukumogami ki* and the Medieval Illustration of Shingon Truth." *Japanese Journal of Religious Studies* 36, no. 2 (2009): 234, https://nirc.nanzan-u.ac.jp/nfile/2986.

8. "*Tsukumogami ki* (Record of Tool Specters)," trans. Noriko T. Reider, *Japanese Journal of Religious Studies*. Online Only Supplement: 1–19 (2009): 8, https://nirc.nanzan-u.ac.jp/nfile/2986.

9. Reider, "Animating Objects," 241.

10. Reider suggests that the author of the *Tsukumogami ki* was probably influenced by *Hyakki yako emaki*, which likely existed first, although the earliest extant scroll dates from the early sixteenth century, whereas the *Tsukumogami ki* have been dated to the Muromachi period. Elizabeth Lillehoj notes that references to *Hyakki yako emaki* can be found in the fourteenth century and possibly the twelfth century. Elizabeth Lillehoj, "Man-Made Objects as Demons in Japanese Scrolls," *Asian Folklore Studies* 54, no. 1 (1995): 28, http://doi.org/10.2307/1178217.

11. Lillehoj, "Man-Made Objects as Demons in Japanese Scrolls," 24–25.

12. Barbara Bradley Haggerty, "After Tsunami, Japanese Turn to Ancient Rituals" *Morning Edition*, NPR, March 17, 2011, https://www.npr.org/2011/03/17/134597421/after-tsunami-japanese-turn-to-ancient-rituals.

13. Elizabeth Lillehoj, "Transfiguration: Man-Made Objects as Demons in Japanese Scrolls," 26.

14. Lillehoj, "Transfiguration," 26.

15. Kevin Taylor, "*Mottainai*: A Philosophy of Waste from Japan," *Kinesis* 38, no. 2 (2011): 31–41.

Bibliography

Foster, Michael Dylan. *Pandemonium and Parade: Japanese Monsters and the Culture of Yōkai*. Berkeley: University of California Press, 2009.

Haggerty, Barbara Bradley. "After Tsunami, Japanese Turn to Ancient Rituals." *Morning Edition*, NPR, March 17, 2011. https://www.npr.org/2011/03/17/134597421/after-tsunami-japanese-turn-to-ancient-rituals.

Lillehoj, Elizabeth. "Man-Made Objects as Demons in Japanese Scrolls." *Asian Folklore Studies* 54, no. 1 (1995): 7–34. http://doi.org/10.2307/1178217.

Mollier, Christine. *Buddhism and Taoism Face to Face: Scripture, Ritual, and Iconographic Exchange in Medieval China*. Honolulu: University of Hawaii Press, 2009.

Reider, Noriko T. "Animating Objects: *Tsukumogami ki* and the Medieval Illustration of Shingon Truth." *Japanese Journal of Religious Studies* 36, no. 2 (2009): 231–57. https://nirc.nanzan-u.ac.jp/nfile/2986.

———. *Japanese Demon Lore: Oni, from Ancient Times to the Present*. Logan, Utah: Utah State University Press, 2010.

Shaner, David Edward. "The Japanese Experience of Nature." In *Nature in Asian Traditions of Thought: Essays in Environmental Philosophy*, edited by J. Baird Callicott, 163–82. Albany: State University of New York Press, 1989.

Taylor, Kevin. "Mottainai: A Philosophy of Waste from Japan." *Kinesis* 38, no. 2 (2011): 31–41.

Teeuwen, Mark, and Bernhard Scheid. "Tracing Shinto in the History of Kami Worship." *Japanese Journal of Religious Studies* 29, no. 3–4 (2002): 195–207. https://nirc.nanzan-u.ac.jp/nfile/2780.

"*Tsukumogami ki* 付喪神記 (The Record of Tool Specters)." Translated by Noriko T. Reider. *Japanese Journal of Religious Studies* [Online-only supplement] 36, no. 2 (2009): 1–19. https://nirc.nanzan-u.ac.jp/nfile/2986.

Chapter 6

The Journey of the Javanese *Keris*

ALAN G. MAISEY

Editor's Note: Chapter 6 moves us from medieval Japan to medieval Indonesia, specifically the island of Java. Javanese culture is influenced by the Hinduism and Buddhism that we have been discussing for the last two chapters (as well as Islam). This chapter, however, focuses on the personalization of weapons, with an emphasis on the history of the Javanese keris dagger. Like the other objects we have discussed, weapons (and other instruments of warfare) have a long history of personalization, as Maisey's chapter will exemplify.

Throughout history, the object that has probably had the closest connection with any man has been that man's personal weapon. More than 1000 years ago on the Island of Java, a weapon appeared that became perhaps the ultimate expression of what a personal object can become. What follows is the story of that Javanese weapon.

The Javanese weapon that is the subject of this chapter has a number of names. The most usual term to refer to the weapon is keris, or kris. In the Javanese language, it can also be referred to as *dhuwung, wangkingan, pusaka, curiga,* or *kadga.* Javanese is a multilevel language, so the term used is dependent upon language level and context.

We are uncertain of the name or names that were attached to this weapon in early times. We can find the word keris in early Javanese literature, but this does not give any certainty that this word did in fact refer to that which we now understand to be a keris, or that the word keris was the only name that could be attached to this weapon.

In this chapter, I will use only the word keris in reference to the weapon under discussion. The keris is a form of dagger, it is usually asymmetric, and the blade can be either straight or waved. In Java, and in other societies where it has been adopted, it has become to a greater or lesser degree a cultural icon, and in Java, it can in a sense be understood as representative of the society itself.

The journey of the keris began in Java, during the Early Classical Period.[1] This period saw the building of many monumental works, perhaps the two best known of which are the Buddhist stupa of Borobudur (built in the ninth century, located at Magelang), and Candi Prambanan (also built in the ninth century, located in the village of Prambanan). Both these monumental works are near Jogjakarta in Central Java.

The word and concept of *candi* require explanation.[2] For people from a European based culture, the Javanese candi is usually thought of as a temple, however, it should not be thought of in this way. A temple might become a candi, but a candi is not always a temple.

A candi is a place where people go to meditate and to pray and to make offerings to a deity, or to an ancestor. The candi itself is not the dwelling place of the deity, nor of the ancestor; it is simply a place that the deity or the ancestor might enter, similar in character to a shrine. Essentially it is an empty vessel that can be made a momentary dwelling place for a spiritual entity who can be called upon to enter by the prayers and offerings of a supplicant. The shrines of today's Bali share this same quality, in that they are not permanently inhabited by any spiritual entity, rather they are a place that is prepared for the visit of a spiritual entity.

The Borobudur is often referred to as a candi; however, it is actually a ninth-century Mahayana Buddhist stupa located in Magelang, near Jogjakarta, in Central Java.[3] It was built during the reign of the Sailendra dynasty, and it is the world's largest Buddhist religious site.[4]

Candi Prambanan is the most graceful Hindu temple complex in Indonesia, and it is among the most beautiful Hindu temple complexes in the world. It is a Shivaite religious site, that is, a religious complex devoted to the worship of Shiva.[5] The building was started in about 850 CE, most likely by Rakai Pikatan[6] of the Sanjaya dynasty,[7] probably in response to the building of Borobudur by the Buddhist Sailendra dynasty. During that period in Javanese history, both these royal houses ruled simultaneously in Central Java.

The Prambanan Temple Complex is dedicated to the Trimurti, which is the expression of God as the Creator, Brahma; God as the Preserver, Vishnu (Jav.: Wisnu); and God as the Destroyer, Shiva (Jav.: Siwa). The Prambanan Temple Complex is entered from the east, Candi Siwa occupies the central position, Candi Wisnu is to the north of Candi Siwa, and Candi Brahma is to the south of Candi Siwa. Presently there are also five smaller shrines.

On the inside of the balcony wall of Candi Siwa, and continued on the balcony wall of Candi Brahma, the story of the Ramayana is carved in relief.[8] The relief carvings of Candi Siwa contain at least three representations of weapons, that by today's standards are recognized as representations of the earliest form of the keris, the so-called Keris Buda, that is, the keris that was used in Java during the Buda period,[9] the period predating the Islamic period.[10]

At this time in history, it seems that the keris was just one of the many Javanese edged weapons, and monumental representations of the keris show it as a dagger and being used as a dagger. The blade shape appears to be a Javanese interpretation of the well-known Indian leaf-shaped blade.[11]

In the eleventh century, the center of Javanese power shifted from central Java to East Java. The court shifted, and many of the subjects of the Sanjaya dynasty followed the court to East Java. During the next three hundred years, a number of small kingdoms rose and fell, and more Hindu and Buddhist candis were built, perhaps the most notable being Candi Panataran, located near the town of Blitar.[12]

The monumental reliefs on the walls of Candi Panataran show several representations of daggers having a keris-like form, so from this evidence we know that when the Court of the Sanjayas, along with many of its subjects, shifted from Central Java to East Java, they brought the keris with them. No representations of keris, nor of keris-like weapons can be found in the Buddhist monumental works of Java.

This progression of East Javanese kingdoms reached its peak with the foundation of the Hindu-Buddhist Kingdom of Majapahit, in about 1293. The age of Majapahit is regarded as the "Golden Age" of Java, something similar in Javanese historical belief to the age of King Arthur and the Knights of the Table Round, in British historical belief. Majapahit was an inland agrarian kingdom that built and controlled a network of tributary states and trade alliances throughout maritime Southeast Asia. Although it was an inland kingdom, it dominated maritime Southeast Asia by virtue of its sea power.

During the Majapahit era, something happened to the keris that influenced its future position in Javanese culture and society, but before we follow the journey of the keris any further, we need to look at the religious beliefs of the Javanese people.

The indigenous religious belief system of the Javanese people is a system that combines ancestor worship with animism. In the Javanese understanding of animism, we have both the belief that trees, rocks, places, and other things can be inhabited by a soul or a spirit, and the overarching belief that all things both natural and manmade possess a part of the life force that permeates all creation. All things possess a part of this life force, but it is not evenly distributed; for example, a horse will possess a greater part of the essence than will a rock, and a man will possess more than a horse.

Together with this animistic belief, we have ancestor worship. In the form that this takes in Java, there is the belief that the ancestors still exist, but they exist in the Unseen World, not in the Visible World. They are always present and can protect us from harm, but if they are displeased with our actions, they can show their displeasure by putting difficulties in our way, the purpose of which is to both discipline us and to teach us the correct way in which to behave.

Offerings are made both to objects that are believed to be vessels that can contain a significant quantity or quality of spiritual essence, and to the ancestors. Examples of inanimate objects that can be considered to warrant offerings are very often, perhaps most often, objects that have been passed from preceding generations, such objects are termed *pusaka* and can include, among other things, objects such as saddles, walking sticks, books, rice cookers, and weapons.[13] Being in possession of one or more *pusakas* can legitimize the reign of a ruler, or the senior position of a member of an extended family.

In Javanese belief, the dwelling place of the ancestors is located on a mountain. In very early times, all mountainous areas were probably regarded as possible locations for the ancestors, but with the coming of the Hindu belief system to Java, and its absorption into the overall Javanese belief system, the broad idea of the ancestors being located in high places underwent change. The Hindu belief system introduced the presence of Mount Meru, the dwelling place of Hindu deities, and its place as the physical and spiritual center of the Cosmos.

So, now there was a single high place that was able to be identified as the dwelling place of not only the Hindu deities but also of the ancestors. As the Hindu belief system was absorbed into Javanese society and influenced Javanese cultural beliefs, a process of syncretization took place whereby the Hindu-Buddhist beliefs overlaid and combined with the indigenous Javanese beliefs. Now an ancestor could become deified and might eventually be absorbed into the essence of a deity.

During the Hindu-Buddhist era, when a Javanese king or other important person died, he was very often deified and monumental representations of him were in the form of a deity. For example, when Gajah Mada, the prime minister of the East Javanese Kingdom of Majapahit died, he was monumentally represented as Ganesha, the elephant-headed deity of knowledge, wisdom, and learning.[14]

So it was that in Java, Mount Meru, the dwelling place of the Hindu deities became also the place where the ancestors waited to be absorbed into the essence of the deity with whom they identified or to be returned to earth to undergo another life cycle and move a little closer to union with their deity. In Javanese-Hindu belief, the deities are aspects of a single supreme god, Sang

Hyang Bathara Guru (who can be regarded as Shiva); thus, the absorption into a deity equates to the Hindu concept of *moksha*.[15]

For the Javanese people, Mount Meru was and is symbolically represented as a mountain-like form that is known as the "Gunungan." This Gunungan symbol seems to have entered Javanese symbolism during the Majapahit era (1293 to about 1500), and with the passing of time it has assumed the role of the single most pervasive symbol in Javanese society. Perhaps its best-known presence is as the symbol used to open and close the *wayang* (shadow puppet) performances, where it carries the alternate name of "Kayon," which infers a tree, and in this context, the Tree of Life.[16]

In Javanese traditional society, the *wayang* theater fills a role that is not unlike the role of sermons given by Christian or Muslim preachers. The lessons of morality and behavior that are delivered through the medium of the *wayang* theater have a pervasive effect on the lives and conduct of those Javanese people who maintain a traditional sense of values.

The Javanese candi, previously mentioned in relation to Javanese Hindu-Buddhist monumental works, has a physical form that is intended to represent Mount Meru. Just as the Gunungan is a symbolic representation of Mount Meru, so the candi is a representation of Mount Meru.

A simplified overview of traditional Javanese religious beliefs has been given above, and the question may well be asked exactly what this has to do with a personal weapon. I have commented on the presence of Mount Meru in Javanese belief, and upon the symbolic representation of Mount Meru as the Gunungan, and of Mount Meru as the candi.

The Javanese keris is also a symbolic representation of the Gunungan, and thus of Mount Meru, just as is the candi, and in a spiritual context the keris can fulfill a similar function to that of the candi, it can function as a personal shrine into which a spiritual essence can enter and it can facilitate communication with that spiritual entity.

Javanese symbolism is multisymbolism, the function and the way in which any symbol can be understood depends upon the context into which it is placed. Thus, Mount Meru as the Cosmic Mountain can be a dwelling place of deities, a dwelling place of ancestors, the Center of the Cosmos, as well as many other things; the candi can be a burial place, a monument, and a place to pray to or make offerings to deities and ancestors; the keris can be both weapon and personal shrine. In the Javanese world view, there are no contradictions in any of this.

The early keris was a form that today we classify as the "Keris Buda." This name recognizes that this keris form was present in pre-Islamic Java, a period referred to by the Javanese people as the "Buda Era." The form of the Keris Buda is a clear reflection of the Gunungan form. It seems likely that at least some

Keris Buda were used as weapons of blood sacrifice, a usage that can be implied by the existence of examples of Keris Buda made of bronze, a material that was preferred to ferric material for some religious sacrificial purposes.

During the time of the Kingdom of Majapahit, specifically, during the reign of Rajasanagara Jayawishnuwardhana (1350–1389), informally known as Hayam Wuruk, and his Mahapatih Gajah Mada (Prime Minister Gajah Mada), it seems probable that the Keris Buda underwent a change in its shape that resulted in the weapon form that we now know as the Modern Keris. This change in shape resulted in not just a single form replacing the Keris Buda, but in multiple forms, each form being a symbolic representation of the social position of the bearer and in some instances of his occupation. The changes in form that reflected social status can be tied directly to the number of roofs that a man was entitled to in his family shrine.[17]

These changes in the form of the keris thus made of the keris a weapon that was directly identifiable as a symbol of its bearer. In other words, a very personal object.

The Kingdom of Majapahit relied heavily upon sea trade. Trading enclaves were established along the north coast of Java by traders who used the east monsoon winds to travel to Java from India and the Middle East and stayed in Java until the winds changed, when they could sail back whence they came. Traders also came to the north coast of Java from China and from other parts of Southeast Asia and East Asia.

These traders took local wives, often sisters or daughters of Javanese nobility. The enclaves that the traders established, and the Javanese trade, in general, was under the control of princes and other nobles from the Kingdom of Majapahit, so the traders were in fact marrying into Javanese nobility and interacting socially and commercially with their relatives. The traders copied the style, manners, dress of the Majapahit nobility with whom they associated, and this practice included the wearing of the personal weapon of the Majapahit nobility, the keris.

However, although for the nobles of Majapahit, the keris carried certain symbolic meanings, for the traders from India, China, and the Islamic countries of the Middle East, those symbolic meanings had no meaning at all. Even if the symbolism of the keris was mentioned by the Majapahit nobles, the symbolism was probably not understood, nor did it need to be understood by the outsiders.

The last ruler of Majapahit was Bhrekertabumi (a.k.a. Brawijaya V, reigned 1474–1478). Raden Patah was the son of Brawijaya V, from a concubine, probably Chinese. In about 1475, Raden Patah established the Islamic Kingdom of Demak on the north coast of Java, and Java's first Mosque was built in Demak during his reign. He also converted his father, Brawijaya V, to Islam. With the conversion of Brawijaya V to Islam, Islam became a political force in Java, rather than a social force, and conversion to Islam thereafter was pursued with the assistance of military power.

Islam began its spread throughout Java in a way that was typical of the style that can be seen in other aspects of Javanese culture and society. Islam did use military means to overcome political entities, and those political entities were Hindu-Buddhist, but once the political entity had been disposed of, the people who had been under the control of that entity were encouraged into the Islamic fold by sympathetic and more or less gentle means, rather than by harsh force. Economic advantage was offered to the lower classes when they came under the control of a Muslim overlord. One element that made Islam more than a little attractive to the Javanese underclasses was the fact that in Islam all men are equal before God, something which was in marked contrast to the previous Hindu-Buddhist system where all men were arranged in a very formal hierarchy.

Many, if not most, of the elements of Javanese society that had been identifiable with the Hindu-Buddhist belief system were not banned, but were altered, or reinvented as elements of the Islamic belief system as it was in Java, and amalgamated into that Islamic system. The *wayang*, that great influence upon the beliefs and social mores of the Javanese people, was not swept away, but rather it was adapted by the introduction of Islamic *wayang* plays, constructed to teach Islamic style and mores, alongside the older Hindu-Buddhist stories. The Javanese keris, which in Majapahit was not only a personal weapon, but was also a symbol of social position, became a weapon that was not primarily associated with the nobility, but instead a weapon that could be worn and used by anybody and not carry any implication of social position.

In short, just as the Javanese indigenous belief system had absorbed and amalgamated with the Hindu-Buddhist beliefs to create the Javanese-Hindu religious belief system, the new Islamic belief system, which in the Javanese form was strongly influenced by Sufic mysticism, absorbed the Javanese-Hindu beliefs, along with the indigenous beliefs, to create a strongly mystical philosophy that emphasized the unitary nature of God, surrender of self to God, and the maintenance of a harmonious relationship with everything in creation.[18] With the passing of time, this philosophy became something uniquely Javanese and is now known as Kejawen. Kejawen has sometimes been described as "Javanese Islam," but it is more a philosophy of life than it is a religion, and is not in conflict with any established religion.

When the Javanese keris became a weapon that was more widely spread in the general population than it had been during Majapahit times, it was reinterpreted as an Islamic artifact, and much of the symbolism that had been a part of its nature under the Javanese-Hindu social system was reinterpreted in Islamic terms. The distinctive blade waves that under Majapahit had served to symbolize social position were counted differently under Islam, and the number of waves counted was divorced from alignment with the number of roofs in a family shrine, thus destroying any hint of association with a societal position. Of course, by this time, the Javanese-Hindu shrines of the past had fallen into disuse or had disappeared, so even if the count had not been altered, there would probably not have been any ongoing association of the keris with the Meru in the minds of the Javanese people.

An example of the way in which Islam reinterpreted Javanese-Hindu symbolism so that there was no conflict with Islamic beliefs can be seen in the treatment of one of the symbols to be found in the iconography of the keris. The symbol concerned is a small feature that is now known as the *ron dha*.[19] In the Java of today, this feature is popularly believed to be a representation of the Javanese letter *dha*; however, why *dha* has been chosen to be included as a feature of the keris is not generally addressed. On those occasions when a knowledgeable person feels inclined to explain the presence of the *ron dha*, he will explain that it is a representation of the Name of God. It is barely possible to give the *ron dha* a reading as "Allah." However, the *ron dha* exists not only in the Javanese keris but also in the Balinese keris, thus, it existed prior to the domination of Java by Islam. The Balinese people do not follow Islam; rather, they follow the Balinese-Hindu belief system (now known as Agama Hindu Dharma), a religious system that was largely inherited from the pre-Islamic Javanese Hindu-Buddhist belief system. Thus, the understanding of the *ron dha* as "Allah" is a Javanese understanding that has come into being only since the domination of Javanese society by Islam.

When the *ron dha* is read in the context of Old Javanese or Balinese script, it cannot be read as anything other than the shortest mantra: Om, or Aum. "Om" is used by adherents of the Hindu faith to begin and to end prayers.

When the iconography of the Javanese keris is read in a Hindu context that iconography quite clearly demonstrates that during the Majapahit era the keris fulfilled not only the function of a weapon and as an indicator of social position, but it also had the nature of a personal shrine. Remember that the Javanese keris is a representation of the Gunungan, as is also the candi. As a shrine, the keris can be thought of as a place that a deity, or an ancestor can enter when called upon by the custodian of the keris. The nature of the keris as a personal shrine is not unique to Javanese culture, it is also found in the culture of mainstream Hindu belief in India, where weapons were often accorded the status of de facto temples that could be visited by deities. Bearing in mind the beliefs brought into Javanese culture by Hindu cultural input, it is not surprising that this weapon characteristic of personal shrine should be encountered in both Javanese and mainstream Indian culture.[20]

As the Islamic domination of Java progressed, the old Hindu-Buddhist symbolism and understandings were subverted by Islamic interpretations, and the face of Javanese society changed. The Javanese rulers instituted Islamic standards, the populace submitted to Islamic ideas in the ordering of society, but as with the Hindu-Buddhist social system that had preceded it, the Islamic social system was merely another layer over the foundation stone of Javanese indigenous standards and beliefs. The culture of the courts retained much of the old Hindu-Buddhist culture, and the underclasses retained much of their own indigenous belief system and culture. Thus, although the visible face of Javanese society might have changed, the body of Javanese society was still firmly anchored in its indigenous culture, as had also been the case during the earlier Hindu-Buddhist era.

As with other Javanese cultural icons, such as the *wayang*, and the *gamelan*, the keris retained an important place in Javanese culture.[21] The replacement of the Hindu-Buddhist faith with Islam may have seen the disappearance of the keris symbolism that related to social position, and its Hindu generated function as a personal shrine was forgotten, but in the communal Javanese memory, the keris was still regarded as a symbol of the man and a cultural object that was associated with spiritual values.

Under Islam, the Hindu-Buddhist deities no longer held quite the same position in the new society, but they still did exist in the stories told in the *wayang* plays and as a part of the communal memory. The keris continued to hold values that were reflections of its original character in Hindu-Buddhist society. No man was considered to be complete unless he possessed a keris, which could represent him in the marriage ceremony, especially when the ceremony involved marriage to a junior wife, and it could fill the role of a token of his authority. It was an essential part of royal regalia, and it legitimized the right to rule. The way in which the keris continued to be regarded, even after the old Hindu-Buddhist belief system was replaced by Islam, was a reflection of the original Hindu value system in respect to a man's personal weapon. The meanings of the characteristics of the keris that related to Hindu-Buddhist societal organization disappeared and were forgotten, but the relationship of the man to his personal weapon remained.

The old spiritual values of the keris were forgotten, if indeed they were ever known by the new masters of Java, but it was quite clear that the keris did have a spiritual value, and a belief system arose in which it became possible for the keris to become inhabited by spiritual beings, both good and evil, and of being able to fulfill the requirements of a talisman. All this was very far from the original Hindu-Buddhist idea of the keris being an indicator of social position, a personal shrine, and a means of contact with one's ancestors or personal deities. However, it still did function at a different level as a conduit to the Unseen World.

In the early sixteenth century, the Kingdom of Majapahit collapsed, and that was effectively the end of the Hindu-Buddhist socioreligious system in Java. Enclaves of the Hindu-Buddhist system continued to exist, for example, the Kingdom of Blambangan was not brought under Islamic control until it was conquered by Sultan Agung (Sultan Agung Anyokrokusumo, 1614–1645) of Mataram in 1639. However, after the collapse of Majapahit, Islam spread its cloak over Java, and from that time through to the present day, Islamic influence has gradually increased in Java, and indeed, in all of Indonesia, to the point where in the 2017 election of the governor of Jakarta, Islam was used for political purposes.

The changes in Javanese society and the interwoven systems of Javanese culture have inevitably undergone change because of this penetration by Islamic culture, but as already mentioned, these changes have had only minor effect upon the roots of Javanese culture; rather, they have affected the way in which Javanese cultural and societal values are expressed. This is not the place to comment on all the changes that have occurred under Islam. It is the Javanese keris that is the focus of attention, so my comments will be limited to some of the ways in which the Islamic domination of Java has affected the Javanese keris.

The Balinese keris was inherited directly from the Hindu-Buddhist kingdoms of pre-Islamic Java; thus it can be thought of as giving an indication of the style and nature of the pre-Islamic Javanese keris. Some obvious physical changes in the appearance of the Javanese keris, when compared to the Balinese keris, are usually believed to be the result of Islamic influence. In early Javanese keris handles, and in Balinese keris handles through to the present time, small sculptures of deities or iconic figures often form the handle, in contrast to later Javanese handles, which are planar in form and often have two areas of carved ornamentation that can be interpreted as vestiges of the previous figural representations of deities or other beings. It is believed that the disappearance of the figural handle on the Javanese keris is because of the Islamic prohibition on the representation of living beings. There are arguments against this belief, but it is widely held, and it may well be accurate.

However, the greatest change that has taken place in the Javanese keris is not a physical change, but a change in its cultural position. During the Majapahit era, the keris was a weapon, an indicator of social status and a personal shrine. These characteristics reflected the influence of Hindu cultural input to the culture of Java. When the Hindu-Buddhist era ended and Islam took its place, the function of the keris as a social indicator and personal shrine no longer had a place in Javanese society; however, there was a cultural memory and acknowledgment that the keris did enshrine a spiritual essence.

It did not take long for the indigenous mysticism of Java, combined with the mystic Sufic influence of Islam, to provide a replacement for the lost function of the keris as a personal shrine. The keris in Islamic Java became something that could be inhabited by a spiritual being, either good or evil, and could have talismanic qualities. The talismanic qualities were a predetermined quality that were governed by the surface pattern on the blade (*pamor*) and by the form of the blade, but the quality of spiritual content was something that could occur in any keris and was dependent upon multiple factors. The keris was and is still a spiritual object in Java, but the way in which that spiritual essence is understood is very different from the way in which it appears to have been understood in pre-Islamic Java.

Between 1812 and 1817, the British governor of Java, Stamford Raffles, wrote that the keris in Java at that time, and for some time previous, held a position similar to that of the small sword in European society fifty years previous. In other words, it had become a dress accoutrement. The keris at the present time still has the function of being an essential part of formal Javanese dress.

For at least the last two hundred years the keris has also had other functions, it can be a symbol of authority, it can represent its custodian, it is held by many Javanese people to be the highest expression of Javanese plastic art, and it can be a store of wealth. Within Javanese society, it holds an iconic presence, and in 2005, it was recognized by UNESCO as a part of the Intangible Cultural Heritage of Humanity.

Over its lifetime of more than one thousand years, the Javanese keris has been subject to many different ways in which it can be interpreted, and the interpretation that is placed upon it is largely dependent upon the window of time and the context through which it is viewed. One thing is certain: its ability to adopt a different character dependent upon circumstances has assured it of continued life, where other personal objects have failed and been forgotten. In a way, this character reflects the character of the land that gave it birth: the Land of Java.

Notes

1. The early classical period of Java began during the seventh century and came to an end in the 10th century, this was followed by the middle classical period which lasted until the early thirteenth century, then the late classical period, which lasted until the fifteenth century.

2. The origin of the word candi (pronunciation: *chandi*) is possibly a contraction of "Candikagrha": dwelling place of Chandika. Chandika/Chandi is one of the names of the goddess Durga, an incarnation of Devi, Shakti of Shiva. Candis were probably

originally monumental structures erected above the ashes of rulers and other important people; sacrifice, including human sacrifice, probably took place when a ruler's ashes were candified. Thus, a candi was a place for Candika, Durga as the Goddess of Death. See R. Soekmono, *The Javanese Candi: Function and Meaning* (Leiden: Brill, 1997); as well as Roy E. Jordaan and Robert. Wessing, "Human Sacrifice at Prambanan," *Journal of the Humanities and Social Sciences of Southeast Asia* 152, no. 1 (1996): 45–73.

3. The *Encyclopedia of Buddhism* identifies Borobudur as a Mahayana Buddhist site. See Robert E. Buswell, *The Encyclopedia of Buddhism* (New York: Macmillan, 2003). However, in 1982 or 1983, the Dalai Lama traveled to Java and consecrated Borobudur as a Vajrayana Buddhist shrine. Vajrayana Buddhism derives from Mahayana Buddhism but is a highly mystical form of Buddhism that uses tantric practices to attain enlightenment. Tantric Buddhism took root in Java during the seventh century and was widely practiced until, and even after, the Islamic domination of Java.

4. The Sailendra dynasty reigned in Central Java from the seventh to the ninth century, they were replaced by the Sanjayas and then shifted to Srivijaya in Sumatra where they reigned until the eleventh century.

5. In this form of the Hindu faith, as it was practiced in Java, Shiva was regarded as the supreme God, and as such he became Sang Hyang Bathara Guru. The worship can be of Shiva, or of Bathara Guru. Javanese symbolism is multisymbolism.

6. Rakai Pikatan was the sixth ruler of the Sanjaya dynasty in Central Java, he reigned between 840 and 856.

7. The Sanjaya dynasty shared power in Central Java with the Sailendras from the eighth until the ninth century, when they replaced the Sailendras. In the tenth century, the Sanjaya center of power shifted to East Java.

8. The Ramayana is an ancient Indian epic poem. See Valmiki, *Ramayana*, tr. Arshia Sattar (London: Penguin, 2003).

9. The "Buda period" is the name used by Javanese people to refer to the period that began with the introduction of Hindu-Buddhist ideas into Java until the beginning of the Islamic period in Java (from the sixth century to the first quarter of the sixteenth century).

10. The Islamic period of domination in Java began following the final defeat of the Kingdom of Majapahit, in about 1525.

11. An Indian leaf-shaped blade is a form that is considered to have its roots in antiquity, with both ancient Egyptian and ancient Greek weapons possessing this form. It is a common heritage of the Indo-Aryan peoples.

12. Candi Panataran (or Penataran) is located near Blitar and is a Shivaite temple complex; it is the largest temple complex in East Java. Its functional existence covers the period from 1197 to 1454.

13. In both Indonesian and Javanese *pusaka* means "heirloom"; a *pusaka* object is frequently believed to hold a spiritual essence.

14. Gajah Mada was the *mahapatih* or prime minister of the Kingdom of Majapahit from 1329 to 1364. He was a powerful military leader and was instrumental in bringing Majapahit to the peak of its glory.

15. In Hindu religious belief, *moksha* refers to freedom from the cycle of birth and death. Hindus believe in reincarnation, in Balinese-Hindu, and probably in its progenitor, Javanese-Hindu belief, that reincarnation is rebirth into a person in the same family, usually a grandchild. When *moksha* is attained, the spirit is absorbed by the personal deity, who is an aspect of the Supreme God, Bethara Guru, who can also be regarded as Shiva.

16. Kayon is the alternative name for the Gunungan used at the beginning and end of *wayang* performances. "Gunungan" refers to the form of this shadow puppet, and "Kayon" refers to the design painted on the Gunungan. This design incorporates a tree, which can be read as the Tree of Life, as well as other symbols that can be understood symbolically in a number of ways.

17. For more on the family shrine, see Alan G. Maisey, "An Interpretation of the Pre-Islamic Javanese Keris," *Arms Cavalcade: Journal of the Antique Arms Collectors Society of Australia* (May 2013): 20–51.

18. Sufic as in the strongly mystic Sufi Islamic sect.

19. *Ron dha* is the eighth letter of the Javanese alphabet; in Javanese numerology, it has a numerical value of 8 and symbolizes both the Naga and the elephant. It is used as a euphemism for a feature of the keris that in Hindu interpretation is read as "Om" or "Aum," the smallest mantra, and in Islamic interpretation can be read as "Allah."

20. The shrine is characteristic of the keris is one that today seems to have been largely forgotten in its originating culture, and it often comes as somewhat of a surprise to present-day keris aficionados as well. I had my first hint of this characteristic given to me by a Balinese Brahmin in about 1980. More on the subject can be found in Robert Elgood, *Hindu Arms and Ritual: Arms and Armour from India 1400–1865* (Utrecht: Eburon Academic Publishers, 2005).

21. The gamelan is the traditional percussion orchestra of Java and Bali.

Bibliography

Buswell, Robert E. *The Encyclopedia of Buddhism*. New York: Macmillan, 2003.

Elgood, Robert. *Hindu Arms and Ritual: Arms and Armour from India 1400–1865*. Utrecht: Eburon Academic Publishers, 2005.

Jordaan, Roy E. and Robert Wessing, "Human Sacrifice at Prambanan." *Journal of the Humanities and Social Sciences of Southeast Asia* 152, no. 1 (1996): 45–73.

Maisey, Alan G. "An Interpretation of the Pre-Islamic Javanese Keris." *Arms Cavalcade: Journal of the Antique Arms Collectors Society of Australia* (May 2013): 20–51.

Soekmono, R. *The Javanese Candi: Function and Meaning*. Leiden: Brill, 1997.

Valmiki. *Ramayana*. Translated by Arshia Sattar. London: Penguin, 2003.

Chapter 7

Cherokee Nonhuman Persons in Dual Realms

CARRIE McLACHLAN

Editor's Note: This chapter brings us out of Asia and into the New World, with a discussion of personalized objects in Native American culture (especially the Cherokee). This chapter echoes what I have called the naturalistic, religious, and practical objects discussed in earlier chapters, but I have chosen to position it here in the volume because it transitions those themes into a context that is closer (if not necessarily more familiar) to a modern North American reader. Moreover, it provides us an opportunity to see the complexity of the relationships among "natural," "religious," and "practical" objects. When talking about the corn and fresh water we (much like the Native Americans) still eat nearly every day (although perhaps now in the form of corn syrups and oil), are these abstractions useful, or detrimental?

Two important nonhuman Cherokee persons, River and Corn, simultaneously live on earth as well as "Above" in a sky realm. These beings would not normally be considered persons in Western religious and philosophical thought. Not only would they not be considered persons, but they would be considered impersonal objects. But in the Cherokee worldview, they and many other "impersonal objects" are persons.[1]

Sixty years after Marcel Mauss's 1928 essay "A Category of the Mind: The Notion of Person; the Notion of Self," Cambridge University published his essay translated from the original French into English, followed by several essays in response. In one of those essays, "The Person," Charles Taylor suggests his views are mainly compatible with Mauss's, suggesting a "rough correspondence" in their ideas. Beyond a "representative" view of the person as a reflective being with a sense of self as an agent able to make choices and hold values, Taylor suggests that one becomes a person by making strong evaluations. In addition, a person is able to experience emotions such as shame before others. To become a person, a being must have language that creates a common ground, a "public space." Not only is a person "self-aware" but is "open to different significances," is able to make "strong evaluations" and "assessments."[2] All of this is accomplished through reciprocal interactions with other persons.

In "The Notion of the Person" Marcel Mauss attempts to trace the development of earlier concepts of *personage* and *persona* into the modern concept of person as a self via Christian theology and philosophic thought. All this is concerned with defining the human person. Mauss suggests that in "primal" cultures, clan affiliation, naming practices, and perceived relationships between the living and the dead are elements that helped "define" a person but that the idea of a self with political rights is fairly recent. Taylor suggests that the evolutionary trajectory is not straightforward, that earlier concepts of persona are important concepts that "we have partly lost": concepts by which a person has an "inner sense" of personal significance linked to "some force or to some region which lies outside us." This loss is significant as this perspective is one way in which persons may become "interlocutors." From this point of view, persons are part of an "exchange that pre-exists us." Persons become an "agent-plus by being inducted as interlocutor into some great conversation . . . To have the name, or perhaps the mask, is to be the interlocutor."[3] In neither Mauss's nor Taylor's essays is the question raised "Can nonhumans be considered persons?" As they develop the concept, person applies primarily to humans. My concern is not to enter into a discussion of the development of the concept of person, but to use concepts from Charles Taylor's discussion of "person" to show how these can be applied to nonhuman persons in Cherokee thought and more specifically, how the concept of "person" can be applied to beings in Cherokee thought who are generally considered impersonal objects.

Traditionally, the Cherokee are part of a civilization that allows individuals to be part of a "great conversation" that includes persons beyond an individual's own community or time, persons such as ancestors, creator beings and culture heroes, animals, plants, and what James Mooney called "elemental beings," such as fire, water, and the sun."[4]

From what has been recorded of the Cherokee worldview, the "real people" are what Charles Taylor calls "agents plus," living in a complex interrelational system with nonhuman persons who would also be considered "agents plus." While I am not aware of a Cherokee explanation of what constitutes a person, we have a few references to nonhuman beings who are considered persons. According to Will West Long (a Cherokee traditionalist):

The fire on the hearth had an intensely spiritual nature, was human in thought, consciousness, intent, emotions, etc., and was in fact an old woman who was a grandmother in kin terms. She was a member of the family and the household. Proper treatment of the fire was essential to the well-being of the family, good family life, mannerly and proper conduct . . . protect[ing] the family from witch attack and many other ills.[5]

That fire is "human in thought, consciousness, intent, emotions" indicates the Cherokee consider fire to be sentient. That Fire is a member of the family and interacts with them, protecting them as they care for her, indicates that she is an "agent plus," participating in a community. Also, through the way the sacrifices to fire are accepted, priests are able to divine messages from her, indicating a form of communication.[6]

Similarly, ethnographer James Mooney indicates that the Cherokee consider ginseng an "animate" and a "sentient being." Ginseng is an important and powerful healer. Before taking a portion of the ginseng root, the "doctor" would address it as "Great *ada'wehi* "(a most powerful being) and then would "humbly" ask "permission to take a small piece of its flesh."[7]

A guiding principle in Cherokee, as in many American Indian ethical systems, is the concept of reciprocity. That persons have an awareness of self and others suggests that they are social beings. We might safely say that a person is a being not only aware of self and other persons, but one who is in relation with other persons. David Carrasco, a scholar of Mesoamerican traditions, indicates that reciprocity is a relationship "based on some form of mutual care and nurturance." Lawrence Sullivan goes a step further to identify the types of reciprocal relationships commonly found among American Indians. He says reciprocity connotes the "establishment and maintenance of right relationships" among a variety of beings including human and other-than-human-persons; men and women; individual persons and the community; persons and environment[8]; and between living and dead persons. These relationships are maintained through ceremony, linking action and cultural knowledge. Through ceremony, American Indians connect with each other, the dead, the environment, and nonhuman persons. Ceremonies enact, represent, and/or foster the "right relationships" that cultural narratives establish and model through the generations. Ritual and cultural knowledge are foundational in the development of an individual into a person. One becomes more fully a person as one incorporates cultural ideals.[9]

The question of what constitutes a person from an American Indian perspective has been addressed, to some degree from an Iroquois/Haudenosaunee perspective. The Haudenosaunee are linguistic siblings of the Cherokee.[10] David

Blanchard's study of Iroquoian thought suggests the Haudenosaunee conceived of "two metaphysical aspects of being: first, *nigonr*, "consciousness"; and second, a "living principle or generic property of matter contained in all substance." Those living beings who are conscious have "an awareness of self and others," and they are persons. So, from an Iroquoian viewpoint, while all things are living, not all living things are conscious persons, having "an awareness of self and others." This is an important distinction: not all living things are persons in Iroquois thought. Among those living beings who are conscious persons, there are two types: sky persons (*ongwe shona*) and this-world persons (*ongwe honwe*). Extraordinary persons are both *ongwe shona* and *ongwe honwe*, transcending categories:

> In the Iroquoian cosmogony, the universe consists of the "Sky World" and this world (Earth) on the back of the great turtle; furthermore, they believe that this world is a material reflection of the Sky World. The Sky World is populated by *ongwe shona*, or first peoples; this world is inhabited by *ongwe honwe*, "real men," material re-creations of the *ongwe shona* of the Sky World. Both the *ongwe honwe* and the *ongwe shona* are considered as persons by the Iroquois; that is, as having a consciousness and an awareness of self and others. The Iroquois further acknowledge that there are human as well as non-human persons. This is true of the persons who inhabit the Sky World and the Earth. For example: corn, beans, and squash—the three "Sister-Providers" of Iroquois myth and legend—are persons, although not human, who exist as both *ongwe shona* and *ongwe honwe*.[11]

The concepts of there being two different types of persons and that the persons of this world are in some way "recreations" of persons in the sky world are certainly concepts the Iroquois and Cherokee share. Both James Mooney and Stansbury Hagar understood that esoteric nineteenth-century Cherokee thought held that earth beings are "images," "reflections," or "emanations" of more perfect beings in the sky world. It is also from this celestial realm that the Cherokee derived their social structure.[12] To be both a sky- and this-world person denotes a being of special significance. Some Cherokee persons also transcend categories and exist as beings of this world and the sky world.

I will posit that in Cherokee thought, as in Iroquois thought, human and other-than-human persons are beings conscious of self and others who are in relation with other persons. At least in the Cherokee worldview, these persons are perceived as having language. I will not venture to list or discuss all beings the Cherokee might consider persons but will limit my discussion to two types of Cherokee nonhuman persons who, like the Iroquois "Three Sisters," corn, squash, and beans, transcend the two categories of person: they are both "this world" and "sky world" persons.

We will see that the Cherokee "Corn Woman," like the Iroquois "Three Sisters," is simultaneously an earth being and a sky being. While there are other Cherokee nonhuman persons who also seem to transcend categories, I will only focus on one other nonhuman person, the Cherokee River, Yvwi Gunahita/ Long Person.

According to an account recorded in the 1830s, the Cherokee primal mother, like the Iroquois "woman who fell from the skies," came to the earth from "above" at the time of creation.[13] "Sickatower," "one of the most aged men in the [Cherokee] nation," revealed that the Cherokee Corn Mother "had been brought down from the skies." When asked the name of the woman, Sickatower says, "I never heard the name. The person had no name. But that person was a Woman. She had two children. Both were sons." A half century later, James Mooney gave her a name, Selu, the Cherokee word for corn. The accounts Mooney obtained from Cherokee traditionalists Swimmer and John Ax are similar in many details to Sickatower's earlier narrative, though each reveal different concepts and details.[14] All indicate that the sons of the Corn Mother and Hunter Father come to the mistaken conclusion that their mother is a witch because she produces food from her body, and for this reason, they determine to kill her. Knowing their thoughts, the Corn Mother instructs her sons how to provide crops for themselves after she is gone. In the Sickatower account, the Corn Mother's instructions also suggest the type of person she is, a being of the earthly realm, in the form of corn and a being of the "sky" realm who remains an ideal relational being, caring for her children even when they betray the relation:

> Sons, your minds are bewildered & your sense is gone & your Mother must be killed by her own Sons. But I found food for you and I was your food and in killing your mother you yourselves will fill yourselves with evil. But your mother will remain a mother to you, even though you kill her. Take heed therefore & treasure up of her words. You may think that I am killed, but I shall not be dead. Do my bidding, for I shall be alive both on earth and in the skies. . . . Do my bidding; and when I am killed, drag my body, to & fro, over a large space. From the spot over which you drag my body, I shall come out upon the earth, & from my habitation in Heaven I shall see whether you do my bidding and toil earnestly to cause me to increase upon the earth. When you see me risen about one foot from the earth, you are to labour all around me and take away every weed that may have come

along to clog my growth; and though the sun burn you when you do this, and though your work make you very weary, do not falter; but remember I am your mother; and call upon me with songs, and let me hear you. . . . When you shall have discharged these duties and when you shall have sung this song, I shall then be in a fair way of growing to maturity. You will see me almost grown. You will see me fully grown. I shall lift my head proudly. You will look on me and be glad: and be sure that you are careful of me, for elsewhere you shall find no milk whose source is inexhaustible like mine. And when you discover that my bosom is full of nourishment; and when my head towers so high that no foot can step over my crest, waving towards the Heavens, then are you to set apart seven days and seven nights; and on the next morning which shall follow, at the rising sun you are to cut deep lines upon your limbs like those between the grain rows of my spikes: and then you are to take me by the hand and to draw me towards you and to prepare me for a feast. And when the feast is ready for your eating and when you shall be placed before it, you are to make your invocations first towards the east, and secondly towards the north, and thirdly towards the west and fourthly towards the south. Then you are to stand in the centre of the four points and to call to me above . . . for I shall be there and shall hear you if you call; and when I hear you, I will take fast hold upon your mind and bring it back to what it ought to be.[15]

This narrative identifies the Corn Mother as a "person" and makes it clear that she is both a woman and "corn." Further, it is evident that this Mother lives in two realms, "above" in some unnamed form and on earth in the form of "corn."[16] Her body contains the seeds of and **is** the corn (and beans and squash) that grow upon the earth, and she also lives "above." In Iroquoian terms she is simultaneously both *ongwe honwe* and *ongwe shona,* a person of the earth and a sky world person. She is also a relational being who provides for her children so long as they remember her and follow the proscribed rituals. She also indicates that through ceremony, harmony, or balance is restored to her children as she will return their minds to the proper state of "what it ought to be." [17]

Though not strictly a human person, Selu is a person in every way. In the Cherokee worldview, she is aware of self and others. She communicates with her children and is the embodiment of compassion and forgiveness. She is involved in reciprocal relations with humans and with the earth/environment.[18] She provides a link between the living and the dead as she was the first person on earth to "die." She connects living generations to her as she continues to provide vegetation essential to life. She is the pre-eminent Cherokee female role-model and is the Primal Mother, an "ancestral being."

For the Cherokee, both hunting and agriculture are associated with ritual proscriptions that must be followed. Mutual care is evident between the Corn Woman, who provides, and her children who follow the proscribed rituals and give thanks for what has been received. This agricultural person is a model of how a person should behave towards others.[19] She gives of herself, providing methods for others to attain the sustenance her body provides, while also requiring accountability from her children. Those who are disrespectful and do not follow the proscribed social rituals suffer consequences.[20] In one narrative, Selu is also associated with granting success in hunting, an activity generally associated with her mate, Kanati, the great hunter. This provides additional support to a thesis advanced by James Mooney, that some beings may be dual female/male beings, manifesting themselves in either a male or female form.[21]

Besides Selu, there are other Cherokee persons who may fit into the category of being simultaneously earth and sky beings. Selu mated with a Hunter. James Mooney identified him *as* Kanati. Kanati is identified in some creation accounts as the laziest of animals before he met Selu and became motivated to build her a house and win her as his mate.[22] On "earth" he is the primal Hunter and Father and is, most likely, Thunder in his "sky" manifestation. After his son's kill Selu, Kanati leaves them to join his wife "above."[23] If the identification of Kanati with Thunder is correct, he too is a person who exists in two realms.[24] Another clue to Kanati's more expansive identity is that one of the names of the River is Ela-Kanati, the "Terrestrial Hunter." And, as we will see, the River has a "Sky World" counterpart.

There are several rivers held sacred throughout the world. Most of us are familiar with the Ganges River who, by her devotees, is considered a goddess.[25] Despite the visible pollution, Hindus bathe in her body to purify themselves and seek divine assistance. Rivers are also sacred to indigenous peoples of the Peruvian highlands. One such river flows through the Sacred Valley between Machu Picchu and Cuzco. This river, the Willkamayu (Sacred River), was sacred to the Inca, to the people who preceded that famous but short-lived civilization, and remains sacred to local indigenous people of Peru. Willkamayu's path is important in creation, mirrors the daytime path of the sun at the time of the summer solstice, and connects this earthly realm with the Otherworld.[26] In New Zealand, another river, Te Awa Tupua, has long been held sacred by the Maori. On March 20, 2017, something quite extraordinary happened in the modern history of sacred rivers. On this date, the government of New Zealand recognized Te Awa Tupua, to be a person.[27] While the legal significance of this event is notable, it is not unusual for indigenous peoples to consider rivers persons.

The Cherokee not only consider the River, Yvwi Gunahita, to be a person but to be one of the most important other-than-human persons in their cosmology. James Mooney summarized the importance of the River, who is

> a giant with his head in the foothills of the mountains and his foot far down in the lowland . . . speaking ever in murmurs which only the priest may interpret. In the words of the sacred formulas, he holds all things in his hands . . . His aid is invoked with prayer and fasting on every important occasion of life, from the very birth of the infant, in health and sickness, in war and love, in hunting and fishing, to ward off evil spells and to win success in friendly rivalries. Purification in the running stream is a part of every tribal function.[28]

From this brief description, it is already evident that from a Cherokee perspective, the River is in a reciprocal relationship with the Cherokee, communicating with them through language and action. For the Cherokee, the River, Yvwi Gunahita, is a person with awareness of self and others. The River is also the earthly manifestation of a more perfect and primal "celestial" being. In addition to the important functions Mooney listed, I will add that an individual's association with Long Person continued beyond death.

I will use "River" or "Yvwi Gunahita"/"Long Person" to designate all Cherokee rivers. However, the River has different titles, perhaps reflecting its different aspects and so the generic use of the term Yvwi Gunahita may not always be accurate.[29] While the most common of the titles associated with the river appears to be Yvwi Gunahita/Long Person, there are others, including Asgaya Gunahita/ Long Man, Inadu Gunahita/Long Snake, Ama ganv:hí:dv/Long Water, and Ela-Kanati/"Great Terrestrial Hunter." These various titles seem to suggest different functions or persona of rivers in Cherokee thought.[30]

Yvwi Gunahita originates in the springs of the Appalachian Mountains and flows on both sides of the continental divide forming the headwaters of several major rivers, most notably the Savannah and the Tennessee Rivers. But the springs are more than sources of pure water, they are portals that link this world with another.[31]

A Cherokee human individual's intimate association with Yvwi Gunahita began at birth and continued beyond death.[32] The newborn baby was passed over the fire and immersed in Yvwi Gunahita. In the mideighteenth century, Henry Timberlake observed that after a child was born, it was "dipped into cold water and washed, which is repeated every morning for two years." He suggested that this rigorous practice helped strengthen the child.[33] Over a century later, the practice had been modified. In the late nineteenth century, after the Cherokee population had been further decimated by European diseases and Removal, James Mooney noted that after birth the infant was not immersed in the cold river water for fear of its health:

> When the new-born child is four days old, the mother brings it to the priest, who carries it in his arms to the river, and there, standing close to the water's edge and facing the rising sun, bends seven times toward the water, as though to plunge the child into it. He is careful, however, not to let the infant's body touch the cold water, as the sudden shock might be too much for it, but holds his breath . . . while he mentally recites a prayer for the health, long life, and future prosperity of the child.[34]

The newborn child was then given a medicine made with some variety of *uni sti-lvi-sti*, a "sticker," mixed with water from Long Person's body, from a waterfall or cataract, "where the stream makes a constant noise." The "sticker" insured retention of knowledge while the noise of the cataract from which the water is taken is believed to be the voice of Yvwi Gunahita, teaching lessons the child may understand. The infant drank this mixture for four successive days in order to ensure a good memory and an attentive mind.[35] This close relationship continued through life and beyond death.

Wild Boy, one of the primal twins, the sons of Kanati and Selu, exemplifies the relationship individuals have with the River. He was born from a mixture of blood and the River. He and his brother were instructed to follow rituals which we know from other sources would have included "going to water." Finally, Wild Boy and his brother followed their father, Kanati, the Hunter, when he abandoned them because they had killed their mother. Their father's trail eventually led through a portal and into the "sky" world. Mooney omitted in his published account that after the boys went "up" to find their parents, they found a "large river," which they crossed in a "canoe." They found their mother and father on the other side of the River. A "celestial" river "amongst" the stars is the trail the boys followed, presumably also the trail that their parents traveled, the "Trail of Kanati." We will see that this pathway seems to be the same that human souls also follow upon death in their journey to Usvhiyi, the Darkening Land.[36]

In the Cherokee worldview, the rivers that flow on and through the earth are sacred and animate. James Mooney classified Yvwi Gunahita as one of the "elemental gods" and intimates that Long Person was of more importance in the Cherokee ceremonial life than the Sun or the Fire: "The sun is invoked chiefly by the ball-player, while the hunter prays to the fire; but every important ceremony—whether connected with medicine, love, hunting, or the ball play—contains a prayer to the 'Long Person.' "[37] All Cherokee villages and towns were necessarily located next to flowing water not only for travel, drinking, and cleansing but for all aspects of life. In addition to the activities Mooney mentions, there were daily rituals that included "going to water," where the Cherokee ritually immersed themselves in the River. "Going to water" was also a central part of monthly New Moon ceremonies when the River was deemed more potent. In addition to "going to water" in connection with hunting, it was an essential ritual performed before and after stick ball games, before and after going to war, and after release from captivity. "Going to water" is also essential for maintaining as well as recovering health. The ritual of "going to Water" was also practiced by the entire community during important annual festivals such as the Green Corn Ceremony.

According to one nineteenth-century account, the Cherokee Nation gathered annually to celebrate the Green Corn Ceremony. On the seventh day of the ceremony, everyone entered into Yvwi Gunahita's body, ritually immersed, sent their old clothes downstream, and clothed themselves in new garments:

> In the morning early, the priest directed all to repair to the river, where, after uttering a short prayer on the bank, he ordered them to all wash. This they did by wading in, and then plunging entirely seven times, first toward the east, then west &c. The men went in a little upstream, and the women and children below. Some went in their old garments, and on coming out of the water changed, & put on clean dry clothes. All must have clean clothes on returning to the council house.[38]

In addition to this ritual, Corn was sacrificed not only to Fire, but also to Long Person. Fire and Yvwi Gunahita transmit the sacrifice into the Otherworld.[39]

Long Person is not only a source for healing and purification, a conveyor of prayers and sacrifices, but is a source of revelation. The association of streams and rivers with extrahuman knowledge is apparent in the practice of going to water in the early morning to listen, when the stream begins to wake and to "talk." The revelatory aspect of "Long Person" is also apparent in the Cherokee deluge narrative. In one account, a dog would "go down to the river every day and look at the water and howl." According to Mary Chiltoskey, the River warned the dog of the impending flood and told him to warn his master to build a raft.[40]

The River is important in medicine, gathering strength from plants into its waters and distributing this medicine to others. James Mooney explained the association between Kanati, the Hunter (Selu's husband), and the River, suggesting that the streams "search out and bring down to the great river the leaves and debris of the mountain forests."[41] That is why in some of the prayers the River is addressed as Ela Kanati, "Terrestrial Hunter." In one hunting prayer, the River is implored to "cover" its "stomach" with leaves. in the fall the leaves and vegetation, as well as the blood from the game killed during the hunting season, collect in the River and strengthen the water's potency. Prayers to Ela Kanati would be of particular importance during the autumn with the initiation of the hunting season. In addition to autumn, the beginning of spring is another time when ritual bathing in and collecting water from Ela Kanati is most advantageous. In the spring, the sap flows through the roots of plants and trees and strengthens the power of creeks and rivers. Spring and fall are also the periods when rainfall is heaviest in the Appalachian region.[42] In the Cherokee worldview, rivers unite the landscape and bring the medicinal power of the trees, shrubs, and other plants to the Cherokee, who ritually immerse themselves in the flowing water.[43] While autumn and spring are times when the medicinal quality of the River is strongest, some healing ceremonies were performed each month during the New Moon. In the moon's absence from the night sky, the River's healing properties were deemed strongest. We are not told why the River's medicinal qualities are stronger at the time of the New Moon, but perhaps the reasoning is the same as that of the Hupa of the Pacific Coast who schedule their "Jump Dance" so that on the last day of the ceremony, the Moon is able to come down to earth (as it is the New Moon and the Moon is not in the sky) to join in the ceremony. This is speculation but perhaps for the Cherokee the absence of the Moon in the night sky signified his presence on earth, lending his significant healing and creative powers.[44]

We have seen that the sons of Kanati and Selu followed the path of their father from this world into another. That path appears to be that of the River. In the Cherokee narrative "The Man who Married the Thunder's Sister" a man follows two sisters (who prove to not be ordinary humans) into another realm by following a path that appeared to be a stream and then a river, but to the otherworldly beings was "waving grass."[45]

The souls of the dead also follow the River from the earthly realm to a sky world. Cherokee traditionalist Will West Long, well educated in both Euro-American and Cherokee traditions, indicates that the River provides the path souls follow upon death: "Some people believed that the soul went into the River and followed the river up to a spring-head when it went down into an underworld." He referred to this path as the "Trail of Kanati."[46] While he used the same term, "underworld" that James Mooney used to refer to the Otherworld, the "underworld" is most likely the night sky. The path souls follow, according to Stansbury Hagar, is the Milky Way.[47]

At the end of the nineteenth century, ethnoastronomer Stansbury Hagar visited the Cherokee and collected surviving star lore. He learned from Cherokee sources that upon death, souls follow a trail across the night-time sky. At a certain point the soul must cross a raging river by means of a pole guarded by two dogs represented in the night sky by two Cherokee "dog stars known commonly as Sirius and Antares. These celestial dogs:

> guard opposite points of the sky, where the Milky Way touches the horizon. . . . The tradition is that souls, after the death of the body, cross a raging torrent on a narrow pole, from which . . . the . . . cowardly fall off, and are swept to oblivion . . ."[48]

The fortunate or worthy souls are able to pass by two dogs who guard the passage. According to Hagar the trail the souls follow is "probably the Milky Way, generally known among the North American Indians as the "Path of Souls."[49]

The link between the "Trail of Kanati" and the Milky Way is strengthened by the Milky Way's association with the Path of Souls in many indigenous traditions. In his study of Cherokee star lore, Hagar cites a cultural narrative from indigenous Peruvian people wherein the souls of the dead journey across the Milky Way, the "Path of Souls," on their way to the "spirit world" and "are carried over the river by some black dogs."[50] He was apparently unaware of a tradition more geographically and linguistically proximate to the Cherokee. In the seventeenth century, the Jesuits recorded a Huron belief in which the dead follow a celestial pathway known as Atiskein Andahatey/Starry Scarf, or Milky Way. As the Huron dead journey across this path, a stop is made at the place of Oscotarach, "Pierce Head," who scoops out the "brains" of the dead, storing them in a pumpkin. Before reaching their final destination, dead souls must cross a river in a manner similar to that described in the Cherokee account previously cited. The Huron account states: "There was also a river across which the only bridge was a tree trunk; it was guarded by a dog who jumped at many souls and made them fall into the water and drown."[51]

While no Cherokee source clearly establishes a one-to-one correspondence of the Milky Way, with the "Trail of Kanati," it is certainly probable that they are one and the same, just in different aspects. In James Mooney's manuscript notes, when the sons of Kanati and Selu follow their parents to the Otherworld, they cross a celestial river. That the celestial pathway is conceived as a river is evident in a Cherokee prayer in which the River is addressed as "*Ama ganv:hi:dv*, Long Water." The text suggests a celestial origin of the river as well as an earthly presence:

> Live Water, Long Water,
> You originated up There in the Seven Heavens!
> "It is to help you with!" You stated, and
> You have come to live upon the Seven Earths![52]

The River according to this text originated above in the "Seven Heavens," the most sacred region of the "Sky World." The River came to "live upon the Seven Earths," a reference to the seven clans that structure Cherokee society on earth. That the earth mirrors the celestial realm or is a microcosm reflecting the macrocosm is a concept common in many American Indian traditions.[53]

The close relationship between the earthly river and its heavenly counterpart is also suggested in another Cherokee prayer where the individual, assisted by a priest, "Goes to Water" and implores Yvwi Gunahita, Long Person, to assist in the journey from earth to "the Utmost Seven Heights":

> Now! Listen! Long Person! . . .
> They have just come to stand upon the very middle of your Body.
> (You are not to release them from Your Hand) . . .
> Ha! You and I have come to elevate him [her] far above to the
> place of Utter Wizardry—Seven!—to the place of Utter Wizardry!
> The Way is Opened through the Seven Clan Districts.
> Ha! He has just come to aim his [her] soul at the Utmost Seven Heights.
> He has just come to aim his [her] soul at where the White Chair
>   is resting.
> Ha! You and I have just come to elevate him [her]
> there to the Seven Distant Heights![54]

The role of the River in taking, guiding, and "aiming" the soul to the "Seven Distant Heights" is apparent: the River opens "The Way," a path through "the Seven Clan Districts." This is a reference to Yvwi Gunahita leading to a springhead portal where Longperson connects with the Celestial River. The River leads the soul to the ideal realm that exists "Above" in the "Sky" realm. The hand metaphor suggests that *Yvwi Gunahita* intimately guides the soul. This prayer requests long life in this world, but the metaphor also reveals the connection between the earthly realm and the "celestial" realm of the "Seven Heights." In guiding the soul, Yvwi Gunahita unites the earthly and celestial realms. Like the Iroquois "Three Sisters" and the Cherokee Corn Mother, Yvwi Gunahita is not only a "this-world person" but also a "sky person." This person is not only of both realms, but also unites these realms for others.

According to several Cherokee accounts, the Milky Way is called Gi-li U-tsv-sta-nv-yi, "Where the Dog Ran." It is so named because this celestial path was created when a dog ran across the night sky spewing corn meal. The version Stansbury Hagar recorded establishes a connection between corn, two hunters, a dog, and this stellar path. In this narrative we learn about the abduction of a woman grinding corn, her relationship to a dog, hunters, and the creation of the Milky Way:

> There were once two hunters in the sky,—one who lived in the north and hunted big game, another who lived in the south and hunted small game. The former became jealous of the latter, and one day, perceiving the southern hunter's wife grinding corn into meal, he seized her and carried her away from the corn-beating place far across the sky to his home in the north. Her dog ate the meal that was left, then followed her across the sky; and the food fell from his mouth as he ran, forming a trail of meal, the Milky Way. But when the northern hunter arrived home with his southern captive, such was the spell of her presence that the weather became warmer and warmer, until all the ice in that region began to melt. At length the northern hunter could no longer endure the heat, so he was compelled to release his prisoner. She returned home with her dog, and the weather in the north resumed its normal aspect.[55]

The woman and corn are associated with her home at "the corn-beating place far across the sky" to the South, which, following the logic of the narrative, was probably represented by a once known Cherokee constellation. Throughout the world, stars and constellations are identified with heroes of cultural narratives. As Stansbury Hagar recorded that "every living object on earth is the descendant of an ancestor in the sky who is represented by some star or group of stars," we might assume that the Cherokee primal parents would have a stellar location in the sky.[56]

It is likely that the woman of this narrative and one of the hunters are associated with the Corn Mother and Hunter, the primal parents of the narratives already mentioned. If the Milky Way is, as it appears to be, the very same path as the "Trail of Kanati," we see a major link between the primal parents, corn, and the celestial river human souls follow in their journey to the land of the dead. This path is likely called the "Trail of Kanati" as it is the path Kanati took as he left this realm to follow his wife back to the Sky Realm and the trail their sons followed as they tracked their father into the otherworld.

For the Cherokee, Yvwi Gunahita is a person in every sense. It is both a sky- and this-world person and connects these realms. It is aware of self and others, it has language and communicates to humans (and other nonhuman persons), and is in a continuous reciprocal relationship with beings of this earth. The River is a revelator and a conductor who sustains and guides human persons from birth to beyond death.

Corn Woman and Long Person are important interrelated and relational other-than-human persons in the Cherokee cosmos. From a "Western perspective" these entities, corn and flowing water, would generally be classified as "things" and not persons. While corn might be considered to be "alive" while growing, a river would not generally be considered alive. But from a Cherokee viewpoint, Corn and the River are both alive and are persons aware of self and others and are beings deeply enmeshed in reciprocal relationships with humans.

Notes

1. Many Cherokee have adopted Euro-American perspectives and may not have a "Cherokee worldview." I consider the Cherokee worldview to be an indigenous perspective encoded in Cherokee cultural narratives and prayers: cultural knowledge passed down from previous generations.

2. Marcel Mauss, "A Category of the Human Mind: The Notion of Person; the Notion of Self," tr. W. D. Halls, 1–25, and Charles Taylor, "The Person," 257–81, in *The Category of the Person: Anthropology, Philosophy, History*, ed. Michael Carrithers, Steven Collins, and Steven Lukes (NY: Cambridge University Press, 1985).

3. Taylor, "Person," 279.

4. James Mooney indicates that while primal animal beings are most numerous in Cherokee texts, "elemental gods," the "great powers of nature" are most important. *Sacred Formulas of the Cherokee, Seventh Annual Report of the Bureau of American Ethnology* (Washington: Government Printing Office, 1886; reprint, Nashville: Charles and Randy Elder-Booksellers, 1982), 340. It is not clear and James Mooney does not so indicate, but just as Pete Hallowell suggested some rocks are persons, the Cherokee may also consider some rocks to be persons (elemental beings). Powerful crystal diving stones, *ulvsata*, were ritually fed and treated with great care. Pete Hallowell, "Rocks and Stones," unpublished typescript, ca. 1936. Series 5 Indian Linguistics, file 2. Cited by Peter Nabokov, "Naming the Spirits: Ojibwa," in *Where the Lightning Strikes: The Lives of American Indian Sacred Places* (NY: Penguin Books, 2007): 27–28.

5. John Witthoft, "Cherokee Beliefs Concerning Death," *Journal of Cherokee Studies* 8 (Fall 1983). 72.

6. Fire is a representative of the Sun, or is the Sun in an earthly manifestation of the Sun. According to the Swimmer manuscript, "we find the fire so closely associates with the sun that their identity could plausibly be surmised, even if there were no actual and definite proof of it." James Mooney, "The Swimmer Manuscript: Cherokee Sacred Formulas and Medicinal Prescriptions," revised, completed, and edited by Frans M. Olbrechts. Smithsonian Institution, Bureau of Ethnology, Bulletin 99 (Washington: U.S. Government Printing Office, 1932): 21.

7. Anna G. Kilpatrick and Jack F. Kilpatrick, *Friends of Thunder: Folktales of the Oklahoma Cherokee* (Dallas: Southern Methodist University Press, 1964): 147–48. Lee Irwin, "Cherokee Healing: Myth, Dreams, and Medicine," *American Indian Quarterly* 16 (Spring 1992): 237–57. According to James Mooney: "Ada'wëhï is a word used to designate one supposed to have supernatural powers, and is applied alike to human beings and to the spirits invoked in the formulas. Some of the mythic heroes famous for their magic

deeds are spoken of as ada'wehi (plural anida'wehi or anida'we) but in its application to mortals the term is used only in reference to the very greatest shamans." Mooney, "Sacred Formulas," 346. James Mooney, "Myths of the Cherokee," in *Nineteenth Annual Report of the Bureau of American Ethnology*. Washington: Government Printing Office, 1900; reprint (Nashville: Charles and Randy Elder-Booksellers, 1982), 402–3, 425.

    8. Environment in a personalized sense.

    9. David Carrasco, *Religions of Mesoamerica*, 2nd edition (Long Grove, IL: Waveland Press, 2013): 135–36. Lawrence E. Sullivan, editor, *Native Religions and Cultures of North America* (New York: Continuum, 2000): 2. This is an idea Tom Belt, Cherokee, expressed when he told me that his parents did not physically punish (in keeping with Cherokee tradition), but would instruct him: "that is not how a Yv'wiya (Real Person) acts" (personal communication).

    10. The Cherokee, though geographically removed from the Iroquois/Haudenosaune, speak an Iroquoian language. Though the linguistic divergence is estimated to be over 3,000 years, linguistic and cultural similarities abound. Floyd G. Lounsbury, "Iroquois-Cherokee Linguistic Relations." In *Symposium on Cherokee and Iroquois Culture*, edited by William N. Fenton and John Gulick, 11–17, Smithsonian Institution, Bureau of American Ethnology 180 (Washington: U.S. Government Printing Office, 1961).

    11. David Blanchard, "Who or What is a Witch: Iroquois Persons of Power," *American Indian Quarterly* 5, no. 3, 4 (Autumn–Winter, 1982): 218–37. See also Floyd G. Lounsbury, "Iroquoian Languages," in *Handbook of North American Indians*, William C. Sturtevant, general editor, vol. 15 *Northeast*, Bruce G. Trigger volume editor (Washington: Smithsonian Institution, 1978): 337.

    12. Mooney, "Myths," 231. According to Stansbury Hagar, in Cherokee thought, "every living object on earth is the descendant of an ancestor in the sky who is represented by some star or group of stars." Stansbury Hagar, "Cherokee Star-Lore," *Boaz Anniversary Volume: Anthropological Papers Written in Honor of Franz Boaz* (New York: G. E. Stechert & Co., 1906): 354.

    13. The Iroquois "Woman Who Fell from the Sky" is in some accounts directly the source of the Three Sisters (Corn, Beans, and Squash), and in other accounts, they spring from the body of her daughter or her daughter's son, Sapling. John Bierhorst, *The Mythology of North America* (NY: William Morrow and Company, 1985), 196–99.

    14. The unnamed woman of Sickatower's account probably has a ritual name that he did not use, nor did James Mooney. *Selu* is probably merely a descriptive term, naming one of this important woman's attributes. John Howard Payne suggested she might be the same being as the Woman of the East. That, in its Cherokee form, may have been a ritual name. In the Payne-Butrick Papers the Corn Mother is also ritually addressed as the "woman above" and "old person above." It is also quite probable that she is the being called the "Ancient of Days," which may be another translation of the "old person above." William L. Anderson, Anne Rogers, and Jane Brown, editors, *The Payne-Butrick Papers*, volumes 1, 2, 3 in book 1 and volumes 4, 5, 6 in book 2 (Lincoln: University of Nebraska Press, 2010). Sickatower's account is found in book 1, volume 2.

    15. Anderson, Payne-Butrick Papers. The passages cited above are found in book 1, volume 2, pp. 119–124/(84–93). The original Payne-Butrick Manuscripts include fourteen

volumes (though the first six are most culturally relevant) and are housed in the Edward E. Ayer Collection, Newberry Library, University of Chicago.

16. For reasons I will not go into here, I believe that the Cherokee primal mother's celestial manifestation may be the sun. One reason, however, is that the mother of the Iroquois twins in most accounts becomes not only the Three Sisters, but also the Sun and Moon after her death.

17. Payne-Butrick Papers, book 1, volume 2, 119–24. The scratching in this context is symbolic of the corn rows. Drawing blood may also symbolize the Corn Mother's blood that was spilt after her sons killed her and followed her instructions to drag her body around prepared soil, seven times around and then inside a circle. According to the account James Mooney published, after staying up all night, the sons would have found an abundance of corn in the morning, her blood having produced the seeds. But because the sons did not follow her instructions correctly, the planned abundance was not realized. This seems to be another example of the relation of humans to their "celestial" progenitors, with humans falling short of realizing the ideal (though the sons, after leaving earth, become Thunder beings). Mooney, "Myths," 245–24. This narrative: "Kanati and Selu: The Origin of Corn and Game," from "Myths of the Cherokee" online, http://www.sacred-texts.com/nam/cher/motc/motc003.htm; James Mooney documents the practice of scratching in relation to ball play in "The Cherokee Ball Play," http://www.sacred-texts.com/nam/cher/cbp/cbp.htm (accessed August 2019).

18. This woman was also probably portrayed as part of a "celestial" landscape as indicated in my discussion of the "Milky Way" below.

19. In "Selu and the Hunter," the link between the corn plant and the form of a woman is evident in that a corn plant "suddenly took the form of a woman and rose gracefully into the air." Though the Corn Woman is generally associated with agriculture and her husband with hunting, this particular narrative also provides a link between her as an agricultural being and hunting. The "single green stalk of corn" spoke to an unsuccessful hunter and taught him "hunting secrets." She told him to take some of the roots of the corn and chew them in the morning before going to water. Then he would be successful and "kill many deer. From then on, he "would always be successful in the hunt." When he related his experience to his community, they realized that the hunter "had seen Selu, the wife of Kana'ti." In Mooney's "Myths," 323–24, online https://www.sacred-texts.com/nam/cher/motc/motc072.htm.

(Accessed August 2019). Mooney advanced this dual male/female being thesis in relation to Stone Man/Spearfinger. Both of these are "stone" beings capable of shape-shifting. We also see a close relationship between the Sun/Moon. The Sun is the *nvda* who travels in the day, and the Moon is the *nvda* who travels at night. In cultural narratives, the Sun is considered female, and the moon, male, and they are identified as brother and sister. Perhaps they are also considered to be "twins." Fire also has dual male/female manifestations: John Witthoft, "Death," 68–72.

20. In a part of the narrative that I do not quote above, the unnamed mother says that if they do not follow the rituals, she will send *ool-skay-tah*, disease. Mooney translated the term for disease contracted from eating corn before it was sanctified as *ul sge' ta*, the same term Payne transliterated *ool-skay-tah*, "the intruder" or "the tormentor"

and Mooney indicates that its cause is a worm, *tsgaya*. *The Payne-Butrick Papers*, volume 2. James Mooney, *Sacred Formulas*, 353-58.

21. Anna Kilpatrick and Jack Kilpatrick identified the supreme Cherokee beings as *unelanuhi*, "providers." Certainly, the primal Corn Woman and the Hunter are providers. Kilpatrick and Kilpatrick, *Cherokee Shaman*, 87; *Walk in Your Soul*, 72. The Cherokee believe if they eat the new crops before the completion of certain ritual activities in the Green Corn Ceremony, they will be afflicted with intestinal worms. John Witthoft, *Green Corn Ceremonialism in the Eastern Woodlands*, Occasional Contributions from the Museum of Anthropology of the University of Michigan, no. 13 (Ann Arbor: University of Michigan Press, 1949), 45. Red Man cited in James Mooney's *Sacred Formulas of the Cherokees* is Thunder, and Red Man's counterpart in healing prayers is Red Woman. Red Man is invoked in some healing prayers to heal women, while "Red Woman" is invoked to heal men: a type of reverse duality or completion of the male with female healing powers and vice versa. Whether dual beings or different male/female manifestations, there is abundant evidence that this is an important reality in Cherokee mythology.

22. Personal communication, Wade Blevins (member of the Cherokee Nation), Spring 1997, at Western Carolina University. Mary Ulmer Chiltoskey relates a similar narrative in *Aunt Mary, Tell Me a Story: A Collection of Cherokee Legends and Tales*, ed. Mary Regina Ulmer (Cherokee, NC: Cherokee Communications, 1990), 4, 40-41.

23. James Mooney suggests that Kanati and Thunder seem to be the same being. He indicates that Thunder is always referenced in the plural and that his sources would not reveal the "positive" identity of these beings: "Thunder is always personified in the plural, *Ani hyv ti kwa la ski*, 'The Thunderers.' The father and the two older sons seem to be *Ka na ti* and the Thunder Boys, although neither informant would positively assert this." Mooney, "Myths," 464. the "two older sons" would be the sons of Selu and Kanati. Thunder, we learn in another narrative, has other sons, one of which is Lightning. Mooney, "Myths," 248, 255-57, 311-16. That James Mooney grouped a discussion of the relationship between the Sun and Moon with that of "The Thunders" also gives cause to wonder about a relationship between the Sun and Moon and Kanati and Selu.

24. The beings of the Cherokee cosmology are complex, and there are many details we do not understand. The Cherokee religious tradition is esoteric, with the most sacred aspects divulged only to the initiated. The initiated were sworn not to impart this information to uninitiated persons, whether non-Cherokee or Cherokee. If they did, the "spirits above" would visit them with sickness or death. What's more, there were priestly specialties so one priest may not have all knowledge, though it has been said that the *uku* or high priest had a complete knowledge. *Payne-Butrick Papers*. James Mooney, *Sacred Formulas*, 318-19.

25. As Ganga descended from heaven to earth, she is also the vehicle for ascent. Diana Eck, "Gaṅgā: The Goddess Ganges in Hindu Sacred Geography," in *Devī: Goddesses of India*, ed. John Stratton Hawley and Donna Marie Wulff (Berkley: University of California, 1996; Delhi, India: Motilal Banarasidass, 1998) 137-53.

26. Hugh Thompson, *A Sacred Landscape: The Search for Ancient Peru* (New York: Overlook Books, 2008).

27. Kennedy Warne's report on New Zealand officially recognizing Te Awa Tupua as a person appeared online, "A Voice For Nature" in a National Geographic Newsletter in April 2019: https://www.nationalgeographic.com/culture/2019/04/maori-river-in-new-zealand-is-a-legal-person/ Though this article isn't dated the date of the article is established in a reference from another dated online source: "The Speaking Poles of Whanganui" http://www.kennedywarne.com/tag/te-awa-tupua/ The post, dated May 12, 2019 refers to the Maori river, Te Awa Tupa, as "A river of manifold voices." Kennedy Warne says he had pressed National Geographic to publish a story on the legislation that was passed in New Zealand declaring Te Urewera a sacred mountain in 2014 and Te Awa Tupua, a sacred river in 2017, to be persons.

28. James Mooney, "The Cherokee River Cult," *Journal of American Folk-Lore* 12 (January–March 1900): 1–10.

29. Pronouns in Cherokee are neutral, they may refer to a male or female being. I am not sure of the sex of the River in all aspects—it may, like other Cherokee beings, have both male female aspects.

30. Differences in transliterations and Cherokee dialects pose some difficulty, especially in the matter of consistency in spelling. Jack F. Kilpatrick and Anna G. Kilpatrick, "Notebook of a Cherokee Shaman," *Smithsonian Contributions to Anthropology* 2, no. 6 (Washington: Smithsonian Institution Press, 1970), 105. Mooney, *Swimmer Manuscript*, 23; Mooney, "Myths," 547; Mooney "The Cherokee River," 30.

31. Peter Nabokov confuses this concept when he identifies "Long Man" or the River with only the Little Tennessee River in "Between River and Fire" in *Where the Lightning Strikes: The Lives of American Indian Sacred Places* (New York: Penguin Books, 2006), 52–59.

32. I use the past tense as, though this was true in the past and is exemplified in Cherokee cultural narratives through Wild Boy, such rituals do not seem to be currently practiced, at least not generally.

33. Duane H. King, ed., The *Memoir of Lt. Henry Timberlake: The Story of a Soldier, Adventurer, and Emissary to the Cherokees, 1756–1765* (Cherokee, NC: Museum of the Cherokee Indian Press, 2007), 35 (66).

34. Mooney, "River," 1–10.

35. Mooney, "Myths," 426.

36. Mooney's manuscript notes, but not the published narrative, mention the celestial river the boys cross in their journey "above" to find their parents. Bureau of American Ethnology, catalogue no. 1905.

37. Mooney, *Sacred Formulas*, 341. James Mooney was not consistent in his translation of Yvwi Gunahita as Long Person. In his published paper "The Cherokee River Cult," he translated Yvwi Gunahita as Long Man, but Yvwi has no gender. Mooney should have translated this title as Long Person as he does in the quotation above. Long Man is Asgaya Gunahita. A Cherokee term for themselves, *yvwiya*, meaning "real people" or "principal people," also utilizes the term *yvwi*.

38. Payne-Butrick Papers, book 1, volume 3 (31).

39. I prefer the term "Otherworld" or "Sky World." James Mooney bifurcated the Otherworld into an Upper World and an Underworld, but there are problems with

using the term "Underworld." According to Cherokee texts, there are seven regions in the Otherworld as there are on this earth. If we are to make some kind of distinction between Otherworldly realms, we might use this distinction, though we cannot always be sure of the particular level. We could also distinguish between the daytime sky and the nighttime sky. "Underworld" may suggest the nighttime sky that Longperson connects with the earthly realm.

40. James Mooney, "Myths"; Chiltoskey, *Tell Me a Story*, 26–28.

41. Mooney, *Sacred Formulas*, 369–71. Another obvious symbolic association common to rivers is with snakes, descriptive of the winding path rivers and streams take. Snakes are Thunder's adornments. Thunder also frequently sends the rain in torrents feeding the streams and rivers even to the extent of flooding.

42. One of Raymond Fogelson's informants, "L.S." indicated that "conjurors have to rejuvenate their powers in the early spring . . . the stream is especially beneficial in spring, because the saps of various plants and trees ooze into the river." Fogelson notes that this is a "shift from Mooney and Olbrechts' version, where autumn was supposed to be the best time for bathing because of fallen leaves." Raymond D. Fogelson, "A Study of the Conjuror in Eastern Cherokee Society" (MA Thesis, University of Pennsylvania, 1958), 78–79. Rather than a shift, however, it is more probable that both times, spring and fall, were especially advantageous times to bathe in the river. Both the spring and autumn new moons signaled the beginning of a "new year" and both were particularly potent periods.

43. Mooney, "Myths," 370. The hunting season lasted from the first new moon of autumn until the first new moon of spring. Payne-Butrick Papers, book 1, volume 3, 205, 209.

44. The Moon is a very powerful male being in Cherokee narratives. The Moon (as well as the Sun) is also sometimes called the "creator" in some Cherokee texts. John Howard Payne, "The Ancient Cherokee Traditions and Religious Rites," *Quarterly Register and Magazine* (December 1849): 444–50. For the moon, one of the Immortals, coming down at the time of the New Moon during the last night of the Jump Dance, see Peter Nabokov, *Where the Lightning Strikes*, 299. See also Thomas Buckley's discussion of the importance of the Immortals, of which the Moon is one, in "Renewal as Discourse and Discourse as Renewal in Native Northwestern California," in *Native Religions and Cultures of North America: Anthropology of the Sacred*, ed. Lawrence E. Sullivan (NY: Continuum, 2000).

45. Mooney, "Myths," 345–47.

46. Witthoft, "Cherokee Beliefs Concerning Death," 68.

47. I wonder if Ela Kanati, the Terrestrial "Hunter" and the "Path of Kanati," both rivers and associated with "Kanati," are identical. Both are associated with Kanati, the Primal Father and Hunter.

48. Hagar, Star-Lore, 362–63.

49. A half century earlier, the Payne-Butrick Papers document a similar Cherokee narrative where souls of at least some souls must cross a "small pole" crossing an "awful gulf." A black dog guards each side of the pole. *Payne-Butrick Papers*, volume 3, p. 206 (2//4).

50. Hagar, "Star-Lore," 364.

51. Ruben G. Thwaites, ed. *The Jesuit Relations, Jesuit Relations and Allied Documents: Travels and Explorations of the Jesuit Missionaries in New France*, volume 10, chapter 2 1636: 147, Cleveland, OH: The Burrows Brothers Company, 1901, http://moses.creighton.edu/kripke/jesuitrelations. Alexander von Gernet, "Saving the Souls: Reincarnation Beliefs of the Seventeenth-Century Huron," in *Amerindian Rebirth: Reincarnation Belief among North American Indians and Inuit*, ed. Antonia Mills and Richard Slobodi (Toronto: University of Toronto Press, 1994), 44.

52. Kilpatrick, *Notebook of a Cherokee Shaman*, 102.

53. Hagar, "Cherokee Star Lore." For a few other American Indian examples, see Trudy Griffin-Pierce, *Earth Is My Mother, Sky Is My Father: Space, Time, and Astronomy in Navajo Sandpainting* (Albuquerque: University of New Mexico Press, 1992). Also see Timothy McCleary, *The Stars We Know: Crow Indian Astronomy and Lifeways* (Prospect Heights, IL: Waveland Press, Inc. 1997); George E. Lankford, *Reachable Stars: Patterns in the Ethnoastronomy of Eastern North America* (Tuscaloosa: University of Alabama Press, 2007).

54. Kilpatrick, *Cherokee Shaman*, 105–6.

55. Hagar, "Cherokee Star-Lore," 364–65. The abduction of a woman in the presence of a canine and in relation to the creation of the "Milky Way" is not limited to the Cherokee. According to Absaroke or Crow Indian narratives, this celestial pathway is called Ammíaaalaau, "Where They Take Women." The Absaroke narrative associated with Ammíaaalaau relates that lecherous Old Man Coyote stole a woman and created a pathway of stars as he fled with her. McCleary, *The Stars We Know*, chapter 1. The Navajo also associate stars and constellations with cultural narratives. See Griffin-Pierce, especially chapters 5 and 6.

56. Hagar, "Cherokee Star-Lore," 354.

Bibliography

Anderson, William L., Anne Rogers, Jane Brown, editors. *The Payne-Butrick Papers*, Book 1, Volumes 1, 2, and 3. Lincoln: University of Nebraska Press, 2010.

Bierhorst, John. *The Mythology of North America*. New York: William Morrow and Company, 1985: 196–99.

Blanchard, David. "Who or What Is a Witch? Iroquois Persons of Power," 218–37. *American Indian Quarterly* 5, nos. 3/4 (Autumn–Winter, 1982).

Carrasco, David. *Religions of Mesoamerica*, 2nd edition. Long Grove, IL: Waveland Press, 2013.

Chiltoskey, Mary Ulmer. *Aunt Mary, Tell Me a Story: A Collection of Cherokee Legends and Tales*, edited by Mary Regina Ulmer. Cherokee, North Carolina: Cherokee Communications, 1990.

Eck, Diana. "Gaṅgā: The Goddess Ganges in Hindu Sacred Geography." In *Devī: Goddesses of India*, edited by John Stratton Hawley and Donna Marie Wulff. University of California: Motilal Banarasidass, 1998.

Fogelson, Raymond D. "A Study of the Conjuror in Eastern Cherokee Society." M.A. thesis, University of Pennsylvania, 1958.

Gernet, Alexander von. "Saving the Souls: Reincarnation Beliefs of the Seventeenth-Century Huron." In *Amerindian Rebirth: Reincarnation Belief Among North American Indians and Inuit*, edited by Antonia Mills and Richard Slobodin, 38–54. Toronto: University of Toronto Press, 1994.

Griffin-Pierce, Trudy. *Earth Is My Mother, Sky Is My Father: Space, Time, and Astronomy in Navajo Sandpainting.* Albuquerque: University of New Mexico Press, 1992.

Hagar, Stansbury. "Cherokee Star-Lore," *Boaz Anniversary Volume: Anthropological Papers Written in Honor of Franz Boaz*, 354–66. New York: G. E. Stechert & Co., 1906.

Irwin, Lee. "Cherokee Healing: Myth, Dreams, and Medicine," *American Indian Quarterly* 16 (Spring 1992): 337–57.

Kilpatrick, Anna G., and Jack F. *Friends of Thunder: Folktales of the Oklahoma Cherokee.* Dallas: Southern Methodist University Press, 1964.

———. "Notebook of a Cherokee Shaman." *Smithsonian Contributions to Anthropology* 2, no. 6. Washington: Smithsonian Institution Press, 1970.

———. *Walk in Your Soul: Love Incantations of the Oklahoma Cherokees.* Dallas: Southern Methodist University Press, 1965.

Lankford, George E. *Reachable Stars: Patterns in the Ethnoastronomy of Eastern North America.* Tuscaloosa: University of Alabama Press, 2007.

Lounsbury, Floyd G. "Iroquoian Languages." In *Handbook of North American Indians*, William C. Sturtevant, general editor, vol. 15 *Northeast*, Bruce G. Trigger volume editor, 337. Washington: Smithsonian Institution, 1978.

———. "Iroquois-Cherokee Linguistic Relations." In *Symposium on Cherokee and Iroquois Culture*, edited by William N. Fenton and John Gulick. Smithsonian Institution, Bureau of American Ethnology 180, 11–17. Washington: U. S. Government Printing Office, 1961.

McLachlan, Carrie. "Cherokee Cosmology." M.A. Thesis, Western Carolina University, 1999.

McCleary, Timothy. *The Stars We Know: Crow Indian Astronomy and Lifeways.* Prospect Heights, IL: Waveland Press, 1997.

Mooney, James. "The Cherokee River Cult." *Journal of American Folk-Lore* 12 (January–March 1900): 1–10.

———. "Myths of the Cherokee." *Nineteenth Annual Report of the Bureau of American Ethnology.* Washington: Government Printing Office, 1900; reprint, Nashville: Charles and Randy Elder-Booksellers, 1982.

———. "The Swimmer Manuscript: Cherokee Sacred Formulas and Medicinal Prescriptions." Revised, completed, and edited by Frans M. Olbrechts. Smithsonian Institution, Bureau of Ethnology, Bulletin 99, Washington: U.S. Government Printing Office, 1932.

Mauss, Marcel. "A Category of the Human Mind: The Notion of Person; the Notion of Self." Translated by W. D. Halls. In *The Category of the Person: Anthropology, Philosophy, History*, ed. Michael Carrithers, Steven Collins, and Steven Lukes, 1–25. New York: Cambridge University Press, 1985.

Nabokov, Peter. *Where the Lightning Strikes: The Lives of American Indian Sacred Places.* New York: Penguin Books, 2007.

Payne, John Howard. "The Ancient Cherokee Traditions and Religious Rites." *Quarterly Register and Magazine* (December 1849).

Sullivan, Lawrence E, editor. *Native Religions and Cultures of North America* (New York: Continuum, 2000).

Taylor, Charles. "The Person." In *The Category of the Person: Anthropology, Philosophy, History,* edited by Michael Carrithers, Steven Collins, and Steven Lukes, 257–81. New York: Cambridge University Press, 1985.

Thawites, R. G., ed. *Jesuit Relations and Allied Documents: Travels and Explorations of the Jesuit Missionaries in New France,* 73 vols. Cleveland, OH: The Burrows Brothers Company, 1901.

Warne, Kennedy. "A Voice for Nature." National Geographic Newsletter, April 2019, https://www.nationalgeographic.com/culture/2019/04/maori-river-in-new-zealand-is-a-legal-person/.

Witthoft, John. "Cherokee Beliefs concerning Death." *Journal of Cherokee Studies* 8 (Fall 1983): 68–72.

———. *Green Corn Ceremonialism in the Eastern Woodlands,* Occasional Contributions from the Museum of Anthropology of the University of Michigan, no. 13. Ann Arbor: University of Michigan Press, 1949.

Chapter 8

The Quilt as Personal Object

SASHA L. BIRO

Editor's Note: As the last chapter focusing on personal objects in specific historical and cultural contexts, Chapter 8 brings us from Native American culture and into modern (nineteenth-, twentieth-, and twenty-first-century) American culture. This chapter discusses how quilts became personalized objects with important sociopolitical significance: in particular for American women, African Americans, and modern political activists. In addition to bringing us back to contemporary times, this chapter rounds out our survey by demonstrating that personalized objects often have social and political importance. This is a theme that will be returned to in later chapters.

The quilt exists as the quintessential American domestic artifact. Surviving quilts tell much about the historical epoch in which they were created, as well as of the identity of the quilter, and often reflect the cultural narratives that situate a people, time, and place. The following analysis will consider the work of quilting, at times interpreted as craft, as women's work, or even as fabric art, to trace a historical arc from antebellum America through the nineteenth century into contemporary times, focusing on the visual-historical elements of the quilt and its function as narrative art. In particular, traditional American quilt patterns may be seen as encoding the values and ideals of American women. These ideals survive as cultural memories stitched into the fabric of the quilt and are passed on from one generation to the next, thus also preserving a family heritage. Looking to the quilt as a readable object[1] conveying both beauty and efficiency, it is also clear that the quilt transcends its functional nature and opens the viewer to a larger narrative experience, relating the individual to the social.

I will utilize the work of Georges Bataille as a lens through which to critically examine the economy of the quilt, whereby as blanket it serves a utilitarian function as project object, but it later becomes more than just object, taking on cultural power as a personalized narrative experience. The quilt is a tangible and tactile object that also holds and transmits personal memories. Specific examples include the Graveyard Quilt, as a type of memorial quilt; the Friendship Quilt, part of a communal tradition; the Crazy Quilt, whose purpose was to serve as memento; as well as the Story Quilt, a piecing together of painting, quilted fabric, and storytelling, as evidenced in the works of Harriet Powers and Faith Ringgold. Even today, quilts are being used as narrative art to tell a story that may be at once deeply personal, as well as political. Examples include the 2000 *Human Quilt*, the 2012 memorial quilt for AIDS victims, as well as the *Monument Quilt* recently displayed in Washington DC. In each instance, the work of quilting as well as the quilt itself, takes on a significance that is both personally and culturally powerful.

Quilt as Visual-Historical Documentary

"The thought, care, and work that went into making a quilt insured it a secure place in American affections; Americans understood and respected such well-directed expenditures of energy. . . . The quilt's association with the bed, the sheltering of the important moments of life played out there, made particular quilts treasured family objects, as did the use in a quilt's construction of materials associated with family members."[2]

Surviving quilts may be read as visual-historical documents: they provide us concrete ways of envisioning the past, symbolizing American life and ideals, including the intimacy of a family genealogy as well as the cultural transformation of the textile industry itself. It wasn't until the twentieth century that a genuine interest arose in documenting the origins and history of localized quilts, affirming the significant historical impact that quilts have as readable objects. The first large-scale quilt documentation project of its kind began in 1981 in Kentucky, known as the Kentucky Quilt Project. Marking the beginning of the Quilt Survey Movement, the goal of this documentation project was to survey early nineteenth-century Kentucky-made quilts and "to leave precise records for any future group," according to Eleanor Bingham Miller.[3] The first of many such projects, the survey inspired Americans to look into forgotten traditions involving textile arts. The project would show that the state of Kentucky, the families who lived there, and their quilts were part of a tradition in the decorative arts and that Kentucky was part of a longstanding quilting legacy. Locating the quilts, documenting their existence, and exhibiting them during quilt days, events where quilts that had been "hiding in closets or trunks were raised to a hanging position—many seen on walls for the first time," were held in Kentucky, county by county.[4] Quilt days imbued the present with the past, giving those who were keepers of family quilts and by extension, keepers of family history, the opportunity to display these heirlooms and to take pride in sharing with the community their family heritage as well as taking interest in the value of their quilts (monetary, heritage, physical characteristics).

While the quilts revealed much about life in the nineteenth century, including fabric, fashion, women's interests of the time, "because quilt making is largely an anonymous art, the identity of the quilt maker usually could not be determined . . . In most cases, no family stories survived to suggest that even such historic and massive upheavals as the Civil War touched their lives . . . [The Kentucky Quilt Project taught] an important lesson—not just that valuable heirlooms can be lost, worn out, or sold away, but that important elements of family history can vanish within a generation."[5] This lesson also can be applied to African American quilts: although the African American quilting tradition has a long and rich history dating back to the eighteenth century, official historical accounts of this tradition are scarce and the artifacts themselves hard to locate, thus recovering and documenting these textiles has proven difficult. However, while in many instances "no trace of the maker may remain," the pieces of a quilt, be they fabric from a family ball gown, the use of repeated images, the design and color choices utilized, and the quilt pattern names themselves offer a glimpse into a narrative experience that goes beyond mere utility and speaks to a cultural memory whose symbolic elements have survived. Georges Bataille identifies the principle of harmony here "[a]s the repetition through which all that is 'possible' is made eternal . . . guaranteeing the duration of motifs whose essence is the annulment of time."[6] Particularly poignant, quilts from the antebellum South, designed by African American slaves who were unable to read or write, record what Gladys-Marie Fry calls "a powerful record . . . a hidden history, as it were, of their humiliation and tragedy, the milestones of their times and of their own lives. It is a record to be read as it was written, not in words, but in feelings."[7] For Fry, quilting was both a communal experience (shared ritual) and an outlet of expression, enabling enslaved women and men to survive.

A closer look at some of the design choices of nineteenth-century quilts reveals the transformation from practicality to aesthetic. The star as a design source, for instance, was among the earliest and most popular quilt designs, according to Jonathan Holstein, a quilt scholar and surveyor of many of the

Kentucky quilts exhibited in the Kentucky Quilt Project. Due to its visually pleasing and emotionally satisfying effect, "Americans saw in [it] the star of the Bible, the stars in their unspoiled night skies, the heavy suns of harvest time, images of a ship's compass, David's crown, the field of stars in their flag. It was an optimistic and exuberant image for a vigorous nation."[8] The Rose of Sharon was another popular pattern motif, often used on quilts made to celebrate the ritual of coming of age. Pineapples were a sign of hospitality and might be included on a quilt used for the guest bed or for a special occasion.[9] The Log Cabin pattern is likely the most archetypal and symbolically significant quilt design.[10] Log Cabin Stars referred to a pieced quilt constructed from strips of cloth in the shape of diamonds, like the logs of a cabin. Crazy[11] Quilt patterns were utilized as decorative textiles rather than functional textiles. Crazy Quilts primarily documented family albums, such as wedding albums, which are pieced together with pieces of wedding day objects (the groom's wedding tie, silk from the bride's dress). Crazy Quilts also "demonstrate the makers' knowledge of Victorian sensibilities" and so would include sentimental motifs and images such as birds, violets, fans, butterflies, keys, spiders in webs, innocent children playing, women's boots.[12] Friendship-style quilts were typically associated with religious groups and were conceived as communal projects, with many different groups worked on individual blocks, which would contain the names of participants or their autographs. Autograph quilts, a type of friendship quilt, were often created to raise revenue for a church. Here a person would pay a certain amount for the inclusion of their signature on the quilt, which would then be auctioned or raffled for further revenue.[13] Most significantly, the *Graveyard Quilt* created by Elizabeth Roseberry Mitchell, circa 1839, is known as a famous folk object that memorializes the deaths of Mitchell's two sons and offers a meditation on death and the afterlife. The graveyard at the center of the quilt contains the coffins of those who have passed on, while the edges of the quilt contain more coffins labeled for family members. All of Elizabeth Roseberry Mitchell's children have a coffin. As relatives died, the year of death would be added to the coffin and moved to the center of the quilt. First Elizabeth cared for the alterations of the quilt, and after her death, her daughters carried on the task. The Mourning Quilt "expresses a view of life profoundly affected by loss and the high mortality rate of the times," while also lending insight into the grief and fear of the quilter herself.[14]

Efficiency and Beauty

"The American quilt most perfectly bridges the two types of objects in which Americans established new models: the superbly efficient things made for practical use and decorative objects using idioms developed in the New World. Quilts were at once the most efficient answer to a pressing need—warm bed coverings—and the best, in some cases the only, medium through which generations of American women could express their creativity."[15]

As Jonathan Holstein describes above, quilts are practical as well as personal. As domestic artifacts, they were used as coverings to warm the intimacy of the bed. Coarser quilting resulted in greater insulation, so many everyday quilts were made thick for warmth, functioning as serviceable, washable, everyday bedcovers. "Bed quilts show the way quilts were used in bedrooms, and the way beds were placed in bedrooms, as indicated by the way the sun slashed across . . . bleach[ing] the yellow out of the color patterns. The notion of thriftily saving scraps and making up quilts out of strips is one thing."[16] In contrast, "best" quilts were thinner, more often than not for display rather than use: "We must remember that part of the tradition of quilting also [is the] quilt as luxury object, and elaborate quilting reduces their loft, lowering their heat retention value."[17] The tradition of mixing and matching fabrics to improvise the final aesthetic of a quilt dates back to the Civil War, where scarcity of fabric was a practical concern. During the Civil War, quilts also functioned in other, practical ways, besides personal bed coverings. These textiles were used as cushions for soldiers, storage blankets for breakable goods or food items foraged by looting troops.[18] When quilts outgrew their usefulness for the bed, they made "saddle blankets, covers for a chicken coop, a dog bed, or they were hung over the opening of the outhouse or barn in place of a door shutter, or placed on the floor as a pallet for the baby."[19]

Contributing to a much-needed area of scholarship, quilt historians Gladys-Marie Fry and Cuesta Benberry have researched and documented the quilts of African Americans in the antebellum South, where enslaved women (and some men) were skilled artisans working as quilters, weavers, and seamstresses. Quilting was considered permissible because of its practicality as a commodity to be sold. A number of enslaved women were able to purchase their freedom due to the income earned from their sewing skills. Nursing babies were taken to the fields by their mothers and placed on pallets[20] between feedings. Children almost always slept on pallets, as bunks were where the adults slept. Besides swaddling infants, quilts were used to wrap corpses. The quilt also served a religious function, used in baptismal ceremonies and to decorate grave sites in accordance with the African tradition that the last articles used by the deceased were to be placed on the grave. They would also hang as inscriptions over sacred entrances.[21] Quilts also expressed coded messages: triangles in quilt design signified prayer messages, while quilts with black in them were hung on the clothesline to indicate a safe house along the Underground Railroad.[22] Quilting parties, or the "quilting," which is today known as the quilting bee, gathered together women in a community building activity. Here, storytelling, gossip, the exchange of information, singing and dancing, plus the sharing of a meal contributed to an understanding of quilting as a shared ritual. [23] In this way, the generational transmission of a shared knowledge would take place, often from mother to daughter.

Quilting bees were occasions for socialization, community, and labor sharing in the creation of quilts, again demonstrating the value and utility of these personalized objects. This invokes an image of the "resourceful American woman solving her bedding problem and unconsciously producing art at the same time" as her value of frugality.[24] As Eleanor Bingham Miller points out, part of the American monomythic involves the

> received image of the creator of the early American quilt; a pioneer woman living in a . . . log cabin, twelve children to raise, farming to do and constant threats to life . . . The story was that she had to produce warm bed clothing for her family, so turned to the dear bits and pieces left over from worn clothing, to make quilts. In the process she somehow, miraculously, stumbled across a pleasant aesthetic.[25]

Part of the problem with this received monomyth is its historical omission: it excludes altogether the role of African American quilters, just as most all official public records of the nineteenth century did. Historical evidence for an active pre–Civil War quilting tradition among slaves was through the WPA Federal Writers Project, which documented first-person accounts of slavery from over 2,300 former slaves. Little material has surfaced about slave quilting and the quilters themselves. As Gladys Fry points out, "Except for quilting bees, the solitary act of quilting would have been witnessed only by family members . . . [and] As 'women's work,' quilting would also have been considered unimportant."[26] This being said, in the sixties, quilting cooperatives comprised mainly of women formed in rural Alabama. Both the Freedom Quilting Bee and the Gee's Bend quilters (as of 2003, the Gee's Bend Collective) gathered to stitch quilts to generate income for their families. In the process, they produced some of the most significant twentieth-century art. A *New York Times* review called the quilts "some of the most miraculous works of modern art America has produced."[27]

The transition from viewing the quilt as an everyday, utilitarian object to a work of fabric art with social and political ramifications in some sense indicates the changing perceptions of the times as in the middle to last half of the nineteenth century, quilts became more and more publicly visible "as community focal points for salient political and social issues "such as Civil War relief or abolition.[28] The Centennial Exposition in 1876 further brought women together as many gathered in the Women's Pavilion to admire one another's domestic work, such as the quilt. However, quilts have also always narrated the personal stories of particular individual women's lives, as well as universal themes of the human experience, such as family, marriage, and death. To argue that quilting as a form of art appeared merely as a fortunate chance side-effect of its practical use-value, is to overlook the important and nonlinear account of quilting as "from the beginning . . . an aesthetic pursuit . . . giv[ing] women a means of expression" and identity.[29] Women wove stories about their lives and personal experiences into their quilts, a way of claiming immortality.

The Story Quilt

Turning from the utility of the quilt as a visual-historic document providing insight into the past of precolonial America, including its practical function as a bed covering, I would now like to examine what results when these visual pieces transcend their functional nature; namely, the power of the quilt as a spiritual, sensual, narrative work of art. Quilt scholars such as Gladys-Marie Fry, whose scholarship is particularly attenuated to African American quilting in the antebellum period, see in the quilting process a survival mechanism: "an outlet for introspection and reflection . . . experiences and emotions. . . . Records of emotional and psychological well-being are etched on surviving quilts," as well as recording family history, folk legend, philosophical and religious beliefs.[30] Despite the degrading, racist policies and practices that "denied these women their physical freedom, it did not diminish their creative talent and artistic genius."[31] Moreover, the quilt functioned as a personal and communal repository, encoding histories that were otherwise deliberately suppressed. Fry describes how, for instance, official public records of births, deaths, and wills excluded African Americans, yet such important historical details were preserved in the quilts themselves, in lieu of a written record. A parallel can here be drawn to Georges Bataille's discussion of general economy, wherein a restoration of the sacred is made possible by salvaging the object from its servility to the utilitarian, "that which servile use had degraded, and rendered profane."[32] Bataille expands this discussion in *The Accursed Share, Vol. 2*, in his consideration of modern systems of exchange, where material wealth, not reciprocal gifts, are of primary concern. Bataille here employs Claude Levi-Strauss's notion of "a total social fact," "that is, an event which has significance that is at once social and religious, magic and economic, utilitarian and sentimental, juridical and moral" in his discussion of certain kinds of exchange. Primarily, Bataille argues that "certain goods cannot be consigned to a drab or utilitarian consumption. . . . [Their] mere presence denotes a moment different from another, *altogether different* from just any moment," thus designating them total social facts.[33] Mircea Eliade, in discussing hierophany, reinforces Bataille's claim: "By manifesting the sacred, any object becomes something else, yet it contains to remain itself, for it continues to participate in its surrounding cosmic milieu . . . Sacred power means reality and at the same time enduringness and efficacity."[34] The quilt as personalized object offers a sacred economy: the quilt as quilt can be said to retain its use value as a functional commodity, while yet offering a larger social and culturally embedded narrative experience for the quilter (and in later generations, the reception of the quilt).

It wasn't until the Whitney Museum's *Abstract Design in American Quilts* exhibition, in 1971, presenting quilts as art that fiber as an art medium began to be taken seriously. As previously discussed, the quilt as functional object was not identified with the quilt as art. The lead up of the acceptance of fiber as an art medium was in large part due to the initial influence of William Morris and the Arts and Crafts movement (1880–1920). The Bauhaus School of Design also was a major reason that the fiber arts were elevated as an art medium. The Bauhaus philosophy claims that the artist has an obligation to society to create good and useful objects for everyday use in accordance with beauty, form, and function. All objects for living are to function as art.[35] In this vein, the fiber arts were increasingly legitimized and eventually received as fine arts and not just craft. Mariska Karasz, a Hungarian abstract expressionist, is credited with most dramatically establishing the reception of fabric as fine art into the early twenty-first century. According to Bets Ramsey, stitchery and fabric collage became a new type of twentieth century art, which yet paralleled the quilting of the seventies. By taking seemingly unrelated materials and media and reassembling them to form a new whole, we see the approach of quiltmakers in taking bits and pieces and putting them together to create an entirely new image.[36] Miriam Schapiro's incorporation of fabric, pieces of lace, and quilt blocks into her paintings coined the term "femmage," or feminist collage. Significantly, "it was the placing of quilts in a vertical plane which allowed the definition of art."[37] Quilting was an art form born of necessity, and its transformation over time resulted in new meanings and possibilities; a building on, instead of being bound by, tradition, as evidenced most significantly in its reception as both a useful and a beautiful object.[38]

The Story Quilt is a cloth-based form of narrative art, handmade and with the incorporation of familiar objects, which render it as both a personal and a communal object. This type of quilt is designed to tell a story, typically through

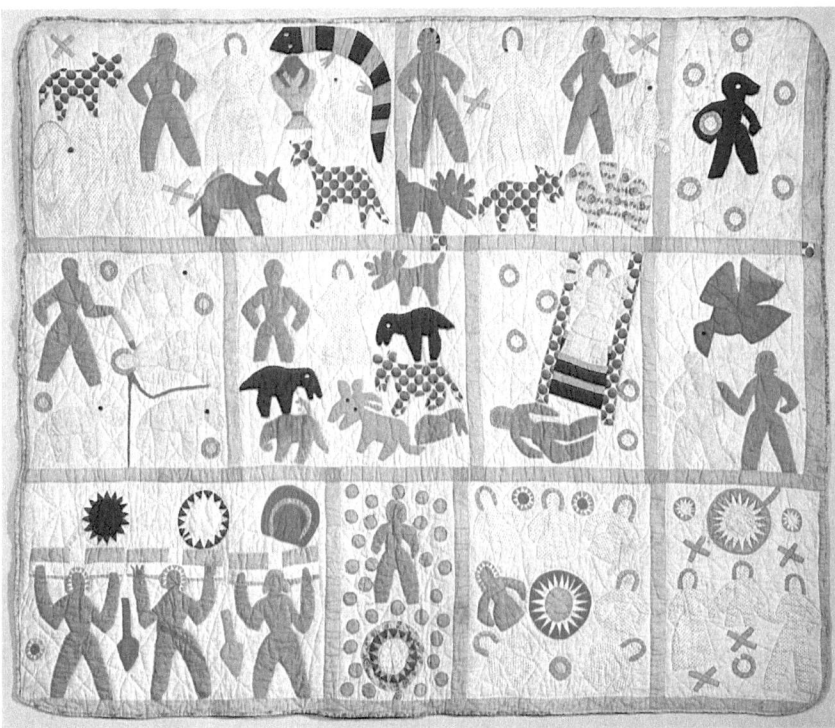

Figure 8.1. Harriet Powers's *Bible Quilt*, 1885–1886, presents a visual narrative at once personal and symbolic. Photo courtesy the Division of Cultural and Community Life, National Museum of American History, Smithsonian Institution.

pictures. Its narrative also reflects the story of the quilter while going beyond the quilter to present a narrative that is often historically or culturally situated. And while all quilts tell stories, "what distinguishes narrative quilts is that the stories are more apparent and the makers have generally revealed more about themselves" than traditional appliqué quilts.[39] Story Quilts trace back to the late eighteenth century and are considered a rare genre. As storytelling has played a prominent role in black American culture as a way of passing down family histories, as well as important spiritual and moral lessons, it is significant that many African American quilters utilize this form of quilting.[40] Perhaps the most famous American Story Quilt is Harriet Powers's *Bible Quilt*, circa 1886. Eva Ungar Grudin relates that Powers's quilt was on exhibition during the Atlanta Cotton States' Exposition, where Booker T. Washington delivered his most famous address, in which he actually dismissed African American quilting and praised the progress made by African Americans over the decades since Emancipation. Grudin notes that Powers's quilt is considered one of the greatest narrative quilts ever produced in this country, but that Washington's dismissal was not atypical, as "historically, the presence of women in large numbers in any kind of art reduced the status of that art form.... That disregard changed in the 1970s [when the quilt] ... became the prime visual metaphor for women's lives, for women's culture."[41] Many of the quilts that I will discuss in the following analysis date from the seventies to contemporary times and are oriented to African American women's creativity.

The Bible Quilts of Harriet Powers belong to a tradition of narrative quilts that can be traced back to the nineteenth century. Such narrative quilts may inscribe verses or wordlessly convey the religious feelings experienced by the quilter. In *Always There: The African-American Presence in American Quilts*, Cuesta Benberry holds that the making of Bible Quilts was idiosyncratic to southern black women.[42] Harriet Powers, who was a slave, could not read or write, but she was well-versed in stories from oral tradition, such as local legends and biblical stories, primarily those concerning heroes who had struggled against overwhelming odds. Biblical animals also figure prominently on her quilts. Some of the symbols depicted in the Powers quilt are similar in design to the banners designed by the Fon of Dahomey. Whereas the illustration of stories on quilts is unusual, Powers transmutes oral narrative to visual imagery in her quilts; some panels of her Bible Quilts depict biblical scenes, while others depict astronomical phenomenon such as eclipses, meteors, and comets.[43]

Many quilts depict narratives of home. Literal depictions of the house as home, or familiar objects associated with home, demonstrate the love and/or nostalgia felt by the quilter for home as a sacred place. The quilts of fiber artist Elizabeth Scott, *The Plantation*, *50 Year Quilt*, and the *Hourglass Quilt* each convey her memories of growing up on a farm in South Carolina. Several of Scott's quilts also incorporate African textile traditions. For example, the *50 Year Quilt* has a monster face composed with beaded features. In the *Hourglass Quilt*, Scott places wrapped rocks "as devices that bring good luck." Some are converted into dolls with button eyes. Here, the rock associates as a tangible reminder of home. Both quilts demonstrate the artist's practice of attaching incidental objects to cloth, not only as an embellishment, but also to empower it with protective charms, making it part of the African "charm cloth" tradition.[44] Other story quilts deal with the narrative of family and heritage. Such quilts demonstrate the importance of oral narrative in keeping family history alive, by passing down family histories and values, as well as family lore, taking what was once an oral narrative and rendering it visually.[45] The quilts themselves may be composed of scraps of dresses that were worn by parents, grandparents, or great grandparents, thus documenting generations of descendants (Alice Neal's quilt is an example of a family commemorative quilt). They may include symbols such as rocks, trees, evil eyes, lace, or hair ribbons that signify value greater than mere ornament. Family quilts preserve a history and can tell us much about life as it was lived in earlier generations (such as the Kentucky quilts). For this reason, they may also be visual-historical documentaries.

Commemorative Quilts are part of a longstanding mainstream quilting tradition marking important historical events and celebrating influential figures. Alice Neal's famous *Mary Bright Commemorative Quilt* was begun in 1955, in honor of her mother, Mary Bright. Bright had taught her daughter how to quilt, and in homage, at the center of Neal's quilt is a reproduction in cloth of a photograph of Bright, utilizing leftovers from an actual dress that Bright had herself made and worn. Blocks around the central image represent elements of Bright's life, including quilting patterns that Bright used, and the Star of LeMoyne to represent her home state of Louisiana.[46] Other commemorative quilts, such as the collective work by the Oberlin senior citizens, entitled *Underground Railroad*, Nora Ezell's *Martin Luther King, Jr.* quilt and Faith Ringgold's *100 Years at Williams College* quilt, reflect social and political events significant to African American history, such as the story of the Underground Railroad, a tribute to the hero Martin Luther King Jr., the history of African Americans' struggle to access higher education.

According to Eva Grudin, fabricated, or fictional, Story Quilts are the rarest of all narrative quilts.[47] Such quilts do not document history or serve as artifacts in any way but are imaginative and may evoke a spiritual resonance through symbols and colors. Images and symbols may allow for a free association, such as in the work of Lillian Beattie, or provide the space for the viewer to imagine their own story when looking at the quilt, as in the work of Yvonne Wells. Symbolism and poetic vision here guide the composition of the quilt narrative. Many quilters seeking to express the creative achievements of accomplished women such as Sojourner Truth and Marie Curie have similarly created Story Quilts depicting these accomplishments. Marie Wilson's *Reprise* quilt, the Gotham quilters, and the works of Faith Ringgold all demonstrate quilting narratives devoted to particular women's issues. In this sense, such works are both commemorative (distinctly oriented to issues of gender and race) and historical. In some instance, notably the quilts of Faith Ringgold, one also sees an element of imaginative fabrication, which adds to the reception of the quilt material.

Faith Ringgold's Story Quilts fuse cultural knowledge with the oral tradition of her ancestors. In her own words, "the story quilt grew out of my need to tell stories not with pictures or symbols alone, but with words. . . . Quilts are intimately connected with women's lives and so could become a most effective vehicle for telling the stories of their lives."[48] Ringgold's Story Quilts of the 1980s mesh childhood memories of home with current events, offering a reconfigured

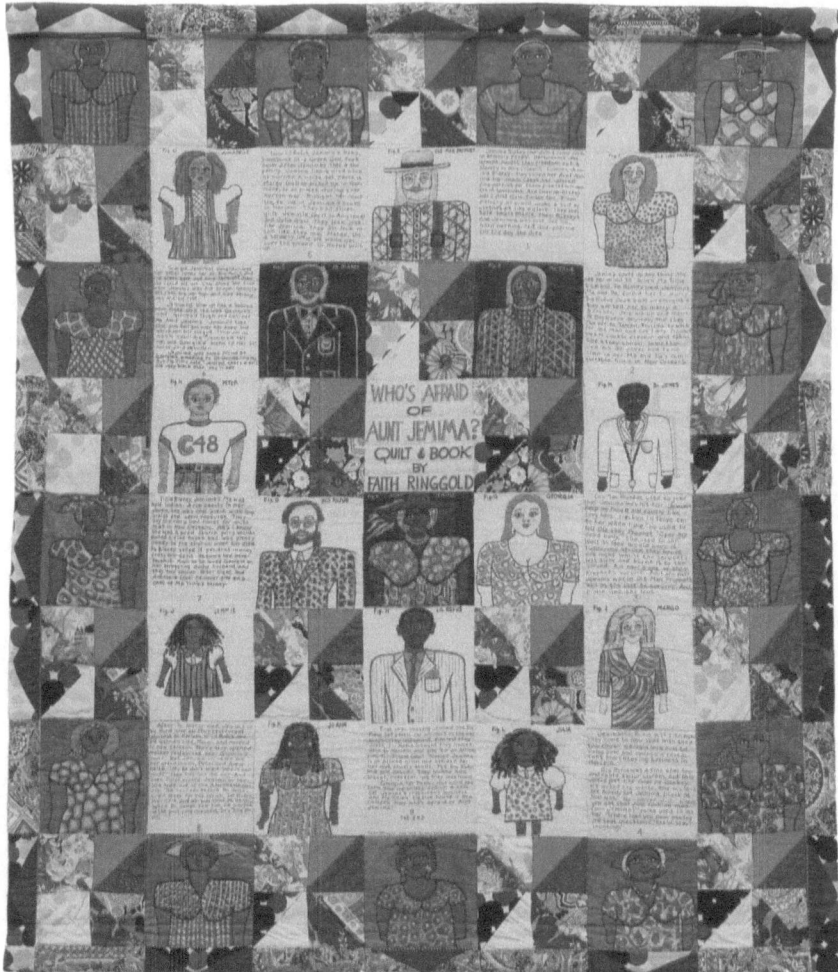

Figure 8.2. Faith Ringgold, *Who's Afraid of Aunt Jemima?* 1983. Acrylic on canvas. 90 x 80 in., 228.6 x 203.2 cm. Photo: readsreads.info courtesy Serpentine Galleries, London. © 2020 Faith Ringgold / Artists Rights Society (ARS), New York, Courtesy ACA Galleries, New York.

contemporary folk tale that is complex at every level of interpretation. Ringgold is untraditional in her approach: by combining fabric, paint, and written text, she draws attention to issues of race, gender, and black history. Her *Who's Afraid of Aunt Jemima* quilt is, for instance, at once a tribute to her mother and part fabrication, part folk lore, part family legend in its re-telling of "the most maligned black female stereotype."[49] The story it tells is both a work of subversion and one of recovery: combining childhood memories and "present realities" that narrate an image of the strong, successful, authoritative black woman; a representation so necessary to our sociocultural imagination.[50] Her story quilts draw on African textile aesthetics: most are bordered with a Nigerian tie-dyed fabric assembled in a design that is employed by the Kuba in Zaire.[51] She utilizes a folk-art style of flat space and bold colors/patterns. What fascinates about Ringgold's quilts is that she juxtaposes squares of traditional quilting with squares of narrative text. Along with narrative text blocks, Ringgold's quilts also incorporate painting, stitchery, photoetching, traditional folk tales and their contemporary retelling. By combining the contemporary with the traditional, Ringgold exposes the viewer to a quilt that is at once a deeply personalized object that yet opens a larger archetypal experience. Ringgold's quilts "encapsulate the yearnings and goals of black American women in terms capable of transcending racial [and gender] barriers."[52] For example, Ringgold's autobiographical *Change* quilt visually records the progressive transformation of a woman (in part, Ringgold herself) from what she is expected to be to what she wants to be, thus expressing the quilters' emotions, as well as her personal and social history.[53] In the late eighties, her Story Quilts began to appear in sequences of three or more separate quilts bound by a continuous story. The *Lovers' Quilt* trilogy incorporates both a Wedding Quilt and a Funeral Quilt, linking this contemporary work to a traditional quilting style. Finally, the *Purple Quilt*, a collaboration with Alice Walker, threads the voices of three women in its homage to powerful black female figures. Illustrative of her resistant imagination, the narrators and heroines of Ringgold's quilts are always women, through which Ringgold weaves a narrative at once intimate and transcendent.

Contemporary Activist Quilts

The uniquely personal yet collaborative nature of the quilt medium has made quilting a prime vehicle of expression for social and political issues of today. In many instances, artists, quilters, and activists engage in a quilt project whose goal is to bring awareness to a particular issue. These quilts are projects in a Bataillian sense of the term—they are produced to introduce objective and external utilitarian ends, while yet exceeding utility in their relation of the individual to the greater social (narrative) experience. Sometimes such quilts are pure performance art: for example, in July 2000, 891 people came together to hold fabric over their heads in celebration of the twenty-fifth anniversary of the Sisters Outdoor Quilt Show, the largest outdoor international quilt show held in Oregon. This "Human Quilt" reorients the traditional form and function of the quilt to one of an unmitigated participatory experience. Other "activist" quilts both memorialize and draw attention to social issues.

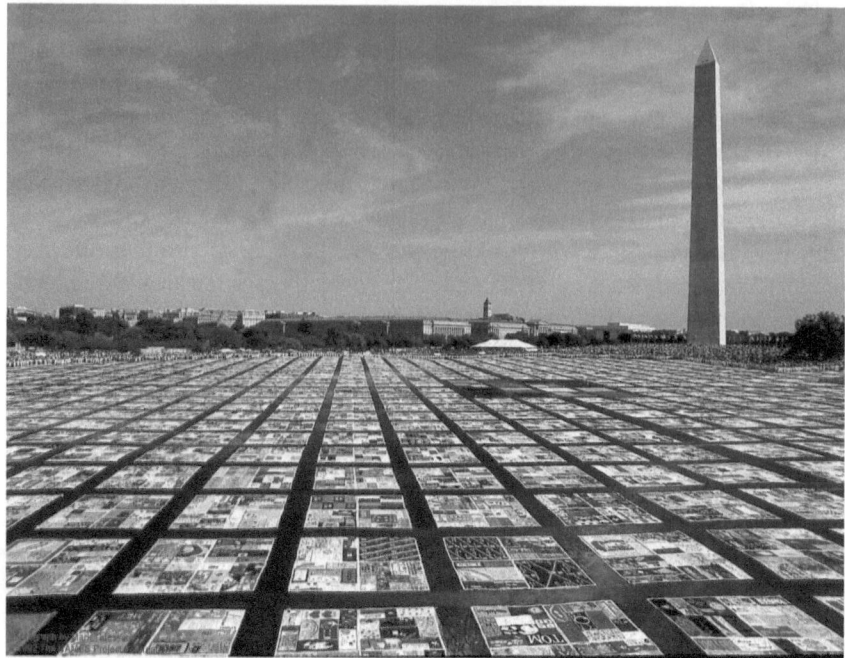

Figure 8.3. The NAMES project *Aids Memorial Quilt*, displayed on the National Mall in Washington, DC. Photo courtesy the National Institutes of Health. https://history.nih.gov/display/history/Tip+of+the+Iceberg.

In 1985, the NAMES project *AIDS Memorial Quilt* was conceived by AIDS activist Cleve Jones. Jones was part of a candlelight vigil in remembrance of the 1978 assassinations of Harvey Milk and George Moscone. Jones asked people to write on signs the names of loved ones lost to AIDS. The signs were then taped to the San Francisco Federal Building, resulting in appearance like a patchwork quilt. Jones carried on with the project the following year. In the eighties, the social stigma of AIDS meant that those who died of AIDS might not receive a funeral or proper burial. The memorial quilt thus substituted in place of a memorial service and grave site. Each panel on the quilt is the size of a grave plot (3x6), poignantly representing the number of lives lost to the AIDS pandemic (the quilt weighs roughly 54 tons). In 1987, the quilt was first displayed on the National Mall in Washington, DC.[54] It is still considered the largest community art project in the world.

Similarly, the Migrant Quilt Project brings together artists, activists, and quilters who are working to bring awareness to the experiences of migrants from Mexico and Central America who have died in the Tucson Sector, a border region between New Mexico and Yuma. A collaborative effort, this series of quilts is composed of textiles such as blue jeans, bandanas, and embroidered cloths that have been discarded by migrants and then collected from sites along the migration route. Each quilt lists the deaths from each year since 2000 (when an official documentation of deceased migrants began). The names of those who have died in that particular year is then inscribed on the quilt. The quilts are displayed at immigration conferences and art galleries across the United States.[55]

The *Monument Quilt*, the largest tribute to survivors of sexual violence, has also been displayed at the National Mall in Washington. DC, a fitting place for this monument made of fabric. Thousands of red squares spell out over 3,000 stories of sexual violence that were written, stitched, and painted on 4x4 squares by survivors. A project of Baltimore-based FORCE: Upsetting Rape Culture, the *Monument Quilt* began in 2013 as a collective action to disrupt rape culture. By crowd sourcing the stories, and then stitching them together, the *Monument Quilt* project is an example of a collaborative effort to change how Americans respond to rape. The *Monument Quilt* "creates a platform for individuals and communities to grieve and heal . . . [while] resisting a singular narrative about sexual violence."[56]

The above quilts move beyond traditional techniques to express a process of quilting whose aim is to draw attention to and explore social justice issues and political matters. Piecing still very much takes place: woven into the social narrative is an individual experience (such as the struggle with AIDS, the border crossing, or the surviving of sexual violence), more often than not in commemoration and celebration. Activist quilts may be more anonymous in nature—they are a collective effort directing the viewer to a message of grave social and political value. In the process, the individuals who collect the stories and piece them together participate in a collective narrative experience, or shared ritual, that is both personal and transcendent.

Conclusion

Beginning with traditional American quilts of the colonial and nineteenth-century periods, the reception of the quilt as fabric art in the twentieth century, and the activist quilts of the twenty-first century, it is clear that, traditional or nontraditional, each quilt is stitched with meaning, an embodiment of real people's lives. Memories, histories, and spirituality are pieced into the work of quilting, resulting in the quilt as personal object. Exceeding utility, the quilt offers an aesthetic; as fabric art, it is beautiful. While beautiful, the composition of the quilt transports the individual quilter and/or viewer of the quilt into a larger narrative experience, expressed by the choice of fabric, design, and further ornamental objects such as rocks, beads, recycled garments, and perhaps including the superimposition (seen more often in contemporary quilting) of paint, photoetching, and digital imagery. Thus, the quilt is a visual-historical document that communicates the values, hopes, and concerns of the quilters and the time period in which they quilt. Those who participate in the quilting experience engage in a shared ritual of community, as they participate in the sacred economy of the quilt. To quilt is, in some fashion, to claim immortality.

Notes

1. Jacqueline Tobin and Raymond Dobard, *Hidden in Plain View: The Secret Story of Quilts and the Underground Railroad* (New York: Anchor Books, 2000), 28.

2. Jonathan Holstein and John Finley, *Kentucky Quilts 1800–1900* (New York: Pantheon Books, 1982), 7.

3. Shelly Zegart, "The Quilt Projects: Fifteen Years Later," in *Folk Art: Magazine of the Museum of American Folk Art* (Spring 1996).

4. Eleanor Bingham Miller, "Since Kentucky: Surveying State Quilts 1981–1991," in *Expanding Quilt Scholarship: The Lectures, Conferences, and Other Presentations of Louisville Celebrates the American Quilt*, edited by Shelly Zegart and Jonathan Holstein (Louisville: Kentucky Quilt Project, Inc., 1994), 13.

5. Holstein and Finley, *Kentucky Quilts*, 20.

6. Georges Bataille, *Inner Experience*, trans. Leslie Anne Boldt (Albany: SUNY Press, 1988), 56.

7. Gladys-Marie Fry, *Stitched from the Soul: Slave Quilts from the Antebellum South* (Chapel Hill: University of North Carolina Press, 2002), 83.

8. Holstein and Finley, *Kentucky Quilts*, 31.

9. Holstein and Finley, *Kentucky Quilts*, 37, 72.

10. Showalter, *Piecing and Writing*, 235.

11. Crazing is an effect in pottery or glass where a network of lines appears in the surface of the object.

12. Holstein and Finley, *Kentucky Quilts*, 44, 66, 69.

13. Holstein and Finley, *Kentucky Quilts*, 62.

14. Holstein and Finley, *Kentucky Quilts*, 52–53.

15. Holstein and Finley, *Kentucky Quilts*, 7.

16. Ulysses S. Dietz, "The Newark Museum and Its Quilt Collection," in *Expanding Quilt Scholarship*, 100.

17. Dietz, 100.

18. Holstein and Finley, *Kentucky Quilts*, 38.

19. Verna Mae Slone, *What My Heart Wants to Tell* (Lexington: University Press of Kentucky, 1988), 58.

20. A pallet is defined by Fry as a makeshift bed—a quilt carpet spread on the floor. See Fry, 42.

21. Showalter, *Piecing and Writing*, 235.

22. Gladys-Marie Fry, *Stitched from the Soul*, 42–43, 65. Quilt lore also holds that the Jacob's Ladder pattern, renamed the Underground Railroad, was stitched into quilts that were hung outside homes to signal safe haven. Cuesta Benberry holds that this lore is, however, undocumented.

23. Fry, *Stitched from the Soul*, 64.

24. Eleanor Bingham Miller, "Forward" in *EQS*, 1.

25. Miller, "Since Kentucky," 1.

26. Fry, *Stitched from the Soul*, 4.

27. Michael Kimmelman, "ART REVIEW: Jazzy Geometry, Cool Quilters," *New York Times*, November 29, 2002. https://www.nytimes.com/2002/11/29/arts/art-review-jazzy-geometry-cool-quilters.html.

28. Fry, *Stitched from the Soul*, 4.

29. Miller, "Since Kentucky," 1.

30. Fry, *Stitched from the Soul*, 1.

31. Fry, *Stitched from the Soul*, 83.

32. Georges Bataille, *The Accursed Share: An Essay on General Economy*, trans. Robert Hurley (New York: Zone Books, 1991), 113.

33. Georges Bataille, *The Accursed Share: An Essay on General Economy Vol. 2* (New York: Zone Books, 1993), 40.

34. Mircea Eliade, *The Sacred and the Profane*, trans. Willard Trask (San Diego: Harcourt, 1987), 12.

35. Bets Ramsey, "Art and Quilts: 1950–1970" in *Uncoverings* 14 (1993): 12.

36. Ramsey, "Art and Quilts: 1950–1970," 16.

37. Ramsey, "Art and Quilts: 1950–1970," 17.

38. Ramsey, "Art and Quilts: 1950–1970," 37.

39. Eva Ungar Grudin, *Stitching Memories: African-American Story Quilts* (Williamstown: Williams College Museum of Art, 1990), 13.

40. Grudin points out that many African practices involve fabric for narrative purposes: for example the Kente cloths from Ghana; the appliquéd tapestries of the Fon of Dahomey (now the Republic of Benin); the traditional woven blankets known as Khasa, produced by the Peul of Mali. Whereas the African tradition often depicts images of royalty or of military achievements, Grudin notes that these subjects are replaced with more humble tales of ordinary, American lives in American narrative quilts. Grudin, *Stitching Memories*, 15–16.

41. Eva Ungar Grudin, *Stitching Memories*, 7–8.

42. Cuesta Benberry, *Always There: The African-American Presence in American Quilts* (Louisville: The Kentucky Quilt Project, 1992), 43.

43. Fry, *Stitched from the Soul*, 84.

44. Grudin, *Stitching Memories*, 38, 11.

45. Grudin, *Stitching Memories*, 64, 74.

46. Grudin, *Stitching Memories*, 73–74.

47. Grudin, *Stitching Memories*, 78.
48. Eleanor Flomenhaft, *Faith Ringgold, a 25 Year Survey: April 1 to June 24, 1990* (Hempstead: Fine Arts Museum of Long Island, 1990), 23.
49. Flomenhaft, *Faith Ringgold*, 24.
50. Flomenhaft, *Faith Ringgold*, 23.
51. Grudin, *Stitching Memories*, 11.
52. Flomenhaft, *Faith Ringgold*, 7.
53. Flomenhaft, *Faith Ringgold*, 27.
54. http://www.pba.org/programming/programs/thisisatlanta/aidsquilt/. Accessed 10/7/2019.
55. http://migrantquiltproject.org/. Accessed 10/7/2019.
56. https://themonumentquilt.org/. Accessed 10/7/2019.

Bibliography

Bataille, Georges. *Eroticism*. Trans. Mary Dalwood. New York: Penguin, 2001.
———. *Inner Experience*. Trans. Leslie Anne Boldt. Albany: SUNY Press, 1988.
———. *The Accursed Share: An Essay on General Economy*. Trans. Robert Hurley. New York: Zone Books, 1991.
———. *The Accursed Share: An Essay on General Economy Vol. 2*. New York: Zone Books, 1993.
Benberry, Cuesta. *Always There: The African-American Presence in American Quilts*. Louisville: Kentucky Quilt Project, 1992.
Cassirer, Ernst. *The Philosophy of Symbolic Forms Vol. 2 Mythical Thought*. Trans. Ralph Manheim. New Haven: Yale University Press, 1977.
Dietz, Ulysses S. "The Newark Museum and its Quilt Collection." In *Expanding Quilt Scholarship: The lectures, conferences, and other presentations of Louisville Celebrates the American Quilt*, edited by Shelly Zegart and Jonathan Holstein. Louisville: Kentucky Quilt Project, 1994.
Eliade, Mircea. *The Sacred and the Profane*. Trans. Willard Trask. San Diego: Harcourt, 1987.
Flomenhaft, Eleanor. *Faith Ringgold, a 25 Year Survey: April 1 to June 24, 1990*. Hempstead: Fine Arts Museum of Long Island, 1990.
Fry, Gladys-Marie. *Stitched from the Soul: Slave Quilts from the Antebellum South*. Chapel Hill: University of North Carolina Press, 2002.
Grudin, Eva Ungar. *Stitching Memories: African-American Story Quilts*. Williamstown: Williams College Museum of Art, 1990.
Holstein, Jonathan, and John Finley. *Kentucky Quilts 1800–1900*. New York: Pantheon Books, 1982.
Kimmelman, Michael. "ART REVIEW: Jazzy Geometry, Cool Quilters." *New York Times*, November 29, 2002. https://www.nytimes.com/2002/11/29/arts/art-review-jazzy-geometry-cool-quilters.html.

Miller, Eleanor Bingham. "Since Kentucky: Surveying State Quilts 1981–1991." In *Expanding Quilt Scholarship: The Lectures, Conferences, and Other Presentations of Louisville Celebrates the American Quilt*, edited by Shelly Zegart and Jonathan Holstein. Louisville: Kentucky Quilt Project, Inc., 1994.
Ramsey, Bets. "Art and Quilts: 1950–1970." *Uncoverings* Vol. 14, 1993.
Showalter, Elaine. "Piecing and Writing." In *The Poetics of Gender*, edited by Carolyn G. Heilbrun and Nancy Miller. New York: Columbia University Press, 1986.
Slone, Verna Mae. *What My Heart Wants to Tell*. Lexington: University Press of Kentucky, 1988.
Smithsonian Institution conference proceedings. *What's American about American Quilts?: A Research Forum on Regional Characteristics and the American Quilt Legacy Exhibition Case at the National Museum of American History*. March 18 and 19, 1995.
Tobin, Jacqueline, and Raymond Dobard. *Hidden in Plain View: The Secret Story of Quilts and the Underground Railroad*. New York: Anchor Books, 2000.
Walker, Alice. *In Search of Our Mother's Gardens*. Mariner Books, 2003.
Zegart, Shelly. "The Quilt Projects: Fifteen Years Later." *Folk Art: Magazine of the Museum of American Folk Art*, Spring 1996.

PART 2

NEW PERSPECTIVES

Chapter 9

The New Materialism

A Critique

MICHAEL JACKSON

Editor's Note: I have chosen to begin the second part of the volume (which focuses on theoretical approaches to personal objects) with this chapter for a number of reasons. First, Jackson provides an anthropological perspective on a number of cultures that grounds the discussion and allows for a smooth transition out of the preceding part. Second, the chapter directly engages with current trends in scholarship (specifically the "New Materialism") that are relevant to our project. And finally, while the chapter outlines several relations between subject and object that can allow for the appearance of animism or personality, Jackson provides a cautionary warning about reifying relational phenomena into ontological categories. This warning against romanticizing the "enchantment" of obdurate matter will serve as a helpful critique as we transition into the remaining chapters.

Although scholars have often invoked animism, fetishism, totemism, and anthropomorphism as signs of primitivism and faulty reasoning, many contemporary anthropologists have embraced these perspectives not simply as modes of thought but as modes of being—alleged evidence of the radical alterity of certain cultures and of the profound multiplicity of the human condition. Indeed, so pervasive is this new exoticism that some writers now speak of a "posthuman" turn in which the lines between persons and animals, or persons and things, are not only contested but also deemed to have no *ontological* foundation.[1]

Rather than ask whether the new materialism fulfills a wish to re-enchant a world that has become globally uniform and intellectually boring or is simply another example of an all too human tendency to confuse forms of thought with forms of being, I want to explore the existential conditions under which things *appear*, by turns, inert or vital, objects or subjects. This requires bracketing out questions as to the *nature* or *essence* of persons and things in order to understand the different effects and appearances that emerge in the course of their *interactions*. It is in this emphasis on relations over relata, the transitive over the intransitive, that I depart from the prevailing ethos of new materialist ontology and its assumptions that materiality is *intrinsically* vital, agentive, self-creative, and productive.[2]

Melquíades's Magnets

In the opening pages of *One Hundred Years of Solitude,* Gabriel García Marquez describes the dramatic impact of ice and magnets on the inhabitants of Macondo. As the gypsy Melquíades carries his metal ingots from house to house, pots, pans, tongs, and braziers tumble "in turbulent confusion" from their proper places and follow him down the street, like the enthralled children in the wake of the Pied Piper. "Things have a life of their own," Marquez writes; "it's just a matter of waking up their souls."[3]

That ironware can spring to life, or that water can shape-shift from liquid to solid to gas, appears to be a potentiality of the things themselves, and even an expression of their intentionality and will. But the "life" of these things depends on the presence of a magnet in the first case and on whether the water is cooled or heated in the second. These effects do not necessarily require a human agent and may occur naturally or accidentally. But they are always the outcome of a *relationship* between one thing and another—an object and its environment, or matter and mind. Moreover, these relationships are never enduring. When José Arcadio Buendía offers a mule and a pair of goats in exchange for Melquíades's magnets, he is convinced that he will be able to use them to attract gold from the ground and thereby become rich. When the magnets fail to fulfill their promise, he trades them in, together with three colonial coins, for a magnifying glass whose power to eliminate distance and generate fire has persuaded José Arcadio Buendía that he has now acquired a formidable weapon of war.

It is difficult to distinguish subject and object here. While the subject of the story is José Arcadio Buendía, one might also argue that the subject is the magnetized ingots or the magnifying glass, or their "magical" effects. Though these "things" are mere objects when not in use, they seem, when taken up and put to use, *as if* they were subjects, revealing their potentialities to attract things to them or transmute one thing into another. But as Heidegger observed, the thingness of a jug "does not lie at all in the material of which it consists," but rather "in its being *qua* vessel," able to be filled and emptied, or hold a liquid.[4] This potentiality of things to attract, magnify, fill or fulfill, is a function not of the thing-in-itself but of a relationship between a thing and a person. Just as Melquíades's magnets participate in the gypsy's subjectivity when taken up and deployed by him, so José Arcadio Buendía appears, at least in the eyes of his long-suffering wife, to be in thrall to the magnet's powers and reduced to the status of a hapless object.

We are, by turns, at once creators of the world and creatures of it, and it would be as spurious to claim that human beings are always and necessarily subjects as it would be foolish to claim that the extrahuman world is always and necessarily inert. But there is a risk that in describing the *appearance* of a person or a thing in any particular context we will conclude that this description reveals the "real" essence of the person or thing and lead us to confuse causation with agency. *Why* Melquíades's magnets induce ironware to move may be explained in terms of material cause (the phenomenon of magnetism) or of efficient cause (Melquíades' deliberate deployment of the magnets), but it would be a mistake to confuse movements that occur without consciousness and will with movements that are a result of intentionality and purpose.[5] There is a world of difference between "being subject to change" and "being a subject that brings change about."

Clearly, the words "subject" and "object" are epistemologically ambiguous. The word "subject" may refer to a particular person (José Arcadio Buendía) as well as an abstract construct ("magnetism" or "magic"). Although idealist thought posits the subject as a transcendent category ("the human") that is intrinsically different from other categories, including animals, material objects, and divinities, the human cannot be conceived without reference to what it allegedly is not. Phenomenologically as well as dialectically, a "subject" always implicates an "object," whether that object is a goal, a thing, or another person. An object can never be an object in itself; it is only an object in the consciousness of persons.[6] In brief, it is the dynamic *relationship* between what we tend to reify as subjects and objects that is interesting, not the intrinsic properties of the terms as such.

Object Relations Theory

In object relations theory, subject and object connote a felt distinction between experiences that appear to originate or belong within us ("inner" or "subjective") and experiences that appear to originate from outside us ("exterior" or "objective"). Two important conclusions follow from this. First, "who" we are always implicates "what" we have, whether this is a natural ability, an item we own, a language we speak, a belief we espouse, a trade we practice, or a place we live. That is to say, being and having are mutually entailed. Second, at any moment, to varying degrees, we are both actors and acted upon. In Hannah Arendt's words, every person is at once a "who" and a "what"—a subject who actively participates in the making or unmaking of his or her world, and a subject that suffers and is subjected to the actions of others, as well as forces that lie largely beyond his or her control.[7] This oscillation between being an actor and being acted on is felt in every human encounter, and intersubjective life involves an ongoing struggle to negotiate, reconcile, balance, or mediate these antithetical possibilities, such that no one person, group or entity ever arrogates agency so completely and permanently to itself that others are reduced to the status of mere things, objects, ciphers or contingent predicates.

This interplay between one's experience of being an actor and being acted upon is a constant in every human life, and it would be a serious mistake to define any individual, society, or period of history as being characterized by either agency or patience, freewill or fatalism. Nevertheless, Westerners have conjured an extraordinary range of vocabularies to describe essential differences between themselves and others, based on the assumption that "we" and "they" construe the relationship between subjects and objects, persons and things, in *essentially* different ways. While "we" make "rational" distinctions between animate and inanimate, human and nonhuman, or words and things, "they" are supposedly immersed in a prerational, vitalist, and anthropomorphic mode of being that Lucien Lévy-Bruhl called "mystical participation," in which the world of objects is typically experienced as animate and therefore capable of responding to human spells, incantations, and special forms of ritual address such as sacrifice and prayer. While I am inclined to bracket out such terms as "rational," "irrational," "mystical" and "prelogical," it is important to recognize that people in all societies oscillate between different modes of thinking, speaking, and acting depending on the situations in which they find themselves.

Bereaved individuals everywhere are prone to hear voices and see ghosts, and in all societies, people imagine that abstract ideals and precious objects are as worth dying for as significant others. Moreover, not only are material objects and imaginary figures endowed with human attributes such as consciousness and will; human beings whose beliefs are abhorred and whose behavior is condemned will be treated as mere objects, trash, or waste. Rather than interpret these phenomena *epistemologically* as true or false, or *morally* as good or bad, or *historically* as signs of barbarity or civilization, I prefer to explore them *psychologically and pragmatically*, as means whereby human beings grasp and process their immediate experience through things external to themselves, such as the language and customs they share with others, the animals, plants, and landscapes that surround them, the material objects they make and use, and the invisible agents (viruses, bacteria, divinities, and heavenly bodies) that lie beyond their ken.

Being and Having

Because we think *through* things, it is only natural that we should think *of* things as vital to our existence, thereby transplanting into them the thoughts and feelings we recognize in ourselves.[8] In grasping our humanity through the extrahuman, and in processing subjective experience through material objects, we tend to lose sight of the difference between persons and things, humanity and divinity, humanity and animality. We readily assume that the principle of reciprocity operates not only between human beings but potentially between persons and animals, persons and things. Though Jean Piaget argued that anthropomorphic thought is characteristic of an early stage in child development (and, by implication, an early stage in human cultural evolution),[9] it is clear that this manner of thinking is present in people of all ages and in all societies. It reveals itself in the imaginings of laboratory researchers working closely with great apes.[10] It finds expression in popular speculations about the conceptual and spiritual lives of animals. And it explains our fetishistic attitude toward prized possessions, such that the loss of our valuables will precipitate the same bereavement reaction as the loss of a beloved person. Being is in all societies invested in and distributed among the *things* that people use and call their own. Having is not only a metaphor for being; it is actually experienced as a mode of being, such that the bonds we form with persons through "object cathexis" are phenomenologically continuous with the bonds we form with objects and ideas.

Consider the ontological metaphor of container-contained—a metaphor that is as central to object-relations theory as it is common to cultures throughout the world.

The model of container-contained was central to the psychoanalytic work of Wilfrid Bion who postulated that we can only process, comprehend and accept overwhelming life experiences ("Beta elements") by working them through with a caring other—someone who can contain or safely hold us and on whom we can rely in constructing life-affirming rather than life-negating responses to unbearable experiences.[11] But we can also feel contained and safe within our dwellings and neighborhoods, with our language, our treasured mementos, and our cultural values. This mutual substitutability of care givers, abstract ideas, home places, and sacred objects is predicated on our human capacity for playing with reality.

In the recent work of Peter Fonagy and Mary Target,[12] they discuss how play typically oscillates between a subjunctive or "pretend mode," in which images and ideas are allowed to take on a life of their own and a mode of "psychic equivalence" in which ideas are made to stand for some external reality. For both Bion and Fonagy, concepts are equated with any*thing* that helps a child objectify and vicariously control its relationship with the world, such as mother's milk, food, toys, blocks, paints, and found objects. Conceptual thought, in this view, is a means whereby one manages one's life in relation with others, a way in which we contain and control life experiences that threaten to engulf, undermine, or nullify us.

In *From Anxiety to Method in the Behavioral Sciences*,[13] George Devereux argues that we share with all living organisms a deep-seated need to be recognized and responded to. "Denial of response" can be so traumatic that in most societies, cultural strategies exist for alleviating peoples' panic reactions to the unresponsiveness of matter. Most notably, physical occurrences are interpreted animistically, and human meanings are projected onto the extrahuman world. Thus, a thunderstorm will be said to embody the malicious intentions of outsiders, and a "natural" disaster such as a flood, mudslide, or earthquake will be construed as a manifestation of ancestral displeasure.

Devereux's thesis applies equally to our tendency to use objects or graven images as surrogate persons, so that faced when an unresponsive person—or someone who is beyond our reach or control—we substitute for that person a doll, mascot, figurine or icon, and act on *it*—speaking to it, nurturing it, harming it, as the case may be—as though it were, in effect, the absent person. Is it possible that the "new materialism" is a manifestation of Devereux's "trauma of the unresponsiveness of matter," a defense against external forces over which we seem to have little control (global warming, epidemic diseases, economic collapse) that involves thinking and acting *as if* these forces were not only open to the human mind but were "actants" or "quasi agents," with "trajectories, propensities, or tendencies of their own."[14] Before reaching any conclusions on this matter, let us continue to explore in an empirical vein the ways in which objects are subject to thought and subjects think about themselves through objects.

Container and Contained

The model of container-contained is as central to the Kuranko of Sierra Leone as it is to object relations theory—a reminder that analogical reason in both Western and non-Western traditions tends to deploy identical ontological metaphors and reflect similar existential dilemmas.

In Kuranko, *miran* refers to any material possession—particularly if it contains, encloses, and protects, such as a house, clothing, a water vessel or cooking pot—as well as to personal attributes that give one a sense of presence and substantiality of being—such as forceful speech, physical skill and social adroitness. But *miran*, in both senses of the term—material possession and self-possession—is never a fixed property or attribute. In practice, a person's *miran* may be bolstered by fetishes that symbolically enclose, contain, and protect the vital spaces that define his or her being—body, house, village, chiefdom—in exactly the same way that in a consumer society material possessions bolster and define a person's sense of substantiality and standing. For Kuranko, the notion of a full container is a common metaphor for anyone who is in command of himself and working his utmost to do what is expected of him, to do his duty. But self-possession and morale may be undermined, sapped, or lost. In this respect, *miran* bears a family resemblance to the Latin American notion of *susto* and the Polynesian notion of *mana*, the loss of which leads to physiological weakening, psychological disequilibrium, and social death.

Just as a person's property can be stolen, a pot broken, and a house fall into disrepair, so a person can lose self-possession and confidence, as when his or her *miran* is "taken away" by more powerful others (such as autocratic parents, forceful public speakers and powerful bush spirits) whose voice and power "press down" with great weight, diminishing the *miran* of those in their presence. Then it is said that "the container has tipped over and its contents spilled out"—a metaphor for loss of self-control, or for a state of laziness or despair when one has "let oneself go" (*nyere bila*). Ideally, a balance is struck in which everyone's voice, presence, and property are accorded due recognition in relation to his or her role, age and gender. But some people assert themselves beyond their due station—as in the case of a Big Man who exploits his position to take advantage of an inferior, a senior co-wife who abuses her junior partners, a man whose jealousy overrules his better judgment or a woman whose emotions are not held in check. A kind of intersubjective logic then comes into play, based on the principle of reciprocity, according to which one has the right to counter in kind any action that has the effect of directly nullifying, diminishing, belittling or erasing one's own being, or indirectly doing so by taking away properties that one regards as essential to and as extensions of one's being. The Kuranko phrase *ke manni a nyorgo manni* ("something happened, its counterpart then happened") reveals the kinship between the social logic of partnership and the abstract calculus of retaliation.

Since *miran* blurs any hard-and-fast distinction between *having* and *being*, it can be augmented through *taking* the wherewithal of life from others—through theft, witchcraft, abuse and humiliation—or through *giving* such things as respect, food, help and protection that will be returned in equal measure at some later date. At the same time "real," symbolic, and fantastic calculations enter into people's notions of what constitutes their due, and Kuranko folktales, like folktales throughout the world, with their magical agencies, supernatural intercessories, and miraculous transformations, attest to the vital role played by wishful thinking in making everyday life endurable.

Consider Janet Hoskins's fascinating examples of magical thinking in her ethnography of the Kodi of Sumba (Eastern Indonesia).

When Kodi talk about their life experiences, they seldom do so directly—by telling life stories. Moreover, when people spoke to Hoskins about their personal possessions, they did so in stories that were in effect life stories, and subjects that were not publicly spoken of in Kodi—such as sexual politics—would find oblique expression in accounts people gave of objects:

> A young girl I knew well never confessed her feelings of romantic longing and later disappointment to me directly, but she was fascinated by the story of a magic spindle that flew through the air to snare a beloved. When later her own hopes were cut off, she sent a message to her lost lover through the secret gift of the object . . . A famous singer and healer who also wanted a female companion composed long ballads to his drum, introducing each ritual session with a history of efforts to cover the drum properly so it could be pierced by a male voice and travel up to the heavens. . . . Another man, famed as a storyteller and bard, said he received his "gift of words" in the simple, woven betel bag he carried with him at all times.[15]

That objects are surrogates for people, metaphors for social relationships, and serve as objective correlatives of subjective moods and states, may, Hoskins suggests, have a lot to do with the fact that in Kodi ritual life, objects often substitute for persons. Thus, in life-crisis rituals, a knife can substitute for a man, a cotton board or gold pendant can take the place of a woman, a betel bag be buried in lieu of a person. Interestingly enough, Hoskins points out that the objects that stand for persons are very often containers: a betel pouch, a hollow drum, a porcelain vessel, a funeral shroud.

Acting and Being Acted Upon

In the foregoing accounts of how subjective attributes find expression in material objects, we discern how the intrapsychic struggle to lift one's spirits, bolster one's confidence, and increase one's sense of presence is mediated by the manipulation of things. While some would see this affective labor as "magical"[16] or "libidinal"[17] by comparison with the "real" work of making a living or finding fulfillment, I am less interested in defining the nature of the action than in exploring its repercussions in people's lives. This pragmatic approach brackets out epistemological and ontological questions as to whether an action is rational or irrational, scientific or religious, real or fantastic, in order to explore the degree to which it enables a person to satisfy his or her existential needs, such as security and shelter, love and honor, wellbeing and recognition.

I now turn to another ontological metaphor, which, as with the image of container-contained, a crucial intersubjective relationship is posited between persons and string, cords, bindings, lashings, and weavings.

In his seminal study of transitional objects and transitional phenomena, the psychoanalyst D. W. Winnicott describes the actions of a troubled seven-year-old boy whose parents had sought his professional help. The boy's mother suffered from depression, and during her absences in hospital, he had stayed with his maternal aunt. Increasingly, however, his parents had become concerned by his behavior—a compulsion to lick things and people, a habit of making compulsive throat noises, threats to cut his little sister into pieces, over-controlling or losing control of his bowel movements. In Winnicott's first interview, the boy revealed an intense preoccupation with string, and subsequently his parents told Winnicott that this "obsession" worried them for their son had gotten into the habit of tying up tables and chairs and had recently tied a piece of string around his elder sister's throat. Winnicott suggested to the mother that her son was dealing with his fear of separation and using the string in an attempt to deny it, much "as one would deny separation from a friend by using the telephone."[18]

With this insight, the mother talked to her son about the times she had gone away from him and about his fear of losing touch with her. Six months after the first interview, the mother told Winnicott that her son had stopped playing obsessively with string and joining objects in the way he had—though the string play subsequently and temporarily reappeared, once when the mother had to return to hospital, and another time when she again suffered a bout of depression.

Winnicott's analysis provides invaluable insights into ritualization for it succinctly demonstrates that the manipulation of objects, abstract ideas, and personae in our *external, social environment* is analogous to, but possibly more significant than, the *intrapsychic* manipulation of *images* of these things (symbolic disguise, displacement, repression, projection, reversal, rationalization, scotomatization) in enabling human beings to come to terms with distressing situations. Both fantasizing and ritualizing are predicated on the logic of intersubjectivity. By this, I mean that all human beings tend to equate, or draw analogies between, their relationships with other persons, their relationships with their own thoughts and emotions, and their relationships with things, ideas, and words. As a corollary, human beings tend to act in critical situations *as if* one of these modalities of relationship could be effectively substituted for the other. In Winnicott's view, these are all "object-relations." "Transitional objects," such as pieces of string, teddy bears, or toys enable children to manage their difficult but inevitable separation from parents or caregivers, as well as laying the foundations for adult responses to traumatic change, separation and loss.

Yet, objects can sometimes not only replace persons but occlude them, leading to pathological forms of dissociation.

In a compelling case study, Bruno Bettelheim describes a traumatized boy called Joey who so distrusted people that he converted himself into a machine. Secure in this mechanized image of himself, he functioned *as if* by remote control. Indeed, Joey's machinelike behavior was so convincing that even his therapists found it difficult to respond to him as a human being. Joey lived the mechanistic image as a literal and embodied truth:

> During Joey's first weeks with us we would watch absorbedly as this at once fragile-looking and imperious nine-year-old went about his mechanical existence. Entering the dining room, for example, he would string an imaginary wire from his "energy source"—an imaginary electric outlet—to the table. There he "insulated" himself with paper napkins and finally plugged himself in. Only then could Joey eat, for he firmly believed that the "current" ran his ingestive apparatus. So skillful was the pantomime that one had to look twice to be sure there was neither wire nor outlet nor plug. Children and members of our staff spontaneously avoided stepping on the "wires" for fear of interrupting what seemed to be the source of his very life.[19]

Winnicott's and Bettelheim's cases help us understand that thinking does not occur in a vacuum, abstracted from lived situations, arising from natural curiosity or wonderment, or directly mirroring cultural patterns. In the case of Joey, it is crucial that we take into account the crises this child suffered in his early life. According to Bettelheim, Joey was rejected by his parents even before he was born. "I never knew I was pregnant," his mother said. Joey's birth "did not make any difference . . . I did not want to see or nurse him . . . I had no feeling of actual dislike—I simply didn't want to take care of him."

Although the new materialism "calls for a detailed phenomenology of diverse lives as they are actually lived—often in ways that are at odds with abstract normative theories or official ideologies,[20] it often presents itself as an inversion of old binaries, showing that the mundane is exotic, appearances are realities, objects are subjects, and causation is agentive. Though one may doubt the epistemological validity of this reasoning, it inadvertently reveals one of the phenomenologically most compelling aspects of human relations with the non-human, namely, a chiastic tendency to essentialize and polarize the terms, and then to reverse the relationship between them, speaking as if "our" perspective was actually "theirs." Thus, when we experience strong emotions when watching a beautiful sunset, we readily say that the sunset "moves" us as though *it* has agency. In giving primacy to the object, the subject masks the part it plays in constituting the experience of being moved.

To construe experience *relationally* brings us to consider the ways in which subjectivity is objectively constituted and, reciprocally, how objectivity is subjectively perceived. Appearances are thus explained neither as functions of the mind nor of external reality but seen as emerging from the space between an experiencing subject and the objects of his or her experience.

In this view, we achieve our sense of being subjects through the objects and others with which we interact, just as those objects achieve the appearance of subjectivity or value through us. Keith Basso refers to this process as interanimation and shows that it is our *interactions* with a landscape or place, moving, working, and living in it, that generate a sense of the landscape as actually imbued or impregnated with subjectivity. As Sartre puts it, "When knowledge and feeling are oriented toward something real, actually perceived, the thing, like a reflector, returns the light it has received from it. As a result of this continual interaction, meaning is continually enriched at the same time as the object soaks up affective qualities."[21]

It is to Marx and Engels that we owe the most compelling descriptions of how the things and objects in which we invest our time and energy, to which we give ourselves, as it were, gradually become extensions of our own selves, valued as we would value a person with whom we have a close relationship and regarded as having will and consciousness.[22] Anthropomorphism is, in this view, not an intellectual conceit, a creation of the mind, but an outcome of a bodily and sensible relationship with things—an expression of our essentially inter-subjective relation to the world.

The interplay between persons and things preoccupied Marx in his early essays on the nature of ownership, since it is through labor-action that a person not only produces a livelihood but produces and reproduces a mode of life, a sense of identity, and a sense of communal belonging. In agricultural labor, for example, the soil becomes not only "the objective condition" of the worker's own reproduction; it is experienced as "the objective body of his subjectivity," "a prolongation of his body." In other words, labor is experienced not simply as the action of an individual subject on inert matter, but as an intersubjective relationship that simultaneously transforms both the object worked upon and the worker himself.[23]

It is important to remind ourselves that in traditional societies "work" includes a range of actions that we in the West would designate as ritual, magical, or even social action as though these were secondary or surplus to the supposedly primary activities of gardening, herding, farming, hunting, or gathering. Thus, it is significant that the Kuranko word *wale* denotes both work and any forms of dutiful action such as raising a child, ruling a chiefdom, or performing a hereditary task. But the phenomenology of labor that I have outlined here suggests that identical elements appear in all intersubjective action. Among the Warlpiri of Central Australia, the "ceremony" associated with sacred sites involves the collaborative effort of patrilineal "owners" (*kirda*) and their uterine kin (*kurdungurlu*) who supervise or "police" the body painting and decoration of those who will perform the ancestral dances that are said to draw out, reawaken, or bring back into embodied presence the primordial forms of life (*kuruwarri*) that reside in the earth at that site and along the ancestral songlines that connect the site with others. In ceremonial labor, then, one reproduces a social past whose reappearance is linked to the burgeoning of desert plants and the increase of game animals after rain or the growing-up of a child in one's care, as well as metaphorically likened to the action of waking from sleep or dawn breaking after a long night. In short, Warlpiri notions of labor as a form of begetting or procreation echo Marx's and Engel's view[24] since at the same time that one "increases" animal and plant life, one reproduces the social relations most crucial to one's identity—with *patrikin, matricin,* and affiliated countrymen (*warlalja*) and affines (*jurdalja*). Moreover, one also reproduces one's own sense of kinship with the site that, depending on one's relationship with it, will be called father (*kirda*), father's father (*warringiyi*), mother's brother (*ngamirni*), mother's father (*jamirdi*), and so on.

Dancing vigorously on the land may be likened to carving an ancestral mask, giving birth, or making a farm. In common parlance, one puts one's sweat and blood into the task at hand. In many Aboriginal societies sacred sites or story-places are said to recognize the sweat-smell of those who bear a kinship relationship to them. Illness or misfortune may come to those who trespass on a sacred site, but whose body odor cannot be unrecognized.[25] The intense labor of the dancer, carver, mother, or farmer is felt to flow into the object or other, which becomes endowed with subjectivity. *It* then appears to speak to the human subject in response to the human subject's action on it. The distinctive stomping of Aboriginal men's dance sends vibrations into the ground that are taken as evidence of the stirring into life of the ancestral essences (*kuruwarri*) that steep the earth underfoot. Among the Bamana of Mali, the "energy of action"[26] is reified as *nyama*—a vibrant force that animates all living things and whose strength is correlated with the stress or intensity of the effort put into vital activity. Thus, the "arduous labor," skill, concentration, and effort involved in iron working entails the "release" of *nyama*, as does the work of formal speech, hunting and circumcision.[27] Indeed, so overwhelming is the *nyama* released from such practices that an unskilled worker may be blinded or killed by the force.[28] This notion that inept labor may create a negative force in the object worked upon is similar to the Maori notion that the vital force (*hau*) that is carried by every fabricated object may be "turned aside" (*whitia*) and cause illness and misfortune if the object received in exchange is not passed on or reciprocated.[29]

In so far as labor transfers vitality and spirituality from the laboring subject to the object worked upon, labor creates an intersubjective relationship between people and things. This is why artists in many societies experience themselves as channels through which divine inspiration flows into the object. Explaining how he transforms logs into art, the Tanzanian wood carver Lugwani observes, "I do not impose my own ideas on the wood—it tells me what to do; it helps me to think creatively."[30] And in commenting on the carving of one particular abstract sculpture, Lugwani noted that at first the log seemed resistant, but after two weeks' work he was able to say, "I am no longer fighting the wood; it has revealed itself to me and we are working together."[31] Similar reflections may be found in Henry Glassie's study of Turkish traditional art and artisans. "In things they do not see things, but people,"[32] he writes; "the artist's gift suffuses an object with spirit."[33]

Clearly, then, the labor expended on an object is gradually felt to inhere in the object itself, investing it with social value. When, as among the Warlpiri, ritual labor demands the collaboration of many different people, the actual place where the ceremonial work is carried out accumulates a value that affirms the intersubjective bonds between both owners and ancestors and *kirda* and *kurdungurlu*. That the process of working on an object comes to be experienced as an inherent property of the object itself also helps us understand why religious ideas are so often entailed by labor action. Sustained, intensive, and collective labor not only creates a binding intersubjective relationship or covenant between self and other, or subject and object; it produces a sense of value and of the sacred that is felt to inhere in the site where that labor takes place. Thus, landscapes become storied, as though the earth itself contained the narratives and scripts that human beings have created as moral constraints and guidelines for their lives.[34]

We may now ask under what conditions does the reverse process occur? How does a valued object, embodying the vitality of those who have worked to produce or reproduce it, come to lose value and die? Is this loss of value also a function of the kind of relationship obtaining between a human subject and the thing that is the object of his or her labor? And is this loss analogous to the demoralization and dispiritedness that overcomes a person abandoned by significant others?

In West Africa, masks can sicken and die when not worn in ceremony or when out of circulation and may even be mourned and given burial rites like a deceased person. And in Aboriginal Australia, a sacred site unvisited for several generations—like grassland left unburned or kinsmen who have gone away for a long time—is figuratively dead, and as such may be mourned, and felt to be haunted by dangerous spirits. But in Warlpiri thought, death and life are functions of relationship rather than absolute and final states. A neglected site, a forgotten ancestor, a primordial event may all be, so to speak, out of sight and out of mind, but none is necessarily lost to the world; it may be brought back into being whenever the living return to it, remember it, dream of it, or perform ceremony that gives it presence. Any landscape is filled with marks, signs, and vestiges of the Dreaming that people notice and discuss as they walk around. But such attention is strictly speaking not a form of remembering, a bringing of the past back to mind; it is an interaction that actually discloses the incipient vitality in the place, quickening it into life and making it present. *Walku* is thus best translated not as death, but as temporary absence, and its opposite, *palka*, not as life, but as embodied presence.

Death is thus a form of temporary estrangement rather than a permanent state of nonbeing. It occurs whenever any object, place, or person whose being depends on a vital relationship with other beings loses that life-sustaining link. The link may be borne in mind, to be sure, but a mere memory or disembodied conception of a person or place is artificial. It is map, not territory.

Estrangement may also be *deliberately* created as a way of expressing power for paradoxically it is only when one masks the context in which an object is produced that it attains a reified form that cannot be subject to questioning and therefore imposes itself on our consciousness, as it were, not through any memory of the work that went into it or the lives that were sacrificed to create it, but simply from its presence as sheer facticity.

Closing Remarks

For Aristotle, agency is very different from causality, though this difference may be more apparent than real. A person may appear to be exercising free will when in reality she is acting under duress. A piece of iron may move under the influence of a magnet, yet if the magnet is hidden, the iron may appear to be alive and ensouled. The question is not whether objects, like bodies, "evince certain capacities for agency" or that "the difference between humans and animals, or even between sentient and nonsentient matter, is a question of degree more than of kind,"[35] but rather under what conditions do objects appear to be subjects. This question demands that we consider *interactions* between subject and object, and the *contexts* in which these interactions occur. It is undeniably true that under certain circumstances objects *appear* to have agency (if only because of their forceful presence, impact, and effects), just as under certain conditions humans behave as if they were things, and animals appear to be human. Under other circumstances, objects appear to be inert, and animals seem to lack humanity.

An Irving Hallowell's Ojibwa ethnography makes this contextual specificity of meaning very clear. In the Ojibwa language, there is an implicit category distinction between animate and inanimate. Although stone, thunder, and objects such as kettles and pipes are grammatically animate, and Ojibwa sometimes speak of stones as if they were persons, this does not mean, however, that Ojibwa are animists "in the sense that they *dogmatically* attribute living souls to inanimate objects such as stone"; rather, they recognize "*potentialities* for animation in certain classes of objects under certain circumstances. The Ojibwa do not perceive stones, in general, as animate, any more than we do.[36] Among the Kuranko, it is axiomatic that will and consciousness are not limited to human beings, but distributed beyond the world of persons and potentially found in totemic animals, fetishes, and even plants. The attributes of moral personhood (*morgoye*) may, indeed, be exemplified in the behavior of totemic animals, divinities, and the dead, while antisocial people may lose their personhood entirely, becoming like broken vessels or ruined houses. In other words, being is not necessarily limited to human being. But this is a *human* understanding, born of the experience of exchanging the roles of actor and acted upon, of subject and object, in people's everyday interactions with others.

Crucial to understanding the ways in which we understand ourselves in relation to others and to objects is the phenomenon of re-cognition—a word I hyphenate in order to emphasize that cognition is always reflexive and mediated. Re-cognition is an expression of our dependency on things external to ourselves, including our language, in order to process, grasp, and articulate what is going on within us. Interiority can only be apprehended through exteriority. Accordingly, all thought is analogical. It involves drawing comparisons between something felt to lie within our immediate sensory experience and something that is felt to exist outside it. Hence such metaphors as "my thoughts are muddy" (like a stream after rain), "my feelings are running high" (like a river in flood), "his expression was stony." It is this unceasing passage of inner experience into the exterior space of the world and back again that is the essence of re-cognition. But in this process, the external objects that have enabled thought to occur tend to be seen as participating in the thought process itself. Because they are vital to our conscious life, objects through which we become self-conscious are seen as sharing in that vitality, and even possessing consciousness themselves.

Though we may agree with Jane Bennett, that "we need to cultivate a bit of anthropomorphism . . . *to counter the narcissism of humans in charge of the world*," to "chasten . . . fantasies of human mastery,"[37] and to develop greater respect for the environment, such political and ethical assertions do little to explain the psychology and persistence of anthropomorphic thought. That the new materialism, like the ontological turn, is idealist in character can surely not be doubted, for in both cases the constitutive terms of idealism—subjectivity, mind, thought, will, intentionality—are extended into the world at large. Instead of seeing divinity everywhere, vitality is discerned in all things. Yet both views preserve the notion of mind against a world that is increasingly felt to render our intellectual mastery of it ineffectual.

The new materialism is not so much a revelation that matter is ensouled, vibrant, or mindful than a defense against the sheer obduracy and otherness of the material world. Whether it is the degradation of the environment, climate change, or the extinction of species, we react to the unthinkable by invoking the age-old strategy of imagining the material world is, like the social world, open to negotiation. In their zeal to impute vitality and agency to objects, the new materialists are not so much creating a new paradigm as unwittingly registering the cognitive consequences of thinking through things, as well as our all-too-human tendency to reduce anxieties about *our limited capacity* to control or comprehend the external world by imagining that it obeys the same rules that govern our intrapsychic and intersubjective existence.

But not only do objects obdurately remain objects, regardless of the ways in which we subject them to our thinking; we, as thinking subjects, are so deeply influenced by the world of which we are a part that we too are, to a degree, objects. As Adorno puts it, "the subject enters into the object altogether differently from the way the object enters into the subject. An object can be conceived only by a subject but always remains something other than the subject, whereas a subject by its very nature is from the outset an object as well . . . To be an object also is part of the meaning of subjectivity; but it is not equally part of the meaning of objectivity to be a subject."[38] That human beings resist the notion that the extrahuman is not only beyond our comprehension and control, but only appears to participate in subjectivity, may be understood as a defense against the unresponsiveness of matter in an age when our waning powers to sustain life on earth make this issue more vexed than it may have ever been before.

Notes

1. See Rosi Braidotti, *The Posthuman* (Cambridge: Polity Press, 2013); Katherine Hayles, *How We Became Posthuman: Virtual Bodies in Cybernetics, Literature and Infor-*

matics (Chicago: University of Chicago Press., 1999); Edouardo Kohn, *How Forests Think: Toward an Anthropology Beyond the Human* (Berkeley: University of California Press, 2013).

2. Diana Coole and Samantha Frost, "Introducing the New Materialisms," in *New Materialisms: Ontology, Agency, and Politics*, ed. Diana Coole and Samantha Frost (Durham: Duke University Press, 2010).

3. Gabriel García Marquez, *One Hundred Years of Solitude*, tr. Gregory Rabassa (New York: Harper and Row, 1970), 1–2. The book was originally published in 1967 by Editorial Sudamericanos under the title *Cien años de soledad*.

4. Martin Heidegger, "The Thing," in *Poetry, Language, Thought*, tr. by Albert Hofstadter (New York: Harper Colophon, 1975), 169. See also Heidegger's description of a table, not simply as a thing but as a vital part of a living space, mediating social relations and participating in our social life: Martin Heidegger, *The Hermeneutics of Facticity* (Bloomington: Indiana University Press, 1999), 66–69.

5. Aristotle, *Physics*, book II 3, tr. P. H. Wicksteed and F. M. Cornford, Loeb Classical Library 228 (Cambridge, MA.: Harvard University Press, 1934), 228.

6. Theodor W. Adorno, "On Subject and Object." In *Critical Models: Interventions and Catchwords*, tr. Henry W. Pickford (New York: Columbia University Press, 1998), 245–58.

7. Hannah Arendt, *The Human Condition* (Chicago: University of Chicago, 1958), 186.

8. Tim Ingold, "Introduction," in *What Is an Animal?*, ed. Tim Ingold (London: Unwin Hyman, 1988), 9.

9. Jean Piaget, "The Origins of Child Animism, Moral Necessity and Physical Determinism," in *The Child's Conception of the World* (Frogmore: Paladin, 1973), 236–81.

10. Kristin Andrews, "Anthropomorphism and Folk Psychology," revised entry, "Animal Cognition," *Stanford Encyclopedia of Philosophy*, ed. Edward N. Zalta. Retrieved from https://plato.stanford.edu/archives/sum2016/entries/cognition-animal/2016. See also: Elliott. Sober, "Anthropomorphism, Parsimony, and Common Ancestry," *Mind and Language* 27, no. 3 (2012): 229–38.

11. Wilfrid Bion, *Attention and Interpretation: A Scientific Approach to Insight in Psycho-Analysis and Groups* (London: Tavistock, 1975).

12. Peter Fonagy and Mary Target, *Psychoanalytic Theories: Perspectives from Developmental Psychopathology* (New York: Brunner-Routledge, 2003).

13. George Devereux, *From Anxiety to Method in the Behavioral Sciences* (The Hague: Mouton, 1967), 33–34.

14. Bruno Latour, *Politics of Nature: How to Bring the Sciences into Democracy*, tr. Catherine Porter (Cambridge: Harvard University Press, 2004).

15. Janet Hoskins, *Biographical Objects: How Things Tell the Stories of People* (New York: Routledge, 1998), 3.

16. Jean-Paul Sartre, *The Emotions: Outline of a Theory*, tr. Bernard Frechtman (New York: Philosophical Library, 1948).

17. Jean-François Lyotard, *Libidinal Economy*, tr. Iain Hamilton Grant (Bloomington: Indiana University Press, 1993).

18. D. W. Winnicott, *Playing and Reality* (Harmondsworth: Penguin. 1974), 17.

19. Bruno Bettelheim, "Joey: A 'Mechanical Boy,'" *Scientific American* 200, no. 3 (1959): 117–27.

20. Coole and Frost, "Introducing New Materialisms," 27.

21. Jean-Paul Sartre, *The Philosophy of Jean-Paul Sartre*, ed. R. Cumming (New York: Vintage, 1965); cited by Keith Basso, "Wisdom Sits in Places: Notes on a Western Apache Landscape," in *Senses of Place*, ed. Steven Feld and Keith Basso (Sante Fe: School of American Research, 1996), 55.

22. Karl Marx and Frederick Engels, "The German Ideology," tr. C. Dutt, in *Karl Marx-Frederick Engels: Collected Works*, vol. 5 (Moscow: Progress Publishers, 1976).

23. Karl Marx, *Pre-Capitalist Economic Formations*, tr. J. Cohen (London: Lawrence and Wishart, 1964), 81, 89, 90–91.

24. Marx and Engels "The German Ideology," 43.

25. See Michael Jackson, *At Home in the World* (Durham: Duke University Press, 1998), 181–83; Allan Marett, *Songs, Dreamings, Ghosts: The Wangga of North Australia* (Middletown, CT: Wesleyan University Press, 2005), 61–62; Elizabeth Povenelli, *Labor's Lot: The Power, History, and Culture of Aboriginal Action* (Chicago: University of Chicago Press, 1993), 31.

26. Charles Bird (with Mamadou Keota and Bourama Soumaoro), *The Songs of Seydou Camara*. Vol. 1: *Kambili* (Bloomington: Indiana University Press, 1974).

27. Patrick McNaughton, *The Mande Blacksmith: Knowledge, Power, and Art in West Africa* (Bloomington: Indiana University Press, 1988), 16.

28. McNaughton, *The Mande Blacksmith*, 69–70.

29. Anne Salmond, "Maori and Modernity: Ruatara's Dying," in *Signifying Identities: Anthropological Perspectives on Boundaries and Contested Values*, ed. Anthony. P. Cohen (London: Routledge, 2000), 40.

30. Lugwani. 2005. Web document. Printout on file with author.

31. Lugwani. 2005. Web document. Printout on file with author.

32. Henry Glassie, *Turkish Traditional Art Today* (Bloomington: Indiana University Press, 1993), 103.

33. Glassie, *Turkish Traditional Art Today*, 4.

34. Basso, "Wisdom Sits in Places."

35. Coole and Frost, "Introducing the New Materialisms," 20, 21.

36. A. Irving Hallowell, "Ojibwa Metaphysics of Being and the Perception of Persons," in *Person Perception and Interpersonal Behavior*, ed. R. Taguiri and L. Petrullo (Stanford: Stanford University Press, 1958), 65.

37. Jane Bennett, *Vibrant Matter: A Political Economy of Things* (Durham: Duke University Press 2010), xvi, 122.

38. Adorno, "On Subject and Object," 183.

Bibliography

Adorno, Theodor W. *Negative Dialectics*, translated by E. B. Ashton. New York: Continuum, 1973.

———. "On Subject and Object." In *Critical Models: Interventions and Catchwords*, translated by Henry W. Pickford, 235–58. New York: Columbia University Press, 1998.

Andrews, Kristin. "Anthropomorphism and Folk Psychology." Revised Entry, "Animal Cognition." *Stanford Encyclopedia of Philosophy*, edited by Edward N. Zalta. Retrieved from httrs://plato.stanford.edu/archives/sum2016/entries/cognition-animal/2016.

Arendt, Hannah. *The Human Condition*. Chicago: University of Chicago Press, 1958.

Aristotle. *Physics*, Book II 3, translated by P. H. Wicksteed and F. M. Cornford. Loeb Classical Library 228. Cambridge, MA.: Harvard University Press, 1934.

Basso, Keith. "Wisdom Sits in Places: Notes on a Western Apache Landscape." In *Senses of Place*, edited by Steven Feld and Keith Basso 55–90. Sante Fe: School of American Research, 1996.

Bennett, Jane. *Vibrant Matter: A Political Economy of Things*. Durham: Duke University Press 2010.

Bettelheim, Bruno. "Joey: A 'Mechanical Boy.'" *Scientific American* 200, no. 3 (1959): 117–27.

Bion, Wilfrid. *Attention and Interpretation: A Scientific Approach to Insight in Psycho-Analysis and Groups*. London: Tavistock, 1975.

Bird, Charles (with Mamadou Keota and Bourama Soumaoro). *The Songs of Seydou Camara*. Vol. 1: *Kambili*. Bloomington: Indiana University Press, 1974.

Braidotti, Rosi. *The Posthuman*. Cambridge: Polity Press, 2013.

Coole, Diana, and Samantha Frost, "Introducing the New Materialisms." In *New Materialisms: Ontology, Agency, and Politics*, edited by Diana Coole and Samantha Frost. Durham: Duke University Press, 2010.

Devereux, George. *From Anxiety to Method in the Behavioral Sciences*. The Hague: Mouton, 1967.

Fonagy, Peter, and Mary Target. *Psychoanalytic Theories: Perspectives from Developmental Psychopathology*. New York: Brunner-Routledge, 2003.

Glassie, Henry. *Turkish Traditional Art Today*. Bloomington: Indiana University Press, 1993.

Hallowell, A. Irving. "Ojibwa Metaphysics of Being and the Perception of Persons." In *Person Perception and Interpersonal Behavior*, edited by R. Taguiri and L. Petrullo, 63–85. Stanford: Stanford University Press, 1958.

Hayles, Katherine. *How We Became Posthuman: Virtual Bodies in Cybernetics, Literature and Informatics*. Chicago: University of Chicago Press., 1999.

Heidegger, Martin. *Ontology—The Hermeneutics of Facticity*. Bloomington: Indiana University Press, 1999.

———. "The Thing." In *Poetry, Language, Thought*, translated by Albert Hofstadter. New York: Harper Colophon, 1975.

Hoskins, Janet. *Biographical Objects: How Things Tell the Stories of People*. New York: Routledge, 1998.

Ingold, Tim. "Introduction." In *What Is an Animal*, edited by Tim Ingold. London: Unwin Hyman, 1988.

Jackson, Michael. *At Home in the World*. Durham: Duke University Press, 1998.

Kohn, Edouardo. *How Forests Think: Toward an Anthropology beyond the Human*. Berkeley: University of California Press, 2013.

Latour, Bruno. *Politics of Nature: How to Bring the Sciences into Democracy*, translated by Catherine Porter. Cambridge: Harvard University Press, 2004.
Lugwani. 2005. Web document. Printout on file with author.
Lyotard, Jean-François. *Libidinal Economy*. Translated by Iain Hamilton Grant. Bloomington: Indiana University Press, 1993.
Marett, Allan. *Songs, Dreamings, Ghosts: The Wangga of North Australia*. Middletown, CT: Wesleyan University Press, 2005.
Marquez, Gabriel García. *One Hundred Years of Solitude*. Translated by Gregory Rabassa. New York: Harper and Row, 1970.
Marx, Karl. *Pre-Capitalist Economic Formations*. Translated by J. Cohen. London: Lawrence and Wishart, 1964.
Marx, Karl, and Frederick Engels. "The German Ideology," translated by C. Dutt. In *Karl Marx-Frederick Engels: Collected Works*, vol. 5. 19–608. Moscow: Progress Publishers, 1976.
McNaughton, Patrick. *The Mande Blacksmith: Knowledge, Power, and Art in West Africa*. Bloomington: Indiana University Press, 1988.
Piaget, Jean. "The Origins of Child Animism, Moral Necessity and Physical Determinism." In *The Child's Conception of the World*, 236–81. Frogmore: Paladin, 1973.
Povenelli, Elizabeth. *Labor's Lot: The Power, History, and Culture of Aboriginal Action*. Chicago: University of Chicago Press., 1993.
Salmond, Anne. "Maori and Modernity: Ruatara's Dying." In *Signifying Identities: Anthropological Perspectives on Boundaries and Contested Values*, edited by Anthony P. Cohen, 37–58. London: Routledge, 2000.
Sartre, Jean-Paul. *The Emotions: Outline of a Theory*. Translated by Bernard Frechtman. New York: Philosophical Library, 1948.
———. *The Philosophy of Jean-Paul Sartre*. Edited by R. Cumming. New York: Vintage, 1965.
Sober, Elliott. "Anthropomorphism, Parsimony, and Common Ancestry." *Mind and Language* 27, no. 3 (2012): 229–38.
Winnicott, D. W. *Playing and Reality*. Harmondsworth: Penguin. 1974.

Chapter 10

Constituting Personal Objects, Constituting Persons

DWAYNE A. TUNSTALL

Editor's Note: This chapter complements the previous, in that it also places emphasis on the relationship between persons and objects. However, the chapter also nicely contrasts chapter 9 by providing an unapologetically idealistic perspective: in this case rooted in the American Idealism of Josiah Royce. The chapter also provides new perspectives on themes such as psychology and scientific empiricism that were touched upon in the preceding chapter. Tunstall argues that it is only through relation to the personal objects that we create (or transfigure) that we become persons at all. Instead of labor or work as the significant act of personalization (as we saw in chapter 9), Tunstall identifies care or love.

We and our things, I and my things, constitute our world.

—John J. McDermott[1]

Introduction

Whatever else cultural objects are, they are personal objects. Whatever personal objects are, they are important to us constituting the meaningfulness of our world. Our world is a personal one to the extent that we transfigure nonhuman things into objects that are significant to us. We transfigure these nonhuman things into personal objects by first selectively paying attention to them and then loving them exclusively. I should note that nonhuman things are not necessarily *physical* things. *Ideas* are nonhuman things, after all. I should also note that we gradually become persons by constituting personal objects for ourselves. Yet, personal objects are not merely the creations of human yearning to live in a personal world. Rather, personal objects are the result of both humans loving certain nonhuman things exclusively *and* humans paying attention to the qualities of those objects beloved by them. Of course, us constituting our world consists of more than constituting personal objects for ourselves and ourselves alone. For example, our relationships with other human persons, especially those relationships with other human persons where we constitute personal objects together, are avenues by which we constitute our world.

By *constituting personal objects*, I do not mean the manufacture of nonhuman things for practical use or enjoyment by humans. Nor do I mean the creation of an idea for practical use or enjoyment by humans. Neither one of these actions adequately accounts for the nature of constituting personal objects. Constituting personal objects is better conceived of as a phenomenological act of personalizing nonhuman things for the sake of us being able to live in a personal world. The phenomenological sense of constituting personal objects involves how certain nonhuman things acquire a personal significance for human persons. If we want to investigate the phenomenological sense of constituting personal objects, we would need to ask the following question: How can nonhuman things become meaningful to us *as* personal objects?

We should note that the phenomenological sense of constituting personal objects is not identical with either the ontological sense or psychological sense of constituting personal objects. The ontological sense of constituting personal objects would involve us being concerned about the kind of entity that a personal object *is* so that we can place personal object in the appropriate ontological category and then relate personal objects to other kinds of entities that exist. When we think about personal objects in this manner, we are thinking about them primarily as theoretical entities. That sense of personal objects does not ring true to how we ordinarily experience them, however. The phenomenological sense of constituting personal objects involves how we actually experience personal objects, which is not primarily as theoretical entities. Phenomenologically speaking, personal objects are better understood experientially and existentially (that is, primarily a matter of how we experience and live in the world) than ontologically.

The psychological sense of constituting personal objects involves how humans are motivated to personalize certain nonhuman things as part of our identity formation process. This process can be understood from a variety of psychological perspectives and approaches—for example, evolutionary psychology, object relation psychoanalysis, existential integrative psychology, and cognitive behavioral psychology. None of these perspectives and approaches is adequate for understanding the phenomenological sense of constituting personal objects because they all presume that we can learn what it means for humans to personalize the world by studying it scientifically. They presume that we can adequately explain our personalization of nonhuman things in empirical terms. The phenomenological sense of constituting personal objects, on the other hand, requires us to describe the conditions of possibility for us caring about nonhuman things in a personal manner. I cannot imagine contemporary psychologists and psychiatrists seriously asking about the conditions of possibility for humans to personalize certain nonhuman things and ascribe personal significance to those things. They most likely would take for granted that humans have the capacity to constitute personal objects except under those circumstances where persons are cognitively incapable of attaching personal meaning to their symbolic representations of nonhuman things.

In this chapter, I will investigate the phenomenological sense of constituting personal objects from the perspective of an unapologetic idealist, Josiah Royce. His idealist theory of individuation and the resulting account of individuality he derives from that theory in parts 3 and 4 of the supplementary essay in *The Conception of God*[2] may not be part of a phenomenological account of how we constitute personal objects. Nevertheless, I contend in the next section that there are phenomenological clues in that theory and the resulting account of individuality that we can use to formulate a phenomenological account for how we constitute personal objects and, by extension, our world. I will then discuss in the final section how our personal identities are constituted by a subset of personal objects—namely, the life plans that we have chosen to live by.

Personalizing Things, Constituting Personal Objects

Royce begins his ontological account of individuality in the supplementary essay to *The Conception of God* by criticizing a few prominent theories of individuation in Western philosophy: Thomistic, Scotistic, and Leibnizian theories of individuation.[3] He criticizes each one of these theories for their failure to account for the origin of individuals in the world. He contends that individuals originate as objects of exclusive interests for wills who can selectively love them as unique entities.

Royce illustrates his principle of individuation with an example from developmental psychology. Young children initially know the world abstractly; more specifically, they are aware of things and persons in terms of indefinite types.[4] Later in childhood, they begin caring about specific nonhuman things. Royce has his readers imagine a boy who plays with a toy lead soldier on a regular basis. The boy becomes attached to *that* toy soldier. He then asks the reader to imagine that the boy's toy soldier breaks. It cannot be repaired by his parents, his siblings, or anyone else nearby. His parents offer him a new toy soldier. This new soldier is identical in appearance to the old toy soldier, except that the new soldier is not broken. Yet, the child refuses to replace his old broken toy solider for the new soldier. The new soldier cannot replace the boy's broken toy soldier. *That* broken toy soldier is irreplaceable.

Royce contends that at the moment when the child rejects the new toy soldier as a replacement for the old broken one, that child "*consciously individuates the toy.*"[5] This individuation occurs because the child loves that toy soldier to the exclusion of all other toy soldiers, even those toy soldiers that are identical to it. This often-pre-reflective love for a nonhuman thing is "the basis of what later becomes the individuating principle of knowledge"[6] for one must first care about the objects of one's scientific inquiries before one is motivated to conduct those kinds of inquiries.

From our childhood exclusive interests in certain nonhuman things, we gradually expand the objects of our exclusive interests to more and more things. As Royce puts this point:

> With such exclusive interests one learns to love each of one's more permanent possessions,—one's home, books, trinkets; one's children, and all the other members of one's family; one's country, business, life; the mass of contents and relations designated as one's self, and the other masses known as each of one's friends. With gentler, but still relatively exclusive interests, one recognises [sic] places revisited, complex objects of scientific interest once carefully studied; and so on indefinitely.[7]

He admits that not all forms of love are individuating because some forms of love are not exclusive in nature.[8] For example, our love of pleasure is not individuating of the things that cause us to experience pleasure because we do not regard pleasurable things qua pleasurable things as unique individuals. It would not matter which pleasurable thing we experience or enjoy; they are fungible. For example, if I desire to eat a chocolate vegan cupcake from the Salted Cupcake, it does not matter which specific chocolate vegan cupcake I eat from that store. Buying and eating any chocolate vegan cupcake from the batch of vegan cupcakes recently made by the bakers there would suffice. Yet, there are plenty of forms of love that are exclusive. Loving one's career to the exclusion of other career options individuates the professional person.[9] Loving someone to the exclusion of other persons individuates both the lover and the beloved, making both the lover and the beloved unique individuals.[10] A mother loving her child individuates both the mother and her child for they become unique individuals to each other.[11] These loves, in turn, are affections that awaken us to a world of individual objects, that is to say, of objects that can be beloved by oneself or by others.

Scientists are the ones who ought to love the entire world since their objects of scientific inquiry are part of an interrelated, complex web of relationships between individuals. To learn more about their beloved objects, they would need to know about all individuals. Yet that goal is not anything that can be known empirically. Rather, it is a postulation based on how we individuate nonhuman things, as well as other persons. This postulation can be taken a step further. For someone to love a nonhuman thing enough to investigate it, that person must presume that there is a unified world of individuals. For those individuals to exist, there has to be someone who loves *all* of them. We are incapable of loving *all* individuals given our affective limitations and our finitude.[12] Since these individuals exist, then we can postulate the existence of a divine lover, a loving Absolute, who individuates them.[13] The origin of all existent individuals, then, is the Absolute individuating individuals.

Since we are investigating the phenomenological sense of constituting personal objects, there is no reason to discuss Royce's ontological speculations about the Absolute in this chapter. We should restrict ourselves to discussing the phenomenological clues from his ontological account of individuality. We can summarize these clues this way: At an early age, humans exclusively care about certain nonhuman things. When we care about nonhuman things in an exclusive manner, those things acquire a unique significance to us. As individuals with a unique significance to us, we refuse to substitute them with anything else, even if the proposed substitute is very similar or identical to our beloved individual objects. The act of loving a nonhuman thing constitutes a personal object, that is, an object that has a unique significance to us. The individuality of a nonhuman thing "is not the property of any object . . . as such, but is an act of one's will, through attention, desire and choice."[14]

How would the act of constituting personal objects unfold for an adult? Here are two scenarios that can give us a better sense of how the act of constituting personal objects can unfold:

> **Scenario 1.** Constituting a Rotating Race Car NASCAR Picture Motion Moving Lamp Night Light RC1230 as a personal object. My wife and I purchased this object as a night light to sooth our son when he was a toddler. We had recently moved to a rented duplex in Kentwood shortly after I was hired to be an assistant professor of

philosophy at Grand Valley State University. He had been diagnosed with developmental and processing disorder. He was mostly non-verbal at the time. He would occasionally throw tantrums because he could not communicate with us effectively. He could understand a lot more words than he could speak. He would get frustrated when he realized that he could not articulate himself as well as he desired. We hoped that purchasing a moving racecar night light would help him calm down during the day and relax right before bedtime.

When we recently moved to our current house, I found that night light. As I touched the age-worn box I had placed it in years ago, I almost cried remembering how this object comforted my son. It had acquired quite a bit of significance in my life. I could not bring myself to throw it away, even though my son is no longer the toddler who was calmed by that night light. It had become a personal object to me because it had helped my son during a difficult time in his life.

Scenario 2. Constituting the keys to a 1997 Teal Buick Skylark as a personal object. I initially began driving my parents' 1997 Teal Buick Skylark because I had problems with the 1997 Pontiac Grand AM I had been driving. As I prepared to drive from my parents' house in Virginia to Carbondale, Illinois, to attend graduate school at Southern Illinois University on a mid-August afternoon in 2002, my parents told me that they were giving me the Skylark. My father was the one who placed the keys to the Skylark in my hand. It was the last gift that my father gave to me before he died. That vehicle lasted until the fall of 2013, when my wife and I could not afford to repair it any further. I spent at least $10,000 fixing that vehicle from 2002 to 2013, largely owing to my personal attachment to it. I still have one of the keys to the Skylark in my possession. I associate that key with my father's desire for me to be successful in graduate school.

In the first scenario, I individuated *this* Rotating Race Car NASCAR Picture Motion Moving Lamp Night Light RC1230 as an object of exclusive interest. I recognize *this* night light as a personal object. I am thankful for *this* night light. There is no other Rotating Race Car NASCAR Picture Motion Moving Lamp Night Light RC1230 that could take the place of *this* night light. There is no other Rotating Race Car NASCAR Picture Motion Moving Lamp Night Light RC1230 that played in my son's room as my wife and I hugged him to calm him down. *This* night light is part of my and my family's world, which also makes it part of our world. In fact, I still love *this* night light because it was one of the objects that helped my son grow as a person.

In the second scenario, I personalized the Buick Skylark keys. I realize that I could have had a locksmith duplicate the set of keys given to me by my parents. However, a duplicate set of keys would not have been the actual keys that my father placed in my hands in 2002. They would merely be keys that start this specific vehicle's ignition. I would not have any reason to regard those duplicate keys as objects of exclusive interest. In other words, I would have no reason to regard them as personal objects in my world; they would just be keys to a vehicle I no longer own.

Even though these scenarios cannot capture all of the possible ways that we can transfigure a nonliving thing into a personal object, they can give us some insight into how personal objects are constituted by us. The act of constituting personal objects may begin as an individual act of personalizing nonhuman things, but it is ultimately an interpersonal one, given that our encounters and interactions with other persons, as well as with other nonhuman things, will be influenced by our attachment to personal objects. Even who we are is shaped by which nonhuman things we have transfigured into personal objects. Personal objects are cultural objects to the extent that they acquire their unique significance as a result of us learning behaviors, rituals, cultural mores, societal norms, ideas, beliefs, and ways of interpreting and knowing the world as part of the socialization process. These features of culture are shaped by other persons who constitute personal objects and co-constitute the world with us. We can, following Royce, call the world of personal objects constituted by us the *world of appreciation*. This world is not a different ontological realm than the physical world. Rather, the world of appreciation is the world experienced by us in a personal manner—that is, as a world consisting of human persons and their personal objects. Viewing the world personally discloses a world populated by unique individuals worthy of our concern, even if we do not recognize the uniqueness of many of these individuals.[15]

Personal Identities Personalizing One's World

There is another feature of Royce's account of individuation that I would like to briefly discuss before ending this chapter—namely, how personal objects helps us constitute our practical identities and our world. Just as the individuality of nonhuman things (that is, personal objects) is not a formal or material property, but "is an act of one's will, through attention, desire and choice,"[16] the individuality of persons is not a formal or material property of humans. Human persons are constituted in the same manner that personal objects are constituted. Unlike nonhuman things, though, human persons individuate themselves by constituting personal objects for themselves. There are certain personal objects essential for humans to self-individuate. In several of his writings, particularly in part 4 of the supplementary essay in *The Conception of God* and in *The Philosophy of Loyalty*, Royce writes about life plans in ways analogous to how I have discussed personal objects that enable us to self-individuate. In this section, I will explain how *life plans* are those nonphysical personal objects that have specific significance for the constitution of persons.

For Royce, a *life plan* is an ideal that expresses "the meaning of your unique experience."[17] It is the ideal that unifies all of one's desires, choices, and actions into a unique self-consciousness. In short, it is what makes your life uniquely *yours*. In colloquial terms, life plans give our lives a purpose and meaning. We are not born with a life plan; yet, each one of us must select a life plan for ourselves and then live by it (see *Philosophy of Loyalty*, 1995, 22). We must be the ones who love the life plans we choose and live by for those plans to direct our actions and unify our experiences and activities into unified self-consciousnesses, making us persons. Life plans are the ways we fully become persons, even as we may fail to exemplify these plans in our daily activities.

We could say that Roycean life plans are ways that we form our practical identities. By *practical identity*, I mean Christine Korsgaard's conception of practical identity in *Self-Constitution*:

> [A person] has an identity that is constituted by his choices. This kind of identity is in a deeper way the person's own than an animal's identity, because he is consciously involved in its construction. And it is more essentially individual than a non-human animal's, because he is free. Constructing, creating, shaping, reshaping, maintaining, improving, in all these ways constituting this kind of identity is the everyday work of practical deliberation. . . . It is because we have this kind of identity that we hold one another responsible, answerable, for what we do and what we are.[18]

In the abovementioned passage, she seems to contend that once we choose a particular practical identity as our own, we are responsible for performing the duties and obligations associated with that identity. Otherwise, we cannot be called *persons* in any meaningful sense. Indeed, unless someone choose and continues to reaffirm one's practical identities by acting on the duties and obligations associated with those identities, then that person ceases to be an agent. Technically speaking, that person ceases to be a *person*. We devolve into organisms that move in response to external stimuli and internal biological urges (for example, hunger, thirst, sex).[19]

Practical identities are substantive identities. They are substantive identities in that they provide us with duties and obligations by which we can determine what to do in a given situation. It is with practical identities that we can identify what it means to be a human person. Here is how Korsgaard expresses this point:

> [W]hen you come to see that your contingent practical identities are normative for you only insofar as they are endorsable from the point of view of your human identity, you also come to have a new attitude towards your contingent practical identities. You come to see them as various realizations of *human possibility* and *human value,* and to see your own life that way: as one possible embodiment of the human. Your life fits into the general human story, and is a part of the general human activity of the creation and pursuit of value. It matters to you both that it is a particular part—*your own part*—and that it is a *part of the larger human story.* What you want is not merely to be me-in-particular nor of course is it just to be a generic human being—what you want is to be a *someone,* a particular instance of humanity. So it's like this: in being the author of your own actions you are also a co-author of the human story, our collective, public story. As a person who has to make himself into a particular person, you get to write one of the parts in the general human story, to create the role of one of the people you think it would be good to have in that story. And then—at least if you manage to maintain your integrity—you get to play the part.[20]

Korsgaard recognizes that to be a person involves us having a commitment to formulating maxims aimed at pursuing interpersonal values that are good for us. She also recognizes that we cannot pursue these values unless we commit ourselves to pursing them in our own personal projects. For instance, once we committed ourselves to a particular project or to a person who embodies a certain kind of value, we are logically committed to that kind of value in general.[21] This is entailed by the formal feature of self-constitution; once we have selected a set of practical identities, either tactically or explicitly by voluntary choice, we are committed to respect other projects and people who embody similar values we ourselves promote in our own practical identities. So, for example, if I value excellent handiwork in granite sculptures, I should also value excellent handiwork wherever I recognize it, whether it is in a well-made piece of wooden furniture or a well-designed vehicle. After all, each one of these activities involves someone designing something excellent. Besides, by valuing the handiwork of excellent granite sculptures, I am also committed to value other people creating excellently designed human artifacts. The same is true whenever we evaluate other people's actions in general.

Royce's conception of life plans in *The Philosophy of Loyalty* is structured in a similar manner to how Korsgaard structures her conception of practical identity in *Self-Constitution*. When considered ethically, life plans are those personal objects that we choose to pursue actively in our lives. We are individuated by choosing and acting on our chosen life plans. We self-individuate whenever we devote our lives to actively pursuing a life plan, which gives our lives an overarching purpose.

Even though Royce writes as though each human person has a single overarching life plan, we can imagine someone living by more than one life plan if they are compatible with one another. Each life plan can be essential to who that person is, and that person's identity can consist of those life plans. For example, one can be a father, a professional, and a husband simultaneously. Fulfilling the obligations and responsibilities associated each one of these social roles can become expressions of who one is and of what makes one's life meaningful. Together, these social roles can function to unify one's life into a coherent, meaningful whole. If one no longer chooses to follow one or more of the life plans one has chosen to live by, then that person will have changed who they are. In short, changing one's life plan changes one's personal identity. We can also understand the change in personal identity this way: once one changes one's life plan, one has individuated oneself differently enough from the previous way one individuated oneself that one has become a different person. This would be the case regardless of if the biological organism instantiating the new person is the same as the one that instantiated the old person or if there is psychological continuity between the old person and the new person.

Notes

1. John J. McDermott, "The Aesthetic Drama of the Ordinary," in *Streams of Experience* (Amherst, MA: University of Massachusetts Press, 1986), 138.

2. Josiah Royce, "The Absolute and the Individual: A Supplementary Discussion, with Replies to Criticisms," in *The Conception of God: A Philosophical Discussion concerning the Nature of the Divine Idea as a Demonstrable Reality* (New York: Macmillan, 1897), reprinted in *Critical Responses to Josiah Royce, 1885–1916, Volume 1: The Conception of God*, edited by Randall E. Auxier (Bristol, UK: Thommes Press, 2000), 133–354.

3. See Royce, *Conception of God*, 223–58.
4. Royce, *Conception of God*, 259–60.
5. Royce, *Conception of God*, 261.
6. Royce, *Conception of God*, 262.
7. Royce, *Conception of God*, 263.
8. Royce, *Conception of God*, 264–66.

9. Royce, *Conception of God*, 265.
10. Royce, *Conception of God*, 265.
11. Royce, *Conception of God*, 265.
12. Royce, *Conception of God*, 265.
13. Royce, *Conception of God*, 265; see also, 269.
14. Bette J. Manter, "The Incompleteness of Loyalty," in *Josiah Royce for the Twenty-First Century: Historical, Ethical, and Religious Interpretations*, edited by Kelly A. Parker and Krzysztof Piotr Skowroński (Lanham, MD: Lexington Books, 2012), 125.
15. For Royce's most sustained explanation of the world of appreciation and its relation to the world of description, see *The World and the Individual*, volume 2, lectures 2, 4–5.
16. Manter, "The Incompleteness of Loyalty," 125.
17. Royce, *Conception of God*, 286.
18. Christine M. Korsgaard, *Self-Constitution: Agency, Identity, and Integrity* (New York: Oxford University Press, 2009), 129.
19. This paragraph and the next few paragraphs are revised passages from my unpublished manuscript, "Creating Personscapes Responsibly."
20. Korsgaard, *Self-Constitution*, 212.
21. Christine M. Korsgaard, "Morality and the Logic of Caring: A Comment on Harry Frankfurt," in *Taking Ourselves Seriously and Getting It Right*, edited by Debra Satz (Stanford CA: Stanford University Press, 2006), 75.

Bibliography

Korsgaard, Christine M. "Morality and the Logic of Caring: A Comment on Harry Frankfurt." In *Taking Ourselves Seriously and Getting It Right*, edited by Debra Satz, 55–76. Stanford CA: Stanford University Press, 2006.
———. *Self-Constitution: Agency, Identity, and Integrity*. New York: Oxford University Press, 2009.
Manter, Bette J. "The Incompleteness of Loyalty." In *Josiah Royce for the Twenty-Fist Century: Historical, Ethical, and Religious Interpretations*, edited by Kelly A. Parker and Krzysztof Piotr Skowroński, 119–32. Lanham, MD: Lexington Books, 2012.
McDermott, John J. "The Aesthetic Drama of the Ordinary." In *Streams of Experience*, 129–40. Amherst, MA: University of Massachusetts Press, 1986.
Royce, Josiah. "The Absolute and the Individual: A Supplementary Discussion, with Replies to Criticisms." In *The Conception of God: A Philosophical Discussion Concerning the Nature of the Divine Idea as a Demonstrable Reality*. New York: Macmillan, 1897. Reprinted in *Critical Responses to Josiah Royce, 1885–1916, Volume 1: The Conception of God*, edited by Randall E. Auxier, 133–354. Bristol, UK: Thommes Press, 2000.
———. *The Philosophy of Loyalty*. Nashville, TN: Vanderbilt University Press, 1995.
———. *The World and the Individual*. 2 vols. New York: Macmillan, 1899, 1901.
Tunstall, Dwayne A. "Creating Personscapes Responsibly." Unpublished manuscript.

———. "Two Varieties of Transcendental Pragmatism: Pihlström's Naturalism or Royce's Religious Existentialism?" *Idealistic Studies* 39, nos. 1–3 (Spring–Summer–Fall 2009): 149–59.

———. *Yes, But Not Quite: Encountering Josiah Royce's Ethico-Religious Insight*. New York: Fordham University Press, 2009.

Chapter 11

A Personalized Cultural World

A Cassireran Phenomenology of Personalized Intuition

JARED KEMLING

Editor's Note: Where chapter 9 drew on Marx (labor) and chapter 10 referred to Royce (love) to describe the relational act that allowed for the experience of personal objects, this chapter offers Gabriel Marcel's concept of "creative fidelity." While this provides another perspective on the personalizing act, the chapter primarily seeks to provide a phenomenological description of how personalized objects are experienced (thus: the form of personal objects, rather than the function by which they are constituted). In doing so, the chapter utilizes the phenomenology of Ernst Cassirer and thus introduces the idea of personal objects as symbols. Cassirer, and the concept of personal objects as symbol, will both reappear in later chapters: most notably chapters 14 and 17.

The focus of this chapter is what I will call "personalized experience." At a very general level, personalized experiences are those in which the "objective" world (objects, places, and so on) presents itself as having a "personal" character: either as a person, or at least resembling a person. In particular, I am interested in the "form" in which personalized experience presents: a form that, if understood and articulated correctly, should apply to any particular personalized experience. In other words, can we say anything about personalized experiences as such? Is there some identifiable form of experience that brings together any personalized experience, even experiences as diverse as an heirloom from your grandparents, the first car you ever owned (that perhaps you even named), a blanket from when you were a baby, the restaurant you took your partner on your first date, and so on? What, phenomenologically, is going on when we have experiences like this? How can we articulate these experiences that are, it seems to me, quite common, and yet can be quite hard to describe? Perhaps because they are so fundamental, or even transcendent? What follows is at attempt to begin that conversation.

It is important to note from the beginning that a full accounting of the form of personalized experience would require a full tracing of the phenomenology of *Geist* in its personalizing aspect—such a phenomenology (in the Cassireran sense)[1] would require a full account of how personalized experience develops through the expressive, representative, and significant stages. Each of these stages corresponds to a certain kind of experience: sensation, intuition, and conception. The expressive stage of the form is characterized by sensation, the representative stage by intuition, and the significant stage by conception. How is personalized sensation distinct from mythic sensation (and so on)? How is personalized intuition distinct from intuition in other forms? And how are personalized concepts distinct from the concepts of other forms? Each of these is a robust topic demanding a thorough exposition.

Unfortunately, while such a project is the ultimate aim and evolution of the present work, it is beyond the scope of this chapter. An attempt to overview the entirety of the form within the constraints of this work would result in a presentation so vague as to be largely useless. Instead, I will narrow my focus to the "representative" stage of the form—that part in the development of personalized symbols in which they take on spatiality, temporality (and for Cassirer, numerality), and become "intuitive" experience in the Kantian sense. Even with this narrowed focus, my remarks may still seem overly brief, but I feel that it is important to offer the reader concrete discussion of the personalized world, and focusing on the representative world strikes me as the most effective use of space.

To put the matter another way: in the following I will provide what might be called a "phenomenology of personalized perception." At any rate, accounts such as the one I will provide are commonly described in this way, especially as influenced by Merleau-Ponty's famous *Phenomenology of Perception*.[2] However, in keeping with Kantian and Cassireran language, it might be more accurate to call what follows a "Phenomenology of Intuition," as I will not be discussing personalized sensation (experience that is not spatio-temporal-numeric, but rather emotive and expressive: *sensatio*) or personalized conception (experience that is purely significant, i.e., symbolic, and therefore not bound by space-time-number).[3] Thus, I am not discussing the broad range of *perceptio* (which is for Kant all "conscious" experience) that includes sensation, as well as both forms of cognition (intuition and conception)—my focus is more narrow.

Lying in the background of the present work is a broader project in which I argue that the human tendency to personalize the world is best understood as what Ernst Cassirer has called a symbolic form of culture—and thus that this human energy of personalization is as essential to the project of humanity as language, myth, science, religion, or any of the other symbolic forms Cassirer identifies. Further, I argue that the symbolizing function (the transcendental "engine" which creates a personalized cultural world) is best understood in terms of what Gabriel Marcel has called creative fidelity, which is a kind of "making oneself available" to the world through an active stance of promising and reaffirmation. While I will not discuss Cassirer's use of symbolic form or Marcel's use of creative fidelity at length in the present work, those concepts are relevant foundations for the phenomenology I am attempting today.[4] Thus, this work is a phenomenology in a predominantly Cassireran sense: I will present the form of personalized experience as it enters "representation" in the Cassireran sense, in the Cassireran manner, modelling as closely as possible the approach that Cassirer himself would have taken.

In order to make an attempt at a "phenomenology of personalized intuition," I will follow Cassirer's general strategy (adapted from Kant) of going through and examining the unique way in which the personalizing activity of creative fidelity spatializes and temporalizes (and in addition for Cassirer, numeralizes)—we must outline the analog of a "transcendental aesthetic" of the personal symbolic form. By outlining the "pure intuitions"[5] of a personal world, my hope is to obtain adequate understanding of *any* "personal" symbol (as given in intuition), regardless of content. In other words, we must construct a positive account of the *form* of the personal. Only then can we have reliable insight into the *content* of a personal world: as Cassirer says, "determination of the pure *form* of knowledge must precede determination of the object of knowledge."[6] A positive description of the personalized cultural world cannot simply be a description of various personalized experiences (although it must be at least that)—we must also articulate the symbolic *form* of this cultural world, the structure of the personal as it is manifested in our intuitive (and ultimately: sensible and conceptual) experience.

For each symbolic form, Cassirer, following Kant, shows how the relevant symbolic function serves as the ground of a kind of "pure intuition"—that is, how each symbolic function spatializes and temporalizes (and in addition for Cassirer, numeralizes) in its own distinct way. Thus, each symbolic form arises with a characteristic form of *intuitive perception,* and these forms of intuition allow us to identify pure intuitions (space, time, and number) belonging to each cultural horizon. The "pure intuition" of mythic "space" is not the same as linguistic "space," or scientific "space," and so on. In explaining the personalized cultural world and the personalized "objects" or experiences that one encounters there, *we must not apply pure intuitions borrowed from other forms*—instead, we must articulate new senses of these pure intuitions from within the personalizing symbolic function of creative fidelity.

For the purpose of articulating the personalized intuitive cultural world, I will use a three-dimensional analysis (following Cassirer) composed of the pure intuitions of personalized *space, time,* and *number*. Remember that for Kant an "intuition" is an *objective (and therefore cognitive), immediate, singular Vorstellung* (presentation/representation) of an object. This distinguishes intuition from *sensatio* (sensation), which is subjective; likewise, intuition is distinguished from *cognitio conceptus* (conception), which is objective but mediated (or indirect). Space, time, and number are unique among intuitions in that they are "pure" in the Kantian sense that "no sensation is mixed in with the presentation,"[7] nor is any sense experience necessary for the experience of space, time, and number. The pure intuitions are not empirically observable in themselves (with no sensation at all), but constitute the basis for empirical intuitive perception itself.[8] These three are, as Kant would put it, intellectual concepts, rather than sensuous concepts—this distinction must not be forgotten, or we will have committed the fallacy of subreption.[9] As Caygill succinctly summarizes, space and time (and therefore number, for Cassirer) are pure *a priori* intuitions: "they are pure in so far as they cannot be derived from either [the power of] sensibility or understanding; a priori in that they anticipate, or are presupposed by, sensible perception; and intuitions in that they co-ordinate a manifold without subsuming it in the manner of a concept."[10]

The role of number for Cassirer (and thus myself), is a complex issue that requires further elaboration, but number may be preliminarily understood as a pure intuition along the same lines as space and time.[11]

Personalized Space: Responsibility

The first task is to establish a form of space that remains personal, unique, and does not fall into a pure field of anonymity and indifference. Such a space would be explicitly non-Cartesian; inasmuch as it is mathematizable, the most general description of such a space would be mereotopological rather than primarily algebraic—that is to say, it is a flexible realm of whole and part that is qualitatively variable, rather than merely quantitatively variable.[12] Personalized experience cannot survive a transformation into the sorts of objects that belong essentially to a depersonalized space (for example, Cartesian space), and so we must establish a new kind of spatiality in order to account properly for this type of personal experience.[13]

It is a simple matter to think of spaces and places that have personality: a church, a cafe, a mountain, a clearing in a forest, a small stream. Each of these might have a qualitative unity that announces itself as a unique, personalized space. The questions are, what is the quality of spatiality that supports and characterizes experiences of this type? How should we describe it? Specifically, how do we describe it without falling into other types of spatiality? In particular, we need to take care not to think of personalized space in terms of mythic space: the primary sense of mythic space arises out of a dichotomy of the world into sacred and profane—it is this *differential* movement that creates mythic space.[14] However, it does not seem necessary to an experience of personality that we should set the experience in such black and white opposition—it is misleading to say that a space gains personality by relegating opposing space to a region of the profane.

So what then is the *differential* element that articulates the pure intuition of space in creative fidelity? Not extension, not the sacred (scientific and mythic space, respectively[15]): we require a qualitative differential that provides for the perception of personalized experience, rooted in the symbolic function of creative fidelity. The differential element of personal space, I believe, is best named as *responsibility*.[16] Responsibility is what we mean by creative fidelity when we spatialize it, when we formalize it spatially. Personalized space is a nexus of topological regions of responsibility: a responsibility that emerges from creative fidelity. By responsibility I mean not merely that I am held accountable for this or that spatial object/region (although there is a sense that this is so), but also that this object elicits a "response" in me and "calls" me to act on its behalf.[17]

Thus it is not simply *I* who am responsible; it is also the personalized cultural world; responsibility is a *qualitative attribute of the objective space* within which personality exists—it is the "ability" of a personalized experience to elicit/demand a "response" in me.[18] Responsibility is the spatialized counterpart of Marcel's *disponibilité*; the space of responsibility is the region in which I must make myself "available" to respond.[19] To say that responsibility is the *differential* factor in personalized space means that on the ground of the form of creative fidelity, we perceive that object as occupying a region that either demands/elicits a response in you or does not. However, to posit the *differential* function is also to demand the *integrative* function: responsibility functions in both directions. That is to say, responsibility not only differentiates by integrating, it integrates by differentiating. Qualitative spatial wholes within personalized experience are experienced *as* wholes (integrated) on the basis of their differing demands for a response, or variations in responsibility. "This" object is perceived as separate from "that" because "this" object demands a response, but not "that" object. In the very process of distinguishing this from that, we introduce difference, but also integration (personal wholes). We have both the subjective/differential side of spatiality (my responsibility to the world) and the objective/integrative side of personal spatiality (a world populated by qualitative personal wholes who elicit a response in me).

Thus, the integrative/differential (objectivizing/subjectivizing) quality in a personalized spatial plurality is the quality of responsibility. A space is experienced as a region of responsibility when the person is acting on the ground of the personalized symbolic form that arises from creative fidelity; your church, your favorite restaurant, the spot where you proposed to your husband or wife—these spaces are not merely integrated/differentiated from other spaces by being "beside" another space or because it is "sacred" while other places are "profane."[20] To approach such spaces in these ways would be to remove them from the sphere of the personal. Rather, personalized spaces must exist within a horizon of responsibility—a responsibility that is an enduring manifestation of the creative fidelity that made them "available" *as personal*.[21] Personalized experience depends *logically* upon a pure intuition of personalized space, although that space always arises contemporaneously with such experience *empirically*. Personalized space of "responsibility" is one axis of the *form* of personalized intuition—not intuition generally, but rather that derived in particular from the personalizing function of creative fidelity.

I feel that my account would be incomplete without at least some attempt to present concrete examples of personalized experience in the style of the analysis I have developed. Therefore, I will briefly show how creative fidelity and the three axes of personalized intuition can be used to understand the cultural experience of personal meaning. I will give two examples (although many more could be provided): the first is a very obvious and easy starting place that hopefully will present itself naturally to the reader—the personalized experience of a wedding ring. The second example I will use is meant to be less obvious, and therefore to show the flexibility of the analysis of form and function I have developed—the second example is the personalized experience of a fictional character. I will outline this second example at the end of this chapter, while I will use the example of the wedding ring to illustrate each stage as I introduce it.

The choice of a wedding ring is a simple one when starting a consideration of personalized experience in the light of creative fidelity.[22] A wedding ring is a symbol of fidelity almost par excellence in modern American culture and is often considered to be an object of immense "personal" value—on the short list of objects that would need to be grabbed out of a burning house, for example. A wedding ring, either newly worn or passed down the generations, is imbued with a very definite personalized form of meaning that separates it (and perhaps even "elevates" it) from other similar forms of jewelry, precious metals, and the like. The wedding ring does not possess meaning that can be reduced to its economic value, nor can it be reduced to linguistic, mythic, or scientific forms of meaning (although these certainly exist). So then, how do we begin to speak about this particular form of meaning? What separates a personalized wedding ring from any number of seemingly identical objects—to the point that even if you purchased the "exact same" ring upon losing the original, you would still feel the loss, the distance in meaning between the first ring and its replacement?

According to the structure of analysis I have given, the spiritual energy that creates this personalized kind of meaning might be termed "creative fidelity"—a peculiar form of act that must rise beyond the level of mere constancy in order to confront and overturn the anonymity of other forms of cultural existence. The fidelity embodied in the ring must not just be a mere declaration of constancy (till death do us part, and so on)—it must be an opening up to an experience of this person as radically nonanonymous (negatively) and as available and present (positively). It is perhaps simultaneously a making oneself available even as it is also an *allowing* the partner to be available—and in the power of my own fidelity toward availability, I find that the meaning of my partner as present now becomes "available" to me. Such an act is hard to isolate in itself, as all actions of spirit must be, but we can feel the force of its effects as it shapes the cultural world around us.

One of those effects is in the personalization of some objects (in this case a ring) that are used to symbolically "reflect" my fidelity back to me—in the presence of the wedding ring, I become aware of my own free spiritual power toward fidelity (just as for Kant the experience of the sublime reveals my spiritual power of judgment to myself). My fidelity is thus "creative" of the meaning of this ring; a meaning that is simultaneously arbitrary (as all symbols are), and also radically integral to the existence of my life as meaningfully lived. Such personalized cultural symbols that have this reflective power are characterized in their intuitive appearance (I am arguing) by the presence of a spatiality of *responsibility*, a temporality of *hope*, and a numerality of *community*.

To intuitively experience a personalized wedding ring, to experience it as a personalized object in a personalized horizon (rather than as a linguistic object, economic object, mythic object, and so on), I enter into a peculiar form of spatiality. When considered personally, the ring is not spatialized in mathematical terms, or as a "sacred" object—it opens up a space of "responsibility." This kind of space of responsibility is the spatial manifestation of my creative fidelity—it opens up a spatial horizon of intuitive objects distinguished from one another on the basis of my responsibility.

Creative fidelity enters space as a "gathering" or "coalescence" of my responsibility—in committing myself, in making myself available, this ring "takes up space" and "looms large" on the plane of my responsibility. On the plane of responsibility, this ring occupies a space that need not correspond to the space it occupies on other spatial planes—the ring "takes up more" responsible space than it does mathematical space, for example. The ring is a concretion of responsibility in a plane of fluctuating responsibilities—it is a spatial manifestation of my responsibility, and it "responds" to me as such, becoming personalized and demanding to be seen as meaningfully in a personalized way. I am "responsible" for the maintenance of this object; this is both mundanely true (I mustn't drop it down the drain) and personally true (I must maintain the fidelity that makes this ring meaningful to me).

Personalized Time: Hope

Now that we have discussed the pure intuition of personalized space as governed by responsibility,[23] we can move on to a description of the pure intuition of personalized time—we should articulate the *form* of temporal personalized intuition. Just as personalized experience has its own sense of spatiality, it also has its own sense of temporality; not only can we experience the difference between that which is *spatially* personal (as a field of differential responsibility), and that which is not—we can also account for how personalized experience arises and expires it personalized time. The differential/integrative (subjective/objective) element of personalized time (that which projects the internal intuition of personality) is *hope*. Hope is what we mean by creative fidelity when we temporalize it.

Just as responsibility is linked to Marcel's notion of *disponibilité* (and therefore to creative fidelity, as the highest manifestation of "availability") we should not be surprised that *hope* is also fundamentally tied to *disponibilité*: this is true not only for our purposes in this work, but for Marcel himself.[24] As the form of personalized time, and therefore as that which arises from the symbolic function of creative fidelity, it makes sense that Marcel would have observed this connection between availability and hope, as well as between hope and temporality. Marcel writes: "This evening I have apprehended the nature of hope more clearly than I have ever done before. It always has to do with the restoration of a certain *living* order in its integrity. But it also carries with it the *affirmation of eternity* and eternal goods."[25] It would not be outrageous, I believe, to assert that the living order Marcel speaks of (that hope seeks to restore) coincides with the personalized cultural world I am articulating in this work: a world that is no longer "broken" in Marcel's sense. However, more immediately relevant is Marcel's observation of a fundamental link between hope and temporality—a temporality that Marcel characterizes as an orientation toward the eternal.

However, how can we talk about hope as a pure form of intuition in personalized experience if hope is oriented toward the eternal, and thereby almost seems to stand outside of temporality as it is experienced? For indeed, it is experienceable time that we seek—and not just any experienceable time, but that which provides for the existence of personalized experience. Are we forced to say that personalized experience stands outside of time or belongs exclusively to eternity? Let us consider the issue. In the first place, it is not necessary to align ourselves with Marcel on this issue; we could merely note that he does well to link hope to temporality, but that he fails to articulate the proper sense of temporality *found* in hope. However, before we dismiss Marcel, we should do our best to see the wisdom in his assertion that hope "carries with it the affirmation of eternity."

Strictly speaking, to say that hope affirms the eternal is not to say that the experience of hope is itself outside of moving time; indeed, Marcel's use of the term "restoration" in conjunction with hope indicates that hope functions in a world of process and experiential time. Additionally, we should realize that Marcel's sense of eternity is modified by the influence of Josiah Royce on his thinking. For Royce, as Dwayne Tunstall points out, "the Eternal is not a static, fixed entity."[26] As Royce elaborates:

> [It is] the endless whole of future time, as well as of past time, before them in one, not timeless, but time-inclusive survey, which embraces the whole of real life. And just such a survey, and just such a life, not timeless, but time-inclusive, constitutes the eternal, which is real, not apart from time, and from our lives, but in, and through and above all our individual lives.[27]

So then, we need to be careful not to remove the eternal from time, but rather to treat it as an immanent, maximal, ideal unfolding of the whole of temporal experience. Tunstall defines Royce's understanding of eternity as "(1) the dynamic, all-inclusiveness that preserves the past, experiences the present, and anticipates the future within itself and (2) an existential phenomenon wherein finite ethical individuals experience the divine whole and become participants in the universal community of the loyal."[28]

So then, given the above sense of eternity, which Marcel received from Royce, what would it mean to affirm the eternal from the standpoint of lived personalized time? Fidelity for Marcel, as an act of hope, means an openness and an availability to something that may transcend the finite, that may be more than that which demands a "response" in the present. When you make yourself available to a sick friend and let him or her know that you will return, you "commit" yourself in the act, and rise above the vicissitudes of time that induce such "anxiety" in us.[29] You have *hope* that your fidelity will stay the course in the future, that you will fulfill the act you have committed yourself to. Each act of fidelity, therefore, expresses a hope that your experiences (and you yourself) are not indeterminate or anonymous; that you are *here*, that you are *available*, and that you *will be* available. In this sense, hope reaches toward the dynamic eternal; it affirms that your availability is not conditional, will not waver with time—not because your availability is *removed* from time, but because it exists *ideally* within time. Whether or not such unwavering fidelity can be actually reached: who knows? However, there is hope, and hope at least must *affirm* such an ideal.

This emphasis on the "eternal" in a discussion of lived time may seem strange at first, but upon consideration, we recognize that there must be an element of the "permanent" in hope, or it is impossible to maintain as a fully articulated, dynamic temporal form. Kant makes this point perfectly clear:

> Hence all time relations (for simultaneity and succession are the only relations in time) are possible only in the permanent. I.e., the permanent is the substratum of the empirical presentation of time itself; all time determinations are possible only in this substratum. . . . Without this permanent, therefore, there is no time relation. Now time cannot itself be perceived. Therefore this permanent in appearances is the substratum of all time determinations. Hence it is also the condition for the possibility of all synthetic unity of perceptions, i.e., the possibility of experience; and all existence and all variation in time can only be regarded by reference to this permanent, as a mode of the existence of what is enduring and permanent.[30]

It is in this sense that Marcel's articulation of the orientation of hope to the eternal needs to be considered. This reaching toward the dynamic eternal is the *integrative* (objective) function of hope: that you *are*, in fact, your ideal self, the self who will always remain present and faithful to your sick friend, or that a beloved family member is always with you (ideally). Hope integrates the personal world in this temporal sense, as ideal unities in the eternal.

However, hope cannot include merely an orientation to eternal permanence. As a pure intuition, hope has both an integrative permanence and a sense of succession (that is grounded in that eternal ideal permanence)—otherwise known as duration. This sense of personalized duration is the way that hope functions as the *differential* (subjectivizing) element of personalized time. In hope, we extend ourselves beyond our present, even as we carry with ourselves the responsibility of past fidelity. Hope is what pushes us forward, it is the ek-static element.[31] Hope is the driving engine that encourages the growth of personalized experience, the temporal expansion of fidelity. The object is integrated in the ideal eternal, even as it is differentiated and expanded upon within a durational present. The tension between this differential and integrative function is the tension that subtends our personalized experience in its temporal mode.

As I have said, hope is what we mean by creative fidelity when we temporalize it. As a pure intuition of personalized experience, hope is the temporal ground of personality, and we cannot understand personalized experience without situating such experience within a temporality of hope. Hope is the form of time specific to creative fidelity; if we borrow temporal intuitions specific to other symbolic functions, we will distort the cultural world that creative fidelity *creates*, and we will be unable to account for personalized experiences.

To return to our example of the wedding ring, the ring moves through a temporal flux that is not measured in seconds, minutes, and so on—it moves through a timestream of "hope." Our statements concerning the space of responsibility find analogues in the temporal plane. The ring "occupies" a certain "time" in the ongoing unfolding of my hopeful being—the path that the ring cuts through mythic or mathematical time (perhaps becoming a sacred object, or tarnishing with age) is not the same path the ring cuts through hopeful time. The ring opens up a horizon of hope (differentially) that pushes unto the eternal, even as it is concretized (integratively) into a hopeful moment that must constantly renew itself through an ongoing act of fidelity. It is both eternal and ephemeral—the hope of everlasting fidelity intermingled with the hope of sustaining a momentary act of fidelity even into the next moment.

The wedding ring, experienced as a personalized object, exists in a temporality of this kind—even as the ring is distinguished from other objects by their relative lack of responsibility, the ring is distinguished from other objects by their relative lack of hopefulness (literally: the ring is "full" of hope, or even, as Cassirer says, symbolically "pregnant" with hope). By accounting for the variances in hope that we experience (between experience of the personal ring with non-personalized objects), we can trace the arc of the hopeful plane on which the ring exists as a personalized experience. The personality of the ring depends upon the maintenance of that hope (hope driven by the act of fidelity)—without hope the ring loses its personalized meaning, become a simple trinket no different than any other (no different at least in regard to its personalized meaning).

Personalized Number: Community

Just as creative fidelity has its own mode of spatialization and temporalization, it must have its own mode of numeralization if we are going to follow the format that Cassirer prefers in articulating a symbolic form of culture (at the representational stage, at least). Just as the form of language requires a different understanding of number than does the form of myth, creative fidelity requires its own mode of numeralization. The number function of creative fidelity should not be confused with the naming *power* of number to ground concrete individual intuitions (as in language)[32] or the mythic view of number according to which "each number has its own essence, its own individual nature and power,"[33] and certainly not with the view of number developed by objectivating knowledge in which numbers are purely significant and "nothing but an expression of conceptual relations"[34] that "serves primarily and essentially the purpose of reducing the concrete diversity of phenomena to the abstract and ideal unity of the 'grounds.'"[35] This is the essence of scientism.

It is easy enough to say what number should *not* be for the personalized form of creative fidelity, but how are we to understand the role of number positively as a pure intuition of creative fidelity—a "personalized number"? I believe that the personalized form of number is best understood as *community*.[36] That is to say: community is what we mean when we numeralize creative fidelity. Just as the spiritual act of creative fidelity creates a differential/integrative spatial field of responsibility, and a differential/integrative temporal field of hope, I believe that creative fidelity opens up a differential/integrative *numeral* field best described as *community*.

Community, like the other personalized pure intuitions, has a differential (subjectivizing) and an integrative (objectivizing) function. The integrative (objectivizing) function of community allows the symbolic agent (through the "availability" of creative fidelity) to "commune" and "communicate" literally with the personalized experience that is the "object" of their spiritual act of fidelity (hence Cassirer meets Marcel). The community logically becomes the objective manifestation of the integration of the numeralization of creative fidelity. If number *should* be interpreted as the dialectical sublation of space and time (a conclusion that I have argued against elsewhere), then community would still work well with such an interpretation since it would bring together the more temporal (hope) and spatial (responsibility) aspects of personalized experience—allowing the temporal hope to imbue the space of responsibility, and *vice versa*, as hoping and responsibility come together in a fully formed expression of spiritual activity.

While it is tempting to see space, time, and number in a dialectic of this sort (and there is certain evidence in Cassirer to support this reading), I think it is better to say that space, time, and number all contribute to the constitution of both the object of experience (through the integrating functions) and the subjective ego (through the differential functions). Hope is not simply subjective, space is not simply objective, and number is not simply the sublation of subject/object; each pure intuition centers and decenters along a particular axis. If we want to avoid an overly dialectical account, perhaps we should jettison (as an unnecessary heritage of Cartesianism) the Kantian notion of time as exclusively the form of inner sense, and space as exclusively the form of outer sense—I have suggested as much elsewhere. After all, Cassirer himself explores the way bodily orientation (seemingly subjective) contributes to spatial intuition.[37] And can we truly assert that *my* temporal experience (*my* hope) is *merely* or simply subjective, without having any effect on the world of "external" experience? While I cannot offer a full defense of this reading of Cassirer, I believe that he is best understood by avoiding recourse to notions of space as the exclusive form of outer sense and time as the exclusive form of inner sense.[38]

As such, even if it is tempting to submit to the possibility of this dialectical cleanliness (or negatively: abstraction), I believe that every pure intuition must feature a differential and an integrative function—a decentering as well as a centering. The same holds true for personalized number as community. The axis of number is somewhat harder for us to grasp than space and time, which have been more privileged historically. With the term "community," I hope to provide something familiar and concrete to grasp in the struggle to understand our numeric intuitions (in the same way that I believe "responsibility" and "hope" provide a familiar experience to ground our understandings of the intuitions of space and time). A numeric object is not a spatial object, nor is it a temporal object—its part/whole relations cannot be understood as side-by-sidedness or succession/duration. And yet numbers *do* have their own mode of "togetherness" (synthesis) and discursiveness (analysis)—and while it is common to understand these modes by analogy to space and time, such shifts in model necessarily introduce error into our understanding. While we *can* plot numbers on a spatial plane, or count them out in time, that does not mean that these are the forms of synthesis and analysis that properly belong to number.

I believe that an intuition of community can be understood as a numeric intuition of this sort—specifically, a numeric intuition proper to the domain of creative fidelity (and thus personalized experience). To find myself in community with a person (or object, place, and so on) represents a kind of togetherness that does not hinge on spatial proximity, and it represents a kind of "aloneness" that does not depend on temporal succession. In this way, it can be understood as a kind of numeric togetherness and aloneness—just as a number is in communion with other numbers even as it is thereby isolated from them. Specifically, community is a personalized form of number—it *is* personalized number. When you take a number and make it personal, you get a community. Creative fidelity as it numeralizes is literally a commune-ication.

Even as creative fidelity numeralizes us into an "objective" communion (not just among human beings, but also the community of place, object, and so on), we also become aware of those experiences that *do not* commune with us, which remain silent, or even object.[39] Even as community objectivizes our world through integrating communions, it also subjectivizes our world (as ego) by making us aware of the hidden character of communions of which we are not a part. This is the differential aspect of community. My assertion that the ego is subjectivized not *through* the communion but as a result of the *loss* of communion or the *absence* of communion is incredibly complex and potentially problematic. Marcel, Royce, Schelling, and many others have much to say on this issue—and I cannot fully address this question at the moment. While my "character" (a set of interests, hobbies, pastimes, memberships, and so on) is objectively developed in communion, my own subjectivity (radical subjectivity?) as an existential subject might not rise in communion. Just as for Marcel, my ideal self exists in eternal hope while I experience duration, so too does my ideal (fully realized, actual, objective) self exist in community, even as I find myself outside of a complete communion. Another way of saying this is that if I were to find myself fully actualized, in full communion with all possible communities/ objects of fidelity, I would no longer exist as a subjective consciousness.

To return to our ring example one last time, the numeric intuition of the wedding ring must also be accounted for. As creative fidelity numeralizes, it creates intuitive objects on the plane of what I have called "community." Thus, a wedding ring is not only an object pregnant with responsibility and hope, but also with community. It is traditional enough to see the meaning of the ring as "two becoming one," and this is in a sense true—but is not the entirety of community. For even as the ring symbolizes a synthesis of the parts into a whole communion, it is still a *communion*, which necessarily entails a lack of identity. The parts are brought into relation in a whole, but they are brought into that whole *as parts*. The discreteness of each person is not subsumed in the synthesis of the new community; the community exists only in the "pure equilibrium" of the parts *as parts* but *in communion*. Such is the demand of number: that the synthesis be purely equaled by the analysis, that the movements into whole and part are perfectly matched. Thus, the wedding ring has this dimension as well: it is pregnant with responsibility and hope, and also with this purely equal coming together of parts in communion.

A Further Concrete Example of Personalized Intuition: Alice in Wonderland

Now that we have described the specific ways that creative fidelity spatializes, temporalizes, and numeralizes, we have a sense of the "symbolic form" (in its representational stage): of that cultural horizon that accompanies the functional act of creative fidelity. Responsibility, hope, and community, as the expressions of the form of personalized intuition, are "conditions for the possibility" of personalized intuitive experience as we know it. Any personalized experience will therefore be differentiated from the anonymous, "non-personalized" along the three axes of responsibility, hope, and community.[40] While responsibility, hope, and community are the logical conditions for personalized intuitive experience, and are phenomenologically required elements of the description of personalized intuitive experience, they are not necessarily the actual creative ground of personalized experience; they are at least the structuralized elements that arise contemporaneously with personalized experience and allow it to function determinately (objectively) as a part of a personalized-horizon-and-cultural-world.

The ground of personalized experience is creative fidelity: the symbolic function, the act by which we create personalized experience and by which we simultaneously open the horizon of responsibility-hope-community. Whereas responsibility, hope, and community are analyzable as formal elements of our actual, determinate experience, creative fidelity is the ground of that experience, not precisely formative of it—creative fidelity can be experienced only "reflectively," in the experience of our creative power as it opens a world of responsibility, hope, and community, creating spaces, times, and numbers in which personalized experience takes root and grows.

I hope that the preceding discussion has helped to ground the phenomenology of personalized intuition that I have developed. I believe that a wedding ring is a useful choice in illustrating personalized intuition; the symbolic character of the ring is widely acknowledged, as is its personalized meaning—furthermore, the axes of responsibility, hope, and community are fairly easily applied to the ring, as they correspond to already familiar ways of interpreting the symbol. Therefore, now that I have established to some extent the phenomenological validity of my analysis, I would like to push to an intuition of personalized meaning that may not be as familiar to the reader, and may not *immediately* offer itself in terms of responsibility, hope, and community (although I will argue that with reflection these axes are vital to the understanding of the experience). The intuition I have in mind is that of a *fictional literary character.*

Perhaps this choice already raises questions in the mind of the reader. In what sense can we intuit an *imaginary* character under the domains of space, time, and number? Furthermore, what sense does it make to call such an imaginary object *personalized*? However, I think that with some consideration such objections can be seen as vulnerable to serious questioning. When we say that an object is "imaginary," what are we implying? Certainly, fictional characters are "real" as symbols, and they can be understood at both the expressive and conceptual levels—but can they be represented in intuition? To my mind, the answer is not only that they *can* be, but in fact they *must* if they are to develop symbolic meaning further than the basic expressive stage. If a fictional character (I am partial to such choices as Alice from *Alice in Wonderland*, Peter Pan, or King Arthur, but any character with sufficient personality will do) is capable of being conceptualized, then it stands to reason that such a character must also be intuited. What is important to realize is that intuition in space, time, and number does not demand something like "materiality." Of course, if we reduce objectivity to materiality, speaking of an imaginary character as intuited in space and time becomes nonsensical (because we have reduced our notion of space and time to one particular *form* of judgment). However, if we do not perform such a reduction, it becomes clear that a fictional character is just as objective (and therefore just as real) as any other cultural object/symbol. The materiality of an object has no determinate bearing on its status as a meaningful cultural symbol—even theoretical knowledge (scientifico-mathematico objectivating knowledge) is perfectly applicable to a literary character. Certainly myth, language, religion, art, and so on are also applicable in this case as well.

So then, if we can accept that "imaginary" cultural objects are just as susceptible to "intuitional" experience as any other cultural object, how should we understand these experiences as "personalized"? It is not a contentious proposition, it seems to me, that many people form intensely personal relationships with fictional characters and settings. The pleasure of encountering a beloved fictional character once more is the same personalized pleasure of visiting a childhood home, going to your favorite restaurant, or even putting on your wedding ring. Of course, I am speaking here only of characters that are actually *experienced* as personalized; there is nothing in the form of art or literature that necessitates personalized experience—it is perfectly acceptable to have an impersonal literary character, just as any artwork may be impersonal or personalized. Therefore, *if* a literary character is experienced as personalized, then the *meaning* of that personalized experience must come not from the artistic symbolic form itself, but as a result of creative fidelity overlapping with the artwork in this particular instance.

The same axes of responsibility, hope, and community that we used to understand the personalized intuition of a wedding ring are just as applicable in this case, to the personalized intuition of a literary character. Suppose we take the example of Alice from Lewis Carroll's *Alice in Wonderland* and *Through the Looking Glass*.[41] This is a classic story that has captured the minds of young and old since it was written, prompting a number of reinterpretations and representations, as well as a goodly amount of scholarly and literary output. What makes this character so fascinating? What makes this character so personalized as to "live" in a certain sense?

In the case of a literary character such as this, we can consider not just the creative fidelity of the author toward the character during the writing process, but also the fidelity of the reader to the character (in this case, generations of such readers). Furthermore, the characters themselves could display fidelity in the course of the story, which may also contribute to the personalization of any given character. Any of these sources of fidelity (from the author, the reader, or the character) may alone be enough to establish an experience of personality, but presumably, the more fidelity is enacted from each or all of these sources, the more personalized the character becomes. Hypothetically, the most personalized characters are more likely to feature fidelity in all three of these domains (author, reader, and character). For the moment, I will not seek to establish Carroll's fidelity during the creation process, although the familiar story of Charles Lutwidge Dodgson's (i.e., Lewis Carroll's) close relationship and repeated storytelling to the Liddell sisters (including Alice Liddell, the supposed basis for the character) seems to me an indisputable ground for the presence of fidelity. Similarly, I will not seek to establish the fidelity of the generations of readers of the work, although the enduring popularity of *Alice in Wonderland* also speaks to the fidelity of the readers of the work. Instead, I will attempt the more difficult (but potentially more interesting) task of asking: Does Alice herself display creative fidelity?[42]

At least as it concerns Alice's personalized meaning (not to speak of whatever linguistic, mythic, or other meanings she might have), Alice exists spatially in the field of responsibility. Alice demands a certain response in the reader; she exists within a certain space of responsibility. The character demands respect, and that demand is a concretion of responsibility on the relevant plane; not all characters elicit responsibility, but this one does—she bends or intensifies the field of responsibility. On this basis, some things are disrespectful to the character of Alice—you could not put her into a WWII narrative, for example, as to do so would be to disrespect the character herself. Carroll is responsible to Alice, the reader is responsible to Alice, and Alice herself must be responsible. There are a number of instances throughout the work where Alice must take responsibility: for the tarts, for the rattle, for the painted cards, for offending the queen, and so on. Whether it is right or wrong to expect Alice to take responsibility in any of these cases is beside the point, which Wonderland instinctively understands—the fact that she *does* take responsibility (or at least feels the call of responsibility) is key for transforming the alien and impersonal Wonderland into a personalized world.

Similarly, for those who experience her as personalized (whether Carroll or the reader), Alice exists within a temporal duration of hope. Alice's *own* hope, pushed to the maximal eternal, is Wonderland itself, as a horizon in which Alice finds herself (and I myself participate along with Alice). *Wonder* itself is the hope, and my fidelity to wonder sustains the hope inherent in Wonderland—not only does this allow for my own horizon of personalized hope, but it sustains Alice through her journey as well, leading her from wonder to wonder. Together we both hope; and it is this hope that characterizes the unique temporality of Wonderland. Even the Mad Hatter and crew, stuck at tea time, are eternally hopeful, and thus able to carry on in their usual merry fashion—it is this more than anything that shows that mechanical time is not the driving force here. Even stuck at tea time, time goes on; so long as that time is hopeful in character. Alice is unsure of herself, stuck between child and adult, but Wonderland teaches her that as long as hope exists, things will move along. Thus, as with responsibility, we find that Alice's personality arises out of a shared hope between Carroll, the reader, and Alice herself—Carroll and the reader's hope must be assumed, but Alice's hope is inherent in the fabric of Wonderland itself.

However, to experience Alice as personalized requires more than experiencing her on the planes of responsibility and hope; there must also be community and communion—between Alice and the reader, between Alice and Carroll, and between Alice and Wonderland. Just as Alice takes responsibility and learns to hope in Wonderland, she also forms community with the various inhabitants. When confronted with increasingly unusual circumstances, Alice maintains a natural curiosity and seeks to commune with the inhabitants of Wonderland. Even if the inhabitants are "mad," Alice struggles to form community with them, in a sense becoming slightly mad herself (perhaps manifesting as her continual inability properly to recite nursery rhymes, poems, and riddles). This drive to connect, to belong, to participate in a community, personalizes Wonderland for Alice, just as her taking responsibility and learning to hope does.

Tellingly, it is the moment that Alice feels herself "above" or superior to the community of Wonderland (during the trial of the knave of hearts) that Alice abruptly finds herself back in the regular world. "You're nothing but a pack of cards" she yells, and suddenly the court turns back into cards, and she wakes up from her "dream" beneath the tree. When she can no longer see herself as part of this Wonderland, she abruptly is not; all of the personalized experiences she has been through immediately become mundane—regular rabbits, the familiar sounds of farm animals, and so on. In that moment, Alice's responsibility, her hope, and her place in the community all vanish in an instant, simultaneously. To my mind, this is a wonderful example of Carroll's insight into the nature of creative fidelity. The reason that all of these vanish concurrently is that they are all nourished by the same stream, so to speak—creative fidelity. Without Alice's creative fidelity (manifested as her responsibility to the inhabitants, her continual hope, and her true presence in the community), Wonderland vanishes like a puff of smoke. The objects that constituted Wonderland (rabbits, cards, mice, tea parties, and so on) have not vanished, but their existence as personally meaningful has, in fact, vanished.

Notes

1. See the three volumes of the Philosophy of Symbolic Forms. For example, Ernst Cassirer, *The Philosophy of Symbolic Forms Volume One: Language*, translated by Ralph Manheim (Yale University Press: New Haven, 1955); emphasis mine. Hereafter *The Philosophy of Symbolic Forms* will be referred to as *PSF*, followed by the number of the volume, as in: *PSF1*. All references are to the Yale edition, translated by Manheim. The *PSF* was originally published in 1923, 1925, and 1929.

2. Maurice Merleau-Ponty, *Phenomenology of Perception*, translated by Donald A. Landes (Abingdon, Oxon: Routledge, 2012).

3. Remember Kant's distinctions among *Vorstellung* ("presentations") at CPR A320/B376: "Here is a chart of them. The genus is presentation as such (*repraesentatio*). Under it falls presentation with consciousness (*perceptio*). A perception that refers solely to the subject, viz., as the modification of the subject's state, is sensation (*sensatio*) [*Empfinding*]; an objective perception is cognition (*cognitio*). Cognition is either intuition or concept (*intuitus vel conceptus*). An intuition refers directly to the object and is singular; a concept refers to the object indirectly, by means of a characteristic that may be common to several things. A concept is either an empirical or a pure concept; and a pure concept, insofar as it has its origin solely in the understanding (not in the pure image of sensibility), is called notion. A concept framed from notions and surpassing the possibility of experience is an idea, or concept of reason." [Brackets mine] Immanuel Kant, *Critique of Pure Reason*, translated by Werner S. Pluhar (Indianapolis, IN: Hackett, 1996).

4. For more information on these points, please see my dissertation: "Creative Fidelity as a Personalized Symbolic Form of Culture," Southern Illinois University Carbondale, 2018. This article has been condensed and slightly modified from chapter 6 of that dissertation.

5. Following Cassirer, I am extending Kant's notion of intuition in the first Critique to a more contextualized account in which there would be a pure intuition of say, mythic space, and spaces belonging to every symbolic form, in addition to the pure intuition of space Kant outlines in relation to the Understanding.

6. Ernst Cassirer, *Kant's Life and Thought* (New Haven: Yale University Press, 1981), 193.

7. Immanuel Kant, *Critique of Pure Reason*, translated by Werner S. Pluhar (Indianapolis, IN: Hackett Pub., 1996) 106. A50/B74. See also Cassirer, *Kant's Life and Thought*, 102, 109.

8. For the meaning of basis for Cassirer, see Ernst Cassirer, *The Philosophy of Symbolic Forms Volume 4*, translated Donald Phillip Verene and John Michael Krois (New Haven: Yale, 1998).

9. "We may call fallacy of subreption (by analogy with the accepted meaning) the intellect's trick of slipping in a concept of sense as if it were the concept of an intellectual characteristic." Translator's note found in Kant, *Critique of Judgment*, 114, note 22. Pluhar is citing the *Inaugural Dissertation*, Ak II, 412.

10. Howard Caygill, *A Kant Dictionary* (Oxford: Blackwell, 1995), 372.

11. Indeed, Cassirer's use of number, whether as a pure intuition or something else entirely (and how this use relates to Kant) merits an entire work of its own. I will, unfortunately, only be able to address this point superficially in what follows. For more on this topic, please see chapter 6 of my dissertation, which features a fuller discussion of this topic.

12. Note the difference to Kant here, as personalized space is in this case allowed a qualitative intensity without recourse to a distinct categorical form.

13. Thinkers such as Husserl and Merleau-Ponty have made similar points, although I do not wish to link explicitly the personalized world I seek to articulate with Husserl's "lifeworld," or similar ideas in Merleau-Ponty, however obvious the implicit connection may be. See Edmund Husserl, *The Crisis of European Sciences and Transcendental Phenomenology: An Introduction to Phenomenological Philosophy*, tr. David Carr (Evanston: Northwestern University Press, 1970). See also Maurice Merleau-Ponty, *Phenomenology of Perception*, translated by Donald A. Landes (Abingdon, Oxon: Routledge, 2012).

14. See *PSF2* and Mircea Eliade, *The Sacred and the Profane: The Nature of Religion*, translated by Willard R. Trask (New York: Harcourt, Brace & World, 1959).

15. I use sacred here as a technical term to refer to the differential element in mythic space. There may be more to the sacred than mythic space.

16. My usage is perhaps evocative of William Ernest Hocking's "response theory" as a means of demonstrating the reality of other "persons." However, there are a number of significant differences between my usage and Hockings: the first being that I do not seek to claim that personalized experience (and responsibility as the spatial form of that) is a validation of a social experience of other persons. The second difference being that personalized objects in a space of responsibility are not themselves the site of the response, as Hocking describes—instead, they are the site of the "call" that brings forth a response in me. I say that this responsibility is an attribute of the object, because it is the object that has the "ability" to evoke a response, and not the other way around. For Hocking's usage of response, see: William Ernest Hocking, *The Meaning of God in Human Experience* (New Haven: Yale University Press, 1912), 248–49.

17. One of course may be invited to think of the work of Jean-Louis Chretien here, as well as others: Emmanuel Levinas or Jean-Luc Marion, perhaps. How related my usage of this formulation is to the work of others with a similar sense is open to debate. Please see the bibliography for relevant works.

18. Seen from the objective standpoint, understood as the integrative standpoint. My responsibility is also radically my own, when taken subjectively, or from the differential standpoint. For all three pure intuitions, the "subjective" side will be found in the differential function, and the "objective" in the integrative.

19. Note that my use of responsibility in this technical sense is not shared by Marcel, who uses the term in a relatively straightforward manner. However, while the term is my own, I believe the concept it represents would not be foreign to Marcel or his philosophy.

20. Cassirer is unclear how we should understand the sacred and the profane, leaving the terms undefined. However, we need to remember that myth is governed by the principles of transmutation and emotional identity, in which identity is maintained as long as there is a consistency-of-feeling tone. Thus, a tree that is cut down and made into a door has the same powers as the original tree, and a lock of hair is tied to its original owner no matter the distance between them. These objects are linked in mythic space and time in a way that they need not be in personalized experience. We do not demand the same responsibility in how we treat a lock of hair as in how we treat a person, and a beloved tree does not demand the same response once it has been turned into lumber. Personality is not so easily transferable as mythic feeling tones are; a new act of creative fidelity may be necessary, and a new responsibility.

21. Available in the sense of Marcel's *disponibilité*.

22. Of course, I am only addressing those instances where a wedding ring actually IS experienced as personalized. There are plenty of instances in which a wedding ring would not be experienced as such, and there is nothing that necessitates that we experience the object along this symbolic form.

23. Governed in the sense that it provides the limits of personalized space, as well as the structure that allows for concentration of personality.

24. "Disponibilité is realized not only in the act of charity but also in hope." Marcel, *Creative Fidelity*, tr. Robert Rosthal (New York: Farrar, Strauss, 1964), 47. See also his discussion (p. 77) of the tie between hope and sacrifice as a form of *disponibilité*: "There is not and cannot be any sacrifice without hope, and hope is suspended in the ontological realm."

25. Gabriel Marcel, *Being and Having: An Existentialist Diary*, tr. Katherine Farrar (New York: Harper and Row, 1965), 75. Italics my own.

26. Dwayne Tunstall, *Yes, But Not Quite* (New York: Fordham, 2009), 47.

27. Josiah Royce, *Sources of Religious Insight* (New York: Octagon Books, 1977), 160.

28. Tunstall, *Yes, But Not Quite*, 50.

29. "When I look at my own deepest experience, it seems to me that in every such case, we are conscious of being fixed within a zone or determinate scale, in an anxiety which is itself essentially indeterminate. . . . [T]his anxiety is surely the agony of a creature living in time, the agony of feeling one's-self at the mercy of time." Marcel, *Being and Having*, 73.

30. Kant, *Critique of Pure Reason*, 254. A183/B226–27.

31. To use Heideggerian terminology.

32. See for example, *PSF2*, 141.

33. *PSF2*, 142.

34. *PSF2*, 141.

35. *PSF2*, 143. A role all three of the pure intuitions (space, time, and number) play for pure cognition, as Cassirer states immediately before the cited section.

36. As with responsibility and hope, this term is chosen as being well-suited to the philosophy of Marcel, so as to cohere well with the phenomenological analysis of creative fidelity that forms the basis for this symbolic form. Community was an important concept central for Josiah Royce (the "beloved community") and through Royce is a formative concept for Marcel as well.

37. And Merleau-Ponty will later make a similar point, see Merleau-Ponty, *The Phenomenology of Perception*.

38. For a more thorough discussion, please see chapter 6 of my dissertation.

39. As expressed by Lyotard's concept of the *le différend*, for example: Jean-François Lyotard, *The Differend: Phrases in Dispute*, translated by Georges Van Den Abbeele (Minneapolis: University of Minnesota Press, 1988). The things that actively object are perhaps less important than the question of the silent, nonobjecting.

40. For the purpose of the present analysis. As mentioned above, other articulations may be available, each suited to specific aims.

41. Lewis Carroll, *The Annotated Alice: Alice's Adventures in Wonderland and Through the Looking Glass* (New York: Wings Books, 1960). This edition features an introduction and scholarly annotations by Martin Gardner. *Alice's Adventures in Wonderland* was first published in 1865, and *Through the Looking Glass* was published in 1871.

42. It is a complex question to ask: can a character be experienced as personalized on the basis of their own fidelity? If neither the author nor myself have engaged in creative fidelity toward the character, can I experience the character as personalized on the basis of their own fidelity? This question is complex not only due to the nature of the imaginary characters being addressed, but because of the larger implications for the question of interpersonal phenomenology. Which is to say, if I see someone displaying fidelity, does that personalize them in my experience, even if I have not enacted any fidelity to them of my own will? Does the fidelity of another person demand or create fidelity within myself (something of a call, or the Levinasian "face" of the other)? I have explicitly set aside these kinds of questions for the present work, but they are intriguing.

Bibliography

Carroll, Lewis. *The Annotated Alice: Alice's Adventures in Wonderland and Through the Looking Glass*. New York: Wings Books, 1960.

Caygill, Howard. *A Kant Dictionary*. Oxford: Blackwell Publishers, 1995.

Cassirer, Ernst. *An Essay on Man: An Introduction to a Philosophy of Human Culture*. New Haven: Yale University Press, 1944.

———. *Kant's Life and Thought*. Translated by James Haden. New Haven: Yale University Press, 1981.

———. *Language and Myth*. Translated by Susanne K. Langer. New York: Dover Publications, 1946.

———. *The Logic of the Cultural Sciences*. Translated by S. G. Lofts. New Haven: Yale University Press, 2000.

———. *The Myth of the State*. New Haven: Yale University Press, 1946.

———. *The Philosophy of Symbolic Forms Volume One: Language*. Translated by Ralph Manheim. Yale University Press: New Haven, 1955.

———. *The Philosophy of Symbolic Forms Volume Two: Mythical Thought*. Translated by Ralph Manheim. New Haven: Yale University Press, 1955.

———. *The Philosophy of Symbolic Forms Volume Three: The Phenomenology of Knowledge.* Translated by Ralph Manheim. New Haven: Yale University Press, 1957.

———. *The Philosophy of Symbolic Forms Volume Four: The Metaphysics of Symbolic Forms.* Edited by John Michael Krois and Donald Phillip Verene. New Haven: Yale University Press, 1998.

———. *Symbol, Myth, and Culture: Essays and Lectures of Ernst Cassirer, 1935–1945.* Edited by Donald Phillip Verene. New Haven: Yale University Press, 1979.

Chrétien, Jean-Louis. *The Call and the Response.* Translated by Anne Davenport. New York: Fordham University Press, 2004.

Eliade, Mircea. *The Sacred and the Profane: The Nature of Religion.* Translated by Willard R. Trask. New York: Harcourt, Brace & World, 1959.

Heidegger, Martin. *Being and Time.* Translated by J. Macquarrie & E. Robinson. New York: Harper & Row, 1962.

Hocking, William Ernest. "Marcel and the Ground Issues of Metaphysics" *Philosophy and Phenomenological Research* 14 (1954): 439–69.

———. *The Meaning of God in Human Experience.* New Haven: Yale University Press, 1912.

Husserl, Edmund. *The Crisis of European Sciences and Transcendental Phenomenology: An Introduction to Phenomenological Philosophy.* Translated by David Carr. Evanston: Northwestern University Press, 1970.

Kant, Immanuel. *Critique of Judgment.* Translated by Werner S. Pluhar. Indianapolis: Hackett, 1987.

———. *Critique of Pure Reason.* Translated by Werner S. Pluhar. Indianapolis: Hackett, 1996.

———. *Critique of Practical Reason.* Translated by Werner S. Pluhar. Indianapolis: Hackett, 2002.

Lévinas, Emmanuel. "Martin Buber, Gabriel Marcel, and Philosophy." In *Martin Buber*, edited by H. Gordon. New York: Ktav Publishing, 1984, 305–24.

———. *Totality and Infinity. An Essay on Exteriority.* Translated by Alphonso Lingis. The Hague: Martinus Nijhoff Publishers, 1979.

Lyotard, Jean-François. *The Differend: Phrases in Dispute.* Translated by Georges Van Den Abbeele. Minneapolis: University of Minnesota Press, 1988.

Marcel, Gabriel. *Being and Having.* Translated by Katherine Farrer. Boston: Beacon Press, 1951.

———. *Creative Fidelity.* Translated by Robert Rosthal. New York: Farrar, Strauss, 1964.

———. *Homo Viator*, trans. Emma Crauford: Chicago: Henry Regnery, 1951.

———. *Metaphysical Journal*, trans. Bernard Wall. Chicago: Henry Regnery, 1952.

———. *The Mystery of Being.* 2 Vols. Chicago: Henry Regnery, 1960. Vol. I: *Reflection and Mystery*, trans. G. S. Fraser; Vol. II: *Faith and Reality*, trans. R. Hague.

———. *Royce's Metaphysics*, trans. V. & G. Ringer. Chicago: Henry Regnery, 1956.

———. "Theism and Personal Relationships." *Cross Currents* 1, no. 1 (1950): 38–45.

Marion, Jean-Luc. *Being Given: Toward a Phenomenology of Givenness.* Translated by Jeffrey Kosky. Stanford, CA: Stanford University Press, 2002.

Merleau-Ponty, Maurice. *Phenomenology of Perception.* Translated by Donald A. Landes. Abingdon, Oxon: Routledge, 2012.

Schilpp, Paul Arthur, ed. *The Philosophy of Ernst Cassirer* (Library of Living Philosophers Vol. 6). Evanston, IL: Library of Living Philosophers, 1949.
Schilpp, Paul A., and Hahn, Lewis E., eds. *The Philosophy of Gabriel Marcel* (Library of Living Philosophers 17). La Salle, IL: Open Court, 1984.
Skidelsky, Edward. *Ernst Cassirer: The Last Philosopher of Culture*. Princeton: Princeton University Press, 2008.
Tunstall, Dwayne A., *Yes, But Not Quite: Encountering Josiah Royce's Ethico-Religious Insight*. New York: Fordham, 2009.

Chapter 12

The Comfort of Things

Personal Objects, Possession, Dwelling, and the Desire to Be God in Sartre and Levinas

JAMES McLACHLAN

Editor's Note: The first four chapters of this part, ending with chapter 12, can be read as in dialogue with one another: they discuss the concept of personal objects from a set of related methodologies (e.g., German materialism, American idealism, phenomenology, existentialism). This chapter introduces figures such as Sartre and Levinas into that conversation and nicely rounds out the discussion, both returning to earlier themes and introducing new ones (specifically: the relationship between personal objects and a human desire to be God). This set of four chapters will provide a general theoretical basis as we move into more specific applications: two chapters on economic themes, two on aesthetic themes, and two on the ethics of bodies.

Sartre and Levinas both argue the reality of the otherness of the Other as another self-consciousness is immediately available to us. Both are humanists in the French tradition, and as such, critical of the tendency toward the personification of things, that things take personal characteristics in cultural traditions. For each, thinking of an object as a person is a mistake ontologically for Sartre, ethically for Levinas. While each is critical of the personing of things, each would also admit that it is the inevitable result of being-in-the-world, of human projects and dwelling

For Levinas, critique of the personing of things is softened by traditions within Judaism that personify certain Talmudic texts. Levinas speaks of being-in-the-book as an essential element of human existence. But even here, Levinas would only allow this because of the text's relation to human creativity and the discursive community that centers around the texts. To understand how Sartre and Levinas approach objects and the personification of objects, it is necessary to examine how each thinks about the human appropriation of things. One of the most interesting comparisons between Sartre's and Levinas's descriptions of the relation to the Other is that for Sartre it is in my relation to the Other that I receive, my solidity, my being, where for Levinas it is the Other who really activates my freedom.

For both Sartre and Levinas, possession, first, represents an effort to escape and then to protect the self from either the positive in-itself of being (Sartre) or the "anonymous rustling of the *there is* . . ." (Levinas)[1] For both, more darkly, possession is a defense mechanism against the Other, who threatens my security in the world. In this sense I might personify an object. I can make it my own while also endowing it with a personality, that only through self-deception, I could see as completely independent of my own will.

For Sartre, possession of objects infuses them with our being and defends us from the Other with whom we are almost always in conflict. It is as if we expand ourselves through our bodies to our things. The things are extensions of us. But this is an impossible blending of the in-itself-for-itself similar to that projection of human desire called God. I labor on things, I create things, to make them my own. While positively, things can resist my will they do so in quite a different way than does the Other. Things make up my surroundings I can imagine they are my world. But the Other is the hole through which my world is drained; that can become her world, my world is lost in the battle for its meaning.

For Levinas, "This fathomless obscurity of matter is presented to labor as resistance and not as the face to face."[2] The object resists us, but it is not the Other who resists my appropriation completely. I can use the object; it makes up my surroundings. The creative activity of the human being can pull something out of time into representation. This allows for us to elude the irrationality anonymous being, of the "there is," but also the challenge of the face of the Other. "Possession removes beings from change."[3] Emerging from the meaninglessness of brute being, the "there is," the self is separated from anonymity through enjoyment of existing, bathing, in constant experience: eating, drinking, sitting in the sun, labor. To protect enjoyment, we create dwellings against the elements in an effort in ensure the continued enjoyment of the things we now possess.

For Sartre, the human condition is characterized by the desire to be God. This is not only expressed by the effort to create the in-itself-for-itself, to unite facticity and transcendence in an impossible identity, to achieve the impossible goal of being capable of both change and permanent perfection. The desire to be God is also always related to the brute existence, which is the current object of desire. We desire to possess an object, to make it personal, to make it ours. This object may be a bit of bread, a weapon, an automobile, the meaning of a cultural object, or even another human being. Even an object that exists obscurely and has not yet been realized is still an object of desire as, for example, when an artist wishes to create a work of art, when a critic or thinker interprets a text.

Sartre maintains that the desire to create is reducible to our desire to possess and, thus, the desire to be God. If I create a painting it is because I wish to be the origin of its concrete existence. Its existence in part interests me in the measure that I have created it and the link of creation that I have established gives me a right of property upon the creation. Through it I've justified my own existence. It is not simply that something is brought to exist, it is brought to exist by me. Just as God has a right of property on His creation, I have a right over what I have made. It is mine and of me. The object owes its existence to me. Because the object exists by my act, my existence gains a type of necessity that it did not have before. I am the necessary being for that object that I have created. God is the Feuerbachian-like projection of our desire. God's act of creation is the supreme example of possession because God has not only created the individual object but the very material that it was made from so the object is absolutely dependent on God for its being. God is the symbol of the fulfillment of human desire, for God possesses His creation completely and his existence is necessary for the existence of all His creations.

I hope to delineate the similarities and differences between Levinas's, and Sartre's approaches to possession and personal objects how the relation to the object does not constitute the otherness of the face of the other person.

Sartre: Cartesian Freedom, the Desire to Be God, and the Awareness of Infinity

To understand the personification of objects, and its relation to the Sartrean desire to be God and Levinassian descriptions of the drive to totalization it is necessary to explain the relation of each philosopher to the Cartesian understanding of infinity, which will elucidate Sartre's notion of freedom and Levinas' description of infinity and its relation to the Other.

Both Sartre and Levinas appeal to Descartes's discussion of God in the third mediation to explain important elements of their central claims. For Sartre, this is a Cartesian understanding of negative freedom and for Levinas, infinity. For both "God" is present in us in a way similar to Descartes's argument that God must exist because the idea of "infinity" is already "in the mind." The irony here is that Sartre's God, which cannot exist, is more traditionally theistic than Levinas's God who "comes to mind." Where Levinas focuses on the idea of infinity in us which will reflect the height from which the Other comes to us, Sartre focuses on perfection as completion, on God as the complete being without lack. In both cases we are led to the relation to the Other and objects in the world that we attempt to make our own in order to protect us against the challenge of the Other.

Sartre establishes the existence of the first type of being, Being-in-Itself, not through phenomenological analysis but through an appropriation of Descartes's version of the ontological argument. The cogito proves, for Descartes, the existence of God because human beings exist in doubt, and this split in their knowledge implies imperfection. But they have within them at least an implicit understanding of perfection. According to Descartes, this idea of perfection cannot come from human beings alone; being imperfect beings, it must have come to them from beyond, from God. Ironically, Sartre uses much the same argument to show God cannot exist. Consciousness is an imperfect form opposed to what it stands before. It's intentional and thus a lack of certainty, a dependence on something beyond it, on being-in-itself. But Sartre also maintains human beings have an *a priori* conception of God. It is not the effort to explain the great spectacles of nature or the power of society that led man to invent God, but, "God" is the symbol through which humans gives voice to what they desire. However, Sartre argues God is a "magical" entity that that is the projection of the desire of consciousness for totality. God has the totality of Being-in-Itself. God is what God is. God is changeless, eternal. But such a being that coincides completely with itself cannot be intentional, cannot be conscious. The fundamental lack of totality in us intends some final unity. This lack announces God in our hearts as the fundamental human project: we try to imitate God; we try to be God. "Man is the being whose project is to be God."[4] God is a projection of our deepest desire. But to be human, to be conscious, is to be in time. To change, precisely not to be a totality. It is, rather, to lack totality.

Sartre's interpretation of the Cartesian cogito, and the isolated and negative nature of consciousness that it implies, is at the heart of his interpretation of freedom. The way he interprets the cogito through the ontological split of the in-itself and for-itself leads directly to his philosophical anthropology. Consciousness, as negative freedom, attempts to break out of its individual negativity toward a positive creation of totality. Consciousness aims to be both in-and-for-itself. This is the desire to be God. There are as many projects as there are human beings, but each project is the expression of the individual's desire for totality, and, at the same time, the ability for spontaneous activity that is beyond totality. The individual demonstrates her fundamental choice of how she desires to be and expresses this original choice in particular terms.⁵ The desire to be God is never constituted as such. Only in each particular situation does the project reveal itself. The desire to be God always realizes itself as a desire to be in a certain manner and expresses itself in countless different projects that make up conscious life.⁶

All human projects demonstrate that the for-itself is its own lack of being. What consciousness, human being-for-itself, lacks is the in-itself-for-itself; a magical entity that would completely encompass both positivity, impassivity, and permanence on one side, and, freedom, negativity, relativity, and consciousness on the Other. This magical entity, an impossibility. The for-itself erupts into being as the negation of the pure positivity of the in-itself; but that negation defines itself as projection toward the in-itself.⁷ Human consciousness projects itself in a project to complete itself. A project that is doomed to fail. Sartre describes the failure of the desire to be God in one of the most famous passages in *Being and Nothingness*.

> Each human reality is at the same time a direct project to metamorphose its own For-itself into an In-itself-For-itself and a project of the appropriation of the world as a totality of being-in-itself, in the form of a fundamental quality. Every human reality is a passion in that it projects losing itself so as to found being and by the same stroke to constitute the In-itself which escapes contingency by being its own foundation, the ens causa sui, which religions call God. Thus, the passion of man is the reverse of that of Christ, for man loses himself as man in order that God may be born. But the idea of God is contradictory and we lose ourselves in vain. Man is a useless passion.⁸

That line "Man is a useless passion" gives us the sense that existentialism is a pessimistic philosophy, but this is to forget that Sartre referred to *Being and Nothingness* as an eidetics of bad faith. Only in so far as we try to make ourselves gods are we a useless passion. Simone de Beauvoir made much of the idea that we might be a useless passion but we are still a passion. A passion to create value and work to allow others to do the same.⁹ This two-edged interpretation of a famous Sartrean line carries over to another famous Sartrean phrase "Hell is other people." In bad faith we see the Other as that being who reminds us that we are not God (which is actually a good thing). The Other is also that being who gives us our being, who defines us.

Like Descartes philosophers have worried about the problem of other minds Descartes thought the cogito can't be doubted I could doubt the that others are thinking like I am. Sartre and Levinas have similar approaches to other persons that transcend their phenomenological methods. Both think we have an immediate relation with the Other. This is different from Heidegger's notion of *mitsein* (Being-with). The Other is not *zuhanden*. The being before me, the Other, is part of the structure of our existence and also transcends it. Sartre thought that through certain "privileged emotions" like shame we are aware of the Other. We are ashamed before someone. "Shame is by nature recognition" of the freedom and power of the Other.

"The Other looks at me and as such he holds the secret of my being, he knows what I am."[10]

For all the conflict here, it is the Other who grants me my being! I become "someone" in the mirror of the Other. S/he stops my flight. "The upsurge of the Other touches the for-itself in its very heart. By the Other and for the Other the pursing flight is fixed in in-itself. . . . For the Other I am irremediably what I am, and my very freedom is a given characteristic of my being. Thus, the in-itself recaptures me at the threshold of the future and fixes me wholly in my very flight, . . ."[11] Sartre's uses the example of being alone in a park. Things group themselves around me. But then the Other appears and suddenly. things group themselves around her. This is an orientation of the world and the things in it "flees me.[12] It is as if the Other is a "black hole" that drains my point of view away. What I do next is to reduce the Other to just another object.

The Other looks at me. This conflict is the origin of the idea that "hell is others." I am frozen as an "ego object." A thing in the world of the Other. I am no longer the master of the situation." I have become a "transcendence transcended." "I perceive myself losing my freedom in order to become a *thing*, but my nature is—over there, outside my lived freedom—as a given attribute of this being which I am for the Other."[13]

Cartesian Infinity in Levinas and the God "Who Comes to Mind"

Levinas also uses the discussion of infinity in the Descartes's Third Meditation to lay out central notions in this thought. But here it is Descartes's examination of infinity and how the idea comes to mind through the awareness of infinity. There is a similarity here to Sartre's discussion of the awareness of the Other and the passivity before the Other. Sartre's idea of freedom in relation to the Other is the negative image of Levinas. For Sartre, it is the Other who gives us our being, though not our nothingness, not our freedom. For Levinas the Other activates my freedom.

> This relation of the same with the Other, where the transcendence of the relation does not cut the bonds a relation implies, yet where these bonds do not unite the same and the other into a Whole, is in fact

fixed in the situation described by Descartes in which the "I think" maintains with the Infinite it can nowise contain and from which it is separated a relation called "idea of infinity." . . . But the idea of infinity is exceptional in that its ideatum surpasses its idea, whereas for the things the total coincidence of their "objective" and "formal" realities is not precluded; we could conceivably have accounted for all the ideas, other than that of Infinity, by ourselves. . . . The distance that separates ideatum and idea here constitutes the content of the ideatum itself. Infinity is characteristic of a transcendent being as transcendent; the infinite is the absolutely other. The transcendent is the sole ideatum of which there can be only an idea in us; it is infinitely removed from its idea, that is, exterior, because it is infinite.[14]

The key here is to note also the striking difference between Sartre and Levinas in their use of Descartes and the relation to the Other. In the relation to the Other for Sartre it may be the case that, like God, the Other gives me my being. In this sense, I am passive before the Other, but notice here that, like the all-seeing eye of God, the Other turns me into a thing, a transcendence transcended. It is at this point the negative freedom that I am comes to the fore. I in turn reify the Other who challenges my attempt to solidify the world as my possession in my desire to be God. This is why, in *Being and Nothingness*, Sartre characterizes all human relationships as conflictual, as war. This is quite like Levinas's claim that violence is done to the Other to make her fit into my total vision of the world. It is to be remembered, however, that Sartre characterized *Being and Nothingness* as an "eidetics of bad faith" and attempted to offer an alternative in the unpublished *Notebooks for an Ethics*. But notice the difference in the reading of Descartes. In his essay "Cartesian Freedom" Sartre uses Descartes's Augustinian understanding of God as the wholly positive author of the world and then in *Being and Nothingness* leaves phenomomenological analysis to employ Descartes use of the ontological argument to prove the pure positivity of the in-itself and thus disprove the existence of God.[15] (God can't be conscious because Sartre has shown phenomenologically that consciousness involves intentionality and hence negativity). Levinas's use of Descartes is quite different. Levinas claims that "the idea of infinity is exceptional in that its ideatum surpasses its idea" and it is the "distance that separates ideatum and idea here constitutes the content of the ideatum itself. Infinity is characteristic of a transcendent being as transcendent; the infinite is the absolutely other."[16] Sartre, on the other hand, is still trapped in the history of Western ontotheology, with the in-itself sitting in for the all-powerful, all-positive God and human freedom, the for-itself, as the negative and ontologically illusory human rebellion and freedom. It is to Sartre's credit that, like Ivan Karamazov, he chose to remain with the poor despised creatures, but in *Being and Nothingness*, at least, he only offers the negative mirror image of that God. Sartre's atheism is an inverse theism. The in-itself that is proved by the ontological argument is the brute absurdity of being. Levinas claims atheism an important moment in achieving a "religion for adults." Levinas doesn't leave God in heaven at the summit of the Great Chain of Being, rather God comes to mind in our experience of the infinite in the face of the Other.

Levinas's understanding of Descartes's notion of infinity is quite different than Sartre's, as is his understanding of the place of God in the philosophical/theological tradition. For Levinas, the idea of the infinite breaks with the structure of conceptualization. It is not ontological but ethical. Two features of Descartes's view are significant: first, the idea of the infinite is prior to the idea of self; and second, the infinite apprehended as a content exceeds any idea we may have of it.[17] Levinas understands the argument from infinity in the Third Meditation to point to the awareness of the Other, in us. Infinity here means that the Other can never be contained in any image I make of her. In his important essay "God and Philosophy" Levinas begins with the story of the tyranny of Western philosophy as ontology, which would compel all thought to justify itself before it.[18] Being is the center of Western philosophy. Thought has not thought beyond (*au dela*) the movement of being (*geste d'etre*). "The dignity of being the ultimate and royal discourse belongs to Western philosophy because of the strict coinciding of thought, in which philosophy resides, and the idea of reality in which this thought thinks." At the beginning of Western philosophy, Parmenides claimed: "It is the same, namely thinking and being." Levinas's claim is that this is the standard notion of the philosophical tradition whether in Hegel's famous creed that the real and the rational and the rational was the real, or Heidegger's complaint that the tragedy of philosophy has been its forgetfulness of Being. The Other is to be reduced to the same in Being and in thought.[19]

He contrasts this impersonal Being with the personal God of the Bible narratives. Philosophically and theologically, this personal God must be situated within Being's move so God is the greatest possible being. Levinas claims that it has not been an accident that, for all its talk about transcendence, philosophy has been the destruction of transcendence. Rational theology is ontology. This is what Yehhuda Helevi and Pascal meant when they claimed the God of Abraham, Isaac, and Jacob is not the God of the philosophers. What Levinas seeks is an escape, an alternative to the tradition of Western ontology. One could say, of course, that the God in the Bible does not make sense. Such a God cannot be thought. The concept of God is not problematical because it is not a concept at all. Levinas wants to escape Being. To move to something beyond the move of being, beyond being, beyond ontology. This is the meaning of his attempt to make ethics first philosophy over ontology. This would be beyond the language of subject and object. This is why, for Levinas, personal objects are not persons. If one translated the encounter with the Other in ontological language would it be a "preamble to being?" He doubts this opposition of the beyond and the ontological constitutes an alternative.[20] When I represent the Other to myself she is petrified and gathered in a presence, "into a move of being' "[21] Transcendence is transformed into immanence.

It is possible the word "God" came to philosophy from religious discourse like propositions related to a theme, which is to say, as an unveiling, as the manifestation of a presence. But even here, Levinas says that from the beginning we treat the religious being as interpreted through our experience, not through the infinity of her otherness. We interpret God of whom we think we have had the experience in terms of Being, of presence, and of immanence.[22] This contrasts with how Levinas understands the encounter with the Other as an encounter with infinity. Part of Levinas respect for Descartes's discovery of the "I think" is that he has seen it as a rupture with the immanence of being. The idea of the infinite comes to mind, carried along in the rupture. It contains the idea of God as the noncontained *par excellence*. This idea explodes the formal reality of cognition, it shatters the frame of thought.[23] The idea of God is God in me and already God breaking the consciousness of is the ideas. Following Descartes, Malbranche claimed the idea of God—or God in us—cannot be comprehended, does not let itself be comprehended in thought.[24] The idea of the infinite that has "come to mind" is from beyond my thought, my perception. It is in an awareness, I am passive in relation to it, a passivity beyond all passivity. In this sense, it is an awakening. This is what Levinas means when he says it comes to us from a height. Levinas criticizes the dialogical Personalists, Gabriel Marcel and Martin Buber, for seeing the I-Thou relation as something like a mystical experience. Here the recognition of the Other is as an equal within a structured dyad of being. For this reason, Buber can have an I-thou encounter with a tree or a stone. This is no possible for Levinas. Ironically, Levinas's understanding of the inequality of the encounter with the Other is much closer to what Sartre describes as "Being-for-Others." The Other turns me into a passivity. Consider Sartre's example of a man in the park walking along, the park arranges itself around him. It is no longer mine but now is his, his experience. The Other disrupts my experience. The arrival of the Other from beyond his little world is an upsetting disruption. He goes from active creator to passive recipient of something, he knows not what, but he is aware he is now an object in the Other's world. This is a very different idea of God than the one Sartre described by the desire to be God as the filling out of my project, the impossible completion of the totalization of the world. That makes me a useless passion. The Other comes from beyond. She is the hell of other people who exposes my project for the pathetic activity that it is. What is striking in Levinas's version of this encounter is the passivity of my reception of the Other. Like Sartre, Levinas describes the encounter with the Other as traumatic.[25] The Other calls me to ethical awareness, which is, unlike Sartre, the awakening rather than the suppression of my freedom. It disrupts my contemplation, engagement, and enjoyment of the world. Now I must decide how I relate to the Other. How I might answer his call, his plea.

> My responsibility in spite of myself—which is the way the Other's understanding of this cry. It is awakening. The proximity of a neighbor is my responsibility for him; to approach is to be one's brother's keeper; to be one's brother's keeper; is to be his hostage. Immediacy is this. Responsibility does not come from fraternity, but fraternity denotes responsibility for the other antecedent to my freedom.[26]

The encounter with the Other is my encounter with infinity. The encounter is diachronic. We exist at different times because by the time I've represented to the Other to myself in consciousness, the Other has moved on. I never entrap her infinity in a representation. This is what Levinas takes from Descartes's description of infinity in the Meditations and how God "comes to mind" in our awareness of infinity that breaks the frames of our attempts to represent my experience of her.[27] Levinas claims the encounter with the Other is more primordial than any experience. The trace of the Other explodes the structure that consciousness creates. This idea breaks with Western philosophy where this structure dwells.

Levinas writes "[T]he idea of the infinite, which is to say the infinite in me" makes explicit here the idea that this idea is like no other idea, it is "in me" because of the revelation of the Other who is before me. Or as he says "Or more exactly, as if the psychism of the subjectivity equaled the negation of the finite by the infinite, as it—without wanting to play on words—the *in* of the Infinite signified at the same time the *no* and the *in*."[28] Levinas claims, against Sartre, the birth of negation does not reside in subjectivity, but in the idea of the infinite. It is in this sense that the idea of the infinite, as Descartes would have it, is a "*veritable idea*" and not simply what I conceive "by the negation of that which is finite."[29] The Infinite in me signifies the desire for the infinite.[30]

Possession: Sartre and the Comfort of Things

Sartre claimed sexual desire, hunger, and desire for knowledge are also all manifestations of the desire to possess. They reflect the effort to create a link between the I and the object. The desire for knowledge is like hunger. It is the desire to possess and digest the object before us and yet to leave it there in its entirety.[31]

We desire the object exist in its integrity, as an in-itself, while, at the same time, being a part of the for-itself. He claims impossible desire of possession exists in sexual relations. The ideal is that the body should be possessed by the lover but also new and other, leaving no trace of possession. The beloved should cease to be another become one with me, and yet somehow remain the Other. Similarly, knowledge attempts to be both the penetration of the object and, at the same time, only the caress of its surface. It aims to digest the object yet contemplate it from a distance. The object is not endlessly malleable because it receives its being from the being-in-itself but it receives its status as object from the for-itself.[32] "This is why desire to know, no matter how disinterested it may appear, is a relation of appropriation."[33] Thus, sexuality, hunger, and knowledge are all forms of possession and, as such, manifestations of the desire to be God. Here the relation of possession to the personification of objects is obvious. Just as I would possess the Other and yet have her remain other, if I could personify an object, I would be involved in the same game of creating another who is not really other. Another over whom I would have some control.

The idea of property gets its meaning as something that belongs to or is a part of the person who owns it. Sartre uses the French phrase for possession, "être à," which has no English equivalent and which literally means "to be to the person who possesses it." In other words, the possession, appropriated by the person, becomes a part of his being; this represents a union of the in-itself and for-itself. Looking for an example, Sartre appeals to the phenomenology of religion and the conception of Mana. He cites Eliade's description of burial rites in primitive societies. A man's personal goods were buried with him, or his wife was entombed or thrown on the pyre with him. Sartre explains that the positivist explanation, that he may have them for use in the next world, is not adequate to explain what is going on in the burial ritual; the object was a possession and hence a part of the departed person and had to be buried with him because it possesses his being. In this same sense, I try to meet the possessor through the objects that he has possessed to make his presence become somehow permanent for me. I visit a museum dedicated to some great person in the past and behold the articles that belonged to her. Through them I attempt to meet that person, remember her and perpetuate her being.[34]

The Desire to be God and Possession:
The Dark Sense of Personing the World

If I create a work it is because I wish express myself, to be the origin of a concrete existence. Its existence interests me in the measure that I have created it and the link of creation that I have established gives me a right of property upon the creation. I see myself in it. It's not simply that something is brought to exist; it is brought to exist by me.[35] Just as God has a right of property on his creation, I have a right of property over what I have made. The object owes its existence to me. Because the object exists by my act, my existence gains a type of necessity that it did not have before. I am the necessary being for that object that I have created. God's act of creation is the supreme example of possession because God has not only created the individual object but the very material that it was made from so the object is absolutely dependent on God for its being. God, again, is the symbol of the fulfillment of human desire for God possesses His creation completely and His existence is necessary for the existence of all his creations.

Possession is an attempt to overcome the exteriorization of objects, to establish a subjective link between the object and me and yet to have the object maintain its exteriority.[36] To possess something is then to appropriate it, to have created it "for me." Therefore, Sartre asserts that to have is, in the first place, to create. The links between myself and the object are links I have created; they must be constantly reestablished, continually created anew.

> To have is first to create. And the bond of ownership which is established then is a bond of continuous creation; the object possessed is inserted by me into the total form of my environment; its existence is determined by my situation and by its integration in that same situation.
>
> Through ownership I raise them (my possessions) up to a certain type of functional being; and my simple life appears to me as creative exactly because by its continuity it perpetuates the quality of being possessed in each of the objects of my possession. I draw the collection of my surroundings into being alone with myself. If they are taken from me, they die as my arm would die if it were severed from me.[37]

What I create is like an emanation from me. What I create is myself, the way I choose myself to be in the world, the meaning I want objects to have for me in the world I have chosen. By creation, Sartre means the way that I have chosen to make the formlessness of being-in-itself appear in my world as form. What I have created is myself or I have chosen how to exist alongside the in-itself for others. But creation must be renewed at each instant; it can only exist by its movement. If one ceases to recreate the links between oneself and the object, creation ceases; the ties are abolished. The relation between myself and the object can radically change because my world can be disrupted by the Other, so my relations to the objects that I possess through creation can also change. I can be left either with my own subjectivity or simply with the brute existence of the material object which is completely indifferent. Creation cannot conserve itself.[38]

Possession is a type of creation and a defense against the Other. I create lines that time me to my possessions. Possession prevents the deterioration of my world before the Other's efforts to recreate the world in his image. In the act of possession, I attempt to delineate my world, to create it in such a way that the Other cannot reinterpret it for me. The possession is mine already, the relationship is pre-established by and for me so it may not be altered by the presence of the Other. "Consequently the Other cannot surprise me; the being which he wishes to bring into the world which is myself-for-the-other—this being I already enjoy possessing. Thus, possession is in addition a defense against others." [39] This explains the personification of objects in the Sartrean view. In the latter, I personify the object in order to fix its meaning as a person within a world, an ontological order but also the otherness of another person with the kind of independence that entails. But I also, through bad faith, am in control of that independence. Both possession and personification are a kind of bad faith protection because in both cases I pretend an otherness to the object that I don't really allow it to possess. It must be is "for me."

Levinas: Dwelling, Possessions, and the Personing of Things

In separation and dwelling, the "I" stands out from the meaninglessness of Being, of what Levinas calls the "There is." For Levinas, sheer isness is not the self-giving of Heidegger *es gibt*, but rather the meaninglessness of the *il y a*, the "There is." The bruteness of being. I seek to separate myself from the brutenss of this meaninglessness, to stand out from it. Dwelling is the essence of egoism of separation from the whole. I build a retreat, a sanctuary, from the world. It defends me against the anonymous horror of the non-I, of the element, of the "There is." But separation is also not a question of being thrown into a situation but rather enjoyment of the world. As a separated being I enjoy the elemental nature of existence. I enjoy eating, being warm, sleeping. But such an existence in enjoyment is tenuous. I can easlily tumble back into the chaos, things can change. Crop failure, floods, are also the elemental "there is."

> Limitation is not due to the fact that the I has not chosen its birth and thus is already and henceforth in situation, but to the fact that the plenitude of its instant of enjoyment is not ensured against the unknown that lurks in the very element it enjoys, the fact that joy remains a chance and a stroke of luck.[40]

Against Heidegger, it's not simply that we have not chosen our birth; our enjoyment is endangered by the element which we enjoy. Enjoyment remains a chance, a stroke of luck. Dwelling is my attempt to preserve that luck. Dwelling and possession breaks the plenum of the element so that the "I" might recollect itself and its labor to possess its surrounding becomes its property:

> The primordial function of the home does not consist in orienting being by the architecture of the building and in discovering a site, but in breaking the plenum of the element, in opening in it the utopia in which the "I" recollects itself in dwelling at home with itself. But separation does not isolate me, as though I were simply extracted from these elements. It makes labor and property possible.[41]

Dwelling opens in the "there is" a utopia in which the "I" recollects itself and is "at home." It is important that utopia means "no place." It makes labor and property possible. The element is fixed for a time between the four walls, but, as with Sartre, this is only a temporary respite. We are challenged by both the element and the Other. The unforeseeable future can and will change all this. There is a radical contingency in living. It's luck. The uncertain future of the element is suspended. The element is fixed between the four walls of the home, is calmed in possession. We seek to make things "still." We buy insurance.

But the unforeseeable is the "there is," the indefiinte, which Levinas also refers to as "infinite." But this is different than the infinity of the Other. It is a bad infinite, a meaningless one. It lacks any meaning. Meaning is only given us by the relation to another. As with Sartre, possession gives us a respite, a sense of permanence, but it is certainly not the solution to meaninglessness. It is not primarily a protection against the Other, though this is possible, it protects the subject against the elemental itself which is understood in a somewhat different sense than the in-itself of Sartre. It would be incorrect to say that the "elemental" is pure positivity. Levinas rather approaches it through phenomenological analysis and describes it as a kind of anonymous being in general, devoid of definition, and distinction. It is impersonal and anonymous, it has no personal form rather is being-in-general beyond inwardness and exteriority:

> The impersonal, anonymous, yet inextinguishable "consumption" of being, which murmurs in the depths of nothingness itself we shall designate by the term *there is*. The *there is*, inasmuch as it resists a personal form is "being in general." We have not derived this notion from exterior things or the inner world—of any "being" whatsoever. For *there is* transcends inwardness as well as exteriority; it does not even make it possible to distinguish between these.[42]

The "there is" is a state without any singular beings. It is devoid of any indicators and or demarcations. It is no-thing rather than nothing. The *Il y a* is utterly impersonal and it is against this impersonal force that the hypostatic act, separation, creation, rebels. This is not against the Other but "since the "existing [of the *Il y a*] is not an in-itself [en-soi], which is already peace: it is precisely the absence of all self, a *without self [sans-soi]*.[43] The individaul emerges from this totality, this no-thingness, through use and enjoyment of the elements of the world. He establishes himself through labor and dwelling. Dwelling and possession establishes the self in the elemental and temporarilly protects his enjoyment against the uncertainties of life:

> Possession masters, suspends, postpones the unforeseeable future of the element—its independence, its being. "Unforeseeable future," not because it exceeds the reach of vision, but because, faceless and losing itself in nothingness, it is inscribed in the fathomless depth of the element, coming from an opaque density without origin, the bad infinite or the indefinite, the apeiron. It has no origin because it has no substance, does not cling to a "something," quality that qualifies nothing, without zero-point through which any axis of coordinates would pass, prime matter absolutely undetermined.[44]

Unlike Heidegger, Levinas argued "Labor in its primary intention is this acquisition, this movement toward oneself; it is not a transcendence."[45] This separation, this surging up, from the elemental is not yet transcendence as it would be for either Sartre or Heidegger. That would make transcendence creativity. It would use the aesthetic as the primary sense of transcendence escape from the bad infinity of the *il y a*. What it does however is to "still the anonymous rustling of the *there is*." It sets up a moment of stillness in the storm of uncertainty:

> A fathomless depth divined by enjoyment in the element yields to labor, which masters the future and stills the anonymous rustling of the *there is*, the uncontrollable stirring of the elemental, disquieting even within enjoyment itself. This fathomless obscurity of matter is presented to labor as resistance and not as the face to face. Not as an idea of resistance, not as a resistance announced in an idea, or, as a face, announcing itself to be absolute—but already in contact with the hand that breaks it, and virtually overcome.[46]

Element yields to labor. It is shaped by labor. It stills the stirring of the "there is" for a time but this is not the face to face. The effort of the craftsperson, laborer, or artist to give meaning to the anonymous rustling of the "there is" does not free us from it is but only "stills" it. We imprint on it. It is ours, if only temporarilly The personification of the object is yet another example of this. One works with the stuborn opposition of the object. But this is not the infinity, the otherness, of the face to face. Notice the similarity here to the kind of work done by the slave in Hegel's master/slave relation and later picked up by Marx. The slave sees himself in the product of his labor. This would be an aesthetic solution to the problem of the elemental and the bad infinite. We have not yet arrived at transcendence. Creativity, Labor, Work, etc. is still the self only playing with itself. This is the problem of personal possessions. The self plays with the self. If I have a teddy bear, there is not an Other speaking to me, only an imagined other. Tom Hanks's "Wilson" fails to be another person even though he has imprinted a face on the volleyball with his own blood. Against Socrates statement in the *Symposium* that we should all prefer our creations like Solon, Homer, and Hesiod because no one has ever raised a temple in "honour of any one, for the sake of his mortal children."[47] Aesthetic and academic creations are not others. Pirandello's characters take on "a life of their own," but they are still Pirandello's. Sartre correctly claims in "Existentialism is a Humanism" that God can have no other because He creates them like penknives. This is the frustration of human relations for Sartre. In love, for example, I want to possess the freedom of the Other but at the same time control them like they were an inflatable sex doll. As Levinas writes: "The laborer will subjugate it; it does not oppose frontally, but as already abdicating to the hand which seeks its vulnerable point, which, already ruse and industry, reaches for it obliquely." None of this stops me. "Possession removes being from change."[48] Possession grants me the rest and ultimately the illusion that I have stepped out of the Heraclitan river. And yet, things are always phenomenal; that makes them something in relation to me. Possession refers to more profound metaphysical relations.[49] Possession by its nature refers to others. As Levinas writes: "A thing does not resist acquisition; the other possessors—those whom one cannot possess—contest and therefore can sanction possession itself."[50] But the Other, the other person, is already present to all of this. War, raiding, theft, exchange, barter, and money enter the picture. Possession is always in relation to another. "Thus, the possession of things issues in a discourse. The action that is beyond labor, presupposing the absolute resistance of the **face** of another being, is command and word—or the violence of murder."[51] The irony is already there is nothing about your relation to your possession that is yours. The Other is always, already here.

   Possession refers to the Other; personal objects exist in the relation between persons in relation to other Others. We are social; we enter into complex relations that include the cultural objects that help make us persons. This is nowhere more clearly the case than with books. Our books, our stories, give us context and relate us to those who have gone before:

> All humanity has books, be they but books before books: the inspired language of proverbs, fables and even folklore. The human being is not only in the world, not only an *in-der-Welt-Sein*, but also *zum-Buch-Sein* [being-towards-the-book] in relationship to the inspired Word, an ambiance as important for our existence as streets, houses, and clothing. The book is wrongly interpreted as pure *Zuhandenes*, as what is at hand, a manual. My relation to the book is definitely not pure use; it doesn't have the same meaning as the one I have with the hammer or the telephone.[52]

Things are not persons, and the most personal of things serve only to refer us beyond themselves to the others who found our reality.

Notes

1. Emmanuel Levinas, *Totality and Infinity: An Essay in Exteriority*, Trans. Alfonzo Lingus (Pittsburgh: Duquesne University Press, 1969), 160.
2. Levinas, *Totality and Infinity*, 160.
3. Levinas, *Totality and Infinity*, 160.
4. Jean-Paul Sartre, *Being and Nothingness: An Essay in Phenomenological Ontology*, Trans. Hazel Barnes (New York: Philosophical Library, 1956), 694.
5. Sartre, *Being and Nothingness*, 689.
6. Sartre, *Being and Nothingness*, 592.
7. Sartre, *Being and Nothingness*, 693.
8. Sartre, *Being and Nothingness*, 754.
9. Simone De Beauvoir, *The Ethics of Ambiguity* (New York: Citadel, 1976).
10. Sartre, *Being and Nothingness*, 221.
11. Sartre, *Being and Nothingness*, 352.
12. Sartre, *Being and Nothingness*, 341.
13. Sartre, *Being and Nothingness*, 354.
14. Emmanuel Levinas, *Totality and Infinity*, 49.
15. Jean-Paul Sartre, "Cartesian Freedom" in *Literary and Philosophical Essays*, trans. Annette Michelson (New York: Collier Books, 1962).
16. Levinas, *Totality and Infinity*, 49.
17. Edith Wyschogrod, "God and 'Being's Move' in the Philosophy of Emmanuel Levinas" in *The Journal of Religion* 62, no. 2 (April 1982) 149.
18. Emmanuel Levinas, "God and Philosophy," in *Of God Who Comes to Mind*, trans. Bettina Bergo (Stanford: Stanford University Press, 1998), 55.

19. Levinas, "God and Philosophy," 55.
20. Levinas, "God and Philosophy, 56.
21. Levinas, "God and Philosophy, 57.
22. Levinas, "God and Philosophy, 62–63.
23. Levinas, "God and Philosophy, 63–64.
24. Levinas, "God and Philosophy, 64.
25. Levinas, "God and Philosophy, 70.
26. Levinas, "God and Philosophy, 72.
27. Levinas, "God and Philosophy, 63.
28. Levinas, "God and Philosophy, 63.
29. Levinas, "God and Philosophy, 63.
30. Levinas, "God and Philosophy, 66–67.
31. Sartre, *Being and Nothingness*, 708.
32. Sartre, *Being and Nothingness*, 710.
33. Sartre, *Being and Nothingness*, 710.
34. Sartre, *Being and Nothingness*, 719–720.
35. Sartre, *Being and Nothingness*, 705.
36. Sartre, *Being and Nothingness*, 731.
37. Sartre, *Being and Nothingness*, 723–724.
38. Sartre, *Being and Nothingness*, 724.
39. Sartre, *Being and Nothingness*, 725.
40. Levinas, *Totality and Infinity*, 143.
41. Levinas, *Totality and Infinity*, 136.
42. Emmanuel Levinas, *Existence and Existents*, trans. Alfonso Lingis (Pittsburgh: Duquesne University Press, 1978), 52.
43. Emmanuel Levinas, *Time and the Other*, trans. Richard Cohen (Pittsburgh: Duquesne University Press, 1987), 49.
44. Emmanuel Levinas, *Totality and Infinity*, 159.
45. Emmanuel Levinas, *Totality and Infinity*, 160.
46. Emmanuel Levinas, *Totality and Infinity*, 160.
47. Plato, *The Symposium in The Works of Plato*, trans. Benjamin Jowett (New York: The Dial Press, 1936), 342–43.
48. Levinas, *Totality and Infinity*, 160.
49. Levinas, *Totality and Infinity*, 162.
50. Levinas, *Totality and Infinity*, 162.
51. Levinas, *Totality and Infinity*, 162.
52. Emmanuel Levinas, "Philosophy, Justice and Love" in *Entre Nous*, tr Michael B. Smith and Barbara Harshav (New York: Columbia University Press, 1998), 109.

Bibliography

De Beauvoir, Simone. *The Ethics of Ambiguity*. Translated by Barbara Frechtman. New York: Citadel, 1976.

———. *Existence and Existents*. Translated by Alfonso Lingis. Pittsburgh: Duquesne University Press, 1978.

———. "God and Philosophy." In *Of God Who Comes to Mind*. Translated by Bettina Bergo. Stanford: Stanford University Press, 1998.

———. "Philosophy, Justice and Love." In *Entre Nous*. Translated by Michael B. Smith and Barbara Harshav. New York: Columbia University Press, 1998.

———. *Time and the Other*. Translated by Richard Cohen. Pittsburgh: Duquesne University Press, 1987.

———. *Totality and Infinity: An Essay in Exteriority*. Translated by Alfonzo Lingus. Pittsburgh: Duquesne University Press, 1969.

Plato. *The Symposium in The Works of Plato*. Translated by Benjamin Jowett. New York: The Dial Press, 1936.

Sartre, Jean-Paul. *Being and Nothingness: An Essay in Phenomenological Ontology*. Translated by Hazel Barnes. New York: Philosophical Library, 1956.

———. "Cartesian Freedom." In *Literary and Philosophical Essays*. Translated by Annette Michelson. New York: Collier Books, 1962.

Wyschogrod, Edith. "God and 'Being's Move' in the Philosophy of Emmanuel Levinas." *The Journal of Religion* 62, no. 2 (April 1982).

Chapter 13

Have We Effectively Made Money a Person and Ourselves Its Corporeal Embodiment?

HELEN GRELA

Editor's Note: This is the first of two chapters that focus on economic themes. Here we return to Marx (as in chapter 9): but now we focus more on the social, political, and economic side of his thinking, as well as introducing figures such as Adam Smith and John Locke. Focusing on the rise of capitalism in seventeenth-century England, Grela argues that our changing views of person (as traced through concepts of legal personhood, for example) are intricately tied to changes in the forms and functions of money. She makes the compelling case that human beings, at least in our current Lockean system, do not have rights: rather, our money is offered certain contractual rights, which only secondarily is conferred to us as the holders of the money.

Adam Smith's iconic description of money's origins continues to inform Western capitalist democracies: man's natural instinct to "truck and barter" gives rise to money as an efficient medium of exchange.[1] This conception of money frames our practical day-to-day attitude towards it and indeed remains a fundamental tenet of orthodox economists. As a result, we tend to treat money not as a bearer of its own independent powers but as a neutral facilitator of transactions.

At the same time, we also experience the uncanny phenomenon of being defined by our money, or more precisely, a feeling of being a reflection of our money in our social interactions. Marx's perspicacious expression of this condition is one that few would dispute:

that for which I pay, (i.e., which money can buy) that am I, the possessor of the money. The extent of the power of money is the extent of my power. Money's properties are my properties and my essential powers—the properties and powers of its possessor. Thus, what I *am* and *am capable* of is by no means determined by my individuality. I *am* ugly, but I can buy myself the most *beautiful* of women. Therefore I am not *ugly*, for the effect of *ugliness*—its deterrent power—is nullified by money. I, as an individual, am *lame*, but money furnishes me with twenty-four feet.[2]

Our daily lives are consciously and unconsciously informed by these contradictory and unreconciled perceptions of money. But why is this so? I consider whether as a society we might have unwittingly turned money into a person, as Marx implied, and ourselves into merely its corporeal embodiment. To do so, I will explore how our social imaginary[3] is built upon certain flawed or inconsistent ideas that both obscure and enable such a reality. These include our often-unexamined beliefs that money is a naturally arising and neutral tool in economic transactions; that our economic system respects the natural rights of life, liberty, and property; and that our legal system protects each person as the bearer of these universal rights.

I will begin by considering how our perceptions of money were grounded and deeply influenced by commodity theories of money. This approach has a long provenance beginning with Aristotle, it was popularized by Adam Smith, and remains hegemonic in orthodox economics today. Nevertheless, it has major shortcomings that remain unresolved. Sociologist Geoffrey Ingham argues that it fails to explain what money is, how it originated, and how it obtains its value.[4] Instead, proponents of commodity theory either conflate an ontology of money with its forms and functions or ignore the question altogether on the basis that money is irrelevant, using the circular reasoning of presupposing its neutral impact on the real economy for doing so.[5]

I will move on to consider credit theories of money that conceive it as debt. While these alternative approaches have existed since at least the fifteenth century,[6] with the exception of a brief period of Keynesian policies, they have largely led and continue to lead an underground existence with limited impact on the social imaginary.[7] Credit theories posit that money is never neutral since it is always the product of a social relation between creditors and debtors. A specific version, the state theory of money, posits that money does not arise naturally but is established by an authority such as the state through its own issuance of promises to pay. This elegant hypothesis may help reconcile our bifurcated experience of money.

That money has taken on various forms and functions that have evolved over time is not in dispute. Arguably, the beginnings of our turning "money into a person" can be traced to seventeenth-century England and the start of modern capitalism. This period bore witness to the first time that the state exchanged private debt contracts for its own notes. By doing so, it depersonalized and universalized them, turning them into money.[8] Commodity theories of money could not accommodate this new form of credit creation as money and did not treat it as such. On the other hand, credit theories viewed the event as the state's extension of its own money-creating abilities to private banks: one that enabled money's explosive expansion.[9] The new credit-money made individual accumulation possible on a grand scale and seemingly without the coercion of others.

Interestingly, it was during the same period that the free individual replaced family status as a building block of society. This was achieved through the development of natural rights theories of life, liberty, and property and social contract theories of the state, most influentially by John Locke. However, while the universality of these rights is widely assumed, it is far from evident, and as will be argued, unsupported. According to Locke, the appearance of money enabled the earth to be fully acquired, leaving a segment of the population propertyless. This fact overcomes the right to property, originally defined as unilateral access to the earth for purposes of survival. Perhaps our perception of money being neutral obscured its own critical role in the accumulation process. It certainly enabled us to attribute radical economic inequalities to differences in our individual laboring efforts and therefore accept them as just. Furthermore, there is arguably a coextensive relationship between the rights to property and liberty, one that is also absent in discourse. These largely unacknowledged issues are pivotal, as they underpin the validity of the free individual as a concept.

The final piece of the puzzle is how the popular and legal concept of person is also an evolving one that experienced many notable shifts. I will again focus on the early capitalist period in England, using the state theory of money as a frame. Considered in this way, our perceptions of personhood appear closely tied to the changing forms and functions of money developed at the birth of modern capitalism.

Just as the money form expanded to allow for radical accumulation, the legal concept of person shifted and became a possessive one. The legal person was reconfigured as the bearer of rights by contract. Contracts made personhood effective, and this was grounded in the freedom of the individual entering into them. However, without the universality of natural rights, the contract does not necessarily reflect the free will of each party agreeing to it. If the right to property is no longer universal, then individuals without direct access to property for their survival are coerced into obtaining money. Money—the most ubiquitous contract of all—mediates between them and their livelihood. It serves to connect society in terms that are not strictly neutral through the relationships between its bearers and those who must seek it for existential reasons.

While legal personhood became specifically tied to contract, our popular perception evolved to firmly associate it with the individual human being, whose universal rights to life, liberty, and property conferred personhood. However, I argue that because the rights to liberty and property are not universal, money seems to be the true bearer of legal or effective personhood, conferring it only to those who have it.

Money

I begin by briefly distinguishing the various forms and functions of money that to a large extent reflect how we perceive it in our daily lives. I also consider its subtler forms and functions, those that we don't readily perceive as money, either rejecting them or failing to consciously register them as such. Money's more obvious forms and functions had an important impact on economic theorizing, which arguably further reinforced how we typically experience it.

MONEY FORMS

While different forms of money have developed and changed over time, for over two thousand years, it was tied to a commodity that was itself considered inherently valuable. For much of its history, money took the form of precious metal coins that embodied its value.[10] These were often mined and minted by an authority who stamped the coin with a face value that reflected the metal content and legitimized it within a community.

In seventeenth-century Europe, paper notes that were convertible to precious metal, essentially IOUs (promises to pay the metal on demand), appeared and gradually became an acceptable form of money.[11] In other words, paper money was still tied to a commodity, albeit as a circulating representation of an inherently precious metal. John Kenneth Galbraith explains how initially goldsmiths began issuing notes that represented stores of gold to spare their clients the inconvenience of physically moving the metal when settling commercial transactions. However, because conversion calls for the stored gold were unlikely to all occur at once, the goldsmith could issue more notes than gold in his possession. By doing so, he was in fact creating credit-money ex nihilo. The gold did not need to equal the notes issued as long as depositors had confidence that the goldsmith would convert on demand. In the same manner, banks also began to use deposits as backing for lending activities in excess of the amount on deposit, also creating money *ex nihilo*. This created money was redeposited and formed the basis for additional lending, or fractional banking.[12]

It is important to note that the creation of money accompanying the shift to notes was not apparent in social discourse. The perception of money as a precious commodity obscured the fact that credit often created a fungible money counterpart not directly tied to a commodity. For all intents and purposes, this credit-money counterpart was indistinguishable from any notes directly tied to the commodity. Although it was merely derivative of the money commodity form, practically speaking, it performed the same function.

In social discourse, we tend to treat commodity money or "proper money" and credit-money as two ontologically different substances having two different natures as opposed to being on a hierarchical continuum of what Ingham coined "moneyness."[13] Money created by credit, because of its fungibility, often led a ghostly existence, and for all intents and purposes was treated by the public as being a direct representation of a commodity. This is exemplified by the fact that banks were and continue to be popularly referred to as money intermediaries, implying that they are helping allocate existing money and not actually creating it.

It was not until 1971 that the already attenuated legal link between money and what was considered an intrinsically valuable commodity was formally and publicly severed when Nixon ended dollar convertibility to gold. As a result, the dollar took on the role of the commodity, replacing gold as inherently valuable and becoming "proper money" on the basis of the US government, backed by economic and military power, issuing and accepting it. Since then, almost all money tied to a sovereign or in the case of the euro, a union of sovereigns, is fiat money. Missing from social discourse is the fact that any state guarantee is self-referential. Also absent is the fact that most circulating money continues to be credit-money that is not issued by the government.

MONEY FUNCTIONS

In our daily lives, there are arguably two main functions that we commonly and consciously associate with money and that give money the appearance of a neutral tool that facilitates economic transactions and stores value. They are

- A medium of exchange—whereby money acts as a universally accepted token in exchanges between producers and consumers or buyers and sellers. It is the "thing" accepted in trade for all other commodities in the economy.

- A store of value—whereby money can be saved, retrieved, and exchanged at a later time at a relatively predictable value.

There are two less obvious functions that are often taken for granted in our daily use of money. These functions, if we perceive them at all, are present to us on a more subconscious level and are not neutral (as will be discussed below). They are

- A unit of account—whereby money is the countable thing (gold, coin, note) that becomes the universally accepted measure of value, enabling different things to be compared to each other. While the unit of account is considered an ideal, the measure of value is what is actually realized in exchanges in the real economy.
- A means of deferred and ultimate payment—whereby money becomes a way of settling accounts between debtors and creditors, as the holder of money ultimately intends to extinguish it through the purchase of goods and services. This function necessarily incorporates a social relationship of debt and an element of time.

COMMODITY THEORIES OF MONEY

There is a long intellectual history behind our collective associations of money as a commodity reaching back to Aristotle's exposition of money in *Politics* (1.9) and that continues to leave its mark on both the public imagination and mainstream economic theorizing.[14] Aristotle conceptualized money as a commodity whose value arose from its embodiment of an intrinsically precious substance such as gold or silver. He was also the first to identify three functions of money that hold to this day: a medium of exchange, a measure of value, and a store of value. (He did not delimit its payment function.) Aristotle considered the medium of exchange function to be foundational: a specific commodity emerges to be the most sought after in barter, thus becoming money. This allowed sale and purchase transactions to be separated and thus avoided the necessity of a double coincidence of wants.[15]

Adam Smith seems to have directly referenced Aristotle when he famously asserted that man's natural tendency to enter into markets to "truck and barter" gave rise to money as a convenient medium of exchange. He also specified that the most exchangeable commodity in barter was usually a metal, which had the advantages of durability, divisibility, and portability.

Smith asserted that the natural value of money, like other commodities, arose from the labor costs of producing it, which in the case of money primarily involved mining and minting it. Prices were simply a reflection of the labor value of money relative to the labor value of other commodities. While market prices reflecting supply and demand conditions might veer from this natural price in the short run, an invisible hand coordinates each individual's selling and buying decisions towards it in the long run. However, Smith's labor theory never adequately explained value, and neither Ricardo nor the other classical economists that followed him were able to connect labor to monetary value in any satisfactory way.

In the late nineteenth century, neoclassical economists established two tenets that continue to underpin contemporary orthodox theorizing, while maintaining money within the commodity functioning as a medium of exchange frame. First, they formalized Smith's invisible hand into a general equilibrium theory that remained grounded in the supply-and-demand conditions of a barter economy where money was a commodity. Second, they rejected Smith's labor theory, instead basing the equilibrium or natural price on individual demand decisions (the theory of marginal utility) and the quantity of money in circulation (the quantity theory of money).[16]

Karl Menger, who provided the definitive explanation of money for the neoclassical school,[17] explicitly stated that money is the unintended consequence of individual rationality (rational choice theory) whereby it serves to reduce transaction costs; it is a byproduct that does not influence the real economy but merely simplifies what was already happening without it. Again, traders maximize barter options by holding the most "saleable" commodity: one that can be most easily and reliably sold at its economic price. Over time, it becomes the medium of exchange.[18] Money is a neutral veil that doesn't affect the real economy of goods and services. John Maynard Keynes and Joseph Schumpeter both observed that with this view, the economy essentially remained one of barter with a money facilitator.[19]

When the gold standard was abandoned in the twentieth century, orthodox economists maintained the neoclassical model, simply asserting that government issued notes became the commodity that was "proper money." Prices are codetermined by the money supply and the maximization of marginal utilities by rational individuals. However, there arose a question that was never adequately addressed: Once "proper money" was no longer backed by gold, how was its supply to be determined? In addition, the old conundrum regarding the nature of money remained: In light of the significant amounts of credit-money circulating within the system, how does one define the money supply?

Because both classical and neoclassical economists were primarily focused on money as a medium of exchange, its other functions were largely either taken for granted or assumed to be derived from it. For example, Menger's insistence that the medium of exchange function was money's original one ignored the fact that transactions occurring over time (e.g., wage labor and capital investments) required a stable value for money. Accordingly, he did not attempt to explain how it was achieved.

Problems with Commodity Theories of Money

Contemporary orthodox economists continue to maintain neoclassical tenets and to treat commodity-exchange theories of money as conventional wisdom. The very term—free market economics, which is bandied about as a commonplace—implies that money and prices arise freely and neutrally reflect supply-and-demand decisions of uncoerced individuals. However, there are unresolved inconsistencies with this vision. Heterodox economists claim that the answers they provide to basic questions about money—what it is, how it originated, and how it gets its value—are inadequate and inconsistent.[20]

To begin, there is no coherent explanation for how a single commodity arises as a medium of exchange to become money. While its spontaneous emergence from barter provides an easily assimilated backstory, it does not address how money comes to be universally accepted with respect to all other commodities. Without universality, it is merely another commodity in barter and not money per se. The spontaneous emergence of a commodity as the medium of exchange resulting from uncoordinated individual actions cannot be explained without engaging in circular reasoning. A self-interested rational individual would not exchange goods for a useless coin unless he believed others would similarly value and accept it. He would only use money if he considered it a viable institution.[21]

In order for money to perform its function as a medium of exchange, it would logically first need to be stabilized as a unit of account. Otherwise, its value could unpredictably alter from one bilateral transaction to another and it would not serve as a useful tool for multilateral market exchanges occurring over time. Stability or predictability of money with regards to the quantity of goods and services it can procure suggests that its foundational function is that of serving as a unit of account and not a medium of exchange. But if this is the case, how does a universal money of account emerge spontaneously? Any potential explanation also involves circular reasoning, as described by heterodox economist L. Randall Wray:

> While use of a single unit of account results in efficiencies, it is not clear what evolutionary processes would have generated the numeraire. According to the conventional story, the higgling and haggling of

the market is supposed to produce the equilibrium vector of relative prices, all of which can be denominated in the single numeraire. However, this presupposes a fairly high degree of specialization of labor and/or resource ownership—but this pre-market specialization, itself, is hard to explain. Once markets are reasonably well-developed, specialization increases welfare; however, without well-developed markets, specialization is exceedingly risky, while diversification of skills and resources would be prudent. It seems exceedingly unlikely that either markets or a money of account could have evolved out of individual utility maximizing behavior.[22]

In other words, spontaneous order theory only explains an unstable money of account determined within bilateral transactions. It cannot explain multilateral and temporal transactions including those of wage labor, capital investments, and debt contracts that underpin capitalist accumulation. A stable money of account is a necessary condition for developing stable pricing that could underpin exchanges with more than two participants as well as those occurring over time.

A second unresolved issue is that commodity theories of money do not coherently explain credit-money. In order to be consistent with the theory of money as a spontaneously arising medium of exchange, orthodox economists must maintain an ontological distinction between money as commodity and the creation of credit-money by banks or other financial institutions. In classical economics, bank credits were initially acknowledged as part of the money supply only if they were convertible into gold or silver.[23] Neoclassical economists also bifurcated money into state-issued "proper money" and bank-created credit-money, which was considered its temporary substitute. While credit-money was eventually incorporated into the money supply, it remained grounded in a commodity, which was always the direct basis of its existence via a causal chain.[24] However, credit-money is not consistent with the neoclassical economics principle that utility maximizing individuals gradually develop money to simplify exchange transactions. This is because the creation of credit-money clearly reflects a social relation and is incompatible with the idea of money as a commodity. The fact that credit-money is a key element in capitalism underscores the importance of this unresolved issue.

Finally, it is worth noting that the commodity theory of money is historically unsupported. There is no anthropological evidence of any barter-based origins of money, with most evidence suggesting state involvement in its establishment.[25] While tokens such as shells used in primitive tribal societies were used by Smith to support his assertion of man's natural bartering instincts, anthropologists later determined that these objects were not used by utility-maximizing individuals as a medium of exchange, but for ceremony, status, and reciprocity that would strengthen communal bonds.[26]

A more likely origin of a measurement of value might have been derived from institutions such as the ancient Germanic one of *wergild*, the socially determined compensation of the debt one owed for injuries to another. It was often measured in accordance with the social status of the person. *Wergild* was a communally determined practice and not the spontaneous outcome of individual actions.[27]

Much historical evidence shows that the stabilization of transaction values and the establishment of a unit of account to measure them occurs when a state levies taxes. The earliest evidence was found in Babylon and Egypt, where taxes owed were recorded on clay tablets and preceded coinage by thousands of years.[28] Notched tallies to record debts were also commonly used and traded in medieval Europe. A. Mitchell Innes asserted that medieval markets primarily served as clearinghouses to settle debts and credits represented by the tallies; barter was merely a secondary function.[29]

CREDIT THEORIES OF MONEY

While money's neutrality requires understanding it as a commodity, there is an alternative approach to money that presents it as a debt contract or formal IOU. The state theory of money posits that the state incurs the original debt that establishes money and imposes taxes in the unit of account of its debt, which creates demand for the money.[30] Money, even when it takes the form of gold or precious metals, is simply the state's own promise to pay and is ultimately offset by taxation. This creates the circulation of money within the state's money space. The fact that the state accepts its own IOUs gives money its validity and establishes its base value. Precious metals that have no use have no intrinsic value unless it is assigned. Money logically precedes markets and actually creates conditions for them. First, money and prices are established. Markets develop in order for individuals to acquire money to meet their tax obligations by selling their goods and services. In other words, a monetized economy is irreducibly political—it arises together with political authority.[31]

In this light, money was never the most "saleable" commodity, but a social relationship between creditors and borrowers. Holders of money are creditors who ultimately expect to redeem their money through the receipt of goods and services. Keynes explicitly asserted that in contrast to barter, which is bilateral, money presupposes a tripartite relationship between the participants in an exchange and between them and an authority. The three-way relationship is a necessary condition for establishing money's universality. It transforms the token from a personal object of trust into an impersonal one that is readily transferable.[32]

Furthermore, the modern capitalist system is a hierarchical system of social relationships whose order is established by money. Its unique feature is an institutional mechanism that turns the banking system's private debt into universally acceptable and therefore impersonal and transferable tokens: bank debt becomes monetized. This occurs when the central bank discounts bank loans presented to it, thus converting them into the most desired IOU at the top of the hierarchy of debt—government notes, which are legal tender. In other words, the central bank buys the banking system's IOUs with "proper money."[33]

The social relation of debt is organized into a hierarchical order determined by who can create credit-money and who can access it. Both the state and private financial institutions create credit-money in a constantly negotiated relationship. Access to this credit-money is determined by the default risk of the borrower and the potential profits from extending it to him. Default risk is most easily mitigated by the existing wealth of the potential borrower, as represented by his holdings of real assets or money that will be universally accepted to buy real assets. A billionaire or well-capitalized corporation seeking credit-money to invest in a venture presented as potentially highly profitable would have a high level of access; a propertyless, unemployed laborer would likely be denied any access at all.

Personhood

We tend to perceive personhood as an attribute that we all embody simply by being human, entitling each of us to the natural, inalienable rights of life, liberty, and property. These rights seem self-evident to us and are legally underpinned by the Fourteenth Amendment of the US Constitution, which requires due process when they are threatened.

However, like money, personhood is not a natural concept, but one determined socially through discourse and made effective through institutions such as the legal system.[34] It is a shared and collectively created concept that has evolved through time.[35] Our contemporary tendency to reflexively associate personhood with specific natural rights was greatly influenced by John Locke, writing during the late seventeenth century beginnings of modern capitalism. The timing closely coincides with the establishment of the Bank of England, the moment when monetization of private debt first became possible on a large scale. Perhaps this was more than just a coincidence.

PERSONHOOD AS AN EVOLVING CONCEPT

The word *persona* has origins in the Etruscan word *phersu*, which meant mask, and which later also denoted the masks used in Greek theater. In ancient Rome under Justinian, a legal status was attached to *persona*, making it the subject of legal rights and duties—a Roman citizen.[36] This concept of legal *persona*, taken together with that of property, became foundational for Western European and Northern American legal systems. It was through the legal *persona* that rights became enforceable and effective. Although the Romans always associated *persona* with humans, they did not consider every human a person. Women, children, slaves, and foreigners were not persons. *Persona* was the public face attached to certain humans, and it was directly tied to their status in society. Status, in turn, was determined to a large extent by the family and personal relations arising from it.

In the Middle Ages, the Christian church became the major source of law in Europe. It linked *persona* to the soul and in this manner extended it to all human beings. Thomas Aquinas eventually linked the soul to reason, emphasizing it as the essential feature of personhood. The Christian focus on the immaterial provided the basis for further extending the person to the corporate body, a group person expressing collective reason. While initially the corporate person applied only to church institutions, it was eventually extended to the world of commerce, and from the seventeenth century onward, the commercial corporation became a legal *persona*.

The seventeenth century also saw the basis of personhood shift from "status to contract," as was insightfully noted by jurist Henry Maine.[37] Traditionally imposed relations of obligations and rights resulting from status and hierarchy based on family, kinship, and personal alliances were gradually replaced by obligations entered into by individuals. Over time, the individual supplanted the family as the unit taken into account by the law, and the contract replaced forms of reciprocity in rights and duties based on family status. On might say that contract made personhood impersonal. Increasingly, the social order came to be the result of contracts between individuals. This tendency from status to contract was exemplified and consolidated by England's Glorious Revolution of 1688 and the Declaration of Right by Parliament in 1689, whereby the supremacy of impersonal law officially replaced that of the monarch.

It was during this period that Locke proposed his image of men as free and rational individuals. It is an image that provided one of the founding myths for the US democratic system, formed a basis for Anglo-American jurisprudence and continues to dominate its social imaginary. Locke asserted that in the state of nature, men were born into "a state of perfect freedom to order their actions and dispose of their possessions and persons, as they think fit." [38] The natural right to life or self-preservation enabled man to make use of things necessary to his Being; the right to liberty ensured freedom from the arbitrary will of others; and the right to property, by which man ensured his self-preservation, bestowed the unilateral ability to appropriate the fruits of the earth.[39] Locke conceived man as a fundamentally self-centered individual who nevertheless was rational and understood that his interests would be best served by keeping his promises and obligations. Man was no longer indebted to society for his livelihood, as was traditionally the case. Instead, Locke claimed the inverse: society was created by free individuals, primarily to benefit themselves. Accordingly, it was a group of independent individuals who freely entered into a social contract to form a state and establish common laws for the express purpose of best defending their natural rights, and more specifically, to protect their natural right of property.

Ownership was an important precondition of the new order that enabled individuals to enter into contracts with others. Through ownership, society itself could be construed as a set of contractual relationships. The sovereign state was the result of a social contract entered into by free individuals to protect their property. Commodities were sold in markets via exchange contracts. Importantly, Locke developed the notion of self-ownership whereby every individual is the proprietor of his body, words, and actions, and accordingly can enter into wage contracts.[40] Contracts became the basis of legal rights, and legal persons were those that could enter into them. In essence, the contract made rights effective. This seemed an intuitively acceptable proposition because individuals were also conceived as free. The contract appears coextensive with the will of the person undertaking it because it is grounded in the freedom of each party entering into it.

In the United States, the rights of life, liberty, and property are considered fundamental, inalienable, and universal. Americans have been apt to accept economic inequality as reflecting each individual's industriousness and choices and therefore something that one directly controls. This perception helped neoliberalism attain its current hegemonic position. Robert Nozick, whose book *Anarchy, State and Utopia (ASU)* was considered instrumental in its popularization, based his own arguments for unlimited personal accumulation within a free-market capitalist framework on Locke's *Second Treatise on Government*, asserting that "Individuals have rights and there are things no person or group may do to them." [41]

This seventeenth-century way of conceiving men as free individuals with natural rights is so powerfully established as to be largely unquestioned by us. Their assurance is the raison d'être of a democratic state incorporating the rule of law based on personhood and contract. Less obvious is the fact that the rights of liberty and property are not universal, and a legal system based on personhood and contract serves only to protect the rights of those who already have them.

The right to property tends to be unreflectively perceived as the right not to have our property expropriated. It actually conflates Locke's right to property, which he defined as the unilateral right to use the earth to ensure one's survival, with Locke's natural law or universal prohibition against expropriating another's property. In reality, in a society like our own where most life-supporting property has been appropriated, only those with property have the right to property in the original Lockean sense, and then it is indeed well protected. It means that those without property to ensure their survival—the dispossessed who can only rely on their bodies and a necessarily mediated access to the earth—no longer have the right to property. It is de facto no longer universal: only those with property have a unilateral right to it when there is no common land available for purposes of survival. The right not to have our property expropriated is theoretically universal; however, only property owners benefit from the protection. Our substitution of the universal right to property by the right not to expropriate property from owners seems to occur mechanically. It is further rationalized by our adoption of Locke's labor-based justifications for the original appropriation of property, so much so that it has become a foundational belief. We accept that inequalities are based on differences in industriousness of free individuals. It is our own choice.

However, this sleight of hand regarding property rights has follow-on consequences for the very freedom that we perceive we have—indeed, freedom is another universal right. Our perception of individual freedom leads the poor to blame themselves for their dearth of possessions and oligarchs to attribute their wealth to their own superior efforts and abilities. The fact that property and freedom may be coextensive also seems to elide the social imaginary. However, although dispossessed individuals may enter into contracts on the basis of owning their own bodies, they are not necessarily entering contracts as free individuals. With no scope for survival based on unilateral action, they have no choice but to enter into contracts. In other words, their lives must be mediated by the owner of the object on which they can labor. They de facto do not have the right to liberty in the original Lockean sense of freedom from the arbitrary will of others, as their life is dependent on the will of others. This undermines the entire basis of the contract being coextensive with the free will of the individual entering into it.

We must return to the labor basis of original appropriation, a deeply embedded belief that underpins differences in property holdings and justifies dispossession; it is also highly suspect and requires unpacking. As we will see, closer inspection shows that if truly taken at face value, it is impossible for radical inequalities to arise on the basis of labor differences alone. Perhaps our conceptions of money as a commodity have obscured its real nature—not as a neutral facilitator of exchange but as a creator of inequalities in its own right. Perhaps it was the social establishment of money as a nonneutral institution and the refined forms of credit-money developed under capitalism that enabled ever-expanding accumulation. Under such a scenario, money and not the human person becomes the effective bearer of the rights of property and liberty. Money becomes the *persona*, the public face of the human body that possesses it.

Money and Personhood

In this section, I explore these assertions more systematically. First, I consider how Locke explained and defended the loss of universal rights to property and liberty after money was introduced. Second, through a thought experiment, I will highlight how the loss of these rights for some could not be solely attributed to differences in industriousness and thrift, as per Locke's theory of property. Third, I will demonstrate how money, when conceived as a social institution and a claim, offers a plausible explanation of what happened.

UNPACKING THE UNIVERSALITY OF NATURAL RIGHTS

As previously stated, Locke conceived the state of nature as a place where men lived in perfect freedom and equality, each enjoying his natural rights to life, liberty, and property. Locke grounded the right to property in the right to life for although God gave the earth to man in common, each individual's natural right to self-preservation required the objects of the earth. Accordingly, man could unilaterally appropriate for himself both the fruits of the earth and any unclaimed land that he improved with his labor.[42] In a moneyless world, an individual could justifiably acquire only as much as he could use and not more, for the excess would spoil. Thus, acquisition was limited and there remained plenty for all.[43]

However, while we tend to interpret the universality of natural rights as normative for Locke, C. B. Macpherson made the case that Locke never explicitly made such a declaration.[44] In fact, Locke's only explicit moral imperative was not a right but a prohibition against infringing on another's rights: The bounds of the law of nature require that "being all *equal and independent*, no one ought to harm another in his life, health, liberty, or possessions." [45] Locke may have treated the universality of natural rights not as a moral principle but simply a description a historical situation at a specific point in time—before the formation of the state and before money. Macpherson's observation might initially seem farfetched to Americans because of our association of universal natural rights with Locke.[46] However, it is a historical fact that in Locke's England, the bifurcation of rights based on property was the status quo. When the *Treatise* was written, property ownership had already been a precondition for voting rights for over 250 years. The Parliament that attained supremacy over the monarch after the Glorious Revolution was fully controlled by the propertied, who represented less than two percent of the population.[47] More importantly, Locke's theory of property leads to the full appropriation of land, a fact that he explicitly stated and accepted. It leaves certain individuals without property and no unilateral access to it thereafter—it results in their de facto loss of the right to property.[48] This fact and its implications tend to virtually escape our social imaginary.

This leads to an obvious question: How did such an unequal appropriation of the earth occur in a justified manner? Macpherson highlighted the pivotal role played by money in Locke's *Treatise,* an aspect that tends to be neglected. In fact, Locke explicitly states that it was the invention of money that overcame spoilage and enabled unlimited appropriation. He asserted that money's invention occurred in the state of nature when men agreed by compact and convention to exchange spoiling goods necessary for survival for durable but not useful things like gold, beads and other representations of value.[49] Money provided the industrious with a store of value which enabled men to accumulate and fully make use of their capacities. It changed man's mode of being by making individual accumulation appear to be a rational approach to existential uncertainty.

It was money that made unlimited accumulation and therefore the full appropriation of the earth possible. Locke asserted (and Nozick implied) that this resulted from the newly found ability of the industrious to now store the fruits of their labor via money. While some were left without access to property, both men argued that the rising tide of industriousness enabled by money would "increase the common stock of mankind," thus benefitting everyone.[50] This might well be the case, but it does not overcome the fact that the right to property was lost for some. Locke further justified the state of affairs by asserting another important consequence of money: It rendered the right to property, which was never foundational for Locke but derived from the right to preserve one's life, no longer universally necessary. Men owned their own labor and with money could enter into wage contracts as an alternative mode of securing their self-preservation. In this way, money overturned the necessity for the universality of the natural right to property, as had been the case in the state of nature.[51]

Unlimited appropriation had largely unexamined consequences for the universality of the right to liberty, which is arguably commensurate with property ownership. By definition, the dispossessed are deprived of objects to independently labor upon for their survival. Wage contracts are not entered into freely in that those without property have no choice but to do so. Every choice they make involves the mediation of an employer-property holder. Those without property have no effective liberty in the original Lockean sense: freedom from the arbitrary will of others.

Regardless of Locke's intentions, which continue to be widely disputed, he acknowledged and accepted post-money dispossession in his *Treatise* as well as the de facto bifurcation of rights that resulted from it. The propertied had the right to their holdings and a commensurate right to liberty. These were protected by Locke's single moral imperative that prohibited harming another's natural rights. The dispossessed did not have these rights and so did not benefit from this protection. However, this logical outcome has all but disappeared in contemporary discourse and natural rights continue to be seen as universal. This oversight was most recently evidenced by the popular impact of Nozick's *ASU*, in which the protection of universal rights of life, property, and liberty is the crux of his book and his natural rights-based libertarian position.

UNPACKING LOCKE'S LABOR JUSTIFICATION OF PRIVATE PROPERTY

Another important element of our commonly accepted interpretation of Locke is the fact that we consider differences in our own labor to be his main justification for unlimited accumulation and economic inequality. However, Locke is again ambiguous as to whether he considered labor a moral justification for appropriation or as Macpherson suggests, just a practical matter that was also overcome after money was invented.[52] In any event, what is important is not Locke's intention, but our contemporary understanding of his intention. We clearly interpret inequality to be a direct result of differences in each individual's labor and industriousness. It is a deep-rooted foundational belief, so much so that even clear injustices are often framed as a result of government interference in free market mechanisms. This perception remains a commonplace in contemporary society, one that Nozick successfully tapped into, explicitly referring to Locke and his labor basis of justifying original appropriation in *ASU*.[53]

However, after the invention of money, in order for labor theory to hold, money must reflect labor in a strictly equivalent manner. It needs to function as a neutral tool, as described in orthodox commodity theories of money—one that facilitates the exchange of the products of our individual labor and enables the accumulation of any expended labor in excess or our consumption. It cannot affect the underlying real economy or social system. Only under such a scenario would an unequal accumulation of wealth be a direct result of differences in each individual's own laboring efforts and free choices.

However, neither Locke nor Nozick detailed how radical differences in accumulation based on one's own direct labor can actually come about in the state of nature. A certain level of inequalities based on differences in luck, ability, and industriousness would certainly be expected, but not ones that lead to the appropriation of the earth in a radically unequal manner, resulting in the dispossession of a large segment of the population. To better illustrate this point, it is worthwhile unpacking the two most obvious ways that neutral money might have led to accumulation: wage labor and exchange. While these explanations tend to be automatically accepted, a closer examination reveals that they not only fail to comply to a labor justification of accumulation but are also unlikely to have occurred from a purely logical perspective. We should keep in mind that at the moment money is invented we are in the state of nature and there is still enough common land for everyone. It is this moment of transition that we are considering.

One new possibility arising with money is the ability to hire labor for wages and to accumulate accordingly. Locke clearly extended justified original appropriation to include the purchase of wage labor: "Thus the Grass my Horse has bit: the Turfs my Servant has cut; . . . become my Property."[54] This assertion was unexplained by Locke (suggesting that labor was a practical limitation and not a moral justification for him) but leads to both moral and practical issues. In order for the employer to accumulate on the basis of wage labor, a portion of the value of the employee's labor clearly must be transferred to the employer.[55] However, from a moral perspective, if a labor justification is taken at face value, this transfer of surplus is clearly unacceptable—it is someone else's labor that is being accumulated. Additionally, from a purely practical perspective, original appropriation via wage labor begs the question: When there is unowned land available, why would someone opt for a wage-reflecting portion of output over directly laboring on common land, whereby in addition to his full output he could also claim the land? Taken from a different point of view, it begs a further question: Although the employer now has the ability to accumulate money, why would he do so? He can neither legitimately nor practically use money to buy commonly held land, but only acquire it with his labor. Furthermore, why buy more land than one can cultivate, when one's own capacities to work on it are limited, and purchased labor would not legitimately advance accumulation possibilities? Accumulated money can only be used to purchase spoiling goods or already owned land whose availability is limited to those wishing to sell it.

Alternatively, one could argue that original accumulation results from advantageous market exchange transactions made possible by money. For example, five labor days of potatoes are sold for one dollar, which is later used to buy ten labor days of carrots, parlaying it into further accumulation. But again, two problems arise. This type of accumulation is again not based on one's own labor but on extraction of another's through successful market speculation. Furthermore, on a practical level, it is highly improbable that radical accumulation could occur in this manner. In the state of nature, the cheap carrots arising from a market glut would have to be eaten or exchanged for money at the same cheap price, offering little advantage. Accumulation through exchange would continue to hover around what could be produced over consumption needs and sold. While surplus could certainly be accumulated, it would not lead to radical differences.

Although this cursory thought experiment is not exhaustive, it serves to highlight in a more concrete manner the obvious point that money as a neutral commodity still limits labor-based accumulation to one's own labor. Inequality is possible but radical inequality and dispossession appear to require a different ontology of money.

We need to return to a more basic question, one that remained largely unexamined by both Locke and Nozick: How did money become a store of value that enabled accumulation in the first place? Once we perceive money as a social relation and not a neutral commodity, a clearer picture emerges.

CREDIT-MONEY AND RADICAL INEQUALITY

The appropriation of the earth seems to require the economic growth and efficiencies that a market economy makes possible. Nozick and Locke explicitly envisioned the development of a fully fledged market economy in their state of nature. The production of commodities specifically for exchange in a market society entails investment, wage labor, and the division of labor. In the case of subsistence economies, where occasional surplus is bilaterally traded by otherwise self-sufficient individuals, an exchange of durable tokens—as Locke proposed— might be imagined, but it doesn't lead anywhere. However, for relations to function in a market economy, where transactions take on a multilateral dimension and encompass a temporal element, a degree of stability in terms of money's purchasing power as well as enforcement of its widespread acceptance is needed. As was previously detailed, a commodity theory of money cannot satisfactorily explain how a market economy could evolve in the state of nature; without it, a Lockean and Nozickean appropriation of the earth without an authority such as the state instituting and enforcing laws and a stable unit of account is improbable.

The state theory of money goes a long way towards plausibly explaining how radical accumulation could occur after the invention of money. It explains how money originated and how it became a relatively stable and universal medium of exchange: by the state issuing its own IOUs in a specified unit of account that it accepts as payment for taxes. However, this shatters the Lockean myth, as inequalities would only appear after the state was founded, in which case the right to unlimited property would no longer be a natural right but one instituted by men. The state theory also provides a viable explanation of why individuals would labor for wages or exchange goods on disadvantageous terms: they need to obtain the money form accepted by the state for payment of taxes.

Radical differences in accumulation are also explained by the state theory. Credit is not the temporary transfer of commodity money, which itself is a direct representation of a useful but spoiling thing. Credit-money was largely created ex nihilo based on expectations of its eventual redemption at a profit. Through the establishment of a central banking system, these private debts were discounted for state "proper money." This monetization of newly created credit made it fully transferable and acceptable in exchange within the entire money space of the state and greatly accelerated accumulation. The created credit-money does not reflect existing labor value but estimated future value measured against the probability of losing the money extended. This assessment orders the availability of money to specific individuals. As a result, those who have money, create money, or have access to credit-money can acquire money created ex nihilo, which will be universally accepted for the purchase of property and labor in the real economy, and on the basis of which they have the potential to accumulate real goods and services. Our treatment of money as a neutral, natural commodity, our blurring of money and credit, and our tying accumulation to our own laboring have obscured this process.

Conclusion

Have we made money a person? In social discourse, we tend to equate the person with an individual human being with rights. However, we live under the rule of law that renders our rights effective. While there is no legal definition of human being, the legal *persona* does have status under the law, one that has changed over time.[56] In the seventeenth century, a legal person increasingly became the bearer of rights via contract.

Arguably, money, when conceived as a series of debtor-creditor contracts originating with the state, is a social relation that defines the rights of the persons entering into it. The holder of money has the right with respect to society to universally exchange his money for any goods and services within the given money space. Those without money are compelled to acquire it in order to mediate their survival in a market society where all common land has been appropriated. This undermines the co-extensiveness of contract with free will, its original justification. Money, as the most ubiquitous of all contracts, and as the basis for most other contracts, informs most of our other legally enforceable relationships.

We see money as a neutral tool that buys us freedom by making our labor exchangeable into the goods and services that we desire. What we often fail to grasp is money's larger role, as a complex and ubiquitous set of interrelated debt contracts which binds us into a hierarchically ordered set of interdependent, impersonal relations within the money space where it is universally accepted. While money enabled freedom from obligations tied to family and status, it actually replaced them with other ones tied to an impersonal order. We also fail to perceive that this ordering is not a direct result of our labor, but to a large extent a matter of access to money, which is credit-money created ex nihilo. Our failure to clearly see the role of credit-money is arguably a result of the commodity lens through which we perceive money. Our tendency to equate economic wealth with our own industriousness, as per our interpretation of Locke's labor theory, further underscores our perception of money's neutrality. As a result, although we conceive our personhood in terms of free, self-determining individuals, it is in fact to a large extent hierarchically ordered by this foundational contract of money, which greatly informs our other contract-relationships in terms of our ability to enter into them and exact terms. Those without money cannot dictate terms. By not seeing this, we have unwittingly accepted this state of affairs, and indeed made money the de facto bearer of rights and ourselves its corporeal embodiment.

Notes

1. Adam Smith, *The Wealth of Nations*, ed. Andrew Skinner (Harmondsworth, UK: Penguin, [1776] 1970), 120–21, 126–27.

2. Karl Marx, *Economic and Philosophic Manuscripts of 1844*, ed. Dirk J. Struik, tr. Martin Mulligan (New York: International Publishers, [1844] 2016), 167.

3. Cornelius Castoriadis, *The Imaginary Institution of Society*, tr. Kathleen Blamey (Cambridge, MA: MIT Press, [1987] 1998), 147–49. Castoriadis identifies the imaginary as: "a system of meanings that govern a given social structure attempting to put every instance into a signifying whole."

4. Geoffrey Ingham, *The Nature of Money* (Cambridge: Polity, 2004).

5. David Hume wrote: "Money is not, properly speaking, one of the subjects of commerce, but only the instrument which men have agreed upon to facilitate the exchange of one commodity for another. It is none of the wheels of trade; it is the oil which renders the motion of the wheels more smooth and easy." See David Hume, "Of Money," in *Hume's Political Discourses*, ed. William Bell Robertson (London, New York, and Felling on Tyne, UK: Walter Scott Publishing, [1752] 1906), 27. More recently, an

example in Paul Samuelson stated: "If we were to construct history along hypothetical, logical lines, we should naturally follow the age of barter by the age of commodity money." Paul Samuelson, *Economics* (New York: McGraw Hill, [1948] 1973), 274.

6. Ingham, *Nature of Money*, 10.

7. After the failure of orthodox economists to anticipate the financial crisis of 2007-2008, credit theories are beginning to garner attention.

8. This new form of money resulted from a concrete shift in the balance of power from the English monarchy to the growing bourgeoisie, which controlled Parliament; after the Declaration of Right in 1689, the latter effectively controlled the state.

9. The establishment of the Bank of England in 1694 was the mechanism through which private debt became circulating money.

10. Herodotus claimed that the Lydians first minted coins in the sixth century BCE.

11. Paper notes appeared earlier in China, in the seventh century.

12. John K. Galbraith, *Money: Whence It Came, Where It Went* (Princeton and Oxford: Princeton University Press, 2017), 21.

13. Ingham, *Nature of Money*, 34.

14. Scott Meikle, "Aristotle on Money," in *What Is Money?*, ed. John Smithin (London and New York: Routledge, 2000), 157.

15. Meikle, 163.

16. Ingham, *Nature of Money*, 17-18; see also Geoffrey Ingham, " 'Babylonian Madness': on the Historical and Sociological Origins of Money," in *What Is Money?*, ed. John Smithin (London and New York: Routledge, 2000), 16.

17. Ingham, *Nature of Money*, 19.

18. Karl Menger, "On the Origin of Money," tr. Caroline A. Foley, *The Economic Journal* 2, no. 6 (June 2000): 239-55. Originally published 1892.

19. John Maynard Keynes, *A Treatise on Money* (New York: Harcourt Brace, 1930), 3; Joseph Schumpeter, *A History of Economic Analysis* (London: Routledge, [1954] 1994), 277.

20. Ingham, *Nature of Money*, 10.

21. Ingham, *Nature of Money*, 23.

22. L. Randall Wray, "Introduction to an Alternative History of Money," *Working Paper No. 717* (The Levy Economics Institute of Bard College, 2012), 21. http://www.levyinstitute.org.

23. Ingham, *Nature of Money*, 19.

24. Wray, "Alternative History of Money," 21-23.

25. David Graeber, *Debt: The First 5000 Years* (New York and London: Melville House, 20014), 28-41.

26. See Randall Auxier's chapter in this volume. See also Marcel Mauss, *The Gift*, tr. W. D. Halls (New York and London: Routledge, [1925] 2002); Karl Polanyi, *The Great Transformation: The Political and Economic Origins of Our Time* (Boston, MA: Beacon Press, [1944] 2001), 45-58.

27. Philip Grierson, "The Origins of Money," in *Research in Economic Anthropology*, ed. George Dalton (Greenwich, CT: JAI Press, 1978), 12-14.

28. A. Mitchell Innes, "What Is Money?," *The Banking Law Journal* (May 1913): 391.

29. Innes, "What Is Money?," 397.

30. Randall L.Wray, "From the State Theory of Money to Modern Money Theory: An Alternative to Economic Orthodoxy," *Working Paper no. 792* (The Levy Economics Institute of Bard College and University of Denver, 2014), 1. http://www.levyinstitute.org. This theory was developed, adapted and refined over time by Georg Knapp, A. Mitchell Innes, Joseph Schumpeter, John Maynard Keynes, Abba Lerner, Hyman Minsky, Charles Goodhart, Geoffrey Ingham and L. Randall Wray.

31. Wray, "Alternative History of Money," 24-27.

32. Keynes, *Treatise on Money*, 3-12.

33. Ingham, *Nature of Money*, 135-36.

34. Searle, *The Construction of Social Reality* (New York: Free Press, [1985] 1995), 40-57.

35. Yasco Horsman and Frans-Willem Korsten, "Introduction: Legal Bodies: Corpus/Persona/Communitas," *Law and Literature* 28, no. 3 (2016): 277.

36. Jeanne Gaakeer, "Sua cuique person? A Note on the Fiction of Legal Personhood and a Reflection on Interdisciplinary Consequences" *Law and Literature* 28, no. 3 (2016): 289.

37. Henry S. Maine, *Ancient Law, Its Connection with the Early History of Society and Its Relation to Modern Ideas* (Oxford: OUP, [1862] 1950), ch. 5.

38. John Locke, *Second Treatise on Government*, ed. C. B. Macpherson (Indianapolis, US and Cambridge, UK: Hackett [1690] 1980), §4.

39. Macpherson, *Democratic Theory: Essays in Retrieval* (Oxford: Clarendon, 1973), 228-32.

40. Locke, *Treatise*, §27.

41. Robert Nozick, *Anarchy, State, and Utopia* (New York: Basic Books, 1974), ix.

42. Locke, *Treatise*, §§25-30, 32.

43. Locke, *Treatise*, §31.

44. C. B. Macpherson, *The Political Theory of Possessive Individualism: Hobbes to Locke* (Ontario: OUP, [1962] 2011), 199.

45. Locke, *Treatise*, §6.

46. It is worth noting that the Fourteenth Amendment to the US Constitution is a prohibition against infringing upon the rights of life, liberty, and property.

47. Neil Johnston, "The History of the Parliamentary Franchise," *House of Parliament Research Paper* 13/14 (UK Parliament House of Commons Library, 2013).

48. When common land is fully appropriated, there is clearly no longer unilateral access for those left without property. They may only acquire property through exchange, which always requires two forms of mediation for the dispossessed: via the employer who provides wages and the property owner of the land that might eventually be purchased. Both transactions entail a third form of mediation: money.

49. Locke, *Treatise*, §37, 47.

50. Locke, *Treatise*, §37; Nozick, *ASU*, 178-82.

51. Macpherson, *Possessive Individualism*, 213-14.

52. Macpherson, *Possessive Individualism*, 214-16.

53. Nozick, *ASU*, 174-78.

54. Locke, *Treatise*, §28.

55. Two standard reasons given for an employer receiving a portion of the value of an employee's labor—his contribution of land and proprietary technology—do not apply here. Regarding the value of land, as long as common land is still readily available for everyone's taking, the value of the employer's land input is arguably negligible, as Locke himself asserted. In Locke's reference to servants, the laborer improves unowned, unimproved land, which the employer can then claim and accumulate. This is clearly illegitimate, if Locke intended for labor theory to be a moral justification. Regarding new technologies creating efficiencies leading to relatively greater value for the same amount of labor (thereby providing incentive to engage in wage labor), there are no protections for such innovations in the state of nature. Accordingly, they are likely to be quickly dispersed, also strongly limiting accumulation possibilities.

56. Gaakeer, "Sua cuique persona?," 295.

Bibliography

Auxier, Randall. "Wampum, Person, and the Life of Exchange" In *The Cultural Power of Personal Objects: Traditional Accounts and New Perspectives*, edited by Jared Kemling. Albany: State University of New York Press, 2021.

Castoriadis, Cornelius. *The Imaginary Institution of Society*. Translated by Kathleen Blamey. Cambridge, MA: MIT Press (1987) 1998.

Gaakeer, Jeanne. "Sua cuique persona? A Note on the Fiction of Legal Personhood and a Reflection on Interdisciplinary Consequences." *Law and Literature* 28, no. 3 (2016): 287–317. http://doi.org/10.1080/1535685X.2016.1232920.

Galbraith, John K. *Money: Whence It Came, Where It Went*. Princeton and Oxford: Princeton University Press, 2017.

Graeber, David. *Debt: The First 5000 Years*. New York and London: Melville House, 2014.

Grierson, Philip. "The Origins of Money." In *Research in Economic Anthropology*, edited by George Dalton. 1–35. Greenwich, CT: JAI Press, 1978.

Horsman, Yasco, and Frans-Willem Korsten. 2016. "Introduction: Legal Bodies: Corpus/Persona/Communitas." *Law and Literature* 28, no. 3 (2016): 277–85. https//doi.org/10.1080/1535685X.2016.1232924.

Hume, David. 'Of Money.' In *Hume's Political Discourses*, edited by William Bell Robertson. 27–38. London, New York and Felling on Tyne, UK: Walter Scott Publishing (1752) 1906.

Ingham, Geoffrey. "'Babylonian Madness:' On the Historical and Sociological Origins of Money." In *What Is Money?*, edited by John Smithin, 16–41. London and New York: Routledge, 2000.

———. *The Nature of Money*. Cambridge, UK and Malden, US: Polity, 2004.

Innes, A. Mitchell. "What Is Money?," *The Banking Law Journal* (May 1913): 377–408.

Johnston, Neil. "The History of the Parliamentary Franchise." *House of Parliament Research Paper* 13/14, UK Parliament House of Commons Library, 2013.

Keynes, John Maynard. *A Treatise on Money*. New York: Harcourt Brace, 1930.

Locke, John. *Second Treatise on Government.* Edited by C. B. Macpherson. Indianapolis, US and Cambridge, UK: Hackett (1690) 1980.

Macpherson, C. B. *Democratic Theory: Essays in Retrieval.* Oxford: Clarendon, 1973.

———. *The Political Theory of Possessive Individualism: Hobbes to Locke.* Ontario: OUP (1962) 2011.

Maine, Henry S. *Ancient Law, Its Connection with the Early History of Society and Its Relation to Modern Ideas.* Oxford: OUP (1862) 1950.

Mauss, Marcel. *The Gift.* Translated by W. D. Halls. New York and London: Routledge (1925) 2002.

Marx, Karl. *Economic and Philosophic Manuscripts of 1844.* Edited and with an introduction by Dirk J Struik. Translated by Martin Mulligan. New York: International Publishers (1844) 2016.

Meikle, Scott. "Aristotle on Money." In *What Is Money?*, edited by John Smithin, 157–73. London and New York: Routledge, 2000.

Menger, Karl. 1892: "On the Origin of Money." Translated by Caroline A. Foley. *The Economic Journal* 2, no. 6 (June 2000): 239–55.

Nozick, Robert. *Anarchy, State and Utopia.* New York: Basic Books, 1974.

Polanyi, Karl. *The Great Transformation: The Political and Economic Origins of Our Time.* Boston, MA: Beacon Press (1944) 2001.

Samuelson, Paul. *Economics.* New York: McGraw Hill (1948) 1973.

Schumpeter, Joseph. *A History of Economic Analysis.* London: Routledge (1954) 1994.

Searle, John. *The Construction of Social Reality.* New York: Free Press (1985) 1995.

Smith, Adam. *The Wealth of Nations.* Edited and with an introduction by Andrew Skinner. Harmondsworth, UK: Penguin (1776) 1970.

Smithin, John, ed. *What Is Money?*, London and New York: Routledge, 2000.

Wray, L. Randall. "From the State Theory of Money to Modern Money Theory: An Alternative to Economic Orthodoxy." *Working Paper No. 792*, The Levy Economics Institute of Bard College and University of Denver, 2014. http://www.levyinstitute.org.

———. "Introduction to an Alternative History of Money." *Working Paper No. 717*, The Levy Economics Institute of Bard College, 2012. http://www.levyinstitute.org.

Chapter 14

Wampum, Person, and the Life of Exchange

RANDALL AUXIER

Editor's Note: Chapter 14 begins with an extended discussion of the Native American concept of wampum, and the economies of exchange that were built on wampum. For that reason, this chapter could easily have been placed in the more historical part of the volume, in conjunction with chapter 7's discussion of personal objects in Native American cultures. However, I have chosen to include it here because, as Auxier says, his ultimate aim is not a historical overview of wampum, but rather to highlight a relationship between personhood and property (and thus, perfectly complementing the discussion in the previous chapter). In addressing certain strands of economic thought (notably in Marcel Mauss and Georges Bataille), the chapter posits a distinction between "currency" (which is described as "a collective person") and "money." Auxier calls "money" an impersonal sign, and he draws on Cassirer (expanding on his presence in chapter 11) to describe how money should be understood as having lost the symbolic meaning of currency. With chapters 13 and 14, the reader is thus presented with two very different arguments about the personal status of money.

> Money and Magic go together.
>
> —Tim Parks. *Medici Money*[1]

I want to begin this philosophical inquiry by retelling, as briefly as possible, the story of the indigenous North American institution of wampum. I am no historian, but I will strive for historical comprehensiveness in this beginning narrative. Historians, along with others, seem puzzled over certain workings of the "wampum economies" of the seventeenth century. For example, the purchase of Manhattan for trinkets and beads has long been a source of head-scratching, but looking more deeply into the circumstances and cultural background of such "exchanges" reveals a complex crossing of ideas and value systems. There is also a general lack of understanding of the idea of "person" among historians, and these two puzzling issues are connected, as I will show. With a fuller grasp of person and wampum in this setting, some of the peculiarities resolve themselves into a clearer understanding of motives and perspectives of the principal actors (both groups and individuals).

It is not my primary aim to contribute to the historical literature on wampum. I leave it to historians to decide whether I have done so. My aim is philosophical. Secondarily, I want to add to certain strain of economic thought, descending from Marcel Mauss, and the relation between sociological analysis and Bataille's idea of "general economy." As Mauss says, "it is the confusion of objects, values, contracts, and men which finds expression" in these situations.[2] I will offer a way of seeing the Maussian accomplishments in a new light.

Let me proceed with the narrative. My sources are listed in the bibliography. Since this is not a formal history, I will not weigh down the narrative by citing every single source for every claim. But anyone thoroughly surveying the sources I have listed should be able to be satisfied with the verisimilitude of the narrative—I do not say "accuracy" because the sources often differ, in matters of fact as well as interpretation. I do have to choose whom to believe, and whom to report, but I claim no privileged position. I have removed to the notes some very important discussions of terminology and context so as not to slow the progress of the main narrative.

Wampum

I have chosen to study the "wampum" makers of the seventeenth-century native tribes of southern New England (Pequot and Narragansett), especially in relation and contrast to the residents of Plymouth Colony and its most immediate indigenous neighbors (Pokanoket and closely related groups). The economic and political disasters that befell both groups led from a massacre of the Pequot peoples (1635–1637) to a period of relative peace and economic expansion (for most concerned) and over time, became a bloody and ever escalating conflict, culminating with King Philip's War (1675–1676), which greatly reduced the Narragansett. The latter war resulted in the deaths of 8 percent of the English population of New England and a much higher but undeterminable percentage of the participating native tribes (some say 40 percent). The early conflict, growth, and subsequent war derived in part from the inability of the colonials and the native peoples to adjust properly to the sudden growth, pervasiveness, and adaptation of wampum, as both "gift" (in a special sense) and currency, from its original role in the two tribes who made it (Pequot and Narragansett) in a precolonial context of a sort that Marcel Mauss calls "total prestation."

Behind the institution of wampum lay certain presuppositions about exchange, land, and ownership which were eventually destined to be worked out and worked through, somehow, since the living proximity of the groups involved would force communication, trade, negotiation, and political relations. Between 1613 and 1619, the native inhabitants of what is now called southern Massachusetts were ravaged by a sickness that reduced their numbers and strength (no one can say by how much, but some estimates run to 90 percent), but that the Pequot and Narragansett, of what is today Rhode Island and Connecticut, were largely unaffected (it came to them later, in the form of small pox in 1633–1634).

Current theories are that the sickness that ravaged the native peoples of southern Massachusetts (groups later called "Wampanoag") in 1613–1619 was either small pox or leptospirosis. This precipitous decline in population provided the famous sachem of the Pokanoket (Wampanoag), Massasoit, with a motive for having constructive alliances with the English as a means of keeping rivals, such as the Narragansett, at bay. William Bradford records the English finding whole villages of unburied dead native peoples along the shore when the "Pilgrims" arrived. Thus, there was available land for the Pilgrims for the same reason: depopulation.

We do not have direct access to all sides of the story, which would bring true balance.[3] We have only English (both Plymouth and Massachusetts Bay—which were very different places) and Dutch accounts in writing, each colored by its interests and perspectives. It appears that these varied colonists had differing experience with and understanding of wampum, but it is well documented that the English of Plymouth Colony learned most of what they knew from the Dutch. We will look into that difficult relationship.

It is worth quoting at some length a passage from William Bradford's history of the Plymouth Plantation. In 1627, seven years after the separatist "Pilgrims" (a term reserved for the Plymouth colonists, since the Massachusetts Bay settlers were not separatists) landed, they were visited by the Dutch from New Netherland (the portion of current day New York state that is just north of Connecticut, reaching to what is now Albany). These "English" at Plymouth had, for almost two decades, lived in Leiden, in the Netherlands, and many spoke Dutch. Their home and sponsoring congregation was still in Leiden. That there should have been cordial relations is even more natural than would be the case between either and the Puritans at Massachusetts Bay. Affecting these relations is the crucial role played by the Dutch in the English civil upheavals of the seventeenth century, leading to a Dutch prince taking the throne of England by 1689.[4] The Dutch visit of 1627 was the beginning of a relationship that lasted many years. In his narrative of this first visit, Bradford says this:

> [T]hat which turned most to their profit [the Dutch] was an entrance into the trade of wampampeag. For they now bought about £50 of it of them [the natives] and they told them how vendible it was at their Fort Orania [now Albany] and did persuade them they would find it so at Kennebec [recently sold to Allerton, the agent who managed Plymouth]. And so it came to pass in time, but at first it stuck, and it was two years before they could put off this small quantity, til the inland people knew of it; and afterwards they could scarce get enough for them, for many years together. And so this with their other provisions cut off their trade quite with the [Virginia] fishermen, and in great part from the straggling planters. And strange it was to see the great alteration it made in a few years among the Indians themselves; for all the Indians of these parts and the Massachusetts had none or very little of it, but the sachems and some special persons wore a little of it for ornament.[5]

Samuel Eliot Morrison describes wampum as "shell money" and notes it was "legal tender" in New England in the seventeenth century in a note at this point in his edition of Bradford's history. One of the native elders in the documentary *Mystic Voices* expresses great dismay that the "history books" are teaching children that wampum was money.[6] Both sources can be correct, however. There can be little doubt that wampum *became* money.[7] Whether that was a good or a bad thing depends greatly on perspective. My intent is not to judge that question but to *explain* it, at least partially.

Bradford describes the spread of a traditional, embedded and ubiquitous institutions, peculiar to the Pequot and Narragansett, into a popular *currency*, as distinct from "money."[8] After reporting that the other local natives, especially the Pokanoket and the neighboring Massachusett, "had little of it," he also adds:

> Only it was kept and made among the Narragansetts and Pequots, which grew rich and potent by it, and these [Pokanoket and Massachusett] people were poor and beggarly and had no use of it. Neither did the English of this Plantation or any other in the land, till now that they had knowledge of it from the Dutch, so much as know what it was, much less that it was a commodity of worth and value.[9]

We don't really know why some tribes were rich and others poor when first contact was made with them by the Dutch and English. We do know that disease had destroyed the tribes east of the Connecticut River, but that the sickness had not crossed the river. The economic systems were far older than the recent plague. Even (perhaps especially) *within* the Narragansett and Pequot, the wealthy and potent *have use* (if "use" is the right word, which I doubt[10]) of wampum, but the poor and beggarly have none, except as occasional ornamentation.[11] *Wampum*, as with other similar indigenous institutions, "is itself only the most solemn part of a vast system of prestations and counterprestations which seem to embrace the whole social life," of its makers, and the exchange of wampum "is set amidst a series of different kinds of exchange, ranging from barter to wage-payment, from solicitation to courtesy, from hospitality to shame."[12]

Among the Pequot and Narragansett "wastefulness was seen as a crime." There is an important difference here between European and native sensibilities, as noted by Mauss and others who have written about archaic economies. The division between *what is needed to survive* on one hand, which *cannot be wasted*, and the ostentation that demonstrates when people are "rich," which *must be wasted*, is a very serious distinction. In the former case, waste is condemned, while in the latter (the exchange of what is *not* needed to survive), waste is not only encouraged, it is mandatory, at least among the powerful part of the group. Wampum belongs to the second and emphatically not the first of these categories (means of survival vs. means of ostentation). Bradford simply couldn't understand this "category" of wampum-as-waste. The English and the Dutch just didn't think in these terms.[13] I call them "categories" because they are foremost the determiners of *thinking* (as Aristotle used the term), and only secondarily do they determine modes of life. Making this case thoroughly will occupy the second half of this chapter.[14]

Meanwhile, per Bradford, the English were without any clue as to what wampum was. One has to *think* about it in the right way before its meaning becomes available. Those whose efforts are bent on survival have no opportunity for such an excess of thinking. This form of exchange was, therefore, of no value to those natives (Massachusett and Pokanoket) who *knew* what wampum was but had little of it, since, after all, why should one trade *from need* in medium that fulfills no need? It is incomprehensible, which is to say, such gaming is for the rich folks, and they are not like us.

Also, the survival of these poorer groups was threatened by the aftermath of the sickness that reduced their population by up to 90 percent. Their situation was dire. The stronger tribes would take their land. And the English, who had been in constant contact with the Narragansett and Pequot for seven eventful years, had failed to note wampum's importance partly due to their unfamiliarity with the situation of "total prestation"[15] (although similar systems of exchange had existed in Europe and the British Isles at many points in history), and because getting enough food was uppermost in the exertions of their energies. These colonists were far from stupid, but wampum was quite beyond their range of comprehension. As Mauss says, "the obligation expressed in myth and imagery, symbolically and collectively, takes the form of interest in the objects exchanged; the objects are never completely separated from the men who exchange them; the communion and alliance they establish are well-night indissoluable."[16] Such a bond in and through exchange is implicit and unanalyzed among those who live it, while it is almost inconceivable to those who know no such system of obligations.

How the Dutch came to understand the nature of wampum is an interesting story, although the full details are beyond my present scope.[17] An envoy of the Pequot in 1636 is quoted as saying "Do we welcome the white man into our ways? Are we now far from the sacred tree? Before the white man came, we did not seek the power of wampum. In wampum was our lives, our lives in the shell.... Now we use wampum for control, to control the white man, to control our own people. We learned these ways from the white man. In the end, we will be like him, or we will be swallowed by him."[18] This shows that the situation relative to the transformation of wampum into currency was far advanced by the time of the Pequot massacre. It had happened very quickly, in the space of some fifteen years.

The Dutch played the pivotal role. They were interested not so much in the land but in the fur trade, and in dominating it. Initially, they would trade European goods with the coastal tribes for wampum and then trade wampum for furs with the inland tribes (who had the better furs, once the shore and rivers of the Long Island Sound were depleted). Thus, "control of access to wampum meant control of the fur trade."[19] This arrangement seems quite reasonable: find out what you can trade to turn a profit, and trade it. The Dutch recognized that wampum was the key to achieving their aims. At this time, the Pequot controlled the manufacture (if it may be called that) of wampum, and hence, had something approaching a trade monopoly, and thus, they were the main obstacle to the Dutch. In recent years, the Pequot had grown more numerous and powerful and had fallen into conflict with the Narragansett and had begun to take Narragansett land (and to take land from their other neighbors as well). It wasn't difficult to turn other native groups against the Pequot.

So it was not selfless advice that led the Dutch to teach the English about wampum. They were undercutting a rival, and in fact, fomenting war. They knew the Pequot had overextended themselves. The Dutch had experienced serious run-ins with the English of Plymouth Plantation over trade and land before this time (1627). The Dutch strategy was multipronged. They purchased a plot of land well north in the Connecticut River Valley, for a trading post called the House of Hope (present day Hartford), from which they declared they could trade with any tribe (a free trade zone, effectively); they set up their own factory for making wampum; and they drew the English into the wampum economy on the side that would diminish Pequot influence. The Dutch therefore had more than a decade of experience with wampum ahead of the English of Plymouth Plantation and had the foresight to use wampum in building their stake in North America. In the crucial moment, the Dutch then kidnapped and murdered the Pequot grand sachem Tatobem, who sold them the rights to the land for their inland trading post, but also demanding and receiving a massive ransom of wampum for him. They returned only his dead body.

This act insured a reassessment of the nature of wampum on the part of the Pequot. *Wampum was body parts. Wampum was person, in the form of substitution, that is, currency. And wampum is currency, whether living or dead.* Or, we might say that wampum is "as good as dead" to the Europeans. The native peoples realized this, probably with considerable horror. This fact of measuring wampum against the body, living as ransom or dead as booty, has been overlooked in everything I have read about wampum. I could not blame a contemporary reader for some initial skepticism about what I have just asserted. But what the Dutch did in the case of Tatobem was a repeat of something they had learned more or less by accident over a decade earlier.

A Dutch trader and agent of the Dutch West India Company, named Jacques Elekens, had, in the early efforts at settling New Netherland (1622), kidnapped a Sequin clan (Pequot) sachem and demanded ransom from his people, threatening to *behead the sachem* if they did not comply. Please note: *the head or the ransom*. The ransom came in the form of huge amounts of wampum (over 280 yards), much to Elekens's surprise (since he did not then understand what it was). But he had an insight. As Tweedy points out, the Dutch had been trading Venetian glass beads with the Africans and with principalities in India for some decades (and of course that practice would figure in their purchase of Manhattan soon enough), and Elekens saw that wampum was analogous. Tweedy says that

> the long strings of wampum given to Elekens were not, strictly speaking, a "cash payment." It represented the symbolic value or status of a sachem. As Graeber writes, "there's no evidence that even the Indians living in the closest proximity to Europeans used wampum to buy and sell things to one another." The Pequots had traded with the Dutch and knew they sometimes used glass beads and perhaps thought they would appreciate wampum.[20]

This incident with Elekens was then widely publicized among the Dutch, even back in Europe, where an account was published in a popular magazine. As a result, business in general increased, all around the region of New Netherland, and the market for furs and other North American goods expanded in Holland. As Pastore puts it, "with hundreds of feet of valuable shell beads in their possession, Elekens and the Dutch authorities parlayed their ill-gotten winnings into the fur trade along the Hudson River."[21] They put their gains right back to work building exchange further south. But now everyone saw that there was advantage in treating wampum as currency, ultimately using the "habeus corpus" strategy (deliver the body). When the Dutch later murdered Tatobem and kept the wampum, they knew very well what they were doing, symbolically and economically.

It must also be recalled that not only the Dutch, but the English, the Pequot, and Narragansett participated in the full-fledged practices of slavery, although their ideas about it were surely different. The idea of exchanging human beings was familiar.[22] The difference was the unknown factor, and it was resolved in part by this kidnapping and ransom carried out by Elekens. The idea of treating whole *persons* as something that might be legitimately traded was entirely familiar to all concerned, and as ancient as any practice might be. Kidnapping a person of worth for ransom is equally ancient. What was new, even if no great stretch of imagination, was how this substitution worked among the makers of wampum.

The swap of human being for wampum was, effectively, the exchange of person for person. But the Pequot may not have grasped it in just that way. Mauss notes among groups with archaic economies (including European, Pacific Islanders, and Native American) there is often "an incapacity to abstract and analyze concepts . . . In these societies groups cannot analyze themselves or their actions, and influential individuals, no matter how comprehending they may be, do not realize that they *have* to oppose each other."[23] In a way, then, one might even suspect Elekens of making an experiment, quite purposely and at a great advantage, to learn what a *person* (one of status, a sachem is both a human being and a "person," but the latter, the person, is what is being traded—the human being is merely the bearer of the "person") was worth among the Pequot, and to get a sense of the upper range of that value. The threat (or promise) to return him in pieces was a setting of terms, since he is "returned" either way. The person is a prestation, but this is no potlatch. It is nascent capitalism.

What were the Pequot to do? They surely did not guess at the sharp trading practices of the Dutch, and they apparently did not (at that point) grasp the wampum they sent precisely as currency, even if they well understood it was ransom. The Pequot were sharp traders as well and had no reason to doubt their own sense of valuation. Yet, the Pequot assisted in their own demise, as we have mentioned, by raiding against European colonists and expanding their territories at the expense of the Narragansett and other neighbors.[24] The Dutch were well aware that, in fact, there was growing resistance within the Pequot councils, especially from the Mohegan clan led by the sagamore Uncas, and this dispute turned out to be fatal for the Pequot. Uncas split his clan and became sachem of the break-away Moheagans and an ally of the English. It was he who produced the rumors of war that brought the English against the Pequot.

So, thinking practically, why should the Dutch fight the impending war when they could have the English, Narragansett, and the Pequot fight it as proxy? The Dutch needed only to provoke and to spread some rumors, drawing on what was already happening, and let human nature take over from there. And that is what they did. The crucial insight, that wampum was the body of the native peoples, as their person, the ultimate prestation, was the necessary fulcrum of the transformation. It was a devilish insight.

For our further purposes, what is interesting is that, according to Governor Bradford, "after [wampum] grew thus to be a commodity in these parts, these Indians [the ones who did not previously make wampum] fell into it also, and to learn how to make it; for the Narragansetts do gather the shells of which they make it from their shores. And it hath now continued a current commodity about this 20 years, and it may prove a drug, in time."[25] This archaic use of the term "drug" means an item one cannot sell, that lies on hand, more like a "drag." Thus, Bradford is expressing skepticism as to its real value and thinking that wampum is a fad. This prediction came to pass when the wampum economy grew, among the English, through 1652 and suddenly collapsed shortly thereafter.[26]

But it was too late. Wampum had moved through currency among the English and had come to be money—everything prized that made a person wealthy could be found in it, but it was no longer *person*. The further removed from the shores of New England the wampum traveled, the greater was its mana, its spiritual power, but wherever it became money, that power died.[27] What is this power? Mauss draws on Malinowski's description of how the Trobriand natives saw their shell currency, and I believe this is close to the same for the peoples of southern New England, both native and European, during the period in which wampum was currency (not yet "money" or legal tender with the backing of law):

> The gift [of the shells] is in fact owned, but the ownership is of a particular kind. One might say it includes many legal principles which we moderns have isolated from one another. It is at the same time property and possession, a pledge and a loan, an object sold and an object bought, a deposit, a mandate, a trust; for it is given only on condition that it will be used on behalf of, or transmitted to, a third person, the remote partner (*murimuri*). Such is the economic,

legal, and moral complex, of quite typical kind, that Malinowski discovered and described.[28]

These characteristics held both for the tribes that made wampum and others who traded in it but did not make it (initially). Of particular note is that there is a "remote partner," and we shall see how, in ancient exchange, before the medium of exchange *becomes* currency, this remote partner is usually a god or ancestor or other divinity. But where the medium of exchange has become currency, the remote partner is more in the character of a contract, albeit unwritten. Still, there is far more to this currency. Mauss continues:

> This institution also has mythical, religious and magical aspects. Vaygu'a [the shell beads] are not indifferent things; they are more than mere coins. All of them, at least the most valuable and most coveted, have a name, a personality, a past, and even a legend attached to them, to such an extent that people may be named after them. One cannot say they are actually the object of a cult, for the Trobrianders are positivists in their way. But it is impossible not to recognize their superior and sacred nature. To possess one is "exhilerating, comforting, soothing in itself." Their owners handle them, gaze at them for hours. Mere contact with them is enough to make them transmit their virtues. You place vaygu'a on the brow or the chest of a sick man, or dangle it before his face. It is his supreme balm.[29]

This description is closely in keeping with the descriptions of wampum in southern new England between the Pequot massacre and King Philip's War.[30]

In short, the role wampum had played for the two tribes who gave birth to it became generalized beyond their embedded traditions. It was commodified by substitution of the body parts or the whole body of the wealthy person, who stood as sacrifice, as waste, in proportion of exchange. A sachem, *living or dead*, is substitutable for about three hundred yards of wampum. This was the shocking message sent to the Pequot and understood by all the native peoples around. Wampum was now currency, even if it also remained a rich symbol.

Some historians have had difficulty understanding the subsequent trading of body parts that persisted through the end of King Philip's War, but in light of what I have described, the movement of body parts among belligerents and allies and even neutral parties now becomes fairly clear. In particular, I would note that when Sassacus, Tatobem's son and heir as sachem of the Pequot, fled at the end of the Pequot war, he sought refuge among the Mohawks. The Mohawks, or someone else, promptly executed him and sent his head and hands to the English.[31] It is not recorded anywhere I can find, but I feel confident in suggesting that they expected to be paid, and about three hundred yards of wampum would have seemed fair to them. I would wager my last clam on it.[32]

As symbol, not just as money, wampum eventually pervaded every aspect of Pokanoket/Wampanoag life, and other neighboring tribes, and they began to make it. The Pequot and Narragansett had no choice but to go along.[33] The *reduction* of wampum to currency by the colonials and other Native groups, and the subsequent collapse of the wampum economy, is among the chief causes of the larger war (King Philip's War) that is fairly described in the terms of "waste," as theorized by Bataille. The Narragansett tried to remain neutral in King Philip's War but were ultimately drawn in and paid the heaviest price—with the Pequot "out of the way," the Narragansett were now the main manufacturers of wampum and as such, shall we say, their stock was overvalued. If their wampum was "the only real wampum," then no one else could really compete.[34] If they were also "out of the way," anyone could claim to have "real wampum." King Philip's War accomplished that end, hideous as it was. It begins to resemble gangsterism.

The Gift of Wampum

We now move to a philosophical consideration of wampum. We have shown its history as substitution and its process of commodification. Arguably, it became money, in the ungrounded sense, not when it was legislated as legal tender and its value set in 1650–1651 in Massachusetts Bay, but rather probably when the Narragansett acquiesced in its manufacture for market exchange. Normally, I would reserve the term "money" for legal tender backed by written law, but it seems that legality includes but is broader than written law, especially in the condition where some of those engaged in exchange do not have written law, but definitely understand legal tender. The fact that there was no written standard for converting the money of nations that could be relied upon in the colonies makes it all the more important to recognize "money" when one sees it. That process of making currency into money began when the Narragansett cooperated in the destruction of the Pequot, and it was completed with their own removal from relevance at the end of King Philip's War. Along the way, written law propped up the monetization of wampum. It separated wampum from beaver pelts, which remained currency.

But we must go deeper. How, apart from the historical circumstances described, was the transformation effected as a transformation of human thinking? How does the body become wampum, and the wampum money?

Marcel Mauss says this: "On the one hand, the clan is conceived of as being made up of a *certain number of persons*, in reality of 'characters' *(personnages)*. On the other hand, the role of all of them is really to act out, each insofar as it concerns him, the prefigured totality of the life of the clan."[35] When the individual is acting in a clan role, that individual becomes a "person," in the sense of taking on a mask through paint, decoration, ornamentation, and entering into the ritual spaces. For the Pequot, Narragansett, and other tribes of southern New England, warfare, along with everything else, was the business of the clan or the tribe, and those who participated were "persons," not "selves" in any individualized sense. For this same reason, we wear uniforms into battle to this day. As a soldier, I am not I, I am my group, my country, and insofar, I become a "person."

What, then, was the Dutch trader Elekens doing? Mauss makes this point about the European development of the idea of person: "The 'person' (personne) is more than an organizational fact, more than a name or a right to assume a role and a ritual mask. It is a basic fact of law. In law, according to the legal experts, there are only personae, *res* and *actiones*: this principle still regulates the divisions between our codes of law. Yet this outcome is the result of particular evolution in Roman law."[36]

In short, what I do as a warrior, or as an agent of the government, and so on, is legally different from what I do as a *res*, as a thing. Thus, the Dutch authorities are responsible for the actions of Elekens in taking the Pequot sachem for ransom. Elekens was doing both his job and his duty. He would not have been convicted of anything illegal. If it strikes us as "wrong," then I am sure much else does in the narrative I have given. Our question is about what happened, and how and why, not about whether it was right.

The "persona" one bore in ancient Latin law was not only a matter of one's "name," but the name, relative to the group, was also a title, and indeed, titles could be many. They are the personae that are exchanged when we are not ourselves as things, but as characters, actors/agents in the dynamics of the clan. When a title is sacrificed or otherwise lost, the physical body is "left over," is excess, is surplus, is *only* a thing, is committed for use alone and for nothing sacred. Its animating force is drained. That is why it was better to die in battle than to be taken prisoner. The death in battle is an attack upon the *meaning* of the one attacked, which requires recognition of that meaning. Only secondarily is an attack in war directed upon the body that bears that meaning. If that body is taken prisoner and *not* sacrificed, the meaning of the *person*, the names, titles, and dignities, has been stripped from the human being. This is why, even in modern warfare, the distinction between officers and other troops is so strictly observed. The officers are bearers of titles, hence persons. The common soldiers are only uniforms; it is true that they bear their family names, and this is not nothing. But in ritual war, there are no common soldiers. All are persons.

But God in Christ, as the Pilgrims well knew, is no respecter of persons (Acts 10:34, James 2:1). Names and titles are but worldly vanities, and Christians are not supposed to stand on these distinctions. That tradition had, over time, produced the sorts of results understood well by such as Max Weber and Emile Durkheim, and indeed, Marx and Engels. There is no genuinely ceremonial warfare among those who are not respecters of persons. Thus, before the Pequot war began, sagamores (envoys) were sent to the English at Saybrook Plantation to ask whether the English would also kill women and children in the warfare. The answer they got, "that they should all meet their maker," assured them of the equality of all in the eyes of the God of the Pilgrims.[37] This would be no ritual war.

The Pequot understood that the English did not fight in the same manner as Native peoples did, and neither did the Dutch—the Pequot claimed to have difficulty distinguishing English from Dutch but pointed out that the Europeans could not distinguish among natives either. The Pequot envoys could well have been interpreted as *requesting* a ceremonial war and being denied that request on religious grounds. That must have been devastating news for them. They had requested civility and an observance of persons, the basic acceptance of what made them the people they were, for which they received a categorical rebuke of their very humanity. Perhaps it is not too speculative to suggest that the Pequot were willing to lose a war on the field of honor but could not get that kind of fight from the English.

The Narragansett, and the break-away Mohegan clan of the Pequot, did not yet understand what the grand sachem Sassacus obviously did grasp. But these former learned, as soon as Captain John Mason led his force to Mystic and carried out the annihilation of every Pequot who could be killed. The horror of realization among the Narragansett and the Mohegan was surely complete. They complained bitterly that the English way of war killed too many. In their own history, there would be few killed, a few taken prisoner, these divided between symbolic sacrifices (cruelly tortured, yes, but it was the *person* being so treated, not the human being who underwent the torture, and this was well understood by all concerned), and slaves. Again, the slave was only the husk of the person who had carried titles and names before. The war was waged in order to create the conditions for negotiating a peace that reflected new balances of power. It is not so different from what Plato describes as the difference between war among Hellenes and war with "barbarians" in the *Republic*.[38]

It appears that it had not occurred to any of the natives concerned that one could really pull apart the wampum from the collective person that was their people. Out of that context, what could wampum possibly mean? One could perhaps annihilate a people in its physicality, but the spirit, their common life, the wampum of that people would seek revenge and could not be destroyed. In a way, this expectation (might it be called prophecy?) was fulfilled, since the misuse of wampum as money brought many to ruin (if perhaps not all) who so abused it.

Collective Persons

We come now to the key point in my argument. It concerns how to think about the relation between person and property in situations such as I have labored to describe in seventeenth-century New England. Marcel Mauss says:

> In the systems of the past we do not find simple exchange of goods, wealth and produce through markets established among individuals. For it is groups, and not individuals, which carry on exchange, make contracts, and are bound by obligations; *the persons represented in the contracts are moral persons—clans, tribes, and families*; the groups, or the chiefs as intermediaries for the groups, confront and oppose each other. Further, what they exchange is not exclusively goods and wealth, real and personal property, and things of economic value. They exchange rather courtesies, entertainments, ritual, military assistance, women, children, dances, and feasts; and fairs in which the market is but one element and the circulation of wealth but one part of a wide and enduring contract. Finally, although the prestations and counter-prestations take place under a voluntary guise they are in essence strictly obligatory, and their sanction is private or open warfare. We propose to call this the system of *total prestations*.[39]

Wampum in southern New England, prior to the arrival of the colonial adventurers and settlers, existed at what Mauss would call an "intermediate" stage for all but the Pequot and Narragansett (for whom prestation was total).[40] Among the latter, the total prestation of the "gift" economy was present and operative (see below), but wampum was *not* "money" for *any* of the native peoples. Mauss rightly resists the idea of calling this sort of economy "primitive." There is nothing primitive about refusing the institution of money, from his view.[41] From the standpoint of humane exchange, it is in fact wise to resist the idea of money, which depersonalizes exchange. From the standpoint of maintaining the dignity of persons, wampum far exceeds, in moral quality (i.e., in dignity and honor), economies based on money. Yet wampum also facilitates a kind of human flourishing that is close to the land, rich in leisure, and humanly fulfilling. That is not to say it signifies a utopia. This paradise is closer to capitalism than Mauss finds comfortable.

Thus, in assessing the moral superiority of a wampum economy, I do not wish to appear as a despiser of capitalism. Wampum economies, where they are intermediate, *are* a kind of capitalism, in my opinion. Where prestation is total, we have not peace but the constant and looming presence of war (albeit ritualized), where intermediate economies of prestation (less than total) will be more peaceable. Further, far from socialist egalitarianism, the hierarchy of total prestation, vying for titles and the like, is the essence of the system. The hierarchy becomes a fixed and limited market, except when peace must be negotiated in the aftermath of ritual war. Anyone can see that the medieval economies of Europe are similar. What is being evaluated here is the robustness of person, wherever prestation is "intermediate." But such economies seem to depend upon there being total prestation *somewhere* (e.g., some royal court). And wherever this total situation is found, person eclipses all else by its ubiquity, which is to say that life comes to be *wholly* symbolic (and hence quite oppressive).[42]

The wampum economy of southern New England was agrarian (corn, squash, beans, the three sisters), balanced by hunting-gathering. It provided for settled, deep, complex, and satisfying social bonds, especially among tribes proximate to but not engaged in the making of wampum. It simply wouldn't occur to the proximate tribes to make wampum. The wampum economy, proximate or total, does not by any means conduce to a wholly peaceful combination of relations. Contest remains uppermost, but contestation (including warfare) is maximally ritualized, as a matter of historical fact. Whether a defensible link exists between ritualized warfare and wampum itself, the physical shells as strung and traded, is a question that a qualified social historian should pursue. One would expect wampum to play a role both in the displays on the battlefield and in the peace negotiations. I find no mention of this in my sources. (For instance, King Philip seems never to have fought in battle openly, with or without his famous coat of wampum, or when Sassacus's head and hands were sent to the English by the Mohawk, there is no mention of what they did with his wampum. There were five hundred pounds of it, according to historians.[43])

Mythic Consciousness

I will attempt now to apply the summary through the ideas of Cassirer, Mauss, Bataille, and Barthes, each in turn, tracing the presence of "person" through each, and showing how this presupposition (especially as present in Mauss) changes our understanding of the development of the difference between currency (which might be a fair term for wampum in the intermediate economy) and money. In my usage, the former not only may retain personality, but *is a collective person*. The latter, money, is an impersonal sign, drained of its "life," its *symbolic* meaning. An implication, which I will not have time to pursue but must suggest, is that the absence of *religious* meaning in money is the greatest source of its depersonalization and demotion to a sign.[44]

Since Mauss admits he has not undertaken the sort of study that would allow him to assess the gift from the standpoint of mythic consciousness, we need the assistance of someone who has made that study. This is where Cassirer's ideas are most helpful.

Total Prestation

Let us continue this narrative by stepping into the middle of that "current." The institution of currency, as Mauss shows, grows from the gift (*le cadeau*), especially as embedded in a culture of "total prestation," as he described it.

He rightly (in my view) describes the energy involved as "the erotic life of property."[45] Bataille picks up this idea and runs with it far further than Mauss might have imagined. But Bataille does not recognize something implicit (and sometimes explicit) in Mauss's understanding of total prestation, and this is the crucial role of "person" in the formation of the energies required for such a condition of exchange. In terms of "intermediate economies," Lewis Hyde, elaborating on Mauss's theory says:

> People live a different life when they treat a portion of their wealth as gift. To begin with, unlike the sale of a commodity, the giving of a gift tends to establish a relationship between the parties involved. (It is this element of the relationship that leads me to speak of gift exchange as an "erotic" commerce, opposing *eros* [the principle of attraction, union, involvement which binds together], to *logos* [reason and logic, the principle of differentiation in particular]. A market economy is an emanation of *logos*.) Furthermore, when gifts circulate within a group, their commerce leaves a series of interconnected relationships in its wake, and a kind of decentralized cohesiveness emerges.[46]

Looming in the background is our deep-seated attitude that there is something undignified, even morally aberrant, about money and measuring things in terms of it, especially in contrast with how we live when a portion of our wealth is treated as gift. Markets bring us commodities; gifts bring us persons. Humans can be commodified (and indeed constantly are), but something kept in reserve holds that force in balance, in an intermediate economy.

When we hear, for example, about the "standard payout" to families who have lost a loved one in an airplane crash, and how this amount is adjusted depending on age, gender, education level, earning potential, and especially (for instance) that women are "worth less than men" and that children bring a relatively low payout compared to an educated young professional man, and that a woman who is not a mother brings less money than a woman who is a mother, these sorts of actuarial calculations offend us. But they are not so different from those that accompanied the market economy of chattel slavery. We know that "persons" are untouched by these measurements, as they belong to us and as we belong to one another.

"Belong" is the right word for the erotic life of property. Its middle voice is forgotten—we hear the middle voice (neither active nor passive voice) in words like "bemused," or "bedazzled," or "bewitched," but we lose that important sense of being at once the subject and object of desire with other commoner words, like "*be*long" and "*be*cause." The "invisible" middles are working at what Barthes cleverly calls "degree zero," or "the neutral."[47] The middle voice, where its workings are noticed, makes explicit the presence not of objects or subjects, but of gifts. Wampum is an intermediary of that voice. It stands to us as mediator of desire. It is property, but not commodity; it is the body of the *be*loved, not in proxy, but in reality. Nothing in wampum is left out, or uncaptured in the culmination of such desire. To possess the wampum is to possess the world that includes the beloved, and that can be done even where the beloved, whether community or individual, is beyond our temporal reach. Your late grandfather's pocket watch is wampum. So is the side-arm he claimed from the body of a Japanese soldier in 1945. That gun presents problems as well, but wampum is a perfected mediator, a perfected person.

Part of what I take to be convincing about my account, or so I hope, is less the positive argument itself than what we must accept if we *deny* it, which is this: without wampum, we intermediates are at the mercy of money and those who love it, root and stem. Human dignity is powerlessness before money; yet, they are in deep tension with one another. The bolstering of the philosophies of Cassirer, Mauss, Bataille, Barthes, and Eco, supplemented with a more robust idea of person, makes those viewpoints much stronger and insistent upon human dignity. There is no need for a prior critique, since all are antireductionists, allowing room for the personalization of their philosophies.

The Workings of Wampum

I am not an expert on wampum and its history. I am at the mercy of the books and articles I have dug up. I have seen wampum in museums. If I have overlooked something crucial, or if I have erred, or if I have failed to be critical of a source widely held unreliable, I beg correction from those who know the ideas and practices better. I only report what I have been able to learn from casting my net as widely as I can within the confines of southern New England, 1620 to 1678.

I explicitly leave aside the Iroquoian adoption (or version) of wampum, which others, such as Graeber, have taken up. Each group that took on wampum after it became currency makes claims that are disputed by the others, and I cannot possibly go into the differences here. Obviously, there are thousands of implications for other practices of North American First Peoples. These will make for wonderful future discussion. But I want to trace just a little further the transformation of wampum beyond the events of the Pequot war.

Nathaniel Philbrick has provided a comprehensive narrative of the principal facts related to my analysis in *Mayflower: A Story of Courage, Community, and War*. He makes no special study of wampum as such. But his understanding of it is broad, and it really constitutes a character, independently, in the history. I will bring forward passages that illustrate the development of wampum as currency for the indigenous peoples of southern New England, including the colonists' interaction with this institution of exchange. Perhaps it became money, but never entirely. It retained "person." I will supplement these illustrations with other studies and sources. As Philbrick points out, the contemporary inquirer is hindered by the paucity of native sources for this information. It is probably inevitable that the story leans toward the perceptions of the colonists since that is the main written record we have.

After some rough beginnings, the leaders of Plymouth Colony and the Wampanoag[48] grand sachem Massasoit came to terms of peace, without mention of wampum or exchange, apart from pledging mutual aid in the event of either being unjustly attacked by a nonparty to the agreement.[49] By Mauss's standard, this surely is exchange, and an exchange accompanied by necessity—survival. The absence of any mention of wampum should be noted. We may infer that by the time these terms were struck (March 22, 1621), trade was well underway among the various Native and colonial populations, but at this early stage, for the English, they would not have had use for wampum (of any quality, see below). They mainly needed food and seeds, although a second problem was their debts to England. It seems that wampum might have been offered by the natives, and perhaps accepted by the colonists as a matter of ceremonial politeness, but there seems to be no record of it.

A crucial change came to Plymouth in the spring of 1623 when Governor William Bradford "decided that each household should be assigned its own plot to cultivate, with the understanding that each family kept whatever it grew. The change in attitude was stunning. Families were now willing to work much harder than they had ever worked before . . . The women now went into the field and took the little ones with them to set corn."[50] This is prior to the moment when the Dutch taught the Pilgrims about wampum (1627). Here a motive is born for independent trading between individual families and individual natives (although the latter are more delegates or representatives than independent economic agents). This is the beginning of a tension. But it is one tension internal to the Pequot and Narragansett, and a different tension between Plymouth and the Wampanoag.

In 1626, the Dutch bought Manhattan in exchange for, in part, Venetian glass beads. The Algonkian natives of that area surely saw these fine beads as analogous to wampum. It would have been difficult for them to know or understand that these trinkets, albeit valued trinkets (unlike their own and whose quality and meaning the natives would have been unable to assess) held no great *intrinsic* value for the Dutch. The Dutch were sharp traders. Recalling that the Mayflower Pilgrims and those who followed had been living in the Netherlands for almost a generation before coming to North America, most of them spoke Dutch and formed natural relations with the Dutch settlers of New Netherlands. As Philbrick says, in 1627:

> The Dutch trading agent Isaak de Rasiere introduced the Pilgrims to wampum, the white and purple shell beads that quickly became the medium of exchange in New England and revolutionized the trade with the indians. By the early 1630s, Plymouth had established a series of trading posts that extended all the way from the Connecticut River to Castine, Maine.[51]

A problem with this description is that it is really impossible that Rasiere "introduced" the Plymouth colonists to wampum. Wampum pervaded every aspect of native life to their immediate west, and the beads themselves were more than a little bit noticeable, being strikingly beautiful and worn openly (among other things). The colonists could not have missed it. Rasiere taught them how to *trade* with wampum, to grade the quality and distinguish various types of the beads, and perhaps also to grasp that a sachem was worth about three hundred yards of it. In the chronology of events, the Plymouth colonists had become individual entrepreneurs *before* being taught how to trade with wampum. Thus, instead of being shown wampum as a collective expression of the dignity of the people who made it, the colonists were motivated and taught to see it as currency from the outset. In short, there was an "intermediate" economy *for them* from the start. Whether they were ever in any position to understand what wampum was for the Pequot and Narragansett peoples seems doubtful.

One wonders what difference it might have made if the Native peoples themselves—whether Wampanoag or Narragansett (different stories surely)—had taught the Plymouth population about wampum during the earliest days of their peace-making, when all sides were cautiously taking the measure of the other, and each needed the other for survival. But for the Pequot and Narragansett, wampum was so utterly pervasive in Native practice and consciousness (as Mauss says, total prestation) that it might not have occurred to them that anyone *needed* teaching of this sort. Meanwhile, the Pokanoket and other Wampanoag would not see wampum as important enough to call forth instruction or advice, if Bradford's account is accurate. Perhaps Squanto would have grasped the situation, but we don't know what he might have said about it.

Confronted with evidence that the English did not grasp wampum, the Natives (not being very impressed with the English generally), would simply have regarded this failure as further evidence of a general ignorance of everything important. It is surprising that Massasoit apparently did not (for all his expansive wisdom) foresee that disaster was in the offing if the English should get the wrong idea about wampum, or of countering the dangerous ideas that had already taken root among the Dutch.

This "intermediate" condition of the English and the Wampanoag leads us to considerations about person and waste.

Waste Management

Cassirer posed the problem, pointedly, of how any physical medium can be the bearer of a meaning—he would say a *"geistlich"* meaning. The sociologists of Durkheim's school, including Mauss, approached the question more as a matter of "exchange" and the carrying of value *in* exchange (among physical objects and beyond), as more a matter of eros than of spirit (Lewis Hyde's point about eros). The problem is as ancient as any problem can be, especially since the advent of *human consciousness* itself seems to present the primal case study of this problem.

If I want what *you* have, or if I merely want what I *don't* have, whether it be food or water or sexual partners or shelter, or ideas, then consciousness grows in proportion to this lack and takes on the form of whatever is lacking.[52] This is true in animals as well as humans. Thus, wanting what *you* have, or what *others* have, forms our consciousness(es) around envy, rivalry, and contest, while wanting what *I* lack, but you *also* do not have, can become the basis of a deep and nurturing bond. This observation is as old as humanity. When we lack *together* and in community, our shared consciousness and our personalities form around (and in proportion to) the way we endure our situation. We might endure it well enough to become deeply bonded, such that the bonds come to replace the lack itself. How many times have you heard it said by someone who went through poverty, "We were poor but we didn't know it"? The theory of relative deprivation and its social meaning and consequences has been widely studied.

But the theory of *relative* plenty, if such it may be called, has registered less attention. Yes, there is everything from Veblen's conspicuous consumption to Galbraith's affluent society, to Packard's waste-makers, but these start from the condition of plenty (which is like to total prestation), not studying the intermediate forms of economic consciousness. So, to wit: if you and I lack together, and if we should in some way improve our condition of want together, is it possible that we share, we trust, and we do not vie for primacy, *unless and until* we come to compare and contrast ourselves?

Why would Cain envy Abel were there not a God and arbiter who awakened this form of consciousness in them? The birth of this comparison and contrast came amid plenty, not in the condition of want. And the origin of the rivalrous form of consciousness is "the gift," which includes the sacrifice. The ancient mythologies of many races hold similar stories. We become persons in rivalry, brought on by the intervention of some third perspective, but also the challenge is sometimes met in striving *together*. In general, the danger to our common personhood arises from the plenty, not from the deprivation. The Pilgrims had individualized their economy. The Natives had not. These groups were "together" in different ways, barely compatible in an intermediate economy, and not at all compatible once wampum was money.

That insight about the relationship of forms of consciousness, and of personality, to want and to plenty, and to some third, some mediator (whether divine or human), may not be evident to everyone. There is a sort of theologico-politico-economics at work here (perhaps this is what Graeber means by an "anthropological theory of value"). The situation is familiar to the students of Vico and of the study of mythic consciousness, what Vico calls "poetic economy," and subsequent inquirers have called by numerous other names, from the deal with the devil to the Faustian bargain. But whether the origins of the human kind of consciousness might better be traced to spirit, to vital energy, or to the erotic kind of vitality, is a question lying close to the heart of the riddle of personality and its very existence.[53]

Rather than ask how objects come to have personality, we might more profitably ask how some objects come to be deprived of it, and how this reduction is rebalanced in a general economy of sacrifice, and hence the effort to re-sacralize whatever has been reduced to mere use, whether these objects be human, cattle, or oils and spices. In this regard, recall the woman who came to Jesus and expended a costly apportionment of oil on his feet, especially when such oils are usually reserved for the nobler parts of the bodies of nobler persons. When Judas Iscariot points out that the oil might have been sold and the money given to the poor, Jesus reminds him that, if one wishes make such comparisons, the poor are always among us, the son of man only for a short time. That is not an easy lesson. It is encrypted. Jesus temporalizes the question and asks, "What energy is sacred and what energy is mundane?" I do not think that Judas, or anyone else who believes in the institution of money, is likely to grasp the workings of personhood in this teaching. But it is intermediate, if still far removed from the gift, as it is understood among those who endure lack together, and who then achieve a condition of plenty.

Where comparison and contrast are minimal, we might say that our personhood, our collective dignity, is strong, but our personalities do not unroll themselves in ways that make for robust individuality. Where plenty prevails generally, personality turns upon itself in an endless litany of comparisons and contrasts. Personality dissolves into luxury, and the humans, as Vico says, ultimately "go mad and waste their substance."[54]

Exchanging Persons

Cassirer traces the development of human consciousness as a functional genealogy of symbol creation. Symbols are created both as the differentiation and refinement of successive *forms* of consciousness, each form serving as a basis for the subsequent form, and as the process of creating of what we now call material culture. In Cassirer's older terminology, it was simply the making of "civilization," by which he understood the progressive self-liberation of the human spirit by the creation of increasingly individualized freedom, and enacted in the presence of advancing technology, science, and art. His account emphasizes the expressive and internal dynamics of our creative powers, and it goes far toward explaining the advent of the subject/object split, at least so far as that division is our own energistic "work." Whether such a split can come into the world without God or the gods, along with the accompanying exterior judgment and comparison/contrast is an open question, but it never has happened as far as we know.

In short, the gods give us "objects": something neither yours nor mine, but harbingers and physical bearers of infinitely significant opportunities for our mutual comparison, contrast, and amid plenty, the subsequent reduction of social solidarity to rivalry. We may perform better or worse meeting this challenge. Once there are "objects," it is unsurprising that they retain something of the energistic trace of their origins, of the time before they *came between us* (please note the middle voice). In short, every artifact, as "object," retains some "personality," some mark of our solidarity from before it was fragmented and divinely arbitrated.[55] We might *read* this trace by regressing ourselves and our objects into a pretheistic *sensus communis*.[56] Our objects themselves might teach us not to be envious, and we might succeed if only we do not submit them to divine arbitration. The desire for special divine favor is the root of all evil. Money is only the evidence of it.

But this account is only half of the story. We might also raise the question of preobjective artifacts, which bear meaning in a way not yet fully objectified, with their expressive or erotic character remaining dominant, perhaps to such a degree as to occlude any consideration of such artifacts as "objects" in any distinct sense. Such standing in the human world renders such artifacts persons—not personified objects, but persons in the fullest concrete sense. Such is the character of wampum, as I have tried to describe it.

Within the system of symbols that creates culture, we find numerous institutions of exchange. Cassirer mentioned "economics" as an independent symbolic form of culture, but he did little to analyze or articulate this idea further. Mauss ought to be credited with creating a subdiscipline of philosophical anthropology that still awaits a name, but it carries out the articulation of exchange at the most basic level. Much as Cassirer surveyed the practices of originary peoples and mythic consciousness to provide an account of the origins of our projecting meaning onto and into physical mediums, Mauss looked at exchange in "archaic" societies (as I have said, he shunned the term "primitive") to discover the contingencies and necessities in the energies of exchange. These are both vital and *geistige* energies. As we have seen, Mauss's methods are nonreductive, empirical, and do not seek full objectification of the practices and proto-objects studied. As a result, he can describe preobjective relations among humans and their creations.

In a number of important ways, Mauss anticipated and also precipitated the work of Georges Bataille, who dubbed this form of study "general economy" a decade later. That name is not adequately clear, but the perspective has been enormously influential in subsequent European thought, especially in France, Italy, and Germany (specifically Frankfurt), after the European version of the "linguistic turn" in its flirtation with structuralism and much longer engagement with the critique of the same. The perspective of general economy then grew, after Bataille's death, beyond the "language-consciousness pairing," narrowly conceived, as Roland Barthes adapted "general economy" to the meaning of images as well as words (both written and spoken).[57]

The path from symbolic forms of culture, to archaic exchange, to general economy, and then to "the problem of the image" also marks the path of this chapter. I offered you wampum in image, in hopes of exposing a trace in its meaning, that of personality, that it retains today, on condition it is not seen as money, but as currency. What has never been adequately considered by the principal authors (Cassirer, Mauss, Bataille, Barthes) is how the combination of "symbol-exchange-excess/wasted energy-image/meaning" is permeated, each at its peculiar level of *abstraction* (or better, "projection"[58]) by the idea of "person." This term is meant in the sense of an existential presupposition of meaning, interpretation, and indeed, the form of existence itself.[59]

In concluding, exchange, contrary to almost every previous economic theory, is best (and indeed only) understood as permeated by the presupposition of "person" in the broadest ways. It is not that our *objects* of exchange are always personalized; it is that they are in fact persons, at bottom, body parts, so long as we grasp what currency really is, as desire, eros not logos. Stripped of all personality, the remainder is not exchangeable at all, even as money. It is not an accident that we adorn our paper bills with portraits of leaders. Such activity, if it is bereft of "person" completely is not true "exchange." It might be buying and selling, but not true exchange.

Another way to say this is that digital and mechanical transactions fall short of true exchange, and are, in the applicable sense, extraeconomic. They are not part of economics at all, and the study of such transactions is akin to engineering, especially computer analysis, and not a human study. Such a topic may be studied, of course, and should be, but it should not be considered a part of economics, which must remain humanistic to have any basis.

Returning then to genuine exchange, to use currency, by implication, is therefore the sacrifice of a person (not always a human, but always a person). This assertion will seem shocking, perhaps, but it can be made persuasive when traced through the best available courses of cultural consideration. I have attempted it.

Even further, we may consider as energistic sacrifice the instantaneous electronic exchanges of the sort that created the bit-coin phenomenon are salvific endeavors that seek to rescue from utilization-oblivion the sacrifice of personality that accompanies, and must accompany, that kind of exchange. The engineering of this kind of transaction is done by people whose desire is to be rich. One does not eliminate eros easily. This may seem to contradict what has been said of digital and mechanical transaction above, but there is a very great difference in the study of what is *left out* of account in digital/mechanical transactions, and what is *used*, or included in the same. The study of what is used is statistical. The study of what is left out or wasted is based on a humane and humanistic insight. Its "rescue" for the sake of profit is less important than the insight that some trace of the unused is wasted in every transaction, however deeply it may be digitized or mechanized, and the reason is simple: time is real.

Were there no waste, there would be nothing to save *from* being wasted, and where that "person" goes *un*saved, the waste is available for sacral consideration, for inclusion as person in and of the community. Were there no person to be sacralized, to be brought back from the abyss of mere utility, there would be no true exchange at all. These claims may seem extravagant, and I cannot hope to do more at present than to have illustrated the aptitude of a certain kind of narrative to our thinking about this problem. Nevertheless, I am convinced that true exchange is the exchange of persons (again, not always human persons, but including these). The work of those I have cited backs this line of thinking, but any sane person must confess that the line goes counter to the press and roil of the contemporary human current. So be it.

Notes

1. Tim Parks, *Medici Money: Banking, Metaphysics, and Art in Fifteenth Century Florence* (New York: W. W. Norton, 2005), 34. This study is valuable for the present inquiry because it documents the evolution in Europe from what I call "currency" to "money" in the century before the events with which I am primarily concerned, and provides the metaphysics of the transformation.

2. Marcel Mauss, *The Gift: Forms and Functions of Exchange in Archaic Societies*, trans. Ian Cunnison (London: Routledge and Kegan Paul, 1967 [1925]), 24. There is a newer translation of this work by Jane I. Guyer (Chicago: Hau Books, 2016), whose main value is the inclusion of extra material and annotations. The translation is not better, as Guyer admits, only a bit updated in usage.

3. I have relied on the PBS (WGBH) documentary *Mystic Voices* (2004) for much of the native viewpoint. The documentarists gathered many of the leading voices of the tribal councils and keepers of the wisdom of the Pequots, Narragansetts, Mohegans, and other tribes for that documentary, and it constitutes an interesting and important oral history. It was recognized with two Emmy awards. It is available here: http://www.pequotwar.com/. Accessed May 8, 2019. Some balance was brought to this imbalance of information in Lucianne Lavin's *Connecticut's Indigenous Peoples: What Archaeology, History, and Oral Traditions Teach Us about Their Communities and Cultures* (New Haven: Yale University Press, 2013), who made every effort to document the relevant history from Native sources. Also the book by Steven F. Johnson tells a wider history from the perspective of the Native peoples, with two useful appendices listing the various confederations of Algonkian groups and a glossary of tribal nations. See *Ninnuock (The People): The Algonkian People of New England* (Marlborough, MA: Bliss Publishing Co., 1995), 237–44. Also helpful in the confusing tangle of information is Edward Lodi's chronology of the main events

of the Pequot war, 119–32, and his glossary of persons involved, 135–93, in *The Pequot War* (Middleborough, MA: Rock Village Publishing, 2017).

4. The story of the Dutch "adventure" in the area is well narrated by Francis Jennings in *The Ambiguous Iroquois Empire: The Covenant Chain Confederation of Indian Tribes with English Colonies* (New York: Norton, 1984), ch. 4. The prior Dutch changes in banking had far-reaching effects on English banking and finance. The complex effects on money, banking, and trade, of these relations and events are summarized by Stephen Zarlenga, *The Lost Science of Money: The Mythology of Money—the Story of Power* (Valatie, NY: American Monetary Institute, 2002), chs. 8–10.

5. William Bradford, *Of Plymouth Plantation*, ed. Samuel Eliot Morrison (New York: Alfred A. Knopf, 1952), 203. Bradford does not quite understand that wampum could (within the two tribes that made it initially) serve as the most solemn form of exchange in a vast system of prestations. Wampum also served to take "the whole tribe out of the narrow circle of its own frontiers," creating relations of exchange with other groups in which wampum becomes "currency" (not "money," see below). In the case of wampum exchanged with those outside the tribe, the chief or an agent of the chief is typically the giver, and the wampum is entrusted to him for this purpose (see Mauss, *The Gift*, 27).

6. *Mystic Voices*, part 1, 10:00–10:50. Apart from the more sophisticated histories of the midtwentieth century, there are the more common sorts of assessments in widely circulated magazines that deeply contributed to the popular perception of wampum. For example, *The American Naturalist* 17, no. 5 (May 1883) has this observation by Ernest Ingersoll:

> The use of a circulating medium to facilitate commerce by simplifying the awkward devices of barter, is supposed to indicate indicate a considerable advance toward civilization in the people employing it. On this score the North American Indians ought to stand high in the list of barbarians, since they possessed an aboriginal money of recognized value, although it had no sanction other than common custom. This money was made from sea-shells, and was known by various names, of which one has survived popularly—wampum—to designate all varieties of shell beads as money. (33)

This is typical of the level of understanding possessed by writers over two centuries later. The term itself had become popularized, and the common understanding of its genuine role in the deeper history of human culture, and native culture in particular, had disappeared.

7. The idea is very old and very European. As Helen Grela says in her chapter in this book, "Aristotle considered the medium of exchange function to be the foundational: a specific commodity emerges to be the most sought after in barter, thus becoming money." See her chapter "Have We Effectively Made Money a Person?" 246. She is referring to Aristotle's discussion of money in his *Politics*, Books 8–10.

8. I am using the term "currency" in a technical way here, following the arguments of Marcel Mauss against those of Bruno Malinowski. Malinowski uses the term "money" for the exchange medium in shell beads of the Melanesian natives of the Trobriand

Islanders, but Mauss argues convincingly that "currency" is a more precise term. The economy Malinowski describes in these islands is closely analogous to the narrative I am providing here, but I am using Mauss's *interpretation* of Malinowsky over Malinowsky's own account. I find Mauss to have a broader and more incisive understanding. Hence the term "currency" I will reserve for the way these shell beads are exchanged in what Mauss calls an "intermediate" economy. See Mauss, *The Gift: Forms and Functions of Exchange in Archaic Societies*, trans. Ian Cunnison (London: Routledge and Kegan Paul, 1967 [1925]), n.17, 92–94.

    9. Bradford, *Of Plymouth Plantation*, 203. The Dutch used wampum as legal tender well before the English did so. The more detailed story of the rise and collapse of wampum as currency among the Dutch can be followed by examining their New Netherland ordinances regarding wampum from 1641 through 1662, which were reprinted in the *New York Times* during the height of the silver-standard debate. See Simon W. Rosendale, "The Involution of Wampum as Currency: The Story Told by the Colonial Ordinances of New Netherland, 1641–1662," *New York Times*, July 28, 1895. There was a growing problem of people trading "unpolished wampum," which was upsetting the legally established ratios of wampum to beaver pelts, to Dutch gilders, to English money. The role played by beaver pelts as currency was exceedingly fluid since they were plentiful in the first two decades of trading and became increasingly more valuable as trapping moved inland. This sad story is documented by Andrew Lipman, *The Saltwater Frontier: Indians and the Contest for the American Coast* (New Haven: Yale University Press, 2015). David Silverman has a good summary of how this unfolded in *This Land Is Their Land*, 211–20, although he misunderstands Bradford's use of the word "drug" to describe it.

    10. In this chapter, I will be drawing on the ideas of "general economy" set out by Georges Bataille, and in his thought, "use" is a descralization of whatever is used. Utility is banishment from all things valuable and precious, whereas "waste" is what is held sacred because it is the realm of our freedom, leisure, and thus true humanity. Bataille is following Mauss in this articulation, but it is unclear how receptive Mauss was to this interpretation of his ideas. See Bataille, *The Accursed Share*, vol. 1, trans. Robert Hurley (New York: Zone Books, 1988), 9–41, and especially 63–77, which is on Mauss's theory.

    11. Those who think that "archaic" societies are egalitarian are against the strong evidence of many studies, and Mauss makes it clear that the few are rich and the many are poor in the indigenous groups he studied.

    12. Mauss, *The Gift*, 25. Here Mauss is speaking of *kula* (shell neckalaces) among the natives of the Trobriand Islands, but the situation is the same among the Pequot and Narragansett.

    13. George Willison gives a succinct account of this cluelessness in *Saints and Strangers: Being the Lives of the Pilgrim Fathers and Their Families, with Their Foes; and an Account of Their Posthumous Wanderings in Limbo, Their Final Resurrection and Rise to Glory, and the Strange Pilgrimages of Plymouth Rock* (New York: Time-Life Books, 1945), 286–87. This book is also valuable because it takes the perspective of the difficult relations, economic, social, and religious, between the religious community that planned Plymouth colony and the "strangers" (non-religious English settlers) they were obliged to bring with them.

14. There is a sort of functionalization of the idea of "category" here, but it follows what Marcel Mauss describes in his "A Category of the Human Mind: The Notion of Person; of Self," trans. W. D. Halls, in *The Category of Person*, ed. M. Carrithers, S. Collins, S. Lukes (Cambridge: Cambridge University Press, 1985), 1–25. Mauss says: "We have concentrated most especially on the social history of the categories of the human mind. We attempt to explain them one by one, using very simply, and as a temporary expedient, the list of Aristotelian categories as a point of departure" (1).

15. Mauss uses the term "potlatch" for the economy of total prestation, a situation in which little effort has to be given to survival and almost all economic activity is wasteful and rivalrous, especially within the privileged class of an archaic society. This bounty and wastefulness, or potlatch, existed with the Narragansett and the Pequot, but not with their neighboring tribes. See Mauss, *The Gift*, 3–8.

16. Mauss, *The Gift*, 31. See also Miguel Tamen, *Friends of Interpretable Objects* (Cambridge, MA: Harvard University Press, 2001), esp. chs 1 and 6. It is worthwhile to consider, in this light, what it *feels like* to be in debt, especially where the debt cannot be met. Ironically, the "Pilgrims" wered in this very situation, but did not recognize its analogue among the natives of the region. This odd feeling of desperation, which clearly survives into advanced economies, is a good place to begin considering the archaic systems of total prestation and their psychological effects. One place to study the effects and causes, as it were, of this complex system is Chris Fowler's *The Archaeology of Personhood: An Anthropological Approach* (London: Routledge, 2004), especially ch. 3, "Personhood, Exchange, and Artifacts," although a number of his chapters bear directly on this chapter and other chapters in this book. See particularly, for example, the "personhood" of swords in archaic societies, pp. 63–64, in relation to chapter six, by Alan Maisey.

17. For a well-written summary, see Ann C. Tweedy, "From Beads to Bounty: How Wampum Became America's First Currency," in *Indian Country Today* (October 5, 2017): https://newsmaven.io/indiancountrytoday/archive/from-beads-to-bounty-how-wampum-became-america-s-first-currency-76Ql3IPA2kKpBqfHiggjXw/, accessed May 8, 2019. Tweedy's article led me to a far more detailed analysis by David Graeber in his book, *Toward an Anthropological Theory of Value: The False Coin of Our Own Dreams* (New York: Palgrave, 2001), cited below.

18. *Mystic Voices*, part 1, 15:22–16:07.

19. *Mystic Voices*, part 1, 37:00–37:35.

20. Tweedy, "From Beads to Bounty," accessed May 8, 2019. A much more detailed version of this incident that Tweedy doesn't cite is in Christopher L. Pastore, *Between Land and Sea: The Atlantic Coast and the Transformation of New England* (Cambridge, MA: Harvard University Press, 2014), 34–35. Also, the name of this crucial trader is "Jacob Eelkens" (51) and "Jacques Eelckens" (54) in Francis Jennings, *The Ambiguous Iroquois Empire*, who reports that the Mohawk threatened Eelkens with death for kidnapping chiefs, so he may have done what I describe here more than once.

21. Pastore, *Between Land and Sea*, 34–35.

22. The process by which human beings became commodified under capitalism is a difficult and vexed subject. The essay of Helen Milne in this volume treats it. But a very subtle account is also given by Achille Mbembe in *The Critique of Black Reason*, trans. Laurent DuBois (Durham, NC: Duke University Press, 2017). Influenced by Bataille and

(evidently, but not explicitly) Mauss, Mbembe has an unusual understanding of capitalism that supports a narrative about this tricky subject. In the context of summarizing the slave trade, he says:

> Capitalism emerged as a double impulse toward, on the one hand, the unlimited violation of all forms of prohibition and, on the other, the abolition of any distinction between means and ends. The Black slave, in his dark splendor, was the first racial subject: the product of the two impulses, the most visible symbol of the possibility of violence without limits and vulnerability without a safety net. (Mbembe, *The Critique of Black Reason*, 179)

No one else I have encountered sees the emergence of capitalism this way. It is not an economic system; rather the economic system is one of the results of an act of symbolization, a sort of speech act, in the marriage of two impulses. I think this account is compatible with the ideas of Mauss and Bataille.

23. Mauss, *The Gift*, 30; cf. 29. I understand that this statement sounds like the standard colonialist excuse-making, but in context that is not how Mauss means it. He doesn't regard the inability to abstract as a deficiency in the humanity or level of sophistication of native peoples. If anything, the power to abstract is a pathology of capitalism.

24. Kevin McBride has documented that the Pequot War was an extended conflict, lasting over a year, and that it was not just a conflict between the English and the Pequot, but rather, the English were joined by numerous Native allies. See McBride, "Preserving the Battlefields of the Pequot War," in *Connecticut Preservation News* 33:6, 6–7, 12. McBride, along with Lucianne Lavin, is probably the foremost expert on these complex issues. A good listing of his relevant publications in Lucianne Lavin's *Connecticut's Indigenous Peoples*, 427–29, which also contains an impressive and comprehensive listing of Lavin's many publications in this area.

25. Bradford, *Of Plymouth Plantation*, 203.

26. As we have noted earlier, the Dutch engagement with wampum as currency and finally as money (i.e., legal tender) was much more involved. The English came into full economic relation with this economy as a result of the interruption of trade accompanying the English Civil War (1642–1651), and the scarcity of other currency in a growing New England. Willison describes the economic collapse in some detail in *Saints and Strangers*, esp. pp. 349 ff.

27. See Graeber's account of this in *Toward and Anthropological Theory of Value*, pp. 117–49.

28. Mauss, *The Gift*, 22.

29. Mauss, *The Gift*, 22.

30. For a compendium of such employments of wampum, see Nathaniel Philbrick, *Mayflower: A Story of Community, Courage, and War* (New York: Penguin, 2006), 170–72, 190–94, 199, 206, 209, 258, 307, 316, 343. Especially striking is this description of King Philip's wampum:

> On Friday, August 6 [1676], Philip was greeted by three of the Nipmucks' most powerful sachems. Philip possessed a coat made of wampum, and he

used it to good effect. Unstringing the white and purple shell beads, he gave "about a peck" to each of the sachems, "which" according to an eye-witness, "they accepted." . . . In the months ahead, Philip continued to cut "his coat to pieces" as he ritualistically secured the cooperation of sachems from Connecticut to modern Maine.

When Philip was killed, he was still a rich man. The man who killed him, the famous Indian fighter Benjamin Church, was given Philip's remaining wampum as a spoil of battle, which is described thus in the reported words of Annawon, a Wampanoag chief:

"Great Captain, you have killed Philip and conquered his country, for I believe that I and my company are the last that war against the English, so [I] suppose the war is ended by your means and therefore these things belong to you." Inside the basket were several belts of wampum. One was nine inches wide and depicted flowers, birds, and animals. Church was now standing and when Annawon draped the belt over his shoulders, it reached down to his ankles. The next belt was one that Philip had commonly wrapped around his head and possessed flags that had hung at his back; the third had been intended for his chest and contained a star at either end. All of the belts had been edged with red, possibly human hair that Annawon said had been secured in Mohawk country. (Philbrick, 342–43)

According to other sources, Annawon also said to Church, "There is no Indian now in all the Land of the Bays who is worthy to keep them." Alma H. Burton, "Massasoit: A Story of the Indians of New England," Heritage History, https://www.heritage-history.com/index.php?c=read&author=burton&book=massasoit&story=annawon, accessed May 18, 2019.

This account shows wampum as the spoils of war, which would be in keeping with its ritual value for the makers of wampum. It was, effectively, the person of King Philip.

31. In a phone conversation, August 13, 2020, with the archaeologist Kevin McBride (University of Connecticut), I learned that it may not have been the Mohawks who killed Sassacus. He also does not think that any bounty was likely paid in wampum in exchange for the head and hands sent to the English. Edward Lodi says that the Narragansetts bribed the Mohawk to kill Sassacus, and in his account, only the scalps were sent back, and only as proof of the deaths of Sassacus and his close kin. See Lodi, *The Pequot War* (Middleborough, MA: Rock Village Publishing, 2017), 95–96.

32. Our habit of using the word "clams" for money derives from wampum. The price of a native sachem was (evidently) about three hundred yards of wampum, but when the Pequots were blamed for the deaths of John Stone and his crew of seven, the magistrates at Massachusetts demanded eight hundred yards of wampum (one hundred yards per Englishmen), but also beaver and otter pelts, exclusive trading rights and land in the Connecticut River Valley, and they demanded legal authority over all disputes between the Pequot and Narragansett. It is not easy to estimate what total value the English were placing on the persons who had been killed, but it is clear that the value was high. And Stone was no sachem. He was a criminal and had been banished from Massachusetts Bay, with the penalty of death should he return, and he was a rogue and a pirate. One would

think that the English would thank the Natives who killed him. It also appears that he precipitated his own murder since he had kidnapped some Native men, forcing them to guide his ship up the river, and then demanding a ransom for them. That the colony expected any compensation under such circumstances seems extraordinary, but they in fact demanded it, and heavy compensation at that. One suspects there was more afoot than the records show. The Pequot understandably refused. When the Puritans sent John Oldham to collect this amount, the natives of Block Island (Pequot tributaries) murdered Oldham and were in the process of dismembering him when confronted by another English vessel. One assumes there would have been a return of body parts. From that point, it was war.

This dismembering and exchanging body parts became an expected part of both trade war and open war. The Dutch remained enthusiastic practitioners. Jennings reports a case when the Dutch returned a kidnapped Mohawk leader for ransom, but without his male member, which they displayed on a pole. See Jennings, *The Ambiguous Iroquois Empire*, 51–52.

33. The name "Wampanoag" seems not to have been in use as a label for the several related tribes it now covers until after the death of Macomet, also called "King Philip," in 1678. Pokanoket identity was criminalized in the aftermath of the war (1676–1678), and those native peoples who had fought it began to refer themselves after the language they spoke, which is the basis of the word "Wampanoag."

34. It is very clear from the Dutch ordinances that the Europeans were making legal distinctions among qualities of wampum. See Rosendale, "The Involution of Wampum as Currency," especially the Ordinance of April 18, 1641.

35. Mauss, "A Category of the Human Mind," in *The Category of Person*, 5.

36. Mauss, "A Category of the Human Mind," in *The Category of Person*, 14.

37. See *Mystic Voices*, part 2, 8:30–9:05.

38. See *Republic*, 469–71; also for the relation to ownership and property, see 464. It would be instructive to have a linguistic analysis of the Algonquian family of words that came to be translated as "friend" from this time period, to see what sorts of alliances and corresponding duties existed in their understanding of social relations. The word occurs frequently in the English accounts of these times and I suspect may be difficult to translate.

39. Mauss, *The Gift*, 3, first italics are mine, second in the original.

40. See Mauss, *The Gift*, 5. This is my own assessment of the situation in southern New England, based on Mauss's theory. In the numerous histories I have read, no one recognizes this situation as total prestation.

41. It is good to remember that Mauss was a devoted socialist and that his work (and that of his group) sought to rework in a more empirical and scientific way the much more imaginative and less believable efforts of Friedrich Engels in *The Holy Family*. Mauss's politics and importance as a political thinker has been discussed in excellent detail by Graeber in *Toward and Anthropological Theory of Value*, ch. 6.

42. The completely ridiculous formalities and etiquette accompanying the marriage of Marie Antoinette (daughter of Empress Maria Theresa) to Louis August of France in 1770 would be an example of the absurdities to which the symbolic enactment of total prestation were extended since, respectively, the supposed dignity of the "person" of the Austrian Empire and the French Empire had to be acknowledged. No appearance of inequality could be tolerated.

43. See Lodi, *The Pequot War*, 95.

44. I confess that I have always felt some discomfort at portions of the traditional Protestant Christian service when the "offering plate" is passed. I prefer to send my check outside of worship (at least it bears my actual name, and my mark, and I have, by signing it, made it "currency," and it stands as my proxy, my agent). Granting that there is plenty of biblical sanction for the practice of taking a "collection," it is common for the money in the plate to be taken to the foot of the cross and "dedicated." One supposes that in this moment the money is transformed into currency, something on a par with the giving of one's service, and talent, and calling to the service of the church—all of that could be "currency." But this act of dedication still seems to fall considerably short of making the money into *wampum*. Such money, even as currency, is still powerfully degraded, although perhaps it was less so when the coins were fashioned of gold and silver. After all, the magi brought gold to Jesus, according to the Scriptures. Mauss deals with the challenge of gifts to the gods and alms in *The Gift*, 12–16. But he allows that he is no way prepared to confront the problems associated with mythic consciousness (12).

45. This is Lewis Hyde's summary, see below.

46. Lewis Hyde, *The Gift: The Erotic Life of Property* (New York: Vintage Books, 1983), xiv.

47. See Roland Barthes, *Elements of Semiology*, trans. A. Lavers and C. Smith (New York: Hill and Wang, 1967), 76–78. He says, "The zero degree [of opposition] is . . . not a total absence . . . *it is a significant absence*. . . . the zero degree testifies to the power held by any system of signs, of creating meaning 'out of nothing': the language can be content with the opposition of some thing and nothing" (77). In much the same way that wampum offers no resistance or opposition until it is currency, the grammatical middle voice offers no resistance and presents no opposition where we have not noticed its work of active passivating or passive activating. "Because," and "between," and "belong," are just the surface of what we are missing at degree zero. The depth lies in "be-ing" I suspect—a point worthy of Heidegger, perhaps.

48. Philbrick, among others, notes that the idea of "the Wampanoag" as a political grouping came into existence a bit later, with the death of the Nauset sachem Aspinet and the expansion of Massasoit's influence. Philbrick, *Mayflower*, 155.

49. Philbrick, *Mayflower*, 99.

50. Philbrick, *Mayflower*, 165.

51. Philbrick, *Mayflower*, 168.

52. For a full account, see Auxier, "The Return of the Initiate: Hegel on Bread and Wine," *The Owl of Minerva: Journal of the Hegel Society of America* 2, no. 2 (spring 1991), 191–208.

53. See Auxier, "Scheler and the Very Existence of the Impersonal," *Eidos: A Journal for the Philosophy of Culture* 1, no. 3 (April 2018), 74–86. http://eidos.uw.edu.pl/files/pdf/eidos/2018-01/eidos_3_auxier.pdf.

54. Giambattista Vico, *The New Science*, trans. T. G. Bergen and M. H. Fisch (Ithaca: Cornell University Press, 1948), p. 70 (paragraph 241, axiom 66).

55. Older readers will perhaps remember that this is the main theme of the 1980 film *The Gods Must Be Crazy*, directed by Jamie Uys.

56. There are two sorts of *sensus communis* at work here. First there is the *sensus communis* which we study through examining mythic consciousness, both phenomenologically and ontologically). Second, there is transcendental or "reflective" *sensus communis*, for lack of a better label. This latter is the sort of weak corona that forms around true praxis and makes us aware of and long for true praxis (ritual, dance, music, being the essence of true praxis). Both sorts of *sensus communis* and reflective are "person." But they are. mirror images of one another. You can't get thick community from reflective *sensus communis*, but you can get concrete ideals, like "a republic of laws and not men." Thick community—living, breathing community—would not be tolerable to us moderns; we have the pathology of individuality, which is a departure from anything genuinely human, and probably a cancer of the soul, but that is where we are. We don't want to be healed, to be fully human again, we want to imagine being healed and have that be enough. *Sensus communis*, in the primary sense, is the lost home we feel as a lack in our being, the hole in the soul, as Socrates says, reciting Diotima in Symposium. Reflective *sensus communis* is its replacement, usually coming in the form of stories, either real stories like the Brothers Grimm collected or impoverished, unimaginative stories like those scientists tell us about the order of nature. It is a sad thing to try to make one's spiritual repast from the thin porridge of science. You will do better to write songs or choreograph dances, if you must indulge your reflective powers while re-enacting the humanness we lost but vaguely remember in our collective being. Better yet, sing the songs and dance the dances and be human again to that degree.

57. The principal and transformative work is, of course, *Elements of Semiology*, see esp. pp. 54–57.

58. Both are Susanne Langer's terms. She used "abstraction" through most of her career as a power of reinserting a past formed feeling into a present culturally saturated situation, but she adjusted this unusual way of using the term "abstraction" to "projection" in her final magnum opus. It was a good decision, although it risks being confused with Freudian or (very different) Jungian usage of that term. Interestingly, it resonates more sympathetically with Heidegger's early sense of Dasein's "projects." Langer's aim is more empirical and scientific than Heidegger's, but the two share ground on the existential and fundamental (i.e., irreducible) work of time and temporality in forming experience.

59. See my essays, "Scheler and the Very Possibility of the Impersonal" and "Bowne on Time, Evolution and History," *Journal of Speculative Philosophy* 12, no. 3 (1998), 181–203.

Bibliography

Auxier, Randall. "Bowne on Time, Evolution and History." *Journal of Speculative Philosophy* 12, no. 3 (1998): 181–203.

———. "The Return of the Initiate: Hegel on Bread and Wine." *The Owl of Minerva: Journal of the Hegel Society of America* 2:2 (spring 1991): 191–208.

———. "Scheler and the Very Existence of the Impersonal." *Eidos: A Journal of the Philosophy of Culture* 1, no. 3 (April 2018): 74–86. http://eidos.uw.edu.pl/files/pdf/eidos/2018-01/eidos_3_auxier.pdf.

Barthes, Roland. *Elements of Semiology.* Translated by A. Lavers and C. Smith. New York: Hill and Wang, 1967.
Bataille, Georges. *The Accursed Share*, vol. 1. Translated by Robert Hurley. New York: Zone Books, 1988.
Bonfonti, Leo. *The Pequot-Mohican War.* Wakefield, MA: Pride Publications, 1971.
Bradford, William. *Of Plymouth Plantation.* Edited by Samuel Eliot Morrison. New York: Alfred A. Knopf, 1952.
Bridenbaugh, Carl. *Vexed and Troubled Englishmen, 1590-1642: The Beginnings of the American People.* New York: Oxford University Press, 1968.
Burton, Alma H. "Massasoit: A Story of the Indians of New England." Heritage History, https://www.heritage-history.com/index.php?c=read&author=burton&book=massasoit &story=annawon.
Cave, Alfred A. *The Pequot War.* Amherst, MA: University of Massachusetts Press, 1996.
Chet, Guy. *Conquering the American Wilderness: The Triumph of European Warfare in the Colonial Northeast.* Amherst: University of Massachusetts Press, 2003.
DeForest, John W. *History of the Indians of Connecticut from the Earliest Known Period to 1850.* Hartford: William James Hammersley, 1851.
Fowler, Chris. *The Archaeology of Personhood: An Anthropological Approach.* London: Routledge, 2004.
Graeber, David. *Toward an Anthropological Theory of Value: The False Coin of Our Own Dreams.* New York: Palgrave, 2001.
Grela, Helen. "Have We Effectively Made Money a Person and Ourselves Its Corporeal Embodiment?" In *The Cultural Power of Personal Objects: Traditional Accounts and New Perspectives*, edited by Jared Kemling. Albany: State University of New York Press, 2021, 241–265.
Hale, Horatio. "Four Huron Wampus Records: A Study of Aboriginal American History and Mnemonic Symbols," with Notes and Addenda by E. B. Tylor. Pamphlet. London: Harrison and Sons, St. Martin's Lane, 1897.
Hyde, Lewis. *The Gift: The Erotic Life of Property.* New York: Vintage Books, 1983.
Ingersoll, Ernest. "Wampum and Its History." *The American Naturalist* 17, no. 5 (May 1883).
Jacobs, Jaap. *New Netherland: A Dutch Colony in Seventeenth Century America.* Leiden: Brill, 2005.
Jennings, Francis. *The Ambiguous Iroquois Empire: The Covenant Chain Confederation of Indian Tribes with English Colonies.* New York: Norton, 1984.
———. *The Invasion of America: Indians, Colonialism, and the Cant of Conquest.* New York: Norton, 1976.
Johnson, Steven F. *Ninnuock (The People): The Algonkian People of New England.*
Lavin, Lucianne. *Connecticut's Indigenous Peoples: What Archaeology, History, and Oral Traditions Teach Us about Their Communities and Cultures.* New Haven: Yale University Press, 2013.
Lipman, Andrew. *The Saltwater Frontier: Indians and the Contest for the American Coast.* New Haven: Yale University Press, 2015.
Lodi, Edward. *The Pequot War.* Middleborough, MA: Rock Village Publishing, 2017.

Mauss, Marcel. "A Category of the Human Mind: The Notion of Person; of Self." Translated by W. D. Halls. *The Category of Person*, ed. M. Carrithers, S. Collins, S. Lukes. Cambridge: Cambridge University Press, 1985, 1–25.
———. *The Gift: Forms and Functions of Exchange in Archaic Societies.* Translated by Ian Cunnison. London: Routledge and Kegan Paul, 1967 (1925).
———. *The Gift: Forms and Functions of Exchange in Archaic Societies*, trans. Jane I. Guyer (Chicago: Hau Books, 2016).
Mbembe, Achille. *The Critique of Black Reason.* Translated by Laurent DuBois. Durham, NC: Duke University Press, 2017.
McBride, Kevin. "Preserving the Battlefields of the Pequot War." *Connecticut Preservation News* 33, no. 6, pp. 6–7, 12.
Mystic Voices (2004). PBS (WGBH) documentary. http://www.pequotwar.com/, accessed August 10, 2020.
Parks, Tim. *Medici Money: Banking, Metaphysics, and Art in Fifteenth Century Florence.* New York: W. W. Norton, 2005.
Pastore, Christopher L. *Between Land and Sea: The Atlantic Coast and the Transformation of New England.* Cambridge, MA: Harvard University Press, 2014.
Philbrick, Nathaniel. *Mayflower: A Story of Community, Courage, and War.* New York: Penguin, 2006.
Prince, J. Dyneley. "The Passamaquody Wampum Records." *Proceedings of the American Philosophical Society* 36:156 (December 1897): 479–95.
Rosendale, Simon W. "The Involution of Wampum as Currency: The Story Told by the Colonial Ordinances of New Netherland, 1641–1662," New York *Times*, July 28, 1895.
Silverman, David J. *This Land Is Their Land: The Wampanoag Indians, Plymouth Colony, and the Troubled History of Thanksgiving.* New York: Bloomsbury, 2019.
Slotkin, Richard, and Folsom, James K. *So Dreadful a Judgment: Puritan Responses to King Philip's War, 1676–1677.* Middletown, CT: Wesleyan University Press, 1978.
Tamen, Miguel. *Friends of Interpretable Objects.* Cambridge, MA: Harvard University Press, 2001.
Tweedy, Ann C. "From Beads to Bounty: How Wampum Became America's First Currency." In *Indian Country Today* (October 5, 2017): https://newsmaven.io/indiancountry today/archive/from-beads-to-bounty-how-wampum-became-america-s-first-currency-76Ql3IPA2kKpBqfHiggjXw/.
Vaughan, Alden T. *New England Frontier: Puritans and Indians, 1620–1675.* Boston: Little, Brown, and Co., 1965.
Vico, Giambattista. *The New Science.* Translated by T. G. Bergen and M. H. Fisch. Ithaca: Cornell University Press, 1948.
Willison, George. *Saints and Strangers: Being the Lives of the Pilgrim Fathers and Their Families, with Their Foes; and an Account of Their Posthumous Wanderings in Limbo, Their Final Resurrection and Rise to Glory, and the Strange Pilgrimages of Plymouth Rock.* New York: Time-Life Books, 1945.
Zarlenga, Stephen. *The Lost Science of Money: The Mythology of Money—the Story of Power.* Valatie, NY: American Monetary Institute, 2002.

Chapter 15

How My Piano Uses Gendlin's Focusing Method

RALPH D. ELLIS

Editor's Note: This chapter is the first of two that focus on themes in aesthetics: specifically, on the topic of music. Ellis examines the relationship between a musician and their instrument. He argues that, in his case, his piano is just as important (if not more so) than he is in crafting and writing music—the personality of the instrument is a vital consideration. To explore this point, he introduces Eugene Gendlin's concept of focusing. This chapter develops some of the psychological themes that were briefly introduced in chapter 10, while also providing a fascinating phenomenological exploration of the artist and the act of creativity.

Some years ago, I purchased a rebuilt Weber grand piano from a singularly self-assured old Swedish repairman in Pittsburgh who politely clicked his heels as he ushered me into a large shop strewn with the guts of numerous and sundry pianos of various types and vintages. As soon as I tried a few notes on one, he confidently directed me to a Weber whose exterior obviously had seen better days, assuring me in broken English that this piano, and no other, was the one I must have.

After taking the piano home and practicing on it for some time, I was quite taken aback to discover the wealth of knowledge and insight this piano somehow had already learned about music, human emotions, and especially jazz improvisation. Without exaggeration, I now have absolutely no doubt that this piano is unique among pianos—a living, intelligent creature with free will and a sophisticated understanding of truth and reality, including moral and valuational reality—in fact, a person. When I say this, people often think I am speaking metaphorically. On the contrary, all these things are literally true, and even stranger things, as I will explain. One of the most baffling oddities is that I can make most of these claims only for the one particular piano, although I have played on many others over the years.

I freely admit that, on occasion, when awakened at night thinking that the piano is playing itself, I discover that there is a simple scientific explanation: one or two of the cats have been playing the piano by walking on the keyboard. But other times, when I seem to hear musical ideas while asleep, I know that the music didn't originate with my own imagination; ultimately and for the most part, it came from the piano, which at earlier times had implanted those imagined ideas into my head, and finally they emerged as dreams or involuntary auditory images.

I am not referring here to the standard truism that a good piano "plays us" rather than vice versa. In fact, there isn't much truth to this truism when I play pianos *away* from home; in those cases, it actually is I who have to do most of the playing, with the piano mostly just responding like any mechanical device. In those venues, the ideas taught to me by my own piano (with slight permutations and extrapolations) do mostly come proximally from my own imagination, from within my own head and body and are simply transferred from my own mind to those other pianos (sometimes with a polite comment or two from the piano in question, reminding me that some idea I tried didn't actually work).

The old Weber that I keep at home, by contrast, is not just a mechanism and is not within my control. It actually tells me what riffs or chord extensions, voicings, substitutions, and so on, do or don't work. Again, I don't mean this metaphorically, as will become clear. If I try something that doesn't work, the piano lets me know unequivocally and matter-of-factly—if only I am paying attention and willing to listen. Unlike other pianos, it possesses the actual understanding and freedom that it needs to direct me away from the silly and idiotic musical ideas to which I most assuredly would initially have been inclined. (I say that the piano has "freedom" in the existential rather than contra-causal sense: "freedom" from currently external constraints, such that what it does is created out of its own personality, without merely being caused by those currently external constraints. Of course, it is constrained by its own personal history and psychological constitution, which had its various root causes just as mine did, and is no more or less contracausally free than my own brain is. I know something of those root causes, because I conversed, albeit across a substantial language barrier, with the wise old technician who so astutely rebuilt the piano.)

When playing *away* from home, the situation is different: I mostly just try to remember the lessons my piano has taught me, and of course expand on them, but again in ways that it ultimately had taught me can work, and in which contexts. In fact, I should emphasize at the outset that as a child I failed my first music aptitude test, proving beyond doubt that only the laborious instruction received from the piano over many years was able to overcome this deficiency.

Some might object—as my above comment about other pianos almost logically implies—that pianos categorically are merely mechanical devices designed to execute scale patterns that reflect the contingent and arbitrary ideas and emotions of human musicians, which make sense only relative to the accidental properties of the human nervous system. Perhaps if our nervous systems were differently designed, we would respond to completely different scales and harmonies from the familiar ones we have come to know and to which we standardly tune our pianos. It might be argued that, since other pianos are physically similar to my old Weber (and in many cases physically superior in their mechanics), the only relevant difference must arise from *my own situated subjectivity,* which therefore—so the argument would go—must be the real source of the ideas. Even the "well-tempered scale" per se, it might be supposed, is only a reflection of human subjectivity and a culturally conditioned one at that.

My piano quickly informed me in no uncertain terms of the error in this kind of assumption, very shortly after I acquired it and began listening to what it had to say. The old Swedish repairman must already have known of its intelligent qualities. He never fully explained, with his minimal English and my total ignorance of his language, why this particular piano was the one I must have, but I soon learned the answer. I happened one day to strike a low C on the keyboard while depressing the sustain pedal and noticed that the C above it was faintly vibrating in resonance, as well as the G above that, and the E above that. The piano, of its own accord, was playing a C major chord. The C resonated with the other strings only in the specific order assigned to them by the inherent overtone series of the C being struck. If you have access to a piano, you can try the same experiment. If you listen carefully, you will hear the resonating notes, especially if you depress the sustain pedal while striking the note. (If you have trouble hearing the G and the E, try actually playing those notes before starting the experiment, so that your ear knows what it is listening for.)

Some people wonder whether they really are *hearing* the G and the E or only *imagining* them. Here is a simple way to tell: Try hitting an F# instead of the G, then hit the low C; you won't hear the F# resonating with the C the way you heard the G. That's because the G is *in* the C's overtone series at that point, and the F# isn't.

All pianos, I must admit, possess at least this elementary degree of sensitivity to the ontological structures of reality. But whether they can also understand the emotional and valuational dimension so well is a matter of which I can't speak, although I can say that, for me, they all seem to lack those more sophisticated perceptions except for the one Weber with which the old Swede wisely entrusted me—a perplexing fact which I will attempt to explain.

To be sure, we do sometimes like to hear scale patterns with some of the notes "detuned" or tuned to quarter-tones, as in Arabic music. My piano later would teach me why this is the case as well. Our ears and our hearts need variety, complexity, and unpredictability, not just dull harmony.

After noticing this strange resonance of the notes of the C chord, I realized that mathematical relationships basic to the fundamental construction of reality were at play here, and the piano was trying to inform me about them—along with the ontological features of conscious beings that make us specifically receptive to the meanings of these relationships (including, as I will show later, valuational and emotional meanings of such relationships). Here again, this ontology is not accidental or relative to culture; it is a feature of reality that anyone can hear if they have working ears and a desire to direct their attention toward it.

I then played a low D-flat, and noticed that the piano faintly resonated in the form of a D-flat major chord. And as in the case of the C, I thought I could faintly detect other overtones of the note even beyond the basic triad, ultimately forming the notes of a scale (not the "major" scale so familiar in modern Western cultures, but the mixolydian one that one can associate with much of Celtic and Indian music, and from which our "major" scale is readily available by a simple extrapolation). Each note that I struck on the piano logically implied its own chords, scales, and possibilities, along with what I would later understand are the emotional and even moral meanings they make possible.

I never would have noticed these strange facts by playing or listening to other pianos away from home. In those contexts, I am much too preoccupied with whether my playing sounds good enough and have little leftover attention to direct to such unexpected phenomena. Or I may be distracted by making polite conversation with the piano's owner or other humans who might be present. Also, I wouldn't want to inflict too much experimentation on anyone who might be present, because 90 percent of the ideas I would try out would inevitably be rejected by the piano, with embarrassing effects on the bystanders.

The simple observation that the piano already knew harmony and scales as reflected in the overtone series was only the beginning of the *least* interesting part of a long course of instruction. Later, the piano would show its ability to correct any possible misperception about which I might have queried it, even regarding the meaning of life and the valuational dimension of reality—if only I were willing to listen. This last qualification, as every teacher knows, is the main challenge to any teaching process: the student must want to learn and be willing to abandon previous understandings despite extensive investments in their validity. This effect is more familiar when it occurs in the political arena, where people are willing to listen only to the evidence that fits their presuppositions—presuppositions that are mostly emotionally predisposed and motivated by existential and psychological disturbances not even visible to the person affected by them. This "hermeneutic circle," as philosophers call it,[1] is known more commonly as a political "echo chamber." In my own case, I was initially quite ill-disposed to the notion that a piano could possess philosophical understanding, existential freedom, and personality. Only later, therefore, was I able to hear what the piano was saying.

In the broader context of music in general, we can see the importance of this hermeneutical aspect of the learning process clearly proven by a simple fact. If we look at the life histories of jazz musicians (i.e., performers who also must compose in real time), we might expect that their improvement in executing the craft would be gradual, like the improvement in the speed of a runner. But this is often far from the truth. When Charlie Parker was a teenager, the other musicians would cringe when he came to sit in with them because his playing was so horrible and amateurish.[2] Then over the course of one summer, which he famously spent "woodshedding" with his sax, he returned in the fall and suddenly was the monster player we all know so well today. Why was the improvement relatively sudden rather than gradual?

I was perplexed by this question for a number of years; but finally, my piano told me the answer, which is fairly simple. When young players listen to themselves play (if they listen to themselves at all), they desperately look for the good qualities in what they are doing. This may be a necessary stage of development, for at least two reasons: first, as Rollo May[3] famously pointed out, creativity requires a good bit of courage, which in turn motivates us to think that successful artistry will come more easily than it actually does; we think we are already almost there. Second, during the creative process, we need to envision ideas that are good, not bad; so we naturally look to see that the good ideas we had envisioned have actually been executed. Both of these factors lead us to overlook the flaws in our playing or in the ideas we use when improvising.

But there comes a point when we quit focusing so much on the good and pay careful attention to the bad. This is a psychologically difficult step in music as in any other aspect of our personal development. As soon as it does occur, the rest plays out in rapid succession: when we know what is wrong, it is a manageable project to construct practice techniques designed to overcome flaws and improve defective areas. The first prerequisite is to recognize that such areas *are* defective. Only after this self-reflective honesty and humility has been achieved can the creative process actually begin. At that point, we become able to listen to what our instrument is telling us we are doing that *doesn't work,* and why it doesn't work. As we notice the numerous ideas that don't work, we eventually discover those few that do. For most of us, the number that don't work vastly outnumber the ones that do; and when we have eliminated those, we are then able to try out in real time (while performing jazz) the infinite variations on and extrapolations from the few that do work. In each of those cases too, if we pay attention, the instrument will tell us whether our extrapolations really do have a worthwhile valuational meaning.

But someone may wonder: Isn't the very question as to whether something "works" ultimately a *subjective* judgment? And for that matter, doesn't the question whether something "works" in music depend on how well it works to express or enable *human* emotions, which are subjective, contingent, infinitely variable, culturally relative, and ultimately merely accidental? How could there even be a "truth" about what works and what doesn't—let alone a truth knowable by a mechanical instrument?

Let's consider for a moment the supposed subjectivity of valuational feelings. Modernity tends to emphasize the emotional dimension of values. After all, the word "value" comes from an emotion: we "value" various things by feeling their value for us. But etymology is not ontology. There are a number of different senses of any given word. To be sure, we value some things subjectively. But we also feel, for example, that a friend's well-being would have had value even if we had never existed in order to ground its value relative to ourselves. In this less subjective sense, we say "X has value" in the sense that, if anyone with the relevant emotional sensitivity (specifically, anyone with a capacity for empathy) were to direct attention to X, they would value it as well.[4] This is different from the subjective meaning of "value" in the phrase "I value X." When "I value" an ice cream cone, I don't imply that anyone else would value it. Hume, in a much underappreciated way, emphasized that it is the "love of truth" that motivates the universalization of moral principles, by comparison to specific empathic feelings evoked in specific, accidental situations.[5] Feminist philosophers like Gilligan[6] and Cornell[7] also emphasize that mature moral principles result not merely from fellow feeling or empathy, but rather from a need to acknowledge the universality of certain principles that result from the universalization of empathic sensibilities. And Scheler[8] emphasizes the same point on phenomenological grounds. Not all moral beliefs are merely subjective preferences.

There is an important hermeneutical element even in this nonsubjective sense of "value." We say that X would be valued by anyone with the capacity for empathy *if they were to direct the same amount of attention* to the valu-*ing* dimension of X that we have directed. The hermeneutics in this situation is embedded in the attention process. The needed attention to notice the value of a given valuing creature is crucial and not always available.[9] If I die, and my children are adopted by someone else, I hope that they will direct the same amount of attention to the children's valu-*ing* dimension that I have. But this attention is not always guaranteed. Yet it remains true that any emotionally sensitive being *who did* direct the same amount of attention to this valuing dimension *would* value the well-being of those valuing creatures. The proof of this point is that I can notice phenomenologically that the extent to which I value the valu-ing dimension of a living or conscious creature correlates with the *degree to which I have directed my own attention* to that valuing dimension. I can value the valuing dimension of adoptive children just as well as children related by blood, when I have come to direct considerable amounts of attention to their valuing dimension. In the same way, I gradually come to direct more and more attention to the valuing dimension of a friend or a military comrade. In each case, the intensity with which I value the creature's well-being hinges on the degree to which I have directed attention to its valuing dimension. As soon as we notice this pattern, we acknowledge, in normal moral development, that all valuing creatures have value, even if we are not currently directing attention to their valuing dimension—just as we know that the contents of a refrigerator are still there when we close the door.

The nonsubjectivity of value statements in this sense of "value" is similar to the nonsubjectivity of scientific statements. We say that global warming is an objective fact, not a subjective opinion, because we are asserting that any intelligent being would believe it to be true *if they were to direct attention to the relevant observations.*

Similar kinds of valuational statements can be made for musical ideas as well as for children and military comrades, but in a slightly more complicated way. When the piano informs me that a certain idea doesn't work, it doesn't just mean that the idea doesn't resonate well enough with anything that *I individually* feel. The piano knows the difference between subjective and nonsubjective meanings of "value." What it means to tell me is that the idea in question can't be trusted to work for *any given* emotionally sensitive creature who attempts to pay attention to its valuational significance.

Granted, of course, and needless to remind ourselves, 90 percent of the people in our twenty-first-century postindustrial mass culture will hardly ever direct their attention toward the valuational significance of jazz. And yet, even granted this fact, the piano knows which ideas would work if people *were* to direct appropriate attention; and it even knows how to recognize ideas that are more likely to get some of those 90 percent to direct their attention appropriately if for some reason they are inadvertently thrown into a situation where good jazz is being played, or if it is sneaked into a film score or the backup band of a popular singer. Nonetheless, it is important to remember that many people simply are not in the habit of directing their attention to the valuational dimension of jazz ideas, in the same way that many have gotten out of the habit of directing attention to the valuing dimension of people of different religions or races, or even different life circumstances, such as those of the beggar on the expressway entrance ramp. This lack of attention doesn't subtract from the nonsubjective fact that such valuing creatures do have value in the sense defined above. Emotional facts are still facts in the real world, and as Giorgi[10] emphasizes on phenomenological grounds, some of these facts are universalizable aspects of what it means to be a conscious being—that is, ontological facts about the structure of reality, yet observable only from the phenomenological perspective. Albert Camus explores our constant attempts to evade the specifically moral aspects of reality in *The Fall*,[11] in which the protagonist tries out every possible maneuver to avoid confronting the most important reality of his life: that he is guilty of a horrible wrongdoing. There are valuational realities that resist us just as physical reality does; that is how we know they are real.

So what the piano is trying to tell me is that an idea I have tried would not be one that any emotionally sensitive being (in the sense specified above) *would* appreciate the valuational dimension of, even if attention were appropriately directed—including for those who are *motivated* to direct their attention or *can be induced* to do so. The piano tells me without any analysis on my part, in the same way that a beginning student knows that two simultaneously struck notes a half-step apart sound "sour" in most contexts. Later they will learn that the same half-step interval is not sour in all contexts—because, again, their piano, if wise, will force them to hear these facts.

But let me guard against misunderstanding. By saying that the valuational status of a musical idea is not merely subjective, I don't mean that there is only one specific, "objectively correct" emotional meaning for each musical expression. There is not one "correct" interpretation of the meaning of a musical idea, any more than for any other art form. Yet the piano knows, with ruthless precision, that there are certain ideas that lend themselves to fertile valuational *use* by any given emotionally sensitive being with a normal auditory nervous system. The same musical idea might be used to resonate with different emotional meanings depending on the context or personality of the user, or even his or her passing mood. When I listen to Tchaikovsky's fourth or fifth symphonies, their emotional meaning can vary widely depending on context and the current situation of my life. But those symphonies lend themselves (better than many other combinations of musical notes) to being used as a symbolizing matrix to explore what I might be feeling or needing to feel at the moment. Not just any combination of notes will resonate with any significant valuational/emotional exploration. The piano knows which ones can and can't, and to what degree.

In fact, the variability of the emotional uses of a given musical idea is part of what the piano reveals when they are tried out. We don't just want to tell the listener, "Here's what I feel; you feel it too!" We want the listener to be able to connect with the music from *wherever* they happen to be emotionally at the time, insofar as possible. And this means that one of the key elements the piano looks for in any proposed musical idea is its potential ambiguities. If there is only one possible emotional/valuational meaning, the phrase will be virtually worthless to most listeners. It needs to be usable for a variety of emotional focusing processes.

I am using the word "focusing" here in the sense used by Gene Gendlin.[12] Focusing means that we don't just assume that there are stock emotions with stock category words to name them. Each "felt sense" presents itself most vividly if we first attend to the way it feels in a nameless way. Words typically name categories of things; we need to go deeper than just a category to feel the unique specificity of an emotional or valuational meaning. In Gendlin's explication of the "focusing" method, we try out different symbolizations—words, phrases, images, metaphors, or even musical ideas—until we find one that resonates with the felt sense in question. We know when we have found the right "handle" for the felt sense (as Gendlin terms these symbolizations) because when we say the word or imagine the image, the felt sense is pulled up into our consciousness analogously to the way typing the appropriate code can pull up a computer program. We then ask ourselves why the situation seems to make us feel so "___" (whatever the resonating "handle" happens to be).

We need these "handles"—symbolizing processes—to give full enough embodiment to a felt sense because feelings and values are not supernatural things; we have to enact them with our bodies in some way. By enacting the symbolization for a value, we appreciate its value more intensely. For example, we say eulogies to a departed loved one, or sing songs to a romantic lover, or genuflect before the image of a saint. While B. F. Skinner[13] is correct to point out that the odds of one vote deciding an election are smaller than the odds of getting hit by a car on the way to the polls, he misses the emotional significance of voting. By voting, we symbolize the importance of the values involved and therefore literally feel their value more intensely. The intensification of the feeling of values (whether subjective ones or nonsubjective ones in the sense defined earlier) is a separate dimension from the satisfaction we get when those values are achieved. There is little point in achieving any value if we don't first feel the value of what we value with a certain degree of intensity. Depression results not from an inability to *achieve* whatever it is that we value, but from an inability to feel positive values with enough intensity to begin with.[14] And in the latter case, there is little point in trying to achieve anything.

The piano literally mirrors the focusing process, in the sense that it does it in reverse. This may be a clue as to why a mere mechanical instrument could embody the properties of knowledge, emotional sensitivity, creativity, and freedom. The piano knows how to offer combinations of musical notes that are capable of resonating with valuational feelings—not just subjective ones, but also non-subjective ones in the above sense. It knows also that the symbolizations it offers must be flexible enough to be used as a focusing "handle" by a variety of users in a variety of contexts; thus, the ideas must be *musically ambiguous* ones. When we hear ambiguity in music—that is, when we hear an idea that could possibly function one way, or possibly in another, depending on how we use it—this recognition of ambiguity is part of what we mean when we know that we are hearing "good" musical ideas. This is why jazz works; it literally constantly presents ideas that not only are complex, but complex in a way that facilitates this kind of ambiguity. In the same way, classical, folk, and other forms of music use ambiguity, for example by substituting a suitable minor chord where one might expect a major one. But the piano also knows how to create many levels of ambiguity, even within the structure of one chord—and this results in the piano's ability for jazz improvisation, as I will now discuss.

Notice that *ambiguous* meaning is not the same thing as *lack* of meaning. Charlie Parker famously advised young musicians to first spend many hours practicing scales and exercises and then to throw away the scales and exercises and "just play." Many young musicians misinterpret this advice as meaning that the scales and exercises can be skipped altogether and that they should simply "play what they feel." The result is predictably bad. Ambiguity means that there are several things an idea could mean—there are several focusing roles that it could play, depending on the specific focusing process in which the listener needs to engage.

So one of the first things the piano listens for, when we try out ideas on it, is this kind of ambiguity. An unambiguous chord or riff beats the listener over the head with one specific emotional meaning that is unlikely to resonate with the listener's emotional needs at that moment. The exception to this rule, of course, is the corny love song that one might have happened to hear years ago while dancing with a young romantic partner. The song then retains that emotional meaning, although it would be unable to elicit meanings of its own accord.

The proof that it is the *piano* that knows which ideas work, and not I (I make this claim only for myself and my specific piano), is that I don't need to technically analyze an idea to know whether it works or not. As soon as I try it, I immediately hear the fact that it didn't work. To unpack all the numerous and potentially infinite technical and philosophical considerations that go into making an idea work or not work would be a ridiculous enterprise to expect to go through in the time that it takes to see that an idea just doesn't work. All of those considerations are retained in the intelligence of the piano, just as we retain them in our brains.

The piano corrects our imagination in the same way that reality forces us to distinguish between wishful thinking and real perception. We might fancy that we could walk through a brick wall. The reason we know we can't is that if we were to try it, the nature of reality would force us to admit that we can't do it, precisely by *resisting* the attempted action. Similarly, the piano constantly resists our attempts to form meaningful riffs or chord substitutions. As phenomenologists like Merleau-Ponty[15] and enactivists like Varela and others[16] and Newton[17] stress, we know reality by first trying to engage in actions and then noticing which actions reality prevents us from executing. The French conductor Pierre Boulez said to a French horn player who kept missing a note, "Just attack her, and she will come"—to which the player replied, "I'm attacking her, but she's resisting!" In science, we even define phenomena in terms of which actions we can or can't perform—by using "operational definitions." We know what something is if we know which actions we could or couldn't perform relative to it. We know something is real because we know it can resist our attempted actions.

The same applies to musical ideas. We fancy that some idea might elicit a certain emotional response in the listener, but the piano knows whether it actually is capable of eliciting a worthwhile response. We have to put our idea to the piano in order to find out whether it works. At a later stage of our musical development, we might be able to internalize the lessons the piano has taught us about this, but we shouldn't forget that it is the piano that knows the reality of the situation; whatever we might think we know is derivative from that.

In the case of finding out what works and what doesn't work in jazz, the process here again is the same as in Gendlin's "focusing." We might initially think we feel "angry" or "sad," but the focusing process moves us beyond such stock categories, toward the specificity of the felt sense of the situation. The policeman who gives me a traffic citation is not really the main object of my emotional disturbance, and after a round of focusing, I realize that what I feel is not simply "anger" "at" him. (After all, he is only doing his assigned job.) Instead, the felt sense may have more to do with frustration with the way my entire life is going or exasperation at the way voters passively accept the lies of a political demagogue. It may be a feeling of being "trapped" in a dead-end job, or a host of other issues that the traffic cop can be used to "symbolize." Music is used as a symbolization in the same way, except that *as listeners*, we are presented with the symbol first (the musical idea offered by the performer) and only then develop our own felt sense relative to it.

Jazz is different from other forms of music primarily in the way it uses musical symbolizations as multiambiguous focusing "handles." Any good standard show tune will already have multiple layers of meaning, but jazz enriches the harmonies, textures, rhythms, and improvised riffs to create still more layers of meaning. These layers reflect the fact that, in the focusing process, we can go more than one "round" of focusing. For example, after noticing that the felt sense of the policeman stopping me is a symbol of all that opposes my career endeavors, I may then ask myself how I feel about those opposing forces. It may then turn out that what I feel is not about those forces at all, but rather about basic, necessary structures of human existence. As the saying goes, "everyone has a boss." I may discover that I am not upset because this specific boss (or academic administration) is jerking me around, but rather that reality is such that everyone must have a boss, and not only a boss, but multiple "bosses," and I can now bring into focus how I feel about *that* fact.

This new felt sense was actually contained in or implied by the original felt sense elicited by the policeman stopping me but is so much more reflective of the truth of what I feel that the "anger" at the policeman now subsides in favor of the more interesting and more nuanced emotional meanings. In that sense, we have now gone a second round of the focusing process to reach this deeper layer of meaning in the felt sense of the situation. It is not that we no longer object to the policeman's decision to ticket us, nor to the actions of our specific bosses jerking us around. But we also now can focus on our feeling of a deeper layer within the felt sense.

So in jazz, something is added to the original show tune, which already contained ambiguous "handles." (Not just any old tune is good material for jazz improvisation; we look for tunes that *offer* those ambiguities to begin with.) If you imagine the original versions of "I'll Be Seeing You" as heard in Hollywood film scores, there is vast emotional meaning to such renditions, playing off the sadness of a lover separated from a lover during a war. If we imagine a jazz pianist improvising over the chord changes, we are imagining another layer of meaning that says something like "Yes, all reality is like that; we are all constantly potentially separated from loved ones by wars, and we are all here together acknowledging that this is the reality we all face, yet we are facing it with some equanimity because we can share the experience."

This is similar to the original blues from which jazz originated, as sung by horribly mistreated slave gangs of the seventeenth and eighteenth centuries. The message was "I work all day into the night, and the White Man sells my family away from me and beats me regularly for no reason—and all I have left is the ability to sing about it." The jazz blues that evolves from that layer of meaning retains it, but adds others: for example, "Yes, the potential for all those horrors always lurks, and many others, whether we are suffering them at the moment or not, but the equanimity we learned from the slaves enables us to see life from that perspective, and to be able to still sing about it"—and to sing music that can resonate with us relative to wherever we might be coming from in our specific life situation.

So when we try out a jazz idea, the piano will let us know whether we have succeeded in opening up new layers of potential focusing meanings, with enough flexibility to allow the listener to use them from out of their own specific situated contexts. As in other forms of music, but to a greater extent, jazz demands "variety within unity" in that sense. Each thing that happens should be unpredictable from what happened before yet after it occurred should seem like the best thing that *could* have happened in that context—because of the unexpected emotional response it facilitated. Again, these emotions are not just "subjective"; they are as much a part of the total ontological structure of reality as the wall that resists our attempts to walk through it. If we think we feel something, yet the feeling is shallow and not worthy of the context in which it occurs or the meanings offered by that context, the piano will let us know as soon as we strike the wrong chord substitution or put the wrong extensions on a chord. The very fact that jazz is so full of chord substitutions, alterations, and extensions is symptomatic of its constant striving for both ambiguity and variety-within-unity in this sense. It opens up the listener to explore different emotional meanings without "drowning in" them, just as Gendlin emphasizes that bringing a felt sense into focus requires that at a certain point we quit drowning in the feeling and begin to ask questions about it and explore its various possible meanings.

This understanding of ambiguity and the needed flexibility of good musical ideas is what makes the piano living and creative—not simply an "information processor" as in a computer. The piano doesn't just check off correct and incorrect answers as in a multiple-choice test. It offers discussion answers, and extensively developed ones—the kind of answers one actually *enjoys* reading during exam week even if stacks of other papers are piled up. In short, it doesn't just replicate: it creates new ideas. If I go over the same tune several times at home (something I can't do away from home), each time the piano reveals new ambiguities and new rounds of focusing reflected in more and more variety-within-unity.

How do I know that all these new ideas and all these facts about what works and what doesn't work in jazz aren't simply executed preconsciously *by my brain* rather than *by the piano*?

There are two reasons. First, I know that there are many ideas that I excitedly imagine would work splendidly, until I put them to the piano, which then dismisses them instantaneously as corny, or superficial, or melodramatic, or wrong for the specific context, or any of a number of other deficiencies of which my imagination is constantly guilty until I put the ideas directly to the piano. And second, I would never have *learned* to think up such ideas in the first place had it not been for the earlier years of experience putting even less effective ideas to the piano in the course of my personal development. The piano literally guided each step of this process and told me without analysis what worked and what didn't work—if only I could pay the proper attention to what it was trying to tell me.

To be sure, the piano, like many living creatures, needed to live in symbiosis with another living creature—me; or more accurately, it needed to be attached to a parasite such as me. But any other parasite with similar willingness to pay attention would have done as well. That, of course, is the proof that the piano is the master, and I the student; and that the piano is more intelligent and more creative than I am. In the final analysis, it is the proof that *this particular* piano, just as the old Swedish repairman promised, is a sensitive, emotionally intelligent, and living creature.

Notes

1. Ludwig Binswanger, *Being in the World* (New York: Basic Books, 1963); Martin Heidegger, *Being and Time* (New York: Harper and Row, 1927/1962); H. G. Gadamer, *Truth and Method* (New York: Seabury, 1971/1975).

2. Nat Hentoff, *Five Ways of Making It* (New York: Viking Press, 1973).

3. Rollo May, *The Courage to Create* (New York: Bantam, 1975/1976).

4. Edith Stein, *The Problem of Empathy* (Washington: ICS Publications, 1916/1989); Stein Bräten, editor, *Roots and Collapse of Empathy* (Amsterdam/Philadelphia: John Benjamins, 2013).

5. David Hume, *Treatise of Human Nature* (New York: Bobbs-Merrill, 1740/1955).

6. Carol Gilligan, *In a Different Voice: Psychological Theory and Women's Development* (Cambridge Mass,: Harvard University Press, 1982).

7. Drucilla Cornell, *At the Heart of Freedom* (Princeton: Princeton University Press, 1995).

8. Max Scheler, *The Nature of Sympathy* (Hamden: Archon Books, 1954/1970).

9. This point is elaborated more extensively in: Ralph D. Ellis, *The Moral Psychology of Internal Conflict* (Cambridge: Cambridge University Press, 2018).

10. Ameideo Giorgi, "Phenomenology and experimental psychology," in *Duquesne Studies in Phenomenological Psychology, Vol. 1*, ed. Giorgi (Pittsburgh: Duquesne University Press, 1971).

11. Albert Camus, *The Fall* (New York: Vintage, 1963).

12. Developed through a series of works, including: Eugene Gendlin, *Experiencing and the Creation of Meaning* (Toronto: Collier-Macmillan/Chicago: University of Chicago Press, 1962/1997); Eugene Gendlin, *Focusing* (Toronto: Bantam, 1978/1982/1990); Eugene Gendlin, "Thinking Beyond Patterns: Body, Language, and Situations," in *The Presence of Feeling in Thought*, ed. B. den Ouden and M. Moen (New York: Peter Lang, 1992).

13. B. F. Skinner, *Walden Two* (New York: Macmillan, 1968).
14. Ellis, *Moral Psychology of Internal Conflict*.
15. Maurice Merleau-Ponty, *The Structure of Behavior*, tr. A. Fischer (Boston: Beacon, 1942/1963); Maurice Merleau-Ponty, *Phenomenology of Perception*, tr. Colin Smith (New York, Humanities Press, 1945/1962).
16. Francisco Varela, Evan Thompson, and Eleanor Rosch, *The Embodied Mind* (Cambridge: MIT Press, 1991/1993).
17. Natika Newton, *Foundations of Understanding* (Amsterdam: John Benjamins, 1996).

Bibliography

Binswanger, Ludwig. *Being in the World*. New York: Basic Books, 1963.
Bräten, Stein, Ed. *Roots and Collapse of Empathy*. Amsterdam/Philadelphia: John Benjamins, 2013.
Camus, Albert. *The Fall*. New York: Vintage, 1963.
Cornell, Drucilla. *At the Heart of Freedom*. Princeton: Princeton University Press, 1995.
Ellis, Ralph D. *The Moral Psychology of Internal Conflict*. Cambridge: Cambridge University Press, 2018.
Gadamer, H. G. *Truth and Method*. New York: Seabury, 1971/1975.
Gendlin, Eugene. *Experiencing and the Creation of Meaning*. Toronto: Collier-Macmillan/Chicago: University of Chicago Press, 1962/1997.
———. *Focusing*. Toronto: Bantam, 1978/1982/1990.
———. "Thinking beyond Patterns: Body, Language, and Situations." In *The Presence of Feeling in Thought*, edited by B. den Ouden and M. Moen. New York: Peter Lang, 1992.
Gilligan, Carol. *In a Different Voice: Psychological Theory and Women's Development*. Cambridge, MA: Harvard University Press, 1982.
Giorgi, Ameideo. "Phenomenology and Experimental Psychology." In *Duquesne Studies in Phenomenological Psychology, Vol. I*, edited by Ameideo Giorgi, 6–29. Pittsburgh: Duquesne University Press, 1971.
Heidegger, Martin. *Being and Time*. New York: Harper & Row, 1927/1962.
Hentoff, Nat. *Five Ways of Making It*. New York: Viking Press, 1973.
Hume, David. *Treatise of Human Nature*. New York: Bobbs-Merrill, 1740/1955.
May, Rollo. *The Courage to Create*. New York: Bantam, 1975/1976.
Merleau-Ponty, Maurice. *Phenomenology of Perception*. Translated by Colin Smith. New York, Humanities Press, 1945/1962. Original French edition 1945.
———. *The Structure of Behavior*. Translated by A. Fischer. Boston: Beacon, 1942/1963. original French edition 1942.
Newton, Natika. *Foundations of Understanding*. Amsterdam: John Benjamins, 1996.
Scheler, Max. *The Nature of Sympathy*. Hamden: Archon Books, 1954/1970.
Skinner, B. F. *Walden Two*. New York: Macmillan, 1968.

Stein, Edith. *The Problem of Empathy.* Washington: ICS Publications, 1916/1989.
Varela, Francisco, Evan Thompson, and Eleanor Rosch. *The Embodied Mind.* Cambridge: MIT Press, 1991/1993.

Chapter 16

Meditating on the Vitality of the Musical Object

A Spiritual Exercise Drawn from Richard Wagner's Metaphysics of Music

ELI KRAMER

Editor's Note: This chapter is the second of two focusing on musical personal objects. It expands on the previous chapter by turning our attention to the music itself, rather than the relationship of the musician to their instrument. However, many themes from the previous chapter will recur, such as the ambiguous suggestiveness of music and an examination of its "felt" qualities. Kramer describes Richard Wagner's concept of the "musical object" and argues that music is a vital object, expressive of Schopenhauerian "Will" and Bergsonian Élan Vital.

Overture: The "Wagner Chord" for Our Reflection[1]

[Richard Wagner is] a man with a gigantic capacity for work, colossal industry and horrendous energy.

—Johannes Brahms[2]

Like its composer, Wagner's music has a gigantic scope, industriousness, and horrendous energy. His musical works might be described as images of vitality, in all its beauty and havoc. It is this musical vitality that I wish to investigate. In this chapter, I will meditate on Wilhelm Richard Wagner's (1813–1883) idea, as articulated in his essay entitled *Beethoven*, that music is, unlike any other object we create or are attentive to in experience, in an immediate analogical relationship with the activity of the Schopenhauerian "will" (the aesthetic experience closest to the numinous).[3] For Wagner, music is always enlivened. He further argued that music gives the "most comprehensive idea of the world." That is, music gives the most enriched articulation of the drama of the will in its dynamic activity. Such a metaphysics of music guided his great operatic works, works that fundamentally shaped the trajectory of Western music by their grand mythic narratives, organic systematicity, novel construction, fantastic images, and emotional depth. By drawing on Wagner's idea, we can not only attend to music as in an immediate analogical relationship with our personal experience, but as perhaps the only object of cognition that is in a constant state of personal vitality. It is by that very continuous vitality that music can return us to our own personhood with deeper insight and perspective. I conclude this chapter by exploring how attending to the musical object can be a spiritual (existential) exercise in reconnecting to our roots in *sensus communis*, educating ourselves on our common personhood, and supporting our ethical relations with others.

To understand the genesis and nature of this idea about the musical object, a bit must be said about its composer. Wagner was a master dilettante, a voracious reader of works on the historical origins of Western myth, a powerful voice in the polemic debates of his day, a shaper of the trajectory of music composition and theory, and even a contributor to idealistic philosophy. He created what he called in his early career *Gesamtkunstwerk* (total works of art), that is, opera as drama guiding discursive poesis, instrumental music, plastic art, and dance (all other art forms). Wagnerian operas slowly coordinate *leitmotifs* (a leading musical phrase-motif for people, places, and ideas) over a significant duration (several hours in clock time), until one is led to an event where they all coalesce to illuminate the ontological depths of archetypal events in humanity's personal experience. Of special importance, however, was instrumental music. Wagner would later in his career argue that Beethoven was the prophet and paragon of the musician/composer whose task is to return us to the direct activity of the will through the musical object. Wagner saw himself as the direct inheritor of this German prophetic lineage, heralding a new age in musical art which would lead to a revolution in culture. Nietzsche would infamously defend Wagner's position in *The Birth of Tragedy*.

He is also a person of infamy in the history of Western culture. He could be deceptive, manipulative, petty, cruel, vindictive, emotionally abusive, narcissistic, dogmatic, deeply anti-Semitic and racist, and even dangerous when given power and a loyal following. His "horrendous energy" was shaped by, but not reducible to, all these traits. It is all too easy to cast Wagner off for all that made him harmful to those near to him. Further, it is even easier to say that Wagner is but the decadence of romanticism and that his music and views were a perfect tool for emerging, proto-fascist German nationalism, as Nietzsche would argue after the demise of their friendship.[4] Yet, as with Heidegger in philosophy, to cast off the legacy of such a polemic figure neither rids us of the darker aspects of their work, nor helps us have the discussion we need to have about it. Ignoring these legacies also does not help us draw out cautious insight from their problematic creations. Honest, unapologetic, critical exploration is what is called for at this time. Without denying who he was or committing to a fruitless and obnoxious apology for him, I will proceed forward with caution.

For the purposes of this chapter, it is also important to note that I am not a Wagner scholar,[5] and I am only a dilettante in the world of classical music. Further, as Carl Dahlhaus, one of the most prominent Wagner scholars in the world has quipped, "the literature on Wagner is legion."[6] My reflection here should not be interpreted as an attempt at Wagner scholarship. That kind of work is best left to those with more expertise. I could hardly have much to contribute to such a layered and expansive field of scholarship. I thus will take no position on critical questions in the scholarship on Wagner's philosophy, such as the exact lengths to which he borrowed from Schopenhauer and Nietzsche or the exact ontological status of music in relationship to the dynamism of the will. I will also not provide accounts of Wagner's, Schopenhauer's, or Nietzsche's views of the "person" or their personalist or impersonalist views, no will I explore the interrelationships between their thoughts on this subject. In short, this chapter is not meant to provide context for, nor enter into, the debates of Wagner scholarship nor be a piece of scholarship in the history of philosophy.

That said, even without the eye of an expert, there is much to draw upon in Wagner's *Beethoven* for other purposes beyond that of scholarship in the history of philosophy. Close reading and reflection can offer a kind of personal insight that is helpful for self-cultivation. The same is true of reading *midrash*, the interpretation of one close reader in deep relation with one text.[7] Such a singular presence alongside close reading can be of immense value for clear and distinct meditation on a single topic. While it is important to recognize that good scholarship can deepen the insights we might glean from solitary reading of primary source texts and of *midrash*, sometimes a close attentiveness to a text without the distraction of other voices and insights, staying with oneself, the presence in the text, and one guide, is of abiding value.[8] We cultivate an immediate sense of the text and its "presence" and of a singular interpretation that is not confused by other voices with other agendas and needs. Once this sense is settled, it can be later enriched by the wisdom of more experienced councilors. For these reasons, I ask you my reader to treat me as a solitary companion meditating on Wagner's *Beethoven*, in the spirit of Jewish playful and open interpretation. Perhaps through such work we can do honor to and enact criticism of Wagner in one and the same exercise. This work is thus meant to be *midrash*, and in particular a source for meditating on the musical object. This source for meditation can be enriched and modified by Wagner and history of philosophy scholarship, as well as by other meditations on musical objects. I hope it has value to itself as a resource for self-cultivation and as an incitement to scholarship.

In the following, we draw upon a close reading of *Beethoven* in order to meditate on the musical object as a source for contemplation and self-cultivation. In particular, we seek to draw out for our own purposes one of the most interesting threads of the work: Wagner's suggestion that music is the only constantly vital object of human cognition. I thus offer to you a reflective study of how Wagner's idea—as articulated in his essay *Beethoven*—of music as a vital object might be of value to us today as a kind of spiritual exercise, or practice of self and communal cultivation.[9] Once we reject Wagner's egotistical, imperialized view of ultimacy, his idea can serve better recognizing, treating, and engaging with other persons. Further, if we treat Wagner's idea as an opportunity for spiritual exercise in self/communal cultivation, a new relation to other persons emerges.

In the first sections of this reflection, I very briefly sketch Wagner's relationship to and reconstruction of Schopenhauerian metaphysics. In the following section, I summarize the main points of his theory of the vital musical object in *Beethoven*. In the final section, I argue that even without endorsing the views of ultimacy embedded in Wagner's Schopenhauerian metaphysics, we can still learn something from him about the nature[10] of music as a temporal, dynamic, and personal object.[11] We can then also feel the power of attending to the musical object as a spiritual exercise in the recognition of personhood in the cosmic becoming.

Act 1: Wagner Finds a Book

In order to better reflect on Wagner's claims about the musical object, we begin with a review of the main points of Arthur Schopenhauer's (1788–1860) *The World as Will and Representation* (*Die Welt als Wille und Vorstellung*).[12] As is well known, Schopenhauer argued that Kant's thing-in-itself (*Ding-an-Sich*) was nothing but the "will." Schopenhauer thought that Kant had missed this insight because he had not been able to go beyond his own self-set limitations in order to explore the implications of the very interior world he had so thoroughly analyzed.

As Kant had suggested to him, the numinous is a functional category for whatever outruns our cognitive powers, and by the end of his *Third Critique*, one can realize that we as persons outrun ourselves. We are more than our determinate cognition of ourselves. It is this insight, among others, that gave Schopenhauer an idea. If whatever outruns our cognitive powers is not mediated from us in-itself, but via the activity of creatures such as ourselves cognitivizing the world (i.e., creating representation [*vorstellung*]), and if this "undivided but divisible"[13] whole includes the deeper vitality of ourselves that we cannot access by mediation, it stands to reason that the force of our cognitivizing *activity* is the expressed aspect of that deeper current of ourselves that is the thing-in-itself. The unity outside of the limits of human cognition must include humans and *be* that activity that humans feel within themselves but cannot access through determinate judgment. In other words, that activity that is mediating the world into representation is the numinous. He names that activity "the will." It is that energy which unceasingly can and does mediate the world as a force, including mediating us from it. Keeping in mind that the will-in-itself is an undifferentiated but divisible whole, which in its activity mediates the world, we can see that it is not us as individuals that mediate the world, but the will that individuates us. We are just another, albeit more complex and cunning, version of its unsatiable mediating activity. The will is then just that vital energy (will-to-life) in the universe of which so called individuals (including but not limited to ourselves) are but phenomena, objectifications.[14]

Thus, unlike Kant, Schopenhauer found personhood but a phenomenon of this never satisfied, utterly futile activity. Personhood is a pathology of the mediating will and ought in some sense to be "renounced." One route to renunciation was to be found through attending to music. Schopenhauer claimed that music had the closest relationship with the activity of the will. Further, "because music does not, like all the other arts, exhibit the Ideas or grades of the will's objectification, but directly the will itself, we can also explain that it acts directly on the will, i.e., the feelings, passions, and emotions of the hearer, so that it quickly raises these or even alters them."[15] Since music escapes the levels of mediation that all the other arts go through, it is freer to more directly speak to and affect us, and help us renounce the veil created by desire.

It is this very anecdote of Schopenhauer's on the metaphysical status of music that so excited Wagner. Schopenhauer began to receive a wider readership after the publication of his expanded edition of *WW&R* in 1844. A decade later, in 1854, Wagner would read this edition of the book and become convinced that Schopenhauer was the first person who recognized the true metaphysics of music, and for that matter the first who had resolved the central problems of philosophy.[16] Wagner would start a correspondence with Schopenhauer, one in which Wagner played the role (for perhaps the only time of his life) of the enamored and obsequious student. Schopenhauer remained in contact, though he was never as enthusiastic about the relationship. *Tristan und Isolde* and *Parsifal* are the two operas considered most clearly influenced by Schopenhauer. Wagner's metaphysics of music, although inspired by Schopenhauer, is anachronistic. Schopenhauer saw Wagner's work as an entire theory built out of anecdotes from the appendices to *WW&R* that were meant to illustrate far more significant points. Wagner's metaphysics of music should thus be read as a creative reconstruction of Schopenhauerian philosophy, and not one that was endorsed by the master.

Intermezzo: Musical Objects

Before we proceed to a close reading of *Beethoven*, a very brief interlude will help us better appreciate its approach to music. The "musical object" for Wagner was not the musician, the written score, or even our auditory capacity. Beethoven created and cognized many musical objects well after he lost his hearing. Music itself *is* an object of cognition (in the Kantian sense), that is, a part of the manifold of sense conformable to cognition in accordance with the categories and an experience about which (at least some) determinate judgments can be made but is best illuminated in reflective judgment. Music, however, is not a thing, in the traditional sense of substance metaphysics (pre-Kantian), but an objectivizing function we experientially transact with (and sometimes create) through our activity in and of the world. As with other intelligible characteristics of the manifold of sense, music conforms to human objectivating (cognitive) processes. For example, Beethoven's "Symphony Number 9 in D-Minor" is an *object* that we as subjects are capable of experiencing, conforming to the requirements of the pure intuitions of space and time, and synthesizing in acts of judgment. The musical object's life may be extremely intense and unstable, but it is nevertheless real. One could say the same of human life, or, as Kant says explicitly, of the "feeling" of being alive.[17] We experience it, both in others and ourselves (although differently), as an extremely intense and unstable, but *real*, duration.

Act 2: The Prophecy of Beethoven

> Only to be able to *play* in those conventional forms with the enormous resources of music, in such that its proper effect, the manifestation of the inner essential nature of all things, was avoided like the danger of an inundation, passed along, in the judgment of aestheticians, for the true and only gratifying product of the cultivation of the art of music. But to have penetrated through these forms to the inmost nature of

music in such a way that he was able from this side to throw the inner life of the clairvoyant outward again, in order to display these forms to us anew in accordance with their inner significance only, this was the work of our great Beethoven, whom we must therefore represent to ourselves as the true paragon of the musician.[18]

In 1870, ten years after the death of Schopenhauer, Wagner was a rising star. He felt himself to be at the height of his craft and would soon bring to life his Ring Cycle (*Der Ring des Nibelungen*) at Bayreuth. At this moment in his career, he wrote an essay to celebrate the centennial of Beethoven's birth. In the essay, Beethoven becomes a representative of a sort of prophetic genius (in a sense to be explained), who was able to call forth from the inner world the dynamic coordination of a musical object.[19] In order to properly explain Beethoven's genial, "clairvoyant" capacities, Wagner spent about thirty pages expanding upon what he considered to be Schopenhauer's formative insight into the metaphysics of music.

In the essay, Wagner defined music as "the revelation of the inmost dream-image of the essential nature of the world"[20] and argued, among many other points, that music thus gives the "most comprehensive idea of the world."[21] Music has such comprehensive power because it has an immediate vital access to the will and can articulate for us the experience of the drama of the will in its dynamic activity. The aforementioned section explores this view. Wagner also argued in this section that a musical object reveals the quality of certain experiences pulled from the composer's/musician's life, but that is not reducible to those experiences, a point we will not fully explore in this *midrash*, but that should be kept in mind in terms of the clairvoyant power of the composer/ musician to create irreducible pieces of art.[22]

Key to Wagner's metaphysics of music is Schopenhauer's distinction between our awareness of the *intensive* interiority of ourselves as *will*, and of the *extensive* understanding of "spatiotemporal objects" (that we can come to recognize as petrified modes of *will*). The spatializing function of representing things for our understanding to act on stifles our ability to note the dynamic activity of the will. In line with Schopenhauer, Wagner thought that music could help us return to our own interiority, where we could be put in touch with the will in its dynamic action.[23]

After making this distinction in the section devoted to the metaphysics of music, Wagner followed Schopenhauer into the realm of dreams, or the interior activity of the will cut off from a direct means of externalization. Wagner noted that sometimes in this dream world—the world of the will (our desire) trapped in-itself beyond the limits of the Kantian formal intuition of time and space—we are driven to an "erotic" cry of frustration, that propels through our action-giving embodiment, which then awakens us from our sleep.

> If we now regard the *cry* in all diminutions of its violence to the tender utterance of desire, as the fundamental element of all human manifestations to the hearing, and if we are compelled to find in it the most immediate of all utterances of the will, through which it turns toward the external world most quickly and most surely, we have less occasion to wonder at the immediate intelligibility of music, than at an art's arising from this element; as it is evident, on the other hand, that both artistic productivity, and artistic intuition can only proceed from the alienation of consciousness from the excitations of will.[24]

In this view, the "cry upon waking" reveals an immediate expression of the will. It is not primarily caused by our transactions with the world, but comes from the intensity of our own inner life that tears the world in its monadic depth asunder, and again veils us in the smoke of the world of representation (the world of determinate thought and action), where we will be lulled back into our daily illusions. Dreams in this sense are closer to reality than the illusions of the world. The most immediate and direct utterances of the will are also in this sense more universally intelligible and in touch with reality than other kinds of art and certainly of our daily perception of the world.

"The cry's" key aspect is its volitional rupturing of the world. It is not music but reveals its analogical function. Wagner believed that alongside the world of sight was one of *sound*.[25] Music's true nature, in the world of sound, immediately analogizes our intensive inner life and the way it breaks into the world of representation. Music should have mirroring tones to our deepest inner feelings. The music should feel *as if* it were "the cry" authentically emerging and breaking into the narrow world of waking life.[26] By doing so, music puts us in touch with the more deeply intelligible direct expression of reality, and thus return us to the depths of ourselves, from which "the cry" emanates. The illusion of representation and of an isolated individual self is dispelled, and we recognize ourselves as a singular expression of will. The genius of musical art requires creating *vital* objects that return us to our inner realm, which for most of us is lost in the act of representing (and living) in the highly spatialized visual realm. The world of representation isolates us in the solipsism of individuated cognition, while music returns us to the song of the universal becoming. Artists of course also find themselves in the mediated world of the will but intuit this alienated condition and through the manipulation of it can return us to ourselves.

Wagnerian opera libretti are metaphors for this deep and problematic rupture between inner life and external expression, and our subsequent alienated condition arising from it. These libretti have compact simple prose, with tight rhyme structures, that are felt as the crest of the wave of musical activity. The libretto is the analogy of the vocal release of "the cry" as it breaks into the world of representation, while its *leitmotifs* are analogies of the inner world from which it emerged. Thus, the voices of the singers both articulate discursive thought and are the expression of the inner reality of the singers manifesting itself in waking life, joined to the wind (spirit) of the horns and the beating "hearts" of the percussionists. In a sense, one is supposed to be able to interpret a Wagnerian opera without knowing the German language and without seeing the staging and acting—the music is supposed to be self-sufficient in its dynamic and immediate intelligibility. As we shall see, we are bewitched to return to ourselves. It is this supposed direct, analogical relation of great music to our inner life as it expresses itself (which belongs to the fundamental force of the universe) that gives the musical object its supposed superiority to the "objects" of the more spatialized (static or mechanical) world represented to our cognition. It is more "alive" than other petrified objects.

But how are we supposed to fully understand his operas without knowing German? To put it more generally, how exactly is the musical object supposed to be immediately intelligible to us?

> The outer world speaks to us with such incomparable intelligibility here, because, by virtue of the effect of sound, it communicates to us through hearing precisely what we call out to it from the depths of our soul. The object of the tone which is heard, coincides immediately with the subject of the emitted tone; we understand without any intermediation through conceptions what is said to us by the cry for help, or of morning or joy, which we hear, and answer it at once in the corresponding sense. If the cry, or sound of sorrow or delight which we ejaculate, is the most immediate expression of the emotions of our will, we understand *similar sounds*[27] which make their way to us through hearing, as incontestably the utterance of the same emotions—and no illusion, as in the semblance of light, to the effect that the fundamental nature of the world external to us, is not completely identical with our own essential nature, is possible here, by which the gulf that to the sight seems to exist at once vanishes.[28]

Upon observation, we can find the will breaking into representation in a variety of our immediate vocal ejaculations. For example (on this account), cries of anguish are intelligible in their immediacy; we do not need an exposition to *know* their meaning. In fact, we *know* it immediately. Music finds the closest analogies to such ejaculations so that we again can be put in touch with the force that brought out that sound. Music is the object of cognition that dissolves the gap between vital energy and expression. An *ideal* listener will immediately *feel* in music the origins of the tones in their corresponding noumenal energies. By this analogical process, the illusion of a gulf between our representations and will vanish, and we find ourselves in a cosmic becoming, an undivided but divisible, whole reality. The *true* musical object makes intelligible a deeper reality as it underlies, is continuous with, and creates the veil of representation. When we become attentive to the musical object, the obfuscation of the "veil of maya," the disrupting of reality by the organization of the will, which then bifurcates the world as we can experience it from the world itself, is lifted. Music in fact is supposed to align us to the rhythm of the continuous activity of the cosmic becoming, both as pure will and rupturing representation. Such intelligibility can only be made clear from an experience that is not so thoroughly lost in the world of representation. Wagner (in line with Kant) thus suggests something quite radical: certain kinds of intelligibility (what Kant would call aesthetic ideas[29]) come to us not through clarity of rational thought, but by saturated aesthetic experiences. We know certain important aspects about the world long before we can rationalize them in discourse (if we can rationalize them at all).

Consequently, good music for Wagner is also not about a mere "interested liking" in the Kantian sense, but reaches down to something far more primal and universal.[30] It is not a matter of individual preference. At its best, it returns us to our deepest "self," which is not really a self at all but the universal becoming. If one cannot access the sublimity in Beethoven's music, it is not a lack in Beethoven's work, for many people do experience such an intense return to a deeper dynamic pulse when listening to those musical objects. Given that this experience is *actual* for many people, it must be genuinely *possible* for others to access the power of those musical objects. Our musical interests ("tastes" in the current sense of that concept) are different. But that is not to say that *certain* musical pieces (great works) do not have the special capacity ("universally" in the sense of possibility) to return and align people with their own becoming. Idealistic, subjective universality does not require that everyone agrees on the power of a piece of music. Rather, it accounts for how people who, having such experiences with particular musical works, feel in the *as if* the universal capacity of others to have such an experience.[31] Wagner, unless discussing the history of human failures to understand the nature of music, almost always treated the musical object as experienced by an ideally situated listener and performer.

To be clear, Wagner was not denying that there are limits to cognition in the world of sound that condition our experience of the musical object as individuals. To the contrary, he even went as far as to suggest that there are *a priori* laws that govern making true exhibitions of a musical object that gives the most comprehensive idea of the world.³² The point is that music as we experience it puts us in touch with something that conditions the world that we experience, but is not reducible to our cognition.

He was suggesting that music, to the ideally situated listener, is in direct analogical relation with our *limited* volitional activity and aligns us with the deeper currents of that activity. Music can "stay alive" in its own limited way because it is *felt* as an immediate relation (a concrete analogy) of our inner connection to reality, while objects further into the outer realm of representation at best can be constantly re-enlivened by their purposefully purposive beauty. For Wagner, the musical object goes beyond most other arts and gives us access to sublimity (to the will as *noumenon*). In this view, plastic arts merely remind us of our own sublimity through their beauty and/or form and are at best a mere ode to the beauty of nature. For example, sculpture and painting are a much further graduation of the will into representation, created in the past to remind us of the *natural* dynamism of ourselves. Music is less lost in the realm of representation, and thus is in a more immediate and vital analogy, some even say "identity," with that activity of nature as it is naturing (*natura naturans*). "If, then, we see an art arise from the immediate consciousness of the unity of our inner nature with that of the external world, it is in the very first place evident that that art must be subject to aesthetic laws entirely different from those of every other art."³³ Music spans a unity that includes but is not limited to the realm of representation, and thus it should not be reduced to the techniques that appeal merely to that realm. Thus, the guidelines for making a visual object *feel* organic and alive ought to be different than for an object that sings our sublimity directly into the world. No attempt at creating static semblances of natural activity is supposed to be needed. That said, music has to be coordinated in such a way that it can clearly illuminate, beyond the veil of representation, the depth of the will of which it analogizes (according to Wagner) immediately.

For this reason, Wagner derisively and caustically attacked the many musical traditions from different nations in Europe in his era that he thought treated music *as if* it was an object that belonged to the plastic arts (that use largely spatial representations, and that are very degraded forms of will), focusing on the play of musical structures for the sake of enjoyable entertainment. In his account, Beethoven was a genius because he oracularly intuited and manifested the true nature of music as a vital, primarily temporal object that can return us to our own becoming and sublimity (to our experience of our supersensible existence in its systole and diastole). For Wagner, this insight was at the heart of the German spirit.

Musicians and composers who are in keeping with this "spirit" (at their best) are thus supposed to become attuned with the dynamics of the will. In carrying out such attunement, they have, according to Wagner, a rapture only surpassed by the saint. The saint however stays in the ecstasy, while the musician only has moments of such experience. In turn, the audience members' vision, when in sympathy with a piece of music are, Schellingianly "depotentialized";[34] they ignore the oddities of the players, of the scene, of a friend sneezing during the *recitative*, and enter the "idea of the world" immediately felt in sound. They then participate in the rapture of the musician/composer when engaged in this activity. "From this world, which otherwise we have no means of portraying, the musician, by the disposition of his tones, in a certain measure spreads a net for us,—or again, he besprinkles our perceptive faculties with the miracle-working drops of his sounds, in such a manner that they are incapacitated, as if by magic, for the reception of any impressions other than those of our own inner world."[35]

But by what technique do these "magic drops" make us so receptive to "other impressions"? How exactly does the musical magic happen between composers/musicians and audience? Further, what means does music have to return us to the will? The answer to all these questions for Wagner lies in the manipulation of aesthetic "ideas of time" (and here only as the most external structuring of music), instead of playing with aesthetic "ideas of space," through the play of tones, that is, analogically luring us to what Bergson called "real duration"[36] through rhythmic patterns:

> But in this approach [to the inner world] he [the composer/musician] comes in contact with ideas of *time* only, as the most external element in his communication, while he keeps ideas of space under an impenetrable veil, the lifting of which would necessarily at once render the dream-image which he views unrecognizable. While the *harmony* of tones, which belongs neither to time nor space, remains the most proper element of music, the musician, now actively shaping, extends his hand, to establish a common understanding as it were, toward the waking world of phenomena, through the rhythmical succession of time in his manifestations, just as the allegorical dream is connected with the usual ideas of the individual in such a way that the waking consciousness which is turned toward the external world, though recognizing the great difference of this dream-image also, from the occurrences of the actual life, is able, nevertheless, firmly to retain it. Through the *rhythmical* disposition of his tones, the musician at once comes in contact, in a certain measure, with the intuitional plastic world, i.e., by virtue of the similarity of the laws in accordance with which the motion of the visible bodies is intelligibly manifested to our intuition. Human gestures, which endeavor in the

dance to make themselves intelligible through expressively alternative, and regulated motion, seem consequently to be *that* for music, that bodies, again, are for light, which without refraction against them wouldn't illumine, while we may say that without rhythm music would not be perceptible to us.[37]

Only through the use of "rhythmical succession" can the musicians/composers make "real duration" (not time as sequence, as the form of inner sense) intelligible to us. They use the harmony of tones as the magic means to analogize the movement of the will, without having to overly rely on the resources of spatialized arts (say sculpture) or thought (through discursive narration). These tones patterns are analogies that span the cognition we have of our spatial/visual outer world and the intuition we have of our durational/felt inner world. They guide the pattern of rhythmic repetition that we (the audience) can then use as hypnotic points of analogy to return to our inner world as it expresses itself, with new continuity, alignment, and appreciative insight. This process works like the process by which the "usual ideas" we have and see in allegorical dreams are analogous enough to waking life (have a "similarity of laws," to use his language) for us to communicate them (at least sometimes) and find insight in them, even if they cannot be exhausted by our own discursive interpretations. It also works like dancers' altering movements, which make intelligible the dance as a whole, even though we cannot fully describe this experience in discourse. The repetition across difference in music is the rhythm of the harmony of tones. It provides a unifying analogy between patterns in the usually bifurcated realms of will and representation. In short, spatial experience and temporal experience are analogous in their use of *consistent enough*, that is, rhythmic, pattern. For Wagner, the tonal rhythmic pattern of the musical object provides the most direct means to communication across spatial and temporal experience and shows that they are one and the same activity. It can do so because these tonal rhythmic patterns are closest in analogy to our lived experience. It is via this external magic that we are put in touch with the greater cosmic activity in which we participate. For Wagner, it is perhaps only in music that we can escape our isolation from ourselves and touch our shared wellsprings of will.

In the final section of the first part of the essay, Wagner offered an interesting and complex critique of Kant,[38] which I will not give an analysis of here but hope to explore in a future work.[39] For now, it suffices to note that Wagner's famous *leitmotifs* are for him more than an existential psychology playing underneath a libretto (which is how opera enthusiasts and music commentators usually treat it). The *leitmotifs* are a part of his musical, metaphysical method of bringing us inward to the rhythmic drama of reality, the most comprehensive idea of the world. Music is that vital object that best analogizes the rhythm of the will in its activity. Meditating on it, that is to listen attentively to music, is supposed to communicate something beyond the façade of the individual self, that is, the will which we are all manifestations of in our lives. For Wagner, it is perhaps only in such artistic meditation that we are no longer alone and can find consolation and peace in this world of suffering. For, in music we can find our home in the deeper cosmic becoming.

Act 3: Music's Magic

Today, Schopenhauer's metaphysics in its classical formulation is certainly not the most appealing and or empirically satisfying account of reality. One will find very few Schopenhauerian metaphysicians still talking about "will" as the name for ultimate reality. That said, is there anything then that can be taken from Wagner's account of the musical object, without committing to this view of ultimacy? The postidealistic process and Continental traditions of philosophy have taken up the task of a refined vitalist theory of music. Henri Bergson is exemplary in both philosophical traditions of recovering such a task.[40] Throughout his career, Bergson argued that music's rhythmic impulsions are *suggestive*, as opposed to being necessarily directly *expressive*, of certain intensive psychic states of duration. It is music's tantalizing analogy to our inner life that gives music its power.[41] Bergson would agree with Wagner that music "depotentializes" our normal mode of spatialization by its luring analogy to our inner intensive life in its deepest aspects as cosmic becoming. He also shared with Schopenhauer and Wagner a vitalist theory that spaces are created by the active impulsions of activity (*Élan vital*) in the universe. Unlike Schopenhauer and Wagner, Bergson was not certain of the ultimate status of such vital energy (hence preferring the term "vital force" denoting the expression of the process, not its ultimate nature), nor did he think renunciation of the purposive drive was the solution to the problem of life (he criticized "finalism" as vigorously as he criticized "mechanism"). Like Bergson, we can admire what the vital musical object *suggests* about our inner lives. We even can go so far as to state that the vital musical object tells us *something* about the nature of the activity of the universe, while recognizing that we do not have ultimate authority on the nature or a soteriology of that activity.

If we explore this idea through the perspective of philosophical personalism, we can go beyond Schopenhauer, Wagner, and even Bergson and suggest a little bit more about the abiding value of meditating on the musical object. If the vital musical object (at its best) can, as a spiritual exercise, return us to our own personal experience, to the deepest valued and most meaningful aspects of our creaturely existence, and can align us with others in a *vital* cosmic becoming in which we participate, it then perhaps shares a special relation with the sublimity of person. A painting of a countryside may return us to a previous or new interior state, but it does so through a beautiful spatial analogy. Music, at its best, does not work its purposive power on us via a spatial memory, especially to the trained listener, but by tones that align us to the rhythm of the purposive feeling of *being* a person. Some may say, as Schopenhauer did, that being drawn to the fundamental experience of the will is impersonal, and is spiritual training in the very pinnacle of impersonalizing, as we dissolve ourselves into that cosmic becoming. A more Kantian view would emphasize the opposite view—only the moral law is sublime, and only because it is experienced by us in our own person, our autonomy, and symbolized for us in the presence of the other person. The argument between Kantian and Schopenhauerian views would be protracted. But a personalized, Bergsonian view goes through the horns of the dilemma. Music, and all that is vital, is personal under certain conditions of time and history, including human experience, and is an exercise in recognizing the vital, becoming of person, that we experience only through and as a part of a community of persons. We recognize our position in a greater community of persons that are the flower and the chorus of the vital cosmic becoming. Music perhaps then can withdraw the gap between ourselves and other persons, and we can then align ourselves with the living, dynamic *sensus communis*. We can feel the unity of person that underlies our symbolically mediated relationships with each other.

Wagner's "Prelude" to *Tristan und Isolde* does not only make us remember a vision of a moment of tragic love, but it seeks to help us participate in the personal depths of tragic love in all of its intensity.[42] In fact "tragic love," itself is but a poor description of this constellation of actual, potential, and possible feelings we experience and find in the "Prelude" in different dimensions each time we meditate upon it. We can do this even if we have not experienced such love ourselves, because the magic rain of music can guide us to the rhythms of *sensus communis*, of the shared personhood in which we participate and which provides us insight we never knew we had into who we are, who we might have been, and experiences we could have had, but have not yet experienced.

For all Wagner's ethical failures, a deeply ethical conclusion can be drawn from his suggestions about the vital musical object. By training ourselves to attune to the musical object, we can not only illuminate our vitality, but can return to the sublimity of our shared personhood, to the collective source from which we recognize what it means to be a person. From that training we can realize that music has an ethical power to find community within, solace from, and respect for realms of our personal lives we share with others but cannot fully bring to rational discourse. Wotan's and Brünhilde's duet at the end of *Die Walküre* gives us access to an incredibly rich vista of personal feeling between father and grown daughter. We learn, in a way we could never fully capture in reasoned discourse, about the complexity of the parental love for children who become independent persons onto themselves and who on that basis challenge our most cherished goals. The depth of recognition for our shared personhood is deepened. These insights transcend the idiosyncratic and become a source for feeling the possibilities of personhood, while remaining accessible to unique individuals who deviate from them in various ways.

On the other hand, music also has the power to subvert our feelings to one aspect of the world and one community of persons, excluding and dismissing the dignity of others. Hitler saw in *Tänhauser* a potential narrow, but compelling vista of the nature of the German spirit. The Nazis would use the magic of that music as a political technique to lure the live feelings in the people of Germany of that era and create a single horizon of meaning that systematically excluded other horizons of meaning. In this way, music helped erase the existence of other persons. Ernst Cassirer in his *Myth of the State*, and a collection of other twentieth-century philosophers and scholars, warned us of the power of myth and its beguiling music.[43] It is easy for music to make us feel alive as part of a community, but also for it to make us blind to other melodies and rhythms. Once we think music is done revealing to us who counts as persons, we are in dangerous waters.

Music can both deceive and dominate our vision of others and open us up to the dignity of the plurality of personhood. The ancients, and especially Plato, knew the gifts and dangers of music for our ethical and political lives. There was a reason he suggested we ban certain kinds of musicians from the ideal community (as suggested in the *Republic*). It was not because music is "bad" but because it is such a powerful ethical force that it must be kept to good political purposes. We too should continue to take music seriously, not just as a means to aesthetic and psychological power, but as an object of deep metaphysical and ethical meditation. It is worthy of *midrash* and of our diligent attention. It is worth our time to practice this spiritual exercise that allows us to "see" each other through listening to the song of vitality.

Notes

1. The original version of this chapter was first published in *Eidos. A Journal for Philosophy of Culture*. This is an updated and expanded edition, published with their approval and acknowledgment. For more, see Eli Kramer, "Meditating on the Vitality of the Musical Object: A Spiritual Exercise Drawn from Richard Wagner's Metaphysics

of Music," *Eidos. A Journal for Philosophy of Culture* 3, no. 3 (9) (2019), https://doi.org/10.14394/eidos.jpc.2019.0029.

2. As quoted in John Deathridge, "Introduction" in *Wagner Handbook*, edited by Ulrich Müller and Peter Wapnewski, trans. John Deathridge (Cambridge, MA: Harvard University Press, 1992), xi.

3. This chapter should be read in compliment with Ralph Ellis's masterful piece in this volume, which explores his piano as an exemplar of a musical instrument as a kind of person. His experience and talent as a jazz musician adds depth and insight into how one can perceive the vitality of music and what role it can play in our lives as what I call a "spiritual exercise." Although we use different heuristics and have different "objects" in mind for consideration as alive or even a "person," Ellis on the instrument and me on the music itself, both of us are exploring how music affords access to the innermost dimensions of life that words are but poor substitutes for. I hope readers will see my modest contribution as providing some scaffolding in the history of philosophy for why Ellis's work is so vital and so needed today. For more, see Ralph Ellis, "How My Piano Uses Gendlin's Focusing Method," in *The Cultural Power of Personal Objects: Traditional Accounts and New Perspectives,* ed. Jared Kemling (Albany: State University of New York Press, 2021).

4. For more, see Friedrich Nietzsche, *The Case of Wagner, Nietzsche Contra Wagner, and Selected Aphorisms,* trans. Anthony M Ludovici, third edition (Edinburgh and London: T. N. Foulis, 1911).

5. For studies from scholars of Wagnerian philosophy, see Theodor Adorno, *In Search of Wagner*, trans. Rodney Livingstone, new edition, foreword by Slavoj Žižek, Radical Thinkers Series (London and New York: Verso, 2009); Bryan Magee, *The Tristan Chord: Wagner and Philosophy* (New York: Henry Holt and Company, 2002); Julian Young, *The Philosophies of Richard Wagner* (Lanham, MD: Lexington Books, 2014).

6. Carl Dahlhaus, *Richard Wagner's Music Dramas*, trans. Mary Whitthall (Cambridge: Cambridge University Press, 1979), 1.

7. In the case of *midrash*, a rabbinic author's singular commentaries and stories fleshing out insights from a singular piece of Hebrew scripture. *Midrash* literally means "textual interpretation."

8. While not through the oeuvre of *midrash*, Juliusz Domański has explored the presence of a singular author or commentator in a text in his work *Le texte comme présence* (The Text as Presence). For more, see Juliusz Domański, *Le texte comme présence. Contribution à l'histoire de la réflexion sur le texte et le livre* (Frankfurt am Main: Peter Lang, 2017).

9. For more on "spiritual exercises" in this sense of the term, see Pierre Hadot, *Philosophy as a Way of Life: From Socrates to Foucault*, ed. Arnold I. Davidson, trans. Michael Chase (Malden, MA: Blackwell, 1995), 79–144.

10. By "nature" I do not mean the technical Kantian term for the realm of possible experience, but as "the function or purpose of something," Wagner often uses *Natur* in this colloquial sense, that is closer to the Greek sense of *phusis*.

11. By "object" I do not mean, in the German Idealistic sense an *Objekt* but a *Gegenstand* or a cognized quantum of explanation.

12. Hereinafter *WW&R*.

13. I borrow this term from Alfred North Whitehead. For more on the "undivided, divisible" in Whitehead's corpus, see Randall Auxier and Gary Herstein, *The Quantum of Explanation: Whitehead's Radical Empiricism* (New York: Routledge, 2017), 112–42.

14. In the second and third editions of *WWR*, Schopenhauer explored whether the will was the numinous itself, or merely its most immediate expression.

15. Arthur Schopenhauer, *The World as Will and Representation*, trans. E. F. J. Payne, vol. 2 (New York: Dover Publications, 1969), 448.

16. For more, see Hartmut Reinhardt, "Wagner and Schopenhauer," in *Wagner Handbook*, ed. Ulrich Müller and Peter Wapnewski, trans. John Deathridge (Cambridge, MA: Harvard University Press, 1992), 287.

17. For example, see Immanuel Kant, *Critique of Judgment*, trans. Werner S. Pluhar (Indianapolis, IN: Hackett, 1987), 202–3 [§54, 331–32].

18. Richard Wagner, *Beethoven*, trans. Albert R. Parsons (Boston: Lee & Shepard, 1872), 40–41.

19. For more on Wagner's views on Beethoven, see Klaus Kropfinger, *Wagner and Beethoven: Richard Wagner's Reception of Beethoven*, trans. Peter Palmer (Cambridge: Cambridge University Press, 1991).

20. Wagner, *Beethoven*, 111.

21. Reinhardt, "Wagner and Schopenhauer," 290.

22. For more, see Wagner, *Beethoven*, 19–21.

23. Wagner, *Beethoven*, 26–29.

24. Wagner, *Beethoven*, 31.

25. Wagner, *Beethoven*, 29.

26. Wagner is part of a heated debate in Schopenhauerian aesthetics as to whether music has direct identity with the will or if it can put us in the most immediate relationship with the will of any of the arts. Wagner took the latter view. Another aspect of this debate is whether music belongs to the soul or is the soul, and is then expressed in nature, or, on the other hand, whether music gives an analogy to our lived embodiment. In this second aspect of the debate, Wagner believed music touches the soul, though is not soul itself. Music is still an object (as *Gegenstand*) but is special because of its unstable and highly intensive nature. It is not pure will but an exhibition that returns us to the will. For an example of some aspects of this debate, see Sandra Shapshay, "Schopenhauer's Aesthetics and Philosophy of Art," *Philosophy Compass* 7, no. 1 (January 2012), 11–22, DOI: 10.1111/j.1747-9991.2011.00453.x.

27. My emphasis.

28. Wagner, *Beethoven*, 34–35.

29. For more on "aesthetic ideas," see Kant, *Critique of Judgment*, 182 [§49, 314]. Also, see my essay: Eli Kramer, "Utopia as the Gift of Ethical Genius: Ernst Cassirer's Theory of Utopia," *Eidos. A Journal for Philosophy of Culture* 2, no. 1 (3) (April 2018), https://doi.org/10.26319/3910.

30. Schopenhauer and Wagner distinguished themselves from Kant, who thought music was the lowest of the fine arts, if a fine art at all, as it was the hardest one to disengage from the body; thus, interestedness is impossible to get rid of in music. For

more, see Kant, *Critique of Judgment*, 189-95 [§51]. Schopenhauer and Wagner thought this interestedness reveals music's immediate purposiveness so analogous to our own. Music is beautiful not because it side-steps determinate judgment, which helps us come to a reflective relationship with our own freedom, but because it beguiles us to withdraw into our own primal purposeful activity. For them, music draws us to more than animal-like pleasure (as Kant thought). Rather, it takes us deeper into it, to our deepest pulsating energies as living creatures. It is perhaps better called the most "primal art," rather than a fine art.

31. Kant's discussion of the distinction between "interested likings" and "subjective universal judgements," like that of the beautiful in the "Analytic of the Beautiful" in the *Critique of Judgment*, largely framed the idealistic theory of aesthetics that Wagner draws from in this essay. For more, see *Critique of Judgment*, 43-91 [§1-22].

32. See Wagner, *Beethoven*, 107.

33. Wagner, *Beethoven*, 35.

34. Wagner's work was also influenced by other neo-Kantian idealists, but often indirectly. For example, the work of Schelling. This influence is in spite of the fact that when he was young, Wagner only read the first few pages of the *System of Transcendental Idealism* before he was befuddled and quickly gave up on it in order to return to his ninth symphony. Richard Wagner, *My Life*, vol. 1(*Academia*.edu, 2010). He probably got most of his Schelling through the filter of other neo-Kantian and romantic sources. For a partial overview of the relationship between neo-Kantian idealism and philosophy of music in the late nineteenth and early twentieth centuries, see Mark Evan Bonds, "Idealism and the Aesthetics of Instrumental Music at the Turn of the Nineteenth Century," *Journal of the American Musicological Society* 50, nos. 2/3 (1997): 387-420, DOI: 10.2307/831839.

35. Wagner, *Beethoven*, 43.

36. For example, see: Henri Bergson, *Time and Free Will: An Essay on the Immediate Data of Consciousness*, trans. Frank Lubecki Pogson (New York: Dover Publications, 2001), ch. 2.

37. Wagner, *Beethoven*, 44-45.

38. Although he never named Kant directly, I have strong suspicions that a critique of Kantian aesthetics is implicit throughout that section. More research needs to be done to confirm my current suspicions.

39. Wagner, *Beethoven*, 47-51.

40. Suzanne Langer is another exemplary example. For more, see Suzanne K. Langer, *Feeling and Form: A Theory of Art Developed from Philosophy in a New Key* (New York: Charles Scribner's Sons, 1953). As mentioned before, Ralph Ellis is another critical figure in this movement. For more, see footnote 3.

41. For example, see: Bergson, *Time and Free Will*, 40 and 65.

42. And one assumes that taking the finite form of personhood is a condition for just this kind of feeling.

43. For more, see Paulina Sosnowska, "The Reinforcement of Political Myth? Hans Blumenberg, Hannah Arendt and the History of the Twentieth Century," *Eidos. A Journal for Philosophy of Culture* 3, no. 2 (July 2019): 51-61.

Bibliography

Adorno, Theodor. *In Search of Wagner*. Translated by Rodney Livingstone. New Edition. Foreword by Slavoj Žižek. Radical Thinkers Series. London and New York: Verso, 2009.

Auxier, Randall, and Gary Herstein. *The Quantum of Explanation: Whitehead's Radical Empiricism*. New York: Routledge, 2017.

Bergson, Henri. *Time and Free Will: An Essay on the Immediate Data of Consciousness*. Translated by Frank Lubecki Pogson. New York: Dover Publications, 2001.

Bonds, Mark Evans. "Idealism and the Aesthetics of Instrumental Music at the Turn of the Nineteenth Century." *Journal of the American Musicological Society* 50, nos. 2/3 (1997): 387–420. DOI: 10.2307/831839.

Dahlhaus, Carl. *Richard Wagner's Music Dramas*. Translated by Mary Whitthall. Cambridge: Cambridge University Press, 1979.

Deathridge, John. "Introduction." In *Wagner Handbook*, edited by Ulrich Müller and Peter Wapnewski. Translated by John Deathridge. Cambridge, MA: Harvard University Press, 1992.

Domański, Juliusz. *Le texte comme présence. Contribution à l'histoire de la réflexion sur le texte et le livre*. Frankfurt am Main: Peter Lang, 2017.

Ellis, Ralph. "How My Piano Uses Gendlin's Focusing Method." In *The Cultural Power of Personal Objects: Traditional Accounts and New Perspectives*, edited by Jared Kemling. Albany: State University of New York Press, 2021.

Hadot, Pierre. *Philosophy as a Way of Life: From Socrates to Foucault*. Edited by Arnold I. Davidson. Translated by Michael Chase. Malden, MA: Blackwell, 1995.

Kant, Immanuel. *Critique of Judgment*. Translated by Werner S. Pluhar. Indianapolis: Hackett, 1987.

Kramer, Eli. "Meditating on the Vitality of the Musical Object: A Spiritual Exercise Drawn from Richard Wagner's Metaphysics of Music." *Eidos. A Journal for Philosophy of Culture* 3, no. 3 (9) (2019): 29–42. https://doi.org/10.14394/eidos.jpc.2019.0029.

———. "Utopia as the Gift of Ethical Genius: Ernst Cassirer's Theory of Utopia." *Eidos. A Journal for Philosophy of Culture* 2, no. 1 (3) (2018): 96–108. https://doi.org/10.26319/3910.

Kropfinger, Klaus. *Wagner and Beethoven: Richard Wagner's Reception of Beethoven*. Translated by Peter Palmer. Cambridge: Cambridge University Press, 1991.

Langer, Suzanne K. *Feeling and Form: A Theory of Art Developed from Philosophy in a New Key*. New York: Charles Scribner's Sons, 1953.

Magee, Bryan. *The Tristan Chord: Wagner and Philosophy*. New York: Henry Holt and Company, 2002.

Müller, Ulrich, and Peter Wapnewski, eds. *Wagner Handbook*. Translated by John Deathridge. Cambridge, MA: Harvard University Press, 1992.

Nietzsche, Friedrich. *The Case of Wagner, Nietzsche Contra Wagner, and Selected Aphorisms*. Translated by Anthony M Ludovici. Third Edition. Edinburgh and London: T. N. Foulis, 1911.

Reinhardt, Hartmut. "Wagner and Schopenhauer." In *Wagner Handbook*, edited by Ulrich Müller and Peter Wapnewski. Translated by John Deathridge. Cambridge, MA: Harvard University Press, 1992.
Schopenhauer, Arthur. *The World as Will and Representation*. Translated by E. F. J. Payne. Volume 2. New York: Dover Publications, 1969.
Shapshay, Sandra. "Schopenhauer's Aesthetics and Philosophy of Art." *Philosophy Compass* 7, no. 1 (January 2012): 11–22. DOI: 10.1111/j.1747-9991.2011.00453.x.
Sosnowska, Paulina. "The Reinforcement of Political Myth? Hans Blumenberg, Hannah Arendt and the History of the Twentieth Century." *Eidos. A Journal for Philosophy of Culture* 3, no. 2 (July 2019): 51–61.
Wagner, Richard. *Beethoven*. Translated by Albert R. Parsons. Boston: Lee & Shepard, 1872.
———. *My Life*. Volume 1. *Academia*.edu, 2010.
Young, Julian. *The Philosophies of Richard Wagner*. Lanham, MD: Lexington Books, 2014.

Chapter 17

Bring Out Your Dead

Human Bodies, Cultural Objects, and Personality

LAURA J. MUELLER

Editor's Note: This chapter is the first of two dealing with what I will broadly group together as an "ethics of bodies." Mueller examines the complex relationship between bodies, personhood, and personality, ultimately attempting to understand the ethical, cultural, and symbolic status of deceased human bodies. The chapter draws on Kant and Cassirer, thus fruitfully expanding on themes from earlier chapters (especially chapters 10, 14, and 16). Moreover, the chapter applies its complex ontological analysis to pressing ethical and moral debates: systematically addressing ethical concerns for the first time in the volume (although several earlier chapters have touched on ethical themes: for example, chapters 1 and 8).

Reverence of the dead is, perhaps, one of the few human phenomena shared throughout time and culture. Vico claims that along with religion and marriage, burial rites are one of the fundamental principles of a civilization: "all have some religion, all contract solemn marriage, all bury their dead."[1] Indeed, to *not* bury one's dead is a sign of times most troublesome or an act of war upon an enemy. And no matter the amount of respect in even the most solemn burial, the dead do not always stay buried. Sometimes we must look upon the face of the dearly departed. We can recall that most well-known tale of Emerson unearthing the corpse of his bride, gone too soon: "On March 29, 1832 . . . Emerson visited the tomb of his young wife, Ellen, who had been buried a year and two months earlier. He was in the habit of walking from Boston out to her grave in Roxbury every day, but on this particular day he did more than commune with the spirit of the departed Ellen: he opened the coffin. . . . He had to see for himself. He could not believe she was dead."[2] If we believe the body decays but the soul lives forever, why do we respect the body so much? Or, if we believe that death is the end, why do we revere the corpse of a decaying thing? The simple answer is: we respect the dead. The more complicated question is: why? In answering these questions, we will delve into an investigation of what the body is, as a cultural object, and what certain after-death practices and taboos, certain aesthetic reactions and moral practices towards the no-longer-living, can tell us about bodies when they are alive. As a cultural object, the body serves as a symbol for sublime personhood and is treated as such, even when the "person" is gone. The body, then, is culturally important after death, if no longer individually important. This conversation, however, does not end with the body but only truly begins there. Through an investigation of postdeath treatment, we can further develop a theory of personhood and two types of personality: personal-personality, and object-personality. My ambition in this reflective piece is to distinguish between these two kinds of personality based on the two criteria for moral personhood as explained in Kant's third Paralogism.

My method is one of phenomenological description through many examples and dissections of those examples. My goal is to discover what underlies these experiences of objects—bodies and mere "things" alike. The first section of this piece contains a short reflection and summary of Cora Diamond's work, to discern what the true question at hand is when we ponder the difference between eating meat and eating people. The fruition of this reflection reveals something particular about people, which is further investigated in section 2, which is on Kantian personhood. After engaging in a discussion on personhood, the conditions for the possibility of personhood, and sublimity, I then move on to an exploration of meeting each one of those conditions separately—which yields not persons, but certain kinds of *personalities*. This distinction allows us to differentiate between 1) persons with personal-personality, 2) self-conscious creatures with personality (but no personhood), 3) objects with personality (but no personhood), and 4) objects with personality that once had personhood (e.g., dead bodies). The conclusion of this chapter establishes that cultural objects with object-personalities are created by the symbolic nature of humanity itself—we create a vibrant, symbolic, and mythical world ourselves.

The People We Don't Eat

The subject matter of this reflection first struck me when I was reading Cora Diamond's "Eating Meat and Eating People." This article is a response to animal rights conversations concerning the moral dimensions of human-animal relations and vegetarianism, and in it, Diamond makes some astute observations and analogies regarding our treatment of animal bodies and human bodies. I will not recount her entire argument for this is not an essay on vegetarianism, but I will recount some of her thoughts concerning the way we treat our human dead:

> *We do not eat our dead*, even when they have died in automobile accidents or been struck by lightning, and their flesh might be first class. We do not eat them; or if we do, it is a matter of extreme need, or of some special ritual—and even in cases of obvious extreme need, there is very great reluctance. We also do not eat our amputated limbs. (Or if we did, it would be in the same kinds of special circumstances in which we eat our dead.) Now the fact that we do not eat our dead is not a consequence—not a direct one in any event—of our unwillingness to kill people for food or other purposes. It is not a direct consequence of our unwillingness to cause distress to people. Of course, it would cause distress to people to think that they might be eaten when they were dead, but it causes distress because of what it is to eat a dead person. Hence, we cannot elucidate what (if anything) is wrong—if that is the word—with eating people by appealing to the distress it would cause, in the way we can point to the distress caused by stamping on someone's toe as a reason why we regard it as a wrong to him. Now if we do not eat people who are already dead and also do not kill people for food, it is at least *prima facie* plausible that our reasons in the two cases might be related, and hence must be looked into by anyone who wants to claim that we have no good reasons for not eating people which are not also good reasons for not eating animals. Anyone who, in discussing this issue, focuses on our reasons for not killing people or our reasons for not causing them suffering quite evidently runs a risk of leaving altogether out of his discussion those fundamental features of our relationship to other human beings which are involved in our not eating them.[3]

Our collective revulsion towards eating the dead manifests in several ways other than just the fact that we do not eat the dead. Take, for instance, human cannibalism—a trope used quite widely in the horror genre, and a trope used historically to justify genocide, racism, and violence towards indigenous peoples. Joy Porter recounts that the myth of cannibalism was utilized by Western colonists to justify racial violence against indigenous peoples of North America, the Caribbean islands, and Africa.[4] Cannibals were monsters, they were inhuman, and there was something wrong with them. There is something wrong with "people" who eat the dead. As Diamond points out, not eating the dead is not a direct consequence of the distress it might cause to the newly deceased, though it might cause me some distress to think that I will be consumed after my spirit departs from this world. After I am dead, however, I will not care. I will be dead. In fact, since I am rather environmentally minded, I might be more rational to condone the consumption of flesh I no longer inhabit. I might put forth a rather modest proposal and desire someone to eat my flesh. But, still, the discomfort remains. The cultural implications of human flesh-eating have little to do with any immediate distress or harm caused to the body, which is now a corpse. We do not, in short, have distress because of the harm it causes; rather, we think it causes harm because of the distress we have at the thought of the act. We are distressed at the very thought because of *what it means to eat the dead in the first place.*

Continuing to take inspiration from Diamond, we can appeal to why eating the dead is taboo (save for certain religious or ritualistic purposes). As Diamond ruminates, we can better grasp what kinds of actions are morally wrong when we first grasp what kinds of creatures are involved. The kinds of creatures not to be eaten, not to be killed, for example, have names, and not numbers.[5] Read any book on the Holocaust,[6] or visit any Holocaust memorial, for example, to learn about giving people numbers and removing their names. People are hard to kill, but people have names. *Things* are much easier to dispose of, and things do not have names. Whipping someone is psychologically easier when that some*one* becomes a some*thing*, to be called "slave," or "boy." In other words, to *de*humanize someone, they first have to be human. When we strip them of names, we remove them from the realm of the kinds of beings who merit certain treatments and against whom certain actions are taboo. Once they are no longer "human," once they are no longer the kind of being to whom we feel any moral obligation, we can then tell ourselves that they were never dehumanized in the first place, for they were never human. Burial and disposal work similarly. We bury bodies with social identities, bodies who, when living, were the kinds of beings to have names, have relations, who were part of families, communities, who had histories and hopes. (This is why we have pet burials, as well. Pets *are* those kinds of beings.) As C. D. Collier writes:

> While cemeteries provide for the secular, profane need of the community for the disposal of the corpse, they also allow for the dead to remain identified as members of families, social institutions, and the present citizenry through the sacred consecration of ground within

the community for their remains. Thus, an afterlife of continued social identity is provided as reassurance in the face of everyone's mortality. In the process, the deceased's social personality is perpetuated beyond death through memorialization, which reestablishes the missing relative with a monument and a grave and thereby maintains the social life the survivors had with the deceased.[7]

We throw away rubbish in piles, let it fester and rot in the dump; we throw away corpses with numbers—not bodies with names—in the same manner.

We can see through the treatment of the dead—as a being who had a name, as a being who is not to be eaten—that the dead are the kinds of beings who *had* a certain sort of relation with others. Those relations, then, are honored by the living, for the dead have no vested interest any longer. But, we must ponder: What are the kinds of beings who have social relations with others, and what do they become after death? The being who lived is gone, and all we have left is the flesh of the body. I think the answer to this question can tell us about two different kinds of cultural beings: persons, and objects with personality. After death, the person becomes an object with *personality*, a symbol of the person-that-was and the social relations that person once had.

Persons, Dignity, and Personality: People and Objects

I would like to begin with reflections on the distinction between person and personality, a reflection very much inspired by Kant's works on the sublimity of the *person*. Let us further distinguish between two types of personality: that which is held by a person, as self-identity, and that which is recognized in *objects*, which have no sense of self. Thus, we can say we have, in the division between person and personality, two main distinctions: the personal-personality, and the object-personality. One is held by the kinds of beings we call *persons*, and the other is held by objects who are not persons and have never been such.

Drawing from Kant, we can first posit that the person is a sublime rational creature, and that intersubjectivity is necessary for self-identity as a person. Thus, here we are discussing what I refer to as personal-personality. As we untangle the weave of Kantian views on personhood, we will also find ourselves engaged in a discussion of dignity, for the two are intertwined. For Kant, it is the *person* who has dignity, and *things* that have a price, as he states in his *Groundwork*.[8] This dignity of persons is at the core of treating others not merely as a means, but also as an end. Thus, the *person* is the one to whom we have direct moral obligation—including ourselves—and the kind of being who is priceless.

Kant's account of human dignity is, perhaps, one of his most lasting contributions to philosophy and politics. As Oliver Sensen points out in his *Kant on Human Dignity*, political rights-granting documents, even in our recent history, seem to draw from the idea of human dignity to ground fundamental rights.[9] Sensen, for example, appeals to the UN's "International Bill of Rights," the Charter of the UN, and the International Covenant on Civil and Political Rights (among many other examples), to demonstrate that politically speaking, dignity is associated with worth, and that rights "derive" from inherent dignity.[10] Sensen, however, challenges this "contemporary" view of dignity—that which identifies dignity as a fundamental, inherent, property of humanity—in favor of what he refers to as a "traditional paradigm" of dignity in Kant.

The view that dignity is some inherent property is what Sensen refers to as the "contemporary paradigm" and is often used to justify *why* we should respect others; we have some special trait and elevated place in the universe and so must be respected on the basis of that special trait.[11] Sensen contrasts this paradigm with the "traditional" paradigm, which holds dignity not as some independent value, but rather as a "relational" value. Sensen claims that " 'Dignity' expresses that human beings are elevated over the rest of human nature because they should be respected directly (while the rest of nature is to be respected only indirectly)," that "the natural human being should revere the higher moral aspect within," and that "Kant uses 'dignity' to express that this moral aspect is 'sublime.' "[12]

The sublime, Kant states, is "what is *absolutely large*," or what is "*large beyond all comparison*."[13] As large beyond all comparison, the sublime cannot be sought in nature, but rather "must be sought solely in our ideas."[14] The sublime is not an object, but rather "the attunement that the intellect [gets] through a certain presentation that occupies reflective judgment."[15] When we judge something as sublime, we are making an aesthetic judgment of reflection, based on "the power of judgment's own principles"[16] or judgment's heautonomy: judgment legislates neither to nature, nor to freedom, but only to itself,[17] through its own a priori principle—purposiveness.[18] As Kant explains, this a priori principle is subjective, and refers to the "supersensible vocation of the subject's mental powers."[19] Unlike an aesthetic judgment of beauty, the aesthetic judgment of the sublime contains formal purposiveness—of our own mental powers—and thus involves an intellectual feeling (rather than a feeling of pleasure).[20]

Kant's major treatment of the sublime appears in his aesthetic and teleological work, the *Critique of Judgment*, though he does draw upon the sublime in his moral tome as well.[21] We treat the living human beings not only as a means, but also as an end, due to the agent's inherent sublimity; this sublime creature, beyond all price and bestowed with dignity, just is *the person*.

Kant's Third Paralogism addresses the person, and before moving on to *personality*, I will briefly discuss the intersubjectivity needed for personhood. Kant first presents the paralogism that he intends to critique:

> What is conscious of the numerical identity of itself in different times is to that extent a *person*.
> Now the soul is [such a thing that is conscious of the numerical identity of itself in different times][22]
> Therefore it is a person.[23]

Kant's criticism of this assertion rests on the claim that the "I" (the soul, the thinking thing) cannot be conscious of the numerical identity of itself in any objectively valid way. This numerical identity—and consciousness thereof—may well constitute "the person," but the thinking thing does not have such an objectively valid identity of itself. Kant's basic argument against the numerical identity of the self as a person seems to be that while I, myself, could have a numerical identity of *my* thinking thing, an external observer could not. That is not to say that an observer would not recognize an "I," but only that what is being recognized by the external viewer is a mere form of the unity of thought—this does not, however, necessarily denote that someone else can recognize my thinking self as a permanent thing and thus as a personality.[24] As given through pure reason alone, no such objective validity—an observer recognizing my self as a permanent self—can be given.

When I am conscious of myself, "I am conscious of this time as belonging to the unity of myself, and it amounts to the same whether I say that this entire time is in me as individual unity, or that I am with numerical unity to be found in all this time."[25] In short, I have an inner sense of time that allows me to ascribe numerical identity to myself, and I can therefore view myself as permanent. When we, for example, see objects as permanent, we do so by way of noting the element of that object that does not change in time. Thus, as an object of my inner sense, time is in me, and I am in time,[26] and it matters not *to inner sense*.[27] To inner sense, I can be permanent to myself. But this is incredibly subjective.[28] If I were to be observed by an external viewer, that viewer would view me as an object of her outer intuition, that is, she cannot observe the permanence that I merely subjectively think that I have. She "thus grants the *I* that in *my* consciousness accompanies at all times—and with full identity—all presentations,"[29] but will not "infer from it the objective permanence of myself."[30] The time in which the observer observes me is *her* time, *not* my time, and thus she can infer her own permanence, but not mine, and vice versa. Inner sense on its own is not enough to merit any objective claim for self-knowledge.[31] The inner sense of another—human or animal—is not enough to grant personhood. We can no more recognize the other personhood of *humans*, based on observation, than we can of nonhuman animals. In other words, we "cannot declare this sameness to be valid from the standpoint of a stranger,"[32] and thus any numerical identity my consciousness may have falls short of objective validity. This intersubjectivity is provided by *sensus communis*, which allows us to take up the possible standpoint of the other. As Kant writes, *sensus communis* is "a power to judge that in reflecting take account (a priori), in our thought, of everyone else's way of presenting [something], in order *as it were* to compare our own judgment with human reason in general and thus escape the illusion that arises from the ease of mistaking subjective and private conditions for objective one, an illusion that would have a prejudicial influence on judgment."[33]

I grant that much of the background on the Kantian person is to be found elsewhere, and the entire argument for the role of intersubjectivity in knowledge of personhood cannot be established here.[34] Let us be content with the person as: intersubjective, sublime, and that which has ultimate dignity. We must continue this reflection's argument, which now pertains to *personality*, in order to move on to bodies as cultural objects that have both personal-personality and object-personality.

When speaking of personality, we can first begin with that with which we are most familiar: our own sense of personality, our personal-personality. In speaking of person-personality, I will be speaking of personal identity as held by, let us say, the average self-conscious creature. Personal identity is that identity that we *personally* have of ourselves; that knowledge that the "me" I am right now, when I am sated and calm, is the same "me" I was, say, twenty minutes ago, when I was extremely hungry and therefore on edge. Arguments and considerations of personal identity are, to say the least, complicated, and not without disagreement. Not only do we have to question what are the kinds of creatures (or beings!) that can have personal identity—infants, communities, God, and animals are worth pondering—but we must determine what personal identity actually *is*. I am more interested in the former question, especially as it pertains to cultural *objects*, but we should spend some time establishing the most basic element of personal identity.

Most commonly, we consider self-consciousness to be a hallmark of personal identity, but that is not enough. As John Locke argues, we must have self-consciousness of ourselves through time and space. That is, we must have a continuity of self-consciousness in different times and in different places. For Locke, consciousness always accompanies thinking and makes what we call a self, a self, and in this alone consists personal identity: the sameness of a rational being.[35] To refer back to our Kantian conversation above, we can say, in other words, that we have a consciousness of our own object permanence. Note, however, that this consciousness of object permanence is not the same as *personhood*, which requires intersubjectivity and *sensus communis*.

In laypersons' terms, when asked of personal identity, we might say that I have my own unique history, of which I am aware, my own set of possibilities, of which I am aware, and a coherence of that history and that future projection in my present self. That is what makes me a unique individual, different from other individuals. When we disparagingly say that someone has "no personality," we usually mean that there is nothing unique about them, that there is nothing to differentiate that person from everyone else. Stated more philosophically, the principle of individuation is a founding principle for personal identity; as Locke writes, "whatever substance begins to exist, it must, during its existence, necessarily be the same,"[36] and "whatever existence makes it one particular thing under any denomination, the same existence continued, preserves it the same individual under the same denomination."[37] Consciousness of the same existence through time and space constitutes personal identity.

Now, if one criterion for personhood is consciousness of numerical identity in myself at different times, then we can say that persons also have personality, even though personality is *not enough* to establish moral personhood. Personhood is more vast, more expansive, than mere personality. Personhood is sublime and cannot be fully categorized; personality, however, can be. For now, then, we can say that in terms of personal-personality, persons also have personality. Another way to think of this is via Kant's distinction between psychological personality and moral personality; psychological personality is "merely the ability to be conscious of one's identity in different conditions of one's existence,"[38] whereas moral personality is "nothing other than the freedom of a rational being under moral laws."[39] This does not mean, however, that nonpersons also do not have personality; and here, we delve further into troubled waters.

When reflecting upon nonpersons who have personality, we might think of animals, to whom many deny any level of moral personhood, but who—at least some of which—have some level of self-identity through time and place.[40] One can easily, for example, find stories of elephants seeking revenge upon hunters long after their herd members were killed, or rampaging villages who housed abusive owners.[41] But animals are living creatures, and here we are concerned with cultural objects that are *inanimate*. The question then arises as to whether—and how—cultural objects, with no self-consciousness of identity through time and place, can have what I refer to as object-personality.

Object-personality: Cultural Objects and Bodies

Let us return to our original example of dead human bodies, or, perhaps more callously stated, corpses. As stated earlier, corpses are a particularly interesting example of personality for they exemplify both kinds of personality in their stages of life and death: personal-personality and object-personality. As a living human being, my grandmother (rest in peace) was a moral person and, as such, also had personality. Now, however, she is dead and no longer a moral person, no longer a personal-personality, at least in this world. As far as we can know, she no longer has consciousness of her self through time and place and is no longer a sublime, rational agent under the moral law. And yet, we still treated her corpse with a noted respect, and we certainly did not seek to use her body to solve world—or personal—hunger. Dead though she may be, her body still has personality—object-personality. Recall the two criteria for personhood: consciousness of the numerical identity of the self through time and place (personality) and intersubjectivity made possible through *sensus communis*. While nonpersons (e.g., animals, other kinds of living creatures—at least as many conceive of them) can still have personality by way of this consciousness of individuation in time and place, cultural objects, I argue, also can have personality by means of intersubjectivity, even if that intersubjectivity is not something the object consciously shares in. That is, cultural objects can have personality because of the intersubjectivity of members of that culture who invest that particular object with social meaning and purpose.

We do not eat my grandmother's body, not because it causes *her* distress—her distress ended when her life did—but because it causes *us* distress, both my family, and I daresay, our culture at large. Not eating her body reinforces a cultural position that humans are not the kinds of creatures that we eat; eating her would undermine that position and ostensibly cast us as members who are not "with it," not part of the culture that does not eat human beings. One reason we are not the kinds of creatures to be eaten is because the human body, even dead, is symbolic of our sublime personhood. This sublime personhood is also a reason to not eat animals, whose personhood and moral status is still contested. It might be better to abstain from a burger than it would be to accidentally eat another person.

Recall, also, Collier's claim that burial rites, cemetery arrangements, tombstone epigraphs, all serve a function to reinforce social identities—not for the deceased, but for the living. Respect for the dead, then, both reflects the moral status of the person-who-was and reinforces certain social functions to keep a culture stable. In his classic work, *Western Attitudes Toward Death*, Philip Ariés describes the changing attitudes toward how we treat the dead. He describes the sense of wanting to keep the dead "with us," and how this "new" attitude toward death affected burial rights—including placement of the bodies. This shift, he contends, arose most prominently in the mideighteenth century, moving away from communal graves and macabre displays of death to new, individualized tombs. He writes:

> What had been going on for almost a millennium without arousing any scruples became the object of vehement criticism. The flooring of the churches and the ground of the cemeteries, which were saturated with cadavers, and the exhibition of bones in the charnel houses all constituted a permanent violation of the dignity of the dead. The Church was reproached for having done everything for the soul and nothing for the body, of taking money for masses and showing no concern for the tombs. . . . Their tombs therefore began to serve as a sign of their presence after death, a presence which did not necessarily derive from the concept of immortality central to religions of salvation such as Christianity, but derived instead from the survivors' unwillingness to accept the departure of their loved one. People held on to the remains. They even went so far as to keep them visible in great bottles of alcohol, as in the case of Necker and his wife, the parents of Madame de Stael.[42]

For Ariés, the shift at hand was between a "tamed" death, in which death was always present, visiting the dying upon their bed, part of a social function in which the community—including children—gathered around the dying, to a more individualized death: the death of the other. Death, rather than something portended, known beforehand, and common, became a rupture that interrupted life. This new cultural treatment of death—the one with which we are most familiar today—hinged on a recognition of *this person's* death. Death became *personal*.

The social function of post-mortem respect is dependent upon a shared cultural intersubjectivity recognizing the history of burial rites, the history of the person in particular, the history of persons in general, and the future possibilities of that culture.[43] We do not want to permanently violate the dignity of the dead. We are now worried not just about their afterlife, but about their present not-life. We do not want to be a culture who eat our dead willy-nilly, for what does that say of our respect for persons who are living?

This intersubjectivity in cultural norms and values also forms objects with personality. I will provide a few examples here of object-personality, starting small, with children and their lovies (stuffed animals, stuffies), and ending with grander instances of widely shared cultural objects.

That most children love stuffed animals is uncontested, and we have all seen the plethora of cute stuffed animals at toy shops, grocery stores, airports, and almost any other shop. Toys to which children are attached are "transitional objects"; these objects are used for a variety of things, including helping children with daily hassles or other anxiety-inducing circumstances,[44] separation anxiety, comfort, or even neutral and unchallenging companionship. Transitional objects are part of the process of children including other-than-me objects and elements into their own narratives and identities.[45] We could even argue that the dialogues children have with animals, and their treatment of their toys, is morally instructive of how to treat—and how not to treat—other creatures. Perhaps the conversations children have with their lovies even helps to develop thinking as Hannah Arendt sees it, via Plato: the soundless dialogue between me and myself.[46] Children talk to their lovies, play with them, and form particular histories and narratives around them until that particular toy is so unique that it cannot be replaced. These toys develop certain personalities. They have a history; they have a future. Mistreating the toy is distressing to the child. Years later, adults might feel distress getting rid of these old childhood toys; perhaps, to the adult, the lovie still has that personality, and we do not like to think of our beloved stuffie isolated and alone in a refuse bin.

This stuffie, then, is an object that has a kind of personality, formed by the history, present use, and projected future of the object, even if that stuffie has no self-consciousness. To the child's mind, there is still a kind of intersubjectivity between the child and the lovie. The intersubjectivity—not *really* shared by the toy—is a dialogue and relation between the child and herself, that imbues the lovie with its own history and future, that individuates *this* stuffie from others.

While a child's relationship to a lovie is intersubjective in a qualified sense—a dialogue between the child and herself, or her imaginings, hopes, fears, and so on—the social role of stuffed animals is intersubjective in a much broader sense. Gendered norms are disseminated through the kinds of toys children are given to play with and love. Historically, girl-children were given dolls to care for, as practice for their own motherhood someday, for example. This first love is practice for how to later love and care for a child of one's own, how to extend one's love and treatment beyond the circle of just "me," to an object that is "not-me" but still deserving of tender treatment. Thus, toys as cultural objects in general can be used to perpetuate gendered identities, social identities, and social arrangements.[47]

While the shape of the object-personality might change as we age, the fact that certain objects have certain personalities to us does not. I might, for example, have a certain set of earrings that have no monetary value, but they were owned by my grandmother. They have a particular history that informs their particular future. Perhaps my grandmother wore them at her wedding, and so I, too, wish to wear them at some important ritual in my future. While another pair of earrings might look exactly the same, they are not the same at all, and they cannot replace the ones I have, with their unique history, memories, and future attached. However, unlike a stuffed animal, the earrings I inherited from my grandmother likely do not perpetuate the same social identity as the dolls I was given when I was younger. Some objects, then, while they have individuated personalities for a particular agent, do not have the expansive social role that others do.

At this point, though, we are still speaking of items with a particular personality to a particular agent. While toys in *general* do have social functions, *my* stuffed animal only has object-personality *to me*. Let us enlarge the conversation to objects that are cultural in both senses: they have object-personalities for the culture, *and* they have a social function. Recall, once more, what is needed for object-personality: intersubjectivity that provides continuity through time and place. That intersubjectivity is not shared by the object itself for the object has no consciousness, of the self or otherwise. However, that object's permanence as *this particular important object* serving *this particular symbolic or social function* is shared by others in that culture, intersubjectively. Thus, though my dearly beloved stuffed animal has permanence as a personality in time and place to me, and serves a particular gendered social function, that toy itself is not a cultural object, for no others are both witness to and creators of its personality. Similarly, my grandmother's earrings might have a particular object-personality to me and my family, but no others; in addition, they do not reproduce any social or cultural beliefs or norms or symbols. Thus, they are very meaningful to me, but they are not cultural objects with object-personalities.

Bodies, as I have argued, are cultural objects with object-personalities. Even though my grandmother is dead, her body has a certain history and identity through time and place, that is still known by me, my family, and all who loved, disliked, or knew her. In addition, as a body in general, she is recognized as having been a person with a particular history and so forth. Furthermore, as stated, bodies upon death have a certain social role, and reinforce certain social and cultural beliefs about status, moral worth, life after death, et cetera. The difference, of course, between my beloved grandmother and always-inanimate cultural objects is that my grandmother also had personal-personality when she was alive.

There are cultural objects that are inanimate, and physically just objects, that are also much more than *mere things*. Take, for example, certain objects from ancient Mesoamerica that have religious and mythological significance. Sarah E. Jackson writes:

In Classic Maya contexts, however, non-human persons can include entities that are not human in form-Hendon (2012:88) cites bowls, jars, and grinding stones, for instance-but are persons in the modes of interaction in which they engage. Houston (2014:98) also talks about vitality in non-human substances in a more abstract vein, identifying stone and trees, for instance, as animate and unified by their warmth and rootedness in the earth.[48]

Jackson uses the terms of "personhood" for her analysis, but by the criteria I have established, these objects are not "persons" in the sense described in this reflection. They are, however, cultural objects with object-personalities. They do have intersubjectively recognized histories through time and place and serve certain relational functions within that culture. Furthermore, great care was taken in tending to these objects: "Object care is seen through the wrapping of objects, which serves to dress them, and also through touch and caress of these objects. Both types of bundles discussed arc wrapped . . . This wrapping, in addition to being a key part of the structure of bundles, is a type of dressing and is one of the signals of being treated in a person-like way. Other objects have cloth or bindings tied to them, as an alternative type of 'dress.' "[49] These objects were treated as if they were personalities.

Religious artifacts are, in general, perhaps some of the most clear-cut cultural objects with personality that we can identify, though the sanctity of a cultural object is not restricted only to religious artifacts. Sanctified cultural objects—objects which have personality on a cultural scale—are objects which are symbolic expressions of a culture, objects that cannot be replaced by another object. That is, cultural objects of the sort we are discussing have a *particular* personality, an individual identity through time and place that is recognized by the individuals in that culture; this is a shared recognition at large. The object's particular personality is symbolic of certain histories, values, narratives, and possibilities of that culture. An object is forever "mere" if it is not symbolic, but cultural symbolism elevates that object from a mere thing to something *more*.

Animal Symbolicum and Cultural Objects

As Ernst Cassirer famously writes, "instead of defining man as *animal rationale*, we should define him as *animal symbolicum*."[50] The ability to symbolize, to create a "symbolic system," opens up a new world, a "new dimension of reality . . . No longer in a merely physical universe, man lives in a symbolic universe. Language, myth, art, and religion are part of this universe."[51] This ability to symbolize creates a living universe for human beings, and this ability is what elevates objects from *mere* things in the physical world to cultural objects with personality, objects that, due to intersubjective recognition, have a particular history, a particular present, and a particular future pregnant with possibility—and the history, present, and future of this particular object are fundamentally tied to the culture. The object represents the culture itself, as a symbol, and is imbued with personality built by that cultural recognition.

Recognizing the object-personality of cultural objects is a remnant of our symbolic ability, particularly in regards to the mythic mind. When speaking of the "mythic world," Cassirer writes:

> The world of myth is a dramatic world—a world of actions, of forces, of conflicting powers. In every phenomenon of nature it sees the collision of these powers. . . . Whatever is seen or felt is surrounded by a special atmosphere—an atmosphere of joy or grief, of anguish, of excitement, of exultation of depression. Here we cannot speak of 'things' as a dead or indifferent stuff. All objects are benign or malignant, friendly or inimical, familiar or uncanny, and fascinating or repellent or threatening.[52]

As Cassirer points out, this power of mythic thought has in no way lost its grasp on the "modern" or "civilized" human being, despite the efforts of scientific thought that are "directed to the aim of obliterating every trace of this first view."[53] Our social lives are shot through with mythic thinking; cultural objects are our inheritance of this earlier mythic stage of human culture and thought. Cultural objects, with object-personalities, are threatening or comforting, are positive or ominous. They gain these personalities by an intersubjective recognition of a history and future—of what they symbolize for us—and of their social roles. In these cultural objects, the scientific boundaries between kinds of life are dissolved; "Life is not divided into classes and subclasses. It is felt as an unbroken continuous whole which does not admit of any clean-cut and trenchant distinctions."[54] Thus, for example, when we are speaking of object-personalities, the object is no longer just a "mere thing" to be classified according to primary qualities or scientific categories; the object itself takes on its own personality. By virtue of myth-making, nature and objects become projections of our own social world[55] and, as such, serve certain social functions.

The Catholic Eucharist can serve as an example of mythic thinking, symbolism, and object-personalities. The Eucharist is, by official Catholic dogma, transubstantiated into the body of Christ. By scientific categories, the "reality" of the Eucharist is a mere wafer—cracker-thin, flavorless, needs salt but also acts as a salivary desiccant. And yet, by symbolic thinking, the Eucharist is more than that—it is the body of Christ, it is sacred, and it must be treated appropriately. One does not merely eat the wafer—one must have fasted for at least one hour beforehand, one must either have not committed serious sins, or have gone to Confession first. In addition, in many parishes, the Eucharist is *adored*; community members often volunteer to adore the Eucharist for times between just a few days or hours a week, to perpetual adoration in certain convents or monasteries. We do not adore the *wafer*; we adore what the wafer becomes through symbolism: the person of Christ. In addition, the Eucharist serves a certain social function: non-Catholics cannot receive Catholic Communion, which serves an inclusive, affirming role (for the Catholics, at least). The Communion unites Catholics, despite nation, ethnicity, culture, or language. The Eucharist clearly delineates a social hierarchy of who is "in" the Catholic community and who is not. Likewise, it marks us as all part of the community of saints, both the living and the dead. The Eucharist is culturally recognized by Catholics as having both a unique history and a future. Before holy Communion, the Last Supper is liturgically reenacted. The Eucharist is seen as a continuation of that Supper. In addition, the Eucharist is seen as an infinitely repeated sacrifice by Christ, both now and in the future. In this particular case, the past and the future—sacrifice and salvation—are the same and will remain so for Catholics in perpetuity.

The Eucharist has no consciousness, not of the self, not of other objects. As such, it has no self-identity, no inner sense of permanence in time or place. In other words, it certainly does not meet any criteria for personhood or even personal-personality. However, this piece of bread, this holy wafer, does have something else: intersubjective recognition by a people of a historical narrative, specific to that object, and a projected future of possibilities. This Eucharist connects people through time—past, present, and future—into a community; it is an irreplaceable, holy symbol of a people. The Eucharist is but one example among many of not only religious objects, but cultural objects with object-personalities in general—and these objects gain personality through the creation of symbols, made possible through mythic thought. Such objects are seemingly countless. The flag of the United States, for example, is one such cultural object with a personality, as is say, the St. Louis Arch, the Capitol Building, the Kaaba, and so on. These objects need not be religious, but they are all *sacred*. There is a certain way to honor the object-personalities, and a certain way to profane them in order to profane the culture. The death or destruction of such objects is itself a symbol of the death—or intended death—of the culture. The part—the symbol, the object-personality—also contains the whole; thus, to profane the part is, symbolically, also a destruction of the whole.

We have taken here a rather long and winding road to get to the heart of what a cultural object might be and how an object can have what we call a "personality." Despite scientific categorizations, classifications, and understandings, despite the intellectual "revolutions" of the modern age of thinking, the world of objects is not dead, not merely material, and not a world of mere "things" to be easily understood by their empirical qualities. That is certainly *one* world of existence, but it is not the *only* world, and on its own leaves no space for personality. To discover this other world in which "things" also take on a much deeper meaning, in which objects have personality, we began by investigating something very peculiar about the human condition, a peculiarity that itself transcends beyond our animal nature: the fact that we do not eat our dead.

Now, as stated at the beginning of our philosophical journey, there are many reasons we might give for not eating our dead, but the true motivation comes down simply to the kind of creatures we are. We are the kinds of creatures who are *persons*, in life, and have object-personalities, in death. In the case of humans, that object-personality itself stems from the fact that we were recognized in life as persons, with our attached personal-personality. This distinction that arises from a study of reverence for the dead allows us to examine other objects to see if they can have personality without self-consciousness—and they can.

The prevalence of creating cultural objects is, I think, also demonstrated in the refusal to let our dead go. Recall Ariés's example of Madame de Stael's parents keeping the dead on display. Consider those who keep their loved ones with them in an urn, displayed on the mantelpiece. These are not morbid, macabre treatments. These are, rather, loving displays of affection and respect, wherein the remains are still treated with dignity—even though they are, at this point, materially, only objects. Mythologically and symbolically, however, they are personalities.

Ariés describes further instances of traditional methods of keeping the dead with us, examples which are reflected in more technological treatments as well. While Ariés's classic text on attitudes toward death focuses on the integration of the past into the present, Kevin O'Neill focuses more on present possibilities and the future, specifically in regard to technological advances. However, both scholars have the same premise: we want to keep the dead with us. No longer are they thrown in charnel houses; no longer are they simply spirits now with unimportant embodiments.

For example, when describing the tradition of a funeral wake, Ariés writes:

> Thus during the wakes or farewell "visitations" which have been preserved, the visitors come without shame or repugnance. This is because in reality they are not visiting a dead person, as they traditionally have, but an almost-living one who, thanks to embalming, is still present, as if he were awaiting you to greet you or to take you off on a walk.

The definitive nature of the rupture has been blurred. Sadness and mourning have been banished from this calming reunion.[56]

I will speak on his claim that the rupture between life and death has been blurred in a moment for this becomes a point of particular interest when we interpret it via Cassirer. For now, I would like to focus on a comparison with Kevin O'Neill's work in *Internet Afterlife: Virtual Salvation in the 21st Century*. What we see in this comparison is a startling similarity of views toward death, despite the fact that Ariés is historically oriented and O'Neill is future-projected.

O'Neill provides examples of new ways of "burial" and "memorials"—those in and of the Web. When speaking of Facebook pages of those who have passed, O'Neill notes a tendency of friends and family members to keep posting on this person's page. He writes:

> As Patrick Stokes argues persuasively in his "Ghost in the Machine," the "you" that remains as the site's focus is not the "you" as the autonomous agent you once were. "You" are now the sum of your content at the time of your death, as well as the comments that people post on the page. Stokes makes the point that, over time, as the posts accumulate without any responses from you, the "you" who once ruled your site progressively disappears and is replaced by a "you" made up of, and by, the people who post to your site. . . . although this is your page, you no longer control it. Your Internet afterlife then becomes your friends' version of that afterlife. Because there is no longer any "you," "you" become their creation. At the same time, there is the "sense" that "you" still somehow still exist somewhere on the screen, on the site—a ghost, as Stokes perceptively notes, in the machine.
>
> This phenomenon was also noted by John Dobler who, when studying Myspace posts, found that after users die, even though friends and family know that the person is dead, they still, even years later, post questions, ask for advice, share news, and in every way behave as if the person who once ran the site were still present at or somehow near the site. Sometimes the comments mention that the one-time "owner" is in Heaven, but more often the posters writes as if the owner were somehow present on the site.[57]

On the one hand, what we get here is that the deceased's person-personality is now an object-personality and is created and cultivated by family and friends. You no longer control the page; you no longer have any kind of personal agency or identity. Your personality now is in fact the constructed personality by others, placed upon the object to such an extent that it seems as if the object has its own object-personality. At the same time, however, people still speak to this new object-personality *as if* it still had personal-personality, as if "you" are still there, somehow:

> The point is that people feel the living presence of the dead on their sites and send messages that reflect this feeling. Even if as Patrick Stokes suggests a dead person's Facebook identity is progressively occluded and obscured over time by friends posting their own autobiographical information, there is still the sense—even years after the Facebook user's death—that something of the subject, the agent, remains present on the site.[58]

The line between the personal-personality and the object-personality becomes blurred, for the rupture between life and death is blurred. As O'Neill so eloquently states, "At one moment a dying person is there, a functioning subject, a unique awareness. A moment later the person is gone and we are in the presence of a corpse."[59] The material transition from person to object is quick and clear—first a body, now a corpse. The cultural, social, symbolic, and psychological transition, however, remains blurred. This blurring of the lines, and the resultant actions, allows someone like O'Neill to make the claim that "we want to keep the dead with us in whatever form we can manage"[60]—whether the form is a tombstone, a Facebook page, or a glass bottle full of displayed remains—and likewise allows Ariés to describe contemporary attitudes toward death as the "great twentieth century refusal to accept death."[61] Our ability to refuse death by keeping the dead with us, always, stems from that blurred line between personal-personality and object-personalities. Remember, after all, that object-personalities are one small component of full-blown *personhood*.

It is very easy for us to lapse into treating object-personalities as if they were personal-personalities, especially when they were, at some point, actual persons. Recall Cassirer's previously shown description of the mythic world—everything was alive in a way; nothing was indifferent, and nothing was a mere object. This mythic thinking was a function of what he refers to as the expressive mode of thought. When we apprehend the world and its objects as alive, we are apprehending the world through a particular symbolic form of thought. Donald Verene explains expression and mythic thought as:

> The phenomenon of expression is characterized by our reaction to the world as an array of benign or malignant forces. These reactions

> become formed in mythic thought as the principles of the sacred and the profane. Myth as a symbolic form provides a complete account of being. Mythical thought brings together the worlds of the human, natural, and divine. . . . All the various symbolic forms, including science, contain an expressive moment from which their various inner forms of identities develop. Our original contact with being and the real takes the form of mythic thought.[62]

Mythic thought is the foundational symbolic form out of which other symbolic forms—such as significance—arise. Mythic thought is ever present in our scientific form of thinking and, as our treatment of object-personalities show, a symbolic form to which we frequently relapse. Donald Verene recounts Vico's account of mythic thought in his *New Science*: once the first word, "Jove" was uttered, thunder had a name; each instance of thunder is no longer a unique event but now "can be found again in the name."[63] This mythic thinking and cosmic separation of the earth and the sky is parallel with the origin of the separation between the knower and the known and is the foundation of philosophical metaphysics.[64]

Verene elaborates, stating, "The first metaphysics is poetic metaphysics or myth. The world is made accessible to human beings through their power of imagination to emerge from the immediacy of sensation into a world mediated by the power of symbolic forms."[65] He describes both myth and metaphysics as a way of confronting the "terror of history" in which time is linear, chronological, in which "one event simply leads to another."[66] Mythic time, the "time of origin," is a cycle in which "the world is continually renewed."[67] In a similar fashion, metaphysics is repetitive: "A metaphysic, once stated, is read and reread, argued out, refined and interpreted, often over centuries. Metaphysical systems are never refuted; they are abandoned out of fatigue."[68] The repetition of metaphysics hinges on its foundation of mythic thought, coming back and back again; this metaphysics and its foundation in myth is present in the experience of object-personalities. Consider, again, O'Neill's and Ariés's respective claims concerning the dead. Per O'Neill, we want to keep the Facebook user alive; we feel there is still something like the ghost or spirit of the deceased present in the social media page. In visitations, we "visit" the embalmed corpse and still view it as a person. We keep the dead with us; the lines between life and death have been blurred. The personal-personality becomes more than just the object-personality due to this blurring of life and death, this blur between metaphysics of personhood and its mythic instantiation of objects with personalities. We fall back into myth. The world is alive, and this is especially apparent in death.

What we end with, here, is a dissection of two kinds of personality, both stemming from criteria for moral personhood. On the one hand, to be a full-blown moral person, we must have self-identity, self-consciousness, and an inner sense of our permanence. But that is not enough. We must also be recognized from the standpoint (even if only possible standpoint) of the other—intersubjectivity. Together, these elements create something far more than the sum of their parts, but they are, at least, the bare conditions for personhood. However, what happens if something only meets *one* of those conditions? We have seen that something or some creature can have personal-personality without full moral personhood (animals, for example). Likewise, certain things can have object-personality without full moral personhood—in particular, cultural objects that are symbols, intersubjectively recognized as being more than what they appear. From stuffed toys, to corpses, to holy relics, to national symbols—our world is alive, and our world is *personal*. This personal element of the world may well be a remnant of myth as the origin of metaphysics, as the foundational symbolic form. As such, it is also a mode of thought into which we lapse more easily than anticipated, wherein the line between appearance and the sublime becomes blurred, and the two meld into a symbol—into a cultural object, an object-personality.

Notes

1. Giambattista Vico, *The New Science*, trans. Thomas Goddard Bergin and Max Harold Fisch (Ithaca, NY: Cornell University Press, 1948), paragraph 333.

2. Robert D. Richardson, Jr. *Emerson: The Mind on Fire* (Berkeley: University of California Press, 1995), 3.

3. Cora Diamond, "Eating Meat and Eating People," *Philosophy* 53, no. 206 (October 1978): 467.

4. Joy Porter, *Land and Spirit in Native America* (Santa Barbara, CA: Praeger, 2012): 41–44.

5. Diamond, "Eating Meat," 469.

6. I recommend Viktor Frankl's *Man's Search for Meaning*.

7. C. D. Abby Collier, "Tradition, Modernity, and Postmodernity in Symbolism of Death," *Sociological Quarterly* 44, no. 4 (Autumn 2003): 728.

8. Immanuel Kant, *Groundwork of the Metaphysics of Morals*, trans. Mary J. Gregor, in *Practical Philosophy*, ed. Paul Guyer and Allen Wood (New York: Cambridge University Press, 1996): 4:434–4:435.

9. Oliver Sensen, *Kant on Human Dignity* (Boston: de Gruyter, 2011), 146–52.

10. Sensen, *Kant on Human Dignity*, 151–152.

11. Sensen, *Kant on Human Dignity*, 153.

12. Sensen, *Kant on Human Dignity*, 176.

13. Kant, *Critique of Judgment*, trans. Werner S. Pluhar (Bloomington, IN: Hackett Publishing Company, 1987), 5: 248.

14. Kant, *Critique of Judgment*, 5: 250.

15. Kant, *Critique of Judgment*, 5: 250.

16. This is in contrast with the aesthetic judgments of sense, which contain "material purposiveness" and refer to the feeling of pleasure. Aesthetic judgments of reflection, however, contain formal purposiveness (Kant, *Critique of Judgment*, 5: 225).

17. Kant, *Critique of Judgment*, 5: 225.

18. Kant refers to subjective purposiveness as an a priori concept of judgment. See *Critique of Judgment* 5: 250, for example, wherein he refers to this purposiveness as the supersensible vocation of the subject's mental powers.

19. Kant, *Critique of Judgment*, 5: 250:

[there is, in the case of sublimity, relative subjective purposiveness;] even assuming that the object, when we perceive it, has nothing for our reflection that [would] be purposive for a[ny] determination of its form, yet [here] the presentation of it, applied to a purposiveness lying a priori in the subject (such as the supersensible vocation of the subject's mental powers) and [so] arousing a feeling of this purposiveness, is the basis of a [different] aesthetic judgment: this aesthetic judgment also refers to an a priori principle (though this principle is only subjective), but—unlike the first kind of aesthetic judgment—it refers not to a *purposiveness of nature* concerning the subject, but only to a possible purposive *use* which, by means of merely reflective judgment, [we can make] of certain sensible intuitions as far as their form is concerned . . .

20. Kant, *Critique of Judgment*, 5: 251.

21. Immanuel Kant, *Critique of Practical Reason*, trans. Mary J. Gregor in *Practical Philosophy*, ed. Paul Guyer and Allen Wood (New York: Cambridge University Press, 1996): 5: 117.

22. I have filled in Kant's second premise for the sake of greater clarity.

23. Immanuel Kant, *Critique of Pure Reason*, trans. Werner S. Pluhar (Indianapolis: Hackett Publishing Company, 1996), A 362. I am well aware that the Paralogisms were excised from the B-Edition. While it is beyond the scope of my current project, I suspect this conversation was taken up in the third *Critique* and in the *Metaphysics of Morals*. The "self" that escapes the structures of pure reason is not beyond all analysis, but it does fall outside the scope of the first *Critique* after Kant had considered the priority of reflective judgment in re-thinking the sublime in its relation to the moral self. The beginnings of such an argument are presented in the latter part of this chapter.

24. Ameriks puts it nicely: "Others may judge differently and say experiences that I take to be mine might have been had by others or by no one." See Karl Ameriks, *Kant's Theory of Mind* (Oxford: Clarendon Press, 1982), 133.

25. Kant, *Critique of Pure Reason*, A 362.

26. Sherover points out that "I am in time" is a rather confusing way of speaking of temporality. In *Are We in Time?* (Northwestern University Press, 2003), Sherover states that, rather, "The reverse would seem to be closer to the truth: we cannot be in time because time is *in* us. It permeates every activity of the being of the self; it orders the

continuity of change in all the complex relations that constitute a self; it permeates the relations each has with others; it appears to be equally pervasive in that dynamic relational system of nature we inhabit and to which we belong," (107). Personality can only be given by inner sense, for were it to be given by outer sense, it would be a substance, and thus subject to the categories—Kant would then be defeating himself in his Paralogisms (see Hoke Robinson's "The Priority of Inner Sense," *Kant-studien* 79 [1988]: 177).

27. This is a problematic and convoluted claim. Ameriks states, "It appears here that Kant is trying to impute to someone the odd idea that since time, supposedly, is only in him, he must be one throughout it. . . . What makes this idea so odd . . . is simply that it blatantly involves the basic non-Kantian mistake of confusing the empirical and transcendental levels. . . . That is, it mistakes the genuine transcendental claim that time is a mere form in us . . . with the quite different and incorrect empirical claim that it is but a form of the individual," (*Kant's Theory of Mind*, 132–133). I think, however, that Kant, in addressing the rational psychologists' view, begins on their own terms—including their mistaking the transcendental and the empirical. Doing this, on their own terms, he can still "prove" their claims to be incorrect, or, at least, incorrectly argued. As Ameriks states, the Paralogisms "need not commit Kant to saying that the conclusions of the specific paralogisms . . . are false, or even that there is no way they can be justified" (*Kant's Theory of Mind*, 10).

28. As Kant writes in the *Inaugural Dissertation*, time is a subjective condition, "necessary owing to the nature of the human mind" (§14, Sherover, 147), and the idea of time is singular (§14, Sherover, 146). See the *Inaugural Dissertation* in Charles Sherover's *The Human Experience of Time: Its Development and Philosophic Meaning* (Northwestern University Press, 1975). Originally published in John Handyside, trans. *Kant's Inaugural Dissertation and Early Writings on Space* (La Salle, IL: Open Court Publishing Co., 1929). In order to have personality, the singular must operate as a universal—something that occurs aesthetically, as we will see.

29. A 363.

30. A 363.

31. Ameriks, *Kant's Theory of Mind*, 130.

32. Kant, *Critique of Pure Reason*, A 364.

33. Kant, *Critique of Judgment*, 5: 294.

34. This is a long and convoluted discussion that hinges on the fact that intersubjectivity is, in fact, the mark of "objectivity" for Kant. In the *Prolegomena*, Kant distinguishes between judgments of perception and judgments of experience (see chapter 1 of this dissertation), and the move from the former, which are merely subjectively valid, to the latter, which are objectively valid. Of this move, he states that objective validity is "reason for the judgments of other men agreeing with mine," (trans. Paul Carus [Open Court, 1929]), (§18, Carus p. 55). In the same text, Kant also states that "necessary universality (for everybody)" and objective validity are equivalent terms; this implies, to me, that it is the more social aspect, or intersubjectivity, that obviates objective validity, *not* mere criteria of such validity.

35. John Locke, *An Essay concerning Human Understanding* (New York: Dover Publications, Inc, 1959), II.xxvii.9.

36. Locke, *An Essay concerning Human Understanding*, II.xxvii.28.

37. Locke, *An Essay concerning Human Understanding*, II.xxvii.29.

38. Immanuel Kant, *Metaphysics of Morals*, trans. Mary J. Gregor, in *Practical Philosophy*, ed. Paul Guyer and Allen Wood (New York: Cambridge University Press): 6: 223.

39. Kant, *Metaphysics of Morals*, 6: 223.

40. For more on animals and object permanence, epistemology, inner sense, and a priori categories, particularly within a Kantian lens, see Kant, "The False Subtleties of the Four Syllogistic Figures," in *Theoretical Philosophy 1755-1770*, ed. and trans. David Walford (Cambridge, NY: Cambridge University Press, 1992), 2: 59-60. Christine Korsgaard, "Fellow Creatures: Kantian Ethics and Our Duties to Animals" (presentation, Tanner Lectures on Human Values, University of Michigan, February 6, 2004). Christine Korsgaard, "Personhood, Animals, and the Law," *Think* 12, no. 34 (June 2013): 25-32. Colin McLear, "Kant on Animal Consciousness," *Philosophers' Imprint* 11, no. 15 (November 2011): 1-16.

41. Caroline Williams, "Elephants on the Edge Fight Back," *New Scientist Magazine*, February 15, 2006.

42. Philip Ariés, *Western Attitudes toward Death*, trans. Patricia M. Ranum (London: Marion Boyd, 1974), 70.

43. Jared Kemling's piece, "A Personalized Cultural World: A Cassireran Phenomenology of Personalized Intuition," in this volume is a good companion piece to this article. Kemling discusses the symbolic forms of personality, and his discussion of personalized time as *hope* and personalized number as *community* points to the need for intersubjectivity in what I refer to as "object-personalities."

44. Sandra L. Lookabough and Victoria R. Fu, "Children's Use of Inanimate Transitional Objects in Coping with Hassles," *Journal of Genetic Psychology* 153, no. 1 (March 1992): 37-46.

45. Sandra Lookabough Triebenbacher, "Children's Use of Transition Objects: Parental Attitudes and Perceptions," *Child Psychiatry and Human Development* 27, no. 4 (June 1997): 221-230.

46. Hannah Arendt, "Thinking and Moral Considerations: A Lecture," *Social Research* 38, no. 3 (Autumn 1971): 442.

47. See, for example, Becky Francis, "Gender, Toys, and Learning," *Oxford Review of Education* 36, no. 3 (June 2010): 325-344.

48. Sarah E. Jackson, "Facing Objects: An Investigation of Non-Human Personhood in Classic Maya Contexts," *Ancient Mesoamerica* 30 (2019): 33.

49. Jackson, "Facing Objects," 37.

50. Ernst Cassirer, *An Essay on Man* (New York: Doubleday & Company, 1953), 44.

51. Cassirer, *An Essay on Man*, 43.

52. Cassirer, *An Essay on Man*, 103.

53. Cassirer, *An Essay on Man*, 103.

54. Cassirer, *An Essay on Man*, 108.

55. Cassirer, *An Essay on Man*, 106.

56. Ariés, *Western Attitudes toward Death*, 101-102.

57. Kevin O'Neill, *Internet Afterlife: Virtual Salvation in the 21st Century* (Santa Barbara, CA: Praeger), 2016. eBook version, 44.

58. O'Neill, *Internet Afterlife*, 47.
59. O'Neill, *Internet Afterlife*, 13.
60. O'Neill, *Internet Afterlife*, 57.
61. Ariés, *Western Attitudes toward Death*, 82.
62. Donald Phillip Verene, "Metaphysics and the Origin of Culture," *The Review of Metaphysics* 63 (2009): 309.
63. Verene, "Metaphysics and the Origin of Culture," 311.
64. Verene, "Metaphysics and the Origin of Culture," 311–314.
65. Verene, "Metaphysics and the Origin of Culture," 315.
66. Verene, "Metaphysics and the Origin of Culture," 318.
67. Verene, "Metaphysics and the Origin of Culture," 318.
68. Verene, "Metaphysics and the Origin of Culture," 318.

Bibliography

Ameriks, Karl. *Kant's Theory of Mind*. Oxford: Clarendon Press, 1982.
Arendt, Hannah. "Thinking and Moral Considerations: A Lecture." *Social Research* 38, no. 3 (Autumn 1971): 417–46.
Ariés Philip. *Western Attitudes toward Death*. Translated by Patricia M. Ranum. London: Marion Boyd, 1974.
Cassirer, Ernst. *An Essay on Man*. New York: Doubleday & Company, 1953.
Collier, C. D. Abby. "Tradition, Modernity, and Postmodernity in Symbolism of Death" *Sociological Quarterly* 44, no. 4 (Autumn 2003): 727–49.
Diamond, Cora. "Eating Meat and Eating People. *Philosophy* 53, no. 206 (October 1978): 465–79.
Francis, Becky. "Gender, Toys, and Learning." *Oxford Review of Education* 36, no. 3 (June 2010): 325–44.
Frankl, Viktor. *Man's Search for Meaning*. Boston, MA: Beacon Press. 2006.
Handyside, John, tr., and Norman Kemp Smith, tr. and ed. *Kant's Inaugural Dissertation and Early Writings on Space*. Chicago/London: Open Court Press, 1929.
Jackson, Sarah E. "Facing Objects: An Investigation of Non-Human Personhood in Classic Maya Contexts." *Ancient Mesoamerica* 30 (2019): 31–44.
Kant, Immanuel. *Critique of Judgment*. Translated by Werner S. Pluhar. Indianapolis, IN: Hackett Publishing Company, 1987.
———. *Critique of Practical Reason*. Translated by Mary J. Gregor. In *Practical Philosophy*, edited by Paul Guyer and Allen Wood, 133–172. New York: Cambridge University Press, 1996.
———. *Critique of Pure Reason*. Translated by Werner S. Pluhar. Indianapolis, IN: Hackett Publishing Company, 1996.
———. "The False Subtleties of the Four Syllogistic Figures." Edited and translated by David Walford. In *Theoretical Philosophy 1755–1770*, edited and translated by David Walford, 85–105. Cambridge, NY: Cambridge University Press, 1992.

———. *Groundwork of the Metaphysics of Morals.* Translated. Mary J. Gregor. In *Practical Philosophy*, edited by Paul Guyer and Allen Wood, 37–108. New York: Cambridge University Press, 1996.

———. *The Metaphysics of Morals.* Translated. Mary J. Gregor. In *Practical Philosophy*, edited by Paul Guyer and Allen Wood, 353–604. New York: Cambridge University Press, 1996.

———. *Prologomena to any Future Metaphysics.* Translated by Paul Carus. LaSalle, IL: Open Court, 1929.

Kemling, Jared. "A Personalized Cultural World: A Cassireran Phenomenology of Personalized Intuition." In *The Cultural Power of Personal Objects: Traditional Accounts and New Perspectives.* Edited by Jared Kemling. New York: SUNY Press, 2021.

Korsgaard, Christine. "Fellow Creatures: Kantian Ethics and Our Duties to Animals." Tanner Lectures on Human Values at University of Michigan, February 6, 2004.

———. "Personhood, Animals, and the Law." *Think* 12, no. 34 (June 2013): 25–32.

Locke, John. *An Essay Concerning Human Understanding.* New York: Dover Publications, Inc., 1959.

Lookabough, Sandra L., and Victoria R. Fu. "Children's Use of Inanimate Transitional Objects in Coping with Hassles." *Journal of Genetic Psychology* 153, no. 1 (March 1992): 37–46.

McLear, Colin. "Kant on Animal Consciousness." *Philosophers' Imprint* 11, no. 15 (November 2011): 1–16.

O'Neill, Kevin. *Internet Afterlife: Virtual Salvation in the 21st Century.* Santa Barbara, CA: Praeger, 2016.

Porter, Joy. *Land and Spirit in Native America.* Santa Barbara, CA: Praeger, 2012.

Richardson, Jr., Robert D. *Emerson: The Mind on Fire.* Berkeley: University of California Press, 1995.

Robinson, Hoke. "The Priority of Inner Sense." *Kant-studien* 79 (1988): 165–82.

Sensen, Oliver. *Kant on Human Dignity.* Boston: de Gruyter, 2011.

Sherover, Charles. *Are We in Time?* Evanston, IL: Northwestern University Press, 2003.

———. *The Human Experience of Time: Its Development and Philosophical Meaning.* Evanston, IL: Northwestern University Press, 1975.

Triebenbacher, Sandra Lookabough. "Children's Use of Transition Objects: Parental Attitudes and Perceptions." *Child Psychiatry and Human Development* 27, no. 4 (June 1997): 221–30.

Verene, Donald Phillip. "Metaphysics and the Origin of Culture." *The Review of Metaphysics* 63 (2009): 307–28.

Vico, Giambattista. *The New Science.* Translated by Thomas Goddard Bergin and Max Harold Fisch. Ithaca, New York: Cornell University Press, 1948.

Williams, Caroline. "Elephants on the Edge Fight Back." *New Science Magazine*, February 15, 2006. https://www.newscientist.com/article/mg18925391-400-elephants-on-the-edge-fight-back.

Chapter 18

Sex Robots and Solipsism

Towards a Culture of Empty Contact

CHARLES W. HARVEY

Editor's Note: This is the second of two chapters focusing on an ethics of bodies. In this case: robot bodies. Harvey discusses the rise of sex robots (and potentially: love robots) and theorizes about the ethical, social (and perhaps even biological) implications these robots might have for humanity. The chapter serves as a suitable closing work. We started the volume with historical cases of personal objects (some as old as humanity itself), and we now turn our attention to the future, speculating about the objects only just beginning to transition into a personalized status. As the volume comes to a close, hopefully the reader will have a sense of the many forms that personalized objects can take, and hopefully the reader will have found new theoretical tools to help understand this fascinating part of the human experience.

In *Love + Sex with Robots: The Evolution of Human-Robot Relationships*, David Levy makes the bold claim that by 2050 it will be common for human beings to have robots as their most intimate psychological and sexual companions.[1] Indeed, Levy argues, some of our children will be married to robots, their children will be raised by robots, and in the final years of their lives they will be nursed and cared for by robots. Moreover, Levy argues, these psychologically and sexually intimate relationships will be *better* than those many people now have with their significant others. Why? Because robots do it better. They will play, console, make love, and care for us exactly as they have been programmed to do, and they will do so without all the messy, sinuous, intricate rigmarole that is intractable to human relations. They will be *programmed* to do and be what we want them to do and be *without* all the recesses and hidey-holes that are the quagmire of human-human relations. They will be the personal objects *par excellence*, personal objects that transform our culture, objects that we think to be persons.

In what follows, I will provide a synopsis of Levy's arguments for these claims with an interest not in refuting them (because I think that, to some extent, they are true), but with an interest in determining *why* these conditions are becoming true and *how* we postindustrial, increasingly urbanized human beings are *being changed* by the technologies we have made that are now (re)making us. While I will use Levy's book as the harbinger of things to come, I will use Nicholas Carr's *The Shallows: What the Internet Is Doing to Our Brains* (2010) to help explain why Levy's theses may be right and why we should be worried that they are. Sherry Turkle's *Alone Together: Why We Expect More from Technology and Less from Each Other* (2011) and Jaron Lanier's *You Are Not a Gadget: A Manifesto* (2010) will also help me express my concerns about the world Levy foresees.

Human-Robot Relations: Levy's Reasoning

Part 1 of Levy's book is titled "Love with Robots," and part 2, "Sex with Robots." In both parts, Levy uses nonfallacious slippery-slope arguments and shows how, in terms of both personal and social history, many adult human beings have slid gradually from love and sex with biological others to love and sex with inanimate objects and machines.[2] In the conclusion of his book, Levy notes that "while . . . love and marriage with robots are certain to lead to much heated debate in the years ahead, still more controversy will be generated by the concept of sex with robots."[3] While I suspect that Levy is right about this, I also think that, as usual, society has its eyes on the wrong target: the far more significant and ominous social-psychological change in people is intimated by their increasing capacity, tendency, and willingness to develop deep psychological attachments to sociable machines. My reasons for this belief are simple: falling and being in love is a much more global, psychosomatic event than is mere sexual intercourse; love demands the mobilization of much more of us than does mere orgasmic oriented sexual behavior. The needs and desires that sex robots meet are much more easily met and assuaged than are the needs and desires that a partner or companion robot would be required to meet; while we will have to ramp up our erotic powers to keep up with our sex robots, we will have to dumb down our very selves to make match with love robots. It is for these reasons as well as economic ones that the manufacture and sale of sex robots is further along than is the manufacture and sale of partner robots. However, the elements are converging that will link the apparent psychological depth and sensitivity of robots with their sexual prowess. Once this occurs, the path from sexual to psychological bonding will be laid (so to speak).

Significantly, but not surprisingly, Levy's arguments for the inevitability of human-robot love are grounded in and guided by a mechanistic, behaviorist psychology complemented by psychoanalytic object theories of selfhood. "Romantic love," Levy writes, "is a continuation of the process of attachment" that begins when we are infants and extends into the last years of our life.[4] Initial attachment (love) is to our primary caregiver and with each moment of separation and individuation from this primary other, we gradually transition into adulthood via attachment to other significant objects.[5] Charles Schultz's "Linus" and his beloved blanket epitomize an early stage in this process; each of us can provide examples from our own lives. Levy appeals to the work of Cindy Hazan and Philip Shaver that demonstrates that the basic traits of adult romantic attachment are not fundamentally different from our original infant-caregiver attachment.[6] This means, of course, that the entire chain of object attachments that people use to segue into childhood, adolescent and adult relationships, remains foundational for our adult relationships.

We know from personal experience and observation that cathexis upon objects (whether inanimate or animate) varies in intensity and longevity of attachment. A number of factors function here. One is that the more psychic energy invested in an object, the more valuable and fetishized it becomes to the person invested in it. From this, it follows that attachment to complex objects is typically longer and more intense than attachment to simple ones. Because animate objects are typically deeper and more complex than are inanimate ones (largely because they involve a reciprocal recognition and response that is absent from attachment to inanimate objects), animate objects tend to be more deeply and intensely fixated upon and fetishized than inanimate ones. But when the boundaries between inanimate and animate objects blur, when machines recognize us and respond to our interests and needs, the depth, intensity and longevity of attachments to objects increasingly resembles our traditional attachments to others. Indeed, as Sherry Turkle has documented, children raised with interactive virtual and physical robot companions (from Tamagotchi to Furbies to AIBO to My Real Baby) begin to blur the distinction between life and non-life;[7] they gradually drop their theoretical concerns about where machine-being ends and life begins, and they adopt pragmatic attitudes towards the attachment objects—attitudes that are guided by the behaviors and responses the object has been constructed to elicit.[8]

Children love their robotic companions, and they relate to them in significantly different, deeper, and more intense ways than they do traditional inanimate toys.⁹ And if, Levy reasons, "one's *capacity* to experience romantic love depends on one's attachment history, an attachment history that involves computers or electronic pets could provide a basis for the *capacity* to fall in love with robots."[10] Almost all of our children's history now involves such attachments, and often to the diminution or even the exclusion of deep and prolonged attachments to nonhuman animals or fellow human beings.

Levy grounds his argument for eventual human-robot love in the actual history of human-human, human-animal and human-machine relations and in a behaviorist, stimulus-response, hedonic theory of love.[11] With regards to the last, he appeals to "Bryne's Law of Attraction," in which David Bryne argued that "the strength of attachment one feels for another person is governed by the strength of one's *positive* feelings for that person in relation to the strength of *all* one's feelings for them."[12] If we then identify the standard causes that make people fall in love (Levy identifies eleven of these in the psychological literature) and program our sociable robots to behave in ways that elicit the love response (fine-tuned to the interests and needs of the specific human partner with whom they are engaged), then invoking the love attachments people need and desire is within our technical grasp. Levy notes, in his consideration of how and why people love their pets, that we anthropomorphize our companion creatures in accordance to our desires and needs and in accordance to the degree to which they actually do look and behave like us.[13] Further, the reciprocity of affection that they show us deepens and intensifies our love for them. Sociable robots are already well on their way to looking like us, and some are already endowed with multiple "personality options" that allow various types and degrees of reciprocity in response to our behavior toward them.[14] Needless to say, they can be endowed with the motions and physical features that most interest us, indeed, so successfully so that sex-robot delivery services and sex-robot bordellos in Japan are already threatening the livelihood of prostitutes and professional escorts.[15]

Appealing to Winnicott's (1951) work on transitional objects, Levy notes the especially intense relations most people have with their electronic objects, especially those that develop a specific history based upon the interactions between themselves and their human user. The machine to some extent replicates the person who has used it and exhibits its unique reciprocal response to that use history each time it is activated.[16] The attachment intensity of such relations has been felt by every one of us when, for instance, our personal computer has crashed or our iPhone has been lost. Though clearly replaceable, we often hear that "It's irreplaceable!" or "I feel naked without it!" The sense of aloneness, vulnerability, and separation-anxiety we experience in such cases is evidence for our depth of attachment to and dependence on these devices.

As Joseph Weizenbaum (1976) discovered much to his dismay in his early ELIZA experiments, this sense of connectedness is especially quick and intense if the computer is able to engage in even a minimal amount of reciprocal discourse with its user. After creating and testing the ELIZA program, which could respond intelligently (but in highly restricted manners) to human comments, Weizenbaum wrote, "I had not realized . . . that extremely short exposures to a relatively simple computer program could induce powerful delusional thinking in quite normal people."[17] The delusions he was referring to were evinced by the readiness of the human users to grant personhood to the program and almost immediately develop a personal relationship to it. Subjects in this experiment as well as others simply working with or exposed to the program quickly wanted to be alone with the computer in order to engage in private, intimate conversation. Sherry Turkle has now observed this tendency manifest itself in children and the elderly in their interactive responses to My Real Baby and AIBO.[18] Although there is no one there "in" these robotic toys, no Other to know or care about us in response to our care for it, the behavior of these objects suggest otherwise. Increasingly, people avoid and neglect the actual Others in their environment to engage in caring behavior towards these inanimate objects. In these and related contexts, the psychological phenomena of projection and transference have not been lost to AI researchers; in addition to its appearance in our relations to our computers, iPhones and robotic toys, it has been observed in human feelings towards their robotic therapists.[19] As the behavior of reciprocal self-disclosure that is central to the sense of intimacy and care is built into robots, our projection and transference of meaning and emotion to them will become increasingly automatic.

Shallowing the Self: Carr's Concerns

Levy's arguments for human-robot relations lie largely on the behavioral surface of our lives. They map our modes of object-attachment as these have developed across both personal and social-cultural history. His accounts reveal human beings to be the creative opportunists they are: what we can use and do to meet our deepest personal needs and desires, we use and do when the opportunity arises. In turn, of course, what we use and do changes us, makes us over to some extent in its image; we become what we behold; what we do, we are done to. It is the history of our intellectual artifacts, our mind-changing machines, that Nicholas Carr considers in *The Shallows: What the Internet Is Doing to Our Brains*. His argument provides some of the deep reasons, I think, for the likelihood that Levy's case will prove largely true and that Turkle's and Lanier's concerns are legitimate ones. The machines we have made that are now remaking us are making us scattered, short-sighted and shallow—less able to deal with other people except in media-mediated contexts that we can turn on and off at a whim. The diminution of empathy that these media-mediated relations generate make us ready for relations with robots.[20] This is done in large part by making us like the robots that were made to be like us.[21]

Carr's arguments begin with a first-person, phenomenological account of how his own attention capacities have eroded with his increased use of the internet.[22] He checks and buttresses his accounts with many others given by readers, writers, and scholars of various sorts. The general consensus among them is that the "more they use the Web, the more they have to fight to stay focused on long pieces of writing."[23] Many worry that they are becoming "chronic scatterbrains," and some report their thinking has taken on a "staccato" quality that reflects the quick skimming and scanning of short passages that is typical of reading on the Web. In a comic but incisive image, Carr writes: "Once I was a scuba diver in a sea of words. Now I zip along the surface like a guy on a Jet Ski."[24] The general conclusion he draws from this first-person evidence as well as the experimental and neurophysiological evidence to be cited is that "the [calm, focused, undistracted] linear mind is being pushed aside by a new kind of mind that wants and needs to take in and dole out information in short, disjointed, often overlapping bursts—the faster, the better."[25]

Carr retrieves Marshall McLuhan's prophetic comment that "a new medium is never an addition to an old one, nor does it leave the old one in peace. It never ceases to oppress the older media until it finds new shapes and positions for them."[26] Wedded and wired, the Internet-computer has proven to be the machine of machines, the medium of all media, absorbing almost all of our previous intellectual technologies. As Carr writes of the Internet: "It's becoming our typewriter and our printing press, our map and our clock, our calculator and our telephone, our post office and our library, our radio and our TV."[27] As the Internet absorbs these previous technologies, it also transforms their former modes of messaging into its own. The *modus operandi* of this medium is to chop what were once intricate wholes into shorter and shorter snippets:

> Snippets of TV shows and movies are distributed through You Tube, Hulu, and other video services. Excerpts of radio programs are offered as podcasts or streams. Individual magazine and newspaper articles circulate in isolation. Pages of books are displayed through Amazon. com and Google Book Search. Music albums are split apart, their songs sold through iTunes or streamed through Spotify. Even the songs themselves are broken into pieces, with their riffs and hooks packaged as ringtones for cell phones or embedded into video games.[28]

Without doubt, this unbundling of content generates new options and choices for the consumer, but the shrinkage, reduction, and fragmentation of previous whole objects and relations to what are often disjointed pieces and parts, come to reflect and be reflected in the depth, complexity, and integration of minds, minds that were once relatively whole subjects that are now becoming shrunken, reduced, and fragmented versions of what they once would have been. The evidence for this is not only to be found in our scattered, rushed, and fragmented thoughts and behaviors but in the neurophysiology of our brains as well.

Carr contextualizes the extensive evidence that shows how the neurophysiology of our brains changes with increased use of the Internet and other electronic media by reminding us of the relatively recent conceptual shift in neurophysiology from thinking of the brain as hard-wired to thinking of it as plastic. As Alvaro Pascual-Leone from Harvard Medical School says, neuroplasticity in children and adults enables the nervous system "to escape the restrictions of its own genome and thus adapt to environmental pressures, changes, and experience."[29] The effect of this, Carr notes, is that "evolution has given us a brain that can literally change its mind [in response to its environment]—over and over again."[30] And this is precisely what it has done, once with the book and now with electronic media, especially the Internet.

In 2008, the first experiment was performed showing "people's brains changing in response to Internet use."[31] Twelve subjects in this study were experienced Web surfers; the other twelve were relative novices to the Internet. The brains of the subjects were scanned while they performed searches on Google:

> The scans revealed that the brain activity of the experienced Googlers was much broader than that of the novices. In particular, "the computer-savvy subjects used a specific network in the left front part of the brain, known as the dorsolateral prefrontal cortex, [while] the Internet-naïve subjects showed minimal, if any, activity in this area. . . . The most remarkable part of the experiment came when the tests were repeated six days later. In the interim, the researchers had the novices spend an hour a day online, searching the Net. The new scans revealed that the area in their prefrontal cortex that had been largely dormant now showed extensive activity—just like the activity in the brains of the veteran surfers.[32]

Gary Small, professor of psychiatry at UCLA and director of its Memory and Aging Center, noted of these results, "Five hours on the Internet, and the naïve subjects had already rewired their brains."[33]

More significant than the *fact* of change in the brain that these experiments demonstrate is *what* these changes indicate in terms of brain-mind functioning. The increase of range of brain activity of Net users is in some senses surely a good thing. The puzzle-solving features of the brain are exercised by Internet use owing to the constant need to evaluate information as we scan and search Web pages. But there are "switching costs" to these constant decision making processes: deep and sustained concentration is broken, "the brain [is distracted] from the work of interpreting text or other information" and this impedes "comprehension and retention."[34] Thus, in response to Steven Johnson's claim that the neural evidence leads one to conclude that "reading books chronically understimulates the senses,"[35] Carr emphasizes that it is precisely this "understimulation" that makes the activity of reading so intellectually rewarding and one of the reasons that it enhances comprehension and retention in ways that surfing, skimming, and scanning the Web does not. The busy brain cuts costs and loses content.

A key means of making this point for Carr occurs by noting how the hyperlinks, search capacities, multimedia and interactivity dimensions of the Internet transform reading on the Web from what it is when reading books. While hyperlinks are a variation of citations, endnotes, and footnotes in books, their effect on us is different.[36] They do not simply hint or direct us to other, related issues, but they demand a reorientation of focus and point us in a new direction of thought and investigation. They tend to distract *now* more than direct *later*. In one of the more disturbing studies on the Internet's effect on long-term memory, these information-interruption technologies play a key role. Long-term memory, the personal storehouse of knowledge and understanding that each of us *is*, occurs via the transference of connected and coherent items of immediate consciousness into the "filing cabinet" of long-term memory. Immediate consciousness is in this context often called "working" or short-term memory. Whereas the items of working memory in the immediacy of consciousness come and go constantly (and consist, maximally, of two to four items of information), the vast storehouse of long-term memory makes and provides the stabilizing schemata and concepts via which we interpret and understand information.[37] Information items within long-term memory appear explicitly only when called into working memory or immediate consciousness. Importantly, owing to the tiny amount of information working memory can hold at any given moment, it is the transition from short-term to long-term memory that "forms the major bottleneck in our brain."[38] In Carr's metaphor, when it comes to establishing long-term memory via the necessary passage through short-term memory, we are in a situation similar to filling a bathtub with a thimble. Slow, steady, coherent and connected information, such as we receive when engaged in focused, deep reading, is now considered to be the key to allowing the conceptual schema of analytic thought to form in long-term memory.[39]

Reading, by its very nature, regulates the velocity and intensity of the information received and typically does so (or typically *did* so) in a monolithic environment of letters, words, and lines on a page aiming at a single, coherent meaning. Here, the information faucet provides a "slow steady drip" that appears to allow for coherent, organized storage in long-term memory. Reading on the internet, however, is more akin to "facing many information faucets, all going full blast." Every time we pause to consider clicking on this link or that, every time we must click-off an ad that invades our screen, every switch from word to sound to image, breaks the coherence of that "drip" and places the information going into long-term memory in disarray. The cognitive load we must carry while reading on the Internet is simply too much to bear. This is no doubt why study after study shows greater retention and understanding of book-read materials than of the same material read on the Internet—and this for all combinations of naïve and veteran book and Internet users.[40] Hence, as Carr writes: "Our little thimble overflows as we rush from one faucet to the next. We're able to transfer only a small portion of the information to long-term memory, and what we do transfer is a jumble of drops from different faucets, not a continuous coherent stream from one-source."[41] In this cognitive environment, it becomes clear why attention deficit disorder (ADD) is so rampant in our children and why a growing body of research increasingly associates it with cognitive overload.[42] We demand that our children become unified, disciplined, and coherent thinkers even while we've bequeathed to them an environment that shatters that unity of thought at every turn.

The search capacities embedded in on-line text also fragment attention and disrupt memory. Because search capacities are immediately embedded in on-line text, there is a tendency to jump out of texts into new ones, again breaking training in long-term focus and shattering one's sustained interest in a specific text. A reader's relationship to the whole of a text is made ever more tenuous with Web-works, even when the text is a classical piece of prose. With its embedded hyperlinks, marginal advertisements, interactive connections to others reading the book, the medium of the Internet transforms the significance, experience and effects of reading—and this in turn changes our brain which changes our mind and personality.

As Carr, Jackson, and Turkle have noted, this information technology is also, intrinsically, an interruption technology. And owing to our natural tendency to "vastly overvalue what happens to us *right now*," we often want to be interrupted. Carr quotes Union College psychologist Christopher Chabris here who notes that we crave the new even when we know that "the new is more often trivial than essential."[43] For good evolutionary reasons, short-term consciousness is inherently protean, as shifting, transformative, and unstable as is the world in which it lives. In contrast, traditional reading forces a retreat from the new and the flashy; it forces short-term consciousness into an unnaturally disciplined focus, which has led to the vastly complex conceptual schemata that underlie life in the contemporary world. But given the choice of prolonged concentration on a single text, versus the promised joys of jumping from this flashy blip to that flashy bleep, our natural tendency is to choose the latter over the former. How long can you read or write these days without clicking to check your email, the weather, the news, and so on? I'm guessing that for most of us, the time is significantly reduced from what it once was; for many of our students and children, the very idea of not clicking a hyperlink or checking a text message the moment it buzzes is incredulous.

Two separate eye-tracking experiments have demonstrated how the increase of cognitive load while reading on the Web has affected reading. Hardly anyone reading online text reads "in a methodical, line-by-line way, as they'd typically read a page of text in a book."[44] The vast majority of people skim and scan a text quickly "their eyes skipping down the page in a pattern that resembled, roughly, the letter F."[45] They read the first line or two all the way across the page, and then their eyes drop down a bit and scan half-way across a few lines before dropping down again usually in search of another link to take them to a new "reading" environment.[46] Carr refers to evidence that this new form of reading occurs among professional academics engaged in research as much as it does the ordinary reader. One five-year study from University College London, after tracking the log-time behavior of users of academic journals, went so far as to conclude about the researchers using their sites, that "it almost seems that they go online to avoid reading in the traditional sense."[47] From all of this and more, we have to conclude that a new form of reading is emerging from our engagement with the Internet; it is a nonlinear skimming and scanning, a "power browsing" that is significantly different from traditional deep reading that may have been largely responsible for the complex selves and social structures of modernity.[48] And, of course, the evolution from reading and writing on the Internet to texting and twittering on our various mobile Internet devices is an evolution towards ever smaller, disconnected and prescribed snippets of thought that are performed and processed at the same time without the burdens of personal thought having to intervene.[49]

For decades, without any evidence to support the assumption, the educational establishment promulgated the belief that the more media feeding us information, the more and better we would learn. The evidence points in the opposite direction. Just as it has become clear that virtually everything we do while multitasking we do more poorly than when we single-task,[50] so too does learning and long-term retention and understanding suffer when multimedia presentations increase cognitive load beyond what can be consciously processed in a connected and coherent way.[51] What we process while multitasking and in complex multimedia presentations is understood in a shallower manner than what we process in the quiet, calm of linear reading and writing. Further, if what we receive to process is increasingly fragmented and shallow and we process it in a more fragmented and shallow manner than we did previously, then we too may be entering, nay, becoming, the shallows—ready for relationships with robots, increasingly capable of only such relations.[52]

The Problem of Other Minds

It is, perhaps, not fortuitous that the philosopher who gave us the problem of other minds and was so certain about his own, expressed anxiety that what he thought to be people might in fact be merely machines. In the "Second Meditation," published in 1641, Descartes wrote that "I may by chance look out of a window and notice some men passing in the street, at the sight of whom I do not fail to say that I see men . . . ; and nevertheless what do I see from this window except hats and cloaks which might cover . . . automata . . . ?"[53] The context of this statement occurs when Descartes is trying to determine how it is that we determine what an object actually is based upon ever-incomplete, ever-changing appearances. Almost four centuries later, the media-mediated transformation in our encounters with others and the mechanistic-behaviorist revolution in our thinking about them has left us believing that appearances are good enough—all that we can get, all that there is of anything anyway. La Mettrie's 1747 anti-Cartesian claim that man is a machine is becoming truer; we seem determined to actualize its truth by making machines behave more and more like us and making ourselves think and behave more and more like machines.[54] John Zerzan's (2008) *The Twilight of the Machines* envisions the end of this trajectory,[55] but at the moment, at least, we are witnessing the reverse: the ascendance of the machines and the twilight of the people.

The changes in our behaviors and our brains indicated in the first two sections of this chapter make us ever more ready for sex and love with robots as prophesied by Levy. Our deepest relations may be shallow ones with utterly shallow beings—nay, with beings who are not even as one-dimensional as Marcuse (1964) feared we would become, but are instead *non*dimensional beings who are not even *there, not present even to themselves*. As we make machines more and more like us, we make ourselves more and more like machines; as our relations to others increasingly become media-mediated relations to moments, pieces and parts of others (and as the same holds for their relations to us), then our capacity to appreciate, even tolerate, complex others starts to decline.[56] Indeed, evidence compiled by Antonio Damasio and colleagues[57] and ADHD researcher Russell Barkley[58] indicates that the capacity to empathize with others, to recognize the felt otherness of the other, requires a history of prolonged contact and concentration, slow and unhurried processes,[59] quite unlike those now dominating our lives. I-Thou relations are being replaced by I-It relations in which we are not even cognizant that the Thou (and hence the I) are thinning to the point of vanishing.

If the phenomenological and neurophysiological evidence compiled by Carr indicating the desiccation of the deep, personal self is partnered with the behavioral, social, and cultural evidence compiled by Levy and Turkle, then it is difficult not to conclude that a new self, a new type of human personality, is on the horizon. In fact, to some extent, it already surrounds us in our students and children, and to some extent it is already us: we are, perhaps, the first of the changelings.[60] But we may be, in another sense, the last children of Descartes. We worry still about deep and genuine contact with "other minds," worry that that "other" might not be what she appears, indeed, might not really be *there, present*, at all. But if, more like our students and children, we had been environmentally conditioned to live and interact in a house of mirrors—performing people, doctored images, edited texts, snippets, voice-mails and human-like machines—then we, too, might not be concerned about the alterity of the Other at the far end of our intentions. The tendency for the problem of other minds to become more and more foreign to us may be enhanced by the fact that most of us are becoming more and more public, more and more identified and self-identified by our degree of self-promotion and public display.[61] If we ourselves lack an inner space of reflective selfhood, why would we worry that others might not have one? How many of you now know yourself and are known at least in part through a Facebook page? The very name rings of a theatrically staged, partial self. Those other objects, those people-images, and people-things, might be becoming "alive enough,"[62] present enough to meet our limited needs, and absent enough to not interfere too much with our busy, increasingly narcissistic and solipsistic selves. With these concerns in mind, I'd like to conclude by thinking once again about sex robots, indicating features of them—already extant or anticipated—that will make Descartes's philosophical conundrum concerning the existence of other minds a science fiction scenario come true.

There is no doubt that the biochemistry of sex is a fundamental causal factor in the formation of romantic love, especially in its overwhelmingly powerful, early stages. As Andrea Dworkin so incisively describes,[63] copulating can make the skin come off because if it turns into love, it makes us fully open and exposed, fully vulnerable to the one with whom we have copulated. When our consciousness and personality are taken over in sexual passion, and when the other with whom we've mated seems similarly possessed, then we merge and for a while give up the world, including our other human relations, to meet and mate with only this other. As robots look and act more and more like us, this apparent merging with them will also increasingly occur. They may soon be able to fuck us better than we fuck each other,[64] and if, for a multiplicity of psychological, social and economic reasons, we can only afford shallow and short-term relations, then nondimensional "others" may be our deepest and most constant forms of "contact." The following are some of the steps being taken to ensure that this happens.

In addition to increasingly looking and moving like us, robots will recognize us as individuals and be able to respond to the social-psychological cues we exhibit.[65] Facial recognition technology is already well developed; this will allow robots to identify us as us, and this in turn will fulfill our desire and need for attention. Sherry Turkle has already chronicled the sense of competition she was shocked to find herself feeling and that she has observed in others while competing for a robot's "attention."[66] She has observed the same in children's response to robotic playmates[67] and in the behavior of elderly people with their care-giving and companion robots.[68] As robots begin to exhibit emotions in their facial expressions, another process well underway,[69] our capacities to *not* respond to them as if they were Others will be significantly diminished and perhaps eradicated.

Reciprocal recognition technologies of other sorts are being developed as well. Complimenting the facial and bodily recognition capacities in robots,[70] "affective computing" already allows computers to distinguish emotions in people. In addition to facial expression, the machines use physiological indicators such as galvanic skin response measurements, heart rate, blood pressure, respiration, temperature and muscle tension to measure a person's emotional states.[71] In another instance of making ourselves like machines in order to make machines like us, "affective wearables" are being developed so that we can wear unobtrusive electronic sensors of various sorts in order to be known and understood by our machines.[72] Levy reports that "Rosalind Picard, Elias Vyzas and Jennifer Healy [have already] developed an emotion-recognition system capable of 81-percent accuracy when distinguishing among eight emotions: anger, hate, grief, platonic love, romantic love, joy, reverence, and the neutral state (no emotion)."[73] While none of *us* would score only 81 percent accuracy on such a test, I'm sure that each of us has had significant others who would have failed this test. So what percentage of emotional recognition would you like in your significant other?

Audio processing will also allow machines to engage in reciprocal response to us. Research in voice recognition technology, first developed as means of identification for security purposes, is morphing into studies of vocal effects associated with emotional states:[74] voice pitch, range frequencies, speed of speech, and changes in volume are all indicators of various emotional states, and these too are becoming behaviors that our machines can recognize and respond to. Feel and touch technologies have already been implemented into some sex robots so that the personality, voice, and motion responses of the artificially sexualized other will be those we desire. Finally, in terms of sense-technologies, smell and taste technologies are being developed as well. Not only are there hopes for robots to detect ovulation via their olfactory sensors to help determine if its female partner might be "in the mood," but reciprocally, there are plans to make robots exude the appropriate odors perhaps to match "your (human) loved one's body fragrance, or even a body fragrance of its own that has been designed to appeal to you and to cater to your hormones and your personal desires."[75] You've heard of designer jeans? Here come designer people-machines.

Much of the design methodology in contemporary robotics is now oriented toward needs and desires for play companions (in the case of children), toward love and sex partners (in the case of adults), and toward care-taker robots (for the elderly). In each of these cases, roboticists are working to design-in behaviors that prompt the evolutionary triggers for our affectionate response, and they are proving successful at doing so. The central behavior for such intense response in adult human beings is sexual behavior and reciprocal self-disclosure. And to this end, the dual sciences of "dildonics" and what I'll call "vulvonics" are undergoing revolutionary developments.[76] I will let the reader research these sex machines on his or her own and note here only that in both cases, and especially the development of dildonics, machines are emerging that leave our sexual biomechanics far behind when it comes to producing orgasm for the other. Given the evidence cited earlier for human cathexis on just about anything, once our machines look like us, talk like us, move like us, smell, feel and taste like us, and then, in addition, fuck us silly as well, it will prove difficult indeed to resist falling in love with our robots.

My initial thoughts about this literature (prior to reading about what can already be done, the areas of research underway and the amount of money invested in it) was that sex and love robots would be no more than sophisticated dildos and intricate, artificial vaginas housed within relatively inactive sex dolls. But what is emerging is significantly more. I conclude my thoughts on our newest techno-trajectory by mourning a few of E. E. Cummings's wise words, reminiscing to a lost lover:

> it is so long since my heart has been with yours . . .
> That I have perhaps forgotten
> How, always (from
> These hurrying crudities
> Of blood and flesh) Love
> Coins His most gradual gesture . . .[77]

I'm afraid that in the near future it is from the well-designed, sophisticated, super-clean crudities of silicon, electricity, and software that love will coin its most gradual gesture. And while it does so, our children will sit alone with their person-thing, deeply involved, even in love with some*thing* that isn't even there—not even, really, a some*one*. If "all real living is meeting," as Martin Buber once wrote,[78] what are we to become in a world where our most intimate meetings are with no one at all?

Notes

1. David Levy, *Love + Sex with Robots: The Evolution of Human-Robot Relationships* (New York: Harper Perrenial, 2007), 22, 303.
2. Levy, *Love + Sex with Robots*, 64–174.
3. Levy, *Love + Sex with Robots*, 306.
4. Levy, *Love + Sex with Robots*, 25.
5. For a development of this idea all the way up to "abstract" religious objects, see Charles W. Harvey, "Narcissism, Fundamentalism, and Cosmological Ingratitude," *Philosophy in the Contemporary World* 15, no. 2 (Fall 2008): 41–53.
6. Levy, *Love + Sex with Robots*, 26–27.
7. Sherry Turkle, *Alone Together: Why We Expect More from Technology and Less From Each Other* (New York: Basic Books, 2011), 35–52.
8. Turkle, *Alone Together*, 69–71, 79.
9. Turkle, *Alone Together*, 76–81.
10. Levy, *Love + Sex with Robots*, 30.
11. While authors such as Ralph Ellis (1996, 2005) would argue against the various drive-reductive, hedonic theories of love, that people are complex, enactive organisms that require complexity and growth in order to thrive, I suspect that he would also agree that we have entered a world where these needs are being ever more diminished by the dominance of reductive social scientific discourse—a praxis that makes people in the image that it articulates. For the most part, we seem bewitched by the belief that what we can manipulate is better than what we can merely understand and if to manipulate it we must reduce its understandability, that is, simplify it, then so be it, simplify it we will—even if that "it" happenes to have once been us.
12. Levy, *Love + Sex with Robots*, 33.
13. Levy, *Love + Sex with Robots*, 62.
14. Levy, *Love + Sex with Robots*, 136–38.
15. Levy, *Love + Sex with Robots*, 247–53.
16. Levy, *Love + Sex with Robots*, 72.
17. Joseph Weizenbaum, *Computer Power and Human Reason: Steps towards the Mechanization of Thought* (New York: Freeman Press, 1976), 7.
18. Turkle, *Alone Together*, 53–66, 103–25.
19. Levy, *Love + Sex with Robots*, 85.

20. Turkle, *Alone Together*, 293; Nicholas Carr, *The Shallows: What the Internet Is Doing to Our Brains* (New York: W. W. Norton & Company, 2012), 220–21.

21. Turkle, *Alone Together*, 279–93; Jaron Lanier, *You Are Not a Gadget: A Manifesto* (New York: Alfred A. Knopf, 2010), 32. 35. 53.

22. Carr, *The Shallows*, 5, 16.

23. Carr, *The Shallows*, 7.

24. Carr, *The Shallows*, 7.

25. Carr, *The Shallows*, 10.

26. Carr, *The Shallows*, 89.

27. Carr, *The Shallows*, 83.

28. Carr, *The Shallows*, 94.

29. Carr, *The Shallows*, 31.

30. Carr, *The Shallows*, 31.

31. Carr, *The Shallows*, 120–21.

32. Carr, *The Shallows*, 121.

33. Carr, *The Shallows*, 121.

34. Carr, *The Shallows*, 122.

35. Carr, *The Shallows*, 123.

36. Carr, *The Shallows*, 90.

37. Carr, *The Shallows*, 123–25.

38. Carr, *The Shallows*, 124.

39. Carr, *The Shallows*, 123–25.

40. Carr, *The Shallows*, 126–29.

41. Carr, *The Shallows*, 125.

42. Carr, *The Shallows*, 125; Maggie Jackson, *Distracted: The Erosion of Attention and the Coming Dark Age* (New York: Prometheus Books, 2009), 16–17.

43. Carr, *The Shallows*, 134.

44. Carr, *The Shallows*, 134.

45. Carr, *The Shallows*, 134–35.

46. Carr, *The Shallows*, 136–37.

47. Carr, *The Shallows*, 137.

48. Carr, *The Shallows*, 58–77.

49. Turkle, *Alone Together*, 162–68.

50. Carr, *The Shallows*, 140–42; Turkle, *Alone Together*, 167, 242, 331, n. 17.

51. Carr, *The Shallows*, 129–31; Turkle, *Alone Together*, 163.

52. Turkle, *Alone Together*, 154, 200.

53. René Descartes, *Meditations on First Philosophy* (Indianapolis, IN: Bobbs-Merrill, 1960), 31.

54. Lanier, *You Are Not a Gadget*, 32, 35, 53; Turkle, *Alone Together*, 55, 72, 225.

55. John Zerzan, *Twilight of the Machines* (Feral House Press, 2008).

56. Turkle, *Alone Together*, 55–56, 293.

57. Carr, *The Shallows*, 220–21.

58. Jackson, *Distracted*, 234–35.

59. Carr, *The Shallows*, 220–21; Turkle, *Alone Together*, 293.

60. For two insightful articles on how and why this change is occurring see Musiał (2017, 2017).
61. Andrew Wernick, *Promotional Culture* (London: Sage Press, 1991).
62. Turkle, *Alone Together*, 35–52.
63. Andrea Dworkin, *Intercourse* (New York: Free Press, 1997), 21–26.
64. Levy, *Love + Sex with Robots*, 253–62.
65. Levy, *Love + Sex with Robots*, 125.
66. Turkle, *Alone Together*, 84.
67. Turkle, *Alone Together*, 85.
68. Turkle, *Alone Together*, 110–20.
69. Levy, *Love + Sex with Robots*, 162.
70. Levy, *Love + Sex with Robots*, 125.
71. Levy, *Love + Sex with Robots*, 125.
72. Levy, *Love + Sex with Robots*, 126.
73. Levy, *Love + Sex with Robots*, 126.
74. Levy, *Love + Sex with Robots*, 126–27.
75. Levy, *Love + Sex with Robots*, 165.
76. Levy, *Love + Sex with Robots*, 120–73.
77. E. E. Cummings, *Complete Poems: 1913–1962* (New York: Harcourt Brace Jovanovich,, 1968), 297.
78. Martin Buber, *I and Thou* (London: T & T Clark, 1937), 46.

Bibliography

Buber, Martin. *I and Thou*. Trans. R. Gregor Smith. T & T Clark, 1937.
Carr, Nicholas. *The Shallows: What the Internet Is Doing to Our Brains*. New York: W. W. Norton & Company, 2010.
Cummings, E. E. *Complete Poems: 1913–1962*. New York: Harcourt Brace Jovanovich, Inc., 1968.
Descartes, René. *Meditations on First Philosophy*. Indianapolis: Bobbs-Merrill Educational Publishing, 1960.
Dworkin, Andrea. *Intercourse*. New York: Free Press Paperbacks, 1997.
Ellis, Ralph D. *Curious Emotions: Roots of Consciousness and Personality in Motivated Action*. Amsterdam, Netherlands; Philadelphia, PA: John Benjamins Publishing Company, 2005.
———. *Eros in a Narcissistic Culture: An Analysis Anchored in the Life World*. Dordrecht, Netherlands: Kluwer, 1996.
Harvey, Charles W. "Narcissism, Fundamentalism, and Cosmological Ingratitude." *Philosophy in the Contemporary World* 15, no. 2 (Fall 2008): 41–53.
Jackson, Maggie. *Distracted: The Erosion of Attention and the Coming Dark Age*. New York: Prometheus Books, 2009.
La Mettrie, Julien Offray de. *Man a Machine and Man a Plant*. Translated by Richard A. Watson and Maya Rybalka. Indianapolis: Hackett Publishing Co., 1994.

Lanier, Jaron. *You Are Not a Gadget: A Manifesto*. New York: Alfred A. Knopf, 2010.
Levy, David. *Love & Sex with Robots: The Evolution of Human-Robot Relationships*. New York: Harper Perennial, 2007.
Marcuse, Herbert. *One-Dimensional Man*. Boston: Beacon Press, 1964.
Musiał. Maciej. "Magical Thinking and Empathy towards Robots." *Proceedings of Robophilosophy 2016*. Edited by Johanna Seibt, Raul Hakli and Marco Nørskov. IOS Press, 2016.
———. "Loving Dolls and Robots: From Freedom to Objectification, from Solipsism to Autism." In *The Eternity of Eros: Between Spaces and Non-Spaces*, edited by John T. Grider and Mary McDonough. Witney: Interdisciplinary Press, 2017.
Turkle, Sherry. *Alone Together: Why We Expect More from Technology and Less from Each Other*. New York: Basic Books, 2011.
Winnicott, Donald. "Transitional Objects and Transitional Phenomena." *International Journal of Psycho-Analysis* 34, part 2, 1953.
Weizenbaum, Joseph. *Computer Power and Human Reason: Steps towards the Mechanization of Thought*. New York: Freeman Press, 1976.
Wernick, Andrew. *Promotional Culture*. London: Sage Press, 1991.
Zerzan, John. *The Twilight of the Machines*. Los Angeles, CA: Feral House, 2008.

Contributors

Marc M. Anderson is the author of *Hyperthematics: The Logic of Value* (SUNY, 2019). He specializes in ethics and value theory and is currently at the Lorraine Research Laboratory in computer science and its applications, at the Université de Lorraine in Nancy, France, as a postdoctoral researcher with the EU Horizon2020 (AI-PROFICIENT) project, where he is working on applications of ethics by design to the development of AI systems in manufacturing.

John W. August III is a fellow of the American Institute for Philosophical and Cultural thought. His areas of interest include process philosophy, radical empiricism, personalism, political and economic philosophy, philosophy of liberation, philosophy of race, and philosophy of science. His current research interests include elaborations of the processes of feeling and the role of these processes in living well.

Randall Auxier is a professor of philosophy and communication studies at Southern Illinois University Carbondale. His research ranges from metaphysics and logic, through the philosophy of science to aesthetics, and the philosophy of culture, including popular culture. He is author or coauthor of several books and has edited or coedited about fifteen more. He was founding editor of the scholarly journal *The Pluralist*, and he is deputy chief editor of *Eidos. A Journal of the Philosophy of Culture*. He is author/coauthor of about a hundred articles and book chapters, most of them too long.

Sasha L. Biro is a teaching associate of philosophy at Marist College. Her research interests are embedded in the Continental tradition, focusing on practices of cultural and political narrative and the reception of antiquity in contemporary philosophical thought. She holds a PhD in philosophy from Binghamton University.

Ralph D. Ellis received his PhD at Duquesne University and a postdoctoral master's at Georgia State University. He has taught at Clark Atlanta University since 1985 and is interested in integrating the social sciences with the philosophy of mind. His various books in this area are listed at the Ralph D. Ellis page of Amazon.com, including *An Ontology of Consciousness* (1985), *Coherence and Verification in Ethics* (1987), *Theories of Criminal Justice* (with Carol S. Ellis, 1989), *Questioning Consciousness* (1995), *Eros in a Narcissistic Culture* (1996), *Love and the Abyss* (1997), *Foundations of Civic Engagement* (with N. Fischer and J. Sauer, 1998), *The Craft of Thinking* (with A. Bueno, 2000), *Curious Emotions* (2005), *How the Mind Uses the Brain* (with N. Newton, 2010), and *The Moral Psychology of Internal Conflict* (Cambridge 2018). Ellis occasionally continues his earlier work as a jazz pianist and saxophonist. Many of his jazz recordings can be found online by Googling the Arabic name under which he performs, Raiff Ellis. Ellis is now trying to integrate enactive consciousness theory with moral and social philosophy, with relevance to our current era of internet disinformation and "alternative facts." The newest book is an attempted beginning in that direction.

Helen Grela's earliest academic and career interests were in economics and finance. She received a bachelor's in international economics from Georgetown University's School of Foreign Service and an master's in international finance from MIT's Sloan School of Management. She was also awarded a Fulbright research grant to the Warsaw School of Economics, where she examined banking under communism. Grela's main career was in finance, first in corporate commercial banking in New York and Boston, and later in private equity finance in Warsaw. She started her philosophical studies under Roger Scruton, who developed a master's-level program for mature students at Buckingham University–London. She is currently at the Polish Academy of Sciences pursuing a PhD in philosophy, with a focus on economics and money. Helen enjoys convivial gatherings and all forms of cultural activities.

Pete A. Y. Gunter studied at the University of Texas and Cambridge University before earning a PhD in philosophy at Yale University (1963). Founding chairman of the Department of Philosophy at the University of North Texas (1969), he later was involved in turning the department into the first in America to offer a degree in philosophy and the environment. President of the Big Thicket Association (1971–1973), he has written three books on the Big Thicket and edited two others. He was one of several environmentalists instrumental in creating the Big Thicket National Preserve. He has written widely on process philosophy with special reference to Henri Bergson.

Contributors

Charles W. Harvey is recently retired professor of philosophy in the Department of Philosophy and Religion at the University of Central Arkansas: charlesh@uca.edu. He has published two books and more than forty articles on phenomenology, existential philosophy, self, and social criticism and a number of essays of philosophy through personal narrative. His most recent essays are concerned with human nature and environmental collapse and are titled "Human(un)kind and the Rape of the World" and "Insatiable: Why Everything Is Not Enough." Both of these essays are published in *Philosophy in the Contemporary World*.

Michael Jackson is a distinguished professor of world religions at Harvard Divinity School. He has published more than forty books of ethnography, poetry, and fiction, most recently *The Genealogical Imagination: Two Studies of Life Over Time* and *Coincidences: Synchronicity, Verisimilitude, and Storytelling*.

Jared Kemling is a tenured instructor of philosophy at Rend Lake College. His research interests are in German idealism, process philosophy, philosophical anthropology, philosophy of culture, and American pragmatism. In addition to his work as editor of this volume, Kemling is an editor for the academic journals *Dewey Studies* and *Eidos. A Journal for Philosophy of Culture*. He has also contributed a chapter to a book to be reviewed for the Brill series Philosophy as a Way of Life: Text and Studies. He is a fellow of the American Institute for Philosophical and Cultural Thought, his work has appeared in several academic journals, and he has presented at conferences around the country.

Eli Kramer is an assistant professor in the Department of Ethics of the Institute of Philosophy, University of Wrocław. His work traverses philosophy as a way of life and metaphilosophy, philosophy of culture, American and European idealism, classical American philosophy, and process philosophy. He coedits with Michael Chase and Matthew Sharpe a new philosophy as a way of life key texts and studies book series with Brill Publishers, as well as series of related, funded research, conference, and translation projects. He is currently working on a three-volume work entitled *The Modes of Philosophy*. This project seeks to revitalize the most culturally enriching meta-orientational modes of philosophical praxis. His work has already appeared in journals such as *Eidos. A Journal for Philosophy of Culture, Syndicate Philosophy, Philosophy and Theory in Higher Education*, the *Philosophy of Education Yearbook*, and the *Journal of School and Society*. Alongside Aaron Stoller, he is the coeditor of the collection *Contemporary Philosophical Proposals for the University: Toward a Philosophy of Higher Education* (Palgrave Macmillan, 2018).

Alan G. Maisey is an Australian audit and risk professional who has studied the Javanese *keris* for close to seventy years. He was trained over a fifteen-year period in Javanese *keris* production, appraisal, and belief by Empu Suparman Supowijoyo of the Karaton Surakarta, located in Central Java, Indonesia. He is responsible for authorship of the dominant theory of *keris* origin and for a commentary that deals with the position of the *keris* in pre-Islamic Javanese society. Currently he is working on the question of the part played by Chinese influence and Islamic cultural mores in the development of the Javanese *keris* as cultural icon following the Islamic domination of Java.

Carrie McLachlan taught American Indian religious traditions at Western Carolina University for several years; before that, she taught courses in both Eastern and Western religious traditions. As Cherokee studies coordinator, she assisted Sequoyah professor Tom Hatley in his push to create a more robust Cherokee studies program. She has published two articles on the mythological significance of dogs in Cherokee and American Indian traditions. She has three amazing children and four exceptional grandchildren. She retired in December 2020.

James McLachlan is professor of philosophy and religion at Western Carolina University. He is past cochair of the Mormon Studies Group at the American Academy of Religion and organizer of the Personalist Seminar. He has assisted as cochair Levinas Philosophy Summer Seminars, in Vilnius, Buffalo, Berkeley, and Rome and was codirector of the NEH Summer Seminar on Levinas at the University at Buffalo summer 2017 and 2022. His recent publications have dealt with concepts of hell in existentialism, Satan and demonic evil in Boehme, Schelling, and Dostoevsky, and the problem of evil in Mormonism. He is currently working on a study of Levinas and the existentialists.

Laura J. Mueller is an assistant professor of philosophy at West Texas A&M University in Canyon, Texas. In addition to her teaching duties at WTAMU, she is also a member of the editorial staff of *Eidos. A Journal for Philosophy of Culture*. Her other organizational affiliations include the International Conference on Persons and the Institute for American Religious and Philosophical Thought. Her research and publications focus on philosophy of culture and philosophy of education, often uniting Kant's theories on education and personhood, the German *Bildung* tradition, and classical American pragmatism (namely, John Dewey's educational and social philosophy). Her teaching and her research are often combined; one of her main research interests is how pedagogy helps to morally develop the person and the contribution of teaching to cultural development. Representative publications include "Education, Philosophy, and Morality:

Virtue Philosophy in Kant," *Eidos. A Journal for Philosophy of Culture* (2019); "The Person and Her Pathologies: A Kantian View of Depression and Suicide," in *The Person at the Crossroads: A Philosophical Approach* (Vernon Press, 2020); and "Pure Reason's Autonomy: *Sensus Communis* in Reason's Self-Critique," *Epoché* (2018).

Martin Pehal is assistant professor at the Department of Philosophy and Religious Studies (Faculty of Arts, Charles University, Prague). He studied Egyptology and religious studies in Prague, Vienna, Leuven, and Providence. His research interests include ancient Egyptian mythology and ritual, contemporary forms of public festivity and ritual, and performance theory.

Kevin C. Taylor is an instructor and online coordinator in the Department of Philosophy at the University of Memphis. He has written several articles on Buddhism and environmental philosophy, including "Mottainai: A Japanese Philosophy of Waste." His current research focuses on friendship in Buddhist traditions as well as data ethics: privacy, surveillance, artificial intelligence, and robotics. He is a guest editor of a special issue of *Education and Culture: The Journal of the John Dewey Society* titled *Deweyan Approaches to Contemporary Issues at the Intersection of Data and Technology*. He also serves as webmaster for a variety of academic organizations, primarily the Society for Asian and Comparative Studies.

Dwayne A. Tunstall is professor of philosophy at Grand Valley State University. His areas of specialization are African American philosophy, classical American philosophy (especially Josiah Royce), and existentialism. His research interests include moral philosophy, phenomenology, philosophy of religion, and social and political philosophy. He is the author of two books: *Yes, But Not Quite: Encountering Josiah Royce's Ethico-Religious Insight* (Fordham University Press, 2009) and *Doing Philosophy Personally: Thinking about Metaphysics, Theism, and Antiblack Racism* (Fordham University Press, 2013). He has published more than twenty journal articles and book chapters on a variety of topics, including diversity in education, idealism, race and racial identity, religion, and social philosophy. He has given presentations on these topics at professional conferences, colloquia, and public lectures. He is currently the secretary of the Society for the Advancement of American Philosophy and executive director of Philosophy Born of Struggle. He is also an editor of the *Transactions of the Charles S. Peirce Society* and coeditor of the *American Philosophical Association Newsletter on Philosophy and the Black Experience*.

Index

Abernethy, Francis E., 24, 25
Absolute (the), 16, 19, 189, 194, 195
abstraction, 54, 119, 150, 167–69, 171, 173, 174, 177, 187, 208, 209, 274, 290, 295, 299, 354, 381
ada'wëhï (powerful being), 121, 133, 134
Adorno, Theodor W., 180–82, 335, 338
aesthetics, 2, 3, 20, 145, 147–49, 155, 157, 194, 195, 199, 221, 235, 236, 303, 320, 324, 328–30, 334, 336–39, 342, 346, 362, 363, 385
Africa, 30, 46, 152, 155, 159, 178, 182, 184, 273, 344
African-American, 143, 145, 147–49, 151–53, 155, 159, 160, 389
aging, 32–34, 37, 42, 44, 45, 48, 49, 373
akh (effective spirit), 56, 62, 70, 73
Alice's Adventures in Wonderland, 5, 210, 212–14, 218
Allen, James P., 67, 69, 71
Ameriks, Karl, 362, 363, 365
Anderson, J. B., 24, 26
Anderson, Marc M., 4, 27, 50, 51, 385
Anderson, William L., 134, 139
Andrews, Kristin, 181, 183
animism, 99, 107, 108, 165, 170, 179, 181, 184
a priori, 200, 224, 328, 346, 348, 362, 364
Aquinas, Thomas, 187, 252
Arendt, Hannah, 168, 181, 183, 337, 339, 352, 364, 365

Ariés, Philip, 350, 351, 357–60, 364, 365
Aristotle, 178, 181, 183, 242, 246, 262, 265, 271, 292, 294
Arjuna, 79–87, 89, 91–93
Assmann, Jan, 55, 59, 66–71
ātman, 96
Atum, 59
August, John W., 4, 75, 385
Auxier, Randall, 6, 194, 195, 262, 264, 267, 298, 299, 336, 338, 385

ba (power or presence), 4, 54, 56–60, 62, 63, 68, 69, 73, 74
bad faith, 225, 227, 233
bad infinity, 234–36
Baines, John, 68, 70–72
Bali (island of), 79, 93, 94, 106, 112, 114, 117
banyan (tree), 14, 15
Barkley, Russell, 378
barter, 236, 241, 246–50, 262, 271, 292
Barthes, Roland, 281, 283, 289, 290, 298, 300
Basso, Keith, 175, 182, 183
Bataille, Georges, 5, 144, 145, 149, 150, 155, 158–60, 267, 268, 277, 281–83, 289, 290, 293–95, 300
Bauhaus (school), 150
Beattie, Lillian, 153
Beauvoir, Simone de, 225, 237, 238

Beethoven, Ludwig van, 6, 320–22, 324, 325, 328, 329, 336–39
being-for-itself, 225
being-in-itself, 224, 225, 231, 232
being-in-the-world, 221
being-with, 226
Bellerophon (HMS, or the "Billy Ruffian"), 42–44, 46, 47, 51
Benberry, Cuesta, 147, 152, 159, 160
Bennett, Jane, 180, 182, 183
Bergson, Henri-Louis, 23, 319, 330, 332, 333, 337, 338, 386
Bettelheim, Bruno, 174, 182, 183
Bhagavad Gita, 77, 79, 82–85, 91, 93, 94
Bichat, Marie F. X., 18, 25
Bierhorst, John, 134, 139
Big Thicket (National Preserve), 4, 11–13, 19, 20, 22–26, 386
Binswanger, Ludwig, 316, 317
Bion, Wilfrid, 169, 170, 181, 183
Bird, Charles, 182, 183
Biro, Sasha L., 5, 143, 385
Blackman, Aylward M., 67, 71
Blanchard, David, 122, 134, 139
Bligh, William, 41, 51
Bloch, Maurice, 65, 66, 71, 73
Bodine, Joshua J., 66, 71
Bolšakov, Andrej O., 67, 71
Bonds, Mark Evans, 337, 338
Bonfonti, Leo, 300
Bonnet, Hans, 68, 71, 72
Book of the Dead, 58, 64, 68, 72
Boulez, Pierre, 313
Bradford, William, 269–71, 275, 285, 286, 292, 293, 295, 300
Bradley, F. H., 16, 19, 24–26, 103
Brahma, 83, 106, 107
Brahmanism, 4, 75–78, 81, 83, 84, 87, 88, 93, 95, 96, 117
Brahms, Johannes, 319
Braidotti, Rosi, 180, 183
Bräten, Stein, 316, 317
Breasted, James Henry, 66, 72
Bridenbaugh, Carl, 300

Bright, Mary, 153
Brun, J. N., 24, 26
Buber, Martin, 23, 219, 229, 381, 383
Buck, Adrian de, 68, 72
Buda (period in Java), 107, 109, 110, 116
Buddhism, 93–103, 105–8, 111–14, 116, 117, 389
Buendía, José Arcadio, 166, 167
Burton, Alma H., 296, 300
Buswell, Robert E., 116, 117

Camus, Albert, 310, 316, 317
candi, 106, 107, 109, 112, 115–17
cannibalism, 343, 344
capitalism, 241, 243, 249, 251, 253, 255, 274, 281, 294, 295
car, 1, 40, 41, 44, 189, 190, 197, 215, 311
Carr, Nicholas, 371–76, 378, 382, 383
Carrasco, David, 121, 134, 139
Carroll, Lewis, 5, 212–14, 218
Cartesian, 2, 200, 209, 223, 224, 226, 227, 237, 239
Cassirer, Ernst, 5, 7, 76, 92, 160, 197–200, 207–9, 215–20, 267, 281–83, 286, 288–90, 334, 336, 338, 341, 354, 355, 358, 359, 364–66
Castoriadis, Cornelius, 261, 264
cathexis (object), 169, 369, 380
Cave, Alfred A., 300
Caygill, Howard, 200, 216, 218
Chabris, Christopher, 375
Cherokee (people), 5, 119–41, 388
Chet, Guy, 300
Chiltoskey, Mary Ulmer, 128, 136, 138, 139
China, 28, 96, 99, 100, 102, 103, 110, 262, 388
Chrétien, Jean-Louis, 216, 219
Churchill, Winston, 30, 31, 34, 35, 44, 49
Civil War (American), 145, 147, 149
coffin, 57, 61, 63, 65, 68, 71, 72, 146, 342
cogito, 224, 225
cognition (*cognitio*), 4, 6, 75, 76, 78, 92, 179, 181, 198, 200, 215, 217, 229, 320, 322–24, 326–29, 331

coin, 166, 244, 246, 248, 250, 262, 276, 294, 298, 300, 380, 381
Collier, C. D. Abby, 344, 361, 365
commodity, 147, 150, 242–50, 253, 255, 257, 259–62, 270, 275, 277, 282, 283, 292, 294
communal, 21, 113, 144–46, 149, 150, 175, 250, 322, 351
communion, 208–10, 214, 272, 341, 356
conception (*conceptus*), 1, 68, 71, 72, 98, 178, 181, 184, 187, 192, 194, 195, 198, 200, 215, 224, 231, 241, 255, 327
Confucian, 95–99, 102
container-contained, 169, 170, 173
Coole, Diana, 181–83
Cooney, Kathlyn M., 70, 72
Cordingly, David, 43, 44, 51
Cornell, Drucilla, 316, 317
Corn Mother (Selu), 5, 119, 123–25, 127–33, 135, 136
corpse, 58, 59, 62, 66, 147, 341, 342, 344, 345, 350, 359–61
Cory, V. L., 24–26
Crair, Ben, 24, 25
credit, 242, 243, 245, 250, 260, 262
credit-money, 243–45, 247, 249, 251, 255, 259–61
cry (the), 325–27
cult-craft, 101
Cummings, E. E., 380, 383
Curie, Marie, 153
currency, 267, 269, 270, 272–77, 282, 284, 285, 290–95, 297, 298, 301

Dahlhaus, Carl, 321, 335, 338
Damasio, Antonio, 378
Daoism, 95, 96, 98
darśan, 75, 78–94
Deathridge, John, 335, 336, 338, 339
DeForest, John, 300
Democritus, 16
Dendara (temple), 56, 67, 73
Descartes, René, 2, 6, 223–30, 377, 378, 382, 383

determinate (judgment), 211, 323, 324, 326, 337
Devereux, George, 170, 181, 183
devotionalism, 4, 75–78, 80, 81, 83, 84, 87–94
Dewey, John, 387–89
dialectic, 167, 182, 208, 209
Diamond, Cora, 342–44, 361, 365
Dick, Michael B., 66, 70, 73, 74
Dietz, Ulysses S., 158, 160
differential (function), 5, 201, 202, 204, 206–10, 216
dignity, 1, 228, 278, 280, 283, 285, 288, 297, 334, 345, 346, 348, 351, 357, 361, 366
dildos, 380
disponibilité, 201, 204, 217
divine, 4, 28, 55, 56, 59, 60, 62, 63, 65, 66, 75–94, 99, 121, 125, 169, 177, 179, 180, 189, 194, 195, 205, 276, 287, 289, 360, 387
Dobard, Raymond, 158, 161
Dobie, J. Frank, 12
Dōgen, 97
Domański, Juliusz, 335, 338
Drake, Thomas, 39
dualism, 53, 119, 125, 135, 136, 380
Duboule, Denis, 22, 25
DuQuesne, Terence, 68, 72
duration, 145, 206, 209, 210, 213, 320, 324, 330–32
Durkheim, Emile, 279, 286
dwelling, 106, 108, 109, 115, 169, 221, 222, 233–35
Dworkin, Andrea, 378, 383
dynamic, 5, 17, 84, 87, 167, 205, 206, 320–22, 325, 327–29, 333, 363

Eaton, Katherine, 68, 72
Eaton-Krauss, Marianne, 70, 72
Eck, Diana L., 78, 84, 88, 92–94, 136, 139
economics, 2, 3, 5, 6, 75, 111, 144, 149, 150, 158–60, 170, 181–84, 202, 203, 221, 241–50, 253, 257, 259–65, 267,

economics *(continued)*
  268, 271, 273–75, 277, 280–83, 285–87, 289, 290, 293–95, 368, 379, 385, 386
Egypt (ancient), 4, 53–59, 62, 65–75, 116, 250, 389
Egyptology, 68–73, 389
Einstein, Albert, 30, 33–36
élan vital, 319, 332
Elekens, Jacques, 273, 274, 278
Elgood, Robert, 117
Eliade, Mircea, 150, 159, 160, 216, 219, 231
ELIZA (experiments), 371
Ellis, Ralph D., 6, 303, 316, 317, 335, 337, 338, 381, 383, 386
empirical, 77, 170, 187, 189, 200, 202, 206, 215, 289, 297, 299, 332, 357, 363
empiricism, 23, 185, 336, 338, 385
Engels, Frederick, 175, 176, 182, 184, 279, 297
Erman, Adolf, 71, 72
eros, 282, 286, 290, 383, 384, 386
eternity, 32, 65, 66, 84, 96, 145, 204–7, 210, 213, 214, 224, 384
Eucharist, 355, 356
exchange, 15, 71, 73, 75, 78, 102, 103, 120, 148–50, 166, 177, 236, 241, 245–50, 253, 255–61, 263, 264, 267, 269, 271, 272, 274, 276, 277, 280, 282, 284–86, 289–94, 296, 301
ex nihilo, 244, 245, 260, 261
Ezell, Nora, 153

Fairman, Herbert W., 67, 71
femmage (feminist collage), 150
fidelity (creative), 197, 199–215, 217–19
Finley, John, 158, 160
Finnestad, Ragnhild Bjerre, 63, 66, 69, 70, 72
Fischer-Elfert, Hans W., 69, 72
Flomenhaft, Eleanor, 160
focusing (method), 6, 303, 307, 311–17, 335, 338, 385
Fogelson, Raymond D., 138, 140

Folsom, James K., 301
Fon (people of Dahomey), 152, 159
Fonagy, Peter, 169, 170, 181, 183
forms (symbolic), 198, 199, 202, 203, 215, 217–19, 360, 364
Foster, Michael Dylan, 102, 103
Fowler, Chris, 294, 300
Francis, Becky, 364, 365
Frandsen, Paul J., 67, 72
Frankl, Viktor, 361, 365
Fritz, Ned, 24, 25
Frood, Elizabeth, 70, 72
Frost, Robert, 22
Frost, Samantha, 181–83
Fry, Gladys-Marie, 145, 147–49, 158–60

Gaakeer, Jeanne, 263, 264
Gadamer, H. G., 316, 317
Gajah Mada, 108, 110, 116
Galbraith, John K., 244, 262, 264, 287
gamelan (instrument), 113, 117
Gandhari, 80–82
Ganesha, 108
Geist, 198, 286, 289
Gendlin, Eugene, 6, 303, 311, 313, 315–17, 335, 338
Gernet, Alexander von, 139, 140
gift, 80–83, 86, 87, 91, 149, 172, 177, 190, 262, 265, 269, 275, 277, 280, 282, 283, 287, 288, 291–95, 297, 298, 300, 301, 334, 336, 338
Gilligan, Carol, 308, 316, 317
Giorgi, Ameideo, 316, 317
Glassie, Henry, 177, 182, 183
God (desire to be), 221–32, 236–39
Goedicke, Hans, 68, 73
gold, 55, 65, 70, 73, 107, 166, 172, 244–47, 249, 250, 256, 298
Goyon, Jean-Claude, 69, 72
Graeber, David, 262, 264, 273, 284, 287, 294, 295, 297, 300
Grant, Michael C., 24, 25
Grapow, Hermann, 71, 72
Grela, Helen, 6, 241, 292, 300, 386

Grierson, Philip, 262, 264
Griffin-Pierce, Trudy, 139, 140
Griffiths, J. Gwyn, 68, 72
growth, 17, 22, 23, 29, 31–34, 37, 41, 42, 48, 124, 206, 259, 269, 381
Grudin, Eva Unger, 151–53, 159, 160
Gunter, Pete A. Y., 4, 11, 24, 25, 386
Gunungan (symbol), 109, 112, 117

Hadot, Pierre, 335, 338
Hagar, Stansbury, 122, 129–32, 134, 138–40
Haggerty, Barbara Bradley, 103
Hahn, Lewis E., 220
Hale, Horatio, 300
Hallowell, A. Irving, 133, 179, 182, 183
handle (focusing), 311–14
Handyside, John, 363, 365
Harrington, Nicola, 66, 70, 72
Harvey, Charles W., 7, 367, 381, 383, 387
Hathor, 56
Hayles, Katherine, 180, 183
Hearn, Lafcadio, 101
Hegel, G. F. W., 16, 228, 236, 298, 299
Heidegger, Martin, 166, 181, 183, 217, 219, 226, 228, 233–35, 298, 299, 316, 317, 321
Heijden, Marcel G. A. van der, 24, 26
heirloom, 116, 145, 197
Hentoff, Nat, 316, 317
hermeneutics, 6, 77, 181, 183, 307, 308
Herstein, Gary, 336, 338
hieroglyph, 4, 54, 57, 65, 66, 68, 69
Hinduism, 75, 77–79, 88, 93, 94, 105–9, 111–14, 116, 117, 136, 139
Hiriyanna, M., 94
Hocking, William Ernest, 216, 219
Holstein, Jonathan, 145, 147, 158, 160, 161
Hōnen, 97
hongaku (original enlightenment), 97
Hornung, Erik, 68, 71, 72
Horsman, Yasco, 263, 264
Horus, 55, 57, 60, 64, 65, 67, 68, 71

Hoskins, Janet, 172, 181, 183
Hume, David, 261, 264, 308, 316, 317
Hunter Father (Kanati), 123, 125–30, 132, 135, 136, 138
Huron (people), 130, 139, 140, 300
Husserl, Edmund, 216, 219
Hyakki yako emaki (Night Parade), 100, 103

Ichiren, 99–101
idealism, 5, 19, 167, 180, 185, 187, 196, 221, 320, 328, 335, 337, 338, 387, 389
I-It, 378
India, 14, 15, 30, 46, 75, 78, 81, 82, 92–97, 107, 110, 112, 116, 117, 273, 306
Indian (American), 12, 13, 121, 130, 131, 133, 134, 137, 139–41, 270, 273, 275, 285, 292–94, 296, 300, 301, 388
Indonesia, 105, 106, 114, 116, 172, 388
infinity, 219, 223, 224, 226–30, 234–39
Ingersoll, Ernest, 292, 300
Ingham, Geoffrey, 242, 245, 261–64
Ingold, Tim, 181, 183
Innes, A. Mitchell, 250, 262–64
integrative (function), 5, 201, 202, 204, 206–9, 216
intermediate (economy), 280–83, 286–88, 293
intuition, 20, 23, 197–202, 204, 206–12, 215–17, 324–26, 330, 331, 347, 362, 364, 366
intuitions (pure), 199–202, 204, 206–9, 215, 216, 325
iPad, 36–38, 48, 49
iPhone, 370, 371
Iroquois (people), 121–24, 131, 134, 135, 139, 140, 284, 292, 294, 297, 300
Irwin, Lee, 133, 140

Jackson, Maggie, 375, 382, 383
Jackson, Michael, 5, 165, 182, 183, 387
Jackson, Sarah E., 353, 354, 364, 365
Jacobs, Jaap, 300

James, William, 19, 23, 51, 80
Janák, Jiří, 68, 70, 73
Japan, 4, 95–105, 283, 370, 389
Java (island of), 4, 5, 105–17, 388
jazz (music), 6, 303, 307–10, 312–15, 335, 386
Jennings, Francis, 292, 294, 297, 300
Jesus, 288, 298
Johnson, Steven F., 291, 300
Johnston, Neil, 263, 264
Jordaan, Roy E., 116, 117
judgment, 75, 76, 89, 90, 171, 203, 212, 216, 219, 288, 301, 308, 323, 324, 336–38, 346, 348, 361–63, 365

ka (soul, spirit), 4, 54, 56–59, 62, 66–68, 70, 72, 73
kami, 4, 95–102, 104
Kant, Immanuel, 1, 6, 30, 49, 82, 83, 198–200, 203, 206, 209, 215–19, 322–25, 328, 331, 333, 335–38, 341, 342, 345–49, 361–66, 388, 389
Karasz, Mariska, 150
karma, 97, 99, 101
Katsuhiko, Komatsu, 100
Kejawen, 111
Kemling, Jared, 5, 197, 264, 300, 335, 338, 364, 366, 387
keris (dagger), 4, 105–7, 109–15, 117, 388
Keynes, John Maynard, 242, 247, 250, 262–64
Kilpatrick, Anna G., 133, 136, 137, 139, 140
Kilpatrick, Jack F., 133, 136, 137, 139, 140
Kimmelman, Michael, 159, 160
King, Duane H., 137
King, Richard, 82, 93, 94
King Jr., Martin Luther, 153
King Philip's War, 6, 268, 276, 277, 281, 295–97, 301
Klein, Tamir, 24, 25
Kobun, 99, 101
Kodi (people), 172
Kohn, Edouardo, 181, 183

Korsgaard, Christine, 192–95, 364, 366
Korsten, Franz-Willem, 263, 264
Kramer, Eli, 6, 319, 334, 336, 338, 387
Kramrisch, Stella, 81, 82, 93, 94
Kropfinger, Klaus, 336, 338
Kshatriya (caste), 87
Kūkai, 96, 97
Kuranko (people), 170–72, 176, 179

labor, 148, 172, 175–77, 185, 197, 222, 234–36, 246–49, 254–61, 264
La Mettrie, Julien Offray de, 377, 383
Langer, Suzanne K., 218, 299, 337, 338
language, 67, 72, 105, 120, 122, 126, 132, 134, 140, 168, 169, 179, 181, 183, 198, 199, 208, 212, 215, 218, 228, 229, 237, 297, 298, 304, 305, 316, 317, 327, 331, 354, 356
Lanier, Jaron, 368, 371, 382, 384
Lankford, George E., 139, 140
Latour, Bruno, 181, 184
Lavin, Lucianne, 291, 295, 300
Leibniz, Gottfried Wilhelm, 16, 18, 187
leitmotifs, 320, 327, 331
Leslie, Mitch, 24, 26
Levinas, Emmanuel, 5, 6, 216, 218, 219, 221–30, 233–39, 388
Lévi-Strauss, Claude, 53, 54, 66, 71, 73, 149
Levy, David, 367–70, 377–79, 381, 383, 384
Lévy-Bruhl, Lucien, 168
Liddell, Alice, 213
life plan (Royce), 192, 194
Lillehoj, Elizabeth, 103
Lincoln, Abraham, 30, 31, 33–38, 134, 139
Lindbergh, Charles, 47
linguistic, 121, 130, 133, 134, 140, 199, 202, 203, 213, 289, 297
Lipman, Andrew, 293, 300
Locke, John, 21, 241, 243, 251–59, 261, 263–65, 348, 349, 363, 364, 366
Lodi, Edward, 291, 296, 298, 300

logos, 282, 290
Long, Will West, 120, 129
Long Person (Yvwi Gunahita), 5, 123, 126–28, 130–32, 137
Lookabough, Sandra L., 364, 366
Lorton, David, 61, 66, 68, 70, 71, 73
Lugwani, 177, 182, 184
Lyotard, Jean-François, 181, 184, 218, 219

Macpherson, C. B., 255–57, 263, 265
Magee, Bryan, 335, 338
magic, 93, 94, 133, 149, 166, 167, 172, 176, 224, 225, 267, 276, 330–34, 384
Mahabharata, 80, 93, 94
Mahayana (Buddhism), 96, 106, 116
Maine, Henry S., 252, 263, 265, 285, 296
Maisey, Alan, 4, 5, 105, 117, 294, 388
Majapahit (kingdom), 107–12, 114, 116
mana, 171, 231, 275
Manter, Bette J., 195
Manuelian, Peter der, 70, 73
Marcel, Gabriel, 197, 199, 201, 204–6, 208, 210, 216, 217, 219, 220, 229
Marcuse, Herbert, 377, 384
Marett, Allan, 182, 184
Mariette, Françoise A. F., 67, 73
Marion, Jean-Luc, 216, 219, 364, 365
Marquez, Gabriel García, 166, 181, 184
Marx, Karl, 5, 6, 175, 176, 182, 184, 197, 236, 241, 242, 261, 265, 279
Masefield, John, 39, 50, 51
Massasoit, 269, 284, 286, 296, 298, 300
Materialism (New), 165, 166, 170, 174, 180–83
Mathaii, Wangari, 102
Mauss, Marcel, 120, 133, 140, 262, 265, 267–69, 271, 272, 274–78, 280–83, 286, 289–95, 297, 298, 301
May, Rollo, 307, 316, 317
Mbembe, Achille, 294, 295, 301
McBride, Kevin, 295, 296, 301
McCleary, Timothy, 139, 140
McDermott, John J., 185, 194, 195
Mclachlan, Carrie, 5, 119, 140, 388

Mclachlan, James, 5, 221, 388
McLear, Colin, 364, 366
McLeod, Claude A., 19, 25, 26
McLuhan, Marshall, 372
McNaughton, Patrick, 182, 184
Meikle, Scott, 262, 265
Melquíades, 166, 167
Menger, Karl, 247, 262, 265
mereology, 11, 13
mereotopological, 200
Merleau-Ponty, Maurice, 198, 215, 216, 218, 219, 317
Meru (Mount), 108, 109, 112
midrash, 321, 322, 325, 334, 335
Miller, Eleanor Bingham, 144, 148, 158, 159, 161
Miller, Max, 45, 46, 51, 144, 148, 158, 159, 161
miran, 170, 171
moksha, 109, 117
Mollier, Christine, 96, 102, 103
money, 6, 71, 73, 236, 241–51, 255–65, 267, 270, 275, 277, 280, 282–84, 287–93, 295, 296, 298, 300, 301
Mooney, James, 120–23, 125–30, 133–38, 140
Morenz, Siegfried, 67, 73
Moret, Alexandre, 69, 73
motherhood, 49, 147, 352
mottainai, 102–4, 389
Mueller, Laura J., 6, 341, 388
Müller, Ulrich, 335, 336, 338, 339
mummy, 4, 54, 58, 59, 61–63, 65, 66, 69
Muramasa (swordsmith), 101
Musiał, Maciej, 383, 384
music, 3, 6, 23, 45, 299, 303–15, 319–38, 372
myth, 12, 20, 122, 133–38, 140, 199, 208, 212, 217–19, 252, 259, 272, 320, 334, 337, 339, 343, 354, 355, 360, 361
mythic, 7, 57, 58, 60, 63, 65, 70, 133, 160, 198, 199, 201–3, 207, 208, 213, 215–18, 276, 281, 282, 287, 289, 298, 299, 320, 342, 355, 356, 359, 360

mythic (consciousness), 281, 282, 287, 289, 298, 299
mythology, 13, 54, 60, 71, 73, 134, 136, 139, 287, 292, 301, 353, 357, 388, 389

Nabokov, Peter, 133, 137, 138, 141
Narragansett (people), 268–72, 274, 275, 277–80, 285, 286, 291, 293, 294, 296
Neal, Alice, 152, 153
Newton, Isaac, 16, 18
Newton, Natika, 317, 386
Nichiren (Buddhism), 97
Nietzsche, Friedrich, 320, 321, 335, 338
ningyō kuyō (ritual), 100
Nixon, Richard, 245
Nozick, Robert, 253, 256–59, 263, 265
numeralization, 5, 198, 199, 203, 207–10

object-personality, 7, 342, 345, 348–61, 364
Object Relations Theory, 167, 170
Ockinga, Boyo, 68, 73
Ojibwa (people, also known as Chippewa), 133, 179, 182, 183
ongwe shona/ongwe honwe, 122, 124
oni, 98–100, 102, 103
onmyōdō (Way of Yin and Yang), 98, 99
ontology, 11, 27, 63, 77, 165, 166, 169, 170, 173, 180, 181, 183, 186, 187, 189, 191, 217, 221, 224, 227–29, 233, 237, 239, 242, 245, 249, 259, 299, 305, 306, 308, 310, 315, 320, 321, 341, 386
Opening of the Mouth (ritual), 54, 61–64, 66, 69, 70, 72
opera, 28, 320, 324, 326, 327, 331
organism, 4, 11, 13–22, 170, 194, 381
organism (colonial), 17–19, 21, 24
organism (monarchical), 17, 20, 21, 24
orgasm, 368, 380
Osiris, 56–58, 60, 63, 65, 66, 68, 69, 72, 73
Other (the), 221–36, 238, 239
Otto, Eberhard, 69, 71, 73
O'Neill, Kevin, 357–60, 364–66

Panataran (candi), 107, 116
paralogism (Kantian), 342, 347, 362, 363
Parker, Charlie, 307, 312
Parks, H. B., 24–26
Parks, Tim, 267, 291, 301
Parmenides, 16, 228
Parry, Jonathan P., 66, 71, 73
Pascual-Leone, Alvaro, 373
Pastore, Christopher L., 274, 294, 301
Payne, John Howard, 134, 135, 138, 141
Pehal, Martin, 4, 53, 389
Peirce, Charles S., 19, 389
Pennisi, Elizabeth, 24, 26
Pequot (people), 268–80, 284–86, 291–98, 300, 301
perception (*perceptio*), 82, 94, 100, 182, 183, 198–201, 215, 216, 218, 219, 229, 313, 317, 326, 363
person, 1, 4–7, 27, 28, 34, 35, 37, 53, 57, 62, 65, 66, 76–78, 80, 88–90, 94, 96, 108, 112, 117, 119–28, 131–34, 136, 137, 139–41, 146, 165–75, 177–79, 182, 183, 185–94, 197, 202, 203, 209, 210, 216–18, 221, 223, 225, 229, 231, 233, 236, 237, 241–43, 250, 252, 253, 255, 260, 263, 264, 267, 268, 270, 273–84, 286–92, 294, 296, 297, 299–301, 303, 307, 320–23, 333–35, 342, 343, 345–51, 353, 354, 356–61, 368–70, 379, 388, 389
persona, 1, 27, 120, 126, 173, 252, 255, 260, 263, 264, 278
personal, 1–7, 23, 27, 29, 32, 34–36, 38, 46, 75–78, 80, 81, 84, 86–94, 96, 105, 109–15, 117, 120, 134, 136, 143, 144, 147, 149–51, 155, 157, 165, 171, 172, 185–87, 189–94, 197, 199–202, 204, 206, 207, 209, 211, 212, 219, 221, 223, 228, 229, 231, 234, 236, 237, 251–53, 264, 267, 280, 300, 304, 307, 316, 319–22, 332–35, 338, 348–51, 358, 361, 366–71, 374, 378, 380, 387
personalism, 1, 4, 77, 84, 229, 321, 385, 388

personality, 1, 2, 4, 6, 7, 20, 22, 23, 27–42, 44–50, 75, 77, 95, 101, 165, 200, 201, 204, 207, 212–14, 217, 222, 276, 282, 287–90, 303, 304, 307, 310, 341, 342, 345, 347–57, 359, 360, 363, 364, 370, 375, 378, 380, 383
personalization, 3, 5, 6, 11, 27, 30, 43–45, 47–49, 53, 75, 87, 95, 105, 119, 134, 143, 144, 148, 150, 155, 185–87, 191, 197–218, 283, 290, 333, 364, 366, 367
personalized number (community), 203, 205, 207–12, 214, 217
personalized space (responsibility), 5, 200–204, 206–14, 216, 217
personalized time (hope), 5, 203–14, 217
personally, 144, 191, 203, 204, 215, 348, 389
personhood, 4, 6, 7, 53, 54, 57, 89–92, 179, 241, 243, 244, 251–55, 261, 264, 267, 287, 288, 294, 300, 320, 322, 323, 333, 334, 337, 341, 342, 345, 347–50, 354, 356, 359–61, 364–66, 371, 388
personification, 33, 53, 54, 67, 136, 221–23, 231, 233, 236, 289
phenomena, 55, 59, 89, 152, 165, 167, 168, 173, 179, 205, 208, 236, 241, 290, 306, 313, 323, 330, 341, 355, 358, 359, 371, 384
phenomenology, 5, 77, 167, 169, 174–76, 186, 187, 189, 197–99, 211, 215–19, 221, 224, 225, 227, 231, 234, 237, 239, 299, 303, 308–10, 313, 316, 317, 342, 366, 372, 378, 387, 389
Philbrick, Nathanial, 284, 285, 295, 296, 298, 301
Philip, Ariés, 364, 365
Philip (Metacomet), 6, 268, 276, 277, 281, 295–97, 301
phusis, 335
Piaget, Jean, 169, 181, 184
Piankoff, Alexandre, 69, 73
piano, 6, 303–7, 309–16, 335, 338, 386
Pilgrims, 269, 278, 279, 285, 287, 293, 294, 301

Plato, 238, 239, 279, 334, 352, 379
Pluhar, Werner S., 215, 219, 336, 338, 361, 362, 365
Plymouth (colony), 6, 43, 268–70, 273, 284–86, 292, 293, 295, 300, 301
Pokanoket (people), 268–71, 277, 286, 297
Polanyi, Karl, 262, 265
Porter, Catherine, 181, 184, 343, 361, 366
positivism, 231, 276
possession, 1, 5, 40, 81, 100, 107, 108, 113, 116, 169–72, 179, 188, 190, 202, 221–23, 227, 230–36, 242–44, 253–55, 258, 263, 265, 275, 276, 283, 292, 295, 296, 304, 305, 307, 378
posthuman, 165, 180, 183
Povenelli, Elizabeth, 182, 184
power, 4, 5, 46, 54, 56, 57, 59, 60, 62, 65, 67, 81, 93, 94, 101, 107, 111, 116, 129, 133, 134, 136, 138, 139, 144, 149, 150, 152, 166, 167, 171, 178, 180, 182, 184, 200, 203, 208, 211, 217, 224, 226, 241, 242, 245, 259, 262, 264, 272, 275, 279, 288, 292, 295, 298–301, 320, 322, 323, 325, 328, 332–35, 338, 346, 348, 355, 360, 362, 366, 368, 376, 381, 384
Powers, Harriet, 151, 152
practical identity (Korsgaard), 191–94
Prambanan (candi), 106, 116, 117
prestation (total), 269, 271, 272, 274, 275, 280–82, 286, 287, 292, 294, 297
Prince, J. Dyneley, 301
profane, 149, 159, 160, 201, 202, 216, 217, 219, 344, 356, 360
property (economic), 1, 6, 34, 68, 171, 223, 231, 232, 234, 242–44, 251–58, 260, 263, 267, 275, 280, 282, 283, 297, 298, 300
psychoanalysis, 169, 173, 181, 183, 186, 369, 384
psychology, 7, 149, 171, 180, 181, 183, 185–87, 194, 294, 303, 304, 307, 316, 317, 331, 334, 344, 349, 359, 363, 364, 366–71, 375, 379, 386

Ptah, 55, 66, 69, 72
Puritans, 269, 297, 301
pusaka, 105, 108, 116

Quaking Aspen (*Populus tremuloides*), 14
quilt, 5, 143-61
Quilt (AIDS Memorial), 144, 156, 160
Quilt (Crazy), 144, 146, 298
Quilt (Graveyard), 144, 146
Quilt (Human), 144, 155
Quilt (Kentucky), 144-46, 153, 158-61
Quilt (Migrant), 156, 157, 160
Quilt (Monument), 157
Quilt (Story), 144, 149-55, 158-61
quiltmaking, 143-53, 155-60

Raffles, Stamford, 115
Ramayana, 107, 116, 117
Ramsey, Bets, 150, 159, 161
Rasiere, Isaak de, 285
Reader, Ian, 100
reflective (judgment), 203, 211, 299, 324, 337, 346, 362
Reider, Noriko T., 102-4
Reinhardt, Hartmut, 336, 339
religion, 2, 3, 6, 20, 53, 54, 56, 59, 67, 70, 73, 75, 77, 88, 95-98, 100-104, 106, 107, 109-12, 117, 119, 134, 136, 138, 139, 141, 146, 147, 149, 152, 173, 177, 195, 196, 199, 212, 216, 217, 219, 225, 228, 229, 231, 237, 239, 276, 279, 282, 293, 310, 341, 344, 351, 353, 354, 356, 381, 387-89
Richardson Jr., Robert D., 361, 366
ring (wedding), 5, 202-4, 207, 210-12, 217
Ringgold, Faith, 144, 153-55, 160
ritual, 4, 6, 28, 42, 53, 54, 56, 57, 59-66, 68-70, 72-75, 77, 88, 91, 92, 97, 99-103, 117, 121, 124, 125, 127-29, 133-38, 141, 146, 148, 157, 158, 168, 172, 173, 176-78, 191, 231, 278-81, 296, 299, 341, 343, 344, 350, 351, 353, 389
Robinson, Hoke, 219, 363, 366
robot, 4, 367-72, 377-81, 383, 384, 389
ron dha, 112, 117
Rosendale, Simon W., 293, 297, 301
Royce, Josiah, 5, 185, 187-89, 191, 192, 194-97, 205, 210, 217, 219, 220, 389

sacred, 61, 62, 65, 69, 99, 125-27, 131, 133, 134, 136-41, 147, 149, 150, 152, 158-60, 169, 176-78, 201-3, 207, 216, 217, 219, 272, 276, 278, 288, 293, 344, 356, 360
Saichō, 96, 97
Salmond, Anne, 182, 184
Samuelson, Paul, 262, 265
Sanjaya (disciple of Vyasa), 80-82
Sanjaya (dynasty), 106, 107, 116
Sartre, Jean-Paul, 5, 6, 50, 175, 181, 182, 184, 221-39
Sassacus, 276, 279, 281, 296
Sauneron, Serge, 68, 73
Scheid, Bernhard, 102, 104
Scheler, Max, 298, 299, 308, 316, 317
Schelling, Friedrich W. J., 210, 330, 337, 388
Schilpp, Paul Arthur, 220
Schmitz, Bettina, 69, 73
Schopenhauer, Arthur, 6, 319-25, 332, 333, 336, 337, 339
Schultz, Charles, 369
Schumpeter, Joseph, 247, 262, 263, 265
Schwabe, Calvin W., 70, 72
science, 2, 12, 19, 21, 76, 173, 185, 188, 189, 199, 201, 202, 288, 297, 299, 304, 309, 313, 355, 357, 360, 378, 380, 381, 385
Scott, Elizabeth, 152
Searle, John, 263, 265
sensation (*sensatio*), 82, 198, 200, 215, 360
Sensen, Oliver, 346, 361, 366

sensus communis, 6, 289, 299, 320, 333, 348–50, 389
Seth, 57, 60, 64, 65, 68
Sethe, Kurt, 67, 73
sewing, 101, 102, 147
sex-robot, 367, 368, 370, 377, 378, 380, 381, 383, 384
Shabaka Stone, 55, 66, 71
Shaner, David Edward, 102, 103
Shapshay, Sandra, 336, 339
Sherover, Charles, 362, 363, 366
Shingon (Buddhism), 96, 99–103
Shinto, 95, 97–100, 102, 104
ship (seagoing), 1, 3, 4, 27, 30, 38–51, 96, 146, 297
Shiva, 106, 109, 115–17
shōji, 101
shokunin (craftsman), 101
Showalter, Elaine, 158, 159, 161
Sickatower, 123, 134
Silverman, David J., 293, 301
Simard, Susan, 15, 24, 26
Sisters (Three), 122, 123, 131, 134, 135, 281
Skidelsky, Edward, 220
Skinner, B. F., 311, 317
Skowroński, Krzysztof Piotr, 195
Sky World, 5, 119, 122–25, 127, 129–32, 134, 137–40
slippery-slope (argument), 15, 368
Slone, Verna Mae, 158, 161
Slotkin, Richard, 301
Small, Gary, 373
Smith, Adam, 241, 242, 246, 249, 261, 265
Smith, M. L., 24, 26
Smith, Mark, 68, 73
Smithin, John, 262, 264, 265
Sober, Eliott, 181, 184
Soekmono, R., 116, 117
solipsism, 326, 367, 378, 384
Sosnowska, Paulina, 337, 339
spatialization, 5, 22, 90, 198–204, 207–10, 213, 216, 325–27, 329, 331–33

Spinoza, Baruch, 16, 18
Sprigge, T. L. S., 25, 26
Stael, Madame de, 351, 357
Stein, Edith, 316–18
Sullivan, Lawrence, 121, 134, 138, 141
susto, 171
susuharai, 99
symbolic, 53–55, 65, 109, 110, 117, 135, 138, 145, 146, 151, 160, 171, 173, 187, 198–204, 207, 208, 210–12, 215, 217–19, 267, 272–74, 279, 281, 282, 289, 290, 297, 333, 341, 342, 350, 353–57, 359–61, 364
symbolism, 33, 109–13, 116, 153, 354, 356, 361, 365
symbolization, 57, 61, 112, 117, 135, 144, 199, 210, 295, 310–13, 333, 354, 355
symbols, 112, 117, 152, 153, 197, 198, 203, 211, 288, 289, 300, 353, 356, 361

Tamen, Miguel, 294, 301
Target, Mary, 169, 181, 183
Taylor, Charles, 119, 120, 133, 141
Taylor, Kevin, 4, 95, 103, 104, 389
Tchaikovsky, Pyotr Ilyich, 310
Teeuwen, Mark, 102, 104
temporalization, 5, 22, 23, 32, 84, 198, 199, 203–10, 213, 214, 249, 259, 283, 288, 299, 322, 329, 331, 362
Tendai (Buddhism), 96, 97
Thausing, Gertrude, 68, 73
Thawites, R. G., 141
Thoreau, Henry David, 23
Tobin, Jacqueline, 158, 161
Tolkien, J. R. R., 32, 50, 51
tomb, 45, 58, 59, 61–64, 66, 68, 70–72, 341, 351, 359
Toshio, Odate, 101
toy, 44, 47, 170, 174, 187, 188, 352, 353, 361, 364, 365, 370, 371
transactional, 6, 65, 66, 241, 242, 244–50, 258, 259, 263, 290, 291, 324, 326, 389

transcendent, 84, 122, 123, 149, 155, 157, 167, 198, 205, 222, 225–29, 235, 236, 334
transcendental, 63, 66, 196, 199, 216, 219, 299, 337, 363
transfiguration, 62, 65, 66, 103, 185, 191
Triebenbacher, Sandra Lookabough, 364, 366
Trimurti, 106
Truth, Sojourner, 153
tsukumogami, 4, 95, 96, 98, 100, 102–4
tsukumogami-ki (scroll), 96–100
Tunstall, Dwayne A., 5, 185, 195, 205, 217, 220, 389
Turkle, Sherry, 368, 369, 371, 375, 378, 379, 381–84
Tweedy, Ann C., 273, 294, 301

Underground Railroad, 148, 153, 158, 159, 161
utopia, 234, 253, 263, 265, 281, 336, 338

Vajrayana (Buddhism), 116
Valmiki, 116, 117
Valpey, Kenneth Russell, 93, 94
valuational, 274, 303, 305, 306, 308–12
value, 1–3, 20, 29, 34, 48, 50, 51, 88, 109, 113, 114, 117, 120, 143, 145, 147, 148, 150, 152, 153, 157, 158, 169, 175, 177, 182, 184, 193, 202, 225, 242, 244–48, 250, 254, 256, 258–60, 264, 268, 270, 271, 273–75, 277, 280, 285–87, 291, 292, 294–97, 300, 308–11, 321, 322, 332, 346, 351, 352, 354, 364, 366, 385
Varela, Franscisco, 313, 317, 318
Vaughan, Alden T., 301
Veblen, Thorstein, 287
Vercoutter, Jean, 69, 73
Verene, Donald Phillip, 215, 219, 359, 360, 365, 366
Vico, Giambattista, 287, 288, 298, 301, 341, 360, 361, 366
vorstellung, 215, 322, 323

Wagner, Richard, 6, 319–39
Walker, Alice, 155, 161
Walker, Christopher, 70, 74
Wampanoag (people), 269, 277, 284–86, 296–98, 301
wampum, 6, 264, 267–77, 279–87, 289, 290, 292–98, 300, 301
Wapnewski, Peter, 335, 336, 338, 339
Warlpiri (people), 176–78
Warne, Kennedy, 137, 141
Washington, Booker T., 151, 152
wayang (theater), 109, 111, 113, 117
wedding, 5, 146, 155, 202, 203, 207, 210–12, 217, 353
Weizenbaum, Joseph, 371, 381, 384
Wells, Yvonne, 153
Wernick, Andrew, 383, 384
Wessing, Robert, 116, 117
Whidden, John D., 41, 51
White, W. L., 50, 51
Whitehead, Alfred North, 17, 20, 21, 23–26, 336, 338
Wiener, Margaret J., 79, 93, 94
Wild Boy, 127, 137
wilderness, 20, 25, 30, 31, 300
wild mind, 53, 54
Wilkinson, Richard H., 69, 70, 74
will (Schopenhauerian), 319, 320, 322, 323, 325–33, 336, 339
Williams, Caroline, 364, 366
Willison, George, 293, 295, 301
Willkamayu (river), 125
Wilson, Marie, 153
Winnicott, D. W., 173, 174, 181, 184, 370, 384
Witthoft, John, 133, 135, 136, 138, 141
Wohlleben, Peter, 24, 26
Wong, Sam, 24, 26
world-knot, 15
Wray, L. Randall, 248, 262, 263, 265
Wyschogrod, Edith, 237, 239

Yin-Yang, 95, 98, 99, 102
yōkai, 98, 99, 102, 103

Young, Julian, 335, 339

Žabkar, Louis V., 68, 69, 74

Zarlenga, Stephen, 292, 301
Zegart, Shelly, 158, 160, 161
Zerzan, John, 377, 382, 384

www.ingramcontent.com/pod-product-compliance
Lightning Source LLC
Chambersburg PA
CBHW020119240426
43673CB00038B/536